John Richcreek

STRUCTURE OF INTELLIGENT JUSTICE

Illustrations by
Linda Givin Fisher

CAMDA
The Publishing Trust
780 Eden Road
Lancaster, Pennsylvania 17601

©1988 Camda
All rights reserved
First printing, 1988
Printed in the United States of America
ISBN 0-9600434-1-1
L.C. No. 87-071747

CONTENTS

*N.B. Each chapter is paged independently;
i.e., page 36.11 = page 11, Chapter 36.*

Contents

Contents

CHAPTER 1

CIVIL RIGHTS
AND YOUR RIGHTS AS A PERSON

A majority in the United States Congress votes aye upon a new bill, and they suddenly alter your personal rights. It happens when your state legislature enacts a new statute and when your city council passes a new ordinance. Though the bill seems light years removed from your personal sphere of life, though it is about welfare programs, seat belt laws, or zoning codes, you are not immune from these alterations. Though entitlement programs entitle selected members of society to some of the government treasury, they disenfranchise all Americans in some of their personal funds.

A court making a decision rearranges your personal catalog of rights. No matter that you are not a participant in the case. And though the permanent effect will depend on the day to day consistency of court decisions, the decision will reach out in every direction and quietly affect you and me.

These comments are also true of actions by the executive branch of government. Each time a government employee grants your request - or denies it; or answers your question; or refuses to answer; or answers honestly; or dishonestly - she shapes and contours your universe of rights. In life, one learns sometimes painfully that one is not governed by laws, those mere strings of words filed away in government offices and law libraries. One is governed by the human beings in the offices, and how they interpret the laws, and how well they comply with the law.

Is there rhyme or reason to those strings of words composing the law? Has there ever been and will there ever be? Can justice emerge crystal pure from a five to four vote of the Supreme Court, or from a 51 to 49 vote in a legislative forum? Is there anywhere in a law library a document setting forth an intelligent set of principles, a standard of justice that helps you determine that a right - a right you claim - fits or fails to fit a sensible pattern of rights; or helps you evaluate the correctness of a court decision or an act of Congress or an officeholder's behavior?

As a fossil hunter sifts bones from stratified mud, daring to propose that man has evolved from more primitive animals, so in this book I will assemble a few bones of American and English law and, as you become familiar with the diggings, you will begin to discern the rudiments of a creature in the process of evolution; a thing of considerable substantiality, having a structure so rational, so practically almost organic as to make you pause a moment in meditative speculation. Here is an evolving thing that might be called an intelligent standard of justice.

As you become acquainted with this remarkable creature, your mind will feel the prickling of a persistent question: What is its origin. Is this organic system of justice one of nature's more exciting phenomena, or is it merely man's greatest intellectual achievement. But I am being extravagant.

From my observations in the field of law, I conclude that this evolving organism has been crudely interrupted in its development, perhaps even fated to extinction in our time. In the case of a creature of such promise, how could this happen? I propose that the rulers of the United States have made a mistake. (In this book, you will become accustomed to my writing of the rulers of the United States.) Our rulers have delegated the making of law to lawyers. In fact, if I were to propose a grand theory of history, I would claim that the decline of all nations - all great nations - begins when rulers put lawyers in charge of making the law.

Well, this is not quite accurate. Rather it is that new rulers careening down the avenues of power are apt to lose perspective. They hear not the eternal riddle rumbling in juristic skies: "What do you wish justice to accomplish?" Is law intended merely to compel a person to do something, or restrain her from doing something else? Nothing more? Or am I asking a pointless question? Isn't it sufficient that justice merely accomplishes justice? Well, answer the question now if you wish, and answer it again after you have read the book.

It is my opinion that the great system of law I will reconstruct for you grew from the brains of great thinkers, some of them lawyers. As for lawyers, it is not that they don't have a place in the legal universe. It is simply unreasonable for laypersons and rulers to entrust their liberties without limit to brilliant professional technicians who have personal desires and ambitions of their own. It is not my wish to dwell on this topic, except in observing that those of you who are not lawyers may consider yourselves challenged to learn how to theorize properly in the law. What I will set before you in the book will probably embarrass me ten years from now. This is the fate of writers. But of one thing I am sure. No intelligent system of justice will ever be devised without considering all the facets of human understanding that I have had to incorporate in this work.

Never before in human history have so many laypersons discussed so many questions of human rights. But what understanding, what disciplined comprehension of law do they bring to these discussions? In elementary school and high school, were we not dragged through twelve years of English and history, with perhaps a smattering of Latin and French? And in college, were we not compelled by general curriculum requirements to broaden our horizons? A taste of psychology and philosophy; physics and biology; economics, ecology and sociology, and a brief dip in art and music? Of course we were, and we were broadened.

And since our educational guardians were aware we would soon be graduated into a baffling universe ruled by law, did they not expose us thoroughly to the details of contract, nuisance, tort, equity, trusts, due process, property, injury, damage and negligence? Did they not sternly insist that we become knowledgeable in the theory of law? Well?

So it is with concern that I say this. If intelligent laywomen and laymen do not soon learn how to theorize properly in the law, we will soon find our system of liberty a thing of rags and tatters.

Like Newton exploring the realm of natural forces, we in this book will investigate a field of force hugging us tight as gravity, and on occasion smashing us as ruthlessly. Our mission is to unlock the mysteries of the legal universe; more precisely, the principles governing people in the United States. But Newton had the advantage of observing an eternal, unchanging system. We on the other hand must try to find order among principles sometimes prevailing and frequently evaporating.

Here I do not refer to the law I propose we should have, but to the law I infer we should have - the law implied by the output of courts and by the product of the Constitutional Convention. Nor do I mean the law implied by each and every court decision. A system derived thus would be no system; it would be chaos. Have not many court decisions, even Supreme Court decisions, been rudely reversed or simply ignored by succeeding courts?

Nevertheless, the book gradually generates a standard of justice - the principles from which you can for the most part determine your rights. Altogether it furnishes a yardstick by which you can judge a court's performance, or the performance of a legislature, or of an officeholder. But it is not a law book. In the code books, you will find statutes that clash with the principles I find, and vacancies of rights where rights should exist. No, this is not a book you can cite in court. My observations, though conforming to current practice for the most part, will deviate sharply from the law in significant instances. If you are going to court in an important case, and though you might not fare well by the efforts of your lawyer, you will not (primed only with this book) fare well without a lawyer.

My friends both liberal and conservative - those locked into the straight and narrow positions of liberalism and conservatism - will refuse to accept my conclusions wholeheartedly. Upon the issues of abortion, Abscam, affirmative action, equal opportunity, and other important issues, my conclusions will not line up tidily in either camp. Internally and practically the conclusions are consistent enough, but their correlation with a liberal-conservative yardstick is zero.

In the book, you will review a wide variety of case decisions, each case being shown to conform - or not to conform - to a developing set of principles, and lo: the principles prove to be an intelligent way to govern a country. This is not to say that a better set of principles does not exist or will never be devised, but the intelligence and magnificence of the theory in this set simply cannot be denied. Governing a country, after all, consists of establishing a standard of behavior among the inhabitants, and many unintelligent standards have been foisted upon the human race. The brilliance that we discover here lies in a hidden set of principles from which a standard of behavior will arise and evolve. It is this set of principles - the standard behind the standard - that we are searching for. If it is intelligent, then we have an intelligent way to govern a country. By the same token, such a set of principles will be the vehicle by which an intelligent person will explore and evaluate her very own universe of rights.

Conceivably this set of principles, breathed into life, might be the beating heart of due process, and due process as it developed in America is nothing other than this organic mechanism, this evolving creature that swims in the depths of law, this phenomenon of which I have been writing.

Blackstone used the phrase civil liberty, and the one word liberty would have been wiser. Later by a hundred years, our Congress enacted some statutes calling them the Civil Rights Acts, and with that our legal system developed a slow leak. Since then we have been dipped, rolled, tarred and feathered in civil rights until we are led to believe that the rights of an American are civil rights. Well, given these last few decades, civil rights is the only label available for an immense carton of jumbled material, an aggregate that cannot be overlooked in a treatment of legal theory.

As a phrase recklessly applied, civil rights has been applied to three different classes of phenomena. First it refers to a batch of legal compositions, the output of government machinery - statutes, court decisions and bureau regulations - roughly the rights themselves; whatever they are. Putting them in a bundle, one might call them the law of civil rights.

Second, civil rights refers to a succession of rebellious movements, the rebels adopting the phrase as a banner for their cause; gay rights, student rights, women's rights are all civil rights. Thus civil rights is a species of political process, and one might say, "Mr. K is a civil rights leader."

Third, the phrase civil rights refers to the kind of situation in which rebellion is generated, the topography of background and environment. The complainants protest as members of a class oppressed by the members of another class. I am speaking of the situations that have inspired all the political movements and all the legal compositions. Thus one says that a cry for equal opportunity lies in the field of civil rights, but one would not classify an eviction suit as a civil rights issue.

Civil rights - this mixture of topical background, political movement and legal composition - creates a dilemma for someone in my position. You see, I wish to construct a model of our legal universe, our structure of law in the United States. I wish to discover the set of principles from which all our law derives; well, not all law. Rather I mean all law conforming to the particular principles that prevailed in this nation for a while. And for purposes of constructing this model, one can't neglect the phenomena of civil rights - the laws, the movements, the topical matter; they are too prominent. And they pose a difficulty. If for a moment we focus on the phenomena of civil rights acted out in court and legislature, and think of them as a series of competitive events - a tennis tournament - we find that American lawmakers have been trying to play tennis on a football field - the field of our traditional legal structure - amid the bump and crush of twenty-two burly football players intent on playing their own game.

Admittedly the tournament has been educational. Finally after a hundred years trying to reach the fifth set and fourth quarter, American jurists have reached a point of crucial decision. They have three options. They can discard civil rights (the legal composition); or they can throw away all their other law books; or they can lose more and more of their dignity. In brief, they must join the football game, or move to a tennis court.

If this is the true state of affairs, and I'll show that it is, how will I build a model of the legal universe? To what federal statutes and court decisions will I adhere? Is civil rights - the legal composition - properly to be tossed aside while I construct a reliable model of American law; or should my model conform to the law of civil rights. In answering this, I am going to suggest that civil rights law has broken down as an instrument for relieving the topical background of civil rights. As a first step in understanding the failure, let us look at the philosophical and psychological environment in which civil rights has bloomed.

Between the topical matter of civil rights and the law of civil rights lies the domain of the civil rights movement, a true social phenomenon. And in examining all the civil rights movements of the 1950's, 60's and

70's, one notices that they swirled within a more broadly sweeping tide of American sentiment. In the thirty years between 1950 and 1980, the people of the United States metamorphosed, and the scene will never be adequately described. Some observers are calling it the liberation of the American ego, others a return to the Dark Ages. Though no new thoughts were thought, old Greek thoughts were re-thrashed by minds that in former generations were bored stiff by philosophical questions. And the mental result is best characterized as statistical. More people than ever before envisioned themselves making the world better for humanity.

A popular brand of existentialism perfused the popular mind, spurring people not merely to talk but to act, and social action became not merely a thematic phrase but a prominent social phenomenon. Peace Corps volunteers, traveling far from home, exported Americanism to "backward" nations, while other volunteers, staying at home, were organized to work in hospitals, or visit the bedfast in their homes, or transport disadvantaged toddlers to nursery school.

Meanwhile rebelling against the "establishment", young people questioned the Vietnam War. Patriotism ebbed. Millions of people, abandoning the country's flag, began pledging allegiance to pure water, pure air and the pristine wilderness. Banding together, they battled smoky chimneys, nuclear generators, strip mines and the wanton slaughter of wild things. The civil rights movement was typical of this new existentialism. People with rights marched with those who claimed to be cheated in the allotment of rights.

Here was the thread of the civil rights movement, segments of the population claiming that other segments had more rights; that rights should be equal. The issues, though clear enough to the mind of a lay person, were legally subtle and twisty. Curing the alleged ills might involve repealing old laws. Worse, it might mean depriving others of their long-treasured rights. With rebels appropriately seeking relief through the courts, lower court decisions were frequently inconclusive. Many appeals rose to the Supreme Court of the United States. Civil rights became this melee of phenomena, the topical background situations, protest movements and legal compositions, lacing themselves into the tissue of American jurisprudence.

A traumatic experience. The job of judges being to hand down decisions, our judges handed them down. But more than once even Supreme Court decisions were relegated to the ash heap. Sometimes they were snubbed by later sittings of the same justices, and sometimes they were cancelled by Congressional action. With civil rights tearing American law into little pieces, citizens watching began to sense the fragility of the system - a system long supposed to be logical and well-structured.

Civil rights as a movement, initially a rebellion of black and white Americans against a brute oppression of blacks, now generated a new fever. Escaping racial bounds, it proliferated and infected quite different segments of the population. The chief symptom was an extreme sensitivity to oppression, and the chief side effect was a growing consciousness of class. Where formerly there were individuals feeling estranged from society as individuals, now they suddenly found themselves members of a class, the whole class demeaned by society.

This step brought benefits to the oppressed. It developed political muscle. Attracting funds, it made court action possible. The "I" of a plaintiff in court action donned the halo of "we". We have the XYZ trait in common, and we are discriminated against as members of the XYZ class. In this development, one discovers a phenomenon partly legal and partly psychological and partly a matter of pure chance. One might call it the class oppression syndrome. In the rising tide of existentialism it inspired mass action, and the rebels, seizing upon the civil rights acts as their wagon to freedom, found there a label for the whole carton of mixed material.

For years black Americans, especially in southern states, have suffered cruel social insult. Obviously many black persons are more talented than many white persons. Yet as a class black persons were given the humbler jobs. Obviously many black persons are cleaner and better mannered than many white persons. Yet white people as a class quarantined black people as though black people were somehow infectious. By private policy, or by custom, and even by law, black persons in many localities were excluded from restaurants, and from hotels, and from theaters. Black children were assigned to schools not attended by whites. Endless is the list of demeaning discrimination; only black people know. But finally they received massive government support.

Witnessing this success, other racial minorities became sensitive to oppression and took up their own cause. Then individuals not racially oriented found cause for class complaint; homosexuals claimed they were oppressed by heterosexuals; students claimed oppression by school administrators. And to a point in time, the rebelling classes sprang from minority segments of the population. Then arose a majority segment of the population - women - who began to sense oppression in every important area of their lives. They were disfavored by employers, pension plans, bankers, military recruiters, inheritance laws, and marriage laws.

Even the civil rights acts had neglected women. "All persons... shall have the same right... as is enjoyed by white citizens." "Hah!" retorted those women who happened to be white citizens. And women were alarmed in reading "All persons shall be entitled to the full and equal enjoyment... of any place of public accommodation, without discrimination or segregation on the grounds of race, color, religion, or national origin." Here was a listing of protected classes, and women had been omitted. To people becoming class conscious, the omission was threatening, and nothing less than a constitutional amendment would suffice. Under massive female pressure, Congress drafted and proposed to the states the Equal Rights Amendment:

"1. Equality of rights under the law shall not be denied or abridged by the United States or by any state on account of sex.

"2. The Congress shall have the power to enforce, by appropriate legislation, the provisions of this Article.

"3. This amendment shall take effect two years after the date of ratification."

It is popularly known as ERA. In case you thought there was more to it, there isn't.

ERA as an issue probably had a greater effect in the population than we recognize. It was explosive in the privacy of the home as well as on the national scene, and we shall never be able to measure the deep-seated effects of the nation's failure to ratify the proposal. It is true that the legal points are subtle. Indeed the implications are so far-reaching and technical that lay people have never been exposed to them. The true issues have never been raised in public debate. Expounding the tortuous points for the general public would have been a hopeless task for the professional.

The fascinations of ERA were saturated with irony. Contrary to the propaganda, the amendment would never improve the status and fate of women. Never was a group more ill-served by legal counsel. "Equality of rights under the law" has a marvelous peal in open forum, and registers a dull thud in an American court. A judge does not know what to do with it.

American courts, as I intend to make clear, listen to two great classes of complaints. The first is, "I have such and such a right, and the defendant is intruding upon it." Rigorously speaking, this complaint is heard in a court of law. The second is, "I have such and such a right, and it should prevail over the defendant's conflicting right." Rigorously speaking, this complaint is heard in a court in equity. I say rigorously speaking because my division of duties between law and equity does not exactly coincide with practice. Notwithstanding, with a little adjustment and tolerance, these two claims cover every case that an American court can listen to.

The point is that you never claim a right on the ground that the other fellow has it. If it is a right that everybody should have, you have it. If a statute deprives you of it, you challenge the statute. And for this you do not need a new Constitutional amendment, or a congressional enactment, or a repeal of the law. Read Chapter 23. Read it now if you wish, and again later.

Discovering the separate roles of law and equity is an adventure in itself. In advance, before entering upon it, an important distinction is appropriate. A court at law will require that plaintiff's claimed right is already established and recognized as a right. On the other hand, though there are complications not added at this time, a court in equity will listen to a plea that a claimed right, though not recognized as a right, should be a right.

Now, the general claim in the ERA movement - the claim we may infer from the wording of the equal rights amendment - is that women have been deprived of certain rights by law. And this happens; it happens even for men. So how should a person proceed to remedy the situation? Usually when a person has a complaint, she goes to a court at law, claiming a recognized right in which she is frustrated. But if she has been deprived of the right by law, she will be doubly frustrated. She is claiming a right that law does not recognize, and for this there is no relief at law. Nevertheless there is relief. She takes her case to equity.

With the government as defendant in the case, let us look at the government's defense. It will argue, "Your Honor, yes, this woman theoretically has this right. But in this instance a certain public principle is involved and, in such a situation, the government has a right to take this particular right away from her. On grounds of public principle, the government's right should prevail."

Confronted with this defense, the plaintiff must argue that her right, on grounds of public principle, should prevail over the government's right. It is a question of right against right - the proper jurisdiction of equity.

In a way, this situation sets out the two-fold task of my book. First note that I have just mentioned rights that should be rights, and theoretical rights, and rights that should prevail over other rights. In other words I have been discussing rights that are not rights, or might not be, and this can not be. There must be something wrong with the word rights; it is not providing a vocabulary for clear thinking and analysis. We need a better vocabulary, better defined for the sake of usefulness, and definition will be a major undertaking in the book.

Second, we find that equity is above the law, and this furnishes the second task for the book. Equity determines when an unrecognized right achieves recognition, and when a right prevails over another right. In other words, equity tells us when a right is a right and when it is not. And since a right established in equity must be recognized by a court of law, equity determines law.

But to what does equity refer for its decision? Not law but principles. And what are these principles? Where are they listed? Who determines them? Is equality the only principle on which rights are established? Does the Constitution declare that equality, as a principle for dealing out rights, will dominate all other principles? These are matters we'll discover along a most amazing path. This then is the second part of our two-fold task. You can never tell what your rights should be unless you have learned the principles from which they spring.

So civil rights, this mixture of phenomena, despite its poor legal conception, will prove to be a boon, forcing us to rediscover and re-evaluate the principles undergirding our system of law.

I will recount a number of incidents in the career of civil rights - the legal phenomena of civil rights - that illustrate what happens when we lose sight of principles.

Obviously, the class oppression syndrome, older than Spartacus, older than history, did not originate in the United States. However, as we currently understand it, civil rights began with the thirteenth, fourteenth, and fifteenth amendments to the Constitution - federal actions taken to compel slave states to strike from their laws the legal disabilities of the blacks.

And usually with the ratification of an amendment, we witness a flood of legislation - our jurists love to say "amendments require implementation" - and the new statutes focus on anticipated infractions of the new amendment. By inversion, a negative reading of the statutes, the new statutes imply how people should act in the light of the amendment. And by a positive reading, they announce how the government will deal with malefactors. The legislative discussion looks to the Constitution, usually the amendment itself, for legal support. For after all, "all legislation must conform to the Constitution."

So the Civil Rights Acts, at least the early ones, stemmed from the thirteenth, fourteenth and fifteenth amendments. Supposedly they derived their constitutionality from them. Happily it can be said that legislation based on the fifteenth amendment - the right of all citizens to vote regardless of race or creed - has not been seriously challenged on constitutional grounds.

But civil rights statutes based on the thirteenth and fourteenth amendments have had rough sailing in the courts. As the record shows, a plaintiff basing his claim on those particular civil rights acts took a significant risk that the acts themselves would be declared unconstitutional! How can this be? Nothing is clearer than the amendments; except for portions. In effect the thirteenth amendment provides that the United States will not recognize the right of any person to keep another person in slavery. It seems simple enough, except for one small difficulty. Our jurists apparently don't have a usable definition for slavery, and, oh, what consequences this has had!

The fourteenth amendment has four major clauses, and it is the fourth that has caused all the trouble: "Every person in the United States will have equal protection of the laws." It is this phrase that leads us to think we all have equal rights. Yes! Everyone in the United States can tell you why equal protection is crucial. And no! No one can tell you what it means, or how it is to be administered, or the connection between equal protection and equal rights.

In 1883, a number of cases were joined together and called the **Civil Rights Cases.** Initially the plaintiffs - blacks - barred from theaters and other public places, had sued under the Civil Rights Act of 1875. The suits being brought in federal courts in several states, the judges conferred. Unable to agree, they asked the Supreme Court to intervene, and the High Court after a very proper analysis declared the act of 1875 unconstitutional. The act was useless, said the justices, for relieving the blacks' complaint. As a result, blacks were barred from hotels, restaurants, places of amusement ... for another fifty or sixty years. Since that decision, other civil rights acts have been used successfully to crush racial barriers. Yet if they are constitutional, no one can give you a convincing reason why the act of 1875 is not.

In 1954, in **Brown v. Board of Education,** the equal protection clause of the fourteenth amendment was used to desegregate schools. The decision was applied to school districts where black and white children were discriminantly assigned to separate schools. In 1955, in a related case sometimes called **Brown II,** the high court greatly expanded the application of the fourteenth amendment, commissioning the lower courts to accelerate desegregation. Equal rights demanded - at least this was the prevailing result of **Brown II** - that every school in a city-wide school system reflect the racial proportions of the entire district. This would apply even when a school happened to be located in a racially monolithic neighborhood, with the students in the school predominantly black or white for that reason.

"Integrating" these schools required that children in such a neighborhood be transported to schools in other neighborhoods. Hundreds of thousands of children across the nation could no longer walk a few blocks to their neighborhood schools; they had to spend hours riding school buses to distant schools. As one might expect, parents complained bitterly, black and white alike, sometimes violently, and eventually Congress enacted legislation bypassing this ruling of the court. People were beginning to question the incisiveness of equal rights as a legal tool in the real world.

To speed the demise of racial discrimination, President Kennedy had proposed a novel approach. Called "affirmative action" its backers argued that black people should enjoy not merely equal treatment with whites but a margin of advantage. They contended that black people had received a poorer education than whites and consequently could not compete with whites in the job market. Nor could they compete successfully for admission to colleges and universities. Occupational and admissions tests, rather than measuring the innate aptitude of the candidates, might reflect a disadvantaged education. Henceforth, according to the Kennedy proposal, government jobs would be filled not on the basis of occupational testing, or apparent skill, but on the proportion of blacks to whites in the recruitment area - the quota system.. To put teeth in the program, the policy would extend to companies doing business with the government, and to all institutions receiving government grants. As for colleges and universities receiving government support, the policy would apply alike to staff hiring and student admissions. At last hopefully the black individual would be placed on equal footing with whites.

Legislation implementing Kennedy's proposal was delayed five years even after his death. It became apparent that the proposal, easy in the proposing, was questionable in legality. Finally it materialized, but only after fierce, destructive rioting by blacks in the late 1960's. It cannot be said that the affirmative action program was born from a calm deliberation of fundamental principles.

Massive as the program became (enforcement commissions were liberally salted across the country) it received a shock in 1978. I am referring to the Supreme Court decision in **Bakke v. Regents of the University of California.** Here was a medical school screening three thousand applicants a year to select the next entering class of one hundred medical students. And to comply with affirmative action requirements, the school had modified its admission procedure. Now the one hundred admissions would include sixteen applicants from the group ordinarily screened out. As it happened, the selected sixteen were from minority races.

From among the rejected applicants steps white man Allan Bakke, claiming racial discrimination. His test scores were higher than the scores of the sixteen. He has been classed as a Caucasian and on that basis rejected. Seeking equal protection of the laws under the fourteenth amendment, his cause is unsinkable. The State of California disguised in university garments has deprived him of his rights. In a relatively rapid escalation of the case, all the courts up to and including the federal Supreme Court affirm the validity of his stand. They order the University of California medical school to admit Bakke.

Judge Tobriner, dissenting in the California Supreme Court decision, said (in paraphrase): "It is illogical. In **Brown**, the fourteenth amendment was used to integrate the schools. In **Bakke** it is used to prevent integration." Thus he accurately evaluated equal rights as a legal device for allotting rights. My own view of **Bakke** is presented in Chapter 37, but do not read it until reaching it in proper sequence. You will not understand there the language developed meantime.

This brief account illustrates the ups and downs of the civil rights acts. Once heralded as beacons of freedom, they have flickered at crucial moments. What is wrong with them? Well, let us study them again.

"All persons... shall have the same right... as is enjoyed by white citizens." Now look; since we are talking about equal rights; do all white citizens have equal rights? I'm white. Will an expensive hotel accommodate me if I belong to the class of whites who can't pay the bill? I'm also over sixty. Will West Point admit me as a cadet? And if I were a white man under eighteen, will a bartender sell me a beer? I am talking about class oppression am I not? If we wish equal rights under the fourteenth amendment, why not "All persons shall have the same right as is enjoyed by the richest, most intelligent citizens regardless of age?" Oh I understand your objection. These are all understandable inequalities. So why do we not write, "All persons shall have the same inequality of rights as enjoyed by white citizens, and will have equal protection of their unequal rights." You see, there is no escape. The route chosen is too easy. A deeper understanding of rights is required - not of equal rights, to be sure - **but of the basis for establishing unequal rights.** The rights of a person winning a suit are favored over his opponent's rights. When we see a person winning the right to sit in a restaurant against the owner's wishes, we witness a right favored over an owner's right to dispose her property as she wishes. Unequal rights! In many ways, the proper establishment of unequal rights are what standards of justice are all about.

Look at another attempt at an easy solution: "All persons shall be entitled to the full and equal enjoyment... of any place of public accomodation, without discrimination or segregation on the grounds of race, color, religion, or national origin." In writing this act, Congress was trying to visualize "class oppression", and was trying to include all classes oppressed. But Congress neglected to include women as a class, and homosexuals, and old people, and young people, and unintelligent people, and intelligent people, and poor people, and rich people, and dissidents, and traitors, and nonconformists, and diseased people, and unlikable people ... and everybody who for one reason or another is discriminated against.

The truth is that not one of us is a member of just one class. You have a skin color; you have an age; you have a religious or non-religious inclination; you like daylight saving time or hate it; you have you very own I.Q.; you have your very own financial status; you have a sexual physique; ...ad infinitum. In fact, if you were to list all the classes to which you belong, you will find that not another person in the country falls into your exact same set of classes. This means you are in a class by yourself!

Frankly Congress, in drafting the civil rights acts, became entangled in words, and the courts were trapped too. All of them should have been pondering principles, not words. Perhaps the budding lawyers of the United States, nurtured mainly on the words of contracts, wills, and trusts, are fed too lean a diet. In the legal profession, words are given exaggerated eminence. Lawyers are disciplined to study each word with a magnifying glass. And if in a suit over a legal document they find the wording deficient, the parties will suffer the consequences of faulty language. Appropriate perhaps for contracts, wills and trusts. Definitely not appropriate for questions of the human spirit.

What actually is the key to the class oppression dilemma? It is "All persons... shall have the same right... as is enjoyed by white citizens." But the key is not in the words; it is in the fact that a white person is a person! She is not a member of a class. She is a person. What Congress meant to write was, "All persons... shall have the rights of a person."

So what are the rights of a person in the United States - this is what we need to learn, and in learning we will find that class oppression complaints are relieved by the very same principles that relieve intensely personal complaints.

What should your rights as a person be? What should your rights be? This is the question.

CHAPTER 2

JUSTICE: LOGIC OR INTUITION?

At the foundation of things, as far as law and government are concerned, we find human conflict, and, with a little reflection, one recognizes conflict as an essence of human existence.

We find today in every land a systematic machinery for settling conflict, and think nothing of it. Imagining prehistoric human settings, with countless scenes of beastlike struggle, we think it normal, this present day machinery for settling conflict. But is it so normal? Recall that those pre-civilization struggles were won time after time by the same dominant individuals. Ponder further that the same sorts of aggressive individuals later succeeded in dominating our organizational machineries. Observe moreover that in a few powerful countries these same domineering individuals have developed government machineries controlling even themselves. And this should alert us that something strange is abroad. Ignoring such a phenomenon would be like Copernicus ignoring the wandering planets.

It is a relevant question. If a person can get what he wants in the absence of law, why establish a system that controls even himself, keeping his own greed within bounds?

So, taking our disputes in an orderly manner to a higher authority, and admitting conflict to be an inescapable fact of life, we must also admit that conflict plays a role in the civilization process. All over the earth, wherever man has found a space big enough for a community, we see this phenomenon of people going to a judge. Here are phenomena seemingly rife as leaves of grass. Yet leaves of grass, far from trivia, are centers of activity more profound that we comprehend, signals of phenomena beyond our wildest imagination, and therefore, to gain a new insight into the law, I propose we view law as a phenomenon, much as a scientist views an intriguing and baffling natural event.

If having never heard of homing pigeons we truck a boxed bird in the dark a hundred miles along a winding road, later to release it and find it flying straight home, we scratch our heads in astonishment. And after a few years, when the bird dies, we record it as a freak. Even as scientists we can go no farther. To try to discover the homing mechanism, we would need to observe many such birds. So when we find a whole race of pigeons with this talent, we speak of it as a phenomenon worth studying. And this is how we should look at this business of people all over the world putting their conflicts in a brief case and carrying them to court.

But are we justified in looking at law and order as a natural phenomenon? Well there are several ways of answering. One could say, "After all, it's just the natural thing to do, so what's there to study?" And there's the approach of the cynic: "There's nothing natural about it. We are seeing a conditioned response; a habit trained into the common mentality by superior minds." Yes, for sake of argument, let's suppose this to be true. But then the question becomes "Why? Why should superior minds go to such trouble? What is the purpose?"

Logic, you say, pure logic. A natural response of superior minds to the environment in which they find themselves. Pardon me; I used that word natural again. I merely meant to say that law and order are imposed on the human scene as the result of pure logic.

If we wish to admit this we are left with a few simple questions. Is it logical that superior minds concern themselves with the disputes of ordinary people? More to the point, what happens when superior minds fight among themselves? Who establishes a tribunal for them, conditioning them to seek a higher authority? And if the whole scenario is a matter of pure logic, why do standards of justice vary so significantly from place to place and time to time? Why doesn't one single standard emerge from the force of pure logic playing on the one fact of human contentiousness?

If proposing a logical genesis for government embroils us in logical difficulties, are we better off proposing that law and order is a natural phenomenon? Am I not taking a too simplistic approach? After all, each nation has a distinctive history, each step explained as a response of leading intellects to their environment, or even as the result of conflicts among those same leading intellects. This, you say, is not a matter for theorizing, it is a matter of getting down to details. I'll agree to that. Certainly we must examine specific cases. And so we look at the system in which we Americans find ourselves, calling it as a first approximation the common law system.

The more closely we look the more likely we will find a jumble of intuition and logic. In fact the common law judge takes a certain pride in confessing he relies as much on instinct as on logic. Instances of instinct will flicker, even blaze magnificently before our eyes in our review of court opinions, and, as natural displays, we will find them equal to the eruption of a Vesuvius or the blossoming of a rose.

But I wish to make a point. If intuition is at all involved in the development of justice, intuition has a machinery. It involves an internal mechanism and an external one, an inner function responding to an external function. Take the homing pigeon. In its brain and body a phenomenon is in progress, and in its outer environment another phenomenon is functioning. The outward display of the homing phenomenon is a response of a hidden inner phenomenon to an obscure outer phenomenon.

So if in a judge's decision-making process, an inner mental program is driven by intuition, what is its cofactor in the outer environment? In this day and age we are constrained to search for this inner function, that outer function. Here after all, in the interaction of inner and outer phenomena, is the total mechanism that has fashioned our standard of justice. To live in such a dynamic field of force without describing it in fundamental terms is to live in the world pre-Newton, pre-Einstein, pre-Freud....

It will be well at this point to define justice, and, as fate wills, I must do so in terms that may displease you. You will agree that we can't confine justice to the idea of "What's right". There are too many ideas of what's right. Nor will I ever succeed in forcing you to accept my idea of what's right, dressed though it might be in high-flung language.

After going 'round and 'round the matter of defining justice, one always returns to the conclusion that justice is whatever a court hands down. It is never theoretical. A court ruling is among the most real sensations experienced by an individual in a civilized environment. To make a definition of justice both exact and general, I will say that **justice is (a) a series of decisions made by a person, (b) affecting the lives of other persons, and (c) backed by irresistable power.** To make it as general as possible, I will let the word person cover not only natural persons singular and plural, but conglomerate persons - organizations - governments. It is interesting that my definition covers every government action; not just court action. It covers legislative and executive acts as well, and it does not exclude acts of tyranny and enslavement.

But this peculiarity is not confined exclusively to my definition of justice. Take an often used one: "Justice is a function of government guaranteeing to every person her own rights," and you still include tyranny and slavery. Tyranny and slavery simply provide fewer rights - for some persons. But more important, repeat my definition, changing just one word. Government (in place of justice) is (a) a series of decisions made by a person, (b) affecting the lives of other persons, and (c) backed by irresistable power - and you will see justice and government defined in the same words. And are justice and government such very different functions after all? Compare two phrases for example, a standard of justice, and a standard of government, and see if they involve two separate and distinct concepts.

I will defend my definition and for introduction I will call upon C. L. Dodgson (Lewis Carroll) for excerpts lifted from the famous trial in his **Alice's Adventures in Wonderland.**

Alice had never been in a court of justice before.... "That's the judge," she said to herself...   The judge by the way was the King.... "And that's the jury box... and those twelve creatures... are the jurors."

..."Herald, read the accusation!" said the King. On this the White Rabbit blew three blasts on the trumpet... and read as follows:

"The Queen of Hearts, she made some tarts... the Knave of Hearts, he stole those tarts...."

"Consider your verdict," the King said to the jury.

"Not yet, not yet!" the Rabbit hastily interrupted. "There's a great deal to come before that!"

Alice felt a very curious sensation... she was beginning to grow larger again....

... one of the guinea pigs cheered, and was immediately suppressed by the officers of the court. (As that is rather a hard word, I will just explain to you how it was done. They had a large canvas bag which tied up at the mouth with strings: into this they slipped the guinea pig, head first, and then sat upon it.)

... "Never mind! said the King.... Call the next witness."

Alice watched the White Rabbit as he fumbled over the list, feeling very curious to see what the next witness would be like, " - for they haven't got much evidence **yet**," she said to herself. Imagine her surprise when the Rabbit read out, at the top of his shrill little voice, the name "Alice!"

... "What do you know about this business?" the King said to Alice.

... "Nothing whatever," said Alice.

"That's very important," the King said, turning to the jury...."

The White Rabbit interrupted: "**Un**important, your majesty means..," he said....

"Unimportant, of course, I meant," the King hastily said. ... Some of the jury wrote it down "important," and some "unimportant," Alice could see this, as she was near enough to look over their slates: "but it doesn't matter a bit," she thought to herself.

At this moment the King, who had been for some time busily writing in his note-book, called out "Silence! and read out from his book, "Rule Forty-two. **All persons more than a mile high to leave the court.**"

Everybody looked at Alice.

"**I'm** not a mile high," said Alice.

"You are," said the King.

"Nearly two miles high," added the Queen.

"Well, I shan't go, at any rate," said Alice; "besides, that's not a regular rule: you invented it just now."

"It's the oldest rule in the book," said the King.

"Then it ought to be Number One," said Alice.

The King turned pale, and shut his note-book hastily. "Consider your verdict," he said to the jury, in a low trembling voice.

... "No, no! said the Queen. "Sentence first - verdict afterwards."

"Stuff and nonsense!" said Alice loudly. "The idea of having the sentence first!"

"Hold your tongue!" said the Queen, turning purple.

"I won't!" said Alice.

"Off with her head!" the Queen shouted at the top of her voice. Nobody moved.

"Who cares for you?" said Alice (she had grown to her full size by this time). "You're nothing but a pack of cards!"

This trial became pure cottage cheese before a decision could be reached. Moreover Mr. Dodgson earlier made it perfectly clear that the blustery royal pair had no power to enforce a decision of any kind. Never would this court utter a decision affecting somebody's life and backed by irresistable power. It was not even a moot court. A moot court at least will reach a decision. So never in any case, including the Knave's, could justice be consummated in this court.

But, you interject, this is obvious. Anyone can see this without the extravagance of a formal definition of justice. And indeed if I had filled in the details; the King intimidating the first witness and letting the second escape; and if you have observed the court "quashing" the guinea pig and by artifice trying to remove Alice from the courtroom, naturally you will declare that justice could not possibly emerge from this trial. The very procedure was unjust. But I warn you; the very habit of using the word "unjust" needs condemning. As I will show, it strangles legal progress.

I will go so far as to propose this: that if in the Knave's trial there had been a verdict and a sentence, and the power to enforce the sentence, and if we would assume the worst - that the Knave was innocent and found guilty, I will contend that justice would have been done! And the point to be gained by such technical hard-headedness is this: that when we say these proceeding are unjust, we are dodging the issue. We really mean that the proceedings do not fit our **idea** of justice, or, putting it more distinctly - the procedure does not conform to our standard of justice.

But we never put it this way. We would develop a loop in our larynx before doing so. We have an unconscious dread. If we put it this way, someone might ask us to elaborate our standard of justice, and that would be too strenuous an ordeal. It's something like this.

Suppose you and a friend are standing outside the courtroom after the knave's trial and you say, "The King should not have tried to remove Alice with that preposterous rule about mile-high people." To which your friend replies, "Right. All relevant testimony should be aired at the trial. Suppressing the truth is not right."

Suppose also that the king, overhearing your conversation, steps up and propounds the forbidden question: "Why shouldn't the truth be suppressed if it suits me?"

Explaining why the truth should not be suppressed is a little like expounding a standard of justice. It opens a practically limitless field of debate. We flinch from it unconsciously, and this is why we never say after a displeasing court decision, "This decision does not conform to my standard of justice." It is so much more pleasant to say, "That was a deplorable violation of justice." Then we can nod grimly to each other and depart, assured that we don't have to explain ourselves to each other, or even to ourselves.

Justifying a standard of justice, supposing you have one, is quite different from justifying a judgment. In a court of law a judge justifies his judgment by reference to the law. In contrast, a judgment in a court in equity creates law; the chancellor in equity does not properly refer to the law. He refers to a manual about making law - a standard of justice - if such a manual exists. So when we go the step farther and attempt to justify the standard of justice itself - supposing we have one - we are talking about yet a third level of rationalization. To illustrate:

Jimmy Jones, fond of strolling through Farmer Brown's forest, does not do it often. He does not beat a path, or trample the ferns, or break down the fence. But Farmer Brown, not liking it, and telling him many times not to enter his land, finally petitions the court to make Jimmy stay off the land.

The judge finds that Brown owns the land and that Jimmy holds no property in it, not even Brown's permission to use it, and the law is quite definite. Jimmy is trespassing. So the judge states his findings and says, "Jimmy, if you persist in walking on Mr. Brown's land, I'll have to find some way to punish you until you stop." Now a case like this might be heard in a criminal court, a subdivision of a court at law. Actually it partakes a little of the function of equity - the power to order someone to refrain from certain actions. But since it is written in statute form, it is in law.

Nor can Jimmy turn it into a court of equity though he might try. For instance, say he defends himself by saying, "Your honor; a woods is a woods. No one else is using it; not even Mr. Brown. I'm not hurting it. I'm simply enjoying God's universe." But this plea will accomplish nothing. If the judge wishes, he may hold his hand over his ears. The law is the law. The law is quite clear on this point. The judge's decision is fully justified. "It is called trespass, Jimmy. If you don't stop, I must do whatever is necessary to stop you."

This is justice as far as this court is concerned. Nor will the judge listen with compassion to Jimmy's plea. Nor will he try to persuade Farmer Brown to relent and permit Jimmy to walk now and then through the woods. The judge must assume (a) that the law of trespass conforms to a standard of justice and (b) that the standard is justifiable. But you will never hear him state the standard in his court and certainly he will not attempt to justify it.

But isn't it somewhere required that the law is justifiable in fundamental terms? What is the general principle behind the law of trespass? What is this thing called private property? And why is private property so precious that the government will marshall all its forces to support Mr. Brown's wishes, his miserly wishes, forbidding the idyllic pursuit of a boy whose drift through the forest is like the flight of a feather?

At this point we are within striking distance of a particular standard of justice, a standard we Americans might consider the essence of "justice". To take advantage of this nearness, let us have the King of Hearts again ask - "Why shouldn't the truth be suppressed if it suits me?" Not that I will try to answer the question but that the debate will be illuminating. Let me make the debate more realistic, removing it from Alice in Wonderland, conducting it in the British-American tradition, in the environment of the common law, under due process. Apparently in this setting our particular standard of justice requires bringing out the facts of a case as completely as possible, for this is the way to learn the truth. Then the king's question can be refined thus, "Why try to establish the truth? What is so important about the truth?" The king, you see, is challenging the standard, attempting to substitute another. And most important, since we are now in the framework of the common law, the king is not a frail playing card. He is all-powerful, and here is the problem. If we are to convince him to hold to the standard, we must persuade him of its advantage to him personally. This you see, in practical terms, is what we must do when we set out to justify a standard of justice. It must appeal to the dominant people of a nation. And though in the effort we see fit to maintain the highest academic purity, this practicality completely distinguishes the effort itself from the academic.

If a particular adversary were to debate the king on this question, with a particular case hanging in the balance, we would find their arguments converging to two separate points. In the king's arguments we would recognize his obvious desire that the truth be suppressed (in this particular case). In his adversary's arguments we would see an obvious desire that the whole truth come out. Inevitably this is always the result when two people try to justify opposing standards of justice, with opposing practical consequences at stake. It all comes down to personal desire. No matter that you marshall regiments of logic all garbed in the bright uniform of law. At bottom they all reflect your personal wishes. Now let us take it another step.

All court decisions have a common two-headed result. A decision can gratify but one party, disappointing the other. This being inevitable, every case yielding a frustrated customer, how can a government get general support for its system of justice? From these two inevitabilities - first that a standard of justice is based upon personal desire, and second that a judgment always creates a loser, we must conclude that even the losing party must find a satisfaction in the final decision. Otherwise about fifty percent of the population will hate the system.

Now this must be a strange satisfaction indeed. It means to me that the system or standard must be coupled to something highly desirable to all parties; so coupled that even the loser realizes some species of profit. Of course, this desirable something, whatever it is, must reside in a different dimension than the practical consequences of the case at hand. And each party's stake in this desirable something must be as great or greater than his stake in any pleading he might ever produce in court. This goes for the king too - if we wish to convince him against his wishes that a production of truth is essential. And if this seems cryptic and a bit abstruse, perhaps one more remark will heighten the effect.

If a nation's standard of justice is coupled to this something else, then justice as practiced in that nation is more than "justice". It is a mechanism enhancing the wealth of all potential litigants, **every individual in the nation,** in this something else. Here is an amazing mechanism if it exists. I think it does. I think it is the heart and soul of what I will for the moment call the common law. To analyze the phenomenon of justice under the common law and to expose this mechanism as explicitly as possible is the task set for this work. It is an example of how to theorize properly in human rights.

CHAPTER 3

DOWN WITH RIGHTS!

I will digress for a moment to discuss the word rights, warning that after this chapter I will shun the word until I deem it purged of its capriciousness.

In our society, and perhaps in others, the words rights and justice suffer from inbreeding. They have been used for so many years to define each other that, like the tigers chasing each other 'round the tree, they have turned to butter. Losing form and shape, and becoming precious to each of us (but only as each of us wishes to understand them), they are not easily brought under control, free of ambiguity.

As words, they have an advantage. Rights and justice are short words, making them sweet, and ultimately commending them to our favor.

Rights have been assigned a critical function in court proceedings. A judge must be able to find a groundwork of rights for the plaintiff before he will summon a defendant to appear and answer a complaint. If the plaintiff fails to state all the essential elements of a proper complaint, the defendant may bring it to the court's attention, and, if the court indeed finds an element missing, it will refuse to listen to the case.

Among these essential elements, two are apparently indispensable. Not easy to characterize in a general mode - there are so many kinds of pleading - the two elements (given a degree of tolerance) can be generalized as follows; first, the plaintiff must describe in her pleading a situation in which the court can detect a right for her. Second, it must be clear from her description that the right was infringed by the defendant, or is being infringed, or is in danger of being infringed.

To illustrate, suppose Shirley comes to court stating (among other things) that (1) while walking on the shoulder of a road, facing traffic, (2) she was struck by a car driven by the defendant. From these statements it is clear that her rights are involved in this case and, if her facts are accurately stated, her rights were violated. And such a case will catch the ear of a court.

But let us consider the same Shirley in an entirely different situation. In this new case she states that she agreed to work in a peach packing shed for four dollars an hour. She states further that after starting work she learned that the other packers were making five dollars an hour. And now she prays the court to compel her employer to pay her five dollars an hour.

A case like this can become amazingly involved. It is simple for Shirley to say, "I have a right to get the same wage that the others are getting." It may seem obvious to her, but the court may have to squint harder to see it. A court cannot use the force of government to make Shirley's employer pay her five dollars an hour just because the court thinks it would be a nice thing for the employer to do, or even if the court thinks it would be an enlightened policy for the employer to adopt. The court must see an infringed right before it can issue an order backed by the troops.

So the court looks in the book of statutes and the reports of past cases, and tries to see if Shirley indeed has a right that is being infringed. Now note that the emphasis in the case is being shifted. The court has actually started to consider a case in which the plaintiff does not have a clearly established right. The debate is not over the claim "My right is being infringed," but over the claim, "My wish in this matter should prevail over the wish of the defendant." The claim of infringement is there, but there can't be an infringement of a right unless the right is established. What we have here is a plaintiff beating on the courthouse door shouting, "The right I'm claiming is really a right, even if you don't find it in the law. And even if you don't think it's a right, you've got to give me a hearing anyway, so I can convince you it's a right."

There was a time when it wouldn't take two seconds for a court to file Shirley's complaint in the waste basket. Today it would take three. The hesitance would be due to the introduction of equal rights in the vocabulary. Only since the civil rights acts became law have we claimed rights on the ground that other people have them. Even if there were actually a valid policy of equal rights in the United States, the case should go to equity. It is a case of rights against rights.

When Shirley asks for the extra dollar per hour, she is asking for a dollar of company money, company property, and one of the important features of property is that a person (including a company) can dispose her property as she wishes. So when Shirley is talking about equal rights, she is really asking the court to give her the company's right to dispose the company's money.

But at this point I wish to make abundantly clear that even equity cannot elevate right above right, cannot even think about it, unless both claimed rights are determined to be rights. So a basic consideration in any case at law or in equity is - Does the party actually have the right that she claims? In Shirley's case is "equal rights" the basis for a right? And even more fundamental is this: If we can't find that the claimed right is acknowledged as a right, how does one establish it as a right? What are the criteria that determine a right. What makes a right a right!

If a careful search of the law does not substantiate a claimed right, the remedy must lie in equity if remedy there is. Unfortunately the duties of law and equity have been merged and confused by both practice and statute in many states. Like judges at law, modern chancellors in equity search statutes and case reports to determine the rights in a case. This is true even of the Supreme Court of the United States in landmark cases. Yes, statutes and court opinions comprise the body of law. But without the most searching induction, they do not disclose the principles by which rights are established, and when the determination of rights is confined to a search of the law, there can arise no new right as a consequence. No combination of recognized rights can be integrated into a new right. In the language of logic, laws derived from laws are derived by the process of deduction, and remain wholly within the field of law already established. The power to make such a derivation falls entirely within the jurisdiction of a court at law. Appropriately, then, it falls entirely outside the jurisdiction of equity. Even in current practice, a bill in equity must include the claim, "There is no relief at law for the plaintiff." So, if new law, new rights are to be created, an arm must reach beyond the limits of law and pull in something from a set of principles transcendent to law. This historically, in the court system, is the special function of equity.

In the absence of a court empowered to perform this function, there can be no development of law, no development of rights save by statute - positive law. But to restrict new law to the creations of legislatures is to invite legal disaster.

Legislators tend to hear only mass complaints, or the desires of the powerful, not the intensely personal complaint of the isolated little man. Legislators frequently are as influenced by the raw numbers of complainers, or the raw power of complainers, as by considerations of "justice". Rarely do they seem to concern themselves with standards of justice, unless we count political leverage as a standard of justice.

Therefore when your courts are confined to deliberations of law, you will find them choking under cascades of legislation. They contemplate a universe of rights marked by a total lack of consistency. In such a situation, the government finds itself with no instrument for hearing a novel isolated complaint - a complaint lacking mass appeal, or the complaint of a person lacking power. And once the crafty-greedy learn that courts have lost their compass, their subterranean thefts expand prodigiously, the mass of unheard complaints mushrooms, a dynamite

3.4

situation for governments. Liberty dies without obituary, in a nation running over with "rights".

Evidently English genius discovered this weakness of purely legislative law, and, by devising equity, layed the groundwork for an orderly development of law. A comparison of their eighteenth and nineteenth century court opinions with succeeding American opinions indicates that Americans have lost the touch for equity. (Perhaps the English by now have lost it too.) Since we parted from English rule, rights in the United States have developed, first, by reference to English law as it developed; this was customary in the United States until the early 1900's. Rights developed, second, by statute, and, as in the case of the civil rights acts, this practice has nearly destroyed the fabric of American jurisprudence. Rights have developed, third, by judges following pure intuition and arriving at excellent decisions. Our tapestry of rights is a patchwork, repatched.

You see, the only way that law can be developed intelligently is by reference to intelligent principles or, as I call it, an intelligent standard of justice. This the English were able to do without defining their standard. Or, if they defined it, they kept it secret. To budding chancellors, by private seminar, they must have passed the technique for creating new rights, probably in serious fireside discussion. But as far as America is concerned, the discipline in equity was disrupted in jumping the ocean.

So we have found a difficulty with the word right at a most critical point in the claim "I should have the right...." Here we are talking about new law without really knowing the why and wherefore of old law. The question "When does a claimed right deserve to become an established right" is a central issue, and the answer must be, "When the claimed right conforms to an accepted standard of justice."

Superficially, the ordinary American philosophy of justice does not diverge too far from this line of reasoning. It is often felt in the United States that the main job of a judge is to determine the rights of the parties. This would imply that justice results from a determination of rights.

But John Quincy Adams gives justice a different genesis. In defending a group of blacks in the celebrated **Armistad** case, he quoted Justinian, "Justice is the perpetual will to secure to everyone his own right." If we follow this lead, we gather that justice is a government trait - a superlative one. The right exists, and justice secures it. From this we gather that rights originate independently - outside of justice - from a different source. And individuals are not secure in their rights unless a will to secure them prevails in the government.

Two superb minds, Adams's and the emperor's, conceiving for

justice a human source within the framework of government, - yet each of these great minds neglected to define the particular system of rights secured by this will. Supposedly the American Adams surveyed the rights emerging from the common law; the Roman Justinian contemplated those engraved in the civil law. Strange. For the civil law easily accomodates slavery. And Adams, were he an attorney in a slave state, would have impeccably observed the rights of slaves and slave-holders in accord with the state code, and would have perpetually striven to secure their rights for them, each for each, respectively.

So Adams and Justinian seem not to have greatly enlightened us on rights and justice, and we test once again the idea that justice emanates from a judicial determination of rights. And it still isn't fundamentally satisfying. A moment's consideration reveals that what we are calling justice is the court's justice, and it emanates from the court's determination of rights. All of which leads us back to the position that justice is what a court hands down.

Thus do we gradually become disenchanted with the words justice and rights as words possessed of any intrinsic value. Taken by themselves, with each defined by the other, we find them to be empty shells filled with any meat we please, and we are reminded of Hugo's **Les Miserables,** our minds chilled by the spectral figure of an unrelenting officer of the law; a soul of integrity; dedicated to justice; a cosmic reminder that a government's standard of justice, though not evil by intention, might not be intelligent either. Given this, we are left thinking vacantly that rights and justice may after all be "relative".

One wonders if the founding fathers didn't come to this conclusion, for the word right appears only once in the original body of the Constitution, and there it is used in an inappropriate rider. Not until the amendments did rights appear in force, and then they appeared so clumsily that they should apologize for having appeared at all.

Why for example does the first amendment read in part, "Congress shall make no law... abridging... the right of the people peaceably to assemble."? Why doesn't it read, "The people will have the right to assemble peaceably."? Ah, you say, this would be theoretically impure. With the people already having the right to assemble peaceably, it would be absurd for the Constitution to provide it.

"Oh," we say. "Then why do we call it a constitutional right?" And there being no appropriate answer, we continue: "Where does the right originate?" And perhaps you will answer, "From the common law," or, "From state law."

To this we reply, "Then what happens if the common law changes its mind, or the state law is repealed, and the right disappears?" And the logical answer: -this would be perfectly legal under the Constitu tion. The amendment does not guarantee the right; it merely provides that Congress will not abridge it if it happens to exist. And this same dialogue is applicable to every so-called "constitutional" right stated in the amendments, even the proposed equal rights amendment - ERA.

It reminds me of the fabled country where beans were a staple in the diet of the people, and the king's counsel wrote a new law for the king to sign, reading, "The king will not deny beans to the people. He will not deny beans to the people on account of race, religion, sex or age."

The law was very popular. The king and his counselors became great favorites among the people. But the king and his counselors neglected to mention that the year's bean crop had been destroyed by beetles. There were no beans to be denied.

So we return to rights and where we get them. But you will forgive me if I gradually disuse the word until I get it under control.

CHAPTER 4

THE COMMON LAW AS PHENOMENON

One should not get an idea that a standard of justice is inviolable. No. A standard of justice and the law never exactly match. Though a government might profess a standard of justice, you will find that law and justice will stray. After all a government is a government; a standard but a standard.

We may then wonder if a standard of justice is useful, and the answer is a resounding yes. On the way to explaining this, I note first that the sort of standard to which I'm referring is not merely a stack of bricks. It is more like a theory of justice. But not a theory telling us what justice ought to be; not a new theory providing a new kind of justice. I refer to a theory like Einstein's or Newton's. It comes from observing the universe of law as though it were a universe of phenomena. From the observations, one formulates a group of propositions from which, hopefully, past legal events might be explained or evaluated, and future ones predicted.

Their universe of observation - the universe of Einstein and Newton - consists of atoms, and stars, and invisible forces. Ours consists of statutes, and court decisions, and executive acts of government - and invisible forces. The giants of science proceeded by assuming an underlying rational system in this madcap physical universe. We, regarding our legal universe, must proceed on the same assumption. But is the assumption warranted? Well, this is a risk we must take, and only at the completion of our labors will we know.

Strangely enough, the deductions from Newton's and Einstein's theories, magnificent as those theories are, don't exactly fit the physical universe in every detail, and this is true of most if not all scientific theories. But stranger still, a good theory is as useful in its "misfitness" as it is in its fitness. For one thing, a truly great theory is absolutely definite.

Thus though today we might ridicule the Ptolemaic theory (it assumed that the sun and stars revolve about the earth), nevertheless sailors and surveyors found it useful over a span of a thousand years. Mathematicians used it to calculate and tabulate the future positions of sun and stars. With the resulting tables, surveyors and navigators could determine their locations on land and sea. The determinations were not quite accurate, but this did not dismay the mathematicians. They simply measured the inaccuracies and furnished the surveyors and navigators with correction tables. As you see, they didn't need to change the theory. If it was inaccurate, it also was definite and, while it did not quite reproduce the universe of observation - the real world - they simply used it as a base line from which to measure the real world. Really that is all we can expect of any theory.

But there is still another equally important way in which a wrong theory can be useful. Since it can be used to deduce and analyze the world of observation, not only by how the theory hits the mark but how it misses it, it follows that if it misses the mark it has helped us discover the influence of invisible factors, factors neglected in our theory; factors to be tracked down and revealed. And the various ways in which the theory misses the mark will furnish clues to the nature of these hidden factors.

From these reflections we gain the proper attitude for viewing a standard of justice.

I have opened up the topic of natural phenomena for several reasons. For one thing, the law deals exclusively with natural pheno- mena who happen to be two-legged animals. Then too, seen from the viewpoint of a scientist, the development of law looks singularly like an evolving universe. The reported cases in a law library, and groups of cases clustered about a particular topic, and fields of law - great categories of legal practice - look suspiciously like planets or stars, and planetary systems, and star clusters and galaxies.

In some ways, the development of law seems as natural as the swinging of a moon around its larger companion, or the falling of an apple. Biologically speaking, there is a great similarity between judges intuitively seeking the "right" and moths fluttering about a lamp, and bees circling with a load of pollen before streaking off toward the hive. I have already mentioned the homing instinct of certain pigeons, and truly the scientific investigation of this instinct has been fascinating. At last the explanation seems at hand.

In this investigation, the results of a particular series of experi- ments were especially intriguing. The observations were made by releasing pigeons one at a time from a plane. With this technique, the investigators could not only record the number of successful homings and clock the journeys, but they could also observe the initial circling of each bird and measure the angle at which it finally committed itself to the homeward flight.

They found the homeward direction of these angles to be remarkably accurate in most cases, but were surprised to find that the accuracy varied with the geographic location of the release. In particular there were specific regions where the pigeons took remarkably wrong courses - all having the same angle of deviation from the true course. It was as though there was something about the geology of the terrain below - perhaps mineral deposits - that dramatically influenced the pigeons' guidance systems. This observation indeed furnished an important clue to one feature of the homing instinct, an extreme sensitivity to variations in the earth's magnetic field.

Similar deviations from the norm must be expected in the world of man-made law, giving clues not only to the principles controlling the norm, but to aberrant features of the particular environment in which the law is operating. This must be kept in mind when one is inducing a standard of justice from the phenomena at hand - the judicial decisions, the legislative and executive acts. Until one has made enough observations to detect patterns, one never knows initially which observations to label "standard" and which to label "deviant". Fortunately in the universe of British-American law, consistent patterns are quickly discerned. It seems safe to suppose that a standard of justice was operative in the developing common law, despite deviations sporadically occurring.

The standard of justice that I will elaborate has been inferred or induced from observations in the common law - that system of law largely developed by the British government beginning after the Norman conquest. I say the British government rather than British judges because in the common law I include statutory law as well as the consequences of case opinions. And for present purposes I will have to extend the common law to include the law of the United States, introducing an ungainly mass of material into our observations. In this country there has been a great amount of legislation deviating strikingly from the standard otherwise inferable from the common law. Of the errant material the civil rights acts are merely the most cosmetically prominent.

One risks fundamental error in using the term common law. The common law at any moment is not what it was fifty or a hundred years earlier. Accordingly justice under the common law is a changing thing. In spite of this, there has been until recently a remarkable constancy to be inferred in the development of the common law. So perhaps the term "spirit of the common law" - a phrase used frequently by jurists - would be more appropriate than "common law" in many places in the text. This is particularly true in referring to a standard of justice to which the common law conforms. It would be more exact to say that the spirit of the common law conforms to this standard of justice. Perhaps when

I use the term common law, the reader can sometimes mentally substitute the phrase "spirit of the common law".

Thus qualified, the term common law is not too inaccurate a term for our purposes, provided we don't forget that the common law is the law that is, and not the law we wish it might be. It is the real world, the universe of our observations, and we must expect it to deviate in significant instances from the model universe produced from our theory of justice.

One other misapprehension introduced by using the term common law, arising for instance from reading that Great Britain and the United States observe a system of common law justice. The assertion neglects the fountain called equity. When our judges and legislators stray from the principles of equity, it is then our nation gets into the most trouble. Really our standard of justice and the principles of equity (not the textbook maxims of equity) are one and the same thing. The spirit of the common law is nothing other than the principles of equity, or so we will find. Therefore when we speak of the grandeur of the common law, we will do well to hear "equity" echo in the recesses of our mind.

In my opinion, no human achievement matches the development of the common law thus viewed. In this opinion, I must bow to more cosmopolitan minds, those steeped also in the civil law, who give equal laurels to the jurists who developed that great system. One cannot overlook the great nations that have adopted the civil law, developing in its atmosphere. But I must trust the students of that system to determine if it springs from the purity of theory that I will reveal in the common law.

In thus praising the creative minds behind all great legal systems, I wish to convey my conviction that we ordinary folk have no comprehension of the difficulties facing our higher authorities in formulating a legal system and putting it in motion. In the case of the common law it is my belief that only a highly invisible cordon of men strung through time, beginning in the court of William the Conqueror, could have conceived and mobilized the legal system I have in mind. Unless such names as Thomas More, Erasmus, Francis Bacon and Isaac Newton were eliminated by exhaustive research, I would include them in the list of contributors. As we will see, the common law has profound anthropological roots - roots deep in the study of man. Yet there is little evidence that practicing judges even in pivotal cases, particularly in America, were aware of this. I cannot imagine that what we will see in the common law was created wholly out of an instinct for justice by judges thus blind.

Yet no one can deny that the common law developed by fits and starts to the perfection it reached in mid-twentieth century. Nor can it be denied that intuition played a controlling part in the development. As

I will amply demonstrate, the perfection of the common law was attained step by step frequently on wholly illogical grounds, yet by means of decisions beautifully attune to a most amazing standard. I must declare if the elegance of the common law has been thus attained, then we witness in its evolution the most awesome natural phenomenon, bar none, appearing in the total universe of which man is aware.

It is this unnatural cooperation of genius and naivete that leaves me uneasy. To my mind it conjures a vision of a secret cabal in England of unsurpassable intellects, building for a future beyond their time. Working anonymously, they built not the completed oak but its germ. For only in this form would it culminate in reality.

My fantasy says these men must have started their work with a simple profound comprehension - the utter impossibility of devising and initiating full blown the system of law they envisioned. The system generating the system was the heritage they left, but that's the task of the book. To prove or disprove what I am imagining would be within the grasp of only the most talented and painstaking historian, and perhaps not even within hers.

Their next step would have been to analyze why the system could not be instituted full blown in their own time, and this must have been a research requiring an inquiry into the motivations and capabilities of men and women at all levels of society. This would have to be attended by prolonged, closeted discussions. Finally, using the facts and relations thus gained, they devised a scheme - not the scheme of law itself - but a scheme that would in time produce the scheme of law. Their scheme was an acorn, so to speak, on its way toward oakhood; created with a skilled working knowledge of the environment in which it would develop over the next thousand years - not the technological environment to be sure - but the environment of human nature. To put it in tree-growing language - they anticipated the diseases and parasites of oaks, the factors of soil and sunlight, and, above all, the touch of those practicing oak cultivators - attorneys, judges, legislators, councillors, and kings.

The splendid aspect of the concept was their understanding that this growth and development had to phenomenalize through the medium of the typical legal mind. Ordinary practitioners would have to be indoctrinated with a few rules and procedures. These worldly novices, facing conflict from a bench and in person, would put together a system of justice unattainable in closeted council; and without knowing exactly how they did it.

Perhaps the era of these lego-anthropologists can be estimated - if they ever existed. When in history we see the legal concepts of property, contract, tort and equity in fetal form, we have probably seen the completion of their work. These legal institutions announce a surfacing system of justice, rooted in depth, though not revealing the supporting matrix beneath.

If such a project ever existed, how can we gauge the perceptiveness of those original minds? Partly by discovering the standard of justice that supports the common law. But more by learning the unsuspected secrets that the common law teaches us about man himself!

CHAPTER 5

INTRODUCING JURISDICTION AND PROPERTY

In **ex parte Warfield**, sometimes heralded as a milestone in the progress of human rights, we are able to observe a case in which a too eager judge set the stage for legal chaos. But **Warfield** gives us an opportunity to raise the curtain on man's most ingenious legal invention - the device called property.

In 1898, Will Morris realized that his wife was enchanted by a certain J. B. Warfield. Vivia and Warfield exchanged letters, strolled together in the park, lunched together and had long discussions in his boarding house. Though the relationship was not yet as intimate as it might be, it was certainly chilling the relationship between Vivia and Will Morris.

Morris, a decent chap entirely civilized, was determined to send Warfield packing. Far from contemplating actions disapproved by government, he took an opposite strategy. Perhaps, he thought, just maybe he could get the government to make Warfield stay away from Vivia.

We all agree that government is strong, making a most effective ally if we can engage it in our behalf. But one can not get the government to listen to every complaint in the world. Take an imaginary Mrs. McNamara bringing her husband to court, complaining, "Your Honor, this man is impossible! I wash his clothes, cook his meals, make his bed... But he won't turn a finger to help me. He won't even take out the garbage. Your Honor, at least make him take out the garbage." Though this case has all the elements of a Greek tragedy, we will find that a court will not listen to it. In fact, Mr. McNamara will not even be required to put up a defense. He need only demur that the court has no jurisdiction - no power over him in this case - and the assenting court will refuse to hear another word from Mrs. McNamara.

It is not that the judge is contemptuous of her feelings or of the humble nature of her request. Indeed he will spend countless hours listening to cases with far less pathos. But here is an instance of cases that surface in every system of justice - the cases that a court will not listen to. Should the government listen to a case in which Green asks government to compel Black to stay away from Green's wife. Can a court tell you who you can write letters to, and who you can take to lunch? In **ex parte Warfield,** these are the central issues. Technically and fundamentally they constitute the issue called jurisdiction.

Certainly things would have been simpler for Will Morris if there was a statute forbidding a man to make friends with another man's wife, but there isn't. And anyhow hasn't Morris picked out the wrong defendant? Would it not be more sensible to order Vivia to stay away from Warfield? Would that not be in line with her marital duties? The trouble is that this would be something like ordering Mr. McNamara to take out the garbage. Often between cases there are differences not apparent to us laymen, with such importance that they determine whether a court will increase the volume of its hearing aid, or turn it off. In a Texas court Judge Richard Morgan listened to Morris's petition to make Warfield stay away from Morris's wife, and granted it. A law-shaking decision.

Part of Morris's request was a familiar one in the courts of that day. He asked damages for alienation of affection, with a little twist. He asked damages for **partial** alienation of affection, a modification with significance becoming apparent later, after several chapters. This was fine with the court, and doesn't seem to have worried Warfield. But Morris's other request was a different matter. He asked the court to order Warfield not to associate with Vivia in any way; not to speak to her or visit with her or write to her or send a message to her. Not even go near her, not even on the public sidewalk - at least anywhere in Texas - even in his boarding house. Meaning that if she went to his boarding house he would have to leave! And the court issued an injunction against Warfield carrying every detail of Morris's petition.

Here was an unprecedented restraint on a man's liberty; by a government pledged to freedom, and it was too much for Warfield to swallow. He continued to visit with Vivia. And Morris went back to court and tattled. And Judge Morgan found Warfield in contempt; fined him $100 and sentenced him to three days in the county jail.

I should point out that **ex parte Warfield** had one foot in a court of law and the other in equity. In earlier chapters I made rough distinctions between the courts of law and equity. I said a case was heard at law if the claimed right was a recognized right not countered by an opposing right. It is heard in equity if it is a case of right against right, in which case a superceding right must be argued into existence. This distinction, a fundamental one, is not always observed in modern practice.

In current procedure, the complaints for money and crimes are regularly assigned to law. Issuing injunctions is a task assigned to equity. Into equity, that is, go cases in which plaintiff asks the court to order the defendant to stop doing something, and Morris's petition for an injunction against Warfield would be heard in equity if heard at all.

To use traditional language, it would be heard in chancery; before a chancellor.

A writ of injunction is a double-barreled device. For one thing the defendant is enjoined to a servitude - definitely a loss of liberty. Purportedly, such a limit on a man's freedom is justified on the premise that someone else is being wronged by his exercise of that freedom. If the person enjoined disobeys the order, he is said to be in contempt of court and is subject to fine or imprisonment. The armed personnel of government may be enlisted to enforce these measures, and this is the other function of injunction. It joins the contemptuous person to the physical power of the government, the executive branch.

Since a court order is backed by this physical power, the propriety of a court using it becomes serious. This is the question of jurisdiction, and Warfield challenged the legality of using government power to separate him from Vivia. He was under no contract to Morris, nor was he Morris's slave or servant. Yet for Morris's benefit the court restricted Warfield's use of the mails, his freedom of speech, his right to use public places, his right to use even his own boarding house. In all pursuits bringing him into correspondence with or proximity to Vivia, he was restricted. And now for Morris's benefit the court would deprive him of $100 and keep him in captivity for three days. Basic is the question; what gives the court jurisdiction in any case?

We may approach the answer by imagining justice to be a vast complex machine composed of many parts, much as a gasoline engine is composed of gears and push rods and electrical components and revolving shafts. Unless its parts are interconnected in very special ways, an engine of this kind is useless. Each part having its own function, the machine as a whole has a quite different function, and therefore each part must be so related and attached to others that all will function as a whole. Though we may say that the function of the entire engine is to power the car, it is not true that powering the car is the function of the spark plug. Its function is to ignite the gas mixture in the cylinder. Nor is powering the car the function of the distributor. Its function is to make the spark plug spark at the right time. Yet there is no engine except as it is composed of all its functioning parts; and the function of all the parts working together is to power the car.

So we may say that the function of the courts - the whole machine - is to resolve conflict. Sometimes in this process the physical force of government is needed, and we ask what will couple this part of the machinery to a particular case and a particular person. In **ex parte Warfield** we see a court issuing a writ of injunction, a device, a part of the machinery. When Warfield did not restrain himself in compliance, we see Morris reporting it to the court. This is part of the machinery. Subsequently the court found Warfield in contempt and applied pressure that Warfield did not like - a fine, a jail sentence - part of the machinery. Now if Warfield refuses to appear at jail voluntarily, a written instruction from the judge will bring the sheriff and the men needed to execute the sentence. This completes the joining of the engine to the person, and will eventually resolve the conflict. But the functioning of the whole process, the proper resolution of the conflict between Morris and Warfield must proceed step by step, no steps omitted, and the proper operation of the entire device is called due process. Really it can be argued that justice and due process are one and the same thing, and a standard of justice is a standard of process.

But what is the part of the whole machine attaching its operation to a particular man called Warfield, bringing its whole maddening weight to bear on him? This is the matter of establishing jurisdiction, really the first step in the machinery of justice, and if it is not properly executed the rest of the process is not only meaningless, it is illegal. A beautifully executed trial with a brilliant decision, and lacking a proper joining of jurisdiction, is a miscarriage of justice. A court before doing anything else must determine absolutely that it may put this human being - this defendant - in the terrifying position of defending himself against the escalation of the monstrous machine named justice.

For hundreds of years in the common law, there was an ingenious device attaching a defendant to due process. It was a device called property. It was explicitly required in equity. If you brought allegations to court lacking the element of property, the judge would hold his hands over his ears and ask the bailiff to help you from the courtroom. As we will see, the element missing in Mrs. McNamara's complaint against her vegetating husband is property.

In its scope the device of property challenges the imagination to its utmost. It is not the narrow little concept that we have been led to believe. It reaches into the deepest recesses of the human soul, at least to the degree that souls engage the universe of mortal existence. The true task of equity through the ages has been to discover the ultimate delicate matter to which the term property can be attached, and it is our task to rediscover that thread of thought. We may begin very humbly by conceiving property not as something to own but as a legal device providing a basis for court action; its function - to establish jurisdiction. One might say accurately that if Black is having an unwanted effect in Green's property, Black may be coupled to a court's jurisdiction. A complaint in court will trigger the attachment.

From its pivotal position in the legal system, we may infer that property is important not only to the parties in a controversy but to the government as well. This we learn from the government's determination not to intervene in a conflict unless it detects the scent of property in the case. At least this was government policy until **ex parte Warfield.**

With Warfield sentenced to jail, his appeal lay in a higher Texas court - the Court of Criminal Appeal, Judge Henderson presiding. Warfield was claiming that Judge Morgan of the lower court had violated "the constitution and the fundamental law of the land", restraining Warfield's "freedom of speech and of locomotion" and his rights "in the pursuit of happiness". Furthermore, Warfield claimed, the court should not even have heard the case. It lacked jurisdiction; no property was involved.

After reviewing the case, Judge Henderson upheld the rulings of Judge Morgan's court. After all, said Henderson, there are such things as personal rights. Surely personal rights deserved a protection equal to that of property rights, and it was time to recognize it.

This statement tells us that Henderson had the narrow under-standing of property. True, his conception of property included more than merely physical things; it included contracts - certain kinds of promises constitute property. He even went further and included marri-age contracts in the idea of property - and a marriage contract is certainly not open to purchase and sale. But he was inexplicably uncertain and ambivalent in this area.

His logic is so confused that a complete critique of his published opinion is beyond the compass of this book. Though he seemingly opened a welcome valve for the flood of civil rights a half-century yet to come, he at the same time prepared the morass in which civil rights would ultimately founder. Unerringly following the precious vein of the common law, he at the same time prepared an acid capable of dissolving the common law. Though his decision exemplified the pure instinct for the common law, his reasoning was tragic.

With a fallaciously limited concept of property, he dismissed the requirement of property as a prerequisite for putting Warfield under his jurisdiction. He proclaimed the dawn of personal rights as a device sufficient for establishing jurisdiction. Yet in **ex parte Warfield** Hen-derson's machinery of justice was firmly grounded in property, and he knew it.

I suppose we must not put too much blame on the judge personally. He was only human; he was subject to the arguments of counsel; and he was immersed in an equity-wide tidal wave of "personal rights". He himself discussed the development at length.

"Formerly," (I extract from his words) "it seemed to be the rule that courts would only interfere where some property right was involved; but now it seems the writ of injunction will be applied to innumerable cases in which really no property right is involved. While the courts appear to adhere to the old rule, yet when we look at the case it is difficult to see any question of property right. We see a vain attempt on the part of the court to adhere to the old doctrine, while it reaches out for the protection of some personal right."

These were not new commentaries. He was but restating a rising tide of opinions on the topic. The drift of juristic thinking was this: to get a case into equity - for engaging equity's power of injunction - attorneys were loosely tacking to the case any feature having the semblance of property. Actually, so the thinking went, the complaints involved interferences with personal matters, not property, and conjuring up a property was juristic trickery unworthy of a great legal system. These personal matters were matters of rights in their own account, and equity jurisdiction - the power of injunction - should be opened up for them independently of any association with property.

This was, as you see, an exhibition of juristic conscience of the highest order. Attorneys and judges saw human feelings and human hopes being trampled, and no remedy in the courts. No one can say that their feelings were not true to the spirit of the common law, but they were getting off course in due process. They had been caught unawares in a crosscurrent of two legalistic tides.

In one trend the courts were slowly but surely extending the privileges of property to increasingly delicate fields of human hopes and endeavors. In the second trend, the narrow layman's view of property was infecting professional ranks. The professionals were losing the inspired view of property that had been the lodestone of equity. Property was being equated with capital assets. Labor politics and the propaganda of socialism were changing human response to this magnificent word. Property was becoming something sordid and, naturally, personal matters and human aspirations seemed alien to matters of "property"; they would have to be protected as a separate class of rights.

It is completely understandable that the correct concept of property was lost as the mass production of lawyers came on line. Property now was what lawyers parceled out in contracts, wills and trusts. And when they began to oppose personal rights to property rights, they became oblivious to the gap opening up in due process. They did not see the legal chaos toward which they were tumbling.

So Henderson decided to call an end to this quibbling about property rights. Henceforth it would be sufficient for jurisdiction in equity merely to claim an injury to personal rights. The English as he noted had accomplished this twenty-five years earlier by the simple process of legislation. Now, said Henderson, without comprehending what he was saying, if a plaintiff claimed injury to his personal rights the court could restrict the personal rights of the defendant! For isn't this what he did to Warfield? And with this step Henderson marched firmly off the brink.

If there was anywhere a case inappropriate for this step, it was **ex parte Warfield.** Will Morris's case against Warfield was firmly based in property. Henderson himself commented on this point and, for that reason alone it is unaccountable that he chose this case for taking the fatal step. It is true that equity in the early days recognized only real estate as a subject of property. But equity's range of vision had widened since then, and property was recognized as existing in contracts and personal belongings, and even in a man's labor.

By the time **Warfield** appeared, the courts had long recognized that a spouse had certain properties in a marriage relationship, this intangible thing. If a married person is disabled by the act of a third person, the spouse has a case for damages. Similarly, courts had long felt justified in granting damages for alienation of affection. Affection as property! Apparently a marriage relationship was something the government felt inclined to protect. A cause for alienation of affection was sufficient to establish jurisdiction in a court of law and, seen in this light, the marriage relationship - a strictly personal territory - exactly fits the requirements of property. By such developments the genius of the common law gradually visualized property as a personal field of human potential that government is inclined to protect.

At a point in his opinion, Henderson summarized the facts of the case, the facts settling him in his decision. In this case, said he (and again I extract), "it cannot be seriously questioned that the principle object of the suit was to preserve the marital relations existing between plaintiff and his spouse as far as may be... and rehabilitate her affections. It was claimed that if defendant's course of conduct was suffered to continue, the marital relations would be destroyed. Among other things, it was alleged that said defendant exercised an undue influence over the wife of plaintiff, and, if suffered to associate with her, it was very likely he would entirely corrupt and lead her astray." To do Henderson credit he had found something he felt like protecting. But he steps onto a path of non-sequiturs that reduced due process to its present state of paralysis in the field of civil rights:

"It occurs to us that the lower court consequently had the power and authority to inhibit said defendant from interfering with plaintiff's wife, and that this was no interference with defendant's inalienable rights to go where he pleased, and to pursue his own happiness in his appointed way, provided such course of conduct didn't interfere with another's right. Nor is there any inconsistency, when thus construed, between the freedom of speech and of the press (Warfield's communications with Vivia) and the sanctity of the marital relation. The law is as much bound to protect the one as the other, and, when both can be constrained in harmony, it is the duty of the courts to protect both."

With this statement Henderson shifts the common law back to the zero point predating 1066. In one sentence he proclaims Warfield's inalienable rights, and then he announces the grounds on which the court can alienate them. He reminds us that the court has a duty to protect equally the rights of both parties if they can be exercised in harmony, overlooking the fact that they need no protection if they are exercised in harmony, and mindless of the fact that he did not feel obliged to protect them equally when his protection was sought. Announcing that the court may interfere with Warfield's pursuit of happiness when Warfield's pursuit interferes with Morris's, the judge fails to explain why he was favoring Morris's pursuit of happiness over Warfield's.

We Americans feeling that court procedure should give equal protection to something, have settled on rights as things to be equally protected. Yet it is obvious in every court case that the court gives its blessing to one party and "puts the other party in a bag and sits on it." And what do we gain by asserting "personal rights"? For when the court is confronted with two sets of conflicting personal rights, it must eventually rule that one set isn't a set of rights after all. Henderson then compounds the confusion by slamming the door on property, blind to the fact that property is the legal device that government uses to give preference to one of the sets of rights. It is for this reason that in Chapter 1 I gave the following statement as the proper complaint for a suit in equity, "I have such and such a right, and it should prevail over the defendant's conflicting right." This is the appropriate issue in equity. Though my contention might invoke anathema from legalistic doctrinaires, nevertheless it is the meat of a claim in equity. Though I will wish to give it tone and substance as I proceed, it is this claim that created the office of equity. Given that a defendant's actions are clearly within her "rights", equity - not law - has jurisdiction over her, and this is the function of a claim in property. If the hearing proves the claim to be justified, then and then only does due process place the power of injunction in the hand of a court.

In real estate how easily we understand that Jimmy Jones is trespassing on Farmer Brown's land. How natural it has become for a court to find a property in land, pronouncing that Jimmy's freedom of locomotion stops at the property line. But how unnatural it seems to us moderns to declare that a marital relationship is property, not to be tampered with by others under the excuse of freedom of speech and of locomotion. So squeezed is the modern understanding of property.

True, I have not explained why the government granted the status of property to the marital relationship; this may require the rest of the book. But when, lately, has anyone demanded to be told why an acre of dirt enclosed by a fence has been given the status of property? We may well ask why we feel a person's relationship to land more sacred than his relationship to his wife. Here we are confronted by some unknown standard of justice awaiting discovery and justification.

So the first thing that Judge Henderson did in declaring his freedom from property was to arbitrarily give the status of property to a particular set of personal rights. He said they sufficed to give his court jurisdiction over Warfield. In this novel action he was fortunate in picking marital rights as his test case.

One wonders what he would have done if brother Warfield had brought the suit, complaining that Morris was tearing up his letters to Vivia and interrupting his luncheons with her and disturbing their strolls through the park. Would such a complaint have sufficed to give the court jurisdiction over Morris? In stripping equity of the property requirement, Henderson stood on safe ground in this particular case. He merely invited his professional descendants to jump off the cliff when "personal rights" next appeared in court.

The fact that we live in a world of moral relativity is the oldest fact in the realm of man, and it does not let courts live in a world without property. They cannot escape the most obvious fact of their operations, that when they grant dominance to one party, they subscribe the oppression of the other. What I will soon begin to demonstrate is that the court's grant of dominance is accurately a grant of property, and a guarantee of liberty within that property. Basically the question is not whether property is required to establish jurisdiction in equity. It is whether equity's grant of property will be arbitrary or in accord with a justifiable standard of justice. This shows us the direction of our task.

Perhaps we can define property so it will be generally useful in resolving conflict, else we must find a more acceptable term. Then from our universe of observation we will derive the general principles guiding courts consciously or unconsciously to their grants of rights and dominance. As I will define them, these principles will constitute the standard of justice of the common law. Finally and most important, we must justify the standard.

CHAPTER 6

INTRODUCING LIBERTY, SERVITUDE, SERVICE

If the common law is an immense embroidered tapestry, partially finished, the tough fabric supporting the elaborate stitching is woven from the early law of landed estates. And the common law of the future, unless Camelot is indeed dead, will continue to be threaded on this basic stuff. Once conceived, this basic set of principles defined liberty in the mightily contested subject matter of land and, as I will laboriously demonstrate in the book, this basic set proves to have all the elements required for projecting liberty into the sublimest regions of human desire.

With the common law rooted in land disputes, there was a time when the word rights was attached only to land. In the beginning only the nobility had rights; only the nobility held land. And recall that our legal heritage starts in the year 1066, with William and his Normans possessing England by force of arms, reducing the islanders literally to slavery. The conquered polyglot islanders were as hapless under the Normans as were American Indians and black slaves under white colonists in America.

The invasion complete, a kind of military code sufficed for law. We assume it was well-suited to the times, knowing the talents of William and his staff. Though English soil and English people were spoils of victory, there was no wild grabbing of the spoils. Soil and people were distributed under strictest feudal control. In Normandy the foot soldier had been summoned to arms as a vassal in the service of his master, his master in turn as vassal to a greater noble. In this manner had the Norman army been gathered, military rank matching feudal rank, feudalism at its best, for in William it had commander-in-chief with lofty purpose and unmatched leadership. Even before the expedition he was in organization and anticipation a powerful monarch, having already gathered for the project a skilled administrative staff, mostly clerics of the church, enthused with plans (practical ones) for a new day and a new realm.

How natural to distribute island and islander according to rank, according to military rank or feudal title; it was all the same. And this is the place to note the essential difference between holding a title to land as we now do, and holding a title to land under fee as then they did. Though today we might say we own land in fee, meaning we may (with certain restrictions and restraints) use it and transfer it as we wish, this is not what fee meant in feudal times. Today's title to land has no connection with the function of ruling. A landholder has no commission to rule. But in Norman-controlled England, the title to land carried with it a responsibility to govern the people who lived there. To grant a title to land under feudalism was to confer a title of nobility. Not only was it a commission to collect taxes for the granting lord, it was a grant of jurisdiction with power to adjudicate the disputes of the lesser nobility and the rank and file of the armed men. English slaves and their troubles were left to their immediate Norman masters, subject to the master's rules and peculiarities. The law was not common to all people.

Thus the distribution of spoils under William constituted a structuring of government, just as a grant of a military commission links the chain of command. William of course was the supreme authority, granting the great counties and jurisdictions, the greatest titles of nobility, assessing taxes from his grantees according to their tax base and according to his needs, and requiring their armed support from time to time. Naturally his own seat of power became the supreme court, himself the chief adjudicator among the great princes.

At the broad base of power were the Norman foot soldiers, remaining armed; and their booty was what they could seize from the conquered. No early law protected the personal effects of the slaves. Stripping the English was, under the circumstances, due process.

True to human nature, the challenge and thrill of the conquering campaign unified the invading army. And now with the goal achieved, with soldiers clustered close to castles of liege lords, human nature asserted itself in other ways. Disputes erupted within the ranks from top to bottom. Barons once eagerly pledging allegiance to the king formed factions challenging the king. It is a practical truism that the survival of a nation is the quintessential concern of a king, peculiar to him alone. His grand army and wealth derive from the system as a whole. But the position of baron or lesser noble tends to split the national structure, particularly when frontier and opportunity are limited. In this situation, wealth increases only by acquiring a neighbor's territory, and it was a natural consequence of island feudalism that land became the chief topic of conflict and the most substantial field for the development of law.

But law is hobbled unless backed by irresistible force, and in feudal England, a king had to gather enough baronial support to give him the balance of power. For a baron to adhere to a monarch, a rare baronic mentality is required. Such a baron must subordinate private interest to a common interest, and nature does not always provide enough such minds to guarantee a balance of power. So it is understandable that the mix and blend of Norman barons and kings varied from generation to generation, and accordingly the power of law in England waxed and waned.

Today in America we live under an all-powerful regime, and we might not realize how valuable this is to us. When for example we buy a piece of land we get a grant of title not fully appreciated. Under the umbrella of title, we actually receive grants of several titles: a title to sell the land if we wish, to bequeath it to whom we wish, to use it as we wish in any lawful pursuit, to rent it to whom we wish. And the sheriff and the court will help us turn back the intrusion of an outsider. But in feudal England a piece of land was held only for life by a vassal. At his death it reverted to his lord. Only with time did lords begin to grant titles to dispose land as vassals wished.

Even stranger to the modern mind, an early title to a piece of land might be a title of "entry and possession". Impressive yes, but a vassal receiving the grant might have to use his own army to evict a tenant already there. Such a title, one might say, was a title of aggression, with the understanding that the overlord would look the other way while the battle was raging. Nor did the title to enter and possess necessarily mean that the grantor would help the vassal fend off future attackers. In fact all such helpful favors depended greatly on the grantor's power at the time.

So, for periods of time and situations when the overlord was weak, I would have to modify my definition of justice. In such periods justice was merely the process of determining and declaring titles. A judgment was not backed by irresistable power.

A remnant of the civil law of the Romans, **jus** (plural **jura**) was the Latin term for title. As you can see, the term justice in its verbal roots signified a decision in title. Developed by brilliant minds, the civil law has long recognized the different kinds of title that we under the common law tend to bundle into one. Thus **jus intrandi** was a title to enter; **jus percipiendi** the title to take possession; **jus habendi** the title to keep possession; and **jus disponendi** the title to dispose of real estate as the title holder wished.

It was only when a vassal acquired the jura of habendi and disponendi that the land could be conceived as his very own, and indeed the root meaning of property is **one's very own.** So property as a word could not have borne much significance until sovereigns began to grant this joint title. It was not an easy step for sovereigns to take, but when they did, a title to land began to look more like a title of property. But a title of property was not yet a grant of liberty. Liberty in land does not become a reality until the protecting power is invincible. Your use of the land, though you hold title, can be frustrated by the intrusions of another; especially if the granting protector can't stop the intruder. So, though you hold title, you might not be completely free to enjoy it.

As we find the Norman lord becoming more powerful (and at the same time more English), we find him issuing a writ of right. And with this document a person dispossessed of land could secure the help of his lord's armed agents to get it back. The appearance of writs of right then was evidence that the government was ready to guarantee a person's liberty in her property. This was the declaration of liberty in its fundamental form. Liberty, within the confines of the common law, means frictionless facility within your property. Given a few chapters, I'll refine this to your delight. Given this, all we need do in determining our liberty is to define our property; the rest follows.

Of course, human happiness depends on much more than can be measured with tape or weighed in scale. So we also recognize that the fields of property must extend far beyond the world of surveyor and engineer. Indeed, it must include the exquisite universe that is the hope and despair of psychologists. Yet I warn you in advance - and this will be the tough meat in the book - property, though approaching the ethereal, must nevertheless be concrete. Material. To preclude chaos, property must fit within the limits of an intelligent set of principles, and this becomes quite an adventure in substantive definition.

In the light of this historical note, one begins to appreciate our modern title to house and home, an awesome bundle of titles. One of them, the pleasant title of liberty in our house, is not merely a title to our use of the house; it is also a title to use the powers of government. In guaranteeing your liberty in your property, the government has placed itself under a service to defend your desires within your property. Given certain conditions, the machinery of government will be brought to bear upon an offender. By seizing jurisdiction, the government transforms an offender into a defendant, and thus by another path we meet again the function of property in the operation of due process.

Having reviewed these concepts in their embryonic form, let us rapidly skip centuries since the Norman invasion. Nobles have discovered that graciousness to English slaves brings its rewards. Spirited slaves, adequately motivated, will bear arms, repel enemies, and plow more land. The lord with loyal slaves grows richer and more powerful. Giving them title to personal belongings, protecting them from rude pillage by his foot soldiers, keeping their wives and daughters inviolate, extending due process to them in their disputes with Normans, compelling even a Norman to keep his end of a bargain with them, so, under the hand of this enlightened self-interested aristocrat, the law governing slaves and Normans starts to become common, the two strains become less distinct, all beginning to work for the common good without knowing it. By such tortuous path, slaves begin to feel part of their world to be their very own. Titles have been issued for the common man, titles not participating in the chain of governmental authority. Titles bringing jurisdiction to the aid of the titleholder - titles of property. Titles pertaining to things other than land.

At the same time the age of commercialism is at hand. Merchants have accumulated peculiar things called capital equipment, inventory, goodwill - things not directly related to land. A process of trading called credit has been intermediated into something called money, and nobles and kings have discovered that money can swell their treasuries faster than oats can, or even silver and gold. Gentry, earls and even kings find it convenient to trade some land for the credit and money of merchants and bankers. So title to land begins to separate itself from the power to rule.

Bankers and merchants, though becoming landholders, are not permitted to raise their own armies and establish their own jurisdictions to protect their wealth. So if commercialism is to bloom, adding its advantages to all parties, these key people must be protected. They must be granted certain liberties in those ephemeral things - capital equipment, inventory and good will. This means that property and due process must attach to those things as well as to land. And since commercialism needs protection in an even stranger thing - commercial agreement - titles of property and due process are attached to certain formalized agreements. Under the name of contract, property now begins to include the subject matter of promises, a truly rarefied substance.

We see titles passing not only by feudal grant but by commercial transaction, a commoner-to-commoner grant giving rise to property as though it had come from on high. Somewhere, during the long transition period, in some chamber of the lego-political mind, there must have been a slow ferment pondering the standard on which to grant property, the basis on which to seize jurisdiction. Some common logic must have been strung through the newly protected fields of human endeavor. A common standard is essential if civilized existence is not to fly apart at the seams. Something tremendous must have taken shape; the central government now all-powerful; yet liberty never greater! Property now has value - even property hard to define, like contracts and goodwill. For of what value to you is your property, if the government cannot guarantee your freedom in it?

Having brought the common law to this stage of development, let us shift the scene across the Atlantic to the United States. Here, though the common law was defiled in the southern states, at least it was stripped of the complications of feudal estates - titles of nobility. In this new setting, and bringing ourselves up to modern times let us broaden our comprehension of property, first as applied to real property. We are witnessing the beginning of Mr. John Brown's farming career;

he has purchased his farm; and we will share some of his experiences as a twentieth century landowner.

We understand that he, having title, has all the lawful uses of his farm; no one else has them unless he grants them permission. It is almost a domain; here he is king, sort of; with the help of government. Whatever legal use of it is conceivable, he has title to it. If he wishes to grow corn, he may. If he wishes to turn his land into an amusement park, he is free to do so (if zoning laws permit). Only in uses requiring license or prohibited by law is his title restricted, except that we will soon discover other limitations, hidden and intriguing, restraining his liberty in this land.

Besides the titles of possession and disposition, the title of use is one of the special functions of title under the common law. Upon purchase, the use of this land has come within Brown's property, and this is sufficient to engage the machinery of government protecting his liberty in this land.

A title to a thing of many uses, such as land, can be split into as many titles as there are uses, a splendid feature. Take Brown's meadow. A choice course for a calvacade of foxhunters, it bridges the gap between neighboring estates of confirmed hunters, and Brown's name on his mail box is hardly dry when the hunting club applies to him for a lease. An old organization, its directors experienced, their contract specifies their exclusive use of the meadow for foxhunting. Their use is limited, however, to the months of September and October, and to a term of five years. Brown himself, anticipating horsepeople galloping wildly over the whole of his farm, insists on a clause stating the boundaries of the hunting area. So, with the amount and timing of rent payments agreed, the lease is signed, and the title of September-October foxhunting for the next five years passes into the hands of the hunting club. Even Brown himself, without the club's permission, cannot hunt foxes there in those periods. But something strange has happened to Brown's property, and he learns about it in the following way.

Potato prices skyrocket in the second year of the lease, and Mrs. Brown needs expensive surgery, and it seems to Brown that planting potatoes on the meadow would produce some sorely needed cash. Realizing he can't keep the hunters off the meadow in September and October, also that potato plants and horses hooves are an unprofitable mix, Brown calculates he can harvest the potatoes before the hunt begins. Forthwith he pursues the potato-growing project, putting the last load of potatoes safely in storage on August 26. On August 27 it starts to rain, and rains for a week. Old county dwellers predict a hunt for the following weekend and they are right. Under the fence comes the fox with the hounds following. Over the fence come the hunters, and then there are flounderings in mud and sounds of anguish. It appears that a field newly dug of potatoes, rained on for a week, is not the firm sod of a meadow and, as the scene fades into history, we record sprained backs, a broken leg for a horse, a huge dry-cleaning bill and, worst of all, an expensively planned and completely spoiled weekend.

Brown the villain, facing a lawsuit threatening to eat up his potato profits, will lose the case. But why? Did the lease provide that he not plant potatoes in the meadow? Did anyone other than he have the potato growing title? In making the lease, did he relinquish anything but the foxhunting title?

The fact is he lost control of countless uses of the meadow when he signed the lease. He lost his liberty in any use interfering in any way with the hunt. Though the titles are still his, he is no longer at liberty to exercise them. He is no longer master of them. Certainly he can pasture his cows on the meadow, but only if he gets them off before the hounds appear. He can take a crop or two of hay from the field. He can use the field for anything that will not interfere with the hunt. And none of these details need be expressed in the lease.

Over a whole set of uses to which this field is naturally adapted, a peculiar cloud settles. Yes the titles are vested in Brown - no one else is entitled to the uses. But though he holds the titles, he can't exercise them. Here is a bundle of uses shelved for the duration. Not belonging to the hunting club, they are subjected to the hunting club's wishes. The titles are subserviated to what has become a dominant use. The hunting club is their master. Though the titles are vested in Brown, the uses are no longer in his property. A strange device called a servitude has settled over Brown's estate in this land.

The hunting club can truly be called master because it holds a bridle on Brown's will in all interfering uses. Indeed if a petroleum company comes to Brown with million dollar prospects for finding oil under the meadow, the two had better consult with the hunting club before starting to drill. Any agreement between them will be subject to the servitude. The hunting club is master of all interfering uses of the meadow.

It is a perfectly logical device, this servitude. For of what value is the lease to the hunters if Brown can use the meadow as he wishes, regardless of the hunt? Even if Brown himself were an avid foxhunter, not leasing the field to the hunting club but reserving it for himself and his hunting friends, he will have to make critical decisions regarding the use of the field. He will not be able to do everything he wishes with the field; one use will clash with another. This is a reality of our world. Where there exists a thing with several uses, some of them are likely to interfere with others. Consider the man needing an anchor for his early morning fishing, and the only thing at hand is his wife's sewing machine. A thing of several uses is a source of conflict not only between men, but within the mind and breast of a single man; he cannot have his cake and eat it too. A servitude, a legal device, merely reflects reality, and its penetration is beyond the comprehension of the uninitiated. A lease for picnicking will master a multi-million dollar construction project, and a common law court will not invalidate the lease on the basis of its lesser value. What the court sees is property, not the dollar value of the property, and that is that.

The term servitude is appropriate for legal use today. Frequently and erroneously it is replaced by the term easement. Sometimes a servitude is called an equitable servitude, and indeed a servitude is usually enforced by the action of a court in equity. The word equitable was added, I suppose, to distinguish servitudes from an undefined nightmare called an involuntary servitude. Of this, more later.

As a legal device, the servitude has a root in civil law and another in feudalism. In feudal times the servitude attended a compulsory personal service, covered more rigorously in the civil law under the term slavery. But we today misapprehend the meaning of the personal servitude under feudalism. We conceive of it as a state of poorly rewarded menial labor, and this conception misses the mark completely.

We know that a vassal was the servant of his lord, but we forget that his lord - unless his lord was king - was vassal and servant of a more powerful noble. Under this system, the vassal served his lord in specific ways. More accurately, the lord held in his servant a well-defined set of uses. Like land, a human is a thing of many uses. The use of a vassal might be that he plow a certain field every year. The use of another vassal might be that he fight mounted and in armor in behalf of his lord. The use of another vassal might be that he attend the lord's court dressed in the latest finery and educated in the latest dance step. Such uses, you see, were services, but they were not servitudes. The servitude was not the use. The servitude was not the activity under-taken in the course of service. It was the bridle held by the lord on all activities the servant might rather undertake. More to the point, it was the master's expectation, enforceable in the master's court and by the master's armed men, that the servant would restrain himself in all his uses of himself that would interfere with the master use. True, the vassal might on occasion ask his master for a leave from service but, if the master was unrelenting, the servant had but one response, "Your servant, master."

With the development of the common law and the refinement of the law of contract, the legal status of servant metamorphosed. Under the feudal system it had been a mode of limited slavery. In the mercantile age, it became a contracted service. Formerly you were placed in service by armed coercion, else happily by feudal grant and your oath of allegiance. Now you entered into service under contract or, as frequently called, indenture. If you worked without contract you were not a servant; you were a hireling. In Victorian America, our cooks and housemaids were not servants, though often called servants; they were hirelings. Not under contract, they could quit without legal prejudice if they wished.

If in eighteenth-century England or America you were truly a servant, your indenture was expressed in a written document. It stated the uses the master had of you and, just as important, the uses you had of him. His uses of you - running errands, collecting bills, working in the shop, whatever the contract provided - were balanced by your uses of him - providing you with room, food and clothing, and sometimes medical expenses. And if you were an apprentice, you had a very important use of him - he had a contractual duty to teach you the skills and secrets of the craft. This was his service to you.

In whatever words the indenture was expressed, prospective master and servant granted uses in themselves to the other, and each use was attended by its flock of servitudes, unexpressed. Inebriation or laziness in a servant interfered with the master's use in the servant. It did not invite dismissal; it constituted breach of contract. And if the master complained in court, the court could jerk the bridle of servitude 'til it hurt. Since the servant had little or no money with which to pay fines, the whip was usual. Nor could the master neglect to teach his craft to the pupil, for the servant could also complain in court. A master could be fined or flogged for not performing his service. We, inclined to pity the plight of the indentured servant, might find that indentures were most difficult, as are modern contracts and criminal laws, on those most disposed to break them.

Vestiges of service, part feudal, part contractual, linger today in many countries. An American woman living abroad is irritated, or amused, by the downstairs maid who refuses to help her with her hair. The American industrialist is disgusted in third world countries when a man hired to turn a valve refuses to push a button. These are relics of earlier times when mistresses and masters held limited and well-defined uses of their servants. To all other uses of the servants, the servants themselves were entitled. In those spheres of activity they were free, and nothing but their services could interfere with their liberties in themselves.

It is worth repeating that a servitude is not the use of the thing - the man for labor, or the land for a golf course. A use, be it the use of a thing or the service of a person, contributes to the pursuit of the user; its function is positive. Conversely, a servitude is negative, restraining a person in a pursuit. As the civil law still teaches: **servitus in faciendo consistere non potest.** A servitude cannot consist of doing.

This is a highly significant distinction, and we will discover that servitudes are magnificent devices for making fine delineations of property. Note, in the case of John Brown's meadow, that his title in his land is not sufficient to define his property. On a gross scale, his title indicates that he can use the meadow as he wishes. But the zoning ordinance is there ahead of him. It takes particular titles of use away from him. It provides restrictions on titles, defining property on a finer scale. And the servitudes created by the foxhunting lease, superimposed on his titles like etching on crystal, create innumerable restraints on his liberty, defining his property on a still finer scale. In fact each of us, before we can spell out our liberty, must become familiar with our particular burden of restrictions and servitudes.

To update the concept of commercial servitudes, observe that the modern contract grants uses and creates servitudes. The contractor who agrees to build your house grants you a use of himself, and we call it performance. A concert singer under contract to a manager-agent has probably granted him the exclusive use of herself for singing in concert, and he in turn sublets this use to specific theaters. And if she attains her best voice when her weight is over 125 pounds, and her best figure when her weight is below 135, he might insist on a contract restricting her to a weight between 125 and 135. She, widely admired as an artist, is nevertheless a servant.

In the case of the human thing, it is difficult for us to distinguish the servitudes that attend the modern contract. Certainly if our singer is scheduled to sing in Los Angeles at 8 PM, she will interfere with her performance by enjoying the Riviera at that time. But if the manager feels like suing her for his losses, he will tend to bring an action under breach of contract, not breach of servitude. Humans can use themselves, and my use of myself in a particular pursuit will frequently interfere with another person's use of me in another pursuit. So when it comes to the use of humans, breach of service and breach of servitude are often the two sides of a single coin.

There is a tendency today in American law to abandon the device of servitudes. Even the English have not been at ease with the term. Certainly the operation of a servitude is not easy to express. The land now occupied by the State of California, having once been under the rule of Mexico, retains some vestiges of the civil law. Try understanding section 806 of the California Civil Code, the only section approaching a definition of servitude, in a brief outburst of sections on servitudes in land: "The extent of a servitude is determined by the terms of the grant, or the nature of the enjoyment by which it was acquired." And if you look up servitudes in a legal dictionary, you will likely find some mutterings about slavery or easements.

In spite of the esoteric and clumsy expression of servitudes in England and America, I have concluded that we cannot divorce the common law from servitudes. Servitudes are phenomenal; very strange; very real. It is worth noting. In a contractual situation, the granted use of oneself or one's thing often is not the source of the greatest anguish. It is the sacrifice of other pursuits, the crowd of invisible servitudes accompanying the grant, that grate the nerves.

To reinforce the meanings of service and servitude, to prepare for what follows, I will conclude this chapter with a miscellany of remarks.

I can think of very few services in the United States today analogous to feudal service, and they are services required by government. There was a time when all able-bodied men could be called out to work on bridges and highways. But now, in the age of asphalt and expensive road machinery, this service has been transformed into an activity called "paying highway taxes". Military service under a draft system is an enforced service, and contemporary enforced services most familiar to civilians are jury duty and the duty to serve as witness.

If it is difficult to describe the effect of servitude upon property, the effect of service is more difficult yet. It is obvious that an enforced service is a material restriction upon liberty. You cannot go freely to a movie at 9 PM if you have been assigned to guard duty for that time. And you cannot go fishing on Monday morning with impunity, if you have been selected to serve on a jury that day. There is no doubt that a service is accompanied by a horde of servitudes.

A year or two ago, a branch of the woman's liberation movement claimed for women a right to be drafted into military service. Those very words were used. If we note that a right is attached to a liberty, and a service is a restriction upon liberty, we hear this group claiming a right to be restricted in their liberty. But of late I have not been hearing this claim.

CHAPTER 7

STARTING TO GENERALIZE PROPERTY

In the preceding chapter, a path became apparent ascending to a general concept of property. Liberty was found to be what a person legally might do within the universe of things. Based on our titles, our liberty is always less than our titles suggest. It is diminished by legal contrivances called servitudes, and occasionally pinched by government-imposed duties. From these beginnings I now must develop the idea of property, exalting it beyond the modern cramped concept of property, for only within our property do we find our freedom protected under law.

There are three modes of freedom; first, the freedom we dream of, a freedom somewhat removed from the world of real facts. Second, the freedom we have, a set of facts sternly set in reality; and third, the kind created by law, the product of all the government activity in which we are immersed. Varying from person to person and changing from day to day, each mode of freedom - freedom dreams, freedom facts, and legal freedom - will play a role in the topic matter called liberty.

We Americans are freedom conscious, we have an urge for it, always wishing more than we have, and, in trying to rationalize it, we usually decide that our urge originates in natural primordial desire. "I want that orange; I want your diamond ring; I want to fly." But delving deeper one learns that desire solely of itself will not generate an urge for freedom. There is a second prerequisite - the existence of more than one human being. There must be at least two. And this circumstance changes a monistic urge into a dualistic one, thus, "I want to fly, and I want you off my back." It takes both desire and human interference to generate an urge for freedom.

Politicians, not always happy to be surrounded with popular freedom urges, have from age to age tried to divert simple desires into compound desires. They teach people to say, "I want to fly, because..," as though desire is grounded in reason.

"I wish to be pure, because my body is the temple of Zeus."

"I wish to raise my child permissively, because I wish to her to be creative."

"I wish for capital to be invested in the state, because I wish an end to the struggle between capital and human welfare."

"I will give up a life of pleasure, because I wish Sparta to be strong."

And so history gives us fleeting glimpses of puritanism, liberalism, socialism, stoicism.... as a basis for government philosophy and rule.

But in reality, desire does not rise from reason; rather reason (so-called) rises from desire. Benjamin Franklin notes this in his autobiography when as a reasonable vegetarian he rationalizes a tasty bit of fish now and again. And rulers, their system of compound desires faltering, eventually change the because clause into an echo clause; "I want that orange because I want that orange," announcing that desire is sufficient unto itself, as though discovering something new. Rarely, however, do they promote hedonism.

Rather they adopt for the nation the Epicurean formula; "Choose pleasures leading to a rational existence; renounce desires leading to a degradation of life." With this we find ourselves still embedded in stoicism, puritanism, socialism. Whatever the tinsel, our ruler is really saying, "I wish you to wish what I wish you to wish," and obviously we witness a silent defection from the ranks. Humans have their own notions of what they wish to desire. Yes, stoicism, puritanism, and socialism are magnificent personal enterprises, but as public projects they always create more political difficulties than they cure.

Brilliantly, without fanfare, the common law solves the problem of what to do with human desire. It establishes a perfect non-idealistic interface between government goals and human desire. The canon of the common law is to be reached only at the most profound level, and so we begin a many chaptered journey, reaching our goal only by attaining a full understanding of what seems at first the aesthetically ugliest topic. Property. We start now to expand our concept of property. There is no other path if we are to comprehend the architecture of the common law. Liberty - liberty under the common law - depends one hundred percent on property.

All the things you dream of, all the projects you might wish to undertake, can be imagined as a space. Imagine an endless suite of rooms, or an underground maze of caverns, or imagine an abstract freeform space curving and twisting in three dimensions, and in this space you wander where you will, when you will. Call it your imaginary project space, and now imagine a second space within it, twisting and curling through it like a long balloon.

In reality you live confined within this inner space, and in it are included only those projects of your imagination that you can undertake with some hope of success. Its walls fragile, these balloon walls, you can push them out here, enlarging your free space, while other people lean against them there and push them in, pinching you into an even smaller space. Flexible, the walls shift continuously, while restraining you like steel. To give this space a name, I will call it your freedom space, without defining it further, and I will not burden it with notions of lawfulness. It is simply the space where you can do what you wish when you wish, and now let us speculate on its dimensions and contents.

If you wish freedom to mean you can do anything you wish, accomplish any dream, then the walls of your freedom space expand to meet the walls of your imaginary project space, and as a thoughtful person you see the absurdity of this. Never will the inner space coincide with the outer. Though you settle in an island paradise, climbing to absolute dominance in your wild kingdom, you will always meet frustration in attempting to make the real world fit your dream world. Endlessly in the real world one finds it necessary to make unwelcome choices, sacrificing good things to obtain other good things, and embracing bad things as a means of diverting other bad things.

The American government constantly reminds us of its wish to secure our freedom, and such promises would be idiotic if the government identified our freedom space with our imaginary project space. And we would be fools to maneuver our government into making such promises. It is reasonable that a legal freedom space reaches out decently in certain directions, pinching back tight in others. Nor can I expect my legal freedom space to equal my completely selfish freedom space, the space of all projects I can undertake, irrespective of what I do to other people. Only the pampered elite of high-rolling tyrants can expect this. But this legal freedom space that we ordinary folk have, this freedom space engineered by government! We dearly wish to know how its outreaches have been determined, and how its inpinchings are justified. We know this much; it all began with property in land.

As England climbed out of feudalism, an anonymous group of thinker-doers uncoupled the strenuous exercise of governing from the passive status of holding a title in land. No longer did a landholder maintain a small army to protect his domain and keep the peace. Really his domain was no longer a domain, for he would not by his own strength protect his possession of it or his freedom in it. Under these circumstances, the government could no longer turn its back on a title holder struggling to maintain her possession of land and her freedom therein. Thenceforth the government must design and mobilize a machinery - due process - for settling disputes.

No longer were physical boundary lines the only topics of due process. The government found it necessary to establish boundary lines in new dimensions, more intangible, protected no less firmly than fence lines on solid turf. What were the limits of freedom for a landowner in his land, and the limits for an outsider, a non-owner. Here we are viewing liberty defined on land, a space in which a titleholder would be absolutely free, a space not land! It was a space composed of the projects the landowner could undertake in connection with his land. Could he dam a stream that ran through his land? Could he pile cow manure on his side of the fence, adjacent to his neighbor's picnic area? A space of permitted projects - this, not the land - was his property.

Moreover this space of projects would be a space from which all other people would be excluded, or something like that. Very difficult to express, like servitudes. An outsider's project, though pursued outside the bounds of the land, could not interfere with the landowner's liberty in her land. What an owner can do, what a non-owner can not do, rises from two sources exactly as the urge for freedom. Source one - desire; and source two - interference with desire. So legal freedom rises from two announcements by government, first a decree telling person A what he may do in his space, and, second, a decree telling all others what they may **not** do relative to what A may do. Here then developing in England was a concept of a liberty space.

Due process as it developed in England can be activated only by an issue rooted in liberty space. But liberty space can be defined only by due process. So which comes first, liberty or due process? The English as you see minted a very valuable coin with a chicken on one side and an egg on the other. But if this seems humorous, notice that chickens and eggs work perfectly.

As we begin to expand the idea of liberty space, to include quite intangible subject matter, note that the basis of expansion is simple. At bottom a dispute over land is a question whether A or B will get to act as she wishes. From the standpoint of a higher authority, it is not the land that's important, it is the desire attached to the land. The ruler holds this desire up to the candle like a jeweler separating diamonds from paste. And this is the common thread supporting the tapestry of the common law. Desire is the context in which land furnished the laboratory for designing and allotting liberty space, and it was in this context that property was conceived, real property as we call it, and in this conception lay the germ of liberty under the common law.

To practice for an expanded concept of property, it is time to start organizing certain aspects of real property already covered. For instance what do we really mean by a title? From experience we already know that a title in real property describes the physical location and boundaries of the land. It lists the encumbrances on the land, encumbrances not really on the land but on the owner, bits of liberty space chopped from the landholders liberty space and acquired by others: easements, liens, leases, and other burdens. But as important as these aspects of title might be, equally important are the unwritten promises of government embedded in a title.

If you acquire a modern title to land, the government will:

a. help you gain possession of it if necessary; help you keep possession of it, and help restore it to you if someone else takes it or uses it against your wishes.

b. restore your legal enjoyment of this project space if the activities of another person interfere with your enjoyment.

c. transfer this government support to any person to whom you grant title in this land.

In other words, the government will protect your liberty space defined on this land, and the function of title is to lay the protective duty on the government.

You will notice first what I earlier said, that in acquiring title you are gaining the strong helping arm of government. You will notice second that these protections relate to that space in which your liberty is defined. And you will notice third that we are talking about a space that the government guarantees to be your very own, free from the interferences of all others, and we are getting very close to the idea of property.

Now concentrate for a moment on a plot of land in a wild uncivilized setting; no government. You covet it and seize it from the deer and rabbits as your very own. Having improved it, ask yourself if you will truly find freedom in using it, and the answer is yes with a very big if. You will be free in using it if you can prevent the intrusions and incursions of others. Even the act of expelling an intruder will interfere with your freedom - your freedom to do what you would rather be doing at the moment. Your freedom in the land will be relative, dependent on your strength and on the strength and cunning of lurking ravagers.

In a civilized state, a land title is worth no more than the strength of the government. The value of your estate in land rests on the dependability of your government. If by a title in land you mean your ability to maintain your freedom in the land, then in an uncivilized state your title is uncertain. If by liberty you mean a secure enjoyment of the land, you can forget liberty in an uncivilized setting. But under a strong government observing the common law, your title to land is the passport to a most rare estate of desire.

To see it more clearly, refer again to John Brown's farm. Note at the far end, over a grassy hill and down a wooded glen, a tiny bit of his land chopped off by a public highway, orphaned, too small for any project presently conceived by Brown, a corner neglected, high in weeds and collecting trash, a corner spotted by Mr. Anthony as a splendid site for a sign advertising his restaurant. Mr. Anthony contracts with a sign builder for the erection of a modest tasteful sign, and he has the weeds and trash removed, all without asking Brown. And Brown, not blind, asks Anthony to remove the sign, and remains obstinate in spite of Anthony's attempts to negotiate. In fact, says Brown, Anthony will remove the sign by May 15 or he, Brown, will cut it up for kindling. And Anthony doesn't; Brown does; and Anthony sues Brown for damages.

As you would expect, Anthony finds the government on Brown's side. Anthony has trespassed, invading a space in which Brown's wishes are supreme. It's law, pure and simple.

Actually, the sign has become part of Brown's legal free space, affixed to his land, hence real property under common law; and to proceed I will need a situation not quite so simple. Instead of a sign on posts sunk deep in the ground, I will say that Anthony's sign was fashioned on a trailer, and, as it was being trailed past Brown's corner, it accidentally uncoupled itself and positioned itself advantageously on Brown's land. Anthony is merely slow in removing it.

Under these circumstances, the sign does not become Brown's property, and though he may remedy the situation peaceably by his own actions, he is not free to harm the sign more than necessary. But if he disposes it on the shoulder of the road, he will be guilty of littering, and trucking it to Anthony's restaurant, parking it on the sidewalk, might bring the same charge. Pushing it into the restaurant might involve unpeaceable action. So if Brown has the junk man haul it away, having duly informed Anthony of his intentions, he is probably safe from any court action attempted by Anthony. With this basis, let us delve a bit into legal philosophy.

The sanctity of a title in land is so entrenched in our thinking that we instinctively deem land to be property, and we would be aghast if anyone challenged us to justify our position on this. "A man's home is his castle" is good enough for us. But there was a time when a king had to justify his protection of a property in land. In particular his arguments had to satisfy barons with a taste for the holdings of lesser folk; barons accustomed to taking what they coveted; especially barons who would challenge even the crown.

Since we are en route not only to deriving a standard of justice but ultimately justifying the standard, and since a standard of justice must be wholly justifiable to powerful and acquisitive persons if they are to submit to it, we can rehearse for this undertaking by referring to John Locke. The following words are taken selectively from his essay **Of Civil Government** and from the chapter entitled "Of Property." The parenthetical comments are mine. Realizing that Locke spoke often with two tongues, we will initially take the extracts at face value - he is writing in pure philosophical mode.

God gave the world to man in common.... He gave it to the use of the industrious and rational....

... cultivating the earth, and having dominion... are joined together. The one gave title to the other. (If one clears the land and cultivates it, he is entitled to dominate it and, if he can dominate it, he can cultivate it as he pleases.)

That was his property which could not be taken from him. (Whatever he can hold against the attempts of all others to seize -- that is the definition of property.)

The measure of property nature has well set by the extent of man's labour.... (The value a man places on a property depends on how much of himself he has invested in it.)

He who appropriates land to himself by his labour, does not lessen, but increase the stock of mankind; for the provisions produced by one acre of enclosed and cultivated land are ten times more than are yielded by an acre lying waste in common.

Read the selections again, for here in brief is my whole thesis. Not that I'm a disciple of Locke, but here in essence you have just read the philosophic rationale for guaranteeing a person's freedom in a specific project space. Does the protection of that person's freedom in that space increase the stock of mankind? That is the question. Here then is a pragmatic basis for establishing and protecting property.

Unfortunately Locke's passages also served to excuse a shameful tragic piracy engulfing England at the time, a practice called enclosure. He has been criticised for trying by verbal trickery to please opposing factions, and in this case the word commons is the villain. To an idealist, Locke seems to be using "commons" to connote the primeval wilderness, and in this sense his arguments are idealistically sound. But as Samuel Johnson's dictionary advises us, commons can have more than one meaning:

"**commons....**
"1. Belonging equally to more than one;
"2. Having no possessor or owner. **Locke;**
"4. Publick; general. **Walton, Addison.**"

Traditionally the commons in England were lands reserved for the food and wood supply of villagers, a matter of ancient custom; even the

Norman conquerers honored it. Though frequently the commons were situate on poor soil poorly cultivated, this was not always the case, and in some areas the sharing of commons reflected a high level of social organization among the "commoners."

Over the course of centuries, however, statutes inched stealthily into English law making it legal for a nobleman to claim property in common lands. He need only fence and cultivate the lands, and they were his. By this process of enclosure the commoner was gradually excluded from the commons, and that was not the full extent of the tragedy. With the passing of feudalism not only did enclosure spread like fire but bondsmen were released from the manor estates. As with the blacks freed in America after the Civil War, this comprised not only a good action - release from bondage - but a bad action - the separation of the newly freed from their source of sustenance. So Locke in his time witnessed tens of thousands cut off from their livelihood, and though his writing, seen on a high plane, explains why powerful men should grant property to productive men, more basely it gave powerful men an excuse for seizing the commons. Read the quotations from Locke again. And now we are in a position to make a distinction of tremendous significance.

Let us suppose that Brown, instead of relieving his sign problem by his own action, had petitioned the court to order Anthony to remove the sign, and Anthony defended his position thus. "Your honor, this man was neglecting the land. It was returning to the wild state. I reclaimed it from weeds and trash, and erected a tasteful sign promoting trade. My actions increased the stock of our community and benefitted the motoring public. My cause is essentially in eminent domain - a confiscation of property for the public good. On this basis I think you should order Mr. Brown to leave my sign alone, and for my part I'll agree to keep the weeds cut, the sign painted, and, in addition, I'll pay Mr. Brown a fair rent.

Lo, the same arguments used by Locke! Property should go to the rational and the productive. But this is not an absolute rule under the common law. In "Brown v. Anthony" the situation is different from the postulates set forth by Locke. The land is neither commons nor wilderness. We are looking at lands to which Brown holds title. Protecting his use and his possession and his right of disposal is a function to which government is pledged under the common law. We are looking at lands in which someone has already invested a great amount of himself. This is **presumed** upon a showing of title. On a certificate of title there is no small print stating: "the government may transfer this title to any person whose use for it has greater economic (or ideologic) (or popular) appeal." Here you see the true meaning of private property. Here you can see a true distinction between the common law and socialistic (or even democratic) law.

Not that Anthony's argument lacks persuasiveness. Eminent domain frequently has been asserted on thinner grounds. Many a court has given many a Mr. Anthony free space, taking it away from the owner, on arguments just as plausible. But in principle here is a dike held by common law judges against violent seas through the ages. And why? Why protect a weed producer against an energetic entrepreneur. Ah why indeed! When you know the reason, you will know the secret of the common law.

The dike was apparently breached in 1968 by **Jones v. Alfred H. Mayers Co.** Eventually with great travail I will show it to be a true common law decision. Unfortunately the jurists involved didn't know why it was a correct decision, and it has been a source of confusion ever since.

In **Jones** a black family was able to force a real estate company to sell them a home in its new subdivision. Freedom of disposing private property. Breached. Yes, this part of the company's free space was surgically removed, but there's an important difference between **Jones** and "Brown v. Anthony", and I assure you I will not neglect the issue. Meanwhile we have reached a vantage point from which to view a significant aspect of property.

If in "Brown v. Anthony" we stipulate that Brown's land is in Brown's property - that Anthony is intruding - we observe here a space of desire where Brown's wishes are beyond challenge, a space that is not the land but rather all the things Brown may do with the land under law and equity. Even his complete neglect of the land is absolutely respected.

If property is viewed in this light, you see here the potential for extending the idea of property into areas of human life far beyond mere physical assets. Property is not something you can put your finger on; it is not tangible. It's a matter of desire and will - **volo.** It's a space of desire in which complete liberty is assigned to an individual; a space where her **volo** is not to be burdened by an intruding **volo.** A person's property is her absolute freedom space under the common law. But her liberty? Her liberty consists of a waiting, powerful, frowning government guaranteeing that her wishes in her free space will not be oppressed by the will of another. The government will bridle an intruding volo if the intruder won't bridle herself.

In our experience we often find two parties pursuing projects within their entitled spaces, and at some point the spaces will intersect each other and the pursuits will interfere with each other. So whose volo will dominate? This is the fundamental case for equity and, when equity makes its decision, the will of the favored party will be allowed to penetrate and master a space otherwise considered to be in the legal freedom space of the disfavored party. What one considers one's liberty space, we learn, is not necessarily one's liberty space - unless one is thinking in terms of the fundamental rules determining liberty space; the standard of justice as perceived in equity.

We know that Farmer Brown's volo is not completely unleashed on his land. Zoning ordinances restrict the reach of his titles, and his fox-hunting servitudes restrain him even within his entitled space, and as we proceed we'll find even stranger bridles on his will. So the land is not his property, and even his titles fail to define his property. His liberty space is smaller than his entitled project space. Government when given good reason will allow other wills to penetrate and dominate portions of his entitled space. If government grants this property holder absolute freedom within this space called property, you can see that the bounds of property must be drawn with great discrimination. The result of a decision in equity is a determination of property - a declaration of exact liberty space - given particular circumstances.

If someone is intruding into the legal freedom space of your desire, (your property generalized - not just in land) the government will exert the force necessary to evict her. First you must show she is exerting an effect within your entitled space. Then the actual eviction materializes through a court order, and, if necessary, a task force. Government in its operation has built a machine actually creating something in the real world, and what it creates is liberty. Relieving oppression within an exact legal freedom space is the business of a court. And this overall operation is called due process.

This is the appropriate place for commenting on the difference between legal freedom and material freedom. We recognize that a burglar in a sleeping household has a material freedom in the contents of the house. Similarly two gangland chiefs may enjoy a material freedom in their respective territories, even approaching legal freedom to the degree they control the government. Perhaps they can deal in drugs as they wish within their territories, even agreeing to split the drug traffic between themselves. However, if one of them invades the territory of the other, the "injured" party cannot catch the attention of a court. He cannot engage the jurisdiction of a court to enforce the "contract"; drug traffic isn't in his legal free space. So while the practice of grabbing freedom space outside the bounds of liberty space sometimes seems to expand a person's material free space, it may actually restrict it.

The Venn diagram of figure 7:1 gives an idea of the various modes of freedom spaces and their relation to one another.

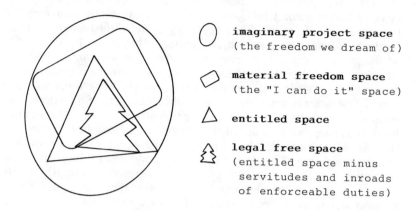

imaginary project space
(the freedom we dream of)

material freedom space
(the "I can do it" space)

entitled space

legal free space
(entitled space minus
servitudes and inroads
of enforceable duties)

Figure 7:1   Relationships Of Various Freedom Spaces

Notice in Figure 7.1 that a portion of your entitled space and legal free space lies outside your material freedom space - beyond your personal capacities. Is this part of your legal project space immaterial to you - worthless as far as you are concerned? No, another important distinction can be made between our "I can do it" space and our legal free space. It has important consequences in court and heightens our respect for our legal freedom.

Imagine for example that you own and live in a two-story house. You, confined to a wheelchair and living alone, cannot use the stairs and, since no one wishes to rent the upper level, it is vacant and unfurnished.

You have no use for it and, as long as you inhabit the house, you have no disposal for it. You have no material freedom in the upper floor. This, however, does not mean your neighbor may mount a ladder from her land to your upper window and camp on your second floor. At your complaint, the government will evict her. She cannot use your incapacity to use it as an argument for her freedom to use it. The government guarantees the free operation of your will not merely in your legal "I can do it" space but in your entire legal free space. This policy not only guarantees our contentment in our space, it is the basis of our economic system. Your neighbor must pay you rent if she wishes to use (with your consent) your upper floor. Never let us unfavorably compare our legal free space under the common law with nature's "I can do it" freedom.

With this elementary analysis of property behind us, perhaps we can give Justinian and John Quincy Adams a more exact terminology for their definition of justice. "Justice," they said, is "the perpetual will to secure to everyone his own right." "Justice," they might have said, "is an assignment of legal freedom space, and the securing of freedom therein." Note, this new definition includes not just the official task of protecting a person's legal freedom space, but the work of defining the space. The latter is precisely the work of creating law. So Justinian and Adams were correct if the word justice is restricted solely to protecting legal free space, without including the work of creating law, and indeed this is the legalistic meaning of justice. This would be appropriate in a government where all law is the result of legislation. Perhaps this was the situation in Rome. But in the English-American system, where the framework of law is constucted of case decisions in equity (even legislation may be tested in equity), I think we may not say the word justice applies only to the protection of rights. If we were to limit ourselves to this definition, we would have to say that the work of equity is not justice.

Sadly, by becoming more definite in our understanding of freedom, we have not escaped the difficulty that we found in the word right. In either definition of justice we leave much unresolved. Not only the common law but every system of law determines legal free space. In a system of law, the legal free space of the governed may be intelligently expanded and extended, or it may be miserably restricted under tyranny or a slave code. In any case, supposing that the "will to secure to each person his right" is in force, it is the legal free space, not the material freedom therein, that is restrictive. It is no star in the crown of a tyrant that, having codified a stingy free space for his subjects, he lends his perpetual will to securing their freedom in that space.

Therefore it is legal freedom space - property - under the common law, that requires our initial attention; freedom follows. Our task is to discover the principles determining property - legal freedom space - particularly at the junctures where clash the project spaces of two or more individuals.

CHAPTER 8

BASIC ENGLISH, BASIC MECHANICS, BASIC QUESTIONS

As a professional field develops, and especially if it develops over a period of centuries, new ideas diverge from old concepts and demand expression, and, as often as not, some of the old words and phrases will be applied indiscriminately to the new concepts. The old concepts are orphaned, left without a means of expression. The words formerly used to express them are now attached to different ideas.

Oncoming youth dutifully learn the technical terms of the profession without always grasping their various historic meanings. The terminology of a discipline seemingly unchanged for centuries, undergoes a continuous unseen flux. As a result, two individuals from diverging schools of thought will debate a point, both using the same key words and phrases, and each will misunderstand the import of the other.

You are perhaps familiar with the difficulties in defining freedom and liberty. Even in professional practice, judges will differ on such highly technical terms as property and servitude, and will misuse two of the most exacting terms in law - injury and damage. Yet justice itself depends on the pregnant content of these words.

Lawyers casually use the word civil to connote several distinctly different ideas. Civil law, the most widely used system of law on earth, differs significantly from the common law. Yet the common law provides a class of lawsuit called a **civil** action, and it has nothing to do with the civil law. Moreover the word civil has been joined in America to the word right, suggesting that perhaps a civil right is different from other rights.

Aside from such professional ambiguity, the adjective **civil** has a secure spot in the lay vocabulary, being frequently applied to a person who behaves intelligently in stressful human-to-human situations. If this usage is rooted in the civil law, perhaps its counterpart in the common law is common decency. And, by mixing lay and professional terminologies, we might describe civilization as a rulerly project teaching men to behave in a civil manner. Perhaps then a civil action in the common law is a teaching device in the civilization process.

Tolerant as we might be with legal terminology, we nevertheless will not make progress without defining a few basic words. For the moment, moreover, it will be profitable to put aside the more heavily loaded language of the law, and cultivate a vocabulary hardly even legal, a few everyday words expressing our ordinary physical and mental activities, and it will be greatly to our advantage to define these precious words in a powerfully general sense.

For instance I will use the word "project" thus, that everything we do is related to a project. Taking a short-cut across someone's lawn is as much a project as building a dam. Even the operation of a legal system is evidence that the government has a project in mind. And if a person is stretched out in a hammock, eyes closed, mind vacant, she is pursuing a project.

In Chapter 13, project will be defined by defining the elements of projects. Until then, an intuitive feel for the idea of projects will suffice. Like points and lines in geometry, projects don't exist except in the mind. A dam finished is no longer a project. It's a dam. And though we might say while building a dam that we're engaged in a project, it would be more accurate to say we're **pursuing** a project.

Similarly, though one might call Jack a project engineer, one should not call Jim a project executive. One should not, that is, if by execution we mean a satisfactory materialization of the thing in the mind. On occasion the building of a projected dam is stopped with the dam half-complete. The projected flight of a golf ball over a pond sometimes ends with a splash. So to say a project is being executed only invites executive embarrassment. Well. Recognizing this, perhaps we may continue calling Jim a project executive.

The person stretched out in a hammock is a weary commuter at the end of a long week. Later hopefully she will be a recreated person, though more sunburned on one side than expected. If, while she is trying to relax, the young people next door tune their stereo at blast volume, she might go to work Monday not a new person but a miserable wreck. Which is to say there are projects, and pursuits of projects, and then there are the results. Sometimes, in analyzing the events leading to lawsuits, these are essential distinctions.

Then there's the word "thing", one of the most general things in our vocabulary, and I will generalize it to the utmost. A "thing", I will say, is a concept that can be functionally associated with a pursuit. A thing is a concept capable of being functional in a pursuit.

This is an immense generalization, and my use of the word

"concept" requires explaining; I'm stretching it to cover not only purely mental ideas but also what we call physical objects. Let me show this to be both logical and practical.

If grinding corn is my project, I know where I can find an undulant expanse of bedrock, smooth enough to walk on and pockmarked here and there with bowl-like depressions. Nearby I can also find stones shaped like cucumbers, useful as pestles. Putting the corn in one of the depressions and pounding it with my pestle I will pursue my project or, as one might say, I will use the rocks to grind my corn.

More abstractly I could say I'm using certain characteristics of the rocks - their size, their shapes, their hardness; I'm using the grasping power of my hand and the swinging power of my arm - to grind the corn. This is reasonable because at this very spot I can also find pieces of pumice, a light porous rock that actually floats, and if I should try to use this rock in my pursuit, the result would be not pulverized corn, but pulverized pumice. So while the word rock smacks of something natural and mineral, it covers an infinite number of concepts - real things with a wide variety of sizes and shapes, and a long list of colors, hardnesses, densities....

Looking at my beater stone, greyish, cucumber-shaped, with finely crystalline surface, very hard, we conceive of it as a solid thing. But if you listen to a physicist describing what it really is, you will wonder what kind of world you are living in. You will learn that the rock consists more of space than anything else. Actually it has no color. Rather it is composed of space vibrations interpreted by our optical system as color, and by our hands as something hard and solid.

Certain physical things can pass through this thing as though it didn't exist, and the only reason it exists to our touch is that our hands are made of a similarly vibrating space tending to exclude this vibrating space we call rock. What we think of as a grey hard rock is something entirely different. And our mental concept of it is more related to how that vibrating space affects us, or how we can use it, than to more fundamental characteristics.

Now true, this is a mental concept with a source outside the mind. The thing that crushes the corn is not the "thing-in-the-mind" but the "thing-of-itself", a concept by which we characterize a particular location in space. An object! So why not use the word object to define the word thing? Well, when we try to define "object", a "thing-of-itself", it's hard to do without using the word thing. And the word thing is exactly what we're trying to define! Looking up "object" in the dictionary, we find it to be (1) some**thing** that exists, or (2) some**thing** capable of being seen, touched, or otherwise sensed, or (3) some**thing** physical or mental of which a subject is cognitively aware. So if we define a thing as an object and an object as some thing, we haven't defined anything.

But we can say that things-of-themselves interact, and concepts that don't interact aren't things-of-themselves. A thing-in-my-mind won't make a pestle grind corn and, if it does, it isn't a thing-in-my-mind. If things interact, they get a "concept" of each other. This puts us on solid ground because we can't use a thing-of-itself unless it interacts with something else. In linking a thing with a project it is our concept of it that we link with the project. In pursuing a project, we inter-engage these concepts as we project their interaction and, if our concepts are accurate, our pursuits will have a best chance to produce the results we wish. If we have no concept of a thing, we can't use it. I will elaborate these ideas further in discussing the word "use".

If I seem to be leading you into an excessively abstract realm of words, think about the almost inexpressible fields of human desire we ask judges to ponder. As I will in time demonstrate, a common law judge may not admit a case, or an element of a case, unless it is material - unless it engages reality. And what we need - what he lacks - is a vocabulary with which we can express the materiality - the sheer mechanics - of a heartfelt situation of hope and despair. So let's practice with the word thing for a minute, remembering that a thing is a concept that can be associated with a pursuit - as a functional element of the pursuit.

Thus not only is a vase a thing, its color and shape are things too. An artist may use the shape of a vase in his still-life, preferring however to use the color of another vase. And he can't possibly use the vase itself in his painting, though it can be used for holding flowers.

A song sung by a shepherd is a thing, even if never written on paper, for it may be heard by others across the valley and relayed throughout the region for the enjoyment of everyone. A complex sonata never performed or noted on paper is a thing, if at night the composer hears it running through his head. A pure thing-in-the-mind, it can be used to give him pleasure in lonely hours. The notation of the music on paper is a different thing, a thing-of-itself, for it can be used by other people in association with a piano, reproducing mind-things in the brains of listeners. But if no one hears him perform the sonata, and if in despair he destroys the notation and commits suicide, the concept ceases as thing. For now no one can associate it with a pursuit, as a functional element of the pursuit. In fact, it ceases as concept.

Similarly a formula for a complex chemical is a thing; even if the inventor has just now conceived it and has not yet put it on paper. He can use the thing-in-the-mind as a model for prescription on paper. Once he has published it and it becomes subject to use by others it takes on a new character, for now it can become the subject of a lawsuit. As you might know, the Latin word **res** (re, rem) and the

French word **chose,** both meaning thing, are important terms in our own legal system. and in this connection we will learn that nothing but a thing can be the subject matter of a lawsuit. Furthermore this thing must be a thing-of-itself; it must be susceptible to the actions of more than one person. Else it cannot be a subject of conflict.

You now can see that words such as liberty, or fraternity, or equality, or "down with despots", or "hang the horsethief" are things. They can be associated functionally with the pursuit of projects. All of which brings us back to the fact that men and women, by acting to phenomenally inter-associate concepts, can produce a lot of results. And if, in all this activity, they don't really understand the phenomena taking place, at least they have a concept of what's going on, and if this concept fits their purposes they are satisfied with their world as they conceive it to be.

So we will find it fruitful to define a thing as a concept that can be functionally associated with a pursuit, remembering that the word concept covers things-of-themselves as well as things-in-the-mind. A piece of land is a thing, and so is the man who holds title, and I suppose even the title is a thing. But is the property - the legal freedom space of the owner - a thing? Can someone use this concept as a functional element of a pursuit? Yes, of course; due process has materialized this concept. A man can associate his property with an action to catch the ear of the court. A pleading lacking the element of property will not get through the front door of a courtroom. A pleading with a basis in property is already half-way through.

The court itself uses property as grounds to attach jurisdiction. Yes, property is a thing; indeed it's a well-honed device; and due process is a machinery built of such devices, interacting functionally in some mysterious project of government, part of our quest. We are looking at the marvelous creations of legal engineers. Property is a thing, and it can be used in pursuing a project in court.

This brings us to the word "use", a bridge helping to carry us from the idea of property in land to the idea of property in the farthest reaches of human aspiration. With this word I have discovered that defining a word is not the same exercise as explaining what it means. Such words as employ, utilize, and exploit will not help us understand the word use. Take the sentence, "I'll use this plow to turn over the soil." If you were to explain to me what this association involves - this functional association of things - you would have to describe the relation between the forward draft of the plow and the excised ribbon of soil; how the plow share gouges out the ribbon of soil and how the moldboard elevates it and coils it over. Even with this you will not have explained how the words "I use this plow..." are affiliated with these physical details. Or, if you wish something simpler, take the sentence, "the cat used the log to cross the brook," and explain to me exactly what the word "use" means.

Digging deeper, we find that the word use includes the idea of purpose. Purpose suggests desire, and before long the words project and pursuit come to mind. Having already threshed through the ideas of projects, pursuits, and things, we are in a better position to grasp the idea of use, thus. **To use a thing means to associate it functionally with a pursuit.** With this step, we can now condense the definition of thing, thus. **A thing is a concept that can be used.** Perhaps you may find many things wrong with this definition, but the book will give it a thorough testing.

When the hunting club members sought the use of Brown's meadow, they had a project in mind. They anticipated the use of a fox, some hounds, and some horses - all things-in-the-mind as far as the project was concerned, and things-of-themselves as far as the pursuit was concerned. That is, there existed real interactions in the real world acting pretty much in conformity with their concepts.

They would also need a hunting course to support the weight of their concepts. The meadow met this requirement, and for this reason they sought the lease. All these things, including the free space(!) - the property - were mentally associated with the design of the project. But for changing the project into reality - pursuing it - all these things had to be inter-associated functionally - phenomenally. If the project was to have a real potential, they had to conceptionalize reliably all the relationships existing among the things - the elements to be inter-associated in the pursuit. And all these ideas that I've taken so long to describe are bound up in one of the smallest verbs of the English language - to use.

Mr. Anthony had a project - to advertise his restaurant. An element of it was a painted sign - a device turning his wish into reality. But a painted wooden sign cannot hang without support in mid-air. A post is needed. And there is a well-known functional relationship between a sign, a post and solid ground, keeping the sign erect and in one place. A particular site is required, and Mr. Anthony decided to associate Mr. Brown's weedy corner with his pursuit. In other words, Mr. Anthony decided to use Brown's land to support his sign.

There was a difficulty, a difficulty one must face when considering not merely use, but legal use. To use, when we consider legal use, requires property - free space - and this was the thing that Mr. Anthony neglected to associate functionally with his pursuit.

These understandings of projects, pursuits, things and uses will supply the means of tying human activity to the legal process. With them we can elevate ourselves into rarer air by rehearsing some hypothetical examples. But first let me refer to my calling a human being a thing, not necessarily a repulsive classification. What is repulsive is the sometime **use** of the human thing. But we must admit that a human can be used in the pursuits of other humans, and therefore is no less a thing than a rock is. Humans are used sometimes legally, sometimes not, yet humans are very special things, and are given very special treatment in the common law.

Thus we picture Mr. Duckweiler using Cantona Lake for his recreation, every day swimming all the way across and back. Too good an opportunity for teenagers Dick and Bill in their daily motorboat race. They can use Duckweiler as a turning marker. Every day, when Mr. Duckweiler is about three-quarters of the way across, they roar off from the pier, give him a taste of their spray, and race home. Undoubtedly they are using him, associating him functionally with their pursuit; but if he wishes to stop them by court action he'll have to establish his position in property. (Even if there's a statute prohibiting this practice, the statute should be grounded in property.) So how do we determine the property? Is the lake in Mr. Duckweiler's free space? Is it in Dick and Bill's free space? Is their use of Mr. Duckweiler in their property? Or are they planting their sign, so to speak, on Duckweiler's land?

We also note that Miss Engel, a shapely secretary, walks to work when the weather is good, striding from the door of her apartment house promptly at seven-forty. And across the street lives Mr. Weatherby, a wholesome young man. Drinking his breakfast coffee by his window, he can use her appearance to check the accuracy of his watch, hah, hah, and Miss Engel doesn't like it. Is he using her? In pursuing his watching project, is he using something to which she holds exclusive title? Is his will - volo - invading a space where her will should reign supreme?

Then there was the unhappy experience of Andrew Wolcott. Introduced to a choice piece of country real estate, and walking over it one evening, he saw from a knoll a breath-taking view - a valley on neighboring land, a mountain beyond - all cast under the spell of a brilliant sunset. Instantly he decided to build his house on this very spot, in his mind's ear projecting the admiring murmurs of distinguished guests. Indeed in less than a year he was occupying a new three hundred thousand dollar home and settling back to enjoy his evenings and weekends.

Now the neighbor whose land formed the apron of Wolcott's view was approached by an advertising agency seeking permission to build on his land the world's largest billboard. And it was done. There it stood for all the motoring public to see, brainlessly annihilating the aesthetics of Wolcott's view. Here, you see, was a situation where the neighbor's real property was desired for two interfering uses, and we anticipate Wolcott hoping a court can be persuaded to order the billboard removed.

We ask if the view was in the legal free space of Wolcott. We ask if the neighbor's air space was in the property of Wolcott, a different question. Then we ask (thinking of Locke): Who - Wolcott or the neighbor - has the greater investment of himself in this air space? What is the relationship of this air space to the landowner; to Wolcott? What are the mechanical or physical details of the relationships? What is the quality of each relationship - the human to thing relationship. We ask if these are proper questions, or does the common law have a ready answer to this situation? For the court must determine to whose will and whim and to whose pursuit it will allot the use of the air space.

These questions we will not answer until later chapters but, to start tying some loose ends together, let us take a step farther into **ex parte Warfield**, the case described in Chapter 5. Given the circumstances of the case, we may assume that J.B. Warfield, chatting with Vivia Morris, taking her to lunch, and so on, was pursuing some sort of a project. Without knowing its particulars, I think we may say that Vivia was one of the functional elements of his pursuit. In short she was a thing, and he was using her. Predicting the eventual outcome of his activities is beyond our ability, but evidently an interim result was a partial breakdown in the Morris marital relationship.

We see Will Morris himself undertaking a multifaceted pursuit; part being to get rid of Warfield, and part being to reestablish the marital relationship between Vivia and himself. This is a rather unemotional way of expressing one of the most complex pursuits that a human being can undertake. But even in Morris's pursuit there can be no doubt; Vivia was a thing. As to those who exult in my admission that Vivia was a thing used by two men, let me remind you that, in this very special sense, both Morris and Warfield were things used by Vivia as well.

Now it so happens, as far as the lawsuit is concerned, that both Morris and Warfield are claiming their uses of Vivia to be properly in their separate and distinct free spaces. So property is at issue and the case is properly in equity. But really it would be improper for either man to claim **Vivia** as the property in question, and it is not accurate to say that each is claiming her as part of his free space. The time has come when we must be more discriminating in what we say.

Recall that a claim in property is a legal device engaging the full power of government to enforce the will of one claimant over the other. Remember that the property and the thing are not equivalents. Rather, property attaches to a person's **relationship** to a thing. Farmer Brown's land was not his property. His legal free space lay in his relationship to the land. His relationship to the land was more honored by government than Mr. Anthony's.

Other than being limited by certain ordinances and servitudes,

Brown is free to use this land as he pleases and, what's more, his pleasure in his freedom is not to be interrupted by any other will - volo - materializing in this free space. Thus a property is defined by what a person can do, and what other people cannot do, with respect to a particular thing. It is a free space for one person and a forbidden space for all others. So it is improper to say that Vivia is anyone's property, even that Vivia is **in** anyone's property. As we will learn later when we get into personal relationships, certain **uses** of Vivia are in any person's property, but only with her consent.

We start with the deceptively simple observation that Will Morris has a relationship with his wife Vivia. Initially calling it a marital relationship, we then begin to remember that every marriage involves a different relationship. There are as many variations in marital relations as there are marriages, each changing from day to day, year to year, decade to decade. So we know very little about the Will-Vivia relationship. But we know this. We know it depends on what each person has put into it, and how each responds to the other.

But Warfield also has a relationship with Vivia. Each had an input; and each has responded to the other. So at the superficial level there is little to distinguish between Vivia's two relationships. However, we can recognize a phenomenal interaction between the two relationships. As Warfield's star waxes in Vivia's sky, Morris's wanes. We may assume that Vivia is not as affectionate toward Morris as once she was. We can imagine a physical coolness. Apparently she spends many recreational moments with Warfield instead of her husband. Perhaps she even neglects the care of her house. In short, her relationship with her husband has been modified by her developing relationship with Warfield.

Now when a person pursues a project, he anticipates the relationships that will hold among all the things associated in the pursuit. His life is staked on the reliability of the relationships. If he is driving a car, he trusts that stepping on the throttle will accelerate the car. Stepping on the brake will slow it down. Imagine a contractor building a dam. He pours cement in a hole and the hole gets bigger! And the more he pours, the bigger it gets. It is a nightmare. And this is happening to Morris. When he steps on the throttle, the car slows down, and, when he pours in cement, the hole gets bigger.

For Warfield, things are rosy. Every move he makes is just what the doctor ordered. And it's not that he bears malice toward Morris; he has no feelings toward Morris. He is only interested in his own pursuits, and Morris's discomfort is purely coincidental.

We are treating Vivia as a thing, and, to the extent of one hundred percent, this is exactly how she is treated in the case report. Later we will learn to appreciate this austerity on the part of a court. But for now we may assume that the court has quietly kept an eye on her. The marriage evidently isn't dead. She still lives with Morris. We will later see that she need answer the judge only, "No. I do not love my husband. I'm no longer interested in his attentions," and the court would wash Morris's claim of property off its hands.

Then how in the world can a court make a decision between two parties each claiming free space in a relationship with a thing? It can do so only if the decision fits the project of government, and this is what the assignment of property is all about. The answer is in Locke: "The measure of property nature has well set by the extent of man's labour....   ...He who appropriates land to himself by his labor does not lessen but increase the common stock of mankind....   ...cultivating the earth and having dominion are joined together. The one gave title to the other." By way of interpretation I have added (changing gender): The value a woman places on her liberty in a her-thing relationship depends on the nature of the bond holding her personally to the relationship. In fact Locke means much more than that. He is saying that an intelligent government will grant the assignment of property to the claimant who's life is most deeply involved in the relationship. That is the general idea. But shaping it into a material, well-defined, workable system is something else.

These profound principles require several chapters for their rationalization, but they nevertheless comprise the structural fabric of the common law. Let us put the general case in the simple setting of real estate once more, and see where it leads.

The pioneer clears the land. He associates it with the pursuit of his projects. Now comes another person injecting an interfering will - volo - into this space (this him-thing relationship between man and land), and the pioneer lays a claim of property before a high authority of great power. At a critical point in the authority's decision-making process, it must ask itself, and answer for itself, three questions: (1) What is the nature of the bond holding this pioneer personally to this piece of land and (2) What is the nature of the bond holding his antagonist personally to this same piece of land, and (3) Which of these bonds, if either, should the government honor with the designation of property?

These of course are questions for equity, not law. However, once property has been assigned for a particular situation - once equity has made the decision - the decision becomes law. And, thereafter, analogous situations are not referred to equity. Properly they are handled in a court of law. So evidently the job of equity is to formulate principles on which property is assigned.

To make a subordinate point quickly, it is becoming clear that a court tends to respect at least the following two kinds of bonds between a person and a thing: (1) rational and responsible effort put by the person into the person-thing relationship and (2) seniority. Nor can a court disregard the effort when the thing is held not by the productive person but by her beneficiary, her donee. Governments honor even dead donors, realizing that potential donors are watching. Apparently the importance of such productive people, and their wishes in the disposition of their property, is not overlooked by an intelligent government.

Returning to the main line of thought, we now present the case of a married man. He associates the woman with the pursuit of projects. Now comes another person interfering with this relationship, and the husband lays a claim in property before the court. At a critical point in the court's decision-making process it must ask itself, and answer for itself, three questions: (1) What is the nature of the bond holding this husband personally to this particular woman, and (2) What is the nature of the bond holding his adversary personally to this particular woman, and (3) Which of these bonds, if either, should the government honor with the designation of property?

By the "nature of the bond", I don't mean something carved in alabaster such as the "marriage vow". From a court in equity we want a probing insight into exactly why each person is clinging to this particular thing. Really. We are talking about the mental attitude of a party and whether an intelligent government will respect it or not.

These are the fundamental questions in a property decision, i.e., where the liberty will lie and on whom the servitude will fall; and making these discoveries and decisions is the true function of equity. I might paraphrase Locke and say, "If a government truly understands human nature, it will grant property to the one whose life is most invested in the thing at stake." And to an extent, as we'll see, the thing at stake is not merely the land, or Vivia. It is the climate of mind in which each antagonist is operating. Does it involve attitudes that a government wishes to cultivate - or to discourage. This is very much the business of government as it intervenes in personal disputes, and lies very close to the spirit of the common law.

We have gone a long way toward generalizing the job of equity, but not the whole way. Let us try framing the abortion issue in the three-question format:

A woman has conceived and now carries a fetus. She wishes to associate this fetus with the pursuit of a project - ridding herself of the fetus itself. Now comes another person injecting his will into this use-space, wishing to interfere with her pursuit, and the mother lays a claim in legal free space before the court. At a critical point in the court's decision-making process, it must ask itself, and answer for itself, three questions: (1) What is the nature of the bond holding this woman personally to this use-space; what climate of mind is involved, what investment of life, and (2) What is the nature of the bond holding her adversary personally to this use-space; what climate of mind, what investment of life, is involved, and (3) Which of these bonds (investments of life, climates of mind) if either, should the government honor with the designation of property?

You see, the questions make one think a bit, but they don't solidify the decision-making process in the abortion issue, and there are many chapters before that point is reached.

Nonetheless we have started to extend the device called property into the electric recesses of human desire and thought. And since a person is legally free within her property, and nowhere else, it follows that her whole freedom without exception is determined by the sum total of her property. This is nothing less than her estate under the common law, and let us not despise property as a word, or as a concept, or as a device, but learn its dimensions and elevate it to its proper place in equity and in the American mind.

CHAPTER 9

INTRODUCING THE COMMON GOOD

I will be pursuing the thesis that, in the universe of the common law, the common good is the basis for assigning property. Note I'm not arguing this **should** be the case but that it **is** the case. I must define the common good, and my definition must be commonly acceptable. From the beginning I emphasize we must think of the common good not as an ideal but as a relentless reality, and this understanding is a chief objective of the present chapter.

Though I have stressed the theoretical aspects of a court decision, I wish also to emphasize its realness; its materiality. Reason and reality; these are two voices usually expressed in every court opinion. But if one of them is missing, it is the voice of reason. The reality is there, at least in the form of previous cases that are (a) relevant and (b) material. And though the judge may try to clothe his decision in theory and logic, he is much more comfortable with the support of precedents; decisions are real. Decisions become law. Theory remains theory.

Nevertheless, the fact that courts advance reasons for their decisions reveals another reality of sorts. Apparently the law is supposed to be rational.

Obviously the first prehistoric court had no background of theory. For the first twenty thousand years of tribal justice we might expect a large variance and contradiction among court decisions. To gain consistency, theory had to catch up with reality. Even now there is a degree of judicial confusion, indicating that reality is still ahead of theory by a nose, and we may wonder if this will ever be reversed. Ideally, the lawmakers have a duty to push theory ahead. Under the common law, due process is in the property of every litigating party, and due process does not include a mistaken judgment - a judgment discordant with all the correct judgments of the legal universe. This means that principles of uniformity must be discernible in this mass of legal data.

This means first, since a court decision is a declaration of freedom space, that there must exist somewhere a rational system for determining freedom space. This is theory. It means second that the tribunal system must have a mechanism for turning this freedom space into reality; materializing it; transforming legal freedom space into liberty -

using the strong arm of government if necessary.

In other words, due process must be perfect or it is not due process. Law must be perfect, meaning that equity must be perfect. Meaning that the theory must be perfect. Meaning that the theory must be in perfect touch with reality!

I've spent much time trying to separate the word property from a misapplied taint of economic materialism. Given the commonplace conception of property, one would be pleased to find a label less burdened with bias. "Freedom space"; one's "roaming territory" where one can "range" freely. These words give imaginative substance to the idea, and be not deceived. As much as we wish to divorce property from the grossly material, it must be material, exactly as trial evidence must be material, exactly as love is material to a developing child.

But property. Free space. Roaming space. Range. Even domain; where one's desire reigns supreme, except that domain signifies one's ability to hold one's range by one's own strength and cunning, not by the strong arm of higher authorities. Nevertheless this space is her very own - the government says so. **Proprietas**; the very word means one's own. It means it is appropriate; proper. It means it fits; it is fitting.

Range isn't bad; it suggests liberty within a given space. To do as one pleases; within limits. Range is easily associated with projects and pursuits, and all these ideas are well-adapted to property. For property stands at the border between desire and the material, and is composed of both. To make it clear, note that a clash of individuals asserting dominance in their free spaces cannot occur if the free spaces are not material. (If you are inclined to challenge this, be patient.) And this is what a court deals with, first, last, and exclusively. The material. And desire.

Dealing then in ranges, free spaces and properties, and standing at the interface between theory and reality, it is here that we find an emerging due process making its early tentative decisions. The court system needs a mechanism by which a space of desire can be elevated to the status of property. A system of elevation is the first requisite of a standard of justice.

At this point I am in the process of building an arch of stone over two pillars. I have placed a couple of stones on top of one pillar, the pillar of property, and they are tilting dangerously inward. I am speaking of constructing a theory and whether the points look convincing as they appear. Now I must take the next risk. I must leave the property side of the arch, going over to the common good pillar. There I will place a couple of inwardly leaning stones, hoping that the arch - the link between common good and property - will in the end display unity and stability.

A badly handled expression, the common good. On various occasions called the general welfare; the commonwealth; the common weal; the public interest; the public good; the public health; res publicus; res populi; and republic; and misused in all these vestments; it is not merely an expression. It is not just a concept. It is the total expression of a society. When intelligently understood, even the mighty heed it, and one may well say that the ultimate definitions of two terms - the common good and property - comprise the entire standard of justice toward which the common law has been straining these nine hundred years.

Decidedly the common good does not mean the good of the state, or the good of the nation. An appeal to the common good does not require a citizen to sacrifice her life that others might live. The idea of the common good has a sublimating influence, but not that sublimating. Nor does the common good mean the **average** good as in the statement, "Some people might be hurt by this legislation, but it's a good bill. It benefits the **average** person." The common good, as with res publicus, bears no relation to the notion of democracy. A government heeding the common good protects the property of each and every person - a concept far greater, and far more difficult to comprehend, and far more difficult to materialize than the concept of democracy. After all, democracy frequently becomes democratic tyranny; a majority oppressing a minority.

But to set the stage for demonstrating the reality of the common good, before working on the common good side of the stone arch, let's project the idea of property to its farthest outreach. This can be done by injecting it into a much heralded, much debated decision - one I have already mentioned - the one handed down in 1968 by the Supreme Court in **Jones v. Alfred H. Mayer Company.**

To many this was a huge stride in the freedom march of black Americans. Already making great progress, at least on the shelves of law libraries, they had gained the government's strong helping arm in many of their efforts. By 1968 they were almost generally accepted in public schools and in service facilities such as buses, hotels, theaters and restaurants. But **Jones v. Mayer** was a cause on a different level. Jones wanted to buy a home in a subdivision of the Mayer Company but, because he was black, the Mayer Company refused to do business with him. Under the guidance of government attorneys, the case was fought through to the Supreme Court. At no time did the Company try to evade the issue - Jones was black, and they didn't want a black family in their tract of homes. The houses were theirs, the title was theirs, and disposition was theirs. It was a matter of private property. They were in their legal free space.

This was not analogous to the situation in which a black person sought and was refused lodging in a hotel. In that situation, the black was protected basically under the innkeepers law, a centuries-old law inherited with the common law from England. An innkeeper, though holding title, is under a duty to serve a traveler's needs in lodging. Regardless of his personal feelings, he is expected to lodge all who apply. His only valid grounds for refusing are (1) he has no vacancy, or (2) the traveler is unwilling or unable to pay the posted rates, or (3) the traveler causes a nuisance or has a reputation for doing so. This duty, imposed upon an innkeeper under regulations governing his operating license, is reasonably associated with the common good.

In early England, a traveler was dependent on innkeepers not only for lodging but for his safety at night. Outside in the night hungry robbers roamed at large, and an unscrupulous innkeeper might bar a traveler unless he paid an exorbitant room charge. A traveler's only alternative would be to quit traveling. But as the mercantile age dawned, travel became vital to the economy, and the legislature soon saw that the free space of the innkeeper should yield to the general welfare.

But in American states harboring slave codes, the common law was shredded to bits and pieces. As an instance, the innkeepers law was reversed in the case of blacks. Innkeepers were forbidden by law to lodge blacks. Came the Civil War and, with blacks emerging from slavery, it was not easy to reweave the common law as one piece of cloth. Congress, trying to remedy the defective systems of the slave states, launched the new Constitutional amendments and enacted the pertinent Civil Rights Acts, but it is amazing what these efforts did not accomplish. And it is amazing how judicial vision was twisted in trying to accomplish anything at all.

As soon as the slave codes were avoided by the fourteenth amendment, the innkeepers law and the logical corollaries would once again be part and parcel of the common law, and the reason blacks weren't given their legal freedom in these spaces was threefold: (1) they didn't know the common law, and (2) the general population didn't know the common law, and (3) no lawyer took the trouble to inform them.

A housing tract, however, is not a service to the public. The developer isn't licensed under the innkeepers law, and prospective purchasers are not travelers seeking refuge for the night. The tract is the private property of the developer, complete with a title of free disposition. In fact, the developer is under no compulsion to sell the houses to anyone except as he is driven by the forces of economics and private gain. For a government to force a householder to sell his house against his will apparently would be an arbitrary encroachment upon the very principles of free space that the government had created, avoiding the very liberty it promised to protect. But the Supreme Court deprived the Mayer Company of its free space in a particular home, ordering that the home be sold to Jones. We can well ask if this was a failure of due process.

In court, Jones contended that a decision in favor of the Mayer Company would perpetuate the stain of slavery, contrary to the thirteenth amendment, and the court agreed. Actually the Court's opinion appears convincing only to those who agree with it, and Justices Harlan and White dissented, calling the action an invasion of private property. We can see their reluctance to concur if we think of this sitting as a hearing in equity, framing the issue in the three-question format introduced in Chapter 8.

A corporation has acquired title to land. It has pursued a home building project, using only things to which it has acquired title. Now comes a stranger wishing to buy one of the houses and, insisting that his wishes dominate the owner's will, seeks a court order subjugating the owner's will to his. At a critical point in the court's decision-making process, the judges must ask themselves and answer for themselves three questions: (1) What is the nature of the bond holding this corporation personally to this particular house and (2) What is the nature of the bond holding Jones personally to this particular house and (3) Which of these bonds should I honor with the designation of property?

Put this way, the Jones case seems pretty thin. The Mayer Company has put time and money at risk in this pursuit, and its bond is strong. On the other hand, the Jones family has put nothing into it; their only bond is the bond of desire, and the common law grants nothing on the basis of mere desire. A government is at all times bombarded by expressions of desire. In every court case, desire rears its head on both sides. In **Jones**, looking at the relative investments of the parties, what possible justification would a court have to subserviate the Company's title of disposal to the whim of Jones? But, said the high court, to refuse to negotiate with a man because he is black is to pin a badge of slavery on him; and the court used "badge of slavery" for the purpose of invoking the power of the thirteenth amendment. I will discuss badges of slavery in another chapter, noting here only that jurists have now swept this phrase under a filing case and are trying to forget they ever used it.

Jones will be with us for many chapters. But my object in mentioning it is to pat the stones of property in their precarious positions and gingerly slip across to the common good. If we are not impressed by the court's logic in this case, can we at least accredit the accuracy of its instinct? My feeling here is that in every case there is a thing-at-stake, and in **Jones** the thing-at-stake was completely overlooked in judicial comment.

In every case the ultimate thing-at-stake is the common good. But in each case we must be able to discover a well-defined relationship between the elements of the case and the common good. It does not suffice merely to say that the decision is "in the common good." Obviously black people should be coupled to the same standard of justice as whites, and obviously this contributes to the common good. But while our intuition tells us that the decision in **Jones** promotes the general welfare, yet there are difficulties. In **Jones** we gave Jones the mastery of a free space carved out by the Mayer Company with great effort and at high risk, and merely because Jones wished it. But, with Jones lacking any visible title and contributing nothing to the effort of developing the houses, it is not easy to see this as the way to "increase the stock of mankind."

To put **Jones** in proper perspective, let us look at the abstract result of the **Jones** decision, what happened on the level of legal theory. Obviously the Mayer Company held the triple title of possession, use, and disposal, and the result of the decision was to put Mayer's title under a servitude to Jone's pursuit, whatever it was, and now the point. It is a different sort of servitude than Farmer Brown experienced under the fox-hunting lease. Brown's was the result of contract, a contract to which he gave his free consent. But the servitude placed by the court on the Mayer Company's title was against the Company's will. It was an involuntary servitude!

Now the thirteenth amendment avoids all involuntary servitudes; all except as punishment for crime; and certainly in **Jones** we are not seeing a criminal sentence; we are seeing a declaration of property. Nor is such an imposition of servitude as we see in **Jones** a rare event. Recall that a court always favors one party and oppresses the other. Every complaint properly heard in equity prays that a defendant's title be placed under an involuntary servitude.

To avert this conflict of terminology, either (1) we must change the wording of the thirteenth amendment, or (2) we must conclude it refers to a different kind of involuntary servitude, or (3) we must propose that the involuntary servitude created by a court decision in property is not really an involuntary servitude. I think the purest theory will embrace the last.

It is not really an involuntary servitude; it promotes the common good. A man of common decency, clearly seeing the common good, will voluntarily impose the same restraint on himself. It's a "common good" servitude. Of course if a court makes a bad decision, destructive to the common good, such a decision does not result in a common good servitude. It's an involuntary servitude, and launches the system on an explosive course. Why explosive? As earlier I suggested in Chapter 8, the thing-at-stake in equity is not the thing that superficially seems to be at stake. In **Jones**, the house at issue does not occupy center stage in the court's mind. Rather the court ponders attitudes and climates of mind as it sees them manifest in plaintiff and defendant. Attitudes are not only at stake in equity, they comprise a large portion of the stock of mankind. With respect to attitudes and climates of mind, and their effect on the "stock of mankind", a court in equity and every court, inasmuch as it reflects equity to the parties, is always sitting on a powder keg. I am about to make this understood in simple elemental terms.

As final preparation for the transition to the topic of the common good, I am going to analyze **Jones** in a most general and abstract sense. The complaint in **Jones** failed to present the most basic element of a cause at law or in equity, a claim of title. A person has no standing as a plaintiff in court if he has not claimed title to a space in which the government has guaranteed freedom of action.

This is the element most commonly missing in civil rights cases. Jurisdiction is invoked on a constitutional or statutory basis without a showing of fundamental entitlement. In all cases, the plaintiff wishes to invade the entitled space of another person, claiming that the amendment or the statute gives him title therein, and, as in **Jones,** the court always fails to provide a satisfying opinion. As I will demonstrate when the time comes, Jones was operating in a space to which he was truly entitled, and the Mayer Company was truly interfering with his liberty there. But all this truth and reason failed to surface in **Jones** and similarly fails in all civil rights cases. As the book proceeds, a tenet of the common law will be shown to be an absolute. A court cannot rationally place a defendant under a servitude in his entitled space unless he is engaged in a project that interferes with the enjoyment of a plaintiff in the plaintiff's entitled space. Evidently the engineers of the common law decided this ages ago. Otherwise a servitude is destructive of the common good.

To put this in terms of the **Jones** case, I must now become abstract in the extreme; we are dealing with a free space for Jones that is completely unknown. In his argument, Jones must show exactly how Mayer's pursuit is interfering with Jones's pursuit in his free space, and now we are doubly abstract. Obviously this interfering pursuit of the Mayer Company is not the pursuit of building and selling houses. If Mayer was not building and selling houses, there would be no house for Jones to buy in the first place. So we must have a pursuit of Jones and a pursuit of Mayers, both within their entitled spaces, and one of them interfering with the other.

Last, there must be a discovery of the thing-at-stake, for the government is going to permit one of the antagonists to go his way, irrespective of the complaints of the other, and will support its favorite with armed force if necessary. Here will be a link between a private thing at stake, very personal, and the common good, and as abstract as I have been, for the sake of generality, it is not as mysterious as all that. We have in the case of the Mayer Company an analogous situation with a handgun.

The owner of the gun holds all title in the gun, and no one else can tell him how to use his gun. But there are restrictions on his use imposed by law, with roots in the common good. Though he has the title of using the gun, he may not use it for murder. And this is exactly the kind of fundamental cause we must find for putting the Mayer Company under servitude in the disposition of its house. In the journey we are about to begin, we'll discover in every true case in equity a remarkable feature: the common good will be promoted if the decision goes one way, and harmed if it goes the other. A decision in equity cannot be made on a quantitative basis - the lesser of two evils, a tally of advantages and disadvantages. The quantitative approach invites the democratic process into the great hall of justice, replacing a razor's edge with the stone hatchet known as majority opinion. We know this much. If the decision is truly in the common good, a decision for Jones by definition must also be good for the Mayer Company.

Having built a tentative foundation for property, we must now examine the basic nature of the common good, with the ultimate objective of learning how property and the common good are intelligently joined in a system of law and justice.

In turning to the topic of the common good, I will quit the abstract and stage a specific setting. Envision an island, a lonely speck in a forgotten sea - populated with two men, castaways, one of them big and tough, one small and tough - an island blessed with regular rains, and smothered in crags and boulders.

For growing crops (the castaways have a bag of viable corn grains) the island fortunately boasts a lone tiny spot of soil at the foot of a ravine and, as events prove, the castaways can grow barely enough to keep themselves alive and healthy. Let me repeat, they can grow barely enough; and what a fascinating complexity is hidden under the term "barely enough". To see it, ask yourself how two people learn to share "barely enough", reminding yourself that barely enough means they are both always hungry and, yes, on the verge of starvation.

One can not assume that they share the food "equally", for barely enough for Scrawn will be less than barely enough for Burl. And to say that they divide the food "fairly" doesn't say anything. The word "fairly" is transcendental; it bears no relation to the material. Not in the least quantitative, it is not even qualitative, and even if it were qualitative, it would have no application to the situation. There's nothing qualitative about barely enough; it is quantitative to the core. To demonstrate this, let us say that Burl can perform twice as much work as Scrawn; he can accomplish twice as much in the same time. On this basis it would seem "fair", out of their harvest of six bushels of corn, to give Burl four bushels and Scrawn two. Given these amounts for a year, they learn to consume each day a 1/365 fraction of their respective allotments.

On these rations, Scrawn finds himself becoming weak - actually starving; ravenous almost beyond control - he isn't getting enough food; not even barely enough. This means, since they are growing barely enough for both, that Burl's allotment is more than barely enough for himself. As they eventually discover, Burl needs not twice as much as Scrawn but only one and one-half times as much. Based on this, a simple exercise in algebra reveals that for each to have barely enough, Burl will have to give Scrawn an extra 2/5 bushel out of his "fair" four-bushel share.

In making these objective judgments we are looking down as from Olympus on these poor fellows. We can imagine ourselves shouting down from our cosmic heights, "Burl, you've got to give Scrawn 2/5ths more of a bushel, or he'll starve to death," and we can also imagine Burl grumbling under his breath, "Go to the devil!"

In trying to persuade Burl, we might suggest to him certain situations in which it will be convenient to have a live, friendly Scrawn at hand. What if Burl gets sick, needing someone to take care of him. And what if another man as big as Burl comes to the island. It would create a situation for murder. There being barely enough food for a big man and a small man, there will not be enough to keep two big men alive and, under these circumstances, a faithful, robust Scrawn would make a most effective ally. Now can you see that both fair rights and equal rights are false idols; what is needed is a system of intelligent rights.

In this example - the simplest of all possible social situations - the combinations of interrelationships between the two socialites are infinite, dependent on a multitude of factors: the health of each man; the intelligence of each man; the personality of each and the frame of mind in which he's operating at a given moment. Make Burl naive and Scrawn shrewd, with the little man getting more than enough and the big man getting weaker and weaker. Even in the absence of an invader, this would be a fatal situation for Scrawn. A calculation from our postulated data will demonstrate that Scrawn by himself has not the ability to raise enough food for himself. If Scrawn's scheming fails to provide barely enough for Burl, he will be laying the groundwork for his own starvation in the following year.

We can begin to glimpse the common good in this mini-nation. It consists not only of the product of the land; it consists of whatever is required to divide the product into the shares required for the healthy survival of both men. We begin to understand that the common good, or commonwealth, or res publicus is not only the product of the land, not merely the rainfall and the size of the farming plot or its fertility. It is the strength of the men. It is their intelligence. At least it is the intelligence of one sufficient to calculate what is best for their joint welfare, and it is his ability to explain his solution to the other. It is their interrelationship, encouraging or discouraging cooperative efforts. It is the climate of mind that prevails in this next to smallest of all possible nations.

Note that the common good may not be "good". If the climate of mind is bad, the common good may plummet. The common good is what it is. Perhaps common matter is a better term than common good, remembering that attitude is fully as material as national resources. Perhaps common treasure is a good term, because treasuries might be well-filled, or medium-filled, or nearly depleted, and because a climate of mind might be like good corn in a storehouse, or a corn-consuming fungus.

But if we preserve the ancient phrase common good, reading into it all these meanings, we remember that the common good is with us always, cultivated or neglected, prolific or shrivelled. It is a dynamic connective tissue, the common good, and if one of the castaways impairs the potential of the other, he impairs his own. They might be conscious or unconscious of their common good or common bad, it makes no difference. The common good is the result of their inter-related efforts. It is the reality of their society.

We are now in a position to draw some interesting conclusions. Suppose for example that Burl is the head of our two-man nation, and suppose he decides to give Scrawn that extra 2/5th bushel of corn. What can we say about this phenomenon? First we can say that he is not sacrificing himself for the good of the nation. Quite the opposite. It is an act in contemplation of his own self-interest. Second, we can observe that intelligence is not the only factor required for promoting the common good. Self-restraint is required. Though intelligence will formulate the theory and express it persuasively, self-restraint is required on the part of a ruler - a material, auto-initiated self-restraint - if theory is to become reality. This is strikingly parallel to the governmental fact that words and theory can construct a system of property, but there must be restraint within the populace - either by self or by government - if property is to be transformed into liberty.

Note here the glimmerings of the common law. Restraint in view of the common good is a common good servitude, and when self-restraint occurs in a powerful head of state like Burl, it's a self-imposed servitude. And with this as a background, we proceed to multiply our Burl-Scrawn population manyfold until it becomes a great nation, with our potentate broadcasting to his subjects, "My friends, I realize I should restrain myself in the interest of the common good. It's a good rule to follow. But I am very powerful and, in the course of my many pursuits, losing sight of the common good, I may wound it. To shield it from calamity, I will establish a tribunal of individuals whom I know to be sensitive to the common good.

"Controversies among you will be referred to this tribunal, and will be resolved in the interest of the common good. For when a person restrains his desires in the interest of the common good he sacrifices nothing. Indeed he gains. And if he sacrifices the common good to his desires, he loses. Therefore the justification of the tribunal system will lie in the promotion of the common good, for then litigation will not produce a favored party and an oppressed party, though this might be the immediate impression and impact, but, in larger perspective, two favored parties!

"Similarly, I will subject even myself to the decrees of the tribunal. My power as judge I separate from myself and give to the tribunal. Their precepts will guide me. Their counsel and public prominence will serve to warn me against my own infractions. Nevertheless to be quite frank, I can overpower all if I wish. Therefore observe that though I vest the intelligence and theory of the common good in the tribunal, it is my personal self-restraint that determines the actual state of the common good in our nation.

"Realizing in my momentary objectivity that my uncontrolled desires can harm me in the body politic, I nevertheless advise you that if I restrain myself in the common good, I will unrelentingly insist that you do the same."

Such sentiments throw light on John Jay's acknowledgement of George Washington in a letter to Jefferson: "It is happy for us that we have a President who regards his own interest as inseparable from the public good."

I have dared to remove the halos from "fair" and "equal". As word-gears in the machinery of justice they do not mesh with reality. We do not look for rights that are fair or equal, but rights that serve the common good. How fundamental it is then that we acquire an unerring image of the common good. Only with this can we hope to reestablish the foundation for an intelligent standard of justice.

CHAPTER 10

INTRODUCING OUR RULERS AND THEIR TREASURE

I now proceed fearlessly to raise a topic inescapable if we are to produce a reliable and viable model of intelligent justice. It is a topic traditionally unwelcome in the United States. Directly put, we in the United States, exactly as every nation needs rulers, have our rulers too. In fancy, a democracy is ruled by the people, as if the word democracy magically transforms a mass of people into something other than a mass of people. Under this illusion we are mystified every day to find our legislators, our councilmen, and our public administrators acting contrary to our voting mandates. So though we condemn the "establishment" and mourn our political ineffectiveness, we threaten in the same breath to make mincemeat of anyone who suggests we are being ruled by monarchs, oligarchs, aristocrats, or dictators, openly or covertly.

Rather than argue the point I will in the book simply assume we are being ruled by a group of rulers, and we'll see if the assumption is productive. If indeed it is accurate, it need not sadden us or incite us to rebellion. It is merely a factor to consider in a realistic analysis of justice. After all, we postulated a ruler for our island castaways and made analytical headway by doing so.

The truth is, I've found no way to understand our system of justice without viewing it from a ruler's perspective. If you will have indulged me in taking this first step, and if you will tolerate a further step, we will observe that the working structure of government - the flesh and blood machinery set up for ruling a nation - is virtually identical across all nations, irrespective of the ideological tinwork that covers it. George Third's England, Rameses II's Egypt, Hitler's Third Reich, Lenin's Russia and the Adams-Jefferson United States display the same governing offices. The outward trappings of monarchy, presidency, politburo, senate or tyrant have little to do with inner government organization. Contact between rulers and people require armies, police, tax assessors, tax collectors, judges, treasurers and jailers. The mechanics of government is the same in all nations, and requires the same tools and devices.

Also at the outset we must admit that rulers are not the men and women who sit conspicuously at the head of organization. For the most part I do not classify departmental officers and their staffs as rulers, unless the truly powerful have let them entirely out of control. Rulers are those who direct the public officers, and who have the capacity to enforce their direction. Nevertheless the body of rulers comprises an indistinct cloud of people - manipulators. It consists of intertwined strands of men and women woven through the fabric of the populace, and certainly includes a number of administration people. In fact it is practically impossible to find the interface where rulers end and non-rulers begin.

In drafting a rough idea of rulership, we can probably agree that there are two broad classes of rulers - I'll call them movers and advisers; the people who can move people, and the people who advise movers about the direction to move in. Naturally some movers act as their own advisers, but movers are primarily movers, born to be movers, and the word "nation" would be an empty crock without them.

Of course nobody but a ruler appreciates the travail of trying to move people. However, the rest of us can catch an inkling of it if we recall that even a single individual, thinking of pursuing a solo project of her own, might never move herself to action. Desiring to phenomenalize her desires, she never acts, and desire without action does not produce results. Between desire and result we infer the existence of a strange function, calling it will or volition. Without it, no action and no result. Projects maybe, but no pursuit.

It is true also of a nation, except that volition can not exist in the non-existent ether enveloping an agglomeration of humans. Volition exists only in an individual, sometimes osmosing and radiating into the mass. That this osmosis occurs is obvious. In no other way can all the elements of a mass move together in a single direction. Before a national step is ever taken, movers must move themselves to move others.

To illustrate, imagine a primitive tribe running short of water, and if there's a sparkling brook just over a hill, the tribe will move itself. It will not need a mover. Spontaneously the people will roam and wander and straggle and stroll over the hill to fetch water. But this isn't a national movement. It's merely the product of individual desire and individual action. And now change the hill to a towering mountain range turgid with rugged slopes, split by treacherous cliffs, swarming with cougars and enemy tribes, and suddenly you face a national problem. Among your thirsty tribal members you will find a few daring souls saving themselves by solo flights through the unfriendly territory. Others will hang around the dusty camp discussing alternatives while the tribe enters the descending path to dehydration and violence. If the tribe is to survive as a tribe under these circumstances, one or more individuals must set it in motion, individuals tying their personal fate irreversibly to the fate of the tribe, and among the characteristics of these individuals we must not fail to perceive a trait in particular: a conviction that they must preserve this social group; for them it constitutes their ultimate treasure. These are the rulers who are movers, and their capacities are not commonplace.

Established movers never lack advisers, and since a mass (if it is to remain a mass) cannot move in more than one direction at a time, and since advisers love to advise movers on direction, a nation is left with a problem. Will their movers take the right advice! Mainly we find them taking the advice most appealing to them, and sometimes this is simply the advice wrapped in the most attractive package. It is on this basis - the power of advisers to sway movers - that I include the mover's advisers in the class of rulers. Elizabeth's earls, Alexandra's Rasputin, Roosevelt's Harry Hopkins. Supreme Court clerks, congressional staffers, friends, mentors, wives, husbands, nepotees, ward heelers - all rulers, though not of the same stuff as movers. Beyond these if you postulate in the shadows the top rulers, here then is your ruling group; omnipresent as a gentle mist from heaven; perhaps individually fleeting as evanescent droplets in the hot sunshine of destiny.

But let us not forget that rulers rule. Meaning they chart and steer the national course for the rest of us. Meaning that government is in their hands. Meaning the law is in their hands. Meaning that our standard of justice will be what they choose. Meaning that the definition of our free space - our property - and our liberty therein - is in their hands. But does it mean that our rights are based on the personal desires of unknown people - not on logic or principle? It means both, and fortunately the two are not necessarily at odds. In any case government decisions are always based on logic and principles of a sort.

To illustrate, imagine yourself a judge in the country of Librador, just recently overrun by the army of neighboring Lahalla, with the president of Lahalla chasing away the president of Librador and taking over the presidency of Librador himself. To you - judge and public servant as you are - your new situation is exactly this: you will henceforth draw your salary (if you draw one at all) from the new government.

Then imagine a day, with the dust of invasion now settled, when your honest but tactless sheriff dances a fellow into your courtroom by his coat collar, protecting him from the flourishing fists of your old friend Senor Manuel Mendes. As the plaintiff's tale unfolds, it seems that this unknown villain has been closeted for a week with Rosa Mendes, age sixteen, whom he has plied with chocolates and a sunken bath in the most expensive suite in your city. Nor does it appear that this was terribly offensive to Rosa.

With his collar now released by the sheriff and regaining his dignity, our unlikely Romeo produces a wallet, being careful not to conceal some very large bank notes, and he places before you, the judge, before your nose an oversized business card showing him to be the Minister of Supply under his excellency the president of Lahalla. And Librador.

Though you are the judge, something tells me your first hunch will be to declare no jurisdiction, dismissing the charges. Unfortunately, Senor Mendes is there and your only refuge is to become a little hazy on the fine points of law. Happily the thought occurs to you that a phone call to the new president will not be amiss.

Now please, for a split second as the reader, don't prejudice yourself against the new president. And back now as the judge, recall that your decisions under the old regime were directed by pure unadulterated political pressure. In those days your decision would have been easy. You ruled in court as you were ordered by the powers behind the throne. But a new day has dawned and you have heard that your new president intends to reestablish the civil law in all its traditional magnificence and, as your adviser, I recommend that you get your standard of justice direct from the new president himself.

Here you are, faced with two opposing parties, and you have to discover who the government wishes to favor. All of which reveals the reality of a judicial decision: our legal free space is shaped by the favor-mentality of our rulers. And even this must be viewed in larger perspective. Remember. Your ruler is not one person, but many people; some visible some not. Some movers. Some advisers. Some operating at a national level. Some local. And, supposing your national rulers to support an enlightened standard of justice, it does not follow that your local ones comply. If national rulers can't control the locals, your local court may follow a pure scratch-my-back standard of justice.

The point is that rulers are preoccupied from the beginning to eternity with the job of picking favorites. Here is a labor that burdens all operations of government - judicial, legislative and executive alike, not to mention the rulers behind the scene.

If a legislator writes a bill, he'll try to justify it to colleague and constituent. But whom is it really intended to benefit, a selected group, or all members of the nation? Either way, he is picking favorites. Lobbyists are rulers to the extent their pursuits are successful. They are picking favorites. A person of extensive financial power who "owns" the government may think he's smart, thinking he has subverted democratic power to his own devices. What rot! He has merely assumed the responsibility for picking favorites. He has put himself in the position of a ruler untrained in the particular vulnerabilities of rulers.

As far as picking favorites is concerned, a judge probably attains his peak objectivity in a suit between two persons not belonging to his power faction. But if one of the parties is a political buddy and the other an outsider, will the judge use the same standard of justice? His worst ordeal probably occurs when both parties are members of his political inner circle; he will have to favor a buddy and oppress a buddy. Does he have a third standard of justice for this situation? We have agreed from the first that conflict is a fact of life. Now we see that the eternal chore of picking favorites among belligerents is a fact of life for those who would rule. Do they have different systems for different combinations of litigants? Or do they have a common law?

So justice - the determination of favorites - reflects the character of rulers in a complex way. If a scratch-my-back mentality pervades the ranks - call it syncophancy or **figism** (meaning the same thing) - it will reveal itself in all the acts of government. Or if there is a rulerly feeling that certain classes deserve special treatment (some call it elitism) we will see it reflected in all operations of government. I call it **tierism.** Finally, a mentality embracing the common good - I call it **holonism** (not the same as holism) - is still a species of favoritism. It is simply a different kind. After all, if a court favors the person who has cleared the land, and disfavors the person who merely craves the land after it has been cleared, you can't deny that this is still a brand of favoritism. That's the reason I don't reserve the word elitism to any one brand of favoritism; all brands produce an elite. They all choose favorites, the very meaning of elite.

From what has been said thus far, we can make three observations. First, the pervading favor-mentality, the actual spirit of the rulers, will determine the whole flavor and output of government - judicial, legislative and administrative. I'll say at this point, though the full significance won't be apparent until a later chapter, the favor-mentality of rulers is the **form** (or mold) of government.

Second, the favor-mentality will have a profound effect on the common good. This dynamic relationship is one of the most exciting phenomena that a social scientist can investigate. Perhaps it is what history is all about. Basically it is what this book is about.

Third, it is obvious to a politically sensitive person that figism and tierism erode the common good. They can have no other effect. It is most easily perceived when one considers that a chief element of the common good is the national climate of mind. Figism and lack of self-restraint are practically synonymous. That holonism as a favor-mentality promotes the common good is beyond question, for this is exactly what I intend this word to mean.

To be accurate, one should not think of figism, tierism and holonism as systems or standards of justice; they are the wellsprings of standards of justice. The resulting standards or systems themselves might be called figity, tieranny and holony or something like that. But figism, tierism and holonism are climates of mind in which rulers are immersed. They might be called political philosophies and this is not irrational if we accept the fact that any philosophy, no matter how cerebral and logical, finds its source in the unthinking personality of the philosopher.

From figism and tierism spring appropriate standards of justice, arising spontaneously, without a need for intermediate theory. Quite the opposite is true for holonism. A standard of justice truly promoting the common good does not rise spontaneously merely from a consuming desire to promote the common good. The intermediate functions between holonism and holony are complex and abstruse though necessarily material, and I will presently illustrate what I mean. In the common law, the functions converting the mentality of holonism into the reality of property and liberty prove to be creations of highest political genius.

Given the personality traits of movers (superlative willpower in an individual is not always accompanied by exemplary self-restraint) it is amazing that we anywhere or at any time find systems of justice sensitive to the common good. Such a system necessarily imposes the same standards on both lions and lambs, and that such a system can exist for long without splintering the ruling clique needs being seen before it is credible. There are of course no reasons to be a ruler except perfectly selfish ones, and they can all be lumped into one. A would-be ruler wishes an especially privileged position in society; he wishes his desires to prevail. And these few words hide an awesome spectrum of desire. In the ranks of rulers it ranges from the most depraved to the most enlightened.

The key to privileged position is the control of political structure, the power to force others to comply with one's wishes. Control and power suggest the strategy of forming a gang, and this requires a system of rewards. Of these the most popular seems to be the system of using government office to favor gang members over outsiders.

Tales of figism thread the tapestries of history. In fact the tapestries of time are mostly woven of this material. It is fully understandable that superior legal systems like Rome's succumbed to the figism of the Caesars. We expect it. But we widen our eyes when we see a common good system emerge from a tieristic government as happened in Norman England. And really it has occurred in most of the advanced nations of the world to a degree, for the common good lies also at the foundation of the civil law. That the emergence of a common good system occurs implies the operation of a natural phenomenon, a natural law; just as natural as figism, though less easily discerned. How might it be explained?

The favor-mentality of a regime is influenced partially by minor rulers who have not yet acquired the exalted positions to which they aspire. Of these some are willing to destroy the whole system if necessary to get what they crave. But there are others even more selfish. Desiring not just power, they crave power worth having when they finally get it; they want a nation bursting with hope and energy, and this begins to make credible the notion that holonism can exist as a yearning in the breast of a ruler.

These people realize that if figism is heads in government, slavery follows. Instinctively they know the mental consequences of slavery, no matter how well disguised it might be. In black slavery in America, the crudest mode of slavery, the consequences were observed by De Tocqueville on his visit to the United States. Taking passage on the Ohio River, he made memoranda that the slave-worked fields on the south bank were not as productive, nor were the farmsteads as prosperous-looking as those on the north bank where the farm hands were hired.

Or consider King Stanislaus of Poland ascending the throne as a young man filled with dreams for reforming his government and reestablishing Poland's former glory. Though more powerful in the 1600's than Russia and Prussia and Austria, Poland in 1772 was easily swallowed by the three and partitioned among them. This blow fell after Stanislaus became king but before he could institute his reforms. The three powers had no wish for a revitalized Poland in their midst. John Adams has translated for us some of Stanislaus's writing. "Our people don't receive the least profit from their labor; we don't treat them as well as we treat our oxen. We draw our luxury from their sweat, and if we want an army to fight our wars, we conscript them. It is no wonder that we lack even the most common artisans that we need. Only where there is liberty will we find ambition and striving."

In the past, aspiring young rulers learned something from John Somers, baron, chief justice, close counselor to the king. Living in England a century before the American Revolution, he reviewed the work of figists in the great stretches of English history under the common law and described their modifications of law and legal practice. Subtle modifications. Bit by bit. Year by year. Slow but surer than a direct attack on the legal system. Each step undetectable except by practiced eyes. Each step coated with sweet chocolate. Great pains taken to disguise the true reason for the legislative amendment, the judicial vagrancy. And when the king's counselor warns the king, the conspirators explain to the king the advantages to him personally. He can use the new amendment to favor his friends. But he doesn't comprehend that this adulteration of due process, this loss of liberty, will destroy the people's confidence in the law and therefore, as Somers wrote, the king will lose his greatest treasure and source of strength - the people's hearts. And then Somers gives figists for all time the warning they never have heeded and never will heed.

Sometimes, he writes, this kind of subversion has proved fatal to the king. But more frequently it has destroyed the very ones who perpetrated the scheme. It is not merely that the king's wrath finally catches up with them. More than that, now that the king and due process have been weakened, the perpetrators have destroyed the source and structure of their own protection and fall prey to the very lawlessness they have created.

Since a spirit of holonism occasionally displays itself in the course of nations, we have evidence that intelligent young staffers, though tempted to join figistic factions, have asked themselves what kind of nation they will inherit under figity. So evidently we may expect to see in government two separate strands of ruling factions, each intent on a different treasure.

Of these, one sees a nation as a lode of ore to be mined dry, her chief concern being to gain control by any means, vacating all thought for the future. To achieve this she enlists others with the same frame of mind - immediacy. A nation is a fig. To be torn apart. To be dangled before others and devoured. This ruler's rationale is simple and direct. It works in the present. It is realistic for the moment. It is human nature. Figism.

When implanted in a gang, such a frame of mind is a crucible and a mold from which emerges the whole character of government. It is a genie that shapes your system of free space, your legislated govern-ment projects, your administration. In such a frame of mind the national level of prosperity cannot help but deteriorate. An immoderate figist takes what he wants when he can get it, caring not that he and his gang might in the end find themselves scraping the bottom of the barrel.

There are other figist societies who consider themselves more sophisticated, giving the people a semblance of liberty, but allowing their gangs to exploit as they choose. Attempting to gain the people's hearts by showmanship, they think to trick the people into productivity and loyalty. Their strategy is to strike at individuals in their more confidential free space, in the affairs they don't tend to discuss with their neighbors. Their inheritances, their trusts, their investments, their debts. And since the troubles of this class of prey don't have mass appeal, the sophisticates calculate that the victims' resistance to plunder will be unorganized and ineffectual. Since material wealth becomes loot in the process, the gangs are well satisfied with their reward system.

The truth is that these raids on individual spaces of freedom take their toll on the nation's climate of mind. As the raiders become more daring and better organized, gaining greater control of government and the legal process, these hidden oppressions proliferate through all segments of society at a dizzying pace. There is reason to believe that people instinctively feel their liberty slipping away, even when they can't express exactly what they have lost, as the princess felt the pea under her mattress. They become disaffected and angry on a scale inconceivable, responding in modes impossible to predict; the very lack of mass appeal keeps the whole turmoil beneath the surface. The joists and girders of the nation become honeycombed with cracks and worm-holes and - most significant - these changes of heart occur not in the people we usually associate with mob violence, but in persons usually productive, usually loyal, with long heads, and usually law-abiding. The greatest treasure of intelligent rulers.

As for the figists themselves, speaking of subconscious psycho-logical responses, their mentality becomes saturate with a clinging vapor of fear and insecurity, and apparently it is relieved only by violence. A year and a half after Hitler's party gained total power, it swam for a day in its own blood. On June 30, 1934 his Brown Shirts and Black Shirts slew from five to seven thousand members of the Nazi party, including many from their own uniformed ranks. These numbers are stated by Churchill. Hitler accused some of his top men of extreme socialism, plotting against him. But there is no real evidence of their scheming, and there is no discernible pattern to the selection of victims. Undoubtedly many of the guards took advantage of the slaugh-ter to settle personal scores, but apparently the murders were random and indiscriminate within the party. The key characteristic of figists is not lack of intelligence, but lack of self-restraint. So naturally when they gain supreme power, free of any reins on their cupidity, there is reason for warlords to eliminate competitors and instill a disciplinary fear in the rest.

Inkeles discusses this methodology as typical of totalitarianism: "In other words terror is a means of instilling anxiety. It is an important part of the pattern that one be unable to find out with certainty what he did wrong. The studied caprice of the terror may be seen in a new light. The non-victim, looking at the actual victim, can never find out why the victim was victimized, because there are different and contradictory reasons for different victims, or **there may have been no reason at all.**"

Three weeks later, Hitler took his case to the Reichstag in a speech lasting two hours. A frightened, stupified legislature heard his words as in a fog. They had been syncophants so many years they no longer had a standard by which they could judge the atrocious act. Hitler brought his arguments to a climax: "Mutinies are suppressed in accordance with laws of iron.... If anyone asks why I did not resort to the regular courts... I say... in this hour I was responsible for the fate of the German people, and thereby I became the Supreme Justiciar of the German people.... I gave the order to shoot those who were ringleaders in this treason... and I further gave the order to burn out down to the raw flesh these ulcers... in our domestic life." John Somers, English baron, could have predicted the Blood Purge of June 30, 1934.

Non-figists - call them holonists - have premonitions of such consequences. Though exploitive like figists, they perhaps have an advantage in depth of perspective. Perhaps not living the debt-ridden existence of the desperate figist, they can afford to look farther down the road. One sign of their sagacity: they don't mentally dehumanize the masses. They note their humanity in breadth and depth, seeing them as individuals responding to rule, responding in unsuspected ways. Responding in ways perhaps contrary to current and fashionable social theory.

The younger holonist looks to the future, to what he will inherit when he comes to power. The older one, at the peak of his career, looks for security as he relinquishes power. So there are reasons, and perfectly sound selfish ones at that, for rulers to look forward to a nation other than figity promises. For them a government must see and treat people as a treasure sensitive to treatment; responding not merely to money matters but to matters of free space as remote from money as a mother from a monster.

Exalted words, but unfortunately they are only words. For if they are to be shaped into an actual system of government, the work ahead is formidable. First comes purely creative brainwork. A standard of favoritism must be formulated that will generate the nation projected by the holonist. The system must have an essential characteristic in particular. It must make so much sense to barons and their more intelligent associates that it will attract to its banner the national balance of power. By making sense I mean that good stout intelligent powerful selfish men and women must be willing to swallow its distinguishing feature - that a judgment favoring an oaf over a baron can increase the treasure even of the baron himself.

By barons I do not mean cardboard and tinsel barons, but cliques of movers and advisors who may actually own the nominal barons. In successfully forming a government in the holonistic mentality, the puller-of-strings must be educated to the fact of his true rulership; that the favor-mentality of the system will have a pronounced effect on the productivity of the subject. This suggests that once the theory - the standard of government - has been devised, the legwork begins. Even the ward heeler must be educated and, if not educatable, disciplined. As in putting together figist machines, all the forces and cunning of political persuasion must be brought into play. In short, movers with surpassing political acumen are required.

To compare the rival political mentalities most succinctly, one might say that the treasure envisioned by figists is the gold of the people, their muscle, and the control of them. The holonists merely add one more ingredient to the formula. The spirit of the people.

But spirit is a word poorly defined and lacking substance, and rulers can not eat and drink spirit. No. The spirit we introduce into the formula must have substance, its gears meshing not only with government and court decisions, but with the welfare of barons. It is not that in analyzing this spirit I am creating a new idea, but that I bring into focus the form that has been shaping the common law all along through the centuries. Therefore as one looks for this consummate conception, this thing, we must think realistically. For in the law one works not only with ideas but with phenomena - with pursuits and conflicts, and with how government activities and court decisions influence the productivity, and loyalty, and fighting power of nation. Here then is the basic problem of legal theory in the common good - to find the machinery of spirit. It's a study in the dynamics and economics of human treasure.

Devising machinery in the treasury of spirit is not easy. A standard of justice with its roots in holonism does not grow on trees. It is all very well for King Stanislaus to wake one morning and proclaim to his chief councillor, "Today we begin a new system of justice. Henceforth we'll be fair to everyone and give relief to the oppressed." Having said this, he will have said exactly nothing. The fact is, a new system of justice simply creates a new class of favorites, hence a new class of the oppressed. Fairness, as we have seen, is a vacuity. Declare justice, if you must, to be the polar star of the nation. But engineering a project in holony is rather more difficult than engineering a trip to a star.

King Stanislaus on his first day, after eating breakfast, throws open the doors of his court, inviting all who want justice to approach, and the first plaintiff to enter is Patricia.

"Your majesty, I want to be in the army, but the recruiting officer said, "A woman in the army!" and laughed at me."

"But Patricia," stammers the king, "I must leave these matters to my generals, and look at the spot you have put me in. If I turn you down, you'll be angry. But if I force my generals to enlist you they may resign, or rebel. Even worse, they might get moody."

It does no good at this point to talk about women's rights. This is the king's opening day and he's just getting acquainted with the difficulties of determining rights. And don't advise Patricia to start a woman's movement to force the king to enlist her in the army. To advise this is to say that desire justifies free space if desire is backed by power. This routes us back to figism.

If the king inducts Patricia because it is the "fair" thing to do, he next must decide how many women to let into the army.

Soon the question becomes not what is fair for women but what is best for the nation. Nor can we escape this question of emphasis by shifting the scene from a simple monarchy to a compound government with a separation of powers and a complex system of rights. In this more sophisticated universe, one cannot long maintain that human "rights" are paramount; that the good of the nation is immaterial or irrelevant. Such a proposition implies that a good standard of justice can produce decisions that are bad for the nation. Perhaps this might be argued successfully from selected premises, but it would be strange to find a government anywhere supporting it.

We are discovering that holonism, far from solving the king's problems, has given him a whole new set of headaches. The next case, I promise, will send him to bed early. Mr. Mancowicz approaches the throne and speaks.

"Your Highness, the Smiths next door have a little son Bobby, whom they are badly abusing. Not that they beat him or scold him, and it's not that they don't prepare good meals for him and keep the refrigerator stocked with milk and fruit. It's that they also keep it stocked with candy. Look at him! He doesn't bother to go to meals; he only eats candy; and they let him. He's a physical wreck!"

The problems rising from this kind of complaint will breed like flies, and this is why the requirements for initiating due process are so strict. Not only have such problems and their solutions determined the limits of our free space, they have determined whether a case should even be heard by a court. Let me list the potential issues of "Mancowicz v. Smith".

a. Do parents have a right to be permissive?
b. Does the boy have a right to eat anything he wants?
c. Does the king have a right to tell parents how to raise their children?
d. Does Mr. Mancowicz have a right, not being personally involved, to bring this case to court?
e. Is it right for the boy to have such a poor diet?
f. How is the common good related to any of these issues?
g. How does the welfare of barons relate to any of these questions?

In this as in all cases, everybody desires something. Mr. Mancowicz wants something. Bobby wants something. Goodness knows what his parents want, but they want something. The king wants something. And I am saying that the key to the decision lies in finding the treasure that everyone wants. Seriously, is the fundamental problem of determining free space like Bobby's problem with candy, thinking that candy is his treasure, when health is his real treasure?

Then Stanislaus might ask, "Isn't it in the national interest that Bobby be healthy?" But then he must ask, "Is it in the national interest that we **force** him to eat good food?" Or, more relevant to the immediate courtroom situation, Stanislaus might ask, "Is it in the national interest that we **force** Mr. and Mrs. Smith to regulate Bobby's diet intelligently?" With this, he will wonder if he should even be listening to such a case, and how to sift hearable cases from unhearable ones.

It was in dealing with such issues that property - legal free space - was conceived and formulated, as well as the principles of jurisdiction, becoming the central foci of due process and the common law. But, seeing the complex lens through which King Stanislaus and all holonists must view a case, we can see the real advantage of figism. The figist needs only to know that he desires political power and that he will use figistic techniques to get it and wield it. He need seek no rational coupling between his standard of justice and an elusive "national treasure", as though such a thing even exists. Poor Stanislaus is stuck with it, this national treasure; supposedly a bond between rulers and people; something that makes them a great people and enlarges his personal wealth and security. As real as the force of gravity. And as difficult to put your finger on.

CHAPTER 11

A STANDARD OF JUSTICE;
THE SCIENTIFIC APPROACH

In the last chapter I postulated that we in the United States as in all nations have rulers, some of them figists - interested in exploiting the here and now; and some holonists - people-users too, but contemplating a somewhat different reality. From the interacting mentality of these men and women springs the character of government, the character of the **acts** of government.

With our body of law varying over the years, and with the blend of figists and holonists incessantly changing, we expect the character of government output to be checkered. Additionally we see nowhere an explicit standard for justice, or for legislation. Perhaps from the Constitution we might derive or infer a standard, but no one has yet expressed it. There are no guideposts to the common good; no compasses, no barometers, no port and starboard for our judges and legislators. Perhaps this has been national policy, this indifference to directional devices, and perhaps it has been wise. Perhaps. But even holonistic judges and legislators, inclined to grope for the common good, will not find it with unerring consistency, especially if their discipline lacks fundamental orientation and instrumentation.

If, given this situation, we propose that our law originates in a rational set of principles, and if then we try to discover its bench marks in each and every act of government, past and present - judicial, legislative and executive - we must fail. The acts of figists almost by definition fit no standard, unless we stipulate that greed and tunnel-vision compose a standard. And the acts of well-meaning but confused holonists fare little better. No. We cannot propose that our law, taken as we find it, unerringly reflects a standard. Our universe of government output is a pudding of incompatible and unblended ingredients.

Nevertheless it has its moments of glory and we, sensing within it a matrix of reason, have but one way to discover this fabric in terms of usable concepts. We must subject ourselves to a peculiar floating frame of mind. It is like the attitude of a detective afloat in a sea of irrelevant clues. It is like a scientist developing theories of how the atom works, knowing that even the atom itself is a supposition!

Actually it matters not at all that atoms exist. The atomic **hypothesis** is sufficient. Over the years, the hypothesis of the atom has been a great hook from which to hang a large assortment of useful relationships, helping us to mentally organize the myriad facts of the physical universe; helping us even to invent things and predict relationships otherwise undetectable - that is, to bring facts into being - facts like radiation therapy that we, absent the hypothesis of the atom, would never attain.

In our case it is pure supposition that a rational standard of justice lies at the basis of our world of law, this world of strange facts; decrees of the judiciary; legislative statutes; administrative fireworks. Particularly today in the United States we are experiencing a truly confused output of governmental facts. We don't know why the confusion exists. We wonder if there is any way to predict its consequences. Then too we wonder if the usefulness of our legal tradition is at an end. Perhaps the law needs restructuring for this new age of ours in which we claim everything to be relative.

There is a branch of astronomy with similar problems. Its practitioners try to make sense of something they can't see - a confused buzzing in their electronic instruments. Electronic signals. Apparently the earth is bombarded incessantly with these things - radio waves and x-rays - originating apparently in the depths of space. From this pudding of noise, the astronomers have extracted raisins of a kind. And from studying these idiotic codes, astronomers have postulated the existence of strange celestial masses, christening them with exotic names - pulsars, quasars, black holes....

If such things exist, we know mostly we can't see them and they aren't like the stars that we see. But gradually they are being described - hypothetically. And gradually these hypotheses are being recognized as facts - inferred facts. At least the hypothetical descriptions are giving us a bigger and more unified picture of our universe, even of our visible universe, than we would have without them.

Yet the dominating fact is that the instruments of these astronomers receive nothing but a jumble of radiated impulses coming from the sky, non-solar, non-visible, this continuous static comprising the facts that astronomers work with. To work they go, girded with faith in the one axiom that science permits: something can not come from nothing. Jumble or not, this buzzing in the electronic telescope is nonetheless a phenomenon. Out there in space things **have** to exist, busy, busy enough to generate all these radio waves and x-rays.

But the output is so confused; with such a huge range and variety of pulses. Is there any orderliness to it? Are the pulses coming from everywhere at random, or are they coming from concentrated spots in the sky? Is a particular sort of pulse coming from one location, and another sort coming from another? Well, perhaps they are coming from things, and maybe there are different sorts of thing. So the first task in analyzing a jumble of signals is to classify them into groups; any set of groups to start with; as though a specific group of signals implies a specific source of signal. And if the first attempt at groupings doesn't make sense, one tries others. And others. Until a grouping becomes meaningful.

And what makes a grouping meaningful? Just this. Its relationships with everything else in the whole world, at least everything we know that is seemingly relevant.

So the astronomer doesn't limit his pondering to the static alone or to astronomy alone. From all available scientific hypotheses from physics and chemistry he tries to postulate what sorts of thing can produce these radio waves and x-rays. From his hypotheses of the known cosmos, he tries to propose how these things might have come into being. He conjures up visions of things and gives them names that fit his visions. Ceaselessly his observations and mental struggles must alternate and interact until they seem to be "meaningful". Then he publishes his ideas for his fellow astronomers to stare at, pick to pieces, and improve on. Like a group of detectives solving a crime, they think: If this happened; and if this were true; and if so and so was here; and if...; and if.... THEN! And the THEN gives meaning to all the relevant facts, and contravenes none. The THEN changes each and every "if" into "yes, it is", and "yes, it so happened", and in place of an assortment of iffy clauses we have established a realm of fact.

But the scientific-minded community, though earnestly debating its pet theories, holds its conclusions tentative. If the theory throws light on everything it touches and contravenes no fact, the theory is fact. But it cannot be held sacred. Never! For it may not make sense with the very next fact we stumble upon.

Never absolutely certain, the scientific method. But who will deny its productiveness.

Turning now to the jumble of facts that we call the law, it would be inappropriate for me to select only those facts that fit my notion of what the law **should** be. Yet science demands structure, and we can begin to group the elements of our legal pudding into raisins and nuts. Or figs. But really one must not forget the matrix of the pudding itself, the matter that holds the whole thing together, the stuff that makes it a pudding and not merely a meaningless aggregation of facts. Thus the astronomers do not concentrate on heavenly bodies and forget the fields

- gravitational, electric, magnetic - in which the bodies are embedded; those elements that make the cosmos a system and not just a hodgepodge.

Except that in law we suspect a mixture of systems, mainly figity and holony, giving rise to the governmental phenomena that we observe. My task of course is to project a system hypothetically consonant with the common good; to test whether there are fair numbers of case decisions that fit such a system; to abstract from real cases some principles of favoritism; to then infer what holonistic rulers deem to be their treasure; finally to develop the functions or couplings that tie the rulers' treasure to the common good; in short to find meaning in the whole supposition. Logic not being sufficient, we find that logic plus meaning equals rationality, and by this route does human conception approach reality.

Arriving at such a conception, we will have something to stare at, to pick to pieces, or to improve; something that we can call a standard of justice. Obviously, considering the jumbled pudding that we observe, what we find cannot be called **the** standard of justice. It cannot even be called the standard of the common law. Whether it is the standard of the **spirit** of the common law is for scholars to determine. Whether it is of interest to rulers - movers and advisers, top and staff and grass roots - is another thing altogether. The most I can do is to propose that it approaches a model of the spirit of the common law, that the common law has direct couplings to the common good, and to define the common good, and to comment that the entire entity is one of the most remarkable I have ever seen. The challenge then is not that you merely find what is wrong with my observations and fabrications, but that you produce a theory of the common law that is better or, much more to the point, that you devise a system purer in theory and more true to human nature, and I dare anyone to devise a reliable theory of law that does not take into consideration all the factors I have considered to this point and will introduce in succeeding pages.

What I am suggesting is not the ideal approach. This isn't Plato and The Republic; not the axiomatic approach, the philosophical approach. It is the scientific approach. The inferential approach. It would be unthinkable without the cosmos of facts composed of case reports in a law library.

The common law is not merely law; not even mere law plus legal history. It is a universe of facts as I will presently elaborate. Beyond that it is a nine hundred year old phenomenon. If a similar phenomenon had occurred in the biological world, the world of plants and animals, biologists would be ecstatic. In studying the evolution of life, they would have not merely frozen mammoths to work with, not merely the fragmented bones of dinosaurs, and fossils of prehistoric ferns. Today before their eyes, walking, swimming, shedding spores would be all the modes of life that ever existed. Around the neck or stem of each creature would dangle a little tag stating not only the date when it first appeared but the names of its evolutionary parents. With such a phenomenon, evolution would not be a theory. It would be a walking, swimming, spore-shedding fact. Not only would each species of creature be a fact, but evolution too would be a fact.

This is exactly what we have in the case reports filling the law library. Thousands of shelves of bibliographed and annotated evolution. But it is even more than that.

Life, displayed in its many shapes, reflects in good part the forces of nature that gave rise to the particular shapes. The dryness of the desert shaped the cactus and horned toad. The wetness of the tropics shaped the balsa and anaconda. The nurture of deep soil shaped the giant oak and the bison. The winds of the mountain top shaped the bristlecone pine. But for the most part the response of life to wind, cold, heat, dryness, wetness and soil chemistry does not react upon and modify these formative physical elements, and the law is different in this respect.

The law itself is a formative mechanism. Its facts are the forces that impact the nation and shape it. In this aspect it forms the environment in which the nation develops. But unlike the interactions between living forms and their natural environment, the response of nation to law reacts back upon the creators of law and justice themselves - the movers and advisers and their staffs, and thereby affects the onspringing development of law, that is, the environment itself. Therefore the common law at any moment of its history has been a force shaping the nation and, at the same time it expresses the evolution of ruler-people relationships over a nine-hundred year span of time in England and America. It is the living evidence of a rulerly pursuit, a pursuit releasing in those two nations the explosion of creative energy and devotion to country so dramatically different from the pallid corpse of Poland that King Stanislaus described.

If today we question the quality of past progress that occurred in England and America, we do not question the creative energy that sprang from the rulers' project. Rather do we question the direction of effort. And if we wish to attribute to the legal structure a mistaken direction of effort, I propose that the source of error lay not so much in the output of courts as in the output of legislators and administrators. The courts, at least before 1950, labored the common law toward holonism. The record of Parliament and Congress is nothing to brag about.

I am proposing that in case decisions, at least before 1950, the common law found the common good. I am maintaining that we now have enough facts on the shelves and a sufficient idea of evolutionary

direction to derive from case decisions the elements of the common
good - what it is; at least its parameters - how to measure it. I am
saying that the principles of evolution are walking around on thousands
of shelves before our very eyes. Raisins in a pudding. Pulsars embedded
in static. Parameters of rulerly treasure. Ready for extraction, abstraction and generalization.

Trying to create such a system of law philosophically would be like
trying to create the cosmos philosophically; like trying to materialize
evolution philosophically. No. We now will be looking at a real body of
data, and trying to find meaning in it.

Though our full corpus of information is comprised of all the acts of
government - legislative, judicial and administrative, I will refer most
often to the signals from the judiciary. They are the clearest. Acts of
legislatures are replete in static, and the output from the executive is
puzzling. Though it bombards us with words seeming to fit our spoken
language - a sort of interstellar communication - the words often seem
remote from facts, and the facts themselves are surprisingly faint and
far between.

Of the signals emanating from courts, we will admit the decisions -
all of them - to be facts. A court decision enters the life of a litigant
with the efficiency of a hammer, or an army tank. But what about
opinions - the spinning of words and ideas - the theories with which
courts support their decisions? Are they facts?

In astronomy it is a fact that a ray of light bends as it passes near a
massive planet. But what of Einstein's theory that predicted this fact?
Is theory a fact? Surely Einstein's theory was not a fact before the
prediction was put to the test. It was an opinion, mathematically
expressed. But when the prediction proved accurate, the theory
became fact - at least in reference to this particular phenomenon. If a
theory states a correct relationship between two sets of phenomena it
is acknowledged to be a fact. An accurate relationship between two
facts is itself a fact. Accurately tell me that A.B. as a child was raised
in a permissive environment and you have told me a fact. Accurately tell
me that A.B. is a non-productive adult and we've got another fact. But
now tell me that permissive child-rearing generates non-productive
adults and you have stated a non-fact. There are too many exceptions.
Even to say that A.B. is non-productive because she was raised
permissively is non-factual. Such a stated relation is an opinion, and
without basis in fact. So it is an opinion that is not a fact.

Similarly, a court opinion is a fact if it shows a true factual
connection between the decision (a fact) and another fact. A figistic
judge who says, "I am favoring A, and I am favoring him because we
play poker together," is stating three facts: (a) the decision (I'm
favoring A); (b) the fact that they play poker together; (c) a true

relationship between (a) and (b). This is what an opinion should be - not really an opinion but a statement of factual relationship.

A judge says, "My decision in A v.B (a fact) will duplicate the decision in C v.D (a fact) because A v.B is exactly analogous to C v.D," and his opinion is a fact only if the two cases are indeed strictly analogous.

If he says "because I **think** the two cases are analogous," he seems to be getting off the hook; he has made a true statement. However for an opinion to be factual, it must be the relationship between the two facts that is a fact, not his hesitance to make a definite statement.

A holonistic judge who says, "I'm favoring A because such a decision promotes the common good," might or might not be giving a factual opinion. If it is to be fact he must exhibit a series of true relationships perfectly coupling his decision to the common good. Alternately he may cite precedent opinions that have already done it. Furthermore his image of the common good must be a true one.

Of course there are other sorts of opinions that are non-facts. There's the figistic judge pretending that "favoring A promotes the common good." The linkage of his decision with the common good is not only a non-fact; it is not his true opinion, so it's not really opinion! Then finally we can find multitudes of case conclusions like that in **ex parte Warfield**, true to holonism, but with opinions completely immaterial, that is, not factual.

So there we see the confusion of signals that we must try to make sense of and, as people learning to be legal scientists, we must pay attention to the decisions, for they are facts. The decisions are the trustworthy phenomena in the legal world, whether they fit the holonistic mold or not.

Already we have postulated our political pulsars and black holes, the sources of our legal facts. They are our rulers, possessed of and possessing differing favor-mentalities. We have already envisioned our fields of natural forces - akin to gravity and magnetism - except that in the legal world we are talking about greed, immediacy, political treasure, the common good, the national treasure. These are the forces that mold the world of law from the stuff of nature.

A scientist, in the process of putting together a worthwhile hypothesis, must go through several cycles of mental legerdemain. First he takes a look at all the facts in his data library. Then he concocts a scheme that will help him envision why the facts are as they are. Then he must find new facts and see if they fit his scheme or not. If they don't, he must modify his scheme to fit all the facts, or throw it away and develop an entirely new scheme. In a complex field this process must be repeated many times before a scheme is found into which all the facts seem to fall sensibly. The whole time, he must be mentally capable of living with hypothesis stacked on hypothesis, yet willing to knock down his whole castle of cards if he meets merely one inconsistency. It is sheer drudgery and stress, and should not be imposed on a reader.

Nevertheless, the final conclusions will mean more to the reader who has a chance to taste the process; to look at real cases at law; to think about simple analogs and fictitious situations; to dip into theory; and to repeat the process several times until the truth begins to emerge spontaneously. Indeed, the criterion is not whether our innumerable hypotheses make sense individually at first, but whether they make sense altogether at the last. This will be our procedure, and you will note that we have begun.

CHAPTER 12

INTRODUCING INJURY AND DAMAGE

In the previous chapter we dipped in the mystic pool of inference - induction. Though sometimes it is called logical induction, I'm not sure it is wholly or even frequently logical. Some think of the topic of scientific approach as the philosophy of science, but I'm inclined to think of it rather as the psychology of science. I exposed you to the topic for several reasons, among others to emphasize the uncertain state of mind that one often must entertain and endure before attaining a meaningful perception of the real world. One must learn to juggle fistfuls of unjustifiable assumptions while awaiting a revelation of the structure of things. Such a masonry of assumptions is like building an arch of stone, the function and position of each rising stone appearing absurd until the last one is in place. Then the arch not only makes sense but supports tons of wall and roof.

We have fairly well shaped a stone we call property. We have roughly quarried a stone called the common good. And now we must start visualizing how these building blocks will ultimately fit together. For instance how does this device called property fit into human conflict on one side, and into a court decision on the other?

In Chapter 19 I will analyze a case decided sixty years ago, the opinion in the case proving to be a non-fact that has influenced succeeding legal decisions to this day. We will need to learn the vocabulary of the case. In the law we enter a world with its own special terminology, and we will have to learn the tags and labels as they are most often applied in the profession. Frankly, however, we must also give them better arch-building characteristics.

A large and important branch of legal practice deals with lawsuits seeking damages. Here the plaintiff claims (1) the defendant in some certain way has impaired plaintiff's welfare and (2) the harm cannot be remedied except by the transfer of an equivalent (usually money) from defendant to plaintiff. If by trial the court finds the plaintiff's claim to be true, finding also that the defendant was indeed responsible for the harm, it will order the defendant to make appropriate restitution. Responsible is a key word, and it aptly opens the door to the legal world we are about to enter.

We have already seen that the common law likes the idea of responsibility. As Locke said, the law favored the man who cleared the land and prepared it in a responsible way for cultivation. In **ex parte Warfield** the court favored the man who seemed to be acting responsibly toward Vivia. Now we find that the law requires responsible action on the part of people who have hurt others.

For learning about damage, I will introduce Mr. Lineweaver on a beautiful morning driving his handsome automobile to an important business meeting. In a busy downtown area, I will spoil his day by introducing Mr. Frick. Mr. Frick, standing on a street corner, is inspired to step off the curb into the pedestrian crosswalk just as Lineweaver's car bears down on the same space. Lineweaver has the green light; Frick has moved against the red. And Lineweaver's car, brakes screeching, crumples Frick frightfully.

Here, to start using our fundamental vocabulary, we witness two men intent each on his own pursuit, each using at the same moment the same thing - a small cross-section of the public highway. At the instant of the collision, we will assign the title of this real property to Lineweaver; he had the green light; and this puts Frick in the position of being an invader; a trespasser. In fact, Frick's invasion of Lineweaver's property is exactly what lawyers call an injury and - get ready - Lineweaver happens to be the injured party in this incident. Frick on the other hand is hurt, wounded, bruised, mashed, broken and lacerated, but he is not injured. All of which provides us with a brief, absolutely accurate definition of injury - an invasion of property.

Moreover Frick, though seriously hurt, wounded, bruised, mashed, broken and lacerated, was not damaged. This is another essential distinction to make. Only an injured person can be damaged. Note then that injury in legal lingo is not synonymous with hurt or harm, nor damage with harm or impairment. We lay people every day misuse these words with great familiarity, but they are not lay terms. They would not exist but for the keen insight of gifted legal engineers. Unfortunately legal practitioners today, bar and bench, use them with ambidextrous ambiguity.

There is no way, if you'll notice, that a person can injure himself - it is absurd to think he can invade his own property. And since he cannot injure himself he cannot, for instance, damage his own automobile. If Mr. Lineweaver independently rams his car into a telephone pole and experiences fender dents, broken elbow, or a heart attack, it is obvious that his potential as a person is in some way diminished. The same is true if his accident causes him to miss an appointment, losing a chance to bid on a contract. But we may not say he damaged himself. Injury was not involved. So what really is damage, and how can we start to generalize the concepts of injury and damage?

In the Lineweaver - Frick collision, I will state arbitrarily that Lineweaver, being injured, is elevated to a new status. He has become a potential candidate for an award of damages. Fender dents, broken elbow, heart attack, loss of a contract, anything that impairs his potential or effectiveness as a person, even if only through thinning his wallet - these are impairments or harms that can be translated into damages. With Frick liable. Note first however that a broken elbow or a lost contract is not damage. A broken elbow is a broken elbow. But what then is damage? And here we will have to be very, very careful.

We can gain insight by equating damage to the shrinkage of an injured person's potential, for instance the loss due to medical costs or the loss in working time. Sometimes even the pain suffered by a victim can be associated with a shrinkage in potential. But whatever pattern the shrinkage assumes, it must be a shrinkage that does not repair itself. A broken elbow, for example, might repair itself. But a loss in working time resulting from a broken elbow is a loss forever. There is no way to make it up. If Lineweaver suffered "a dreadful shock" in the collision, he could not collect damages for it; that is, he couldn't unless he could show that the shock had somehow reduced his future potential as a person.

As satisfying and general as is this view of damage, and as useful as it is in analyzing many situations, we should not limit ourselves to this view. Damage viewed as a shrinkage of potential is really a **parameter** of damage; a means of measuring it, so that an equivalent in reparations - damages - can be transferred from the liable person to the impaired person. If the impairment happens to be a permanent paralysis of the victim's legs, it is obvious that damages cannot repair the harm. So the transfer of money is intended to compensate for it, sort of, and for that reason it is called an equivalent. For the practical purpose of assessing damages, the view of damage as a shrinkage of potential (connected with injury) is useful, and so we must retain this idea as we proceed. But damage in the common law is more profound than this, and to gain a vantage point for glimpsing a more fundamental meaning, we will leave the topic of damage for the moment, returning to it at the very end of the chapter.

So Mr. Frick is hospitalized in a critical condition with multiple fractures while Mr. Lineweaver, missing an appointment, has lost a contract. Naturally our sympathy lies with Frick, but Lineweaver is the one who can sue and win.

If Frick is a person of responsibility with a sense of common decency, he will realize, when he has recovered, that he "damaged" Lineweaver. Moreover we will learn that damage to a person is also damage to the common good. In shrinking a person's potential it shrinks the common good as well. The potential of a person and the potential of a nation are strongly coupled. The connection becomes graphic if you imagine Lineweaver and Frick to be the Burl and Scrawn of our distant isle, Scrawn acting so carelessly as to push a boulder off a cliff with Burl directly below.

If we suppose a nation to have rulers, certain assumptions about damage make sense. If the law holds a person responsible for his acts, we may infer that the rulers deem a climate of irresponsibility to imperil their treasure. If we find that all classes of people are held equally responsible for their action (no elite) we may infer that the rulers have a holonistic streak in their character. If court rulings stress responsibility - if they assess damages equivalent to damage, and possibly punitive damages as well - we may infer that the rulers not only wish to repair damage but to instill responsibility as a part of the national intuition. In other words, damages is an instructional technique. And there is another point to be made here.

If a high level of potential is to be maintained in a nation, it is obvious that rulers themselves must be exemplary in their self-restraint, perhaps greatly contrary to their natural inclinations. How keenly they feel it, then, when their subjects act otherwise. Here we catch a second glimpse of the common good - a sense of responsibility, a sense of restraint - traits to be cultivated in a nation; something promoting a high level of the general welfare; something evidently treasured by the mighty. Is it of this kind of stuff - stuff like responsibility and self-restraint - that the nation's treasure is composed? Well, for the moment we must concentrate on Lineweaver and Frick.

Property has a powerful function in due process, once the boundaries of a property are determined, yet no task requires a more delicate touch than the task of establishing property lines. If Lineweaver could have stopped his car before hitting Frick, he should have done so. If a trial court finds that Lineweaver could have stopped in time, the court will redraft the property lines for the moment of the accident. The use of the crosswalk will be switched from Lineweaver's free space to Frick's. Green light or no, Lineweaver would be invading Frick's property.

The common law holds a person's body to be a fundamental subject of property for the person. The fence line runs through all the points at which you can touch him. No one, without his consent, may lay even a finger on this surface unless it is physically impossible to evade the contact. Therefore we may say without error that the green light gave Lineweaver a title to the crosswalk, except for the portion occupied by

Frick's body. Lineweaver was not at liberty legally, say, to hit Frick to "teach him a lesson". He was under a common good servitude not to touch Frick's body if at all possible. If he could stop, the Frick body-space in the crosswalk was excluded from Lineweaver's free space.

Then what is it in this particular accident that frees Lineweaver from responsibility, and binds Frick to it? It is not that Lineweaver had the green light and Frick the red. It is that Lineweaver was trapped into hitting Frick.

It is almost mandatory on a city boulevard that a driver maintain a practical rate of speed. A dawdling car is a hazard, and if all cars as a matter of policy moved at a snail's pace, the traffic jam would become so dense that motion would halt. The streets of the city could not hold all the vehicles destined to pass that way. Even pedestrians trying to cross the street would have to climb over the cars. That this can happen can be shown mathematically, and it sometimes occurs.

The necessity to maintain speed conspires with a basic law of physics, causing trouble for drivers. A car's velocity, combined with its weight, generates a complexity called momentum, and a singular feature of momentum is that it can't be extinguished instantly - pouf! Time and distance are required to completely drain the energy out of momentum; to brake the car to a full stop. So Lineweaver was trapped by traffic practicalities and the laws of physics into a certain minimum braking space, and if Frick steps into that space, Lineweaver is trapped into hitting him. Now we must proceed in our analysis even more cautiously or we will overlook a critical element of injury. We must examine more closely the walls of the trap, for if Lineweaver is to escape responsibility for Frick's impaired potential, he must be trapped by a will other than his own. Now what do I mean?

In this particular case Lineweaver, driving in the proper lane, observing the traffic signals and maintaining a practical velocity, was in his legal free space. Maintaining the minimum braking space was within his property. True, a wall of the trap was his own will, for he was engaged in a pursuit of his own, but his will was operating within his property. No pursuit is ever fully under control, and if a person could be held responsible merely because he is engaged in a pursuit of his own, everybody would stay in bed and never get up; and for rulers this would be an unacceptable state of affairs. So injury is not just a matter of will, it is a matter of whose will is operating in whose free space.

So while Lineweaver was thus in motion, partly under his own free will and partly constrained to a moving trap, the trap was suddenly tripped by Frick's unexpected waltz into the street. Lineweaver was helpless. Things were out of his hands. Upon analysis, Frick has fallen victim to his own will, and the event materialized in Lineweaver's free space. Lineweaver's will was entirely neutralized under the circumstances. But there's still another pitfall in this land of injury.

What if Lineweaver had been driving too fast - over and above the practical speed? In such a case the minimum braking distance would not be established by a practical speed momentum but by a reckless speed momentum - a result completely caused by Lineweaver's own will. This new and larger minimum braking distance is not within his property; the braking space extends beyond the common good braking space. If now he hits Frick, yes, he has been trapped by circumstances. But the circumstances have been created by his own will extending beyond his legal free space, and under this variation of the story we see Lineweaver's will invading Frick's bodily free space. Lineweaver injures Frick! And this would be true even if Frick has stepped out against the red light.

But as I initially told the story, Frick's bodily free space was not invaded by Lineweaver's will. The intersection of Frick and crosswalk and Lineweaver's braking space was brought about by Frick's will. Lineweaver's will had been shoved into an empty closet by the course of events, and the door slammed shut.

I mentioned that Lineweaver was under a common good servitude, a duty of self-restraint, not to lay even a finger on Frick if he could help it. And did he violate his servitude? Obviously not; he could not help what he did. No; a servitude - the self-restraint that is involved - is a matter of will. A person is bound to a servitude to the extent his will is free. But if his will has been neutralized by the acts of others, it is not reasonable that the law holds him responsible for the consequences.

I have stated that no pursuit is entirely under control. If a car is put into motion, it cannot be stopped "at will". It becomes a charged device, constrained to inexorable laws not made by man. An archer, wishing to embed an arrow in the center of a target, places the arrow in the bow, pulls it taut, takes aim, and releases. This describes what the archer does. But the action of the bow and arrow is something else, and this is true of every man-manipulated phenomenon. A pursuer does something, and something else happens. This is the magical feature of every device, whether it is a hammer or a phoned order to your stockbroker. In the case of the bowman we will probably see, a second after the release, the arrow sticking from the center of the target, and the bowman will say he hit the bull's eye. But he didn't. He put an arrow in the bow, pulled it taut, aimed, and let go. What he did was to charge a device and trigger it. In charging it, he had good control of his actions. But as the device discharges - as the bow springs and the arrow flies - it is completely out of the bowman's control. Yet the life of that arrow as it flies consists of the bowman's will.

His project is "arrow in bull's eye". But his will is the mysterious difference between project and flying arrow. If as a result of his actions the arrow leaves his free space and tragedy results, it is a result of his will. It is not of course a result of his intention - his projected wish - but of his will, and he is responsible even though the arrow is out of his control the instant he releases it.

We are now ready to see the marvels of property and injury as conceived in the common law, and can begin with a simple story about a little girl named Nancy.

Her project this morning is to walk to the store for some candy. Her device of locomotion is her own body, a marvelous device. In this pursuit each step is a mini-project of its own. In walking, a person falls forward as though to fall on her face. But before falling very far she places a foot forward and catches herself. Such a series of fallings and catchings is what we call walking. As you may have noticed when Nancy was learning to walk, her fallings and catchings were jerky and sometimes there were fallings without catchings, but now she walks smoothly.

Since the walking device consists of herself, and since she is using the public sidewalk, and since she is observing her common good servitudes towards the free space of others, she is operating completely within her property. And now comes Timmy from the other direction.

Timmy's project this morning is to have some fun. As he approaches Nancy he waves and greets her with a smile and, just as he passes her, he suddenly sticks his foot out sideways. Timed well, it catches her foot coming forward to keep her from falling in her regular walking pattern. So she falls and we call it being tripped.

"After all," jokes Timmy with his friends later, "her broken tooth was her own fault. She was under her own motion - falling and catching herself, falling and catching herself; only once she didn't catch herself. But her broken tooth was due to her own momentum and the law of gravity and the hardness of concrete. She made a charged device of herself and went out of control.

The truth is he touched her foot without her permission and thereby invaded her property. By his act of will he trapped her; he deprived her of her volition in her own free space. Her fate was the result of his will. She became a thing used in a project of his. We will learn that a claim of entrapment is required for all claims of injury. And now we approach the naked truth of injury.

Since Timmy invaded Nancy's property without her permission, we are witnessing injury. But also for a split second her will was impressed to bow to his will in her own free space! For a second he was her master, and this is exactly the state of servitude. Not only that, this was not a contractual servitude or a common good servitude. He seized this advantage without her consent. So we are witnessing a pure case of involuntary servitude! And now we come to understand that injury and involuntary servitude are labels for the same state of affairs.

Sadly for simplicity, the involuntary servitude here described is not the condition called involuntary servitude in the thirteenth amendment, but I treat that in a separate chapter.

You will recall that I opened the topic of servitudes with a fable in real property: Farmer Brown renting his meadow to a fox-hunting club and subjecting himself to a silent but confining company of servitudes. Here under his ownership was a piece of land, a thing of innumerable uses, some of them not even conceived. And by owning it "in fee" he held title to all its legal uses; meaning that if anyone was to enjoy them it would be Brown or someone who had his permission. One of these uses - fox-hunting - he let to others for money, a contracted use. And now, though he still held title to all the other uses, he could not exercise any that would interfere with the contracted use. This had become a master use, simply a matter of applying pure logic to the nature of things, and the hunting club became Brown's master as far as all interfering uses were concerned. Yes, Brown can plant potatoes on the meadow - if he gets the master's permission. What a galling experience this is when an owner first discovers he can't exercise a use to which he and only he holds title. His will is under the bridle of her who holds the master title. He must restrain himself in perhaps his fondest desires. If he doesn't, the master can carry a complaint to court and enforce her will. A servitude, even a contractual, perfectly legal one, can test a man's soul.

But if it has a dark side, it also has a bright side. True, the hunting club members can't use the meadow for baseball or picnics or any activity other than fox-hunting. For fox-hunting, however, the servitudes perfectly clear away all stumbling blocks and encumbrances and outright frustrations. Nothing may interfere with the foxhunters' enjoyment in it. Within this space their will is guaranteed freedom from friction. Within its boundaries their legal freedom is unblemished, protected by government. Here is a freedom not possible in uncivilized nature, and indeed it is possible only in the domain of an overwhelmingly powerful government.

Then too I have mentioned another kind of servitude, one seemingly imposed on us without our explicit agreement - the common good servitude. Under such a device, though we have the title of use, we have not the liberty of use. Though we own our city lot, own the pile of leaves we've raked up, and own the matches, we may not set fire to the leaves. Why? Well of course, if there is a city ordinance against it, we have a restricted title; the title of burning leaves has been snipped from our general title in fee. On the other hand even if such an ordinance has not been enacted in our town; if we hold a title in leaf burning; a court might well put this title under a servitude restraining us in this use, a common good servitude. Frequently a restrictive statute or ordinance is enacted though a common good servitude has already been established in the area of conflict, if only to make the government's position crystal clear to people who have difficulty in perceiving common good servitudes. But it is important to note that a law restricting title, if it is to be consistent with the common law, must have the same justification as an injunction in equity, a declaration of servitude; the result must have the effect of promoting the common good.

Or if our neighbors are playing their record player too loudly on their patio in spite of our protests, and if we take the trouble to complain in court, the government will order them to decrease the volume. Obviously the sound created in their free space leaks out of bounds, and though a moderate leakage is tolerable, there is a limit. Above this limit we, sitting in our own free space, feel our space suddenly shrink under a torrent of sound. As a space for quiet meditation it is shattered. As an environment for quiet conversation it is crippled. Like an arrow fleeing the target area and causing a tragedy, our neighbors have released a charged device that escapes control, invading the free space of others. If we do nothing to abate this nuisance, if perhaps we do not wish to take them to court, our will bows to theirs in the space of our own property, the exact circumstance of involuntary servitude.

Here is an opportunity to make an educational digression in our journey. Suppose our neighbors, taken to court, happen to be personal friends not only of the judge but of our own lawyer, and suppose this little clique inclined to figism. Suppose the professionals marshall their comments and arguments to make it appear to us that our neighbors' loud record-playing is completely within their property and we lose the case. With such a decision, the neighbors can continue to saturate our air space with their sound. We must continue to bow the knee in our free space, and the plain fact is that the strong arm of government has been used to trap us in involuntary servitude.

It is a double-layered, doubly agonizing trap. Not only do people of common decency recognize intuitively a dishonorable act of government, but they get a sense of entrapment on an entirely different plane. If we were all living in a jungle and our neighbors insisted on beating their tom-toms in the middle of the night, we would have two fairly practical methods of abating the nuisance; with our tomahawks; applied first to the tom-toms and that failing, to their heads. But here in "civilization" if we carry our hammers to the neighbors' patio with dire intent, we can expect to be surrounded on all sides next day by blue uniforms. Under these conditions we are worse off with government than without. If even a contractual servitude can be galling to a person, a person who probably entered the contract with great expectations, imagine what happens to the mood of a person confined to an involuntary servitude by government. Here truly is corrosion in the ruler's treasure.

We can now begin to organize the concepts of property, injury, liberty and damage in general form. As we have seen, property is free space, the special volition space where the government allows the owner's will to range freely. Then injury is the material appearance of another human will - volo - uninvited in that space.

We say that government guarantees our freedom in our property, but this is an over-simplified way of expressing a quite different function. Since injury exists in the real world, it is clear that the government does not without fail prevent invasions of property. The space of our actual liberty does not always coincide with the space of our legally declared liberty. All that government can really do is to pledge that it will evict the intruding will if, under due process, injury is found to exist. Injury turns out to be a pinching of the liberty guaranteed by government. So due process and the pledge of protection turn out to be identities except for this difference; the pledge is the project of government, and due process is the government's pursuit of the project. The law, as we realistically recognize does not protect our liberty except to the extent that threat of punishment deters people in their greedy and reckless pursuits. A court does not shield except in certain injunctions and declaratory judgments. Rather it **relieves**, and relief comes through due process, and it follows that our liberty under the common law consists of our government-declared liberty in our property, **plus** due process. If we in England and America wish to define our liberty under law and equity, this is it.

Now we are prepared to discuss damage in depth. Until now I have identified damage as the injury-related reduction of a person's potential, a reduction lingering even after the conditions of injury have been extinguished - the Invader has withdrawn. With the aid of the elementary vocabulary developed thus far, we can note that damage represents a permanent reduction of one's potential within one's property.

Damage being a residual incident of an injury, and injury representing an alien will discharging uninvited in a person's property, damage is the ghost of that alien will remaining even after the will itself has flown. It is the will of the injurer that has somehow crystallized in the free space of the victim, lingering on and on, infecting and debilitating the victim in her subsequent rightful pursuits. It imposes on the victim a persisting involuntary servitude that will never be truly relieved.

This makes theoretic difficulties for the government. Here is a persistent lingering of an intruding will; and a government pledged to protect liberty finds itself helpless to restore that devastated range of legal freedom. To the government, damage is a damnable intrusion into its own pursuit.

Here I cannot help but be intrigued by the fact that the word damage has the same language roots as damnation. And pondering it I must wonder if our ancient forbearers in the common law were not better abstractionists and generalists than we. At first one supposes that it is the victim of damage who is damned by his affliction and finally saved by an award of damages. Some such root connection between words is to be expected when we consider the high scholarship, much of it embodied in the clergy that attended English courts beginning in 1066. We know there was a close interaction between church and state as they developed in Norman England. The separation between church and state was not so much a blank wall as an exquisitely drafted property line. It defined separate free spaces for the two authorities as they labored in the vineyard of the human spirit. Why wouldn't the theory of one authority have its parallel in the theory of the other, and why wouldn't damnation in the church have its analog in the law?

It might then be clever of us to remember who the damned is in the church. It is not the victim of the sin but the sinner. And who in the Middle Ages was the beneficiary of indulgences? Not the victim but the sinner; by virtue of atonement. Even the money paid for an indulgence went not to the victim but to the clergy, and the clergy in turn represented the sinner before the bar of heaven. Indeed, against whom was the sin committed? Not the victim, but God, his law and his kingdom. The sinner had not exerted self-restraint; he had been contemptuous of his servitudes under canon law.

Damage, then, in the law; why does it not signify that the perpetrator of the harm has fallen from grace in the eyes of the secular rulers? For rulers it is not so much that the sinner's lack of restraint has impaired a fellow-human, a victim perhaps purely by chance. It is that she has impaired the common good, the ruler's treasure. This is the sin that the law sees in damage. Atone for your sin, woman; assume responsibility for the consequences of your acts. Pay an equivalent and restore yourself to grace.

Certainly a payment for indulgence was an equivalent; the blacker the sin the more money to save the sinner from hell. So also with damages, the only difference being that the state is sagacious enough to transfer the equivalent to the victim. As with buying indulgences, the damage-equivalent in no way saves the victim from the particular pit into which he has been cast. In no way does it bring back an arm or a leg or health or a dead husband or mother. Conceivably then this is the theory of damage, but what about damages - the equivalent? What from a ruler's point of view is the function of damages.

To answer, one might first ask how the common good will be promoted by damages. To be sure, the common good is wounded by the shrinkage of potential in a member of the nation. But a payment of money, though it may re-elevate the member's shrunken potential, sort of, will not of itself elevate the common good in the least. In elevating the potential of the victim, it reduces the potential of the losing defendant. It takes from Peter to pay Paul. As far as the common good is concerned, the transfer of money in payment of damages adds up to zero. In damage the impairment of the common good is forever, and damages does not repair it.

But the common good will be in even greater danger of erosion if people find they need not take responsibility for the consequences of their acts. It is reasonable then to believe that the rulerly purpose of damages is to instill in people a sense of common decency. It teaches them to be more careful in releasing charged devices into the environment. And damages has other good effects from a ruler's point of view. Potential victims, the mass of the people as a whole, feel the supporting arm of government all about. Their urge to circulate, to create, is not dampened by a social environment in which people can act as irresponsibly as they choose. If damages cannot cure common good ailments, at least it is a good dose of preventive medicine.

We have then three views of damage, and perhaps each has an essential role to play in due process. First it is an estimation of a person's irreversible shrinkage in legal potential, a shrinkage linked to an invasion of his free space. This idea of damage furnishes a parameter, a yardstick, for measuring the shrinkage of the common good, the nation's potential. Thus damage is a guide to damages, a money equivalent.

Second, damage can be viewed as the remnant of an alien will remaining to haunt the victim; a ghost that cannot be exorcised. As a sin cannot be erased from the records of the universe, so damage. It can only be atoned. This view of damage supplies part of the most critical test we have for detecting the presence of damage in a case; part I, has there been injury - has the free space of the plaintiff been invaded somehow by the will of the defendant, and part II, is the will of the defendant still lingering materially, in crystalized form, in the free space of the plaintiff, diminishing her real liberty there, her legal potential as a person?

In the third view of damage, the sinner is before the bar of the common good and atonement is required. The common good requires the astringent of discipline. An equivalent is demanded. It will free her conscience from guilt (whether she is aware of her conscience or not). It will remind all others to be cautious in pursuing their projects. The common good is vulnerable to reckless action.

The eyes of damages peer in many directions. Not only does damages measure shrinkage in potential, it measures the attitude of the sinner. Was her mind steeped in malice as she took the action that led to injury and damage? Was there contempt for the common good? Or was the affair an unfortunate coincidence of events precipitating upon a lover of the common good? In the latter case, it is sufficient that damage reflect only the shrinkage in potential. But recklessness or maliciousness will switch a punitive program into operation. Damages in excess of an equivalent will be charged against the defendant, increasing in proportion to her wilful lack of self-restraint.

The eyes of damages also see incalcitrance, numbness to discipline. How heavy a slap is required to teach the sinner a lesson? In making this estimate, it will often be the personal assets of the defendant that are taken into account. It is assumed that the greater her wealth, the more insensitive she will be to a light monetary slap. On the other hand, the amount of damages must not be greater than she can bear. After all her attitude, not only the attitude of the plaintiff, is part of the common good and, in all these decisions, it is the common good that must be kept in mind.

Taking all these matters under consideration, it would seem to me that the ultimate argument for damages is not an appeal to the court's sympathy for the victim of damage. It is the argument that the ruler's treasure has been diminished; the common good has been impaired; and the common good will be in danger of even greater erosion if this occasion is not used to teach the watching public a sensible lesson in caution and self-restraint. People must learn that they will be held responsible for the consequences of their actions. And this, I imagine, is rather sound policy on the part of rulers.

CHAPTER 13

THE BASIC ELEMENTS OF
PROJECTS AND PURSUITS

Perhaps now we can begin to discern the possible shape of our arch of justice. It seems that property is a base on which to set injury and damage and, taken together, property and injury provide a base on which to erect due process. Property and due process, taken together, then provide a basis for our legal freedom and in fact, when put into action, they materialize our legal freedom.

So, in civilized countries, and particularly in those dominated by holonistic rulers, each of us strolls casually about a marvellous estate of her very own, our estates being assemblies of our properties - our legal free spaces; being all the things we can do under law, and more: being our legal freedom - the things we **may** do, even if we don't have the physical capacity to phenomenalize them. We stroll casually about our estates; that is, we stroll casually unless we get the uneasy feeling that another will - volo - is taking liberties, or is haunting us (materially) in our freedom space; without our permission; and then we lose our casual attitude. We begin to feel the stress and even the anger that attends the slightest of injuries. We feel the oppression. Then, if we but knock and seek, the government will come to our aid and relieve our oppression and restore our potential.

In any event, our estate consists of all the uses to which we hold title, including the use of government machinery under due process, **minus** the services and servitudes to which we will be held under law and equity. Here in the title of use I am including the titles of possession and disposal, and this is a reasonable inclusion for literary purposes. Possessing something - keeping it where you can see and touch it, and disposing something - transferring it to the ownership of another, are kinds of uses at least for the sake of generalization. And with this we have a completely general definition of our estate - our complete collection of properties - the space of our legal freedom.

As I have stated, injury is an invasion of property. In injury, the will of a person has an unwelcome effect in the freedom space of another. Given this, the two primary claims in a claim of injury are (1) the plaintiff has within her property a particular project space and (2) an activity of the defendant is having an uninvited effect in that space. If the only point at issue is the second claim, we have only a trial of fact, a case in law. But if property is at issue, we might have a case in equity.

In a case purely in equity, there will be no issue raised as to the unwelcome effect; the defendant will admit it. There will be a challenge of property lines. The defendant will claim she is acting within her entitled space. And to be purely in equity, this will be a historically new challenge - one for which there is no analogous precedent. That such challenges are sometimes sustained indicate that estates are expandable and contractable by actions in equity. This frames our main quest in this book: on what grounds - by what precepts of justice - may a court change property lines? More fundamentally: what justifies - what is the rationale for - a property line in the first place?

Estates: entitlements, services and servitudes. A gun is a subject of property. I buy one, meaning that I acquire the exclusive titles of possession, use and disposal or, more generally, uses. For me now owning a gun, the field is wide open for all the uses to which guns can be applied. Except I may not use it to harm another person (except under special circumstances). I may not fire it within city limits (unless I do so on a licensed shooting range). I may not use it to shoot deer (except between November 13 and December 1) (and never if I'm seated in a car on public highway) (and never a doe) (without special permission from the game commission). Somewhere there exists within all these uses and exceptions, and restrictions, and exceptions to restrictions, my title in the use of this gun.

My neighbors are out of town, and one night I see a person crawling into their window. A bullet fired by me from my gun hits him in the thigh. It turns out that he has promised my neighbors to check the house while they are away. He forgot to bring the key with him that night, and he sues me for damages.

Much of the time in cases involving guns, the issues are issues of fact. Was the plaintiff hit; was the gun fired by the defendant; what is the measure of damage; and many such cases are handled in a court of law. Yet the issue may not be solely a question of fact. For instance, the difference between murder and justifiable homicide is basically a question of property. In murder, the defendant acted outside his free space. In justifiable homicide he acted within his free space. The decision will depend on certain kinds of facts, the kind a court uses to determine property. So the case against me might be a matter for equity. And while most courts other than municipal courts now wear both robes - equity and law - the judge is not truly observing due process unless he initially analyzes the case on the basis of two primary issues: (1) Is it clear that plaintiff was within his property or were both plaintiff and defendant acting within their entitled spaces and will it be necessary to declare which of the spaces will be given the designation of property? (2) Is it clear that there was injury, that is, an invasion of property? And injury cannot be made an issue until the question of property is put to rest.

In the case in which I shot the window-crawler, there is no doubt about the materiality of my will in the shooting. But did hitting him constitute injury? This question cannot be resolved until it is decided that my will was having an effect in his freedom space. A set of facts must be discovered that spells property for him or me. And, with property ascertained, the question of injury - did my will have an effect in his property (providing it was his property) - can be put at issue.

Perhaps this shooting situation has occurred so many times that the law is quite clear on the topic. Certain sets of facts place the defendant in his property; other sets place him in the plaintiff's property. But if the particular facts don't line up on a historically established property line, we see a primary issue not at law but in equity. This should be discovered early in the litigation for it determines how a jury will fit into the proceedings. Due process never permits a jury to make a property decision. This power is given only to a judge in equity. And true equity will provide a judge especially trained and talented in property decisions, for remember, an equity decision reaches out beyond the pale of the law. A mere knowledge of law does not qualify a person in equity. Placing a person under a servitude in his own entitled space is a very serious action.

The damage case in which property lines are uncertain poses a knotty difficulty. Suppose the judge decides I was outside my property in firing at the window-crawler, but suppose also that this issue was a true issue for equity; no judge had ever previously determined that a person in my position and acting as I did was outside her free space. How then can a court hold me responsible for my action? How could I be expected to restrain myself in firing if it cost a learned judge many midnight hours to decide that I had acted contrary to the common good? How had I sinned? How could I be damned? Fundamentally, can injury and damage be found in a case if property is determined **after** the fateful transaction? An important question for rulers, for if damages are not levied in such a case, how will the property lines be engraved in the public mind, and how will public sensitivity to the common good be sharpened?

We are not ready to answer this question. First we must gather other tools, more vocabulary for describing property. As precise as our terminology in property and freedom is becoming, it must take another leap in incisiveness. Several fundamental words need definition if we are to express the complex thoughts that demand expression. We now begin to build a vocabulary to use for labeling the basic elements of property, and first we must have names for the basic elements of projects and pursuits. The reasons will become clear.

I have already said that Farmer Brown's land is not his property. Land, or vases and television sets do not belong to people. They are their own selves. They can exist (once created) though we ourselves disappear from the earth. Then what is Mr. Brown's property as it pertains to this land? Well, it might be said that his property is his relationship to the land, a government-defined, government-protected relationship. More specifically I might say that his property consists of all the ways in which he may use the land. (Use, including possession and disposal.) But one finds that the word "use" is poorly defined in connection with legal functions, specifically property. In fact, before we can define property in a manner useful for analyzing our more complex cases in human rights, we must define other words linked to concepts that might be called the elements of property.

A thing can be a subject of property, in the sense that a thing-of-itself can be the subject of a dispute. A thing-of-itself is subject to being used by more than one person, but this is not true of a thing-in-the-mind. A pleasant daydream is a thing and subject to being used by the dreamer to pass time. But it is a thing-in-the-mind and therefore can not be used by anyone else. It is not a subject of property. And while a person's daydreaming project can be frustrated by the actions of another, the daydream itself cannot be the subject of the dispute.

What has this to do with Farmer Brown's land? First and last, it is not Farmer Brown's land. We have here merely an expression truncated for brevity and non-technical communication. What we call Farmer Brown's land is a piece of land in Calhoun County particularly situate in the southwest quarter of section 27 township 11 north, range 2 east, and in legal terms it also happens to be a subject of property. Moreover it so happens that on March 23, 1927 John Brown holds title to said land and also holds properties in it that do not precisely coincide with the title. For instance we know that for two months of the year he does not hold a fox-hunting property in it; he has assigned this property to others. Nor does he hold a property in any use of the land that will interfere with the fox-hunting use.

But let us withdraw from the complex world of property for a chapter, and dwell in the relatively simple world of projects and pursuits. Projects after all are what we use things for, and if we do not understand projects we will never understand property.

I now commence the first truly disciplinary section of the book, and it is not the last. To take full advantage of the book, you must grit your teeth and familiarize yourself thoroughly with how I use six words that label the basic elements of pursuits and projects.

As you will recall, a project is at the bottom of every human action. Even the scratching of an eyebrow is evidence of a project of some kind. Also at the bottom of every dispute we find a conflict of projects. And since the potential for conflict is at bottom the reason for producing a system of property, we see the link between projects and the court system. Indeed, the elements of projects must form part of the language of property, and for that reason our concept of projects requires an analysis into components or elements.

For the sake of analysis, we may say that projects have "elements". In the case of a particular personalized project, one of the elements is the person in whose mind the project is projected; it is reasonable that a project cannot exist without a projecter. We can call this person the **projecter** if she is merely thinking about the project, and the **pursuer** if she has initiated action in pursuit of it.

A project also has an **objective,** an immediate one. The immediate objective of Farmer Brown is to materialize a crop of potatoes stored in the barn. He wants to grow potatoes on that meadow in Calhoun County and store them in the barn. These activities require a use of that particular land, and we need not inquire into his ulterior objectives such as the provision of money for his wife's operation.

A projecter must envision a thing to use in pursuing the project, for example the meadow. This thing to be used is the **subject** of the project. There can't be a project without contemplating the use of something, perhaps many things, and this thing or these things to be used I will call the subject or subjects of the project.

So I have suggested three elements of a project: the projecter or pursuer, the objective, and the subject to be used, and it would be easy to say that the fourth and final element of every project is the actual use of the subject. This seems to make sense; the pursuer uses a subject to attain her objective. But it will be better to reserve "use" for another application. So I will call the fourth element of a project the **loading** of the subject. The loading is the set of acts brought to bear on a subject by a pursuer with a view to materializing her objective. The archer pulls on the bow and releases the arrow and lo! The arrow flies. You suddenly push down on the earth with your feet and lo! You go up in the air. You scribble some marks on a piece of paper and put it where your executor will find it and lo! When you die your money will be distributed here and there more or less as you directed in your scribblings. Loading, when you come right down to it, is a pursuer's attempt to load her will in material form into the subject of a project. Perhaps even now you can see the relation between use and loading in the two statements, "She uses the subject to attain her objective," and "She loads the subject with a view to materializing her objective."

We say John Brown grows potatoes on the meadow, but he really doesn't. What he really does is to perform a series of acts that interact with the space identified with the meadow. In consequence, the soil becomes soft and crumbly; it becomes charged with pieces of seed potatoes and chemical fertilizers; and after a short period of time shoots emerge and develop into healthy potato plants. We observe him swinging a hoe, and later note a trail of wilting weeds in his wake. He powders the plants with a queer smelling dust, and in a day or two we see the carcasses of bugs scattered about on the ground. When during a dry period the plants begin to droop he causes water to run in the furrows between the plants and mysteriously the plants revive. In the autumn the plants become yellow and withered and soon we see Brown causing some heavy machinery to roll slowly back and forth over the field. Magically the soil gets soft and crumbly again; the plants become crushed and half-buried; and potatoes appear in a truck driven along-side. When the truck is full it is driven off to the barn and lo! When this has occurred several times, the objective of Brown's project has materialized! A crop of potatoes is stored in the barn.

But he didn't **grow** potatoes. He performed many acts, thus loading the space of the meadow with his will, and as a consequence the total environment became more or less conducive to the growth and harvest of potatoes.

We say he used the meadow to grow potatoes, and this is true. But we are in the process of analyzing the elements of "use". To tell the truth, the meadow to Brown was a device. Remember devices? With a device you do something and something else happens. The archer does something to a bow and arrow, but the bow and arrow do something else.

We are being quite fundamental and general in this terminology. In Brown's project, the meadow was truly a subject. It was subjected to Brown's actions; to his will. Exactly as the people of a nation are the subjects of rulers in rulerly projects. When rulers act as rulers, they load the people, expecting the people to react. They put the arrow into the bow, draw it taut, aim and release, hoping that the people will react and discharge as anticipated; as projected; according to the laws of demo-psychology. In this way people are devices; subjects in the projects of rulers; engaged in projects having rulerly objectives. And in this sense, rulers are people-users.

So what is meant by the use of something, as in "A good use of this computer is to type routine communications"? In this sense a use is: (a) the set of all loadings... (b) that a projecter might execute... (c) to induce the subjects of the use... (d) to materialize a particular objective.

Example: a use of this automobile is: (a) the set of all loadings... (b) that a driver might execute... (c) to induce the automobile... (d) to get him to the beach.

Note that the elements of projects can be grouped in various ways. For example, the idea of use that I have just defined is composed of the subject, the objective and the loading. The driver is not particularized. Driving the car to the beach is a **use** of the automobile. In this sense, the use is abstract with respect to the pursuer; it is not a particularized project. So a use and a project are not equivalent.

Consider the sentence, "Grinding corn would be a good use for the hollow depression in this rock." It specifies the subject (hollow depression), implies a particular objective (ground corn), and takes the loading process for granted as a matter of experience. But the pursuer remains in the abstract for the moment. However, if you take the sentence, "If anybody is going to use the cavity in this rock for grinding corn, that person is going to be me," you are viewing a perfectly particularized project - a use plus a particular projecter. And we see not only all the elements of a project but all the elements of a potential dispute.

An objective is never a thing-of-itself. It is always at the end of the rainbow. It is always ahead of the pursuer; always projected. A pursuer is real. A subject is real. And so is an actual loading. The pursuer never executes a project; she executes a loading. If the pursuer ever catches up with the objective, or something like it, or something quite different, it is no longer an objective. It's a result.

I have been tempted to group together the subject, the pursuer and the loading, calling them the operational elements of a pursuit, but this would not be accurate. One can not omit the objective from such a grouping though its operational aspect is not obvious. In a project, the projecter anticipates the acts that she will load into the subject or into a complex of subjects. These are acts that are not completely definite but form a sort of space of loadings from which she will choose those seemingly appropriate to promote the progress of the pursuit. If one considers the use of a particular piece of land, the anticipated loadings for growing corn are quite different from those required for transforming it into a golf course, and so we may say that the objective is operational in a project or a pursuit. It gives a more or less rational shape to the space of loadings to be associated with the project or pursuit. Apparently it is operational in spite of the fact that it is never anything else than a thing-in-the-mind.

Finally, we can place loading in a group by itself. The actual loading of a subject by a person, it is this that transforms a project into a pursuit. It is this, the activation of a loading, that calls for the will - volo - of the projecter, transforming her into a pursuer. Without this, the object of desire will never materialize.

I wish to make a critical phone call, and at the same time wish not to. My finger hesitates before it dials the number. Though the words of the communication project are complete in the mind, the dialing is the first step in the loading process, requiring an act of will. I do it. The familiar voice at the other end sounds reassuring. Briefly we greet each other and I ask a few questions oblique to my true purpose. But will I really order that $10,000 worth of stock? This will be the next step in the project if it is to maintain status as pursuit. This simple act of ordering will load a rather complicated device - the device of investment - and I don't really know what the result will be. In any event, the loading of a subject always changes the subject itself - the pulling of the bow changes the bow - and it will be the inner reaction of the subject to its inner change that will produce the result of the pursuit. A bow under stress can even sometimes break.

For practice with this new vocabulary, let us dwell upon the elements of projects and pursuits at monotonous length, and view them in a multitude of lights; perhaps actually becoming accustomed to this stiff, inflexible, and absolutely essential terminology.

First, to review the dull catalog list of project elements, the view we have already covered, adding one or two comments. There is always the immediate **objective**, without which a project is wholly vacuous. There is the **subject**, the thing fastened upon by the roving eye of the projecter, to be subjected to her will. And then there is the **loading**, sometimes contemplated in advance, sometimes not; that indeterminate bundle of acts that she will impose upon the subject, with an eye to the objective. These three elements taken together form the **use**, and here's the point: a use, when associated with a particular subject, can be fought over. A particularized project, leaving the prospective pursuer in the abstract, can be the topic of a dispute. Take a bowl-like depression in a rock, with a pestle-like stone lying nearby, both adaptable to poundings; and corn meal as an objective. They suggest a use to the human mind and can inspire hair-pulling and fingernail scratching.

When you ponder a use and a projecter in various degrees of abstraction, you have a project in the abstract. Example: "If we had a car we could drive to the beach." But given a specific use - a specific car, rational loadings, and the beach in mind - plus a specific projecter - a driver - you have the capacity for results. And when the driver turns the key and starts the engine - when the pursuer loads the subject - you've got dynamite.

A use is always in the abstract, even if there is a specific subject in view - because it leaves the pursuer dangling in the abstract. This is true whether we put it in the form of a noun - "A senior center would be a perfect use for this building" - or in the form of a verb - "This building could be used as a senior center."

But what about the expression, "He is using the hammer to break windows"? There is nothing abstract about that. "The hammer can be used to break windows." That is abstract. But, "He is using it." That is concrete. And, in this concrete sense, **use** means almost what **load** means. "He is so loading the hammer that it is breaking windows." By this we mean that he is injecting his will into the hammer in the form of momentum, and proximity to glass.

We might use "use" in both senses and we would communicate fairly well. But by using use for something that can be fought over - subject plus loading plus objective - we have something corresponding to **res** and **chose** in the law. And by substituting **load** for the other use of use, we not only escape ambiguity but gain a much greater advantage. We use a word for which we do not have an intuitive feel. It's a word that requires filling in the details. "He's using the hammer to break windows." I understand you. But, "He's so loading the hammer that it's breaking windows." I guess you had better fill me in on that. It is like the difference between, "That court decision is a miscarriage of justice," and "That court decision doesn't fit my idea of justice." The mind snaps shut on the first statement, but the ears prick up on the second, and this is exactly what we need in a precise analysis of a case.

Pursuing our exercise in projects and pursuits, looking at them in different lights, we can look at them in the light of desire. The project itself is related to the desires of the projecter. The objective of a project is practically identical to the related desire of the projecter. The specific subject is the thing that the projecter desires to engage intimately with his project. On the other hand, the loading of a subject might not directly reflect the desire of the projecter. I might not wish to load my racing legs onto a narrow plank crossing a terrifying chasm. But if that is the only way to escape a rhinoceros, I will initiate the loading.

Indeed in many loadings there is a conflict between desire and will, as for instance one might hesitate to commence a lawsuit, and this is usually due to at least two conflicting desires in the projecter. Nevertheless desire is the ultimate force that pushes the loading button of a pursuit. It is desire, the desire latent in the elements of projects and pursuits, that is frustrated by interferences, giving rise to anger and rebellion. If on the other hand such desire is confronted by overwhelming resistance as by a powerful individual or government, it frequently succumbs to a passive acceptance of fate and a sort of living death, and the potential for these natural human reactions are the very reasons inspiring intelligent rulers to devise systems spelling out property, injury and due process.

Lastly, we look at projects and pursuits in the light of the **functional** aspect of the elements. A particular subject, for instance, might occupy center stage in the eyes of a projecter because it is well adapted to her project, both to her convenience in loading it and to her objective. A bouldery hillside is not as good as a meadow for potato-growing and fox-hunting. Nevertheless, even with the most suitable of subjects, a projecter often has to adjust his objective to the limitations of the subject. In wet years, the soil of the meadow may be water-logged; moldy for potatoes; treacherous for riding to the hounds. Such possibilities are anticipated by experienced farmers and hunters, and projectively taken into account. In sum they compose the **potential** of the subject for the materialization or phenomenalization of the objective. And if the hopes of the projecter are in some way bound to a particular subject, the potential of the projecter himself depends critically on the potential of the subject. If a farmer owns only a meadow, he must adapt all his farming hopes to its potential, and in exactly such fashion does the treasure of a ruler accumulate or crumble. His projects depend on the inanimate subject matter of his realm and on the potential of his human subject matter, his subjects. In this aspect of the elements, if we see the wasting of subjects at all levels, we see the potential of damage; to a person; to the common good; to a ruler.

Further, in the light of function, it can be said that the characteristics of a particular subject not only determine the kinds of objectives that can be associated with it (one does not make airplanes of lead), they determine the kind of loadings appropriately to be applied. Making a statue of marble requires a different loading than making a statue of bronze. Functionally, all the elements of projects are bound together, and the niceties of loading are frequently critical in the success or failure of a pursuit. A television advertisement is a loading of viewer minds in the public relations pursuit of a company, and a slight variation in composition or execution can produce a tremendous difference in results. Indeed, it is often the fine tuning of loading that is frustrated by the bungling impact of an intruder.

Now I turn your attention from the project itself to its activation; to the attempts of the projecter (now pursuer) to phenomenalize the thing-in-the-mind, that is, to materialize the objective. Depending on the reliability of his preconceptions as a projecter, and on his skills as a pursuer, he might load the subject effectively, or he might not. He might apply too heavy a hand, or too light. He might perform all the required loadings, or only part of them, or none.

And the subject responds in accord with its nature. The soil of the meadow, too wet when Brown plows in the spring, turns up in big ugly lumps instead of the wonderful crumbly mulch that plants love. If this is the year he plants potatoes, neglecting his fox-hunting servitude, the riders come over the fence in September expecting turf - a turf springing back from the stab of their horses hooves, keeping the horses air-born as the steeds of Apollo. But no, instead of turf there awaits the mire of a dug-up sodden potato field. True, the hooves stab the ground, and go down, and keep going down, and fail to come up. The meadow fails to respond as expected to this loading. Its characteristics have been altered. Its potential for the hunt has been reduced to zero.

So in the pursuit of a project we see the loadings of the pursuer, the response of the subject, and the consequences, and the consequences might be a material reproduction of the objective, and they might not. And what is left for us to examine about projects and pursuits? The review and evaluation of what we have done in a given pursuit and what has happened.

We size up the results and compare them with our objectives. We try to find the reasons for our successes and failures; we attribute them to how well we estimated the suitability of the subject, to how accurately we predicted its response to our loadings. We judge how skillfully we loaded it. And finally we might wonder if the potential of the subject or the effectiveness of our actions had been diminished by the intrusions of others - others who had no business interfering with the phenomenalization of our project. Here then are the elements of projects and pursuits, and the various meanings they have to us as hopeful mortals.

CHAPTER 14

THE BASIC ELEMENTS OF PROPERTY

The rules of property can be sorted into three groups: First, the rules determining the class of persons (pursuers) to whom a use of a particular thing is assigned. Farmer Brown holds title to all potato growing projects connected with Tract ABC in Calhoun County. All persons hold title to the strolling use of McKinley Park. All citizens 18 years of age and over hold title to the use of polls in Presidential elections.

Second, the rules limiting objectives for projects. Unlicensed persons may not use their hot water heaters for distilling alcoholic beverages. No person may use her automobile for maiming another person.

Third, the rules defining the space of loadings applicable to specific subject matter. On the public highway, a driver may not so load his throttle that the speed of his car exceeds 55 miles per hour. A person may not so load her record player with electricity that the sound intrudes into the enjoyment space of others. A teacher may apply a hairbrush to her own offspring for telling a lie, but not to a pupil in her classroom.

The academic classification just stated is not particularly useful. In fact, the rules would be meaningless without the little examples. But having stated the rules, I can use them as tools for expressing the essential idea of property, and here I start to trace property into the transcendental world gained by the common law.

The purpose of the rules of property is to prepare a very special place for you. If in relation to a specific subject you are (1) in the provided class of pursuers and (2) staying within the provided space of objectives and (3) properly limiting your loading of the subject, you are in a space in which your every desire will be protected by government, applying all its power if necessary.

What a statement! Really, if this very special space embodies the idea of property, then my term "legal freedom space" is wholly inadequate. The very best word indeed is "property" - a space of your very own - and we should educate ourselves to appreciate this word. Yes, one might substitute for property the term freedom space, but "protected desire space" is more accurate.

And now, having practiced a bit with the vocabulary, I will abruptly abandon the world of the abstract, for governments labor only in the world of the concrete.

The device called "title" transforms the legal abstract into legal meat. To enter the space called property, we must use the gate called title; there's no other entrance.

We may imagine the idea of property germinating on an early British manor, in the well-tilled soil of title. Here, where Sir Brian Keswick governs a small jurisdiction, we find a fertile meadow that many plowmen would like to use. Perhaps as I describe the situation, you will have preconceptions of Farmer Brown; different times; different land.

"Alan," says Sir Brian to his favorite yeoman, "I'm going to grant you the potato growing use of the meadow, reserving the fox-hunting use for myself and friends. We'll keep to this a number of years. And, since the uses tend to interfere with each other, we'll divide the meadow into several fields and schedule a reasonable rotation of the uses every two or three years.

"Anyhow," he continues, "we'll agree that you won't grow potatoes on the fields assigned to fox-hunting, and I won't run the horses over your plantings. We'll further understand that you won't be personally obligated to grow potatoes for the year; you can return the use to me, and I'll reassign it. I wish to have the disposal.

"Understand that I will protect your use. I'll chase away anyone who tries to grow potatoes on the fields assigned to you. I'll put a stop to anyone interfering with your operations. And if anyone harms the crops, I'll thump them. Just let me know.

What Keswick has done is to grant Alan title to the potato growing use of the meadow, and note that his statement covers all the elements of a project. It includes an assignment to a particular pursuer - Alan. It specifies the subject - the meadow - and the objective - a crop of potatoes. The permissable loadings - plowing, planting, hoeing, harvesting - are implied by the objective. Loadings are assumed to bear a reasonable relationship to the objective. Keswick would be outraged to find Alan conducting a religious revival on the meadow, collecting donations on the pretext that the Lord will bless the potato crop. When we see these ingredients assembled, we know that Keswick has instituted something quite definite. He has established a particularized project complete with pursuer, subject, objective and loadings. Observe further, it is not a contractual title. Alan is not obligated to plant potatoes. He may plant or not, as he wishes.

Since Keswick represents government in this jurisdiction, his grant creates a joint government-civilian project. Keswick wants potatoes, and he wants Alan in charge of production. The project reflects two sets of desires -government's and Alan's.

Furthermore, to keep the pursuit free of intrusion, Keswick has pledged his powers of physical force. The project - and Alan - have Keswick's armed services at their command. This is an element of Alan's title, making the project exclusive to Alan. It makes it private. Private enterprise is a government project. And this is what materializes Alan's freedom in this project space.

So we have here all the rudimentary elements of modern title, and this particular grant from Keswick to Alan has an added element - the protection from interference. This is a step toward property, and I'll discuss it presently.

Thus title in a way represents a government pursuit. It is a device in a government project to protect private enterprise. The government wants private enterprise for some reason. Or putting it more basically, the government wants enterprise, and title is a means of promoting it.

In this you see, we are thinking about projects on a different plane, from a ruler's point of view. Perhaps entering this phase a bit prematurely, let's look into it briefly.

If title is a device in a transcendant government project, what are the elements of the project - the **government** project. Who is the pursuer, and what is the subject? What are the loadings, and what is the objective? Briefly. A pursuit being a reflection of desire, a pursuer cannot be an abstract something called "the government". Government, being nothing more than a piece of machinery, is incapable of desire. Only living individuals possess desire, and therefore (I say it for you), the true pursuers in a government project are the rulers.

The subject? Well, in Keswick's case, the subject is comprised of everything involved in a potato-growing project. All these things are in Sir Brian's domain. The meadow is subject to his will. The objective matches his desire. But more than these, Alan himself bows to Sir Brian's will, responding to his courtesies. And Sir Brian wills that Alan manages the loadings on the meadow. Therefore Alan is a subject in Keswick's project, and as you see, the entire potato growing project, this rulerly project on a different plane - complete with pursuer, subject, loading, and objective - comprises the profile of the title of the more elevated project.

So title is not a dead thing filed away in a recorder's office. Title is composed of (1) at least two human beings, a ruler and his subject, and (2) the things elevating a ruler's potential in the real world, and (3) the promise of power safeguarding this potential.

What are the loadings that Sir Brian will exert on this subject matter? Will he put his hand to the plow or take his turn spading potatoes in the autumn? Hardly. No. His loadings will be upon the human element of title - Alan the plowman. And what are the loadings that he will exert on Alan? As I will show, the loadings of the common law follow an extremely simple and mature principle. First and second, the loadings are appropriate demonstrations by Sir Brian of his over-whelming power and absolute integrity - what Sir Brian promises, he fulfills. These are not necessarily loadings directly on Alan but on others; Alan merely senses them in the atmosphere; they are the environment in which Alan develops. Other than that the loadings are null - nothing. Oh, there will be a property tax, a quiet hint of rulerly interest. Other than that - complete freedom of action within property. Complete guarantee of title. Complete protection of freedom and title.

What kind of loadings are these! What kind of loadings are **no** loadings? Why, it is simple. They are the loadings that rulers deem to be conducive to their objectives? And what is their objective? That's easy to answer. Their objective is Omega! If these simple statements require elaboration, well, there is the rest of the book.

It will become obvious that the rulers' Omega is not merely potatoes. Common law rulers are not merely calculating the potato crop. Note, they protect even the title in a neglected weed patch. Evidently they wish to protect not only the entitled project of their subject-projecter,but, for some reason, her every desire within the entitled space.

When Jimmy Jones floats through Farmer Brown's forest, he is not bothering Farmer Brown except in one particular: - Brown's wishes. Brown desires that Jimmy **not** be in his forest, and this evokes the magic of trespass. Not that Jimmy interferes with a pursuit of Brown; Brown never floats through his own forest. But only one person is entitled to float in that forest; only one entitled to grant that use to others; and it is Brown. And on this seemingly trivial basis the government will exert all the force necessary to protect this space of desire for Brown.

It is true that most titles are not printed on sales slips or deeds. The right to stroll through public parks or walk on public streets might be granted by ordinance or public dedication, or simply distilled into being by decisions of common law courts. Parents seem to have an unwritten title to the space of rearing their children, a title gathering dust and tatters of late. Nor is it necessary that a person carry an owner's certificate for a dress made by her own hands from her own fabric. Moreover every legal code recites the entitlement of every person to personal safety and bodily freedom, and yes, even the pursuit of happiness seems to be tagged with a sort of title, though we will soon see its limitations.

Under the common law there is an absolutely unbending rule of title. Every thing must have an owner. It applies to every blade of grass and grain of sand, every rusted piece of junk and every diamond bracelet. If no one claims past ownership, the new owner is he or she who claims it first, and this title is as good as the title to a castle that has been in the family for six hundred years. In the seedbed of the common law, after the conquest of England by the Normans, you held title (if you were a Norman) to whatever you could take and possess by the sword. You need only meet William's feudal arrangements. So if you trace an English title back until you can trace no farther, the deed may refer to the earliest holder as holding by "prescription", as though title had come from on High. It means that the title emerged from that ancient bloody mist. Given that seizure, title was conveyed from that time to this by a fairly regular process. One gained and held the title under feudal grant, or, as commercialism developed, by paying money for it.

In the modern world, beyond these titles to subject matter conveyed to you by gift, commercial transaction, or public dedication, you now have title to the use of your own body and the creations springing from your mental and physical efforts. You have title to even more intangible matter - your personal relations, your social relations, and the training of your children. To these I will devote much space. The legal world bursts with rules of title and restrictions upon title. You have a right to pursuits you might not even be aware of. Still I repeat. Entitled space is not identical to property. As you are now learning, your property - your protected desire space - is smaller than your entitled space.

As we learned from Farmer Brown's experience, the chief factor reducing one's entitled space is the legal device called servitude. A less definite factor is the effect of one's duties. Near the end of Chapter 7, I used a Venn diagram to depict a primitive idea of title and property. It bears repeating:

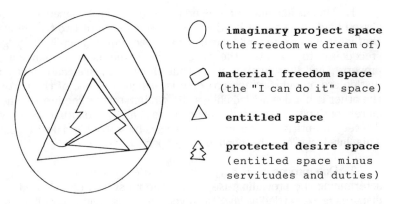

imaginary project space
(the freedom we dream of)

material freedom space
(the "I can do it" space)

entitled space

protected desire space
(entitled space minus
servitudes and duties)

And now we must really roll up our sleeves and get down to work.

With what has been said about title thus far, it is possible to list **the elements of title:**

1. The assignment of title. To be valid a title must be assigned to a person or a class of persons in accord with the rules of assignment; that is, by gift or purchase; or by recognition that the assignee has created the subject matter of the title; or by statute, ordinance and public dedication; or by a person claiming a thing having no other apparent owner; or by the rules implied by common law judgments; or by a court's declaration of title in a specific suit.

2. The profile of title, namely the use to which title is granted and the person to whom it is granted. Since the use consists of the subject, and the loadings to which the subject may be subjected, and the objectives for which the subject may be used, and since the grantee is the entitled projecter or pursuer, the profile consists of a particularized project complete with an assigned pursuer. The profile identifies the very pursuer, the very subject, the very loadings permitted and the very objective approved under the title.

3. Due process. As a result of the government's guarantee of title, due process becomes an element of title. Under due process, the government has a duty to protect the entitled person's enjoyment of the entitled space, though only to the extent that the particular enjoyment does not breach the principles of equity. A complaint in court that title has been violated has the function of invoking due process. In harmony with this, it is the function of title to define an entitled space - the profile of title - so precisely that a violation is easily detected. Once violation is manifest, the function of due process is to sweep the intruding will, the intruding loading, out of the plaintiff's entitled space.

Enumerating the elements of title lays the groundwork for listing **the elements of property,** and they are:

1. The assignment of property. Property is assigned only to a person holding a valid title. But when the pursuits of two title holders conflict in a space to which both are entitled, equity is called in to give precedence to one over the other. The result is an assignment of property, and it is in this arena that the most passionate pleas for justice are brought. When property is assigned to one of the parties, the other is not disentitled unless the circumstances require it. She is merely put under a servitude sufficient to remedy the situation. As you can see, an entitled space might not always be a protected desire space. This label can only be applied to property.

2. Due process. Today, when entitled uses clash, the rules determining the prevailing use are for the most part established. The dispute can be settled at law. However when the case is novel, with no solution at law, one of the clashing uses will be placed under servitude, a very serious matter. The judge in such a case must refer to the principles of equity.

3. **Servitude.** This is both a positive and a negative component of property. To the title-holder placed under servitude it is negative, depriving him of a portion of his entitled project space. It is positive to the person whose project is favored, although it does not add to his entitled space. It affirms his entitled space as his property; I have called it a protected desire space. Though entitled space grows out of the principles of equity, a servitude restricting it rises from the same principles, invoked by a special situation.

4. **Service.** This generates a restraint on freedom in one's entitled space, rising from a government duty impressed on a person. The effect reflects the inability of a person to be in two places at one time, or to have her cake and eat it too. If you are called into armed service, it will be impossible to go to your business office every day, though you are entitled to do so.

5. **The profile of property.** Based on the profile of title, complete with title-holder, subject, objective and appropriate loadings, but the profile of title is indented by the inroads of servitude and duty, and the result is the profile of property. Not as constant as a profile of title, the profile of property changes from situation to situation, and, in a particular case, the task of equity is to describe exactly how a party's profile of property differs from her profile of title.

Having in hand a vocabulary for expressing title and property, based on the elements of projects, we now have tools for expressing surprisingly difficult situations in a surprisingly clear mode, tools that we otherwise lack.

When we are discussing a specific title or property, it is important to cover each and every element of the involved project. This will become clearer. A reason for thinking in terms of projects: title is often partitioned to accomodate particular projects. Example: Brown sold the fox-hunting project (a title to it) to the hunting club. The same subject, the land, was involved, but different objectives; hence different loadings.

With a simple example, let us become accustomed to the vocabulary of this space called property.

Mrs. Rinaldo is a very talented person. Though involved in many pursuits, she herself is a subject in the pursuits of many others. She is hired as receptionist in a real estate office. She is a consenting subject in a marital relationship. She is in debt for her automobile, hence a subject in the interest-collecting pursuit of a bank. She is under contract to sing every Sunday in the First Congregational Church, a subject of a church project, a device into which the congregation loads money, and out comes song. This what we mean when we say the church uses her as a singer.

We are in the habit of calling Mrs. Rinaldo a free person. Free to go where she wishes. Free to spend her money as she wishes. Free to flirt lightly with real estate clients if she likes. Free to stay in bed of a morning if she wishes. She is entitled to pursue all these projects, and free to load the subject matter as nicely as she chooses; but only within that space called her property. So what is her property?

In describing it, you might attempt to count off all the projects to which she is entitled, but what servitudes must she observe? To what services is she bound? What are the properties of others in her? These are some of the problems that people face in trying to determine the shape of their estates, the profiles of their properties.

Let us continue to walk idly through the landscape of property for a while, surveying old matters in a new language. You have acquired title to a particular use in Mr. Gianetti's huge spread of land - the barley growing use. You now the titleholder, the approved projecter-pursuer in this particular project, what is your entitled space in the land, and what is your property in the land?

Let us say that another person has acquired the use of the land in his search for underground oil fields. A third person has permission to use the land for winter-pasturing his sheep. And a fourth has bought a long narrow easement for the purpose of erecting and maintaining electrical transmission lines. It is possible to partition the entire title in land use into as many titles as there are uses of the land.

Your entitled space consists of all the loadings you might exert on the land consistent with growing barley. In addition, your entitled space includes your use of government in preventing other people from pursuing the same project on the same land. Mr. Gianetti, after selling the barley-growing title to you, is no longer in a position to sell it to another person. If he does, the second person may not grow barley there as long as you are the entitled pursuer. Priority of title prevails.

But your property is not the same as your entitled space. Before you bought the barley-growing rights, the sheep man had the winter pasture rights, and his pasturing title covers the period from November through April inclusive. Therefore, though you prefer to plant barley in early March, you will have to wait until the first of May, and this will cut into your yield and profit. Mr. Gianetti, in selling the pasture rights, placed himself under a servitude not to interfere with the pasturing project. This removed a piece of freedom space from his property, and he could not sell you what he did not own. Mr. Gianetti's servitude falls upon your barley-growing project.

It is after your barley is growing that the electric power company applies to Mr. Gianetti for the power line rights. In erecting the towers and stringing the wires they will have to build an access road to their tract, cutting across your barley planting. In addition, their construction will destroy a wide strip of your planting.

Having sold the company the transmission line title, Mr. Gianetti cannot deny them access to the tract, even if the contract of sale does not explicitly provide it. But you, having played no part in the transaction, can you prevent the coming destruction to your barley? Yes. These are interfering projects. Though the objectives are not the same, the loadings are mutually interfering, hence are covered by due process. You have the senior title, purchased without servitude to the power transmission title, and someone - Gianetti or the power company - will have to buy from you the space of loadings in which there will be interference.

It can be seen that mutual loading interferences will also occur between the electric company pursuit and the oil drilling pursuit, and hopefully the conflict will be resolved according to an intelligent standard of justice. It appears that when you buy "rights", they depend not only on your entitled space but on other people's titles. Your rights depend on your title, but with variations. More accurately, they depend on your property.

Strictly limited title. This is exactly the meaning of easement. Under the powerline title, the company has the right to use the land, but not the right to sell the land. It has the right to sell the use, unless this was expressly denied, but only the use that it has. It cannot sell the use of the tract to a telephone company for a telephone line. So in all these matters we are talking in terms of the profile of title or the profile of property, and when we ask of a person, "What property are you buying?" we might be asking something that he can not state in detail. A precise answer would require a detailed description not only of the projects to which he would be entitled, but the loadings in which he would have to restrain himself. We would be asking not only for the profile of his title but the profile of his property.

By a back door, we have arrived at a point where we can begin to define rights in a fairly satisfactory manner. A right is a person's projected loading within her property. On Mr. Gianetti's land, the power company is entitled to build the transmission line, but it hasn't the right. If it starts loading the land without your permission, you can invoke due process to halt it. And how do you mobilize due process? By loading a proper complaint into the court machinery. The rules of court dictate how a court should respond to such a loading. So we come to a preliminary definition of right. Your right is a projected loading in your property. This is not my final statement on right, but if you insist on something definite, this is it.

Does Warfield have a right to load Vivia with free lunches and sweet nothings? Do the motor boat boys have a right to load the water around Mr. Duckweiler with their speeding boats? Does Mr. Wolcott's neighbor have the right to load the airspace between Wolcott and his view with the world's biggest billboard? Does Mr. Weatherby have a right to load his window and Miss Engle's mind with the image of his eyes looking at her? Does Patricia have a right to load King Stanislaus's army with herself?

If a person's contemplated action constitutes a loading within her property, then she has a right to initiate it. So how does she determine if her project is within her property? She first determines the profile of her desired project. What is the subject matter she wishes to load? Has it been assigned to her? What loadings does she wish to apply to the subject, and what is her objective, and is she entitled to them? If to this point everything is affirmative, she may conclude that her project is within her entitled space. She then asks if she is under any servitude restraining her from acting as she wishes to act. Servitudes are perplexing components, and I will deal with them in detail. Finally, she asks herself if she is under a service or duty conflicting with her project. Besides certain services demanded by government, I will conclude by a tortuous path that her only duties are her fiduciary duties. If she has title to her desired project space, free of servitude and duty, then the project is within her property. She has the right to go ahead.

But what if someone else is standing in her way, interfering with her enjoyment of her liberty space? She may call upon the government to act in her behalf. But what if the other person seems to be staying and acting within his own entitled space - within his rights? Ah. This is a main reason for writing a book like this. Some of the most difficult cases in court are those seeking a declaration of servitude or a declaration of duty. It is the servitude or the discovery of duty that puts the finest of touches on project approval, and tailors the project to the projecter. Are our courts today able to construct a reliable profile of property? This is the critique we seek.

Here above all is the chief idea to grasp. When your finger is firmly on property, it is firmly on injury as well. And, until you have your finger firmly on property, you cannot reliably determine injury. Excepting the final chapters, this is what the rest of the book is about.

CHAPTER 15

A UNIFIED CONCEPT OF POTENTIAL, FREEDOM, LIBERTY, PROPERTY, RIGHTS, AND INJURY

In preparing to read this chapter, find a space adapted to comfort, seclusion and concentration. It will not be light reading, and I sound a second warning. In this chapter I will pursue an analysis not found elsewhere to my knowledge. You will meet precise definitions for concepts like rights and liberty, concepts that no two people have ever defined in harmony. Perhaps you will be offended that my definitions do not fit your concepts, but look at it this way. I am dividing the real world of projects and competition into analytical elements and spaces, and I have to find a vocabulary for expressing them. I could have given them exotic names, and this chapter would have read like computer language. Instead I have used familiar words, but remember; they are merely labels for the elements or spaces. They are not sacred. So please accept them as labels, names for the concept spaces to which I have applied them. Be not distracted if they stray from your cherished ideas and ideals. Someday a true legal scientist will design better labels, and even a better system of spaces.

The title of this chapter presents six words that I have earlier used. Three of them - property, rights, and injury - we know to be weighty in juristic halls. Two more, freedom and liberty, at least furnish the excuse for government, and many of its problems. The remaining word, potential, rarely appears in legal discussion.

For this chapter you will want a unifying frame of mind, and the shortest path is this. Ask yourself what is injured in injury, and what is damaged in damage. Answers like freedom, liberty, property, rights and potential will come naturally to mind, these are injured and damaged, and thus do we instinctively sense a structural matrix, tying these words together.

What is injured... what is damaged. I phrased it thus with premeditation, and I think it is phrased incorrectly. In studying this topic, I have gradually come to feel this: We corrupt injury and damage when we make verbs of them. In injury I am not sure we injure something, or in damage we damage something. It's like sin, but we haven't corrupted sin so completely. We say we sin **against** Scott Smith; we don't say we **sin** Scott Smith. However we say we "injure" Scott Smith and, in doing so, we may be grammatically and theoretically abusive.

Fundamentally we commit acts and they turn out to be sin in God's order of things. The same with injury and damage in the legal universe. Sin, injury and damage are rents in the garments of the great. They are not transitive actions, my action affecting you. Law, it is true, relates them to transitive action - my action affecting you - but the words sin, injury, and damage do not express the mechanics of the transaction. And this is our goal in this chapter and the next: an understanding of what is transpiring **mechanically speaking** in the world of freedom and potential when we label it injury and damage.

I am convinced that the brains generating the common law were riveted on effectiveness - the effectiveness of the people they wished to govern, and on two aspects of a person's effectiveness; first on something we might call potential (I have used such a term) and second on something quite different - her freedom. It is obvious that a person inhabits a space called potential and another called freedom, and this habitation is independent of law. She has a condition of potential and a condition of freedom whether or not she dwells within a system of law. Take a very able person climbing palm trees for coconuts, cliffs for eggs, and into thatched openings for murder and theft.

She can dig soil for potatoes, marshland for clams, and old men for trinkets. She can make love, corn cakes and babies. Her capabilities can be listed ad infinitum. They comprise her potential.

Her potential includes things other than herself, subjects that she can load according to her objectives. A dagger is helpful for murder, a spade for digging clams, a mortar and pestle for grinding corn, and a man for starting the baby-making process. Give her these; her potential climbs. Take them away and it dwindles.

Her freedom is something else. Her freedom - and here I'm not speaking of her legal freedom but of her real, material, freedom - is limited by her potential. If for some reason she can not climb trees, then she is not free to do so. And though she is perfectly able to dig clams, she hasn't the freedom if someone prevents her. So her freedom is bounded by her potential and her competitors, and by one more thing - the peculiarities of time and space. Though she can do a million things, she has on this earth only time for five hundred thousand. For this reason, the notions of time and speed are so precious to mankind.

If we wish to point out a dynamic difference between potential and freedom, we might say that potential lacks the two factors, time and desire. "I could do it if I wanted to and had the time" - this is a statement of potential. But the idea of freedom loses an essential dimension if it is not tinged with at least a wisp of desire.

Basically we could more or less define her freedom (her real freedom) with this statement: "She is free to pursue project X if, at this moment, she wishes to pursue it, and can." In confusion, one might say, "I would do it if I wanted to; - therefore I'm free to do it," and this is a bad syllogism. (Remember, I'm defining labels.) In such a statement, one is talking about potential, not freedom. One is not doing "it" because one is doing something else; one wishes to do something else at this moment; and as a result one is not really free to do "it".

Thus the strictures of time and space weigh upon us. Thus our preferences among time-screened projects sternly determine the space of our freedom - our real freedom as distinguished from our potential. One may have the potential to become a good lawyer and a good doctor. But one's freedom to become both a successful lawyer and a successful doctor during one lifetime is greatly restricted.

I will attempt to organize these ideas with the use of Venn diagrams. You will see an initial resemblance to the former diagrams. The rectangle of Figure 15:1 represents the space of every project that everybody in the world can imagine themselves doing; not only the projects possible but those impossible; - like - sitting on a cloud. It might be called dreamland; partly realizable and partly unrealizable; but I will call it the imaginary project space.

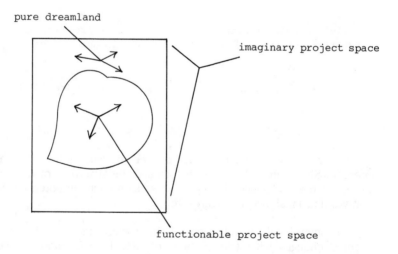

pure dreamland

imaginary project space

functionable project space

Figure 15:1

The heartshaped area holds the possible projects. I will call it the functionable project space - the set of all projects in the world that actually can be realized, materialized, phenomenalized - projects for which the necessary subjects and functional loadings exist; - realizable dreamland.

Now Emily is merely an individual - she is not the entire human race - and she does not have the ability to pursue all the projects in realizable dreamland. So Figure 15:2 duplicates the functionable project space and depicts within it the portion within Emily's capacity; the space of her potential. Here are the pursuits she has the capacity to undertake if she wishes to - not counting the restrictions of time and competition.

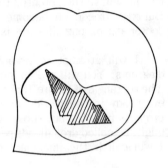

Emily's potential within the   Emily's freedom space
functionable project space   within her potential

Figure 15:2   Figure 15:3

As I have explained, Emily is not free to completely realize her potential. She is limited by competitors and the strictures of time and space; her freedom space of projects is smaller than her potential; it's relative size is shown in Figure 15:3

To comprehend the full scope of this topic, remember that one's potential changes with the fortunes of life. Like an amoeba one's potential changes its size and shape, and crawls about over the space of functionable projects. Not only that; one's competitors and desires vary with time; so one's freedom space is also fluid, shifting about within the space of one's potential. Additionally one discovers how immoderately a Venn diagram oversimplifies the human universe. One's potential is not really a continent in an ocean of conceivable projects. It is an archipelago of islands scattered through this region - each island having or not having an included space of freedom, and creeping about and blinking in and out as the case might be.

Now, given a person's potential, let us look at her freedom more closely. In Figure 15:4, I show the ideal freedom of two persons A and B. By ideal freedom I do not refer to dreamland, I refer to their real freedom, **absent competition.** Each, as she chooses the pursuits of her ideal freedom, is limited only by her potential, and by space and time.

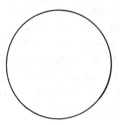 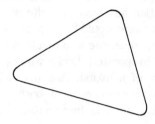

A's space of ideal freedom   B's space of ideal freedom

Figure 15:4

But here by "space" I am referring, of course, to a set of things and projects - real things. We are within the space of realizable projects. And when we place these spaces of ideal freedom within the real world, they are likely to overlap (Figure 15:5 A). This might occur when A and B both wish to load one certain thing, each in her own project, and at the same time. To load it mutually is either physically impossible or they don't like the idea, and a competition for this space is initiated. Then if B is able to dominate A in the space of competition, B's space of freedom remains about the same, approximating her ideal freedom, but A's freedom takes the shape shown in Figure 15:5 B. Comparing it with Figure 15:4 shows the bite taken by B from A's ideal freedom.

space of   A's resulting
competition   freedom

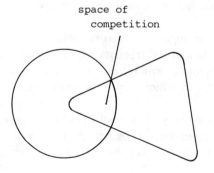 

Figure 15:5A   **Figure 15:5B**

Tholda wishes relief for her fingers, raw and sore from scratching the soil of her planting place. So, finding a fallen limb and a sharp stone, and spending two days in hard scraping, she shapes a digging stick, and now she can make a garden twice as big. Her potential has increased. But Hilda steals the digging stick, and we ask, has Hilda's potential soared, and has Tholda's plunged? No. Strangely enough, Tholda's creation has increased the potential of both. First, without a digging stick there would be no potential for theft. Second, Tholda's potential did not decrease as a result of the theft; it was her freedom in using it that evaporated. Locke was right; improving raw nature increases the stock of mankind. And now when Hilda clumsily breaks the digging stick, the potential of both women decreases. Freedom to use the digging stick is immaterial. The potential is gone.

Even when Hilda possesses the digging stick, it is still within Tholda's potential; but there is a barrier between it and her use of it. Not an impossible barrier, yet enough to decrease her freedom in using it. Since the spade exists, it is within her potential. The question is, who will use it. A matter of competition. And this is exactly what distinguishes freedom from ideal freedom.

It is haunting to reflect. All things within the range of a person's use are within her potential. It hints that all things are common to all people who move within the same space of effectiveness. It becomes clear. Only law and competition will decide who will enjoy the subject matter within this common space of potential.

Thus far the discussion of potential and freedom has been kept separate from questions of legality. Potential and freedom are realities in both civilized and uncivilized states. Now we will wish to study this same space of competition, but with an overlay of law.

In Figure 15:6, I show again the functionable project space, emphasizing not Emily's potential and freedom but spaces quite different - first, the space of projects to which Emily is entitled, and, within that, the space of projects in which Emily is propertied.

Note that Emily's entitled space lies wholly within the universe of functionable projects; the government does not grant titles in impossible dreams. Moreover her property lies entirely within her entitled space; the government does not recognize a person's claim of property in a project unless she is entitled to the project. As you already know, the bits and chunks of entitled space cut from her property represent servitudes and duties restraining her from certain entitled uses.

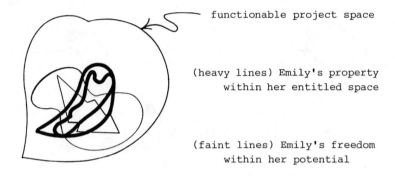

functionable project space

(heavy lines) Emily's property
within her entitled space

(faint lines) Emily's freedom
within her potential

Figure 15:6

By faint lines in Figure 15:6, I have reproduced Emily's potential and freedom. Note the considerable failure of overlap between Emily's potential-freedom spaces and her title-property spaces. We understand perfectly. In a state of law, there are projects she can pursue but may not. Conversely there are projects in which she is fully entitled, unencumbered by servitudes but for which she lacks the potential or freedom. Fortunately there are spaces in which her freedom and property join hands. If there were not, she would need special permission to greet a person, or to go to bed.

So there we have these various spaces and intersections of spaces, and it is how a government treats them, especially in competitive situations, that is so important to each of us.

In Figures 15:7 A B C, for visual ease, I reshape the project spaces, calling them the project spaces of Lydia.

Beginning with two potential-freedom spaces in Figure 15:7A and one property space in Figure 15:7B, and superimposing them in Figure 15:7C, the number of Lydia's distinguishable project spaces suddenly

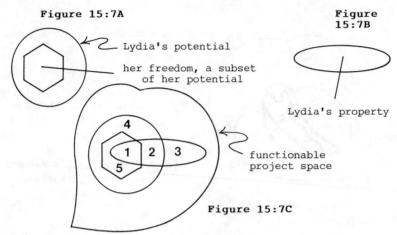

Figure 15:7A

Lydia's potential

her freedom, a subset of her potential

4

1 2 3

5

functionable project space

Figure 15:7B

Lydia's property

Figure 15:7C

rockets to ten. This is because each intersection of spaces has a distinct character. Study the following list carefully, relative to the spaces in Figure 15:7C.

(a) spaces 1 + 2 + 4 + 5 = Lydia's potential.

(b) spaces 1 + 5   = her freedom.

(c) spaces 1 + 2 + 3   = her property.

(d) spaces 4 + 5   = her unpropertied potential; her illegal potential.

(e) space 4   = her unpropertied, non-free potential; projects illegal and beyond her wishes or time limits or competitive ability.

(f) space 5   = her unpropertied freedom; illegal projects that she undertakes freely

(g) spaces 1 + 2   = her propertied potential; her legal potential.

(h) space 1   = her propertied freedom; legal projects that she undertakes freely

(i) space 2   = her propertied non-free potential; legal projects beyond her wishes or time limits or competitive ability.

(j) space 3   = her property beyond her potential.

If this seems excessively complicating, remember this is the world we live in. This is why legal decisions are sometimes torture. Actually there is an added complication not shown in Figure 15:7, and, when I introduce it, the whole concept will fall beautifully into place. I will now begin an effort to find a space to call liberty. Liberty is a different word than freedom, and we might as well make use of it. Perhaps you will be delighted with the way I apply it.

Freedom and property, though both mapped upon the space of functionable projects, are different in kind. Freedom is a phenomenal situation. It exists, small or large, shriveled or prodigious; it is concrete. One is free in a project or not. But property is a government decree. It attaches certain things, certain loadings, certain projects - in a legal sense - to certain persons or classes of persons. In the invisible book of government, the rules of property comprise a chapter. But there is another chapter called due process, and now I will define due process. Due process is a set of statements telling us what the government will do for us in various subdivisions of the functionable project space. More accurately, they tell us what government will do for us in a particular subset of our potential.

In the common law we find no such formal set of statements. The chapter of due process is not explicit. If we want to know what the government will do for us - beyond statutory statements - we must infer it; and we must hypothesize upon the areas of life in which it will do it. What I am preparing is a structure upon which to hang these inferences and hypotheses.

From what body of information are we to draw these inferences and base these hypotheses? As you can guess, our body of data consists of all those shelves and shelves of case reports in a law library. As a matter of fact, a full set of case reports and due process in the United States are identities. They are one and the same thing. Let me give you an example of inferring due process.

In Figure 15:7, spaces 4 and 5 comprise Lydia's unpropertied potential - her illegal potential. If she engages in illicit practices, they are mapped in space 5 - her illegal freedom. Space 4 is that portion of her illegal potential lying dormant; she could pursue a project in space 4 if she chose and had the time. So we ask what the government will do for Lydia in spaces 4 and 5 and the answer of course is nothing at all.

If she uses her shed for distilling 80-proof medecine and someone steals her inventory, the government will do nothing to help her. And if the sheriff brings charges against her for illegal loadings and illegal objectives, she will have no defense. Toward Lydia's activities in space 5, the statements of due process are quite negative. Is not this a true inference, a reliable hypothesis that we can draw from all the records of cases in the United States? Taken in this sense, it is a statement from government telling us what it will do for us in the space outside our property.

I have classed due process as an element of property, and so it is. But it is more than that. It is the interface where property is coupled to reality. It is the rule of justice.

Property is no more than words, a decree of sorts, but due process, duly observed by a court, is the operation by which government enforces its decree. Yes, property can be mapped on the space of projects, but in the unwritten chapter of due process, property attains another dimension, the dimension of government action. Meaning that in due process we are entering the space of government pursuits.

As in Figure 15:8 I show very simplistically, due process, founded on the loading space of property, pushes property into another dimension. The difference between property with and without due process is like Manhattan Island with and without skyscrapers. The implicit statements of due process - what the government will do for us in our various project spaces - we must infer from the whole body of law. And now we must discover the exact content of these statements.

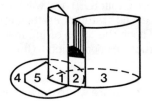

the various statements of due process, based on various subdivisions of the functionable project space

Figure 15:8. Statements Of Due Process.

I have defined due process as the set of statements telling us what the government will do for us in a particular subset of our potential, and now I should identify this segment.

In Figure 15:9A I show the ideal freedom spaces of P and Q and how they overlap, forming a space of competition. In Figure 15:9B I have reproduced the same spaces, but over them I have laid the properties of P and Q.

Notice that the space where competition is occurring lies outside Q's property and wholly within P's property. This is the space on which the eyes and ears of due process concentrate. To be precise, it is the portion of our ideal freedom lying within our property and in which an outsider is competing with us. Let me be more explicit.

Figure 15:9A   Figure 15:9B

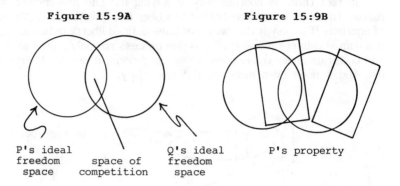

P's ideal   Q's ideal   P's property
freedom   space of   freedom
space   competition   space

In Figure 15:7 I did not depict the ideal freedom space of Lydia. It would have been too complicating. But the distinction between freedom and ideal freedom must not be neglected. To show its importance, I'll now reveal Lydia to be a sweet elderly person living alone. A nephew, visiting her frequently, always threatens her with physical harm, and always leaves with a large part of her pension income in his pocket. This determined the size of Lydia's freedom shown in Figure 15:7, and reproduced in Figure 15:10. Were it not for the nephew's extortion, her freedom space would be larger, shown by the dashed line in Figure 15:10. If this is the only factor depressing Lydia's freedom, we can see that the dashed line describes her ideal freedom and that what I called her freedom is merely the portion left when the nephew departs.

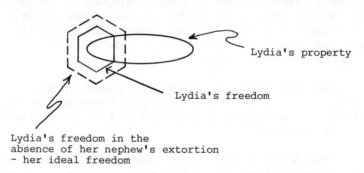

Lydia's property

Lydia's freedom

Lydia's freedom in the
absence of her nephew's extortion
- her ideal freedom

Figure 15:10

Finally she calls the police, and the government puts an end to the extortion. Her freedom increases. Truly her freedom is greater under the operation of due process. And now we may ask what the government says it will do for us - its statement of due process. It tells us it will protect for us the portion of our ideal freedom lying within our property.

In fact there is another way of saying it. The government will restore that part of our **liberty** that has been disrupted by the activities of another. If we say it this way, we have defined liberty to be our ideal freedom within our property. Thus due process not only states what it will do for us under these competitive conditions, it defines liberty for us. And it does even more. It defines injury.

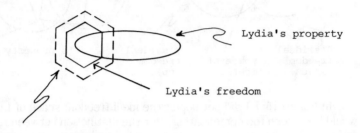

Lydia's property

Lydia's freedom

Lydia's freedom in the
absence of her nephew's extortion
- her ideal freedom

Figure 15:10

For look; the government cannot intervene in Lydia's case unless it hears claims of property and injury - this too is a statement of due process. Property is here in Lydia's case, and so is the court's intervention - we know from all those shelves of case reports that the government will intervene. It is an inference that will not fail. So we know that injury - as the government understands it - must have occurred. And what was the injury?

Well, what did the nephew do? He chopped off part of Lydia's liberty - part of her ideal freedom that lay within her property. Therefore reducing a person's liberty - as I have defined it here - constitutes injury.

A technicality or two before proceeding. It is common to hear in legal parlance that injury is an infringement of property. Poorly phrased. Property is invulnerable. As a decree of government, it can not be infringed. Freedom, however, can be infringed. This is phenomenally possible and liberty, being mechanically like one's freedom, is susceptible to infringement. The difference between property and liberty is like the difference between a contract to build a house and the materialization of the house by the contractor. The contract cannot be impeded; the materialization can. The phrase "an invasion of property" is fairly apt, at least it is descriptive. Since your liberty is within your property, the antagonist infringing your liberty has in a manner of speaking invaded your property.

So an infringement of liberty constitutes injury. But we can not yet define injury to be an infringement of liberty. We cannot call them identical until we have enlarged the idea of liberty. With this we step out of the space of our freedom into another space, and for this space due process has prepared another statement.

Lydia Abercrombie cannot possibly climb her apple tree. It is not within her potential, and therefore not within her freedom, even her ideal freedom. Yet if Willie Fitz-Hugh is in the tree, the police will chase him out if Lydia asks them to. Lydia's claim of property is secure, and we know the police will act, but Lydia's freedom is not at stake. Willie has not infringed her freedom in the least. So what is the basis of injury?

One sees that Willie is loading a subject that, under the rules of title, is assigned exclusively to the loading of Mrs. Abercrombie. Or to those with her permission to load it. He is usurping her place as the rightful commissioner of loading. He is enjoying her use.

Figure 15:7 has been reproduced again as Figure 15:11. We are talking about space 3, that part of Lydia's property lying beyond her potential. We know that injury is present, else the government will not act to relieve her, and there is but one inference to be made, a magnificent statement of due process, applying to this particular situation.

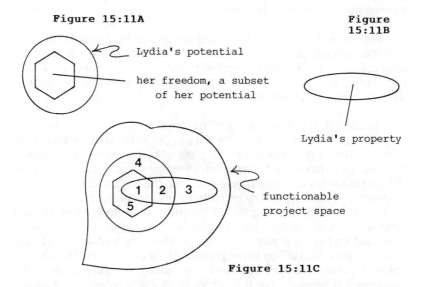

Figure 15:11A

Figure 15:11B

Lydia's potential

her freedom, a subset of her potential

Lydia's property

4
1 2 3
5

functionable project space

Figure 15:11C

Willie is using something that Mrs. Abercrombie wishes him not to use, and it is a something to which she is entitled. We are observing a function coupled to the plane of projects, yet on a different level. It would be easier to understand if Willie's use simply interfered with a pursuit of hers. For instance he is always in the tree whenever her guests gather beneath it for an afternoon tea party. In the case at hand he seems not to be infringing her liberty. He is merely countering her wishes as to who will load her apple tree, and now we reach the climax of this analysis.

Above every project in the space of your property, regardless of your ability or your wish to undertake the pursuit, the government erects a space of pure desire for you and you alone, assigning the title of loadings to your desire. In this space where your every wish prevails, a loading without your permission constitutes injury. Instantly upon an unpermitted loading and upon your complaint in court, the government will intervene and enforce your wish. One sees here a competition not in the space of ideal freedom. It is a confrontation between the pure desire of the property owner and the ideal freedom of the adversary. Injury here does not seem to be an infringement of liberty, but it is; for I will enlarge the concept and definition of liberty. Thus:

The choice of loading in a space of property is a liberty of the property owner. If someone other than a property owner uses an element of the property without the owner's permission, he diminishes the owner's liberty. He makes a choice that is the owner's to make. With this understanding we can maintain our definition. An infringement of liberty is injury. Injury is an infringement of liberty. Identities. No infringement of liberty, no injury.

With this, I believe we have almost captured liberty in its entirety. Our liberty consists of (a) our ideal freedom within the space of our property, i.e., our material freedom in our property, unencumbered by competitive interference and (b) our free determination of loadings in the space of our property.

An addendum to the concept of free choice of loadings is pertinent. The concept embraces all the elements of projects. By free choice we mean the owner may select the subjects of the property to be loaded, the loadings to be exerted upon them, the objectives of the loadings and the particular persons to execute or direct the loadings. Therefore by free choice of loadings we imply the free choice of projects, and we may draw this conclusion. A grant of property is, among other things, equivalent to a commission to choose the projects that will be exercised within the property. This is practically equivalent to a feudal estate. It puts Alan O'Day in the position of Sir Brian Keswick, with the difference that Alan may not use force against his competitors (with important exceptions). But it has the decided advantage that Alan can call upon the most powerful force in the land.

So our liberty consists of (a) our ideal freedom in our property and

(b) our free determination of projects in the space of our property, and part (b) has dimensions not included in the liberty of ideal freedom. It embraces functionable project spaces beyond even the personal potential of the estate-holder. Each portion of our liberty protects project areas that the other does not cover. They admirably supplement each other. We will find that infringements of liberty thus defined will include all injuries to be found anywhere, anytime, within the universe of the common law.

I have illustrated some profound ideas with simple examples, but later chapters will show how amazingly these definitions will throw light on some of the truly difficult issues that judges have been asked to decide in the American story.

You should recognize that I am not defining injury and liberty from grand transcendental principles. I have not in this chapter engaged with theory but with facts. I have pinned names on real spaces. I have described what happened between Mrs. Abercrombie and her nephew. I have reported what the government would undoubtedly do under the circumstances. The elements of property are derived from what is easily observed. I have simply placed names on concepts that are common in human experience, and have defined them in relation to each other. From these observations sprang my definitions of injury and liberty, and these definitions require testing for their usefulness. We will give them a considerable testing in the remainder of the book, with ample opportunity to revise or reject them as we proceed.

I have not dealt here with principles; there has been no attempt to justify the rules of due process. I have treated the mechanics of due process at the interface between property and the real world of human activity. It is the empirical approach for comprehending the structural basis of law in the United States. In concluding this chapter, I want to fit "rights" into the scheme so far expounded.

In the last chapter, I finally concluded that "a right is a loading in which you are propertied." This conclusion rises from the expression "I have a right to do this... I have a right to do that." To do something is precisely what I mean by a loading, and a loading implies a subject of loading. Thus, "I have a right to this job," implies, say, a desk and chair in an office - equipment that you can load with parts of your body; and a range of activities to which you can apply yourself with consequence. Your claim implies that you are entitled to these loadings and are under no servitudes restraining you from exercising them. Even if you do not own the desk, the chair, the office or the business, you are claiming some principle by which the government will protect your participation in these matters. In loading them you will be within the space of your property; at least this is your contention when you say, "I have a right to this job." So it does not seem inappropriate to say that a right is a loading in which you are propertied.

Thus the fox-hunters don't own Farmer Brown's land; they have a right to ride over it with fox-hunting as an objective. They have a property - a space of projects - that includes the loadings pertinent to fox-hunting. Really when it comes to basics it is impossible to distinguish between right and property. Nevertheless there is a slight intuitive distinction between them, and some clues to its nature. The first clue is the common use of the phrase "infringement of a right" and the second is the fact that one frequently uses the expression, "I have the right to...(do this thing)", using it especially when one feels one is being frustrated or challenged in the right. These usages suggest to me that in using the word right, one is trying to ride a fence between liberty and property. If right is property, then right cannot be infringed. If right is liberty then it can be infringed. Property is not action. It is a decree. If it is a decree it can't be frustrated, it can only be held in contempt; and material contempt is in the eyes of the legal gods - precisely injury.

Therefore if right is property, it cannot be frustrated. Only the pursuit of the rightful project can be frustrated. Only liberty - as far as due process is concerned - is vulnerable to frustration, and thus directly associable with injury.

Here may be a source of confusion in popular movements, and in legal procedure as well. Ambiguity in the word right permits legal arguments to slide past each other without meshing productively. In discussion a person should be aware that we sometimes use right to mean liberty and sometimes to mean property. When it means liberty, one is discussing something that can be infringed. When it means property, it can't.

Perhaps it is a tactically useful phrase: "I have a right to XYZ." Before your opponent responds, he must pause to grasp what you mean, and you have a chance to wonder what you mean. It can mean "I have a property that includes project XYZ." Or it can mean "The government should grant me a property in XYZ" Or, "I have a liberty in XYZ and someone is infringing my liberty."

Actually we can be quite specific now. The expression "I **should** have a right... " means "I don't have the right, but the government should place this use within my property." The expression "I **have** the right... " has two meanings. First, in a popular forum, it might mean the same as "I should have the right... ". But when the person is sure of his claimed right, as in "I have a right to a college education," it means "the use of the college facilities is within my property." Do you see how the latter way of putting it gives one a clearer picture of the legal problem one is facing?

I have done my best with the word right, but my best is none too good. If after this in the book I use the word right, I think it will most of the time signify a propertied loading. But I really do not believe I could define the word even for a group of my most congenial friends, without losing their friendship and respect. Look at one of the most common usages today, "I have a right to be free from ...." In Antieau's 1978 supplement we find a number of cases listed, purportedly establishing these various rights: the right to be free from an establishment of religion, the right to be free from an unlawful arrest, the right to liberty, the right to be free from cruel and unusual punishment. What does it mean, a right to be free? If you are in your property, you are free or else. This is the voice of due process. What this phrase tells me, this phrase "I have a right to be free from..." is this. You are not sure where your property lies, or of what it consists, and no lawyer has been able to tell you. And putting an end to this state of affairs is what this book is all about.

CHAPTER 16

UNIFICATION CONTINUED: DAMAGE, POTENTIAL, PROJECT EFFECTIVENESS, DAMAGES, MONEY

Having derived in Chapter 15 a strict definition of liberty, I could pinpoint injury very simply and exactly. Injury is an infringement of liberty. Damage now needs fitting into the system of project spaces. Damage, I said in Chapter 12, represents a permanent reduction of one's potential within one's property. Well, as an intuitive effort, the analysis of Chapter 12 was productive. Sometimes in starting a conversation one is limited to gutteralizing and slapping one's chest. Obviously in the damage phenomenon something is reduced; something like potential; but what, exactly? Is it potential, or freedom, or liberty or property, or what?

To begin, let us analyze "Lydia Abercrombie v. Nephew". Knowing we must search for injury before claiming damage, we ask what the injury was in "Abercrombie v. Nephew". What was the specific liberty that the nephew infringed? And we find it was Lydia's liberty to determine how her money was to be disposed. Under due process this liberty was assigned to Lydia and to no other. But her nephew's forcible extraction of her money deprived her of this liberty.

Associated with the injury was a loss of money, and it is important to understand that this loss was not an essential factor in the injury. To grasp this, let the nephew spend the money for antiques. Let him give Lydia the antiques and, with their dramatic increase in value, let him explain to the world that he acted as he did to protect her from inflation. Financially her situation is greatly improved. Nevertheless injury occurred. She was deprived of her liberty of disposal. Behavior such as the nephew's can be enjoined. Disposing Lydia's money is in her property; not the nephew's.

We strongly feel that loss of money is damage, and so it is when associated with theft or robbery or extortion. In such cases it seems hardly worth while to distinguish the damage from the injury. If you take money forcibly or by stealth, it would seem that deprivation is a natural consequence, an indivisible transaction. If one gets, the other loses. If you perpetrate the injury, the harm ensues; and one is tempted to say the injury causes the damage. But this is not a reliable concept. True, the legal connection between injury and damage is tough as steel, but the causal connection is surprising fragile.

In "Lineweaver v. Frick", Frick absent-mindedly stepped into the path of Lineweaver's car, and became chargeable with staggering damages. Frick's action "caused" Lineweaver to lose a contract. So easy to say. But how easy to turn the tables. Change but one of the circumstances - let Lineweaver drive five miles per hour faster. Let Frick step off the curb and, magically, he will not be the defendant. He will be the plaintiff. On Lineweaver, not Frick, the wrath of the gods will fall. Still, was it not Frick's stepping off the curb that caused the accident?

I am not saying that injury and damage are causally independent. It is a matter of understanding their true relation. Upon analysis it will be found that damage and the related injury always have two elements in common. First, as phenomena they both occur in the victim's property. Second, they both have roots in the same contributory act - the act of a person not the victim. And note for future reference the word contributory.

Your son digs a hole in the dirt, and the dirt is at the edge of a public road running in front of your house. Night comes, and a pedestrian's foot falls upon the hole space; an ankle is twisted. Medical bills follow, the pedestrian loses working time, and you (or your insurer) will pay damages.

What was the injury? Well, the hole was in a sidewalk (legally, to be a sidewalk, a sidewalk need not be paved - the common law presumes a walkway safe for pedestrians, paved or not, at the side of every public street). The world of pedestrians (or the government their agent) has the liberty of deciding whether holes shall be dug in a sidewalk. In the digging of this particular hole, their wishes were not sought and determined. Their liberty was infringed. This was the injury. The act of digging the hole was not the injury. It was the mechanism of injury. Depriving pedestrians (or the government their agent) of their liberty to determine the loadings in their property - this was the injury. And the act of hole-digging also contributed to the twisted ankle. Both the liberty and the ankle were in the pedestrian's property. Both were distorted as a result of one and the same set of acts. The word "contributory" is a key word, better than "cause."

In many ways we find the world to be a cocked and loaded gun pointed at each of us. For tragedy to happen, the world lacks only the pulled trigger. Understanding this is basic to understanding damage and responsibility. The world is a complex set of things intermeshed with functional relationships. It is a hodge-podge of harm-causing functional sequences. Fortunately, in most of the harm-causing sequences, an essential element is missing - a thing or an energizing action is missing - a thing or an action that will complete the functioning of the harm-causing sequence. In thousands of situations tragedy is impending IF... if an element - a thing or an energizing action - is added to the brew; contributed to the reactive chain.

Nancy walks to the candy store. In walking she leans forward almost to the point of falling, but, in walking, her coordinated footwork keeps her from falling. As she walks, she is surrounded by the forces of gravity and momentum. She is surrounded by soft insupportive air and hard supportive concrete. She is vulnerable to the relations between hard concrete and brittle teeth. If you decide to interfere with the forward motion of her foot, you can bet on the result. As she journeys to the store, the causal sequence resulting in a broken tooth is almost complete at each step. If the sequence is completed by the act of another, deliberate or not, and if the act happens also to infringe Nancy's liberty, we are in the presence of damage.

Take the fact that the world teems with small children. At age two they are seen running about exploring their world, and I propose the following experiment. Build a swimming pool in this world of children. Build no fence to discourage them from reaching the pool. Yes, you might propose such an experiment, but you won't pursue it. Every experienced person with any sense can predict the outcome.

Here we are; surrounded by a world of things and relationships, a world of action and reaction. A part of this world consists of human minds responding to what they see and feel. Human nature forms an element in many harm-causing sequences. Do this. Add that. And one can establish odds on the results.

People are at every moment balanced on the brinks of a hundred precipices, and a careless bump tips them over. These are the circumstances and mechanisms of damage. "Open your eyes to the harm-causing sequences that surround you. A reckless action might contribute a missing element completing a harmful chain of reactions. Direct your actions. Know where your next step will fall if it's to be a safe step. Make sure it falls there." This is the message of damages.

"If you act voluntarily, and if your act contributes an essential element to a causal sequence, you will be held responsible for the consequences. If a consequence of your act perpetrates injury, and if the person whose liberty is infringed is harmed as a result of your act, I'll pronounce damage, and I will assess damages against you." This is the voice of due process.

These are the mechanics of damage, and I have successfully

evaded the question of what damage is. Yes, I made progress along this line in Chapter 12, but we must understand damage in terms of project spaces, if we wish our analyses of difficult cases to be reliable. In Chapter 12 I discussed the three faces of damage. Damage, first, I said, represents the shrinkage of a person's potential. A shrinkage of a person's potential, I said, is also a shrinkage of the nation's potential.

Next, I said, damage can be viewed as the ghost of an alien will lingering on in the property of the victim, eternally constraining her freedom. It is a loading crystallized in her property, impossible to evict.

And finally damage is an affront to the gods, a shadow cast by a transgression on their system of property. In this context, damages is analogous to hell. It might get you if you contribute to injury. And as due process teaches us, this threat is not empty.

The first view of damage, a shrinkage of potential, appears to locate it in the system of project spaces, and seemingly it fits. A person gets a twisted ankle, and for a period she cannot pursue her preferred projects. Her potential has been reduced. Medical bills pile up. Work time is lost. Add these up and you derive an amount called damages.

But look. If damage represents a loss of potential, why do we compute it in medical bills and loss of time on the job. Does loss of money measure a victim's full loss of potential? Does it measure the fact that he can't play tennis, he can't take his scout troop on a hike in the hills, he's not free from pain, he can't sleep at night? Does money loss tell us anything about the reduction of his project space, except in projects related to money-making? These questions have been raised in court. Should damages be assessed for loss of recreational activities, for pain, for mental anguish, for loss of activities that cannot be measured in money?

Nevertheless money is central in damages. It is called an equivalent, but is it truly? Egad! Money damages seems a poor equivalent for the loss of an arm or an eye. The idea sometimes seems reasonable. Take two men both victims in the same automobile accident; both requiring the same period of recuperation. One of them works for six dollars an hour, the other for twenty. Should damages be proportionate to earning power? Usually due process says yes. Like Humpty Dumpty, the person suffering harm should be placed back on a wall of the financial height he fell from - even if he can't be put back together.

But what about the many cases in which plaintiffs were not profitably employed before the accident. Though they had been earning nothing, they recovered damages for lost time. The principle cited: - recovery is for loss of time, and loss of fictional earnings is a means of determining the value of the lost time!

Something is missing from this formula. The man earning twenty dollars per hour gets more in damages than the man earning six, but the man earning six gets no more than the man earning nothing.

We can make it more confusing. As the result of an automobile accident, Martin Santino's leg had to be amputated. Martin was a passenger in his friend's car, and the driver of the other car was at fault. So far, so good, but there were special circumstances. Martin had previously lost two arms and a leg, and his remaining leg, the one lost in this case, was already paralyzed. And Martin was not working.

Should he receive damages for more than his medical bills? Should he receive damages for lost time? Should he receive less damages for lost time than the unemployed person with two good arms and two good legs? What are we talking about anyway? What is the basic unit that has been lost forever, for which money is an equivalent?

Loss of time is an interesting concept. To completely master it, we would have to discover what time is. Is time equivalent to potential, or freedom, or what? Time, however, I will keep on a purely intuitional level, merely a prime consideration in our lives. In a very real way, time seems to make the difference between our potential and our ideal freedom. Let's explore the difference.

In primitive non-legal surroundings, a person steals your spade and breaks it by accident. It reduces your freedom. It interferes with your vegetable growing pursuit. But the impact on your effectiveness is greater than merely reducing your freedom. It reduces your potential. You will have to fashion another spade, and the time required for this task will reduce your freedom for pursuing other projects. So stealings and breakages have a way of reducing people's time for pursuing preferred projects.

But note that we began this discussion with a broken spade - a loss of potential, and we regain the potential by paying in freedom. To make a new spade, we had to give up other projects. There seems to be a confusion here between potential and freedom. Is there a flaw in my system of project spaces and, if so, can it be mended?

By one's potential I mean of course the set of all projects one can undertake; the projects for which one has the capacity - not taking competition or the limitations of time into consideration. Grossly oversimplifying, suppose your potential project space consists of six projects E,F,G,H,J,K. Assume that, for the period of the next month, you can undertake any three projects; no more; each project consuming about ten days. For example you can pursue FGK as a project combination, but not FGJK. Assume further that the combination must consist of different projects , no two the same, not EEG or HJJ. Given these rules, how many different sets of projects might you pursue in the next month? Assembling all the possible combinations - EFG,EFH...HJK, etc. - you will find there are twenty.

Don't deceive yourself that you have a greater choice than this; that you can limit yourself to just one or two projects per month, doing nothing the rest of the time; that you can add to the set of twenty three-project combinations all the one-project and two-project combinations. Doing nothing is a project, and if it happens to be in your project space of six, it is already accounted for in your set of twenty combinations.

If we did not know better, we would consider the set of twenty project combinations to represent your ideal freedom. True, you are limited by time to only three projects per month. But you are free to choose the combination that you will pursue, and it is tempting to think that our freedom - our ideal freedom - consists of our freedom of choice, as it ranges among the combinations of projects available to us. So it seems as though time makes the difference between our potential and our ideal freedom.

Except that time is not the only factor limiting a set of projects. One's effectiveness is also a factor. By improving your skills you might pursue not three but four projects a month. Thus, though time is definitely a factor, the set of twenty project combinations remains more closely related to your potential than to your freedom. For this reason I will call the set of twenty combinations your **per unit time potential**, and I will call your full project space of six projects your **time-free potential.**

What then is your freedom? Your freedom, like it or not, is EFG or EGH or GJK, or whatever combination of projects you choose to pursue and start to pursue and continue to pursue. Your freedom is what you do. Your potential, be it your time-free potential or your per unit time potential, is in the realm of projects. But your freedom is in the realm of reality, the realm of pursuits, the realm of action. You are free to do "it" only if you have chosen to do it and are doing it. You are going to argue with me, but remember; I am labeling a space that exists. There can be no argument. In the next day, or the next week, or the next month you will be able to undertake only a limited number of projects. You cannot undertake all the projects of your potential. And you will be able to undertake them only if you are ideally free. And it is into this space that you will most intensely resent the intrusion of others. And it is this space for which I need a label. And you will find some day, if a name and a substantial respect is not devoted to this space, you and your neighbors will be deprived of their freedom, and, without a well-defined label, they will have no way to express it. All these matters I will make clear chapter by chapter, but at this point it is important that we understand exactly what we are talking about when we are tossing these labels about.

Project E we will say is your"do nothing" project. Project F is a project in which you make a spade, and G is a project in which you use a spade. With the spade stolen and broken, your time-free potential is reduced. Since you cannot engage in G, your time-free potential now consists of only E,F,H,J,K - five projects instead of six. You will also discover, if you care to make the calculations, that your per unit time potential has been reduced from twenty combinations to ten. The whole set of combinations involving G has evaporated. But has your freedom been reduced?

To find a satisfactory answer for this, we must pass beyond the land of Venn diagrams. By Venn diagrams in Chapter 15, I depicted a person's space of freedom as a large sub-continent in the sea of potential. To convey a more realistic idea, I suggested that the space of freedom is not really continental, but rather an archipelago. It is composed of islands scattered through the space of potential. But now we must provide a new dimension for expressing the idea of freedom.

Suppose we represent your time-free potential by a circular grouping of letters as shown in Figure 16:1(a). Your desires and projections can range freely among the six projects. On this space it is impossible to depict your per unit time potential. A single combination of projects, EGJ, is outlined in Figure 16:1(b). Three, EFG, KEF, and GKJ are outlined in Figure 16:1(c). In Figure 16:1(d), an attempt has been made to outline a few more; and depicting all twenty combinations would be unintelligible.

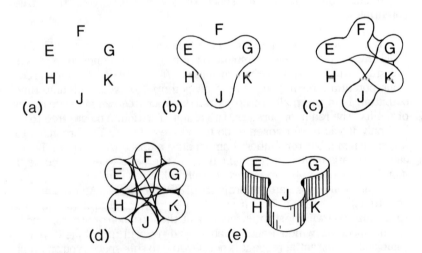

Figure 16:1. Potential, Choice, And Freedom.

Now suppose you choose to pursue combination EGJ as shown in Figure 16:1(b). Is this your freedom? No, it is not. It is your choice, and as such it remains in the land of your potential; still in the land of desire; of projects. To realize your freedom, you must exert your will in this loading space. You must act. In acting, you materialize (or fail to materialize) your freedom. In dealing in the coin of freedom, we are no longer talking about the flat two-dimensional plane of potential projects. We are pushing the EGJ combination into another realm, another dimension, as illustrated in Figure 16:1(e). It is just like the difference between property and liberty. It is the difference between Manhattan Island without and with skyscrapers. At this point we will neglect the factor of human interference. We are talking about your ideal freedom. So we know you will be free in pursuing EGJ. But your freedom will not exist until you are acting effectively in the pursuit itself.

But what about my freedom of choice, you ask. I am free, you say, to choose among the twenty project combinations. Therefore I am free before I act. And my freedom of choice is an immensely precious commodity.

With this we are forced to a sobering conclusion. Our so-called freedom of choice is a non-entity, an inanity. It is incompetent, irrelevant and immaterial. It is a burst bubble. It has the peal of a plastic bell.

Let us suppose you are ideally free. You have selected EGJ, and you are acting effectively in its pursuit. You might have selected EFK, GHJ or any of the others, with the same results as far as freedom is concerned. Your per unit time potential was there - your twenty combinations of projects to choose from - and we find that your so-called freedom of choice was merely your per unit time potential.

The choice was all within your brain, and no one can steal from you your freedom of choice. They can rob you of your potential, but not your freedom of choice. Freedom of choice is nothing other than your per unit time potential - the combinations of projects available to you in a given period of time - and this is not an independent space. It depends on the length of the time period. It depends on your efficiency or effectiveness. And it depends above all on your potential, a space that can be diminished, disrupted and distorted by others but, given your potential, your freedom of choice is an abstraction swirling within your own mind, and constitutes nothing material of which you might be deprived. One can simply look it up in an algebra book under the topics of permutations and combinations.

Certainly by freedom of choice we do not mean the freedom of a pauper to choose between cruising to Tahiti and wintering on the Riviera. He is free to dream, if you wish to call it freedom, but when I write about freedom I am thinking of a space more real. Let's face it.

There is no reason to give your allegiance to a government merely because it promises to protect your freedom of choice.

Since you are still not fully convinced, I'll deliver my last argument. Let us assume that there is something real that we can call freedom of choice. Of your per unit time potential you have chosen the EGJ combination, and have started to pursue this choice. While thus engaged you find that the actions of another person are frustrating you in your chosen pursuits. So you are not free to pursue EGJ effectively. Instead of your freedom as shown in Figure 16:2(a), you have a freedom looking more like Figure 16:2(b).

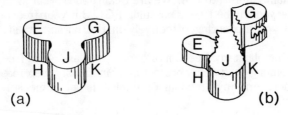

(a)   (b)

Figure 16:2. Freedom And Frustrated Freedom.

What good did it do you to have "freedom of choice"? More aptly, what good does it do you for someone to protect your freedom of choice. In short, you want protection for your potential and protection for your freedom - the combination of projects to which you have committed yourself, and it is in exchange for these commodities, not "freedom of choice", that you will give your allegiance to a government.

Here is a strange consequence of this analysis. When the thief stole your spade, it was still within your potential, though less effectively so. When he broke it, he eliminated it from your potential, and from his too for that matter. But he didn't reduce your freedom! Your freedom lies in the effective application of your will to a project within your potential. It is nonsense to say that a pauper is not free to eat breakfast at the Ritz. He simply lacks the potential. On the other hand, a human cuckoo in a clock with but a single project in his head is as free in his performance within his potential, given that no one interferes with him, as an absolute monarch with a thousand servants pursuing ten thousand projects.

But if your spade is unbroken, though stolen, and your potential has not been reduced, and your freedom has not been reduced, what has been reduced? This question strikes at the heart of our investigation.

The thing reduced is your effectiveness, and the same is true upon the breaking of the spade. Actually your potential is not reduced even upon the breaking of the spade, if material is at hand for the making of another. For look: you have project F in your potential - the ability to make spades. Hence project G - the project of using spades is still within your potential.

The difference is this. Previously you could pursue say projects EGH during the month, and attain the objectives of three projects. But now, during the next month - if you wish to pursue project G - digging your vegetable garden - you must first pursue project F - making your spade. Your must pursue F and G, two projects, in order to obtain the objective of just one project - digging your vegetable garden. This then is how the spade-breaker has affected your life, and there are several ways of expressing it. It is as though he has shortened your life. He has decreased the number of pursuits you will pursue during your life - the number of preferred pursuits to be accurate, and you feel it deeply. You find yourself constrained to a pursuit - making a spade - in which you wouldn't engage were it not for this fellow's interference. You are suffering the intrusion of his will into, well... Not exactly your potential; not exactly your freedom. But, as a result of his actions, you have lost some of your effectiveness in pursuing objectives, and this hurts.

One reaches the same conclusion if one loses potential irretrievably. Your original spade was made of the only suitable piece of material within your effective range. It was unique. The loss of a leg, though infinitely more dear, is in the same class of loss. You have lost your effectiveness in them not merely for the next month, but for life. Time and life, for a human, are inseparable, and time is an essential element in the phenomenon of damage.

But money! How is money tied to damage? Do we limit our desire for effectiveness merely to money-making or money-spending projects? Suppose Mr. Lagomarsino inactivated for a year by an accident, winning damages based on losing a year's work. But before the accident, he had decided to take the year off without pay. He would spend a year traveling with his dying daughter. This is the project he wished to pursue during the lost year, and how can damages in mode money be called an equivalent!

But a year's work is the rulers' treasure, you say, testing me. "A year's work is a measure of Mr. Lagomarsino's effectiveness - a measure of the nation's wealth." Is it indeed? Well, that comes under the topic of justifying the law, and our present task is to understand damage and project spaces. Without this we cannot approach the topic of justification.

At this point in our progress we must be content reflecting that our rulers have found some sort of treasure in the liberty of their people. This became evident in our treatment of injury. And evidently this rulerly interest extends into damage. And now we catch our first true glimpse of this province.

In the case of **Dandoy v. Oswald**, Oswald dumped earth on Dandoy's land. In trial it was determined that the land was not actually harmed, and nominal damages ($1.00) were assessed for technical trespass. That's all. But the Appeals Court modified the judgment. Oswald, it held, should either remove the soil or pay damages equal to the cost of removal. To hold otherwise, said the court, "would be to decide that an owner of land may be compelled to accept a change in the physical condition of his property, or else perform the work of restoration at his own expense." In effect the court was saying, "To leave the soil there and assess nominal damages would be like telling Mrs. Abercrombie that Willie could stay in her apple tree as long as he liked. "Willie; pay Mrs. Abercrombie $1.00. Technically you have trespassed." The Dandoy case reflected not only an infringement of liberty to begin with, it was a loading that would persist. It would be a continuing injury. The will of the loader would linger on, infringing forever the liberty of the owner in his property.

The effect on the land? Negligible. So where is the effect? We will find it in the mind of the owner! Something the government doesn't like is happening in the mind of the owner. And it is here, in this mental sphere, I propose, that the sobering phenomenon occurs; the phenomenon to which the government applies the term damage.

Damage then is not crystallized injury; it is not an alien will haunting the property of another. These are **signals** of damage.

What are we seeing? We are seeing a government-created alarm system. In property, liberty, injury, we are seeing the working parts of an ingenious instrument, an instrument alerting government that an unwelcome phenomenon is occurring in a human mind. A persistent injury, a crystallized injury is a red light. Given this signal, an officer of government should recognize that damage stalks in the shadows.

Do we see injury in a case? Do we see a loss of project effectiveness, and does it result from the same act that perpetrated the injury? If we do, we may infer damage. This is the voice of a ruler. Given damage, the government will assess damages. Money. Now how in the world does money fit into a scheme like this? It fits for this reason; money is a **mode** of project effectiveness!

To illustrate this let us say a trip to Europe is within your potential. But, it is not within your one-month set of projects; it is within your fifteen year set. If you resolve to save money for the next fifteen years, you will have to sacrifice other pursuits during that time. But this does not mean you will surrender your freedom. This is your freedom. An exercise of your effectiveness in a preferred project is your freedom.

Nor does saving money diminish your per unit time potential. At any moment you can change your mind about the trip, and choose another set of pursuits for the days ahead. In fact, having saved some money, you can now pursue more projects - more money-spending projects - than you could had you not saved the money. In saving, your project effectiveness accumulates. Over a period of time you will pile up bits of project effectiveness, these being pieces-of-eight. With respect to projects requiring money, extra money allows us to squeeze more pursuits into a given period of time. Money is a pile, large or small, of project effectiveness.

I wish to make this more precise. To do this, I will make the EFGHJK project space more realistic. Until now, I have specified three projects a month, each consuming a third of a month; about ten days. Now we will agree that each pursuit consumes the number of days shown in Table 1.

Table 1.

Project Name	No. Of Days Required
E	2
F	4
G	6
H	8
J	10
K	12

I will also change the rules for determining project combinations. Any combination of projects can be pursued during a month, provided that the total time required by the chosen projects adds up to exactly thirty days. We will also permit projects duplicated any number of times during the month, within the thirty day restriction. Some possible combinations meeting these rules are: HJK, EFGHJ, EFGEFGG, JJJ, GGGGG, FFFFFFFE, KKG. Each of the examples consumes exactly thirty days.

If project F is the spade-making project, it would seem silly for a person to pursue mostly F. He leaves no time for digging in his garden, or eating, fishing, making his bed, and cleaning his clothes. It would be silly unless other people want his spades, want them so much that, in exchange for his spades, they will dig his garden, give him some fish, make his bed, and clean his clothes. By trading, you see, he can achieve a number of objectives, though executing loadings in but one or two projects.

Suppose further he is more effective than anyone else in making spades. And there are others more effective than he in projects G,H,J,K. If he pursues combination FFFFFFFE for a month and trades spades for G's, H's, J's, and K's, he finds he can achieve FGHHJJKKE during the thirty days. Achieving this by his own efforts would require seventy-two days! Trading has increased his project effectiveness, and the project effectiveness of his trading partners too.

Instead of trading spades for G,H,J,K's, suppose he trades spades for enough money to buy G,H,J,K's. No, make it even more realistic. His money will buy combinations of goods and services from a wide variety of goods and services. Call these combinations S1, S2, S3... each S a different set of goods and services, not just one good or service, and make the list of sets practically endless. With this I will show you that money is not only a measure of project effectiveness. It is a storage of project effectiveness. And this is only the beginning, for we will see that money is project effectiveness in material mode.

This month he sells all his spades, and, with his money receipts, purchases and enjoys S1 S2 S3, a collection of S sets. Next month he again sells all his production of spades, saving a portion of his money and enjoying only S1 S2. The following month, having again sold all his spades, he has the capacity once more to enjoy another S1 S2 S3, and he still has the money equivalent of another S3, saved from the previous month. Possibly S3 + S3 are the equivalent of S4, a trip to Atlantic City, an excursion not within his one month project effectiveness. So by saving money he has carried a bit of project effectiveness from an earlier period of time to a later period. This is a chief benefit of money, providing a means of storing and accumulating project effectiveness, and allowing us to amass it for preferred times and preferred objectives. But how can we call money effective? What makes it effective?

On my bookshelf is a textbook saying, "the possession of money gives the owner or producer a claim on production," and this is inaccurate. Money is not a claim on production, and this is not the source of its effectiveness. You cannot make an owner or producer sell an item to you (unless of course she has offered it generally at a stated price). Money's attractiveness is the source of its effectiveness. Money has enticement value, and by offering it to people you can coax them to join you in your pursuits.

Often we state it oppositely. We say that people display their wares to entice money from you. But really money is the true attraction. Not that people do not produce in anticipation of your needs and desires, and try to guide you in choosing your purchases. But their enterprise is motivated by the attractiveness of your money. Money is effective because it's attractive, and attractive because it's effective. It is attractive not because it represents project effectiveness. It is attractive because it IS project effectiveness. It is effective because it is attractive. A loss of money, you see, is a loss of project effectiveness.

Now you can see in legal theory the meeting and joining of two profound material facts. Money is project effectiveness, and damage is linked to a loss in project effectiveness. We can trust the keen minds of our legal forbearers. Not calling damages a "substitute" or "surrogate" or "alternate", they called it an equivalent, and so it is. As we know, lead is not a substitute for gold. On a weighing scale it is an equivalent. In the coin of gravity it is an equivalent. So money, in the coin of project effectiveness, is an equivalent.

We are not talking about the force field of gravity, but the force field of project effectiveness - a force field of human psychology. Certainly there are losses in project effectiveness that cannot be measured in money. But a loss of money hurts; it too is project effectiveness. Money damages hits where it hurts. In this way it is an equivalent.

In Chapter 12, I observed that damages does not remedy a loss in the common good. A loss in project effectiveness is a loss forever. A payment of damages, as far as the common good is concerned - the common good of the here and now - balances out to zero. Damages, as far as rulers are concerned, looks to the future. We go no deeper than this in this chapter. Rulers pay attention to a loss in effectiveness coupled with injury. For them it signals damage. For them it signals a disturbing frame of mind. As to why damage concerns them, and what damage really is, is a development requiring the rest of the book.

Some valuable conclusions can be drawn at this stage. Damage is signalled by various situations - a crystallized infringement of liberty. The dumping of soil on farm land, with no actual impairment. Or it may be signalled by a seemingly reparable loss of potential - a fence broken in a drunken car chase. Here the irreparable loss is the loss of time for society as a whole, turning its attention to restoring a fence, when the carpenters might be employed in a more productive project. Sometimes damage is signalled by an easily calculable loss of money - medical bills and loss of working time. And sometimes it is signalled by the irreplaceable loss of a Mona Lisa, or a once-in-a-lifetime opportunity, or a human limb. But in all cases, the common unit of loss is project effectiveness; the sense of powerlessness; perhaps powerless rage.

In damages, the principle of compensating the victim, taking all cases into account, is left with little significance. It can be applied only in an ideal textbook case - where the loss can be actually calculated in money. But a malefactor can never pay for destroying a commercial airliner, and, conversely, a billion dollar corporation will feel no pain paying compensatory damages due to a single fatally defective electric toaster. We all know that nothing will replace a lost loved one, and certainly strict compensation will not distinguish a malicious act from an innocent act resulting accidentally in harm.

Besides the compensatory aspect of damages, damages represents a government attempt to safeguard the common good of the future, and it seems to have three modes of action. To the victim suffering the loss of project effectiveness, damages is the voice of government saying, "I understand your feelings." This simple statement by an omnipotent authority has a salutory effect on the common good. Second, damages is the teaching method adopted by government to show a person causing harm how it feels to lose project effectiveness. Third, it is the way government suggests to the population as a whole that it is smart to be careful; government holds us responsible for contributing to a harm-causing sequence.

Under due process, damages may be determined by juries, a wise policy. Given the complexity of the decision, one supposes a judge will painstakingly instruct the jury in the purpose of damages.

As a final thought on the teaching value of damages, one wonders about the immunity afforded by liability insurance. Should insurance be permitted to take all the sting out of damages? Remember, we are thinking about intelligent justice.

CHAPTER 17

A MECHANICAL ANALYSIS OF INJURY

Now I am committed to strict definitions of property, liberty and injury, and they will have to conform to all the statutes on the books, all the case reports. Well, not all, of course. Not all statutes and court decisions are consistent with each other. Nevertheless a working hypothesis of legal principles should display fitness to the body of law. It must conform to many decisions and statutes. It must illuminate the flaws in poor decisions. It must corroborate the rightness of good decisions - decisions supported perhaps by defective opinions.

A person's property, I have said, is the set of all the projects in which the government guarantees, under due process, absolute liberty to the person. Due process itself is a two-tiered instrument. First it is a book telling us, among other things, exactly what our liberty is. Secondly it is the will of a very strong government clearing away all infringements of our liberty.

Due process places the power of government at a person's beck and call. It adds the government's potential to her own potential - within the range of her liberty - and this added potential generates for her a freedom far beyond her freedom in a lawless state. Not only is she guaranteed the freedom to load as she pleases within her property, but she has the denial of all loadings within that range due to the actions of others.

This latter bit of liberty has tremendous economic value. Though she might not have the physical ability to pick apples from her apple tree she can, with the government's help, prevent others from picking them. By this means they are forced to pay her for the liberty of picking and enjoying the apples. So the government has extended her potential and freedom into projects that would be beyond her capacity in a "state of nature". Thus government enhances her project effectiveness.

Remember that property is composed not only of subjects but of loadings defined upon the subjects. Through contract a person might obtain the picking of the apples but not the eating. Or not having the picking of them, he might obtain the marketing. Property is defined as much by loadings as by subject matter; and sometimes the loadings are defined by objectives (John Smith rents the use of the Lakeside Marina for an art show). And sometimes a court will recognize that loadings are defined merely by the nature of the subject, as in "Yes, you may use my new carving knife." (Implication: "for carving a roast, not scraping plaster off bricks.")

It is also of course essential that a person is attached to a property, and therefore I say that property is defined upon particularized projects - particularized as to the entitled projector, sometime pursuer. It is important when we are talking about a specific property, a specific loading space, a specific liberty, that we not forget to consider each and all of the elements - subject, loading, objective and projecter. And nowhere are the elements more important than in an analysis of injury.

Due process defines our liberty to consist of (a) our ideal freedom in our property and (b) our unrestricted determination of loadings in the loading space of our property. Injury, then, is perpetrated by an infringement of our liberty. Your "injury space" is your liberty space - your property. In no other space can you be injured. Having made these distinctions, there remains the question of how a liberty is infringed. Here I am addressing a question of pure mechanics. What constitutes infringement? Putting it as a cunning person might put it - "How can I infringe the liberty of X so craftily that no one can say with certainty that it constitutes injury?" One finds there to be a variety of mechanisms through which one's liberty might be infringed. Many remaining chapters explore some of the highly obscure almost occult mechanisms. For that task I will now lay a foundation for categorizing such mechanisms.

In a game of tennis you use several subjects: some balls; your racket; the court marked with lines; the net; a high enclosing fence to corral your balls; and last but not least your opponent and her racket. The game of tennis arises from the actions and reactions that occur between you and these subjects and one other item - the set of devices known as the rules of tennis.

You trigger the energy of your arm, your arm loads the racket with momentum, the racket loads the ball with momentum, and the ball loads the net with the energy of your arm. The net saps the momentum of the ball and the action stops momentarily. Reconsider.

As the ball hits the net, it is loaded with your will. Not your intentions probably, but with your will for it was your will that triggered the energy of your arm. The stopping of the action therefore is a consequence of your will, for your will is loaded not only into the crude triggering of energy but into your manner of guiding the racket. You are engaged in a pursuit; you have objectives: and your pleasure in the game derives in great part from how well the results of your loadings match your objectives.

When the ball hits the net, a device called a set of rules takes effect. Not a physical device, it nevertheless has an effect, depending on the will of the players to follow the rules. The rule is activated - loaded - by the ball hitting the net. It is also loaded by the point score, the game score and the set score as they have accumulated to this point. It is also loaded with a certain amount of reason and experience. Like a computer it reacts with an output, telling you and your opponent what to do next. Should you serve again or should your opponent serve? Should you move to the other side of the court or should you put a towel around your neck and call it a match? All these instructions are part of the rules. If you don't act accordingly, you are not playing the game of tennis.

For a public park there are written or perhaps unwritten rules governing who is to use the tennis court. Generally speaking you wait your turn and, when it is your turn, you and your opponent have the exclusive use of the court, meaning that you may load it with all the loadings consistent with tennis. No one else may thus load it (during your turn) without your consent. And no one else may so cause a load within this space that your liberty within it is restricted. The loading of the court for tennis, for the term of your turn, has become part of your estate.

As you play, a prankster insists on standing between you and the net. "I can stay here if I want," he says. "It's public property." But he is mistaken. As a member of the human race he is entitled to use the park, but with limitations. In this case for example, he has no title to the court for the term of your turn, and he may not interfere with your enjoyment of this project space.

But he is persistent. No longer standing within the lines of the court, he stands near the fence and within it; interfering not at all with your play. Nevertheless at your request a policeman will remove him. He is loading the court against your wishes.

The policeman leaves and the prankster gets bolder. Not only does he enter the court but he catches your racket just as you start to swing at the ball; an added infringement of your liberty. Not only is he loading the court but he's loading you. And you, now and forever, are a subject of title in no one else's project without your consent (certain government services excepted). Your body is reserved for your own exclusive use.

Each injury perpetrated by the prankster has been through trespass, and I stress the preposition "through". I did not say that the injury was trespass or that trespass was the name of the injury. I make here two or three distinctions not always observed in legal practice. First the injury is not the act that perpetrates the injury, the injury starts purely and simply with the infringement of liberty. Second, in analyzing a situation for an infringement of liberty, the infringement is not always easy to discern or discover and one must learn how to analyze the case mechanistically if one is to determine exactly how the act of the injurer engages and infringes the project space or loading space in question.

In trespass, the perpetrator is operating completely outside his entitled space. He is using something to which he is not entitled. In the case of the prankster, in each prank he loaded a subject in property assigned to you and your tennis companion, but the various loadings impacted your liberty in distinguishable ways.

When the prankster merely stood close to the fence within the court, without interfering, the impact on you was not physical. He was merely loading the court without your permission, like Jimmy Jones floating through Farmer Brown's forest. You might contend that his presence was distracting, or that he might suddenly interfere, or that you might run into him, but a court will not require an explanation of your wishes in the matter. In injury, mode trespass, your liberty is mapped one-to-one on the space of your desire. At your call the government will evict the trespasser.

When the prankster stood between you and the net, we see a different mechanism of infringement. It still originates in trespass, but interference is involved. In standing between you and the net, he changed the shape of the court. Your potential in achieving your objectives in accord with the rules has been decreased. He has changed the shape of your project space, and I will call this mechanism of injury distortion. This is a case of distortion through trespass, meaning that the mechanism of infringement was not only an unentitled use of something in the complainant's entitled space, it had the added effect of changing the functional relationships within that space.

Notice that a pursuit can be frustrated in ways directly related to the elements of projects and pursuits. You can interfere with the pursuer - catch her arm. You can alter the subject, it won't respond to the pursuer as it normally would - puncture the tennis balls. This is distortion. You can influence the loading itself, separate the pursuer from the subject - steal the ball. This we might call deprivation and remain within traditional terminology. In a more general sense it is an alteration of the pursuer's project space - still distortion. In this sense, catching the pursuer's arm is also an alteration of her project space; distortion.

Really all injury is distortion of a project space; and isn't this what is meant by an infringement of liberty? But if it helps to categorize special cases of distortion such as deprivation, is there a special category into which we can place this case of catching the pursuer's arm? For a second while the prankster caught your arm during a forehand swing, he annulled the capacity of your will to materialize your desire. For a second you were his captive. These are the exact conditions of capture, the decapacitating of a person's will - momentary in this case to be sure - but capture nonetheless, and you will be amazed later to discover how capture insinuates itself into the fabric of modern society. As you will see, there will be advantages in classifying injury as to the mechanistic impact of the injurious act on the entitled project space of the complainant.

It is clear that injury could exist in early times when there were only titles - jura; before property was conceived. Injuries were violations of jura. We might even imagine that the feudal lord looked upon an injury to a vassal as something more than a mere infringement of the vassal's uses. He might take it personally. An injury showed disrespect for the feudal lord himself, the person who created the title. It tokened a contempt for the lord's grant of title. Injury, in the world ruled by law, was the psychological equivalent of immoral in the world ruled by social convention, or sin in the world of the gods.

In the primitive world of the common law, still emerging from feudalism, there could be only two mechanisms of injury - trespass and breach of service. Aside from breach of service, no injury was possible save by person B's intentional use of a subject to which person A was entitled. Only a thing-of-itself can be loaded, and there are only two elements of a project that are things-of-themselves, the projecter or pursuer, and the subject.

If Sir Brian Keswick held full title to all pursuits that might be associated with his meadow, he held among all the rest the title of "walking-on-the-land". Therefore someone else walking on the land without Sir Brian's permission was usurping a use belonging to Sir Brian. It was an injury through trespass.

If Keswick granted Alan O'Day his freedom, it meant that Alan now held title to all uses in himself. Even the laying of a finger on Alan, a loading without permission, is trespass. So if another lord captured Alan, it was effected through trespass for how can you capture a person unless you lay a finger on him? If the marauder stole Alan's spade, it was necessary to lay a finger on it - deprivation through trespass. And if the robber baron tried to enslave Alan, what else could it be than injury through trespass for does not slavery involving the loading of a subject - the use of a person - without her permission?

So titles - jura - were the basis for injury but, having established this system, the creators of the common law began to discover that a person can load another person's loading space by action at a distance. Ingenious people could interfere with other people's pursuits without a trace of trespass. Intentional use was missing and the harmful act could not be identified with injury - the mechanical tie-in was defective. The malefactor could not be coupled with jurisdiction, hence relief was unavailable. Undoubtedly the common law, as probably with all systems of law, has developed under the pressure of new and devious mechanisms of injury.

The prankster on the tennis court, having been escorted by the police from the court for the third time is told he will be jailed if he enters the court again, and he complies. He merely sits on a bench outside the court and blows a shrill whistle each time you prepare to hit the ball, and there is no way you can pin trespass on him. He is within his entitled space. There are no statutory restrictions on whistle-blowing and he is using nothing belonging to which you and your tennis partner are entitled. He merely completely disrupts your concentration, your loadings and your pleasure. It is nuisance, and we will find that all injury can be pleaded under the two general mechanisms, trespass and nuisance. But it is not easy to put a finger on nuisance. That is the beauty of it for an unconscionable perpetrator. Can it be pinned down with certainty? You will see.

With this brief reconnaisance of injury, we will now begin to see the rough outline of a cause - a presentation that a court will listen to - a cause for clamping jurisdiction on a defendant, a cause for court action against the defendant. It will be a general cause, one covering both trespass and nuisance - all mechanisms of injury. First the court must see a loading space to which the plaintiff is entitled. Second the court must be shown that a loading has been made in this space, contrary to the wishes of the plaintiff; and the court must see and comprehend the material mechanism of the intrusive loading - how it was loaded with the defendant's will. Third - and this spells the difference between an entitled loading space and a propertied loading space, the court must see that the plaintiff is not under a servitude or a service to the defendant, a situation that in effect annuls the plaintiff's claimed liberty in his entitled space. For if there is no liberty, there cannot be injury. But if all these elements are present in a case, injury is presumed, and there is cause for relief.

I will put these elements in a format to which we can refer:

The General Format of Injury

A government operating under the common law will favor a plaintiff with a remedy if in the plaintiff's case it finds each of the following elements:

(a) The plaintiff is entitled to a certain loading space.

(b) There is (or has been, or is likely to be) a loading in the space, adverse to the wishes of the plaintiff and loaded with the will of the defendant.

(c) Plaintiff's title in said loading space is not under a servitude or a service to the defendant that justifies the adverse loading.

This format is not without defects and deficiencies, but it is useful for our immediate purposes, and a little practice in using it will enable us to better understand its deficiencies as they appear.

If you remember Mrs. McNamara's prayer that the court order her husband to take out the garbage, observe now that her claim lacks the very first element in the general format of injury; she is not entitled to her husband as a subject in any project of hers. Not unless she has his consent. The marriage license is not a contract that places him in service to her, except the service of maintaining and supporting her in her illness and disability, and she is under the same sole obligation to him. He is not a subject to which she is entitled, and the court has no cause for ordering a relief for Mrs. McNamara's complaint. Having no remedy available, there is no reason for the court even to hear the case. No person in a common law country will be forced to act against her wishes as the subject in the project of another (except in certain government projects).

Having now the format of injury and a little grasp of trespass - the usurpation of another person's uses, we will quickly step into the world of the indirect mechanism of injury, the world of nuisance. For this step we have at hand a fictitious case tailor-made for a discussion in nuisance. As outlined in Chapter 12, our neighbors have been in the habit of playing their record player very loudly on their patio and we, sitting in our own backyard, can no longer enjoy a quiet conversation with each other. We have asked them to lower the sound and they have responded with insolence. So we have taken them to court, and now we present our complaint along the lines of the general format of injury.

(a) We are certainly entitled to pursue a quiet conversation in our own backyard. Our voices are our own, and so is the airspace. We are entitled to the loading we make of the airspace. We are entitled to the objective. So using the air for communicating with each other is a protected loading space for us.

(b) However, this same air is loaded with vibrations caused by our neighbors wilfully playing their record player very loudly. In fact this loading completely changes the nature of our airspace, making it ill-adapted as a subject in our pursuit.

(c) There is no contract between us subserviating our wishes to theirs in this matter, nor have we contracted our airspace to them for their loading in this fashion.

As I have described the situation under the format of injury, the impact of our neighbors' loadings on our project space is clearly in the mode of distortion; they have altered our subject matter. There is no doubt about the chain of cause and effect - the causal sequence - leading from the operation of their will to the loading of our space with disruptive vibrations. But they try to be shrewd. "Your honor," they argue, "plaintiffs claim that our will has penetrated the fence between our yards; they claim that the effect of our will prevents their will from operating freely in their free space. But consider the result, your honor, if you force us to turn down the volume of our record player. Remember that it's our record player, our patio, and our air space that we are using. We are operating completely in our entitled space. And if under these circumstances you compel us to lower our sound, it means that plaintiff's will has penetrated into our loading space and, with the aid of your strong arm, the plaintiff's will will be dominating our will in our entitled space, holding us in involuntary servitude."

Here in our neighbors' defense we see a key signature of nuisance. It is not so much the indirect nature of the mechanism - the actor is not using anything belonging to the complainant - but as often as not the actor is acting completely within her entitled space. Merely a byproduct of her activity happens to creep into the complainant's space.

Here also, in observing that injury is present yet trespass is not, we see an advantage in adding the term loading to our terminology, supplementing the term using. Trespass is always a using of the complainant's project space. The trespasser injects himself into the status of the entitled person, and in the early days it was by showing non-use that clever nuisancers could escape the clutches of due process. In a system of justice lacking the idea of indirect loading, our record-playing people could defend themselves with the claim, "We are not using anything to which the plaintiffs are entitled. We are not laying a finger on anything in their space."

But what about their defense that a decision in our favor will place their will in their entitled space in servitude to our will? Actually it is ineffective. We in our complaint have stated an injurious situation: their record-playing pursuit is distorting our entitled air-space. But their defense statement does not describe a case of injury; they are describing a result of due process. Let us see what due process is telling us.

This fictitious case is typical of the common law handling of nuisance, and I think we can discern here a principle. When we see two pursuits, both parties operating completely within their entitled spaces, and just one of the pursuits generating an impact in the other person's space, the intrusive pursuit will be put under a servitude to the non-intrusive pursuit. And now we know what an injury through nuisance is; it is a situation in which a person is generating an effect in the entitled space of another, though without using anything belonging to the other. This is nuisance whether or not the perpetrator is operating within his own entitled space.

So in nuisance as in trespass we see the will of person A having an effect in the entitled desire space of person B, and since there are only two ways in which an act can have an effect in a loading space - (1) by direct use of the subject matter and (2) by an indirect loading on the subject matter - there are only two mechanisms of injury - trespass and nuisance. This is indeed a hypothesis worth testing and test it we will, with perhaps a bit of refinement as well.

The general format of injury with the aid of the term "loading" enables us to more easily detect injury in a case of nuisance. In certainty of detection it places nuisance on a par with trespass. Getting down to basics, cause and effect, the causal sequence, it asks if there was an effect in an entitled loading space; an impact; and if so how did it originate? Can it be traced to a phenomenon of will other than the will of the plaintiff?

But still it will be essential to distinguish between trespass and nuisance in another way if we wish to understand a most enlightening difference between them. Historically and today, trespass is a violation of title. The trespasser is usurping the position of the entitled pursuer. Trespass where it exists is always intentional. There is no way you can use something without intending to use it. Trespass is a violation, a contempt of title. Nuisance, then, is a violation of... what?

Before answering, I will pose another question, one that may seem absurdly academic, yet it has been profoundly instrumental in the development of every system of law since the earliest hint of civilization. What is it that safeguards your legal desire space for you?

Physically, under law, it is the strong arm of government, but now I want to get into the esoteric reaches of legal strategy. In the Mosaic law, for instance, we see torrents of "thou shalts" and "thou shalt nots" and these in a way are mental signposts protecting people's legal desire spaces. The point I wish to approach is this. In this world the government has not assigned to each of us a supervisor watching our every move and keeping us within our assigned liberty spaces. The only restraint preventing us from infringing the liberty of another is a purely mental mechanism within ourselves. The Mosaic law attempts to put this inner restraint in the form of a voice, the voice of an all-seeing God, a strategy recognizing the fact that nothing shields loading spaces except inner restraints. More often than not, the protection that a government boasts is not a shielding. In most cases the government does not arrive on the scene until the harm has been done. The government does not shield so much as relieve and restore.

The feudal law was not greatly different from Mosaic law in this aspect. It merely substituted the voice of a worldly lord for the voice of God. In the place of "thou shalt" feudal law put "service", and in the place of "thou shalt not" it put "servitude". In the place of "sin of omission" and "sin of commission" it put "breach of service" and "breach of servitude". But the English mind never really liked the idea of service and servitude; it associated these terms with the Norman invasion and subsequent slavery. And as England climbed out of feudalism, the terms service and servitude were transformed into affirmative and negative duties. One obeyed the law because it was one's duty to do so. And if your will intruded into another person's loading space, it was a breach of duty. This development was an outgrowth of a school of thought, a school of thought recognizing inner restraints as the true guardians of the common law, concluding that an inner voice should be instituted as an element of due process. With the voice of God gone, and the voice of the feudal lord as well, now it became the voice of duty that shielded people's loading spaces. And "breach of duty" was the alarm that made justices sit upright on their benches; the device that invoked jurisdiction.

So here is my question. Is this the prevailing school of thought in the common law today, and should it be? Is this the way the common law proceeds today? Does it say, "Today between ten and eleven a.m. Miss Torres and Mr. Guajardo will be entitled to the north tennis court and no one "should" violate their title - no one "should" infringe their liberty in this space"? Should and should not, you see, are the voices of duty.

This of course is precisely the way tort operates, and tort certainly dominates common law procedure in cases seeking damages. Tort raggedly overlaps the field of negligence (negligence referring to neglect of duty) and the general procedure in tort/negligence is to look for a breach of duty. This, if found, is presumed to be the equivalent of injury.

It appears to me there is another school of the common law, viewing duty as a disposable contrivance. Its thinking would be this. "First, I see property. Second I see injury. And third where there is injury, the government will find a remedy for it." Duty is not an element.

Let me criticize the duty approach like this. In the kitchen freezer is a box of popsicles to be equally shared among all the children. But one of the children persists in helping himself to popsicles in the absence of a sharing experience. On such an occasion there are two strategies for Mother. She can say to the child, "A good little boy will not get into the popsicles all by himself, and I will spank the little boy who does." Or she can say merely, "I will spank the little boy who gets into the popsicles." The first method is a double-barreled attack. First it appeals to the boy's conscience - to his sense of duty. Next it talks about the mechanism of due process. The second method is brief and to the point.

Nobody will deny that conscience, a sense of duty and self-restraint are effective in keeping law and order. Indeed, they are the only true shields of our assigned loading spaces. But the common law does not listen to a case unless self-restraint (or breach of duty) has failed or is likely to fail. Being a good boy is not a factor in a case at court. There is a defendant whose actions have had an injurious perhaps damaging result, perhaps intentionally, perhaps accidentally. The question is not one of duty but one of (a) property (b) injury (c) due process.

"But," says our old school of thought, "Why not keep the sense of duty central in the court procedure? It cannot hurt. It might help. It provides valuable training and psychological conditioning."

It's like this. The mother says to the little boy, "Tommy, you have a duty not to take what belongs to your brothers and sisters, and if you take them you will not be doing your duty. You'll be breaking it." But Tommy, taking more popsicles anyway, is brought to trial and what will he be charged with - breaking his duty or taking the popsicles? "Well, what's the difference," asks the old school of thought. "It is the same thing."

Let us say that breach of duty and injury are the same thing. All right, we can go two ways. Injury we have been able to define as an infringement of liberty, an invasion of entitled loading space. Therefore we could define breach of duty to be an invasion of entitled loading space, though the word duty itself is irrelevant to the definition, adding nothing to our understanding of injury. Or we can reverse the procedure and define injury as breach of duty, and all we need do now is to define breach of duty.

I should explain that I am not talking about affirmative duties such as jury duty, or the duty imposed by a probate court on the executor of an estate, or the duty of a fiduciary to tell a trusting soul all the bad aspects of a project. I am talking about negative duties - "Tommy, you have a duty **not** to take popsicles that are **not** yours." And I am talking about ad hoc duties - "If you dig a hole in a public sidewalk, you have a duty to patch it up before someone steps in it and twists her ankle." - Duties that never turn up until they turn up in court. My position will become clear in Chapter 19.

So take a piece of paper if you wish, and compose a definition for this kind of duty. I defy you to do it without first delineating a property. But this is what courts have been trying to do ever since they became attracted to the procedure called tort/negligence.

I am proposing that a sense of duty, and conscience, and the voice of God, and common decency, and the fear of retribution, though the greatest - indeed the only shields of our protected loading spaces, have no relation to court procedure. The government protects our loading space only when the facts show that it is likely to be invaded, and more frequently only in the sense that it has been invaded and must be restored. Therefore the job of the court first of all is to discover infringement in the case. To do this it must discover the loading space - the arena of invasion. A mature common law, it seems to me, does not say to the people: "don't produce a loading in the loading space of another." It says (a) this is what I mean by a loading space, (b) this is what I mean by injury, and (c) this is the procedure to which I will subject you if someone charges you with an injury."

Therefore, I say, though our legal loading space might be shielded by a sense of duty or self-restraint, our "protection" in the governmental sense of the word is by due process. Due process relieves and restores. Perhaps due process raises in people's minds a mechanical spectre of retribution sufficient to have a beneficial effect in the future, but due process itself comes into play only when the spectre has failed to shield. Which means that due process is called into action by a violation of loading space, or a threat of violation. And this brings us back to the point that trespass is a violation of title. And nuisance is a violation of... what?

Nuisance is a violation of servitude, and this needs examination in depth.

It is clear that a finding of nuisance creates an occasion for the court to declare a servitude. In the case of "Quiet Conversation v. Loud Music" the loud music interferes with the quiet conversation but the quiet conversation does not interfere with the loud music. So the court declares that the title to load the air with loud music is under a servitude to the right to enjoy a quiet conversation. As a result the truth emerges. The loud music playing is in the neighbors' entitled space, but not in their property.

But in this action of the court isn't the court creating a servitude? And, if so, how can nuisance be a violation of servitude? And the answer is that the court decree does not create a servitude, it **declares** a servitude. The servitude pre-existed the case. It existed in the form of a principle. A servitude preventing nuisance is not the kind of servitude created by equity after a period of profound deliberation. Though nuisance is usually handled in equity, it need not be. It is a mechanical, automatic procedure not requiring the weighty considerations of equity.

In hearing the case we run our finger down the general format of injury, asking:
(1) Is the plaintiff entitled to the loading space in question?
(2) Is there a loading in the space that is (a) adverse to the wishes of plaintiff and (b) charged with the will of the defendant?
(3) Is plaintiff's said title free of servitudes and services to the defendant that would justify the adverse loading?

If all the answers to the questions are affirmative, injury is present. Then we ask:
(4) Does the adverse loading constitute a use of the plaintiff's loading space? If the answer is yes, the injury has occurred through trespass, and the relief is the complete eviction of the adverse loading agent. If the answer is no, the injury is through nuisance, and the defendant must cease whatever pursuit has resulted in the adverse loading. If his loadings are entirely within his entitled space, then it is obvious that they are under whatever servitude, self-restraint, is

required to prevent the undesirable effects in the plaintiff's space. This is the simplest of all principles, and if the defendant has not learned it, time that he did.

We find ourselves in a space of beautiful theory that could not have evolved by chance. We might ask, for instance, why we limit the remedy in nuisance to an elimination of only that loading that happens to interfere with the plaintiff's enjoyment of her space. We will not demand, for example, that our neighbors keep their music so low that not a hint of sound penetrates into our yard. Why not create free of nuisance the same perfect space of desire that is free from trespass? Well, remember that a servitude is a burden on an entitled space. The "intruder" is after all operating within his titles, a situation recognized by the Romans in the civil law. "Servitus civiliter exercanda est." - "A servitude must be so used as to cause as little inconvenience as possible." Almost but not quite, these Latin words say, "A servitude is an exercise in civility."

At this point it will be illuminating to ask, "If Farmer Brown's potato planting in the meadow caused grief to the fox-hunters, did he violate a title or a servitude? Did he occasion injury through trespass or nuisance?" And the answer is that it was an instance of nuisance.

But didn't the fox-hunters have the use of the meadow for fox-hunting (YES) and didn't he use it for potatoes (YES) and therefore wasn't it trespass? No.

Title is fixed to a project. If you have modern title in fee, you have title to all the projects not specifically assigned to others. For the hunting club the pursuers were the members, the subject was the meadow, the objective was fox-hunting, and the loadings were all loadings consistent with the objective. This was the loading space to which the members were entitled. They had the use of the meadow for fox-hunting. The only way that Brown could trespass in their property would be to hunt fox on the meadow. Holding otherwise in fee, he was entitled to all other uses, growing potatoes among them. He was entitled to this project, including the use of the meadow therefor, and the hunters had no title therein.

Both parties were operating in their entitled loading spaces, and the projects were mutually interfering. By the contractual nature of the lease, the hunting title mastered all interfering uses, and Brown's resulting servitude excluded his exercise of these uses from his property. His potato pursuit produced injury through violation of servitude. Nuisance.

In "Fox-Hunting Club v. Brown" we have an absolutely logical servitude, generated by the limitations of nature and practical business considerations, a contractual servitude. I have suggested also the existence of "common good" servitudes - restraints for the good of one and all. All such servitudes are sound, and free from figism by virtue of pure reason, or at least by definition. But what of the nuisance servitude. Though due process operates automatically in a case of nuisance, and on a purely cause and effect basis, is the nuisance servitude free from figism? Is there a chance that "someone up there" in legal heaven prefers quiet conversation to loud music? Or put it another way. Is it truly holonistic? Does it lead to a higher common good? For instance, it would be impossible to prove that quiet conversation is better for the common good than is loud music.

Undoubtedly nuisance generates friction between parties, and equity historically has undertaken hearings in nuisance. This undertaking equity would not do unless the government found it to be practical. Nuisance decisions were likely given to equity because the automatic nature of the decision wasn't recognized, and also in observance of the rule that only equity may issue injunctions - pronounce servitudes.

It is possible that the principle of nuisance is grounded directly not on considerations of the common good but in the rather more ancient justice of the peace function - simply keeping the peace. It is said that the pre-Norman English were great family-feuders, and their rulers had to enforce the keeping-peace function of government simply to prevent able inhabitants from annihilating each other.

Obviously arguments occur in life that ruffle the quiet waters of society, and it seems reasonable that the government might enter such a dispute even if violence has not erupted. Perhaps it has not erupted merely because the oppressed party is opposed to violence, and perhaps rulers respect this trait, at least in domestic matters. And while such a climate of mind definitely contributes to a climate of peace, who will say that it does not also have a favorable effect on the common good.

I would like to call the nuisance servitude a common decency servitude, much as the Romans might call it an exercise in civility. A person with a great reserve of self-restraint will put up with a lot of nuisance, but the time will come when he can no longer afford to be patient. People lacking a sense of common decency, if unchecked, become bolder and bolder in their intrusions until the victim of their indecency fights back. Thus a common decency servitude has much in common with a keeping-the-peace servitude, and, when you think about it, inter-family mayhem cannot be claimed to promote the common good.

Inevitably after a court case of nuisance, the losing defendant will retire in a huff. Realistically we have a title-holder who finds himself mastered by the will of another person. So we cannot expect that perfect peace will prevail in the wake of a nuisance decision. In these cases, it is the job of the court to decide if nuisance exists and, if it does, to "put the guinea-pig in a bag, head-first, and sit on it." What is required then is a consistent procedure for settling the dispute; an impartial procedure; a logical one; one that cannot reasonably incite a cry of "figism". And the general format of injury, with an addendum for separating trespass and nuisance, fills the bill.

In analyzing nuisance in this chapter, I have but suggested the impact of nuisance on the loading space of the injured party. In "Quiet Conversation v. Loud Music" the impact was in the mode of distortion. The varieties of nuisance and trespass, and distinguishing between them, furnish the fascinating and formidable problems of due process, as we shall see. But let us not overlook this great coherent structure of the common law. Trespass is a violation of title, nuisance a violation of servitude, and together, title and servitude compose property! And thus simply does due process protect liberty by recognizing these two huge all inclusive and mutually exclusive categories of injury.

CHAPTER 18

THE REALM OF PROJECT EFFECTIVENESS:
CONTRACT, SERVICE, INJURY, DAMAGE, MONEY

This is a good place to introduce contract - the topic of contracts. The ramifications of contract are immense. Money, for instance, is a contract.

It is a promise to everyone who accepts it - accepts it as a gift, or in payment for goods or services rendered; meaning you. The dollar bill in your pocketbook is a promise someone has made to you. What! Money a promise? Who made it! And what is the promise? And is it important? And is he keeping his promise? And, if not, are you being hurt? And, if so, can he be made to keep his promise?

Money, or so dictionaries and textbooks tell us, is (a) a medium of exchange; (b) a measure of value; (c) a store of value. And defining money like this is like defining grass as food for sheep. It doesn't tell us what money is, or grass. It merely lists some activities in which money and grass are used.

In Chapter 16 I showed that money is project effectiveness, but that's not the whole story. Money is a contract; an implied contract. More accurately it is the documentary evidence of a contracted service. Indeed the attractiveness of money and its project effectiveness depend on how closely the contractor fulfills her contracted service. This aspect of money is not usually acknowledged by economists.

Money cannot be fully understood without a basic understanding of contract, and this goes deeper than learning the six classic elements of contract (offer and acceptance, parties, consideration, consent, form, and legality). Comprehending contract means understanding it in terms of project spaces - potential, property, liberty, project effectiveness... Understood in this way, the topic of contract becomes a central mart where we get a deeper understanding of our whole lego-economic universe.

Generally, a contract is an inter-person agreement that the govern-ment will enforce. A contract rises from a set of statements describing a strange two-way project. Take for instance a contract to build a house. The instrument of contract, the set of statements on paper, commits the builder to perform a batch of loadings resulting in a house, but the house isn't his objective. His objective is to enlarge his bank account. Hopefully, by measuring and sawing and hammering, the result of his loadings will be money in the bank.

On the other hand, the prospective owner's objective is to have title to a real house, a particular house; to have possession, use and disposal. But she doesn't anticipate herself measuring and sawing and hammering. Counting on the effectiveness of money, she will visit a banker, sign a piece of paper, sign some checks and lo! A house will appear, complete with a document naming her as owner. In signing a contract each party - contractor and prospective owner - binds herself to a service to make the other party's objective materialize!

You might call a contract a transactional project. The parties are identified in the instrument, and each party will execute the loadings consistent with the other party's objective. This is something like a title. A title, you will recall, is fundamentally a joint project between government and titleholder. Sir Brian Keswick and Alan O'Day undertook a potato-growing project on the meadow. But there is a difference between a title and a contract in modern times. Alan O'Day (or Farmer Brown) doesn't have to do anything with his land if he doesn't want to. A contract is different.

Moreover a contract has a feature that distinguishes it from a mere project. A project has a result. Rather, the pursuit of a project has a result. The result might faithfully materialize the objective, or it might be frightfully disappointing, and this is not at all characteristic of a contract. In consequence of entering a contract, each party must faithfully materialize the objective of the other - the objectives expressly stated in the instrument. If a party fails in her service we hear noises like non-performance or breach of contract, and they spell injury and maybe damage.

"A will build a house for B on lot C, and B will pay A $100,000 when A gives B the deed to the completed house." This generates a contract. It secures A's objective - a supply of money; but what about B. There are many shapes and structures of houses, an eternity of completion dates, and from this contract we may expect disappointment and conflict. There is a very low probability that the objective as expressed in the instrument, if and when materialized, will match the picture of perfection filling the prospective owner's mind.

What has a person lost when the results of the contractor's loadings don't match her stated objectives? This is the question that makes us search for the basic meaning of contract. What is the coin of contract? In making a contract, what does each party surrender in terms of potential, liberty, project effectiveness, and what does each receive. What does a party lose if the other party doesn't perform.

Suppose you are the housebuilder. As a person you have a potential. There are many projects you might perform over the next several months, but you are not free to undertake your entire potential. Time is a limiting factor. Your project effectiveness is a limiting factor. Under these limitations your potential is reduced to subsets of your potential. You see before you a space composed of possible combinations of projects, your per unit time potential. Given reality and a specific period of time, only one of these combinations of projects is available to you. And now you enter a contract with B to build her a specific house within a designated period of time. If you honor your agreement, you will be surrendering something. Something about your project space will be reduced. And you may be sure, knowing the government's view of contract, that you will honor your commitment or lose an equivalent. Are you losing your liberty when you sign the instrument? Are you losing your project effectiveness? What in terms of project spaces is reduced when you pledge your service under contract?

In many ways it seems that a pledge of service reduces one's freedom and, if so, it reduces a portion of one's liberty. It reduces the space where one's property and ideal freedom overlap. Let's test this proposal.

If you enter a contract to build a house during the next three months, and if you are a contractor who personally supervises construction, you will probably find time for a game of golf now and then, but it would seem foolish for you to undertake a cruise around the world. What does due process say about it?

A cruise around the world is not an illegal project. You will pay for your ticket with your own money. You'll be free to take the cruise. So why would it not be within your property and consequently within your liberty? On the other hand wouldn't you think that the prospective homeowner hearing of your plans could obtain a court injunction against your trip? If a court will restrain you in such a pursuit, it follows that it is not within your liberty - your protected desire space.

Recall that a service is not a servitudo. If we could class service as servitude, we could say that the servitude removes from your property all pursuits that interfere with your service. Being out of your property, they are also out of your liberty. But this won't work. Interference is a positive, phenomenal interaction. Loud music interferes with quiet conversation. A prankster on the tennis court interferes with your play. Planting potatoes on the meadow adversely distorts the ground for fox-hunting purposes. Though it is common for us to say, "Don't let your play interfere with your work," it is a mistaken figure of speech. In no way can your play interfere with your work. You have simply made a choice among the project combinations of your per unit time potential. We cannot cut away pieces of your property by calling your service a servitude.

We can reach this conclusion another way. If the court can enjoin your trip on the basis that the trip will interfere with your service, it can enjoin you from "doing nothing" on the basis that doing nothing will interfere with your service. In other words, the court could force you by injunction to perform your service. In the civil law this would be impossible. In the civil law **servitus in faciendo consistere non potest** - "a servitude cannot consist of doing." In the civil law a servitude is a restraint upon action. It is entirely negative. What does due process say about it? Here is a region of the common law left completely undefined except by implication.

Let us say that due process says something like this: Your liberty consists of (a) your ideal freedom within your property and (b) your free determination of loadings within your property (c) excepting Beta. You are familiar with statements (a) and (b), and by Beta I mean a sentiment that I will now try to express. "You should not engage yourself in a combination of pursuits that makes it impossible for you to fulfill your contracted services." Or, "You have a duty not to undertake a combination of pursuits that will preclude a performance of your services." These are equivalent statements. They are indigenous to the thinking of tort and negligence. If you study (c) you will see that the common law creates a servitude of "doing" if it works this way. Under (c) the government can force you to perform the services you have agreed to perform.

However, due process does not work this way. Though your cruise destroys the possibility of your completing the house on time, due process will not enjoin you from cruising about the world. If it did it would run into theoretical and practical difficulties. Suppose (1) you contract to build a house, (2) your presence at the site is essential to performance and (3) you buy a ticket for a world cruise. According to Beta, the third statement of the liberty statement, going on the cruise is excluded from your liberty.

If you are not at liberty to take the cruise, you cannot be injured in this enterprise. If on this trip a cruise company employee causes you to fall and break a leg, you will have no recourse at law. The fragrance of the old school of duty. "You had a duty not to take the cruise; you were not in your property; you were a bad boy; you are excluded from our protection."

No. Due process will protect you in your cruising pursuit. It is within your property, and therefore within your liberty. The (a) and (b) statements of liberty stand firm, but (c) - Beta - is incompatible with the common law. Note here a fundamental difference in the functioning of contractual services and servitudes. A servitude removes portions of your entitled space from your property. Your property is smaller than your entitled space. A servitude reduces your liberty. A contractual service does not.

This section of the discussion started with a question: what does a person give up when she signs an instrument of contract. Committing oneself to a contract is a commitment to a service, and the answer to the question will provide a basic understanding of what a service is. So far the answer has been negative. We know what a service is not. It is not a reduction in liberty. Due process will not command the perform-ance of a contractual service. Perhaps we might then ask what due process demands of a person who fails to perform.

It might assess damages, indicating that the court has pronounced damage in the case, signifying that the plaintiff has been injured, meaning that the plaintiff's liberty has been infringed.

And this is strange! Can A perpetrate injury in B's space without exceeding her own liberty? In trespass, A uses a subject belonging to B. In this A is certainly outside her entitled space, therefore outside her property and liberty. And in nuisance, though A might be operating within her entitlements, the nuisance servitude has sliced from her property - hence from her liberty - the contested portion of her entitled space. Now in breach of service, due process finds that A has exceeded her liberty, though we have also concluded that A's commitment to service has not reduced her liberty. Can a non-performer be within her liberty and outside her liberty at the same time? What kind of absurdity have we stumbled upon here?

We were happier looking at the plaintiff's side of the case. If the plaintiff was injured (there is no practical way of eluding "injure" as a verb) we may draw one of two inferences. First that the defendant interfered with the plaintiff's ideal freedom in her property or, second, that the defendant determined a loading in plaintiff's property without plaintiff's consent. This introduces a second inconsistency. The plain-tiff having paid no money, the house not having been built, how can the plaintiff have freedom, hence liberty, in a house that doesn't exist. How then can she be injured in this space? A loading space must contain something to load. Can property, hence liberty, hence injury, exist in the absence of a subject of property? And the answer is no.

But due process sees injury in breach of contract. Therefore she sees a liberty that has been infringed. Therefore she must presume property and, therefore, she must presume the existence of a subject of property.

I have said that the service of a contracting party is to materialize the objective of the other party. Time is important. Either the contract designates the date of completion or a court upon petition will establish a reasonable date. What can we conclude from all these facts?

I think they tell us that due process has a policy about contractual objectives; about the materialization of contractual objectives - a house for example. Due process says that the house exists as of the specified completion date. It exists, that is, as a liberty space for the prospective owner. Yet perhaps it does not actually exist in a usable shape, or perhaps it does not exist in the shape specified in the contract. If this is true, then the entitled project space of the prospective owner has been altered, distorted, and the will of the contractor has contributed to these circumstances.

After all, take Y's house that has been burned to ashes as a consequence of W's activity. Y's liberty in the house has been infringed. Though the house no longer exists, the injury persists; the will of W lingers crystallized in this space where the owner otherwise would be exercising her liberty. The liberty space exists though the house is altered or destroyed. There is no difference between this and the house not yet completed or completed incorrectly. In both there has been a distortion of the subject matter of the project space, and the distortion is loaded with a will other than that of the owner or prospective owner. Such a variance perpetrates injury, and if a loss of the plaintiff's project effectiveness results damages will be assessed.

Then evidently in a contracted service the government makes three presumptions. First that a specified property exists for each party on the date provided and under the conditions provided. Second that a variation from the specifications signals injury perpetrated by the other party. Third that a contracting party in entering the contract has given full consideration to these legal presumptions and to the consequences of not performing as agreed. Now this is what we wished to discover, the effect of a contractual service upon a contracting party. It can now be expressed in terms of project spaces.

Refer once again to your simplified project space EFGHJK - your potential - and to your per unit time potential of twenty project combinations - EFG, EGH and so forth. Having this potential you now resolve to pursue a certain project H in the course of the next month. What is the effect upon your potential? It means first that every project combination you might choose will contain project H, and there are not twenty of these but ten. So in resolving to pursue H, you have cut your potential time-set in half. More importantly, however, it means that your project effectiveness in your preferred projects has been cut to two projects per month instead of three. By this I mean that though you have resolved to pursue H during the month, you may find when facing reality that you will wish to pursue another combination, say GJK instead of HJK. So a resolution to pursue a certain project reduces your project effectiveness in preferred projects, and this is what occurs when you commit your services under contract.

But this is an iffy reduction. New Year's resolutions are notorious failures, and so are many others. These however are not resolutions. They are statements of resolution. If by resolution we mean an act of will, a resolution is necessarily successful. If you resolve to pursue H, you pursue H regardless of your preferences, and your project effectiveness in preferred projects is diminished. There is not enough time.

Resolve is an inner attitude. On the other hand a pledge is an outward representation of an inner attitude. Pledge might be true or deceitful. Integrity is an appropriate word to introduce here. By integrity we mean that the pledge and the resolve are identities; that the outward representation is the equivalent of the inner attitude. And evidently the message we get from due process says the government likes integrity. The effect of due process in the contractual situation is this: if you don't reduce your project effectiveness in your preferred projects to fit the requirements of your pledged projects, due process will do it for you.

This is the exact effect of due process. If you don't complete the house on time, due process will give you a choice. You may either complete the house or pay another builder to do it. Either way you will lose project effectiveness in preferred projects. Nor does this ruling represent damages. It is called specific performance. The principle is that a pledge of service is a pledge to sacrifice your effectiveness in preferred projects and "By Gad Sir, You'll Do It."

Continued failure to perform is a persistent injury and renders the defaulter vulnerable to charges of damage. Damage through persistent non-performance or through distortional performance presents all the variations and difficulties that we have faced already in treating damage, and is solved generally through the same medium - the loss in project effectiveness suffered by the injured party. And now you will begin to see the full power of project effectiveness as a medium of exchange in the law.

How can one say that the non-completion of a house can perpetrate damage, and here I am not thinking of the economic losses that might be associated. I am thinking of the silent rage that occurs in response to a breach of faith. Here we again meet the person who was awarded damages for lost time in recuperation, though perhaps not suffering financially as a function of lost time. Yes, the prospective owner of the incomplete house does not have the enjoyment of the house. However, she has not yet borrowed the money; she has not yet paid any of her own money; and she is living comfortably in a leased home with rent payments less than her anticipated payments for her new home. Though not financially hurt, nevertheless she has as a contracting party surrendered some of her own project effectiveness.

She has spent time planning the house and speaking to several contractors about it. Having signed the contract she has surrendered the possibility of signing with a late-coming contractor who will build the house for less money. She has not spent her downpayment money on other projects that might render her incapable of performing her own pledged service under the contract. Perhaps she gave up a trip in August with a friend, expecting to move into her new house in August. In short, in anticipation of her pledged service and the builder's pledge, she has voluntarily reduced her effectiveness in preferred projects. She has acted with integrity.

This is the true consideration that she has given to the other party - sacrificing some of her project effectiveness. And due process will award damages in return. The government seems to have a policy of awarding damages to palliate feelings of lost effectiveness, especially since it will also impress the injuring party how it feels to lose project effectiveness. In addition, depending on the defaulter's financial standing, there may be an amount added to sting the defaulting contractor to be sure that he gets the message. Evidently the government wants him to know that the government doesn't like a situation in which a person is sitting on another person's propertied effectiveness. And all this is independent of economic compensation and punitive damages.

Now of course, a plaintiff must make a good demonstration of consideration. She must have held up her end of the bargain. She must have shown good faith. If she herself has gone flitting about independently of completion dates, spending money without regard for her contractual obligations, and losing her credit standing - if she cannot show that she has lost project effectiveness in consideration of her contractual pledges, the defendant will have a perfect defense for his actions.

This analysis of contract can illuminate for us the whole field of liberty and injury. Refer to the paragraph second above where I wrote, "...the government does not like the situation where a person is sitting on another person's propertied effectiveness." Here is the signal of damage. The ghost of the perpetrator's will has crystallized in the loading space of the victim. But this is not merely a prerequisite for damage, it is also the essence of injury.

To understand this, let us grasp freedom and project effectiveness as clearly as possible. Regarding the per unit time potential, EFG, EJK... etc., of twenty combinations of projects, three projects per combination, I said that your project effectiveness is EFG, or FGH, etc. More generally, your project effectiveness is measured by what you can accomplish in projects in a given period of time. Strangely, I said also that your ideal freedom consists of EFG, or FGH, etc. Certainly your freedom rises from your facility in realizing your project effectiveness. But it begins to appear that the term project effectiveness is ambiguous. In one sense it connotes potential. It is what you might do if you select a project combination and pursue it. On the other hand it is not what you might do but what you are actually doing and accomplishing. In this sense it is the equivalent of your freedom and, if no one is interfering with your freedom, it is the equivalent of your ideal freedom.

It will be helpful to observe if one makes the time frame small enough, that one's freedom and one's project effectiveness consist of exactly one project. This does not apply to mighty rulers who direct the progress of many pursuits in any given period of time. However it applies to every person, including a mighty ruler, if we restrict our observations to pursuits in which the pursuer is making her own loadings directly. What I am pointing out is that one might undertake and accomplish HJK during a period of a month, but for the period of the next second one may undertake only H or J or K. Certainly you will not accomplish, say, J during the second (unless it is the ultimate moment of completion). What you will accomplish is to apply yourself to a loading, and you will accomplish during the second what you would expect to accomplish, given your project effectiveness.

We have arrived at a point of understanding where it is difficult to distinguish between freedom and project effectiveness. In a sense, project effectiveness is identical to the realization of project effectiveness, and this is identical to freedom. My struggle is to determine if the word freedom and the term project effectiveness are interchangeable. If they are we can say that your liberty consists of your ideal project effectiveness within your property. That's all there is to it as long as it is understood that (1) by ideal project effectiveness we mean project effectiveness untrammeled by another human being and (2) by project effectiveness we don't mean project effectiveness in the sense of potential, we mean project effectiveness in action and (3) by project effectiveness we refer also to one's free determination of loadings; is one or isn't one effective in determining the loadings in one's property.

With this step we see injury - infringement of liberty - as a reduction of your project effectiveness within your property. As a generalization it does not seem to introduce error into our understanding of the legal universe. It is a powerful generalization because it unifies the concepts of injury and damage. Both subsist in reductions of project effectiveness, and evidently the government doesn't like such reductions. Injury becomes qualitative damage. Black and white. Has project effectiveness been reduced? Yes or no. Damage becomes quantitative injury - if project effectiveness has been reduced, how much has it been reduced and how permanent is the reduction.

With this generalization the format of injury can be modified and gains crispness:

(1) Is the plaintiff entitled to a certain claimed project space?
(2) Is there a loading in the claimed space, charged with the will of the defendant and reducing the project effectiveness of the plaintiff?
(3) Is plaintiff's title free of services and servitudes that justify the adverse loading?

If all answers to the above are affirmative, then injury is present, and we must determine if the mechanism is trespass or nuisance. We ask if the defendant has intentionally used a subject in plaintiff's project space. If he has, then the injury is through trespass; if not, through nuisance. Damage and damages are then determined as discussed earlier. (But the format of injury is not yet in its final form.)

The aptness of interchanging the terms freedom and project effectiveness can also be tested by applying them to money. Money clearly is project effectiveness, but is money freedom? Here the ambiguity of project effectiveness, one leg in potential and one in freedom, is its beauty. Money in the act of being spent is the epitome of active project effectiveness, project effectiveness in action. It accomplishes worlds. Hence the spending of money is an exercise in freedom. However, money stored is a form of potential project effectiveness and, by definition, potential cannot be expressed by the term freedom. Therefore, to maintain definitional structure, we cannot adequately describe money by associating it solely with freedom.

So, if we adopt the word project effectiveness in the format of injury and also in our understanding of money, we flirt with ambiguity. Perhaps this can be relieved by attaching "active" or "potential" to the term project effectiveness when a distinction needs to be drawn. It's worth a try. If we go this route, we can actually drop the word freedom from our technical vocabulary. Ideal freedom becomes our ideal active project effectiveness and freedom becomes our active project effectiveness. Well, perhaps it isn't worth the effort. Freedom is a good word if we know what it means, and now we know.

At the beginning of the chapter, I announced somewhat imperiously the contractual nature of money. To describe how money is a pledge of service is a fascinating task, but it requires more pages than I will allot. Nevertheless I should explain myself. The line separating the economic world and the legal world can be drawn through the point called money; money is an essential element of both worlds. I will give the basics in a few paragraphs.

Money is not evidence of one contract, but two. The basic pledge is that of a producer who has received a valuable good or service from another person but has yet to perform his service in return. Such a remnant of contract is called a debt. It is evidenced by a written instrument called a note. There was a time when there was a large open trade in producer notes. You could trade your firewood note for some other person's note for two bushels of wheat. A risk in holding a producer's note lay in the possibility that he might hand out too many notes; so many that paying them all - say, in firewood - was beyond his project effectiveness. He would not be able to honor all of them. Many of the notes would become worthless, or worth less.

The second pledge is that of a central banking system who in effect collects everybody's producer notes, handing back bank notes. The pledge of the central bank people is that they will maintain behind the scenes the number of producer notes, no more, that will match the project effectiveness of the producers. By this supervision they will maintain the value of the producer notes, hence of the bank notes, the bank notes becoming the medium by which the producer notes are valued and exchanged. If in your lifetime you find that the value of money is diminishing - the phenomenon we call inflation - it indicates that the banking people are not keeping their pledge. Inflation, one might say, is a signal of distortionary performance, but so far no one has sued the banking system for breach of contract. The supervisory function comes under the Constitutional powers of Congress: "to regulate the value (of money)", but Congress seems to have defaulted.

The effect is real. Suppose you work in a computer factory. By working, you have surrendered a large part of your project effectiveness. Instead of accepting computers in return, or a producer's note to pay you in computers, you agree to accept bank notes on the assumption that the bank notes will retain their value. In being paid in money, you have received a fair return in project effectiveness for the project effectiveness you surrendered to the work. As long as the notes retain their attractiveness, your store of project effectiveness will be secure. But if too many producer's notes get into the banking system, the bank notes (money) begin to lose their attractiveness. Your money is no longer as effective as it once was. You have to pay more of it for an overcoat than if you had bought the coat when you first received the money. You have lost part of the project effectiveness you surrendered to your job. The banking system has not performed as it contracted to perform. Project effectiveness is the coin of both the legal world and the economic world.

CHAPTER 19

PALSGRAF IN A NEW LANGUAGE

We have now gathered the legal tools needed to solve the riddle of **Palsgraf v. Long Island Railroad Company.** Completed in the courts in 1928, it was "the most famous tort case of modern times," or so Noonan calls it in his book **Persons and Masks of the Law.** The final opinion in **Palsgraf** was written by Benjamin Cardozo, chief of the seven-judge New York Court of Appeals. Quoting Noonan again, Cardozo was "the most justly celebrated of American common-law judges." To Cardozo's mind this opinion in **Palsgraf** was, I suspect, a doctoral thesis; he intended it to end an era of confusion in tort and negligence. The case was reviewed in journal after journal, becoming widely used in the classrooms of the nation's law schools. However Noonan, in spite of his tribute to Cardozo, offers an opposing solution to the case and deals not too kindly with the chief.

During the period of her life in which the accident occurred, Helen Palsgraf lived in a basement apartment in New York City. As a cleaning woman in the apartment house she earned thirty-five or forty dollars a month, and with this income she supported herself and three daughters.

Apparently with this income in those fairy-tale times one could plan a day at the beach. So for a hot Sunday morning, August 24, 1924, history locates Mrs. Palsgraf on a crowded railroad platform, and with her were her younger daughters Lillian, age 12, and Elizabeth, age 15. Standing next to a tall weighing scales at the rear of the platform, with Lillian off buying a newspaper, Helen mused inattentively as a standing train took on passengers and began moving out of the station. Suddenly there was an eruption of smoke and explosive noises; then panic. Destructive things, human and inhuman, hurtled toward Helen Palsgraf and swirled around her, and at the height of the tumult the scales toppled and scraped down her side.

Two men had tried to catch the departing train, the faster one boarding without incident and the other having a lot of difficulty. Carrying under his arm a very large bundle wrapped in newspaper, he made a desperate effort to board, and only with the help of two railroad employees did he succeed. A trainman on board leaned down to pull him up and a platform officer, running with him, tried to boost him on board. At this the bundle was dislodged, falling into the narrow space between platform and train. It contained fireworks and they ignited. Later during the trial and in the written opinions, lawyers and witnesses and judges expressed the event in terms of an explosion. Everyone seemed to assume that an explosion had occurred and that it had broken the glass on the platform scales, knocking them over on Mrs. Palsgraf. With calmer hindsight reviewers have concluded that the scales were toppled not by an explosion but by the panicked crowd. Actually one gathers in reading Mrs. Palsgraf's testimony that the noise sounded more like fireworks, not an explosion. However she described the crucial moment as "Flying glass... a ball of fire came and we were choked in smoke, and I says "Elizabeth turn your back," and with that the scale blew and hit me on the side."

Though battered and bruised, she suffered a more serious result. A stammer developed that refused to go away; and for this she and her attorney sought $50,000 from the railroad as damages.

A case of this sort is usually handled under the label of tort, with a subheading of negligence. A tort is "any wrong, not consisting in mere breach of contract, for which the law undertakes to give to the injured party some appropriate remedy against the wrong-doer." This description given in 1899 by a California judge is still used in textbooks. As a guide to tort, it's about as helpful as the mother sheep's answer when her lamb sought information on what to eat. "We sheep," she said, "eat anything that's food."

If you read enough cases in tort, you'll realize that a tort at bottom is an act that has a damaging result. In our new terminology it means there had to be an impairment of project effectiveness associated with injury. Then with a little thought you will realize there must be three parts to a tort case. First there must a determination that the plaintiff suffered injury as a result of the defendant's act. In the second part (to be undertaken only if the first determination is affirmative) there is a marshalling of facts to determine that there was, stemming from the contributory act, a persisting impairment of the plaintiff's project effectiveness. Then if these findings are affirmative, the third part of the case becomes significant - a determination of the damage equivalent, usually in terms of money - the damages.

Decisions about damage and damages rest entirely on a determination of facts and, if a jury has heard the case and has been properly instructed in the pertinent law, these decisions can be committed to a jury. But this isn't necessarily true for the first part of the case - the determination of injury. True, injury can usually be handled at law, as a trial of facts. Sometimes however a determination of injury will depend on a decision in property - who was in whose free space at the critical moment - and if the law isn't clear in the case, the property decision must be made by a judge in equity. Never, if due process is being observed, is this decision delegated to a jury.

However, it has become established practice to hear a suit for damages in a court at law. The requirement of property as the basis of injury is overlooked. The equitable undertones of the case are muffled. Jurisdiction in equity is not invoked. A jury is frequently seated to hear the facts, and consequently the court will make a serious error. It will charge the jury with the task of making a ruling in equity, and this is what happened in the trial court in **Palsgraf.**

It is clear, no matter what legal language we use, that Mrs. Palsgraf suffered injury and damage. Her very own loading space was invaded by the will of another, and the invasion lingered in the shape of a stammer. Her project effectiveness was diminished. All established as fact at the trial.

While she was standing quietly on the railroad platform, she reposed entirely within her property. Caught by the unexpected on-slaught of eruption, incapacitated by smoke, fettered to a child at her side and paralyzed by separation from her other child, she was trapped helpless amid pandemonium, her will rendered inoperative. In the course of pursuits of other people, charged devices had been released - roman candles, tumbling humans - things shooting about like mis-directed arrows. They penetrated her very own loading space and dominated her there. They withdrew, and left her - distorted. All fact, as plain as day. But at this point juridical thinking became mired in the swamp of negligence theory, and it will be well for us to follow the professionals into that dark fen for a moment. What indeed were the complexities of the case, and how were they handled by the judiciary?

There was an undoubted culprit - the man carrying the fireworks; but he got away. And as for the madding crowd, they would never be held responsible for Mrs. Palsgraf's stammer. Though they bumped and buffeted her, and perhaps caused the scales to fall on her, they had become unthinking incompetents, charged with blind adrenalin, trig-gered by the misdirected wills of others.

Only the railroad employees can be caught and blamed, and if they are found at fault their employer will be held responsible. So the railroad company became the defendant, and the contribution of the trainmen to the accident became the pivotal issue.

Judge Humphrey presiding, a jury seated, the trial was held in Brooklyn in 1927 - three years after the accident. Before I present some fascinating critical testimony, I want to describe Judge Humphrey's charge to the jury at the conclusion of the hearing. With the arguments closed, the judge spoke to the jury. First he told them there was no dispute as to the facts. Then in a few well-chosen words he recalled the events of the accident. Third he stated the plaintiff's complaint in simple language: she claimed that the railroad employees had acted negligently. It was not in failing to examine the contents of the bundle, but they had been unprofessional in handling the man carrying the bundle. Lastly Judge Humphrey presented the issue and the charge.

In paraphrase he said, "Did the trainmen do something they should not have done? Did they fail to do something they should have done? If so and if Mrs. Palsgraf met with her injuries (sic) as a result, then she is entitled to recover. So if you, the jury, find under these guidelines that the railroad company is liable, then determine the amount that the plaintiff is entitled to recover."

Here was a jury properly to be charged with a commission to determine the facts; yet Judge Humphrey began by telling them there were no issues of fact. He compensated for it by giving them his own job - determining the law. "Did the trainmen do something...?" This would be a commission to determine facts. But, "Should they have done it?" is a commission to determine the law.

It is not my intention to be hard on the judge. He was caught in the quicksand of negligence, trying only to give the proceedings a semblance of rationality. Besides, observe his correctness. Before giving the jury a charge to assess damages, he told them to find damage if it was there to be found. And before doing that, he said, they should determine if the trainmen did something they should not have done. This was roughly equivalent to telling them to determine if injury had occurred.

The feet of negligence as a cause of action are embedded in the idiom of tort, creating a major semantic handicap. Every text on tort states: "tort is a violation of a legal duty owed by the defendant to the plaintiff"; and there the trouble starts. People always seem to have difficulty putting their fingers on the legal duty and, for a given case, the duty in question usually ends up being what the defendant did or didn't do, depending on whether the judge or jury thinks he should or should not have done it. And the court ends up looking like a puppy marching forward, tail in mouth.

Recognizing this, a few modern jurists have tried to minimize the legal duty aspect of negligence, without finding a good way to do it. To do it the legal profession would have to abandon the cause of negligence. After all, what is being neglected in a case of negligence if not duty?

So it was Judge Humphrey's job to discover the legal duty of the trainmen toward Mrs. Palsgraf, and he solved his problem ingeniously.

He stripped it of its professional terminology and dressed it in laymen's language - "What should they have done; what should they not have done?" And he tossed his job into the jury's lap.

In Chapter 17, I suggested that the idea of duty is alien to the spirit of the common law. There are exceptions to this - the fiduciary duty and certain services to government, and I will in later chapters discuss the fiduciary duty at length. The idea of duty presently criticized is the vaporous duty of the ordinary negligence case. I maintain that instead of telling us what we should or should not do, the common law tells us what we may do; it delineates our free space. Nor does it say, "You have a duty to stay out of the free space of other people." It says, "If it appears under due process that you are in Mrs. MacGregor's garden patch, I'll chase you out. And if it appears that you have been there and stepped on a cabbage, I'll thump you."

I don't want to dwell on this point at this time. What we will want is to gradually relieve due process of this indigestible lump - ad hoc duty; and we can do this by discovering that **Palsgraf** has nothing to do with "what they should (or shouldn't) have done". It has to do with "what they did". It was a case of injury through nuisance, with associated distortion of a project space. Persisting distortion. Damage.

So when the arguments had been completed, and Judge Humphrey was charging the jury with finding negligence if it was there to be found, we might ask what he really asking them to do. He was saying, "Determine if the trainmen injured Mrs. Palsgraf. And you might as well define injury for me, while you're at it. To do that, I think you'll have to dig into this matter called property. And along the way, maybe you had better tell us what we mean by negligence, and like good chaps, figure out this thing called duty, will you?"

So we have here the spectacle of twelve laymen from Brooklyn - no women - being commissioned to create a legal structure supposedly assembled over the last nine hundred years by the best minds in England and America. These ordinary (?) men did it in two and one-half hours, including time for lunch; and during this time they also decided that the railroad should pay damages in the amount of $6000.

The decision by this remarkable jury was not the end of Palsgraf in the legal world, it was the beginning. It would be heard on appeal in two higher courts and, in the wake of Cardozo's opinion, it would command an inestimable expenditure of time in erudite review, research, analysis, debate and publication. Without even the facts I've presented thus far, it was argued hotly for twenty years. During those twenty years, while Cardozo's opinion was exerting its greatest influence in the legal world, the "facts" were drawn from the opinions stated in the appellate reports, and unfortunately they were not only insufficient for realistic debate, they were inaccurate.

Then a textbook by Scott and Simpson (later succeeded by Scott and Kent) included the full verbatim transcription of the trial in Humphrey's court. The authors supplied a quiet comment: "... this case is of considerable importance in the development of the law of torts."

What we will never have, and what would be most precious, is a record of the jury's discussion. What did they think the trainmen did that they shouldn't? And what did the trainmen fail to do that they should have done? How would we, sixty years later, rate the system of shoulds and shouldn'ts developed by this jury in less than two and one-half hours?

The railroad company, having lost the first round, quickly took the jury's decision to the Appellate Division of the Supreme Court of the State of New York, and lost the second round. The jury was upheld by three of the five justices. For the majority, Justice Seeger wrote that the trainmen had caused the accident by knocking the bundle from the arm of the boarding passenger. The judge speculated on the jury's deliberations: "The jury might well find that... the passenger... trying to board a moving train was negligent, and... the defendant's employ-ees... assisting him... were also negligent. ...they might better have... warned him not to board the moving train." These were conscientious thoughts, concentrating not on what the trainmen did but on what they "might better have" done. All properly cast in the mode of negligence.

Presiding Justice Lazansky, dissenting, admitted that these acts might warrant a finding of negligence but, he argued, they didn't constitute proximate cause; by themselves they would not have re-sulted in harm to Mrs. Palgraf. There was an "independent intervening act". The stage had been act by the negligence of the passenger who carried an unmarked package of explosives into a crowded public place.

The slim majority of justices, it seems, were adhering to an older rule of justice - strict accountability. Strict accountability was simple. If the defendant had committed a negligent act, and if the act contributed to a harm-causing sequence of events, the defendant was held liable. But Justice Lazansky was depending on a newer, more sophisticated rationale - a consideration of independent intervening acts. It enables a judge to enter the maze of negligence and exit through the same entrance, upside down. However, Lazansky makes us face a missing piece in the puzzle: the role of the passenger with the bundle too big to get his arm around.

A witness at the trial - Mr. Gerhardt - had described in bold relief the two men's dash for the train. He had become aware of them before the fireworks began, for the one with the bundle had hit Mrs. Gerhardt "in the stomach" as he ran through the crowd. When the fireworks were over, Mr. Gerhardt wanted to take a railroad officer aboard the train and identify the man. "But they wouldn't do it, they wouldn't hold the train, they let the train stop but the train continued right on again."

The principle that Justice Lazansky tried to apply can be illustrated this way. Suppose a car stalls on the highway and the engine refuses to start. So the driver leaves it standing on the road and goes for help. Meanwhile another car, driven recklessly and much too fast, comes around the bend and hits the stalled car. It ricochets across the road and hurts a passing pedestrian. Given these circumstances, who is responsible for harming the pedestrian? Well, one can apply several negligence theories and reach opposing conclusions. One of them, the one held by Lazansky, holds that the harm to the pedestrian was caused by the driver who left her car standing on the road. Even though the moving car was being driven negligently, and though it was the activating instrument in the harm-causing sequence, the stalled car was the essential link between the speeding car and the pedestrian. In the absence of the stalled car, the accident would not have occurred. The act of leaving the car on the road was an independent intervening act. It was the proximate cause, the act of negligence that actually caused the harm. This said Lazansky was the situation in **Palsgraf**. Though the trainmen were the activating instruments, the man carrying the fireworks into the station performed the independent intervening act. His act of negligence "superceded" the trainmen's acts of negligence. It was the proximate cause.

The difficulty is that many jurists turn the theory inside out. To them, the intervening act intervenes **in time** between a prior act of negligence and the harm done; the independent intervening act occurs **after** another element of the causal sequence. Thus the stalled car sets up a potential accident, but another act of negligence intervenes - the act of driving a car recklessly and too fast. This then is the independent intervening act and the proximate cause.

Nor has the confusion ended since **Palsgraf**. In **Premo v. Grigg** (1965), Premo and his wife were cleaning Grigg's restaurant at night. He drew a bucket of hot water and placed it on the floor. Their 4-year-old daughter, playing while they worked, fell into it and was fatally scalded. Premo sued Grigg, claiming he was negligent in allowing the water heater to be set to such a high temperature. Though one might say that the stage was set by the scalding temperature of the water, the court held that the act of filling the bucket and placing it on the floor was an independent intervening act; the proximate cause. It is not that I disagree with the court's decision; I am just illustrating the looseness with which these phrases are tossed about.

When Cardozo entered **Palsgraf** this was the failure in definitude that plagued the cause of negligence, and this was the technical problem he set out to solve.

The railroad company, noting it had lost its first appeal by only one judge, and noting that judicial confusion has its charms, took its case to the New York Court of Appeals. There Chief Justice Cardozo penned his famous thesis and carried three of his six associates with him. This was enough to reverse the jury's decision, cancel the award of $6000 for Mrs. Palsgraf, charge her with all court costs, and leave her to pay her medical expenses on her own. The railroad company won the third round, and Helen Palsgraf and Attorney Wood came to the end of their rope.

Cardozo's solution to the dilemma was ingenious. Had he been more convincing, his work would have been no less a landmark in the journals of negligence, but I doubt that **Palsgraf** would have become, to quote Noonan's quote of Dean Prosser, "the most discussed and debated" tort case. The Cardozo result, later known as the Palsgraf theory, was fairly well expressed by the chief justice, but I want to express it in a more rigorous and elementary format, as follows:

1. Negligence requires a showing of proximate cause. That is, the plaintiff must establish the whole sequence of phenomena linking a negligent act of the defendant to the harm suffered by the plaintiff. Sometimes there are two or more negligent acts in a causal sequence, each independent of the others, attributable to separate persons, and a dispute will arise as to which of them is the true proximate cause of the harm.

In **Palsgraf** the patron brought the fireworks into the entrainment situation; the platform officer jostled his arm, causing the bundle to fall; the situation was conducive to the ignition of fireworks, and ignition occurred. As a direct result of the causal sequence, Mrs. Palsgraf partially lost her ability to articulate her speech. Thus the facts of the harm-causing sequence are established and complete.

2. Note there are two independent candidates for proximate cause: the acts of the boarding patron, and those of the trainmen; and it is not possible to conclude that one supercedes the other as to proximateness. So we must look for another criterion if liability is to be properly distributed among the parties.

3. Recall now that a proximate cause in negligence must have its source in a negligent act (or a negligent failure to act), so perhaps we can eliminate a candidate for proximate cause by finding it is not a negligent act after all. Obviously a person cannot be held negligent in a duty unless she actually has the duty in the first place. Negligence is not an abstract concept. It relates to specific duties owed by specific persons to other persons. Negligence is a specific breach of a specific duty. If you can find a link between negligence and a specific harm, you have a proximate cause. But if there is no duty, there cannot be negligence. And if an act isn't negligent, it cannot be called a proximate cause in a negligence case. Therefore look for the duty before you

involve yourself in the question of proximate cause. This is a logical way to proceed in a case in which there are more than one candidate for proximate cause.

4. If the initial step is to look for the duty, a rigorous definition of legal duty is required, and the basis for rigor is right before our eyes: a person cannot be considered negligent of a duty unless she is aware of the duty. But now we must define the phrase "aware of a duty".

Since there are two general modes of negligence - a negligent act, and a negligent failure to act, we must recognize two general modes of duty - (a) a duty to restrain ourselves in certain kinds of acts, and (b) a duty to act positively in certain kinds of situations. Relying on a wide experience and a wide reading in law, we may express these duties in the following conclusive words:

(a) **Duty of restraint:** If one or more elements of a potential harm-causing sequence exist within the effective range of a person's activities, and if she is aware of them or has a duty to search for them, then she should restrain herself from any act that might complete the causal sequence. (If two adults are standing on the brink of Grand Canyon, then each should restrain herself from playfully pushing the other in the direction of the canyon.)

(b) **Duty of Affirmative Action:** If a person has so acted as to materialize or activate an element of a harm-causing sequence, and if she is aware (or has a duty to be aware) of the existence of other elements that might complete the sequence, then she should act affirmatively in a way that will annul the possibility of such a completion. (If a person's car has stalled on the road, she should get it off the road or effectively warn oncoming motorists.)

Having Cardozo's thesis, we ourselves can apply it to **Palsgraf.** We see immediately that the boarding passenger, having brought the fireworks into the station, had a duty to act affirmatively in every possible way to preclude ignition. He must have been fully aware that he was supplying a crucial element to a potential harm-causing sequence. The possibilities for forseeable mishaps were everywhere. Slowly should he walk. Loudly should he proclaim the presence of the peril. Earnestly should he consult with the authorities. Yet he took not a single step to preclude catastrophe. His action (in the absence of a superceding intervening act) must be considered a proximate cause of the accident.

The only other candidate for proximate cause was the activity of the trainmen in helping the passenger aboard. But they were not aware of the fireworks. True, there were people on the platform. True, the trainmen were assisting a passenger in a rather dangerous adventure. But there were no visible elements in the situation linking their actions with the other passengers on the platform. Therefore they had no duty to restrain themselves in helping the passenger aboard except perhaps with respect to him personally. This is what Cardozo said. With respect to this specific act, they had no duty of restraint with respect to anyone other than this one specific person.

If there is no duty, there can be no neglect. If there's no neglect, proximate cause cannot be charged. Q.E.D.

Some professionals will disagree with my reconstruction of the Palsgraf theory, and even Cardozo might not like to see it expressed so rigorously. However I am not claiming that this is what the Palsgraf theory should be. I'm claiming that this is what it is. I'm claiming that this is what it must be, given Cardozo's own application of it in **Palsgraf.**

Unfortunately, Cardozo's solution did not provide the legal world with a firm path through the bog of negligence. It introduced other quicksands. For instance, regarding the man with the fireworks I made this assumptive statement: "He must have been fully aware that he was supplying a crucial element to a potential harm-causing sequence." But what if he was not aware of it? What if it never occurred to him that his fireworks might be subjected to high friction? Indeed, what if he did not realize that high friction could ignite fireworks? What if we are talking about a very simple man with a lot of fireworks and a high sense of urgency? If a man does not understand causal sequences, can duty exist? Can duty, any more than negligence, exist in the abstract?

So we come to a refinement, post Cardozo, of "awareness of duty". It is expressed, "A person should be aware of a duty if a reasonable or prudent person would be aware of it." This sounds reasonable except that ...should ...if ... would   ... are guideposts to the land of abstract. "I SHOULD be AWARE of "X" IF a REASONABLE person WOULD be," is a statement abstract in at least six dimensions. Therefore duty can exist in the abstract. Therefore negligence can. And so much for the rationalization of duty.

The reasonable person refinement is persuasive on the proposition that it will catch the person clever enough to plead ignorance. But it gives him another loophole. Now he can ask, "What do you mean by "reasonable"? Surely you can't expect everybody to be a genius!" It can be argued that sometimes the perception of risk in a situation requires more than reason. It might require experience, even instruction, and perhaps a rare inductive imagination. By this line of thought we come to the refinement of the refinement, and under this modern doctrine we learn that a person has a duty if an "ordinarily reasonable" person would be aware of it. The doctrine is often expressed as "liability depends on the foreseeability of unreasonable risk by a person using ordinary reason or prudence". And, armed with this, the contemporary jurist is led to believe he can now approach the question of negligence with a reasonably cautious broadmindedness.

The criterion of foreseeability is insidious. It invites the attitude, "What I don't know will be good for me." It doesn't discourage recklessness. A man shooting a bullet into a thicket and maiming a person, and released from liability on the premise that it's not likely that a person would be in the thicket, will not grasp the possibility that a person might on occasion actually be there. This is an essential ingredient of recklessness; taking an action with unforeseeable consequences; regardless. If an ulterior purpose for damages is to minimize future loss in the commonwealth, then a liability for damages that depends on the "foreseeability of the harm" will defeat it. In real, non-abstract life a government faces this policy decision: "How are you going to make people more sensitive - keeping their eyes open and their minds alert - to the possibility that their action might complete a harm-causing sequence?"

In wandering into the land of duty and negligence, the courts have prepared a paradise for figity. Under modern negligence "theory" lawyers and judges can make a complex case conclude any way they wish, and they can transform a simple case into a complex one. Experience tells us that some people are blind to the common good, and now we can see a fundamental defect of figism. In not thumping certain favorites - in not holding them responsible for their destructive acts - a government creates a rapidly proliferating class of people, blind and remaining blind to the common good, and reaching right down into the grass roots. You can see here a policy decision to be made, a decision for rulers, present and prospective.

I've shown to this point some difficulties in treating a dispute by the duty-negligence procedure, and it would seem reasonable to try cases by causes other than negligence. I will now show that Palsgraf was a case of injury materially contributing to harm; injury with an origin in nuisance, and culminating in persistent distortion. I will show that the will of the railroad company intruded upon Helen Palgraf's very own loading space and crystallized there.

Let us quickly thumb through the general format of injury:

(a) Has there been a loading space to which Helen Palsgraf was entitled? Answer: yes. (b) And was this (the bombardment with fireworks) loading adverse to her wishes? Answer: yes. And (c) Was this loading a consequence of the will of the trainmen? Answer: possibly no. Yes, an impact was made on her body without her permission. However the loading of the trainmen's will into the situation is an uncertain point, an issue to be discussed.
(d) Was Helen Palsgraf under a service or servitude to the railroad that justified the adverse loading? Answer: no. The railway made no claims to such services or servitudes.

We can say immediately that Mrs. Palsgraf's pursuit - that of waiting quietly to take a train to the beach - in no way interfered with the railway company's mass transit pursuit. To the contrary, the two pursuits were in complete harmony with each other. But can we say truthfully that the smoke and eruptions of fireworks, and the stamped- ing crowd - the things that had such a material impact on Mrs. Palsgraf - embodied the will of the trainmen, hence the will of the company? Or should we conclude that the company - its employees - was trapped into the Palsgraf affair? Was its will reduced to zero under the circum- stances? This is the issue. The involvement of the will of the trainmen or the company is the only issue in **Palsgraf**.

There is no doubt about the vital presence, in the Palsgraf incident, of the will of the running train-chaser. On that August Sunday he was busy materializing a project. We can safely assume, though without knowing his ulterior objective, that his immediate objective was to get himself and his fireworks onto the train. We know that he loaded himself with the bundle, he made the loadings that located the bundle and himself on the train platform, he loaded the trainmen with himself and his problem, and he loaded the train with himself, less bundle.

As to carrying fireworks into the station, as to his entitlement to that project, Judge Seeger touched upon it. " ...it does not appear that the provisions of the Greater New York Charter were violated."

If after acquiring the fireworks, this prospective passenger had merely placed them in his closet at home, he would have created a situation saturated with his will. Though we cannot say he charged the fireworks - this had been done by the manufacturers - he would have been charging his closet and his house and now, by bringing them to the railroad station, he was adding a charged element to a potentially harmful situation. He placed the fireworks wrapped in newspaper in the midst of a milling, bumping crowd, spotted with glowing cigarettes and cigars. He made of himself a transport vehicle with an inadequate suspension mechanism - an arm that couldn't quite reach around the bundle. Not enough that the whole thing - bundle plus man - was a charged device, he now added an unwieldy momentum to the device; he ran with it. Finally he undertook to launch the whole infernal device across the narrow space between platform and train, a jaw of slithering steel and toothy concrete understrung with steel wheels whining on steel rails, his aim - to attach himself and his unstable charge to the train by means of an unreliable gadget composed of a hand and arm.

Every gear and lever of this entire situation was connected and bolted together by this man's will. But he has eluded the wrath of the law, and perhaps it is well he did. His escape focused the uneasy attention of the legal world on the railroad company. Did there exist in the fire and terror of that August Sunday the quiet operation of a will that almost went unnoticed?

The Long Island Railroad Company was engaged in a continuing commercial pursuit. By providing public transportation the officers and stockholders hoped to make money. Though they placed charged devices - their trains - in the midst of the public, their pursuit was not an uncivil one. In fact it was approved and encouraged by the rulers of the region and the Helen Palsgrafs as well. To that extent the rulers and the Helen Palsgrafs were partners in this project of putting charged devices into the midst of the public.

But they were junior partners, meaning that the railroad people understood their creature's potential for harm better than the patrons did. They pledged themselves to keep it under control. They were the ones who could anticipate and prevent the catastrophes that might result from the railroad operations.

Surely people had been hurt many times trying to board moving trains. Surely as a measure of safety the top executives could order the conductor to shut and fasten all doors before giving the engineer the go signal. Surely by printed signs in the station and warnings on tickets, the company could notify all patrons that boarding a moving train was prohibited. All such measures would forestall a number of tragedies. All this was true, and it applied to the boarding passenger, but how was it functionally related to Helen Palsgraf standing quietly far from the tracks? This was Cardozo's question, a valid one, and the answer lies in a little enterprise that the Long Island Railroad Company had on the side.

Not an evil pursuit; quite the opposite. It comes from railroad people thinking they are serving the public. It comes from the thought that a patron left behind by a train might be left frantic in some kind of an emergency. It comes from the fact that you can't stop trains for late-comers. Havoc would spread through the system. Time schedules would become shambles. On a busy day a train would never leave a busy station. Considering everything, isn't it a practical and commonly decent policy to assist a desperate patron to board a departing train?

Here then is a little subproject undertaken mutually by railroad people and gasping train chasers. It is an extra service contracted on the spur of the moment between railroad and boarder. It is a joint venture in which both parties are full partners and in which the rulers and Helen Palsgrafs of the region are not subscribers. The trainmen know the danger, and the boarder sees and hears it just as keenly. Under his twinkling feet he sees the perilous shear between moving train and immovable platform, and he hears the squeal of steel on steel.

To the mind of Benjamin Cardozo the trainman if responsible to anyone is responsible to the person he is pulling aboard. But is this reasonable? If the boarder trips and gets mangled, where is the injury. He has welcomed the trainman into his loading space. During the run for the coach, an implied contract has been signed and sealed. Says the patron to the trainman, "If you'll be good enough to help me on board, I'll surrender my title to my personal safety. Helping me on board is now an element of your very own loading space." The acceptance of the contract by the railroad company - for surely this act of the trainman is a policy of the company - does not imply a guarantee of safety. The only way the railroad company can injure the patron, once the contract is made, is breach of contract; failing to make the effort.

Well, this is debatable. In any case in this joint venture, each partner accepts the other "as is". It is not a matter of the trainmen being unaware of the fireworks. In effect, the trainmen said to the boarder, "Buddy, we don't care even if you have a loaded machine gun in that bundle; we're going to help you on board if that's what you wish." This is a policy of the railroad. An action of will. Executed by the trainmen. Whatever happens, the wills of both boarder and railroad company are loaded into the causal sequence and the consequences.

This is the basis of partnership liability. Each partner is responsible in full for the liabilities of the venture. A partner is not absolved of liability on the excuse that she did not foresee the monster created by the union of forces. The fact is that the wills of both parties are engaged fully in the undertaking, and the government presumes that each partner has in advance thoroughly investigated the trustworthiness of the other.

For critical seconds, August 24, 1924, Mrs. Palsgraf was engulfed by the materialized wills of the railroad company and the boarder; not by their intentions, but by their wills; without her permission. And when the intrusive wills receded, they left her project effectiveness diminished.

But am I making an erroneous assumption in **Palsgraf**? Is it possible that the railroad company was not a full partner in the boarding venture? Suppose that the passenger had already set foot on the train before the trainmen started to help him. He was hanging on with a hand, close to falling into the shearing gap beneath. Could the trainmen refuse to help? Were they not trapped into helping? If so, it might not be their will that invaded Mrs. Palsgraf's loading space. They were merely responding in the highest climate of mind to a fellow creature in danger. What about this? Here, first, is Cardozo's recitation of the crucial moment. "The other man, carrying a package, jumped aboard the car, but seemed unsteady as if about to fall. A guard on the car, who had held the door open, reached forward to help him in, and another guard on the platform pushed from behind."

On this version have most of the debates on **Palsgraf** relied. But Cardozo recited the facts incorrectly. Listen to Mr. Gerhardt, trial witness, answering the questions of Attorney Wood.

Q. ...you say the train was in motion? A. Yes, sir.

Q. And there was a guard on the train? A. A guard on the train.

Q. And a platform man on the platform? A. Yes, sir.

Q. And each tried to assist this man to get on the train? A. Yes, because the other fellow was on already.

Q. And which man hit the arm that carried the bundle; the platform man or the guard? A. The platform man.

Q. He had hold of the right arm of the Italian? A. Yes, he tried to assist him on and he was trying to grab the train.

This indicates not an attempt to save a man in danger of falling, but an implied offer and acceptance of a joint venture. The results of the ensuing cross-examination are confusing. From them one might derive Chief Justice Cardozo's version. But Gerhardt's original statement was corroborated by the testimony of Mrs. Gerhardt and Lillian Palsgraf who, though distant from her mother, retained in her memory a distinct picture of the event.

However for the sake of argument, let us give the railroad people the fullest benefit of the doubt. Let us say that the boarder was in trouble; hanging on for dear life. And now we ask if the railroad people were trapped by his will into their attempt to help. Trapped perhaps they were, but were they trapped by wills other than their own? Was there a standing invitation for desperate boarders to board moving trains? Was this a railroad policy? Here was a key question: was the door of the train car closed when the train got under way, or was it open? If it was open we must assume that the company's will was loaded into this event. It welcomed last minute boarders. If under this circumstance it was trapped into rescuing them, it was trapped by its own wilful policy.

Cardozo's version of the crucial moment states that the car door was open during the rescue operation. But had it been closed prior to that?

This is a key question, and due to the genius of "ordinary" men we have a basis for getting at the facts. There was an exchange between a juror and Judge Humphrey, one that occurred after the judge had given his charge to the jury and just before the jury left for the jury room.

Juror No. 1: Your honor, may I ask a question? There was no evidence to show whether the door was shut at the time the train left, or the door was closed before the train went in motion. There has been nothing shown in the case. Am I permitted to ask that question?

The Court: Well, what have you to say about it?

Mr. Wood (for Palsgraf): I don't see that it makes any difference.

Mr. McNamara (for defendant): In view of the question of the juror, I ask your honor to charge the jury that the fact that the door of the train - .

The Court: There is no evidence that the door of the train was closed, or the gate of the door was closed - the gate of the platform was closed. There was no evidence that it was closed. You may retire, gentlemen."

This is amazing. A juror asked the key question to the whole riddle. With this we can better judge the quality of the jury's deliberations. It looks as though the twelve ordinary men did a pretty good job in two and one-half hours, including time for lunch. Scott and Kent comment on the trial, "Perhaps neither party did a very good job in drafting the pleadings or in the conduct of the trial." One must also contemplate their remark, quoted earlier: "...this case is of considerable importance in the development of the law of torts."

We have in **Palsgraf** the most widely debated case in the history of torts, complete with duty, negligence, proximate cause, independent intervening act, ordinarily reasonable people and the foreseeability of unreasonable risk. But how simple the case really is when one understands the elements of property and the mechanics of injury. It is a case of nuisance with associated persisting distortion and loss of project effectiveness.

CHAPTER 20

WHAT JUSTICE SEES AND WEIGHS

I have spent a number of past chapters developing a basic language for due process. In those chapters I have unscrewed the nuts and bolts of pursuit and conflict; I have tried to find the wave-length of complaints that fit the radio reception band of the courts. In short, I have been treating the legal world like an engineering problem.

But as we become legal technicians we must not lose the grander vision. "Why justice?" we might ask, and I intend to break away from gear boxes, surveying instruments and electronic switches to dwell on this higher plane for a while. And though I will draw conclusions that will seem excessively romantic to a magistrate in a police court, nonetheless they illuminate his true situation. Though the question "Why Justice?" examines the hidden principles of equity, the vision of equity filters down to every case, even to the humblest court in the land.

Recalling the white-robed figure of Justice, blindfolded and raising her scales, we might ask our question in a different way. "What," we might ask, "does Justice see; and what does she weigh?" Surely she is not blind to everything and, though her eyes are covered, at least she must be pondering something in her mind's eye. As for the scales, we suspect she may weigh whatever she pleases. But we also suspect that she will weigh whatever seems very precious to her at the moment.

To answer the question in general mode, one would like to imagine that she sees and weighs things that a supremely intelligent being would see and weigh. But she has a human figure. Moreover if I am to view Justice in a truly general mood, I must declare despite all opposition that she personifies any standard of justice that our rulers might choose. This allows for example that the figure of Justice is blind to the common good, and weighs only the figistic advantages in favoring one party over the other.

So much for generalization.

I have in earlier chapters suggested matters to which the courts are blind; at least matters that they don't hear. For one thing they are deaf to a case unless the plaintiff lays claim to a loading space of her very own, claiming in the same breath a particular infringement of that space by the named defendant. I earlier asserted, for instance, that a court would not listen to Mrs. McNamara when she laid before it a petition to compel Mr. McNamara to take out the garbage. This attitude of the court becomes understandable when we recognize that Mr. McNamara is not a subject in her property. Nor is he under a contractual service to take out the garbage. No one has invaded her property and infringed her liberty; she has not been injured.

We are not unsympathetic. We know there can be true pathos in a McNamara situation, the marriage, say of a responsible woman and an irresponsible man. But we are facing the question of what the government will force a person to do to satisfy another person's wishes. Is pathos sufficient?

Noonan, in **Persons and Masks of the Law**, makes definite proposals about what Justice should see. Like me, though for different reasons, he is dissatisfied with Cardozo's ruling in **Palsgraf**. In analyzing **Palsgraf**, Noonan pursues the theme of his book: a judge places too much stress upon being objective. During the hearing of a case, a judge places a mask over his own ego; he places hoods over the persons before the bench - all to preserve a semblance of impartiality. But in the process he strips a cause of its humanity, and as a result reaches erroneous conclusions.

Noonan's argument is persuasive in his chapter on slavery in Virginia and, having gained high ground, he attacks **Palsgraf**. In **Palsgraf** he sees the wealth of the railroad and the pitiful plight of Helen Palsgraf. He sees Cardozo blind to the person of Mrs. Palsgraf and almost suggests that Cardozo could not erase the money effectiveness of a railroad from his subconscious eye. Cardozo failed to see Mrs. Palsgraf's struggle to support three children, the strain and expenses of four years in litigation, and he failed to hear her debilitating stammer. He should have perceived these facts, says Noonan. Justice should not blind herself to the human aspects of a case. A decision should be made with a sympathetic understanding of the relative positions of plaintiff and defendant. But I cannot support such a solution for **Palsgraf**.

In the **Armistad** case, John Quincy Adams criticized the government for observing sympathy, not justice. Sympathy for the whites, as he put it, and antipathy toward the blacks. In **Palsgraf** Noonan advocates sympathy for Mrs. Palsgraf and antipathy toward the powerful railroad company. Extrapolating this policy to my fictitious case of Lineweaver and Frick, Noonan would look at Frick's mangled body and at Lineweaver's mere loss of a contract and permit this comparison to overrule the fact that it was Frick who invaded Lineweaver's property. Or to put it more concretely, what would Noonan have decided in **Palsgraf** if Helen had been an heiress to millions of dollars and the railroad close to bankruptcy, with stockholders mostly widows and pensioners?

I support Noonan absolutely in saying that Justice must see the human element in a case. Yet we must admit many human elements in a case; many desires, many hopes, many admirable attitudes, many sordid ones. Suppose for example that Mrs. Palsgraf's stammer was a sham. Sham springs from a human element. If discovered it would shatter her case. Yet should we allow sham to snuff out our sympathy for her poverty? Or let's cut the cake with a keener knife and suppose that the railroad was not really responsible for the accident. The car door is closed, the man with the fireworks catching the boarding bar, clinging desperately to the accelerating train, and the trainmen trapped by conscience into opening the car door and assisting him. The bundle drops and ignites and Helen is deprived of clear speech.

By collecting fares, the railroad company is in a position to charge a little more, enough to accumulate a fund for just such accidents. This is Noonan's exact proposal and it reveals his fine concern for human welfare. He is, however, proposing a function properly legislative, not judicial.

Let a man in a restaurant choke on a piece of lettuce, with brain damage as a result. Why shouldn't the restaurant owner, with money collected from his business, help offset the gentleman's loss of effectiveness? Well he should, says Noonan, unless the man and his family have plenty of money. You see, the emphasis has shifted to human welfare completely disassociated from property and injury. We have departed the topic of responsibility and embarked on a redistribution of wealth. We have been derailed from the pursuit of a national training program training people to be alert to the harm-causing sequences with which we are all surrounded, using damages as a very effective training device. Let the courts adopt redistribution of wealth as a cause and you establish a policy depriving defendants of property without due process. Damages would be assessed in the absence of injury.

It is unfailingly true that aiding a distressed person will enhance the national treasure. But to do so by abusing damages and placing fault on a person not at fault is to confuse due process and finally destroy it.

I suggest that the separation of powers be kept razor sharp. Let the courts hear cases involving infringements of liberty. Let the legislature and the welfare department of the executive hear cases of distress in which injury is not an issue; where appropriation, entitlement, redistribution of project effectiveness are the issues. It is clear that Noonan's proposal, confusing infringement and pathos, is antithetic to the standard of justice that I am expounding. I think the adoption of such a proposal would encourage figity in sheep's clothing.

If we let Justice peek at relative assets for charitable reasons, she may become charmed by what she sees. A judgment of injury based on relative wealth is alien to a judgment based on an infringement of liberty.

However, it is easy to be critical of someone like Noonan who is trying to express what Justice should see. It is easy to assert what Justice should not see. To express what she should see is like pulling light out of a black hole. Yet we cannot evade the question "What should Justice see?" We must pursue it aggressively. It is not that Justice fails to see the human elements of a case. In a truly difficult case, Justice must look beyond titles and easily defined infringements. She must look into the innermost recesses of the human soul. Unfortunately, while a theoretical Justice might have 20-20 vision in this sphere, a mortal judge may be prone to ocular affliction. Let us take class oppression cases as an example.

It is agreed that courts have difficulty in determining what they should and shouldn't see in class oppression cases. For example it is often said that a court should not see the color of a person's skin. But then the "affirmative action" school maintains that we must see the black's skin color if we are to compensate her for past inequities. In fact we can learn much about judicial vision by reviewing the history of the black thrust in the United States.

It is common knowledge that black people as slaves were completely invisible in court; they had no property; no loading space of their very own. Therefore they could not be injured. We need but a few quotations of court opinions from Wheeler:
"They are generally considered, not as persons, but as things. **Bynum v. Bostwick** (1812).
"...the witness was properly rejected. There is no instance in which a negro has been permitted to give evidence, except in cases of absolute necessity; nor indeed has this court ever recognized the propriety of admitting them in any case where the rights of whites are concerned. **White v. Helmes** (1821).
"Our slaves can do nothing in their own right; can hold no property. **Brandon v. Merchants' Bank of Huntsville** (1828).
"...slaves are, in every respect, except as to descents and wills, personalty. They go to the administrator, and may be assets in his hands for payment of debts." **Sneed v. Ewing** (1831)."

With the coming of emancipation for the blacks after the Civil War, their legal helplessness became a salient feature of their new situation. Since slavery would have been illegal under the common law, it had been necessary for southern jurists, both judicial and legislative, to weave another system of law into the common law. This adulteration, known today as the slave code, though thoroughly disjoint with the common law, was nevertheless law and had to be cancelled by positive law if the effects of the slave code were to be abolished. This was the aim and legal effect of the thirteenth amendment (1865) of the federal Constitution. Other legal disabilities of the blacks were remedied by the first clause of the fourteenth amendment (1868) declaring all persons born in the United States to be citizens. This in effect included all blacks. And finally the fifteenth amendment was ratified (1870) compelling every state to permit these new citizens to vote under the same set of qualifications as all other citizens (how difficult it is to phrase such a sentiment effectively).

Constitutional amendments meant nothing to greedy whites taking advantage of helpless blacks. The amendments simply escaped the notice of biased whites who wished to keep the blacks "in their place". So to give the courts grounds for jurisdiction in cases of racial discrimination, Congress enacted a series of statutes called the Civil Rights Acts, giving the Justice Department power to prosecute the complaints of blacks and giving courts power to impose penalties for misconduct under the acts. Congress has continued to the present to produce civil rights acts in connection with various species of class oppression, and it seems that nothing in our legal history has confused the judicial process so much as has this particular stream of legislation. This I have mentioned before.

The Civil Rights Acts created a slough into which the black movement plunged and disappeared for fifty years. In no case is this better illustrated than in the **Civil Rights Cases**, decided in 1883. I introduced this set of cases in an earlier chapter, and now I will examine it in depth. It joined five separate cases from as many states and placed them before the Supreme Court of the United States. Of the joined black complainants, two had been denied hotel lodging, two had been denied admittance to theaters, and one had been barred from the ladies' parlor car on a railroad train. The case well illustrates how the blacks were rendered invisible to Justice by the technicalities of legal practice.

The Solicitor General of the United States, prosecuting the case for the blacks, grounded his pleading on the Civil Rights Act of 1875. This act exacted a penalty against inns, public conveyances and places of amusement that turned away a prospective customer by reason of her race. None of the defendants denied their discriminatory actions, their defense was simply that the Civil Rights Act of 1875 was unconstitutional. They contended that it was not truly supported by the thirteenth and fourteenth amendments as previously supposed, and therefore they had done nothing wrong. The various lower federal courts had failed to agree on the constitutionality of the act, and the question was taken to the Supreme Court.

So the question before the court was not whether the blacks should have been accomodated by the proprietors of the various businesses. It was a question of whether the Civil Rights Act of 1875 was constitutional or not; a purely technical matter. Of course the causes of the blacks would evaporate if the act were to be declared unconstitutional, but this would be merely incidental; nothing personal. Thus though the controversy was generated by the visible features of the plaintiffs, they the plaintiffs - features, humanity, and all - became completely invisible to the court. And the court, with a perfectly sound and well-reasoned opinion, declared that no authority supporting the act can be found in either the thirteenth or fourteenth amendment and **"no other authority supporting it being suggested"** the act must necessarily be declared void.

The act is of course constitutional, but the court chose not to think beyond the pleadings and arguments of the Solicitor General. The case for the blacks was so mismanaged by the United States that it would be impossible in a few words to describe the fiasco accurately. But this mismanagement is not unusual. All along, the United States has handled "equal rights" awkwardly. For some reason it has tried to treat class oppression cases by positive law - constitutional amendments, legislation - when all along the solutions are implicit in equity. The all-too-frequent effect of civil rights has been to change class oppression cases into battles over the meanings of clauses and provisions, not an opportunity to exercise and apply great principles. And during these hours and years of verbal legerdemain there quietly and invisibly sits in the courtroom a group of plaintiffs whose liberties have been infringed.

Actually Justice Bradley's opinion, speaking for the majority of the Supreme Court justices, was a declaration of freedom for the blacks, and it went completely unheard. It is unfortunate, he said, that there is no relief for the plaintiffs on the grounds they have chosen. Nevertheless, he continued, black people have exactly the same standing in the common law and equity as anyone else. If they have been injured, let them use the procedure that has been proposed for all free men under our legal system. Let them proceed by civil action in the courts of their states.

In a sense we may say that the common law is rooted in slavery. It began to glimmer while the English were still slaves to the Normans. The road out of slavery and the evolution of the common law represent an inseparable parallel development, and it is apparent that powerful people promoted it with a mystifying intensity of purpose. You might say that the resulting genius of the common law lies in its capacity to dismiss from society, almost with nonchalance, the slightest stain of slavery.

But in weaving the slave code into the common law, the new world lawyers learned to be cute with words. By means of words they intended not merely that Justice peek through her blindfold at skin color, they intended to distort her inner vision as well. How thorough their work was. Cleverness with words seems to have become addictive in American law. Despite the best of intentions on the part of legislators, perverse words insinuate themselves in statutes sliding a silk screen between the common law and the inner eye of Justice. Even as our nation tries to alleviate class oppression, it seems that a word-caused astigmatism continues to plague the perceptiveness of Justice. For this reason, the opinions of the old English courts, as they handled certain questions of slavery, are especially enlightening.

Helen Catteral in the first volume of her exhaustive **Judicial Cases Concerning American Slavery and the Negro** presents as background a number of cases from the English courts. The first is the familiar quotation from **Cartwright's Case** of 1569: "In the Eleventh of Elizabeth, one Cartwright brought a slave from Russia, and would scourge him, for which he was questioned; and it was resolved that England was too pure an air for Slaves to breath in." Analysis pales before the vision that we see here, the complete harmony between opinion and decision. One can only comment that the chancellor's field of vision was certainly not cluttered with the words of statutes and constitutional amendments. But what was he seeing?

Slavery was already dead in England; the chancellor merely put the lid on the coffin. Afterward, only when visitors from America brought their slaves with them did English courts catch an ill wind. A slave it seems sometimes took the visit as an opportunity to apply for her freedom. To counter, the owner would seek a writ of habeas corpus on grounds that the English court lacked jurisdiction. It was a matter of forcibly escorting the black to the owner's terra firma where the case would be properly disposed of.

These cases had varied results. Occasionally the decision hinged on whether the slave was a Christian. Sometimes the English court would recognize the colonial law as binding. During that era there was a theory that colonial law could absorb the complexion of native law. Since in the new world the Indians practiced slavery, the English government would countenance the practice among colonists.

In the case of **Smith v. Gould** a different criterion was applied. The court reasoned that since a man may own property, he could not be the subject of property. In still another case, the court freed the slave of a foreign visitor on grounds that the common law does not distinguish between negroes and other men. Really it was as simple as that, except that the decision did not tackle the issue of jurisdiction.

So we see in English courts, in this very narrow class of complaints, a bit of hazy insight, a sort of ocular misangularity. But 200 years after **Cartwright,** the eve of the American Revolution, 1769, Lord Chief Justice Mansfield, in the case of **Somerset v. Stewart,** found the exact focal length of the problem.

Stewart had brought his slave with him on a visit to England, and Somerset didn't wish to return to the island colony of Jamaica in Caribbean America. At the time of the court action, Somerset was being held in irons on board ship in an English harbor with the ship's master awaiting instructions from the court. Stewart sought to return Somerset to the jurisdiction of Jamaica on a writ of habeas corpus, his pleading stating, "The slave departed and refused to serve; whereupon he was kept, to be sold abroad." Somerset's appeal reached the ears of the highest court in England.

Since the dispute seemed to involve the ownership of a property, and since the property was held under the laws of Jamaica, Mansfield might have remanded the case to that jurisdiction and gone about his business. In such an act his visual field would be governed by the niceties of protocol between English courts, one in the mother country, one in a colony. But Mansfield's court had been the birthplace of equity, and other images were filling his line of vision. He caught a larger view and he saw the impact of his act upon the universe of English society. The execution of a writ of habeas corpus is itself an act; the act of an omnipotent government. In seizing a human figure and returning it to Jamaica, Mansfield would be displaying his power over the person of a human, and this per se is jurisdiction. In exercising such power, Mansfield was bound to the principles of equity, but such an order in effect would force a human to remain in slavery. This would be the undoubted result of a trial in Jamaica.

Such an act on a court's part, said Mansfield, "must be recognized by the law of the country where it is used. ...the state of slavery is of such a nature, that it is incapable of being introduced on any reasons, moral or political; but only by positive law.... It is so odious, that nothing can be suffered to support it, but positive law. Whatever inconveniences therefore may follow from a decision, I cannot say this case is allowed or approved by the law of England; and therefore the black must be discharged."

This was nothing less than absolutely clear vision. In looking at Somerset, Mansfield was seeing a human adult - skin color invisible - who sought nothing more than the property guaranteed to all noncriminal adults in England, the loading space of their own bodies. In Stewart the slave-owner he saw an individual who wished to dominate that loading space. And if he executed the writ of habeas corpus he saw an act that he had vowed never to do - the forcing of a man to submit to the will of another.

But if Mansfield was looking at the total situation, we might ask how the common good of England would be enhanced by freeing a foreign black man on English soil? I'll introduce the answer with a thought from Joseph Wood Krutch's **If You Don't Mind My Saying So**, and I'll paraphrase it as follows:

"The Puritans forbade bearbaiting, but not because it gave pain to the bears. They forebade it because it gave pleasure to the spectators. And to this day the Puritan logic is also that of the Roman Church, based on St. Thomas: cruelty to animals is wrong, not because animals have rights but because cruelty corrupts men."

Here you will notice we have gone beyond rights. We have entered the grounds where rights are established. Here is the private observatory of equity. Among the ideas I'm trying to express is that the greatest judges in equity are not necessarily brilliant technicians (though Mansfield was); but they have the ability to see in their mind's eye how the nation will react to a court decision.

There is a gift among humans that sees the pain caused by an injurious intrusion into the life of another human. And there is another gift; more rare; the gift of seeing what happens to the soul of a spectator when she observes that an intrusion is enforced by the power structure of her community. Though a court be blind to the situation, it does not follow that the bystander is mentally inert to the report from the courtroom. "There but for the grace of God go I" expresses a bystander's reaction to her fleeting glimpse of the power of government. A scene in which an intrusion is supported by such power sends a tremor through the human frame. Though the mind may not comprehend what's happening within it, the scene shapes attitudes all the same.

We don't like to admit it, but in every human heart there's a dream of owning slaves and, simultaneously, a dread of personal enslavement. Witnessing enslavement in a cleverly subtle guise brings a flicker of a grin to the corner of our mouth, and a stab in our stomach. If you don't believe me, test your own response to the man who liked Dickens in Evelyn Waugh's **A Handful of Dust.** It was condensed in the June 1978 Readers Digest.

Mansfield, as an intelligent member of England's body of rulers, could not afford to be blind to this element of the case. From the writings of predecessor John Somers he had probably extracted this message, "When influential people little by little subvert the standard of justice and gradually legalize injury they create a system, backed by the power of government, that can swallow themselves."

Note then the great range of vision open to Justice. If she removes her blindfold she sees the whiteness of a person, or a narrow concept of property, or the assets of a person, or correct protocol among fellow jurists, or pleasant relations with the "colonies". If behind her blindfold she becomes visually confused, she sees words or the absence of words in a written law, and frets over their import. If she gains visual clarity she sees human desires in conflict and, weighing them in a strange balance, determines where her true treasure lies. On the horizon of her vision stands her jurisdictive act, the fact materialized by her decision, and she foresees the phenomenal effect it will have on the psychology of the nation.

There remains a question unanswered. Was sympathy for Somerset a factor in Mansfield's decision? The truth is that sympathy is an emotion wholly unfit for freedom. Let me explain.

Blacks were not held in slavery by chains of iron. Of chains there were many, all composed of flesh and blood. The first chain was their own human ability to anticipate punishment. Animals can be conditioned to act as their trainers wish them to act, but humans can anticipate punishment without having ever experienced it. Though the slave code was introduced on the premise that blacks were not human, half of the laws depended for their effectiveness on the human understanding of the blacks. All law in fact depends on the human power of anticipation.

Another set of slave chains were applied indirectly. Half of the slave laws were directed at controlling the behavior of whites! Under provision for punishment, a free white was required to report a black apparently running away. A tradesman, though proud of engaging in free enterprise, would be punished if he traded with a black except as an emissary of her master. And a clergyman, free to do God's work according to his conscience, would be punished if he officiated at the marriage of a black without the owner's consent. Even the Constitution forged part of this chain. The rulers of free sovereign non-slave states were required under the Constitution to commit the very act that Mansfield refused to commit. They were required to return an escaping black to the jurisdiction of the owner's state.

Another chain was wrought of the reasoning ability of the owner. Given this, slave code lawyers found it unnecessary to take away the owner's right to free his slave. In Virginia, three words in the index of the Justice of the Peace Manual made black and slave legally identical. A black set free by her owner was an abandoned thing; an abandoned subject of property. By a bizarre reversion to common law - every thing must have an owner - she could be claimed by the first person who discovered she had no owner. Being black, she was automatically the claimant's slave. Though he might not want a slave, he would be mad not to claim her, there was a ready cash market for these things. Though the owner might wish to free his slave, the act would be idiotic.

There was no end to the subtlety of these flesh and blood chains. Blacks there were who would try to escape, defying all fear and all reason. But Matthew, powerful and manly as he was, had wife Linda and daughter Susan. Though he had the capacity to escape to the frontier and survive, he would never leave his loved ones behind in slavery, nor would he expose them to the dangers and hardships of the escape. Thus did the system use Matthew's own intelligence, his affection and sense of responsibility, to keep him enslaved. The very system that denied this man's humanity used the greatest of his human traits to bar him from freedom.

We can learn something about the human mechanism from this little story, and we'll run across this little trick in modern times. In holding Matthew to slavery, the system did not reduce his desire to escape, nor his ability to escape. It attacked his will, that mysterious function marking the difference between project and pursuit.

Now we come to the point, the final chain that held the black in slavery. As you know, there actually was a legal gateway to freedom for a slave. Her mistress could renounce her ownership of her black friend and convey her to a state having no legal provision for slavery. But now the imagination of the mistress leaped into the future. How would her friend be treated in this new land? What if she spent her money before she found employment? Who would take care of her if she fell ill? Under the burden of such thoughts did a slave owner slowly abandon her emancipation project and decide to keep her friend at her side. Sympathy, you see - the ability to feel the suffering, physical and mental, of another person - was the bar to the black's only legal gateway to freedom. If Lord Mansfield had operated from sympathy instead of observing Somerset's desires within his very own loading space, he might have wondered how Somerset would survive set free in England. Operating from sympathy, Mansfield might well have returned Somerset to Jamaica.

The Supreme Court of the United States has had to combat this very kind of sympathy. In 1977, as a result of the court's decision in **Halderman v. Pennhurst State School and Hospital,** a ponderous state program was disassembled and laid to rest. The mentally retarded inmates of a state institution were returned to their home communities, and the Commonwealth of Pennsyvania was ordered to provide them with training and care within those communities. The court asserted that there were only three justifiable causes for confining a mentally inferior person to an institution: first if and when she presented a danger to herself; second if and when she presented a danger to others; and third if and when she needed training and received it in the institution. It was not sufficient to argue that she should be confined "for her own good". If the dangers were not a factor and treatment or training was not provided, there was no justification for confining the inmates. "Thus," said the court, "on the basis of this record we find that the retarded at Pennhurst have been and presently are being denied their Equal Protection Rights as guaranteed by the Fourteenth Amendment to the Constitution." The appeal to the fourteenth amendment was superfluous. Nevertheless, this is as apt an application of the amendment as we'll find.

Mansfield would have viewed the case in more fundamental terms.

He would have seen each retarded person as a loading space owned by the person herself, and he would have seen Pennhurst as a person trying to impose her will on this loading space. In cases more complex, Mansfield would have looked beyond law. He would have observed the mental attitudes operating in plaintiff and defendant. He would have seen the awesome power of government enforcing an intrusion or warding it off, and he would sense the reaction of the nation to this spectacle of power. Like John Somers he would discern under the guise of "sympathy for the disadvantaged" a potential for legalized injury. The phrase "for his own good" might become a camouflaged path to enslavement.

A chancellor in equity should have the gift of visualizing the psychological forces operating in plaintiff, defendant, and watching nation. As you will see, it is in the universe of the psyche that the common law finds its justification.

CHAPTER 21

THE COMMON GOOD AND THE TRUE
CONSTITUTION OF THE UNITED STATES

Throughout this writing I have insisted on an unseen link between our law and the common good. Yet where is it written that our lawmakers must heed the common good? I haven't presented evidence demonstrating that judges and legislators in the United States are under a mandate to tie their actions to the common good.

Such a mandate, even if it exists, certainly would not make life easier for judges. The business of locating the latitude and longitude of the common good can be an excruciating task. The common good has a way of hiding in a thick fog. To give shape to the common good is a main goal in writing the book, and I must now show, if possible, that the founding fathers actually intended that all acts of government in the United States - legislative, executive, judicial - be justified in the light of the common good. In other words let us ask if blindfolded Justice in the United States is under a legal duty to keep always in her mind's eye a true image of the common good and steer directly there.

First, since American law refers historically to the common law of England, we may ask if the common law of England embraces the common good as a lodestone, a guiding star. The historian Cantor, in writing his readable and scholarly book **The English** devoted much thought to the topics of liberty and the common law. If we look at the parade of English kings and Parliaments, prime ministers and theologians, wars and civil wars, commercial development and industrial revolution, we can't understand what we are seeing without referring event by event to English tides in liberty and law. Says Cantor:

"The seventeenth-century constitutional struggles are really a series of conflicts fought around the idea of liberty. From this tangled cluster one idea ultimately triumphed in England - an idea of... astonishing simplicity.... In England, liberty is... whatever the king-in-Parliament says it is. But beyond this conclusion lies a whole complex of ideas of what liberty is and ought to be - a web of strands rooted in several distinct sources.... ... specifically to two significant foundations, the common law and religious ideals.
"... The common law idea of liberty is, just as Coke said it was, enshrined in Magna Carta. ... Liberty in England is nothing more than

the right to have what is due to you under the law. ... The only universal right is the procedural one of due process, a protection available... to all men.

"... The common law idea of liberty is antithetic to equality. In Magna Carta... liberty and property are virtually synonymous. ... Due process is a superb protection for what you already have.... ... The common law assumes that the rights granted to men are very disparate, but among them is one universal right - the right to have what belongs to you under the law.

"... This is the fundamental concept of English liberty; it is the only idea of liberty that appears in every century, the only one to survive unvanquished. ... Any challenges or modifications will come... out of medieval Christianity or, in the seventeenth century, from ideas of medieval Christianity that have been reworked into secular forms."

Cantor, you will notice, had to use the same words we have been busy with - the common law, property, liberty, due process. But what about the common good?

He describes how theology and philosophy contributed to the common law, as an example - "the doctrine propounded by St. Thomas Aquinas, the thirteenth century philosopher.... ... restated around 1600 by the brilliant Anglican theologian, Richard Hooker. ... To man's law is assigned a place within the grand structure of the universe. Due process is the reflection of natural law, which is itself a reflection of divine law. ... The only aim of government is to serve man and the common good."

There we have a statement linking due process and the common good. But does it suffice, put as it is by a theologian, not by a government manual? Worse, the statement is contaminated by the term "natural law", not a bad term, but open to so many interpretations and misinterpretations. Pulled from the blue into the general forum, it can't help but weaken Hooker's argument. It is a term I've tried to circumvent 'til now. Its character has been divisive in the field of legal philosophy. It is indefinite. In the view of many people, natural rights are the same as natural desires. "If Donna really wants Maxwell, she has a right to take him away from his wife." This must have been Jeremy Bentham's perception of what people mean by natural rights. An English contemporary of Thomas Jefferson, Bentham wrote in his **Theory of Legislation, "Natural law, natural rights**, are two kinds of fiction.... (Natural law means) general inclinations of men... from which must proceed the establishment of... law. ...What there is natural in men is... faculties. But to call these... faculties, natural rights, is... to put language in opposition to itself."

Bentham's statement is the correct rebuttal to the argument that desire makes right. In this he probably shows his displeasure with Blackstone's use of "natural liberty" as the basis of "civil liberty". But in this Blackstone really did not embrace the idea that desire makes right. "But every man," he says, "when he enters into society, gives up a part of his natural liberty, as the price of so valuable a purchase.... ... therefore... civil liberty... is no other than natural liberty so far restrained by human laws... as is necessary and expedient for the general advantage of the public." There is, I think, no real disagreement between Bentham and Blackstone. It's that their vocabulary is too wobbly. Of course Bentham is right in maintaining that rights don't exist outside of law, and while Blackstone evades the adjective "natural" in connection with rights, he uses the phrase "absolute rights" with exactly the same meaning. But even by absolute rights he does not mean that desire makes right; he means the freedom to act as one wishes, tempered only by one's innate sense of good and evil. This restraint, he maintains, is by the "law of nature".

Here, I believe - in natural law - lies the crux of the debate; not in natural rights. Is there anything to natural law? What is it in the first place? Is it an exudation from outer space? There is but one sense in which I will credit it, and in this sense I will put natural law at the very foundation of the common law. There is a natural psychological law that operates in humans living among humans. Let a man fail to observe common decency toward other men, and any treasure he possesses in the minds of other humans will disappear pearl by pearl. The loss mounts and becomes complex when several men form a power structure oppressing other men at will. Strange things happen to the minds of the oppressed. This is a natural function, as natural as the law of gravity.

In contrast, let such a power clique discover this natural law; let them develop a power structure in harmony with it; and this new legal environment will have an amazing psychological effect in the subjects of this experimental project. But the point to be made here is that, as this more intelligent power structure develops, certain kinds of right are seen to emerge in the evolving legal system. And these rights, since they arise from a rationale based on natural phenomena, can be called natural rights - rights based on human nature.

Calling them natural, however, is not essential. What they are, is rights. The essential part is to understand the relation of governmental law to natural law for there is a cast steel relationship between them, whether or not rulers heed it.

To imagine that the greatest of Greek and Roman minds did not understand the meaning of natural law is to be obtuse ourselves. A natural law is a relationship between phenomena that one observes again and again. If you release a cup from your hand, it falls. If it hits the floor, it breaks. If you rub a cat's fur the wrong way, it radiates. If you leave a stone in the sun, it gets hot. If A then B; not logic but phenomenal interrelationships. If between two phenomena I perceive a relationship that never fails, I call the relationship a natural law.

Cicero, when he spoke of natural law, did not mean a message in the stars perceived intuitively; he meant exactly what I have just written. If the ancients attributed natural law to God, it was simply their way of saying that the origin of natural forces is beyond human discernment. And no idea is truer.

Said Cicero, "There is this law that has not been made by men but is a part of their nature." According to him, when man uses accurate reasoning along the paths marked out by nature, he arrives at true law. Wrote Alexander Hamilton: "The sacred rights of mankind are not to be rummaged for among old parchments or musty records. They are written, as with a sunbeam, in the whole volume of human nature, by the hand of the divinity itself." A fairly constant observation, I would say, to have held over a span of 1700 years.

We know also that Cicero was aware of the thing that most accurately reflected government, the public thing, the res publica. Tacitus brought it even closer, the utilitas publica - the nation's loading space; the usefulness of the nation; the effectiveness of the nation! Rome having reached and passed beyond the pinnacle of stately success, how clearly these men could see the result of rulerly conduct. The res publica reflects the natural reactions of the people to the quality of rule. The wealth of the nation, people and rulers alike, is vested in the utilitas publica. (For these classical references I am indebted to Dr. Robert Lisle of James Madison University, Department of Foreign Languages, and his in-house paper "The Classical Content of Political Thought in Eighteenth-Century America".)

Take these relationships; go now to William the Conqueror and his successors, and look with an intelligent rulerly eye at a backward feudal civilization; and consider the intelligent clerics and scholastics who comprise an essential portion of your administration. You see the possibility that philosophers and theologians can give receptive movers something worth thinking about. Though the theory tying rule to common good is not expressed openly and in detail by the ruling class of England, we know the germ is there. Then let us ask if it grew. Did it take root? Was it put into effect? Did it become fact? Specifically, can we find a legal practitioner in England who, in logically expounding the English system of justice, drew a connection between rights or liberty and the common good? We are not talking about theory now. No natural laws or natural rights. Just "Law -> Common Good". A definite, functional statement.

We can learn much about the logical structure of ideas from dictionaries. We would in any event wish to refer to some of the older dictionaries. We will wish to grasp the meaning of words as the founding fathers used them; not that we wish to ape our progenitors. We simply do not wish to lose the wealth of ideas that might be there. We have good reason to refer to the legal dictionaries of the 1700's, and Samuel

Johnson's dictionary as well. They were available to the founding fathers. I have referred to Blount, Cowel, Cunningham, Jacob and Student's, as well as Dundas's **Feudal Law**, all published in England. They were all the founding fathers had.

There is little to gain in looking up the word "right". If and when it is treated in an eighteenth-century legal dictionary, the meaning is so restricted it could not have been a significant feature of the legal landscape. As for liberty, Dundas and Blount don't bother to define it. With Cowel it is a "Privilege held by Grant of Prescription whereby Man enjoy some Benefit or Favour beyond the ordinary Subject." This we recognize as the feudal meaning of liberty - a special privilege held by members of the nobility and royalty.

Jacob echoes Cowel but fortunately goes farther: "But in a more general Signification, Liberty is said to be a Power to do as one thinks fit; unless restrained by the Law of the Land. The Laws of England, in all Cases, favour **Liberty**, which is counted very precious, not only in Respect of the Profit which every one obtains by his **Liberty**; but also in **Respect of the Publick**." Do you remember Blackstone, publishing fifty years later? "... civil liberty... is not other than natural liberty so far restrained by human laws... as is necessary and expedient for the general advantage of the public." Notice in both quotations the word "public(k)". Jacob, not I, put emphasis on "Respect of the Publick". Their meaning in using the word is essential, and it is not the twentieth century meaning.

Unfortunately none of the legal dictionaries, even Jacob's, defined it. But like the founding fathers we can turn to Samuel Johnson. A portion of his quote from Davenant, treating public as a noun, begins to sharpen one's curiosity. "... those nations are most liable to be over-run and conquered, where the people are rich, and where, for want of good conduct, the **publick** is poor." Apparently the people and the public are not identities.

Treating public as an adjective, Johnson gives us as a meaning: "Regarding not private interest, but the good of the community." Then he quotes South: "All nations that grew great out of little or nothing, did so merely by the **publick** mindedness of particular persons." And he quotes Atterbury: "A good magistrate must be endued with a **publick** spirit, that is, with such an excellent temper, as sets him loose from all selfish views, and makes him endeavor towards promoting the common good."

So, putting Jacob and Johnson together we learn that liberty is precious not only to the individual whose liberty it is, but to everyone around her. Her liberty is precious to everyone in the community, commoner, nobleman, king, for her liberty enhances the common good. And here let us be careful for surely the liberty to maraud at large will never enhance the common good; only a certain kind of liberty will do it. In fact, if we are to achieve this kind of liberty, we must define liberty in "Respect of the Publick". We must arrive ultimately at one and only one formula. The liberty of each person is a precious commodity for everyone in the community, if it is defined with respect to the common good. And protected with an iron will and a mailed fist.

Finally we find a little icing on the cake. Both Cunningham and Student in defining "Commonweal" show that the justification of English law lies wholly in the common good. "Commonweal is understood in our law to be **bonum publicum** (public good), and is a thing much favoured; and therefore the law doth tolerate many things to be done for **common good**, which otherwise might not be done: and hence it is that monopolies are void in law, and that... covenants to restrain free trade, tillage or the like, are adjudged void."

Monopoly, resulting from free enterprise, represents freedom. But in view of the common good, the power to monopolize is not a liberty. The common good is the difference between freedom and liberty. There can be no doubt; the common good is at the very heart of the common law of England.

Now we must cross the Atlantic Ocean, and perhaps cross a legal gap as well. Is there a legal link between the common law of England and law in the United States? It is true that the code of every state in the United States expressly embraces, in one way or another, the common law of England, and it is true also of the federal code and even that of the District of Columbia. But the expressions are so wrapped in mufflers and mittens that one wonders how binding the linkage is. For example the Civil Code of California puts it this way: "The common law of England, so far as it is not repugnant to or inconsistent with the Constitution of the United States, or the Constitution or laws of this State, is the rule of decision in all the courts of this State." Such a statement, it seems to me, is an assertion that California law is wholly independent of the English methods and results. Does that mean that American law is independent of the common good?

And there are other difficulties. It is not enough that Cantor insists: "In England, liberty is... whatever the king-in-Parliament says it is," and the matter of reconciling this with Jacob's liberty, the kind promoting the common good. There is the matter of the American colonies defecting from the English king and rejecting monarchy in their own systems of government. Yet we learn from the writings of American patriots that they were proud of their heritage of liberty as Englishmen.

The bridge across this gap is furnished by Cunningham's legal dictionary, in his definition of prerogative: "... a word of large extent (including) all the rights and privileges which by law the king hath, as head and chief of the commonwealth, and as entrusted with the execution of the laws. The nature of our constitution is that of a limited monarchy, in which the legislative power is lodged in the king, Lords and Commons; but the king is intrusted with the executive part, and from whom all justice is said to flow; hence he is styled the head of the commonwealth, supreme governor, **parens patriae** Ec., but still he is to make the law of the land the will of his government; that being the measure of his power, as of the subjects' obedience: for as the law asserts, maintains, and provides for the safety of the king's royal crown and dignity, and all his just rights, revenues, powers, and prerogatives; so it likewise declares and asserts the rights and liberties of the subject....

"Hence it hath been established as a rule, that all prerogatives must be for the advantage and good of the people, otherwise they ought not to be allowed by the law."

So there is no missing link after all. Though "In England, liberty is... whatever the king-in-Parliament says it is," the king himself must be ruled by considerations of the common good. I think we can say that it was to this principle that our founding fathers were loyal when as British colonists they were loyal to the crown. And when they rebelled, they did not rebel against this concept of the crown but against the king's breach of the principle. What was the first fact that the Declaration of Independence submitted "to a candid world"? -"He (the King) has refused his Assent to Laws, the most wholesome and necessary for the public good."

But were the founders themselves true to the principle? If they pledged allegiance to the principle of the common good, then wouldn't we expect them to include it in our written Constitution? Yes we would, and so they did. They embedded it in the heart of the Constitution, the one and only indispensable portion of the Constitution; the most neglected canon of the instrument. The preamble.

"We the People of the United States, in order to form a more perfect Union, establish Justice, insure domestic Tranquillity, promote the general Welfare, and secure the Blessings of Liberty to ourselves and our Posterity, do ordain and establish this Constitution for the United States of America."

When you see the word "general" don't give it the popular misty more-or-less for the most part fairly prevalent better than average meaning that we modern non-mathematicians give it. To mathematicians, and to the intelligent people of the age of reason, general means universal. It means "without exception". And "general Welfare" in pragmatic terms means the common good. What promotes the common good promotes the general welfare.

The preamble is often brushed aside as a corsage "pinned on the nose of a workhorse". Nonsense! It is the very genius that controls the beast. Jurists are apt to recite the doctrine that the preamble grants no powers and establishes no right. How wrong they are. It draws every property line for every person in the country, including presidents, congressmen and judges. It governs every power and right conferred by every other portion of the Constitution. It places all government personnel under an awesome burden of services and servitudes. And talk about power! It empowers every citizen to invoke due process and jurisdiction to question in court the legality of any act of government. It goes the whole distance. It furnishes her grounds for challenging any provision of the Constitution itself - Article or Amendment. If the act or provision controverts the sense of the preamble, it is illegal!

Take for example the Constitutional provision reading, "The Congress shall have Power to lay and collect taxes... " Well may we ask the purpose for which it may collect taxes. And is there no limit upon this power? Go back to the days when the people of the states were reviewing this clause for ratification. Can we imagine any person of substance supporting it unless there were strict limits on this power? So he questions his legislator about it, and what will the legislator say?

"Only in the preamble, my dear Sir, do we find these limitations and, believe me, the preamble is controlling. It provides Congress with power to lay and collect taxes for the purposes of forming a more perfect union, establishing justice, insuring domestic tranquillity, promoting the general welfare, providing for the common defense, and doing whatever is necessary to secure the blessings of liberty to us and our children. And these are the only purposes for which Congress can lay and collect taxes.

"Now I will admit, my dear Sir, that a provision for the common defense will hardly put a lid on the taxing power of Congress. But Congress must also take under consideration the domestic tranquillity, the general welfare, and the preservation of liberty - these other provisions of the preamble. It is well known that an excess of taxes causes a general unrest. It is also true that an excess of taxes will diminish the level of the general welfare. And it is certain that bleeding the people will eventually result in a complete loss of liberty.

"The point is, Sir, that if Congress enacts a bill tending to make the Union less perfect, or weakening the administration of justice, or provoking a significant unrest, or weakening the common defense, or impairing the general welfare, or destroying the fabric of liberty, it creates an illegal statute; one properly challenged in a court in equity. The other powers of Congress as well -- borrowing money, regulating commerce, regulating the value of money, declaring war, calling out the militia, all; all are similarly governed by the statement of intention labelled "preamble"."

In effect, the preamble says, "There are certain purposes, and these are the only ones, justifying an establishment of a federal government. These purposes are: U,V,W,X.... These are our intentions in establishing this government. These are the standards to which the government will conform. And we entrust ourselves into the hands of the federal government on the premise that it will observe the standards. We put our project effectiveness in the hands of government with the understanding that government will safeguard and promote it." At least this is the sense of "We the People of the United States...."

Such a preamble might be the introductory remarks of a contract or a trust. Often in contracts and trusts particular provisions will prove to be uncertain. They may clash. Something important will be omitted. To meet such situations a contractor or trustor will brace his instrument with general statements of his intentions - what he wishes to accomplish. If interested parties later have difficulty interpreting particular provisions, they will refer to the statements of intention. They ask which interpretation of the uncertain provisions most match the intentions. The statements of intention will govern the express provisions, and this is the exact function of the preamble to the Constitution. It is a controlling statement. The balance of the Constitution derives from it, expressing mostly operational functions. Whatever is not in the preamble is really a proposal of a plan of government that will help achieve the intentions of "We the People".

There is another interpretation of the source of the preamble. "We the people" may actually be "We the rulers of the United States... ". When one thinks realistically of the make-up and complexion of the Convention, and whom the participants must have represented, and that the ratifiers would be the members of state conventions in each state, one understands that the sources of the Constitution were the people who understood ruling. The preamble then stated their intentions and that these would be the guidelines of government that they expected their administrators - legislators, executives, judges - to follow. Their own will, and their ability to control the machinery of government are another matter. As I said earlier, there are projects, and pursuits of projects, and results. But at least we can talk about projects - intentions.

As the preamble controls the powers of Congress, so it controls the powers of the President - his command of the armed forces, his power to grant pardons, make treaties, appoint ambassadors and Supreme Court justices, not to mention his powers of administering the government generally. A federal judge too, at any level, must relate his decision to the multiform objectives projected by the preamble. What must Justice see in America? She must see the Union and its perfection; the establishment of justice; domestic peace; the common defense; the common good; the consequences of liberty thus defined.

And the constitutionality of an Article or Section of the Constitution must be scrutinized and qualified in the light of the preamble. Does the freedom of the press in a particular instance threaten to undermine the national defense. If so, the freedom of the press must be denied in the instance.

The preamble brings a sobering thought to our attention: In the United States, the standard of justice is not wholly holonistic. Our governors are entrusted with objectives other than the common good. We have already found that a nuisance decision is basically a keeping-the-peace decision, a common good decision only as an ultimate effect. The Constitution, we see, in its domestic tranquillity clause, has provided for nuisance decisions.

But there will be occasions in which conflicts will occur among the various intentions expressed in the preamble. Congress and the President, in meeting their common defense duties, must sacrifice individual liberty and safety, hence the common good. The good of the nation and the common good are separate and distinct considerations. Nevertheless they are delicately balanced. Though defense is necessary for the survival of the nation, and perhaps for the survival of holonity, an unwise lurch into war can cripple the common good beyond repair.

The tragedy embedded in the Constitution is its provision for slavery in the southern states. The objective of forming a more perfect Union dictated a tolerance of slavery. There would have been no union of thirteen states had slavery been prohibited. But the initial toleration almost destroyed the Union, and it was the more perfect Union clause that enabled the President to order a federal attack upon the seceding states. This time the clause eradicated the blot of slavery from the American scene. It purified a system of liberty based upon the common good. But lives were sacrificed. Perhaps after all an effort to materialize holonity and to preserve it, even if individuals are sacrificed, is a promotion of the common good. The trick is to get the consent of those whom you would sacrifice, and you will be successful only with those who have a strong feeling for the common good, a sense that the government is tending it.

I will not attempt to prove the general welfare identical to the common good. In fact as I will propose in Chapter 55, there are good phenomenal reasons for distinguishing them. But there is a special bonus in learning that the general welfare does not mean the "average good" or "good of the nation" or "what the majority wants". These phrases do not express the intention of the founding fathers, and should not be permitted to express ours. In forging the Constitution and while it was being ratified, there was a continuous referral by movers and advisors to a three volume treatise written by John Adams. Called **Defence of the Constitutions of the United States** (referring to the several new state constitutions) the first volume appeared in 1787 just in time for the Constitutional Convention. The other two volumes appeared the next year during the debates over ratification.

At the time, Adams was our minister to the Court of St. James, separated physically from a labor most precious to him, the legal establishment of a new nation; the Constitutional Convention. Many proposals for structuring the new government were afloat. Some from Europe were widely publicized in America and gaining popularity. But to minds well-educated in the history of nations, they were dangerous.

Many shrewd men saw an advantage in a weak United States. Among these were some accustomed to controlling their small political worlds in townships and colonies. With England out of the way, they saw bigger worlds. Others were the movers and advisors of England, France and Spain, nations with plans for their own occupation of North America. Their strategists were fully in tune with any poorly conceived constitution of government for the United States.

Working feverishly to combat these influences, using English libraries, consulting with the best English legal minds, drawing from his ambassadorial contacts with Europe as a whole and from his own thorough acquaintance with the classics, Adams wrote a compendium of histories of European governments. His pounding theme was the domestic unrest, the bloodshed, the deterioration of national welfare and the eventual subjugation of countries who had the very political structures being proposed and popularized for the new government of the United States.

In his haste to publish, and in his desire to amass as much damning evidence as possible, Adams produced a work deficient in what we call "readability". He himself apologizes for his redundancy and the obvious lack of editing. Nonetheless, the **Defence** contains jewels of political insight, even flashes of keen humor and, most of all, it gives us the thinking of the men who guided the writing of the Constitution. For though the toils of research and composition were Adams's, today's scholars believe that the **Defence** represents not his novel contribution to the thinking of the founding fathers, but a commitment to express the thinking of the best minds among them, and to present the results in compelling form.

Several passages disclose the central position of the common good in the minds of the founding fathers. At one point he juggles the ideas of two contemporaries, Richard Price the English clergyman and political essayist, and A.R.J.Turgot a French nobleman. It was Turgot's published criticisms of the state constitutions that Adams used as an adversarial setting for the **Defence.** Frequently in the **Defence** Adams expresses admiration for Price and contempt for Turgot. But at one point (Vol I p122-123) he uses the writings of both to advantage.

Price had defined civil liberty as "the power of a... society to govern itself... by a majority in a collective body or by fair representation." He then said, "Legitimate government consist only in the dominion of equal laws made with common consent."

Adams pinpoints the defect in this formula. "I shall cheerfully agree with Mr. Turgot," he says, "that... even equal laws made by common consent may deprive the minority of their rights. A society by a majority may govern itself... so as to oppress the minority. Therefore we must add to Dr. Price's ideas of equal laws by common consent this other: - for the general interest or the public good."

By the time he reached Volume III, Adams was drawing into a tight braid the individual threads of government, law, republic, property, liberty, and common good. It is clear that when the English and Americans used the terms general interest, public good, general welfare, common good, commonwealth, they had in mind the same concept as that of the Romans Cicero and Tacitus when they used the terms res publicus or utilitas publica. Now in Volume III, relating the res publicus or res populi to a theory of government, Adams made a uniquely searching statement in political-legal theory, giving us a clear insight into the founding fathers' minds when, by means of the preamble, they put the onus of the general welfare upon the personnel of government.

"Res populi, and the original meaning of the word republic, would be no other than a government, in which the property of the people predominated and governed; and that it had more relation to property than liberty: it signified a government, in which the property of the public, or people, and of every one of them, was secured and protected by law. This idea indeed implies liberty; because property cannot be secure, unless the man be at liberty to acquire, use or part with it, at his discretion, and unless he have his personal liberty of life and limb, motion and rest, for that purpose: it implies, moreover, that the property and liberty of all men, not merely of a majority, should be safe; for the people, or public, comprehends more than a majority, it comprehends all and every individual; and the property of every citizen is a part of the public property, as each citizen is part of the public, people, or community. The property, therefore, of every man has a share in government, and is more powerful than any citizen, or party of citizens; it is governed only by the law."

In this statement of Adams we see the authoritative definition of the general welfare. Here are stated the required relationships between government, property and the common good. Property is to be defined within these principles. Defined thus, if we allow the property of just one person to be sacrificed, we erode the welfare of all - universally; without exception.

This defines the condition that the preamble places on every function of government. It defines the property, the legal liberty, the loading space of government. It is from this statement - the principle behind it - that due process emerges. It reveals, given the provisions of the preamble, that most of the constitutional amendments are the mere babbling of babes. Here finally, in this statement of Adams, if you care to look into it, is the difference between life under communism and life under the common law; the difference between communism and holonism.

There is much more in this statement than meets the casual eye, but we must proceed. We have an important engagement. As we have just learned, the basis for entrusting the United States government with immense powers is the premise that it will use them only in the interests of the common good, tempered with essential pursuits in the common defense and maintaining the peace. All these powers end, however, at the line where state powers begin, and the question now is this: given that the federal government has a legal duty to act in the interest of the common good, what will prevent the states from using their powers to enforce fascist or communist regimes? In this issue we stand at the crossroads of states' rights. We are amazed at the boldness of the thirteenth and fourteenth amendments. They tell the states that they may not have slave laws; they may not enact a law that deprives a person of her loading space without due process. For special cases they tell the states to observe the common good. But the founding fathers took this fork in the road long before the post-Civil War amendments. We don't see it because we insist on our watered down interpretation of their words.

In Article IV Section 4, the founding fathers provided that "The United States shall guarantee to every State in this Union a Republican Form of Government.... " In this we moderns think the founders promised the people in every state an elected state government with a separation of powers and a representative legislature. But no interpretation of this clause could be farther from the founders' intent.

You have seen in Adams's statement exactly what the founders considered to be a true republic. It is a state in which the people's liberty resides in their property, and their property is defined in the light of the common good. If they were using the language of this book, they would say that a republic is a holonity, a holonistically governed community. Note the importance of the word republican to them. In drafting the Constitution they had adopted the somewhat outdated practice of capitalizing their nouns. Rarely did they capitalize adjectives, but when they did the reason was self-evident. And if it was not self-evident, you can wager they did it to honor the principle that the adjective represented. They capitalized Republican.

The word that confuses us is the word "form". They were guaranteeing the republican form of government. And doesn't that mean a "form" like the one set out in the Constitution for the federal government - elected legislators and executives, and so forth? But you know, that sounds strange when you think about it: that they guaranteed a **form** of government. Wouldn't it have been better to have guaranteed for every state a **republic**? After all, are not there many dictatorships that parade under a republican **form** of government?

We must realize that when we speak of representative government, or elected officials, or separation of powers, we are in a different dimension of concepts than when we speak of republic as the founders used it. In spite of the way your dictionary or encyclopedia defines the word, you should know that the founders used republic to express a **principle** of government. On the other hand the phrases democracy, representative government, elected officials, monarchy, oligarchy, refer to the operational structure of government. A democracy might be a republic, if the majority were constantly common-good-minded. A monarchy or an oligarchy might be a republic if the rulers happened to have holonistic frames of mind.

It is clear that the founders did not intend to constitute a democracy for the United States. They intended to found a mixed government. The House of Representatives was intended to register the complaints and needs of the powerful mass of the people. The Senate was intended to represent the intelligent asset-managers of the country. And the President was intended to represent the highest ideal of the chief magistrate. As the head of the nation he was supposed to be the final arbiter, watchdog of the common good - an elected monarch, no less.

The mixed government (all this is explained forcefully in Adams's **Defence**) taps the best features of the elemental governmental structures - democracy, aristocracy and monarchy. History has shown that whenever democracy became the prevailing structure of government, the unreasonable demands of the majority drove the aristocracy to seek control and, whenever the aristocracy got control, their excesses incited the people to rebellion. A monarchy never lasted long unless, as in England, the monarch acted as a balance between the aristocrats and the masses. The most fruitful government was one in which the power of brains and the power of mass were balanced in a head who constantly kept his eye on the common good. A balance of powers, when it occurred in history, produced the most creative nation. A balance then was the structure of government best suited for the requirements of the preamble. It was the structure best suited to serve the republican principle. It was a structure of government, but not a form of government.

The key to the thrust of Article IV Section 4 is the founders' understanding of the word "Form". For them it did not mean shape, or structure, or mode. As in our modern unabridged dictionaries, Samuel

Johnson's treatment of "form" is extensive in range and depth. He begins with popular, simplistic meanings and gradually delves into the more technical and philosophic ones. Some of his quotations on form approach the esoteric, even eerie. Generally in relation to complex ideas, we may say that the form of a thing is the source of a thing's characteristics. Roughly it is like our use of the word form in the building industry. A form is the mold into which concrete is poured and takes its shape. Even more closely analogous, a person's genetic inheritance plus her environment is the form from which her bodily traits and her mentality develop.

As Johnson goes deeper and deeper, we find the idea of form becoming more definitely the molder or shaper or essence of things. When we reach definition 13, he states form to be "a formal cause; that which gives essence," and quotes Bacon: "They inferred, if the world were a living creature, it had a soul and spirit, by which they did not intend God, for they did admit of a deity besides, but only the soul or essential **form** of the universe." Thus today we might say that there are forces in the universe - electric, gravitational, magnetic - and their operation generates the structure of the universe as it appears to us; the forces are the **form** of the universe.

As we might find in our modern dictionaries, these ideas were proposed by the classic philosophers, with whom such men as Adams and Jefferson were thoroughly familiar. To Plato and Aristotle, form was the essential nature of a thing that determined its kind or species. To Kant, according to Webster, form was a mental factor that molded reality into meaningful experience. Kant had done much of his work before our founders sharpened their pens. Frankly I do not know that the American politicians had become familiar with Kant, but I think Kant had a genius for using words not just to suit his concepts but to reveal the wealth of ideas historically embodied in them.

Therefore when the founding fathers wrote "The United States shall guarantee to every State in this Union a Republican Form of Government," there is every reason to believe that by "a Republican Form of Government" they meant the essential spirit of ruling from which the highest common good would arise. This of course is the definition of holonism. This "form" refers to a particular climate of mind among rulers, and that is exactly what the United States is pledged to materialize in every state!

Even apart from our misconception that republic refers to a particular structure of government, the word republic is fated to have an unhappy life. John Adams's marvellously basic definition of republic was undoubtedly the concept held in the formative days by the most gifted leaders of the United States. Unfortunately it wasn't the true definition of republic. Rather did it define the highest ideal of republic. As Adams himself says, "But of all the words, in all languages, perhaps there has been none so much abused... as the words **republic, commonwealth,** and **popular state.**

"In the **Rerum Publicarum Collectio,** of which there are fifty and odd volumes... France, Spain, Portugal, and the empires... Babylonian, Persian, Greek... Roman... Ottoman, are all denominated republics. If, indeed, a republic signifies nothing but public affairs, it is equally applicable to all nations...." And of course this is still true today. I wonder if there is a nation on earth not calling itself a republic. And each is correct in doing so!

As I have said, the common good, the res publica, the national thing, the nation's project effectiveness is what exists. As Adams said, the common good in some nations might well be the general poverty. The common good is social reality whether it is a soaring eagle or a ball of lead. The trouble with republic we must admit starts with the very few governments who want to elevate the res populi in their nation to the highest possible level. And our founding fathers wanted just that. And that's what they wished republic to mean. That is why they provided that "The United States shall guarantee to every State in this Union a Republican Form of Government". The difficulty is that we have no word meaning "a state dedicated to promoting the general welfare". And if we say we'll redefine republic to mean exactly that, we are faced with the fact that we must live among nations who will continue to refer to themselves as republics though their movers and advisers have no intention of promoting the general welfare.

It was in recognition of this situation that I coined the word holonism, meaning one for all and all for one, a way of viewing the whole thing in perspective without losing sight of the individual. But holonism I'm afraid is a word that will always ring with an academic hollowness. It will never be part of a pledge of allegiance. Yet holonism is exactly what the founders meant by a "Republican Form of Government" and a holonity is exactly what they meant by a republic - a state dedicated to promoting the general welfare.

It appears then that, as with the word civil and some others, we must be of large enough mind to tolerate more than one meaning for republic. When we come to the Constitution we must suppose republic to mean a state dedicated to the highest common good - the High Commons, so to speak. When we pledge allegiance to the republic, it would be well to mentally assert "We pledge allegiance to the flag of the United States of America, and to the Republican Form for which it stands...."

For in the United States we do not pledge allegiance to a thing; we pledge allegiance to that spirit that generates the highest common good. Since a spirit, to be phenomenalized, must be associated with matter, human matter, we pledge allegiance to the rulers who possess that spirit. And if in a showdown, men and women are sacrificed to save holonistic rulers - if the common good is sacrificed for the common defense - it is still an action to promote the common good, for without holonistic rulers the High Commons cannot materialize. Even as lives are sacrificed for such a purpose, the common good rises again.

Never will there be found a purer or more complete constitution of government than we find in the preamble; the preamble alone. The preamble is our constitution. The spirit of the preamble, when materialized in rulers, is our constitutional form of government.

CHAPTER 22

INVOLUNTARY SERVITUDE AND THE CAREER
OF THE THIRTEENTH AMENDMENT

Amendment XIII (1865)

Section 1. Neither slavery nor involuntary servitude, except
as a punishment for crime whereof the party shall have been
duly convicted, shall exist within the United States, or any
place subject to their jurisdiction.

Section 2. Congress shall have power to enforce this article
by appropriate action.

Our judicial system's overall performance in freeing black people
from discrimination is regrettable. All in all, it provides damning
evidence that our jurists have lost sight of basic principles. In most
cases they have relied on the thirteenth amendment, and the most
frequently raised professional issue has been the interpretation of the
phrase "involuntary servitude". I have searched the origin of the
phrase. Some of my readings and findings are scattered throughout the
book, but the central thread of the search is presented in this chapter.
In the chapter after next, I begin the study of personal relations, the
true key to non-discrimination. It is appropriate that we here dispose of
statutory law as the bridge to freedom.

In previous chapters, we have tried to discover what Justice "sees"
in a case and what she weighs in her balance scale. I'm speaking of
Justice wedded to common law. She sees injury. And if the entitled
spaces of the opposing parties overlap, pinching their enjoyment of
these spaces, and the easy solution of nuisance does not apply, Justice
closely examines the attitudes of the opposing parties as they relate to
their conflicting pursuits, weighing them in the gravitational field of the
common good.

But under the influence of the civil rights phenomena, Justice's
vision has seemed to be blurred. When blacks were slaves, a judge first
had to see blacks as black as a prerequisite for rendering them invisible.
Now he is supposed to see only persons, not skin color, except that on
occasion as in school bussing he is asked to see blacks as blacks en
route to seeing them as non-blacks, and under the affirmative action
rules he is expected to see a black person as black.

We observed in the **Civil Rights Cases** how the United States managed to render the black plaintiffs completely invisible; the attorneys were permitted to transform the plaintiffs' pleading into a constitutional issue. That was in 1883. Exactly twenty years later, in **United States v. Morris,** the federal district judge successfully saw people as people though they happened to be black. The defendants were charged with attempting by various means, including intimidation, to prevent plaintiffs from leasing certain farming lands. The case was brought under the Civil Rights Act of 1866, an older one than the one tested in the **Civil Rights Cases.** Section 1982 of the United States Code, the condensed version of this act, reads: "All citizens of the United States shall have the same right, in every state and territory, as is enjoyed by white citizens thereof to inherit, purchase, lease, sell, hold and convey real and personal property." As in the **Civil Rights Cases,** the defendants in **U.S. v. Morris** claimed the act to be unconstitutional. In particular, they claimed it was not supported by the thirteenth amendment. Judge Trieber ruled against them.

In effect this was a reversal of the Supreme Court ruling in the **Civil Rights Cases,** and it was a reversal by a lower court, the act of a federal district judge in Arkansas. In the earlier case the Civil Rights Act of 1875 was at stake. Was it justified by the thirteenth and fourteenth amendments? The act provided that "all persons... shall be entitled to the... enjoyment of the accomodations... of inns, public conveyances on land or water, theatres, and other places of public amusement; subject only to... conditions... applicable alike to citizens of every race and color." The Supreme Court said this act was not supported by these amendments. Said Justice Bradley in regard to the thirteenth amendment, "The only question... is, whether the refusal to any persons of the accomodations of an inn, or a public conveyance, or a place of amusement... does inflict upon such persons any manner of servitude, or form of slavery, as those terms are understood in this country?" The Court's conclusion: "...we are forced to the conclusion that such an act of refusal has nothing to do with slavery or involuntary servitude...."

Judge Trieber contradicted that argument without advertising the fact. He quoted Supreme Court Justice Field's dissent in the famous **Slaughterhouse Cases** of 1873: "The abolition of slavery and involuntary servitude was intended to... give (everyone) the right to pursue the ordinary avocations of life without other restraints than such as affects all others.... A prohibition to him to pursue certain callings... and to reside in places where others are permitted to live, would place him... in a condition of servitude." The **Slaughterhouse Cases** did not involve race, so that seems to generalize Field's statement. In quoting Justice Fields, Judge Trieber was dipping into minority opinion, but that apparently didn't disturb him. "In my opinion," he said, "Congress has the power, under the provisions of the thirteenth amendment, to protect citizens of the United States in the enjoyment of those rights which are fundamental and belong to every citizen, if the deprivation of these privilieges is solely on account of his race or color, as a denial of such privileges is an element of servitude within the meaning of that amendment." And evidently his opinion was finalized as the law of the case; it was not appealed.

As you see, the divergence between the two court decisions rose from a difference of opinion on how liberally one may interpret the phrase "slavery and involuntary servitude." Trieber's interpretation marked a high point, a lone upward spike, for the thirteenth amendment as a general declaration of liberty, and for the next 65 years the words were as narrowly construed as possible. In 1916, in **Butler v. Perry**, the Supreme Court asserted that the term "involuntary servitude", as used in the thirteenth amendment, "was intended to cover those forms of compulsory labor akin to African slavery...." And in 1935, in **Crews v. Lundquist**, the Supreme Court of Illinois maintained that involuntary servitude means, "the condition of one who is compelled by force... and against his will to labor for another whether he is paid or not."

The death throes of the liberal interpretation of slavery and involuntary servitude were over by 1947 as evidenced by the report of the President's Committee on Civil Rights. Here was a group of intellectuals as influential and highly acclaimed as will ever be assembled for such a purpose in the United States. Note the narrow reach of the thirteenth amendment in their perception:

"... As recently as 1944, the Supreme Court struck down as a violation of the thirteenth amendment... an Alabama statute which enabled employers to force employees (on account of wage advances) to continue to work for them under threat of criminal punishment.

"... In 1945, the Department of Justice prosecuted a case in which a Negro woman and her ten year old son had been held in captivity by a Mississippi farmer. Forced to work on a farm by day, they were locked in a crude, windowless, chimneyless cabin by night."

"... Where large numbers of people are frightened, uneducated, and underprivileged, the dangers of involuntary servitude remain. If economic conditions deteriorate, a more general recurrence of peonage may be anticipated."

With this perception of the thirteenth amendment, how could it support any bill in civil rights. There is nothing here that reaches for equal opportunity. And the epoch of civil rights was about to break on the horizon. Many academic papers have been written on the words slavery and involuntary servitude as used in the thirteenth amendment. Much has been made of speeches made in Congress debating the passage of the civil rights acts, proposing a wide scope of enablement by the amendment. However in the end it is the words of the amendment that count, not the words of the debate.

All that we have are the words slavery and involuntary servitude.

Of the meaning of slavery there has been little debate; it is the meaning of involuntary servitude that has spurred controversy. Where there is technical uncertainty in the words of a legal document, they should be construed in the context of the entire document. In the case of the thirteenth amendment we would have to try to discover what the ordinary state legislator understood by the words involuntary servitude. After all, he was the one who had to vote for or against ratification. As you recall, I have in an earlier chapter equated involuntary servitude with injury. If this were applicable to the thirteenth amendment, we would have a statement that neither slavery or injury will exist in the United States. For educated draftsmen to draft such a statement would be for them to say that common law judges had been saying nothing for centuries.

The drafters' acquaintance with the phrase "involuntary servitude" undoubtedly started with their reading of the Northwest Ordinance of 1787, or perhaps its predecessor of 1784. To that constitution of government for the Northwest Territories, we can trace almost the exact language of the thirteenth amendment. The parent document was written in the hand of Thomas Jefferson. We are speaking of a plan proposed by a committee of the Continental Congress.

Before the proposal was presented on the floor, I find no trace of the phrase involuntary servitude. In the Journals of the Continental Congress we find motions to delete the provision prohibiting slavery and involuntary servitude, but the terminology itself was not debated. One would think that the members in their correspondence would make an allusion to the phrase, but I have not been able to find it.

None of the many English law dictionaries then available defined even the word servitude, much less involuntary servitude. The index of Blackstone's **Commentaries** (1765) doesn't contain it. Only in John Dundas's glossary to his **Feudal Law** have I found, "Servitudes, are Burdens Affecting Property and Rights." But this was Scot law, conforming more to the civil law than to the common law. It is possible that legal technicians shunned the word because then, as now, it seemed emotional rather than technical. After the Normans enslaved the English, the British jurists have never been legally happy with the word servitude. This didn't bother Samuel Johnson. His dictionary (1783) merely states:

"Servitude. s. [**servitus.** Latin.]
1. slavery; state of a slave; dependance. **South.**
2. servants collectively. **Milton.**"

and really this was all that Jefferson and the other members of the Continental Congress had.

We don't find the term involuntary servitude in earlier documents.

It is not in our oldest American documents, though the word "liberty" was freely used. Take for example the Maryland Charter of 1632, whereby the king granted to his Maryland colonists "... all Privileges, Franchises and Liberties... freely, quietly, and peaceably to have and possess... without Impediment, Molestation, Vexation...; any Statute, Ordinance, or Provision to the contrary thereof, notwithstanding." If in our loading spaces we must live by words alone, give me the Maryland Charter any day in preference to the thirteenth and fourteenth amendments.

Nor does the phrase appear in the Justice of the Peace manuals used in the colonies. Boyer, in his journal article **The Justice of the Peace in England and America from 1506 to 1776,** gives us an idea of the central position held by justices of the peace and their manuals. In England, "By the beginning of the seventeenth century, the justices of the peace had become the de facto rulers of the counties."

In America, "the colonists were confronted with a different environment.... The Virginia assembly usually assigned the justice of the peace the task of enforcing the laws dealing with hunting, hog-stealing, Indians, runaways, servants, slaves, and tobacco. The Virginia justice also spent much of his time supervising the morals of his fellow-citizens; adultery, barretry, buggery, bastardy, bigamy, marriage, and religion all came under the purview of his office." By the end of the seventeenth century, "their jurisdiction in criminal cases had been extended to all but capital cases, and in civil cases all monetary restrictions had been lifted."

And what law did the justices refer to? Almost all of them referred to "Michael Dalton's **The Countrey Justice,** which first appeared in 1618," written, published, and printed in England. In England, as well as in America, "For over a hundred years he was the most widely quoted authority, and many of his successors actually plagiarized from his work."

The environs of New York, Pennsylvania, New Jersey and Delaware were in the very early days governed by the Duke of York's Laws of 1664, which "read very much like a justice of the peace manual." The first truly American work was not published until 1736. This was **The Office and Authority of a Justice of Peace** by George Webb, a justice of the peace in Virginia. This was followed by manuals for South Carolina (Simpson, 1761) and North Carolina (Davis, 1774).

In the northern states, the office of the justice "did not differ substantially from those of his English equivalent." The southern justice, on the other hand, "was granted many new responsibilities and was given more independence of action during the eighteenth century. This was especially true in his dealings with the growing slave population. It is therefore not surprising that the three original justice of the peace manuals produced in colonial America were all written by southern justices."

I have referred to these works. They all legalize certain conditions that we might call involuntary servitude, but they do not use the word servitude. They speak of service. From Dalton's legal manual, we may infer much about the economic conditions of the day. "Every Justice of Peace... may cause all such... persons... to work by the day... for the saving of Corn and Hay, and may upon their refusal imprison them in the Stocks by the space of two days and one night.

"Any one Justice of Peace (upon complaint to him made) may compell any person meet... to be bound as an Apprentice...." The "persons" Dalton was referring to were the masses of people released from the manors, displaced by enclosure, and wandering about England with no means of making a living, and little incentive for doing so. J.H.Plumb, in **England in the Eighteenth Century**, gives us a graphic picture of the times. People swarmed into the cities. "All houses and cellars were desperately overcrowded - ten to a room were common in Manchester.... ... small pox, typhus, typhoid... made death a commonplace...." "they dig... large holes or pits in which they put many of the bodies... and (they) are not covered till filled...." "

Is it a wonder that these people would do anything to come to America? William O. Douglas in **An Almanac of Liberty** makes a diary entry for the Englishman John Harrower who, in 1774, became an articled school teacher to a Virginia family: "This day I being reduced to the last shilling was obliged to engage to go to Virginia for four years as a schoolteacher for Bedd, Board, washing and five pounds during the whole time." But remember, this wasn't involuntary. He was entering a contracted service.

Chumbley has a chapter "Labor" in his book **Colonial Justice in Virginia**. "Indentured servants comprised the earliest labor class in the Virginia Colony.... Ordinarily the contract of indenture between master and servant was drawn up before the servant left England.... ... servants ... were classed with neither slaves nor hirelings."

Though we have been taught in elementary school to be disgusted with the existence of indentured labor in the colonies, we might have looked at it quite differently if we had been one of those miserable creatures wandering homeless in England. For all we know, a boy might have felt as though he were entering heaven if he were lucky enough to be apprenticed under the indenture form that Dalton provides in his manual:

"This Indenture... witnesseth, that __(M)__ and __(N)__, overseers for the poor... by and with the consent of Sir __(P)__ and __(Q)__, Esquire, two of his Majesties Justices of Peace... have...

put, placed and bound (John Jones) being a poor fatherless and Mother-less child, as an Apprentice with (Richard Ward), Baker. And... with him... to dwell... until (he) shall come to... age of 24 years (if it be a Woman, then until her age of 21 years, or the time of her Marriage)....
... the said (John Jones) shall... his Master well and faithfully serve in all such lawful business as (he) shall be put unto, according to his power, wit and ability.... And the same (Richard Ward)... promiseth (to teach and inform) the said (John Jones) in the craft, mystery, and occupation the which he useth, after the best manner that he can or may.... And also during all the said term to find unto the said Apprentice, Meat, Drink, Linnen, Woolen, Hose, Shooes, and other things needfull or meet...."

Jeremy Bentham in **Theory of Legislation,** like Blackstone, has a chapter, "Master and Servant", and, like Blackstone, nothing on servitude. But he gives us the theory of apprenticeship. "Aside from the question of slavery, there is not much to be said as to the condition of **master,** and the correlative conditions... of **servants.** All these conditions are a matter of contract." Then he presents a few words from which we draw a clearer insight. Not only can the master take the apprentice to court for breach of performance, but the apprentice can complain in court if the master does not perform as the indenture provides. In particular, the master is in service to the apprentice in regard to thoroughly teaching him all the skills of the vocation.

There were hirelings who might be called free men. They might live apart from their employer's home. They could quit at any time if they wished. But in many cases their dwellings were cold huts, their pay barely kept them alive, and if they quit they might not find another job. On the other hand the servant slept in his master's house. His appearance, as he went about town on errands or attended customers in the shop, had a way of reflecting upon his master's prosperity and habits of mind. For masters with little pride, Virginia very early drew up laws protecting the welfare of servants.

To those fleeing from the old world, indentured service in the new must have seemed like emerging from a snake pit. And their sea passage would be paid by the new master! Sometimes such people - desperate - would put their lives in the hands of a ship's captain and sail without contract. Somehow or other the colonies would have to find a place for them. Then too there must have been the rascal who promised to pay for his passage as soon as he earned the money, intending to do nothing of the sort. But the captain had his orders. Immigration was big business for otherwise empty ships. Just as Indonesians and Cubans are the "boat people" of today and Pilgrims were the boat people of the seventeenth century, the indentured class were the boat people of the eighteenth. The colonies were England's dumping grounds for her unwanted. And actually the colonies suffered from this burden.

Thus we find under "Servants" in **The Practical Justice of the Peace and Parrish** by William Simpson of South Carolina: "Where any person...(is) imported into this province without being under indenture or contract, and (is) unable or unwilling to pay for (his) passage, it shall be lawful for the importer... of such person, before any of his Majesty's justices of the peace... to take an indenture... in consideration of said passage money, to serve the said importer or his assigns five years...." If such a person refused, he could be carried before any two justices of the peace, who would determine and certify in writing the appropriate conditions of the indenture; "which certificate is sufficient in law to bind every such person according to the tenour thereof, and transferable in as full... manner **as if an indenture had been voluntarily executed.**" Notice the words on which I have placed emphasis.

So after the American Revolution, in the Continental Congress, a committee was appointed to prepare a plan for the temporary government of the western territory. Committee members were Thomas Jefferson of Virginia, Jeremiah Chase of Maryland and David Howell of Rhode Island. Their plan called for a gradual formation of new states in the territory. From it eventually were formed the states of Ohio, Indiana, Illinois, Michigan, Wisconsin, and part of Minnesota. Among the principles presented in the committee's resolution on March 1, 1784 was:

"5. that after the year 1800 of the Christian era, there shall be neither slavery nor involuntary servitude in any of the said States, otherwise than in punishment of crimes, whereof the party shall have been duly convicted to have been personally guilty."

This you see is the exact sense of the thirteenth amendment. It became Article the Sixth of the Northwest Ordinance of 1787.

Thomas Jefferson had undoubtedly familiarized himself with every charter, state constitution and justice of the peace manual that had appeared in the new English-speaking world. From 1776 to 1786 he was busy drafting bills for the Virginia legislature. In this work his attention was engaged in every topic, including the care of the poor, the slave laws for the new state, and the laws governing masters and servants. In not one of these bills, reproduced in Princeton University's **The Papers of Thomas Jefferson**, can I find the word servitude. In fact in the index of this collection, the word does not appear except to index the word in the Northwest Ordinance.

In the Duke of York's Book of Laws, Jefferson undoubtedly found: "No Christian shall be kept in Bondslavery villenage or Captivity, Except such who shall be Judged thereunto by Authority, or such as willingly have sould, or shall sell themselves...." This forbade slavery and permitted contracted service. Noting these exceptions, we may infer that enforced service was prohibited. Such enforced service is after all slavery though perhaps limited in the services required.

Jefferson could refer to Virginia's own Bill of Rights, adopted June 12, 1776, having been composed by that staunch bill-of-rights man, George Mason. Look how Mason cleverly permitted slavery: "... all men... have certain inherent rights, of which, when they enter into a state of society, they cannot, by any compact, deprive their posterity; namely, the enjoyment of life and liberty...." When a black was imported into Virginia society, her status was not due to her compact but to her captivity. Thereafter she could not by compact deprive her posterity of their rights. She was legally incompetent to execute a compact. The enslavement of her child was logically pure. Since all of the slave's attributes were in the loading space of her owner, her fetus, her child, was in the loading space of her owner, and her child would never be **not** her child. Mason's provision for human rights might prevent white parents from selling their children into indentured service, but it did not conflict with Virginia's slave laws.

The constitutions of the thirteen original states, excepting Rhode Island, predated the Northwest Ordinance, but while some of them prohibited slavery, there was no mention of involuntary servitude. However, Vermont produced something novel. Not being a colony, and claimed piecemeal by the states of Massachusetts, New Hampshire and New York, Vermont was nevertheless a state in her own mind, and in 1777 her good people wrote and accepted for themselves a state constitution. In it was a passage asserting, "... that all men... have certain... inalienable rights, amongst which are the enjoying and defending life and liberty.... Therefore, no male person... ought to be holden by law, to serve any person, as a servant, slave or apprentice, after he arrives to the age of twenty-one years, nor female... after she arrives to the age of eighteen years, unless they are bound by their own consent, after they arrive to such age, or bound by law, for the payment of debts, damages, fines, costs, or the like."

There, full blown, is the logical intermediate to Jefferson's phrasing, and it would be like Jefferson to reduce it to the essentials. The question is does the Vermont expression give us an accurate interpretation of Jefferson's "involuntary servitude" or did he wish to generalize the prohibition to include all injury.

In the Princeton publication of his writings we find, written in his hand probably in 1789 (Vol.14 p.496), "To reduce a man to slavery, to buy him, to sell him, to retain him in servitude are real crimes, crimes worse than thefts." But these are not necessarily his sentiments. They represent his soon deserted project to translate a work from the French - **Reflections on the Slavery of Negroes** - by Schwartz, the self-styled "Condorcet".

In **The Writings of Thomas Jefferson** published in 1904 by the

Thomas Jefferson Memorial Association, in a section entitled "Miscel-
laneous Papers" (Vol.XVII p64 et seq.) you will find a passage in which
he uses the word servitude twice. He explains the indentured servant
situation in America much as I have described it - the horrors of life in
England, the burden of excessive immigration in the new states, and he
excuses the position of the United States under the circumstances; "so
mild was this form of servitude... " yet "The American Governments
are censured for permitting this species of servitude, which lays the
foundation of the happiness of these people."

Although Jefferson certainly understood the technical import of
the word servitude, it is clear that he used the word in its popular,
Johnsonian, sense in his writings. He was always careful to expose and
defend his thought processes. If he wished a prohibition of involuntary
servitude to mean an all-embracing declaration of liberty under the
common law, we would find him explicitly defining his new phrase at
some point in his correspondence. So in the Northwest Ordinance we
see the word servitude used in its everyday sense, ready for immediate
application, and the word involuntary is self-explanatory. Perhaps it
was suggested by the provision in Simpson's justice of the peace manual
by which a court could order an immigrant into service in payment of
passage, issuing a certificate of servitude as sufficient in law as if it had
been an indenture "voluntarily executed". Involuntary servitude, thus
understood, means nothing more nor less than limited modes of slavery.

After all, there was no need to interpret the clause in the
Northwest Ordinance as a general declaration of freedom. The committee had already provided for legal liberty. In the Ordinance of 1787 it
appears as Article the Second:

"The inhabitants of the said territory shall always be entitled to
the benefits of the writ of habeas corpus, and of the trial by jury; of a
proportionate representation of the people in the legislature, and of
judicial proceedings according to the course of the common law; all
persons shall be bailable unless for capital offenses, where the proof
shall be evident, or the presumption great; all fines shall be moderate,
and no cruel or unusual punishments shall be inflicted; no man shall be
deprived of his liberty or property but by the judgment of his peers, or
the law of the land; and should the public exigencies make it necessary
for the common preservation to take any person's property, or to
demand his particular services, full compensation shall be made for the
same; - and in the just preservation of rights and property it is
understood and declared, that no law ought ever to be made, or have
force in the said territory, that shall in any manner whatever interfere
with, or affect private contracts or engagements, bona fide and without
fraud previously formed."

This a splendid statement. Only one is more pure, more basic and
more comprehensive - at least as stated in an American constitution of

government and that is in the preamble to the Constitution, executed two months later. Actually, given Article the Second of the Northwest Ordinance - read it again carefully - the prohibitions against slavery and involuntary servitude were superfluous. Perhaps they were added as reminders to those who had forgotten that legally under the common law there is no way that slavery can exist. The preamble rather than providing the detailed clauses provided the form - the spirit - the intentions, from which such clauses necessarily derive.

Similarly, given the preamble, the thirteenth amendment is superfluous, but it served in its time as a trumpet call. Slavery before the Civil War had been permitted by the founding fathers in order to form a more perfect Union. Given the Civil War, the federal government had demonstrated other means for preserving the Union. Now the pursuit of a more perfect Union could converge with the pursuit of promoting the general welfare. "States, listen," said the thirteenth amendment. "Slave laws and involuntary indentures will now be dishonored by the United States government."

There is no need for the thirteenth amendment to mean more, given the context of the Constitution. Our liberty, meaning enjoyment of property plus relief from injury under due process, derives from the preamble and from Article IV Section 4. After the Civil War the United States was free to guarantee a holonistic form of government to every state. Such a pursuit was no longer in servitude to the pursuit of forming a more perfect Union.

So I must acknowledge two definitions for involuntary servitude. The first is my theoretically pure definition; involuntary servitude is identical to injury, and to that extent it is a superflous phrase. Psychologically it helps us recognize that where we see injury we see a person bowing to the will of an intruder, and in her very own legal free space. This is a sound, useful comprehension of injury.

The other definition of involuntary servitude is the one we should use in interpreting the thirteenth amendment; it is a limited mode of slavery; slavery with a limited set of services. For any other use, for class oppression relief, it is bad. It is terminologically adulterate, semantically unstable, legally vulnerable, theoretically unreliable.

So we proceed to 1968. It is time for **Jones v. Alfred H. Mayer Company**, and the Supreme Court justices have decided to force the Mayer Company to sell Jones the house he desired. They have done it on the ground of the thirteenth amendment! Sidestepping the issue of involuntary servitude, they have replaced "slavery and involuntary servitude" with a phrase used in the congressional debate over the bill proposing the Civil Rights Act of 1866. Justice Stewart, writing the majority opinion, declared that the thirteenth amendment empowered Congress to abolish the "badges and incidents of slavery". This is an emotional phrase whose heritage is not known to me, though I have seen a quotation of Samuel Adams using it in connection with the impressment of colonists into the British military service. Stewart declared further that Congress could determine what such badges and incidents might be. He said that Congress, in the Civil Rights Act of 1866, asserted that a refusal to sell a person a house because he was black was burdening him with the badges and incidents of slavery. This must be one of the more brazen and insupportable interpolations of meaning in the history of the common law, but Stewart goes even farther. This, he said, was what Judge Bradley said in the **Civil Rights Cases.** How Bradley must have groaned in his grave! He had said the opposite. What a lesson Bradley could have given Stewart in legal history, legal terminology, and legal propriety.

And what a lesson Stewart could have given Bradley in what Justice should see!

When it comes right down to it, we have three opinions - Bradley's in the **Civil Rights Cases,** Trieber's in **U.S. v. Morris,** and Stewart's in **Jones** - all devoting much space to the interpretation of the thirteenth amendment. We have Bradley disagreeing with the other two, and Bradley much the most correct in his arguments. But the application of the thirteenth amendment was not their basic disagreement. Their basic differences lay in what they thought Justice should see.

Bradley was true to a school of thought that says a court should limit its field of vision to the framework of the pleading. In the **Civil Rights Cases** the defense was correct; the thirteenth and fourteenth amendments did not support the Civil Rights Act of 1875 and "no other ground of authority for its passage being suggested, (the act) must necessarily be declared void...." Bradley's faithfulness to his school had trapped him into an absurdity. Worse, it blinded him to the fact that discrimination was at large, with the common good at stake.

The same irrelevant issue of constitutionality was brought to Trieber in the district court in **U.S. v. Morris** and to the Supreme Court in **Jones,** and both courts gave the pleadings their due lip service. But in the final analysis, the courts did not rely on the thirteenth amendment to relieve the plaintiffs. The gist of Trieber's last sentence was, "It is indisputable that the right to lease land is a fundamental right, inherent in every free citizen...." and it was on this ground that he supported the black plaintiff. It had no relation to the pleadings or to the thirteenth amendment, and it is an inaccurate statement, but at least he was taking his eyes off the small print.

In the **Jones** opinion, after an extended attempt to connect the civil rights act to the thirteenth amendment, Stewart apparently was still not satisfied with his own argument. He did the most reasonable thing he could do under the circumstances. He quoted John Marshall's maxim on constitutionality, delivered in **McCullough v. Maryland**: "Let the end be legitimate, let it be within the scope of the constitution, and all means which are appropriate, which are plainly adapted to that end, which are not prohibited, but consist with the letter and spirit of the constitutional, are constitutional." With this, in effect, Stewart threw the thirteenth amendment out the window.

Assuredly the courts in **U.S. v. Morris** and **Jones** were looking in the right direction; they were looking at the obvious facts, and climates of mind, and the common good. Nevertheless something solid is missing from their arguments. Unless we find something better, worthy complaints will be left unrelieved, and, equally as bad, relief will be granted in cases where it should not, oppressing the wrong party. We get a hint from the dissenting justices in **Jones.** The thrust of their dissent was this: if the government forces the Mayer Company to dispose of its property against its wishes, the company is impressed into involuntary servitude! The company would be bowing to Jone's will, and in its very own legal loading space. Here is involuntary servitude in both meanings of the phrase. It is contrary to the thirteenth amendment, the very amendment used to support Jones's case.

What is missing in Jones's case? An allegation of property. Is there a right to buy a house? No. There is no right to buy a house. No person, no matter how classed, has a right to buy anything. The two parties must have agreed contractually to a transaction before the government will compel a defaulting party to perform. No person can go up to the owner of a thing saying, "I wish to buy that thing," and enlist the government to force the sale. There is no right to buy. No. Due process says that Jones, if his case is to be heard, must (a) claim title to the space of a pursuit and (b) claim an infringement of his liberty within that space.

Certainly the Mayer Company's house is not a subject assigned to Jones as part of his estate. House A, being in the free space of the company, is not in the free space of Jones. Yet we are asked to find that the Mayer Company's title to dispose of its house should be put under a servitude to some project of Jones. If a court is to make the decision made in Jones, these are the essential conditions of the case. A court has no remedy unless it sees for Jones a title to a project, including subject, use and objective, and unless it sees in the Mayer company's action a result that interferes with, and should not interfere with, Jones's entitled project. If a court is to invoke jurisdiction and find cause for relief, it must see both title and injury. This we will find for **Jones.** I promise.

CHAPTER 23

EQUAL RIGHTS FOR WOMEN

Many books have been written on the topic of equal rights for women and, hoping this book will supply the tools for coping with the many aspects of the topic, I will not address it directly. However, you will wish to be acquainted with **Ritchie v. People**, decided March 14, 1895, and for the most part I will permit Judge Magruder of the Supreme Court of Illinois to speak for himself.

William E. Ritchie had been found guilty by a justice of the peace in Cook County. Having violated the eight-hour law, he was fined five dollars and costs. He appealed to the criminal court of Cook County and lost, whereupon the case was brought to the Supreme Court of the state by writ of error. The Attorney General of the State of Illinois represented the People, charging that on a certain day in February, 1894, Richie employed a certain adult female in a factory for more than eight hours. In 1893, there had been an act passed by the Illinois legislature declaring under section 5 that "no female shall be employed in any factory or work shop more than eight hours in any one day or 48 hours in any one week." Punishment for violation was provided in Section 8 as follows: "Any person, firm or corporation, who fails to comply... shall be fined not less than three dollars, nor more than one hundred dollars for each offense."

It was claimed by Ritchie's counsel that Section 5 was unconstitutional; it imposed unwarranted restrictions upon the right to contract. On the other hand the Attorney General claimed that the section is a sanitary provision, and justifiable as an exercise of the police power of the state.

I will extract some of the passages from Judge Magruder's opinion word for word. I will use the word appellant to mean Ritchie, and the term Attorney General to mean the counsel for the people. Instead of citing the texts and opinions referred to by the judge, I will insert the word "Citation" parenthetically in their place.

Magruder, J. "Does the provision in question restrict the right to contract? The words, "no female shall be employed," import action on the part of two persons.... First, that no manufacturer or proprietor of a factory shall employ any female therein for more than eight hours in one day; and, second, that no female shall consent to be so employed. ... In other words, they are prohibited, the one from contracting to employ, and the other from contracting to be employed, otherwise than as directed. (Citation.) ... It follows that section 5 does limit and restrict the right of the manufacturer and his employee to contract with each other with reference to the hours of labor.

"Is the restriction thus imposed an infringement upon the constitutional rights of the manufacturer and the employee? Section 2 of article 2 of the constitution of Illinois provides that "no person shall be deprived of life, liberty or property, without due process of law." A number of cases have arisen within recent years in which the courts have had occasion to consider this provision... and its meaning has been quite clearly defined. The privilege of contracting is both a liberty and property right. (Citation.) Liberty includes the right to acquire property, and that means and includes the right to make and enforce contracts. (Citation.) ... Labor is property, and the laborer has the same right to sell his labor, and to contract with reference thereto, as has any other property owner. In this country the legislature has no power to prevent persons who are competent from making their own contracts, nor can it interfere with the freedom of contract between the workman and the employer. ... (Citations.)

"... The legislature has no right to deprive one class of persons of privileges allowed to other persons under like conditions. ... If one man is deprived of the right to contract as he has hitherto done under the law, and as others are still allowed to do by the law, he is deprived of both liberty and property.... In line with these principles, it has been held that it is not competent, under the constitution, for the legislature to single out owners and employers of a particular class, and provide that they shall bear burdens not imposed on other owners of property or employers of labor, and prohibit them from making contracts which other owners or employers are permitted to make. (Citations.)

"Applying these principles to the consideration of section 5, wo are led irresistably to the conclusion that it is an unconstitutional and void enactment.

"... If the act be construed as applying to manufacturers of all kinds of products, there is no good reason why the prohibition should be directed against manufacturers and their employees, and not against merchants, or builders, or contractors, or carriers, or farmers, or persons engaged in other branches of industry, and their employees therein. Women employed by manufacturers are forbidden by section 5 to make contracts to labor longer than eight hours in a day, while women employed as saleswomen in stores, or as domestic servants, or as bookkeepers, or stenographers, or typewriters... are at liberty to contract for as many hours of labor in a day as they choose. The manner in which the section thus discriminates against one class of employers and employees, and in favor of all others, places it in opposition to the constitutional guaranties hereinbefore discussed, and so renders it invalid.

"But aside from its partial and discriminatory character, this enactment is a purely arbitrary restriction upon the rights of the citizen to control his or her own time and faculties. It substitutes the judgment of the legislature for the judgment of the employer and employee in a matter in which they are competent to agree with each other. It assumes to dictate to what extent the capacity to labor may be exercised by the employee, and takes away the right of private judgment as to the amount and duration of the labor to be put forth in a specified period. Where the legislature thus undertakes to impose an unreasonable and unnecessary burden upon any one citizen or class of citizens it transcends the authority entrusted to it by the constitution, even though it imposes the same burden upon all other citizens or classes of citizens. General laws may be as tyrannical as partial laws.

"... But it is claimed by the Attorney General that this section can be sustained as an exercise of the police power of the state. The police power of the state is that power which enables it to promote the health, comfort, safety, and welfare of society. It is very broad and farreaching, but is not without its limitations. Legislative acts passed in pursuance of it must not be in conflict with the constitution, and must have some relation to the ends sought to be accomplished. ... It cannot invade the rights of persons and property under the guise of a mere police regulation; and where such an act takes away the property of a citizen or interferes with his personal liberty, it is the province of the courts to determine whether it is really an appropriate measure for the promotion of the comfort, safety, and welfare of society. (Citation.) There is nothing in the title of the act of 1893 to indicate that it is a sanitary measure. ... there is nothing in the nature of the employment contemplated by the act which is in itself unhealthy or unlawful or injurious to the public morals or welfare. ... ...

"... ... It is sought to sustain the act as an exercise of the police power upon the alleged ground that it is designed to protect woman on account of her sex and physique. It will not be denied that woman is entitled to the same rights, under the constitution, to make contracts with reference to her labor, as are secured thereby to men. The first section of the fourteenth amendment to the constitution of the United States provides: "No state shall make or enforce any law which shall abridge the privileges or immunities of citizens of the United States, nor shall any state deprive any person of life, liberty, or property without due process of law, nor deny to any person within its jurisdiction the equal protection of the law." It has been held that a woman is both a "citizen" and a "person" within the meaning of this section. (Citation.) ... As a "citizen," woman has the right to acquire and possess property of every kind. As a "person," she has the right to claim the benefit of the constitutional provision that she shall not be deprived of life, liberty, or property without due process of law. Involved in these rights thus guarantied to her is the right to make and enforce contracts. The law accords to her, as to every other citizen, the right to gain a livelihood by intelligence, honesty, and industry in the arts, the sciences, the professions, or other vocations. Before the law, her right to a choice of vocations cannot be said to be denied or abridged on account of sex. (Citation.) The tendency of legislation in this state has been to recognize the rights of woman in the particulars here specified. The act of 1867... (chapter 48 of the Revised Statutes of Illinois)... by the use of the words "he or she," plainly declares that no woman shall be prevented by anything therein contained from working as many hours overtime or extra hours as she may agree.... An act approved March 22, 1872, entitled "An act to secure freedom in the selection of an occupation, etc. ", provides that "no person shall be precluded or debarred from any occupation, profession or employment (except military) on account of sex." (Citation.) The married woman's act of 1874 authorizes a married woman to sue and be sued without joining her husband, and provides that contracts may be made and liabilities incurred by her and enforced against her to the same extent and in the same manner as if she were unmarried; and that she may receive, use, and possess her own earnings, and sue for the same in her own name, free from the interference of her husband or his creditors. (Citation.)

... As a general rule, it is the province of the legislature to determine what regulations are necessary to protect the public health and secure the public safety and welfare. But, inasmuch as sex is no bar, under the constitution and the law, to the endowment of woman with the fundamental and inalienable rights of liberty and property, which include the right to make her own contracts, the mere fact of sex will not justify the legislature in putting forth the police power of the state for the purpose of limiting her exercise of those rights, unless the courts are able to see that there is some fair, just, and reasonable connection between such limitation and the public health, safety, or welfare proposed to be secured by it. (Citation.)

"The Attorney General refers to statements in the textbooks recognizing the propriety of regulations which forbid women to engage in certain kinds of work altogether. ... Attention is also called to the above-mentioned act of March 22, 1872, which makes an exception of military service, and provides that nothing in the act shall be construed as requiring any woman to work on streets or roads, or serve on juries. But, without stopping to comment upon measures of this character, it is sufficient to say that what is said in reference to them has no application to the act of 1893. That act is not based upon the theory that the manufacture of clothing, wearing apparel, and other articles is an improper occupation for women to be engaged in. ... On the contrary, it recognizes such places as proper for them to work in by permitting their labor therein during eight hours of each day. ... But the police power of each state can only be permitted to limit or abridge such a fundamental right as the right to make contracts when the exercise of such power is necessary to promote the health, comfort, welfare, or safety of society or the public; and it is questionable whether it can be exercised to prevent injury to the individual engaged in a particular calling. The court of appeals of New York, in passing upon the validity of an act "to improve the public health by prohibiting the manufacture of cigars and preparation of tobacco in any form in tenement houses"... has said: "To justify this law, it would not be sufficient that the use of tobacco may be injurious to some people, or that its manufacture may be injurious to those who are engaged in its preparation and manufacture; but it would have to be injurious to the public health." Tiedeman, in his work on Limitations of Police Power, says: "In so far as the employment of a certain class in a particular occupation may threaten or inflict damage upon the public or third persons, there can be no doubt as to the constitutionality of any statute which prohibits their prosecution of that trade. But it is questionable, except in the case of minors, whether the prohibition can rest upon the claim that the employment will prove hurtful to those employed. ... (Citation.)

"We are also referred to statements made in some of the textbooks to the effect that the legislature may limit the hours of labor of women in manufacturing establishments. (Citations.) These statements appear to be based entirely upon decision of the supreme court of Massachusetts in Com. v. Hamilton Manufacturing Co.... ... But the Massachusetts case is not in line with current authority, as it assumes that the police power is practically without limitation. ... The reasoning of the opinion in the Massachusetts case cited does not seem to us to be sound. ... We cannot more appropriately close the discussion of this branch of the case than by quoting, and adopting as our own, the following words of the New York court of appeals in **Re Jacab**, supra "When a health law is challenged in the courts as unconstitutional on the ground that it arbitrarily interferes with personal liberty and private property, without due process of law, the courts must be able to see that it has at least in fact some relation to the public health, that the public health is the end actually aimed at, and that it is appropriate and adapted to that end. This we have not been able to see in this law, and we must, therefore, pronounce it unconstitutional and void. In reaching this conclusion we have not been unmindful that the power which courts possess to condemn legislated acts which are in conflict with the supreme law should be exercised with great caution, and even with reluctance. But, as said by Chancellor Kent (1 Comm. 450): "It is only by the free exercise of this power that courts of justice are enabled to repel assaults and to protect every part of the government and every member of the community from undue and destructive innovations upon their charter rights.""""

CHAPTER 24

PERSONAL RELATIONS I:
INTRODUCTION

By personal relations, I mean your relations with your loved ones, with your neighbors, with your community. And to generalize it, I also mean your relations as a businessman with your buying public, and your relations as a performer with those on whom you wish to make a unique impression. Have you ever felt that someone is intruding on a very precious, carefully nurtured relationship? Is it possible that the common law has been able to create a space of property for you in this area of life? I go even farther.

I propose at the heart of the civil rights - class oppression phenomena, an interference with personal relations, and I propose that the common law possesses a classic mechanism of relief. It requires demonstrating, this mechanism of personal relations; the project space involved - the subject, the loading and the objectives, and we now begin a several chapter exploration of the field, the field of personal relations, the property granted to your efforts in establishing fruitful relations with your human kind. And first I wish to position civil rights in its proper niche in the legal universe.

A person's civil right is not her charter of freedom from class oppression. To the contrary, class oppression can be set in concrete by a code of civil rights. If you have a legal system providing for slavery and "unfair" justice, you have a system of civil rights providing for slavery and "unfair" justice. So the thirteenth and fourteenth amendments don't protect civil rights, they declare federal war on systems of civil rights that provide for slavery and "undue" process.

But what do we mean by slavery and "undue" process? Take a contractor fulfilling a contract and losing money every day, or the man drafted into the army. Are they not slaves? Doubtless many of us have felt victimized by an unfair person, an unfair justice. Slaves we are, oppressed by "undue" process, or so we reason. But argue we might forever on the topic and never be satisfied. Yet in America the matter has been determined for us; hopefully for all time. We turn to the preamble. By slavery and "undue" process we mean any use of a human being and any legal procedure that rings a bad note in the carillon of preamblar objectives - domestic tranquillity, common defense, general welfare, and - Lord help us - a more perfect Union.

In enacting the civil rights acts, our legislators attempted to spell out rules of private behavior. They confounded their legal creations by including in their design a self-destruct mechanism; they grounded their proposals on the thirteenth and fourteenth amendments. But rules of private behavior cannot be grounded on the thirteenth and fourteenth amendments. Those amendments do not apply to private behavior, they apply to whole systems of law. In outlawing slavery and undue process, they dictate legislative behavior, judicial behavior, and executive behavior, but not private behavior.

At rock bottom, the civil rights acts symbolize intellectual failure. They beat a retreat to the ancient citadel of implied duty. Creating not a single right, they concern themselves entirely with what people may not do. Apparently the theory is that if you can be fined for barring a person from XYZ, you have a duty to admit her to XYZ. Shades of tort and negligence! What has happened to basic common law procedure - defining free space; defining injury; and providing due process. At what point has the intellectual failure occurred? The civil rights leaders have not defined the legal free space in which the complainant is being oppressed. The complainant wishes to get into the grandstand to see the horse races, but the owner of the turf club doesn't want her there. So the civil rights act says she is entitled to go there. But she has no title to the turf club, and without title there cannot be injury, and if jurisdiction is seized over the defendant, we witness undue process.

The missing element in a court hearing of class oppression is an allegation of property; missing are the details of the loading space to which the oppressed individual claims title, the pursuit that the plaintiff asks the court to honor, honoring it above the defendant's traditionally honored property. Going to the horse races? Is that the pursuit that the court will honor above the ownership of expensive real estate? If so, why can't Willy Fitz-Hugh stay in Lydia Abercrombie's apple tree? Why can't Jimmy Jones float through Farmer Brown's forest? After all these are cases of class oppression. Willy and Jimmy are in the class of non-owners.

Having taken exception to the sanctimony with which we regard "civil rights", I now take exception even to the phrase class oppression. It is not a bad term; people are sometimes oppressed by way of classification. But it is not a good term either; it suggests that a class can be oppressed, and this is impossible. Like a species, a class is an abstraction existing only in the mind. Individuals exist, fish or human. But a class does not exist. What happens is this. If you place before a human mind a number of individuals with traits in common, it will classify them; often for predictive purposes, and often unreliably. But the point is that individuals exist; so individuals can be oppressed. A class does not exist except in the mind and can't be oppressed. If we do not make this distinction, we will not find the remedy for class oppression.

Now we must look at the word oppression, for it too can fool us. Oppression is always bad in the eyes of the oppressed. But if a talented criminal feels oppressed by due process, should society view such oppression as bad? Oppression, if we are not careful, can assume a guise of unqualified evil in the popular mind, setting the stage for a grab-fest in civil rights.

The social democrat might not view oppression in the light of the preamble. Society might be split on the question of loud music v. quiet conversation, but Justice is unequivocal in the matter; the loud music lover will be oppressed. Society might take sides in Morris v. Warfield, but a wedded loading space will be deemed property by the courts, at least for another year or two. And take Mrs. McNamara. Surely she feels oppressed. If something needs doing around the house, it is she who must do it, and I think a majority of Americans including judges will sympathize with her. But a court will refuse to hear the case. Never will it make a slave of Mr. McNamara for the sake of relieving Mrs. McNamara's feelings of oppression.

What I am saying is this; that though not all oppression is injury, it is natural that each of us wishes our oppressions to be deemed injury. It is here the issues of class oppression become confused. When the protester says, "I demand my civil rights," he makes an ambiguous statement. Does he mean he is being injured, or is he asking that his oppression be deemed injury? The distinction is crucial; the ambiguity can be fatal to his cause. Too often the history of a class oppression case is this. When a right is claimed in the name of a specific statute, the statute has been found to be unconstitutional. On the other hand when the complainant claims he should have the right, not having it, and the case goes directly to equity, or to the legislature, an attempt is made to ground the case in law and this simply will not work. If you claim you should have the right, you admit that your oppression is not injury, that the oppression is legal. And in such a case there is no appeal to law. The appeal must be to the principles that govern the law. In "civil rights" cases, the basics have been forgotten.

The class oppression movements swelled with the tide of "personal" rights, and they have been beached high and dry. How can we be of help? By going back to fundamentals and framing their complaint in a mode that due process understands.

First of all, a complainant must lay claim to a loading space - a pursuit - complete with subject, loadings and objective. She must claim either that this loading space is already in her property - that she is being injured - and there you have a case at law; or she must claim that she is seeking the title of property for this loading space - she is asking that the label of injury be attached to her oppression - and there you have a case in equity.

And what must be her grounds if she seeks a grant of property for her loading space? Well, if she seeks a right that she thinks she should have, her appeal is to the preamble. To be both general and specific, she must appeal to the common good. She will rarely have an appeal in behalf of a more perfect Union or the common defense. These causes are practically reserved for the use of the government.

To the poorly disciplined eye, **Jones v. Alfred H. Mayer Company** was a novel case. No lawyer in his right mind would undertake such a project, seeking a decree ordering the Mayer Company to sell its property to a person with whom the company did not wish to do business. As a class oppression case it was novel, and it provides a typical example of how a class oppression case turns out. Typically the court gave a wholly leaky excuse for its decision. Fortunately, as often happens, the decision was the correct one. So all we lack is a rational support for the decision.

Typically, the case as presented lacked all the elements of a claim in property. What was the loading space that Jones wanted? What was the subject to which he wished clear title? In no way could he claim the house as his entitled subject. What was his projected use of this unknown subject? And what was his objective? Surely, the objective of dwelling in a house to which he had no title could not be honored by a court. So all in all what was the loading space for which Jones was seeking the label of property? This was the missing element in his case. This is the first claim in every case in law or equity, and this is the first point to be raised in every class oppression case. A man, old or young, has no claim to a position, a desk, a salary as his propertied space in an employer's office, unless a contract exists to that effect. Without a contract, a claim to a job must be found in a different sphere than mere money and business.

Finally in **Jones** - typical again of class oppression suits, the government was asked not only to honor the pursuit of Jones, whatever it was; it was asked to dishonor the time-honored title of disposal; the right of a property owner to grant use, possession, disposal to whom he pleased. In **Jones** the title was held by the Mayer Company. In job opportunity cases, the title to the job is held not by the candidate but by the employer. In equal education complaints, the title of admission to a college is held not by the applicant but by the institution. In every class oppression case, the defendant will be exercising a use to which she is traditionally entitled. This is the element of a suit in equity that makes a decision in equity a breed apart.

But the point now to be made is this; the **Jones** case, typical of class oppression cases yet so novel as to be regarded as a new stride in civil liberty, was not in the least novel as a case in personal relations. Not that a case in personal relations is simple. To a judge, a case in personal relations will be one of his greatest challenges. What more fragile **chose** than personal relations? So delicate on occasion that no one in the court room recognizes the case as a case in personal relations. Yet to a government it will be the most consequential case of all. A history of oppressed pursuits in worthy personal relations can destroy the substructure of a nation like nothing else. Understanding the field of personal relations is the ultimate education in the law. How do you couple due process to such impalpable matter? How dare we try to engage such intangible pursuits with the red muscle of government? Yet the facts indicate that the common law can accomplish exactly this. It contains both the theory and the machinery; and these accomplishments I am willing to nominate as the greatest of human achievements.

The California Civil Code Section 43 reads: "Besides the personal rights mentioned or recognized in the Government Code, every person has, subject to the qualifications and restrictions provided by law, the right of protection from bodily restraint or harm, from personal insult, from defamation, and from injury to his personal relations."

As in many similar attempts to put the common law into coded form, Section 43 sounds expansive, seems protective, probably does as much harm as good and rather little of either. However we applaud it for reminding us that the government will protect us from injury to our personal relations. It implies that personal relations have indeed been granted the status of property. And now all we need do is to learn what this means.

Obviously personal relations isn't like personal effects, or even personal rights. Personal relations doesn't mean the relation of a person to himself personally. It means her relations to another person or to other people. We will learn that we can reliably expand the field of personal relations to include relations that aren't at first glance personal. Relations that we might call social or community are really personal. As with other abstractions like species and classes, you cannot have a relation to a community; only to the individuals of the community. A relationship to a community is a person-to-person relationship even if the individuals don't know each other personally. Similarly the public relations of a professional singer and the goodwill of a washing machine manufacturer are person-to-person relations. A liking or dislike for a rubber tire or a public figure cannot exist in a community. It can exist only in the minds of the individuals of the community. Public relations are personal relations, mass produced.

But the most significant generality in the field of personal relations is that the phrase personal relations has two connotations, both valid, and each requiring a distinct treatment. The difference is precisely the difference between "P.R." and goodwill. P.R. (public relations) is a project or a pursuit. In contrast, goodwill is the objective of the project, and hopefully the result of the pursuit.

Clearly a personal relation is an objective or a result. This is our primary understanding of it. It is the relationship that exists between two persons. It is the thing that is precious, or on occasion unsavory. If it is precious, it is the thing that government will protect. It comes close to being a thing that property can attach to. As in **ex parte Warfield,** a personal relationship can be a focus of conflict. It can become the subject matter of a suit in law or equity. As an existing relationship, it can be used, fitting our definition of a thing. Goodwill can be used by a corporation to sell its refrigerators. A personal relation with a neighbor can be used to borrow his egg-beater. The goodwill toward a person existing in the mind of another is recognized by the law as a **res**, a **chose**, a **thing**, and this is philosophically and scientifically sound.

But personal relations as an objective or as the result of a pursuit does not fully cover the territory comprising the field of personal relations. For just as public relations can be P.R. - a pursuit, and also it can be goodwill - the result, so personal relations can be a pursuit. Personal relations can be a pursuit to establish personal relations, and the personal relations, once established, can be used to borrow an egg beater. Personal relations can be a pursuit, and when the objective is attained, the personal relationship so attained can be the **subject** of a separate pursuit; it is something that can be used, and this is a most important distinction to make. We will find that the government will protect not only the personal relation that is a thing; it will protect the personal relation that is a pursuit. This is true whether the pursuit is on the P.R. level, the social level, or the intimate level.

We tend to think that government protects things, subjects of property, but not pursuits. One indeed may ask whether a pursuit is a thing, and under my definition it isn't. So one may ask how it can possibly serve as the subject of a suit, and this I will not try to answer. The fact is that government pays special attention to pursuits in personal relations, so they might as well be things.

No doubt a pursuit, properly defined and particularized is an elemental profile of property. A loading space has a subject, a use and an objective, as well as the projecter or pursuer. In protecting a loading space, we are protecting a pursuit. But the thing used in a pursuit - the subject - must be considered a fundamental element. It is of high consequence in the field of conflict, hence law. The subject is inescapably and eternally the focus of conflict. So we find one mode of personal relations to be a pursuit, one that the government will protect, and we must ask what are we using in this pursuit; what is the subject upon which we are exerting our will? And are we entitled to the use of this subject?

If protecting a pursuit seems like a strange task for government, especially when a subject is indistinct or when there might be a question of title, the following example will dispel some of the strangeness. We have learned that Farmer Brown can by court action, prevent Jimmy Jones from strolling harmlessly through his woods. And he can prevent Mr. Anthony from erecting a sign on the little weedpatch by the highway. But Brown will meet his match in Sheila Rienzi.

She is his neighbor and more than once he has warned her not to pick ox-eye daisies in his pasture by the road. So she is driving by one day, eying the daisies, and notices a small boy running full-tilt across the pasture. Peter who lives a farm away, is five years old and a blythe spirit. To Sheila's mind flashes a picture too dreadful to dwell on. In Peter's line of travel, behind a thin fringe of trees, a precipice plummets to a river below. In a glance, Sheila assesses the situation; the pasture gate is closed and chained and Brown, up by his house, is watching her like a hawk. Like lightning she crashes the gate and is bumping across the pasture, cows jumping in all directions, and Brown is already calling his lawyer.

But Sheila is not trespassing; she is in her legal free space. Here is a situation where the pursuit determines the property. No time here for niceties. For such an occasion the government gives everyone a title in this land, restricted of course to the objective at hand and the loadings required for the purpose. But we may be sure that Sheila's liberty in the pursuit will be confirmed by the government, and no court will ever caution her against doing it a second time. Brown's title ends at the borders of the project space and he is under a servitude not to interfere. (Paying for the gate is a problem left for the reader.)

We may be sure that at one time there was a case like this in equity, and property lines were re-surveyed to meet the specific circumstances. By such action a principle emerged and became law. In the instant, we might call it "precedence of bodily safety", but as important as such an understanding might be, it is not razor sharp for the more difficult cases. Fortunately for equity there is a principle that I will illustrate in a later chapter, and I dare say it can be applied in every case that properly appears in equity. It provides the infinitely keen cutting edge. "Observe the climates of mind in the opposing parties."

We can respect Sheila's climate of mind in trying to rescue Peter. And compare to it Mr. Brown's climate of mind. Is this a man who would prevent a rescue attempt for the sake of preserving the sanctity of title? If so, there is no way that a government can respect his obstructive pursuit. Let a government reflect that the government is the source of title in the first place, and it will resolve never to grant a title precluding a rescue attempt. How better can we learn that property is never in a thing. It is in a pursuit, and only in a thing as the thing relates to a pursuit; as the thing contributes to the material requirements of a loading space.

In this example we touch the perimeters of personal relations. A rescue attempt has features in common with honorable pursuits in personal relations. In Sheila we observe a sensitivity to the human bond. In contrast, looking at Farmer Brown and making him for the moment the meanest of clods, one sees in him no capacity for personal relations of any kind.

With this introduction, I will now take you with me on a tour of personal relations. Here is a branch of law where judges have made the most splendid decisions, and on the most impossible grounds. In this and the following chapters, we'll see if we can make personal relations a science.

To this point we have acquired a few helpful legal tools. We have a firm grip on property and the format of injury. How better now to get started than wading once more into **ex parte Warfield.** Marital relations certainly come under the heading of personal relations. So let us see where we get when we apply the format of injury to **ex parte Warfield.**

1. Is plaintiff Morris entitled to a certain loading space? (What; the marital relation?)
2. Is there a loading in the space that (a) reduces Morris's project effectiveness in the space and (b) is charged with the will of defendant Warfield?
3. Is Morris's title free of servitude and service that would justify Warfield's adverse loading?

If all the answers are positive, injury is present, and we proceed to determine trespass or nuisance. If the adverse loading (Warfield's friendship with Vivia) constitutes a use of Morris's loading space, then injury is through trespass. Otherwise injury is through nuisance.

Now let us become more specific. As long as Vivia does not run kicking and screaming out of the Morris home, we must assume she consents to her husband's personal presence, at least a bit of it, in her life. Never, mind you, is it the marriage certificate that entitles him to pursue a relationship with her. It's her free consent. It is her consent and not any other factor that makes her a part of his loading space. We can answer yes to question 1 of the injury format. The wedding relation - not as a thing but as a pursuit - wooing Vivia; not possessing her but somehow loading her to establish a wholesome marital relation; this is in Will Morris's entitled loading space; as long as she does not order him to desist.

What is the subject of the loading, the subject of the pursuit, the subject of title? It can be nothing other than Vivia, and obviously the answer to question 2 is yes. There is another loading impacting on subject Vivia, a loading reducing Will Morris's effectiveness in his wooing, and charged with the will of defendant Warfield. And yes to question 3 as well. Morris is under no servitude or service to Warfield giving Warfield a right-of-way in this loading space.

But can we say that injury exists? Is not Vivia also in the entitled loading space of Warfield? As long as she willingly receives his advances in companionship, he is entitled to load her with such advances. No law exists forbidding a man to write letters to a woman; stroll with her in the park; chat with her over a bacon and tomato sandwich, as long as she consents freely. So Warfield is not using something belonging exclusively to Morris, and we can't call his loading by the name trespass.

Almost we might call it nuisance. Interference is certainly present. Both men are operating in their entitled spaces, and while Morris isn't particularly successful in thwarting Warfield's pursuit, other than through court action, Warfield's operations are certainly throwing a monkey wrench into Morris's machinery. Vivia no longer responds to him as she once did. If it is injury through nuisance we can be more specific; it is distortion. Warfield's pursuit has altered Vivia's nature as a subject in Morris's entitled pursuit. If it is nuisance, the result is automatic; the judge need not choose sides on the basis of his tastes. One and only one party is interfering in the pursuit of the other and must be put under servitude; a keeping-the-peace action. Really how pure and simple this conclusion would be. If Vivia does not like it, she has complete freedom of action. She may tell Morris to desist and she may leave him. No longer then is she in his entitled loading space, and Warfield may do whatever he likes.

But what if Vivia is not this decisive. What if the pursuits are mutually interfering. There might be something in Morris's personal presence at supper that prevents Vivia from sharing her finest thoughts with Warfield at lunch. Given a mutual interference, is it something that both men will have to accept? Or is there a property at stake? Are there grounds for Justice clamping jurisdiction on one or the other of these men if he happens to be the defendant?

Judge Henderson's logic - personal rights, property rights go jump - is sieve-like. In baling the boat he jettisoned the rudder. It is not a matter of personal rights. In the absence of interference, both men are entitled to their pursuits. On an occasion of interference it is a question of which pursuit, if either, will government protect. If the particular question has never been raised before, it's a question of property, a matter for equity. But for this set of circumstances the principle has been settled for years. The marriage pursuit is the master pursuit and the alienating pursuit is in servitude. Actually, were it not for the rule of practice (injunctions must issue from equity), it is a case for law.

It leaves us with a problem; intellectual, valid and material. Why is the marital pursuit given the preference! This question must not be left wanting a conclusive rationale. We must establish it absolutely, on grounds suitable for resolving all the most disturbing questions that confront a court. In pursuing this objective, we will skirt the boundary between law and equity. Such a hedging tactic is thrust upon us by the nature of the data we must work with. The courts themselves are uncertain of the distinction. Yet it will be essential, as we proceed, to clarify the proper functions of the two courts, and I wish now to make a distinction between the two courts. For this it will be helpful, trivial as it may seem, to draw a parallel between our legal system and a sport such as football. The court at law may be compared to the referee on the field. He judges the infraction and establishes the remedy by referring to the established rules. But is there not a football commission that determines the rules? Of course; yes; and such a commission is analogous to a court in equity. There is a slight difference because legislatures also devise rules, and they may not always agree with equity. But equity is the authority of last resort.

Making up rules is not the commission's only job. Making up rules is in fact relatively easy. More difficult is the job, when the occasion demands, of justifying the rules that the commission itself has devised. And this, in the field of justice, is equity's most difficult job. This it always does in connection with a case before it. It never involves itself in a moot case, never in ivory tower isolation from a material conflict, and its logic is heard only in its opinion in the case report - the only logic recognized to have weight in the court system.

I bring this up because I must more and more immerse the reader in the task of justifying the law. Obviously it is more difficult than the parallel task in football, but equity's practice has made its own task doubly difficult, and I refer particularly to practice in the United States. In contrast to the rules of football, the particular rule of law that applies to a particular case is frequently impossible to find. Opinions are frequently diffuse, and decisions in quite similar cases do not always agree. Really in a case one might become so happy to have discovered a rule, one might forget to inquire whether it is a reasonable rule. Therefore I say we will be skirting the boundary between law and equity. Much of the time we will be trying to discover the rules. In this we will be acting as referees in the field. But more and more we must face the task of justification. In this we will be acting as academicians in equity.

CHAPTER 25

PERSONAL RELATIONS II:
NAME AND FAME

In this chapter, pursuing the line of research introduced in the preceding chapter, we will observe the work of equity in four cases. In these I will not attempt to derive the principles justifying the rules. It will be enough merely to try to find the rules. **Dandini** and **Hodecker** are cases touching upon marital relations and community relations. **Edison** and **Brown Chemical** involve commercial reputation. For the sake of generality, they all can be positioned in the field of personal relations. To be more direct, we can also place them in the subfield "name and fame". Reputation.

In 1948 in **Dandini v. Dandini,** by a 3 to 2 vote, a California District Court of Appeal affirmed that Mr. Dandini was properly bound under a rather strange court decree: he had been ordered not to marry. This was not the first instance of litigation between Lillian and A.O.Dandini. In 1942 she had sued him for separate maintenance. In 1946, February 13, the court finalized their separation, ordering A.O. to pay her $150 a month. In March he set up a temporary residence in Nevada for purposes of getting a divorce. He got it on June 3, and returned to California the next day. On June 28, back in Nevada, he married Juliana Sesenna.

On the day before the wedding, Lillian filed her bill for injunction in the Superior Court in San Francisco, stating "defendant is now about to enter a pretended marriage with one Juliana Sesenna...; that if said pretended marriage... is permitted to take place... defendant A.O.Dandini will cause said Juliana... to be represented as his wife and... said actions will cause plaintiff... chagrin, worry... and public ridicule; ... if said marriage ceremony is permitted to take place the defendant will expend money for the said Juliana... to the detriment of plaintiff's... support... from defendant...."

On July 3 a hearing was held, and Mr. Dandini did not appear. On

July 11 the court decreed that his Nevada divorce was void. Moreover the court placed A.O. permanently under an injunction not to remarry - anywhere. It should be noted that A.O. had not paid a cent toward Lillian's support in this whole period.

The lower court and the appeal court of California had a tightwire to walk. At stake was the recognition of divorce and remarriage in the sister state of Nevada. There was also the question of how far the injunctive power of a California court can reach. Did it have the power to declare a man's remarriage invalid everywhere, in every state, and successfully enforce it? This is a far reach. But it was true that Lillian had not submitted to the jurisdiction of the Nevada court. Given this, the Nevada court had no power to reach across the Nevada-California border and deprive her of her property. For also at stake was her property in A.O. Dandini. This was acquired through the court award of support. In effect this bound A.O. in service to her for this purpose.

It came down to this. If a California court recognized a Nevada decree reaching beyond Nevadan jurisdiction; if it recognized for Juliana Sesenna her right of support as Dandini's new wife; it would in effect be dishonoring the property of support it had awarded to Lillian. It would be depriving her of property by undue process. A.O. had admitted he could not support two women. And depriving Lillian of property without due process was contrary to the fourteenth amendment. It was contrary to the law of every state. Really, the injunction was not so much an order commanding Dandini not to remarry. Rather it was a notice that California would enforce Lillian's claim to support, not Juliana's. It would deny any such right for a new wife. And it would reach throughout the United States if necessary to enforce its position.

In arguing its affirming opinion, the District Court of Appeal walked its tightwire neatly and professionally. Its path to decision was well marked by case law. Yet for some reason the court, after meticulously tying up its package and delivering it, felt compelled to express itself in the field of personal rights. Apparently Lillian's attorney argued that his client, being the true wife, merited the status of wife in the community. This, according to the argument, was a personal right that the government protected, and it would support an injunction restraining Dandini from remarrying. Attorneys and judges feel uneasy about the power of injunction. For support of an injunction they tend to pack too many odds and ends into their arguments. In its opinion, the appeals court had already relied heavily on some pertinent New York cases; but now it said:

"Apparently, under New York law, it was necessary to find that a property right was in jeopardy before an injunction would issue.... It should be pointed out that in California there is no such rigid require-ment.... Whatever confusion may have existed... was set at rest in the well-reasoned and unanimous decision of the Supreme Court (of California) in **Orloff v. Los Angeles Turf Club....** In that case the court held that equity will protect by injunction not only property rights, but, in a proper case, personal rights. This furnishes an additional reason why the injunction properly issued in the present case, **particularly when the direct and important interest of the plaintiff in preserving her status as the wife of the defendant is considered.**"I have inserted emphasis on these last words, not because they represent my sentiments, but to ask you to keep them in mind.

Using **Orloff** as a citation was eventful. It furnished an instance in which a class oppression decision was used to support a decision in a marital dispute. My intent already stated is to proceed in roughly the inverse direction. I will show that class oppression properly finds relief as a claim in personal relations. At least we can see how important it is that consistency reigns within and across all fields of law. A decision in one field of law is often used as a precedent for a decision in another.

Unfortunately the **Orloff** opinion was not well-reasoned. Fortunately the decision was correct. But our question in **Dandini** is this: what is the rule? May we quote Justice Peters when he says that an injunction will issue to protect "the direct and important interest of (Lillian Dandini) in preserving her status as the wife of the defendant"? Judge Henderson protected Morris's pursuit of the marriage relationship in **ex parte Warfield.** Are we talking about the same thing? We need more facts.

Justice Peters did not cite **Hodecker v. Stricker** when he said, "Apparently, under New York law, it was necessary to find that a property right was in jeopardy before an injunction would issue...." **Hodecker v. Stricker**, New York, 1896, was the exact equivalent of what **Dandini** would have been if Lillian's support property was not involved; If only her personal right in the status of wife was at stake. In **Hodecker,** the Supreme Court of New York told Anna Hodecker that she did not have an exclusive right to her husband's name. Anna was the lawful wife of Frederick Hodecker. But Frederick was living with Emma Stricker, and Emma was calling herself Mrs. Frederick Hodecker. In her complaint, Anna stated that this appropriation of her name scandalized, defamed and humiliated her in the community, and greatly distressed her in mind. Like Lillian Dandini, though earlier by fifty years, she was claiming that her status as true wife should be protected. But the Supreme Court of New York denied the protection. Judge Bradley said that Mrs. Anna Hodecker had no property in Frederick's name, and refused to listen to the case.

Are we seeing callousness in 1896 and sensitivity in 1948? Are we witnessing a general shift in government sentiment, or are we witnessing legal inconsistency? Are we seeing an improper stress on property in 1896, or a misreading of the rules in 1948? Is **Hodecker,** New York, 1896, by not recognizing marital status, being inconsistent with **ex parte**

Warfield, Texas, 1899, in which marital status was honored, and is **Dandini**, California, 1948 (honoring marital status) consistent with **ex parte Warfield**?

We are talking about names here, and the importance that people place upon names in the community. We are also talking about reputation, and the close connection in people's minds between names and reputations. In marital status we are talking about the name and reputation of a person in the community, and in the marital relationship we are talking about personal relations. So there are these threads, you see, running between personal relations, names, and fame. Do you remember Jacob's (1727 A.D.) little addendum to the ordinary definition of the common law, "And it is the common birthright, that the Subject hath for the Safe-guard and Defence, not only of his Goods, Lands, and Revenues; but of his Wife and Children, Body, Fame, and Life also." Quite a statement. So in **Dandini** and **Hodecker** we are asking in a way what the government will safeguard in the way of fame; about the broader personal relationship of a person with the individuals of a community.

If class oppression decisions must be consistent with personal relations decisions, business relations decisions also must join this sorority of reason. And since disputes over names, reputations and public relations in the field of business have long kept the courts busy, we can turn for information to cases in that corner of the legal universe. What there do the courts protect in the way of names and fame?

Helpfully the transition from marital status to business relations is not strained. We understand Mrs. Frederick Hodecker's embarrassment when she discovers an unmarried Mrs. Frederick Hodecker living with Mr. Hodecker. Equally we understand the annoyance of the people at Brown's Iron Bitters when they discovered in 1881 that Brown's Iron Tonic, manufactured by another company, was appearing on the same shelves in drug stores. It appeared only two years after they introduced their Bitters. In both cases men with the name Brown were associated with the products, but Bitters Brown stayed with his company, and Tonic Brown withdrew from partnership with Meyer two years after putting the product on stream. So we have the Brown Chemical Company suing to have the exclusive use of "Brown's Iron..." and we see **Brown Chemical Company v. Meyer** finding its way up to the Supreme Court of the United States, and a final decision in 1891.

The word Iron is generic, said the Supreme Court, and cannot be monopolized. Furthermore, said the court, there is no way we can prevent a person from putting her own name on the product she manufactures. That left a sole issue, could the name Brown be transferred to a successor whose name was not Brown. "What's in a name" is the name of the game, and the court had a very good answer. Evidently, said the court, Brown's Iron Tonic gained a good reputation during the two years when E.L.Brown was with the company. In commercial language, it acquired goodwill and therefore became a property distinguishable from the attachment to Mr. E.L.Brown's name. As such it could be transferred exactly as any property may be.

We have in **Brown Chemical** a true case for equity. The court recognized for the Brown Chemical Company a title in the name Brown's Iron, and a title in it also for Meyer. The question was, should the court honor one title over the other; give one mastery and enjoin the other to servitude; and the answer was no. Confusion over the names might occur in the public mind, and annoyance between the competitors. But both titles were there; both manufacturers had cultivated the commons honorably; there was no evidence that the tonic people were trying to imitate the bitters label. So there were no grounds on which the government could favor one over the other.

This seems a sound decision, well-reasoned, and is a rule beginning to appear? Is it possible that a name in itself is not greatly important. The important factor - what Justice sees - is the person's relation to the general public, and how she uses the name. It is the connection between name and fame that a court considers worth protecting, if it is worth protecting. This is the element of property, if property there is. Two Mrs. Frederick Hodeckers, one married to Fred, one not. Is there anything here worth protecting?

Before making a judgment in **Hodecker v. Stricker** it will be worthwhile to study **Edison v. Edison Polyform Mfg. Co.** The distinction and confusion between personal rights and property rights began, as much as anywhere, in the realm of names and pictures. The juristic problem, as one might divine, was to discover when a party's name or picture was associated with a loading space that a government should protect. Juristic intuition whispered that a name or pictoral image should represent something of value before being included in a person's exclusive legal free space. In attaching value to property, the term "valuable property" at the turn of the century was becoming identified with "valuable asset", and jurists were succumbing to this popular confusion.

Nevertheless a hesitance remained. As Vice-Chancellor Stevens put it in 1907, "It may, at times, have become a matter of doubt whether what was called "property" was really such, and whether the injury... was not so "shadowy" as to be incapable of judicial cognizance; but still the criterion was always injury to property rights. It is to be noted, however, that the insignificance of the right from a pecuniary standpoint does not always bar relief." He expressed this in the Court of Chancery of New Jersey, in the case of **Edison v. Edison Polyform Mfg. Co.** As with others of his brethren, the Vice-Chancellor was feeling his way along a precipitous ledge, knowing instinctively there were loading spaces yet to be declared free and protected; realizing also, still intuitively, that if he didn't keep a firm grip on property - whatever property might be - he would tumble off into legal chaos.

Thomas Alva Edison was suing to have his name and picture removed from the label of a proprietary liniment. Years earlier he had concocted a liniment for relieving a facial pain with which he was afflicted. In 1879 he had mentioned it to a visitor in his factory who subsequently bought Edison's rights in it, and later the rights passed through several hands. So did the name of the company organized to make and sell it - the Edison Polyform Mfg. Co.

The liquid was being marketed in a bottle bearing on its label a likeness of Mr. Edison and the following words: "Edison's Polyform. I certify that this preparation is compounded according to the formula devised and used by myself. Thos. A. Edison." A leading circumstance must have been the fact that the medecine no longer contained the most potent ingredient of Edison's formula - morphine. The Vice-Chancellor's opinion does not go into details but I imagine that Edison's Polyform - so-called - was no longer effective.

Vice-Chancellor Stevens probably wished to make of this case a pure, classic issue. Is a person's name her own property, a person's likeness her own property? It was not claimed by the defense that Edison had assigned title to his name and likeness to go with the medecine; Edison claimed that he did not; and Stevens would not allow it to become a factor in the case. He wanted a landmark case in names and picture images, and his review was extensive. He cited cases, mostly English, in which prominent names had been used in connection with retail goods, and the bearers of the names had complained. In some cases an injunction issued against the use, in other cases not, and the Vice-Chancellor seems not to have discovered a rule in his reading. Nor did the situation seem covered by the fair trade laws; Edison was not marketing a competing product.

Conceivably the use of his name would subject Edison to financial risk. He might be sued if the medecine happened to harm a user; and injunctions had occasionally been issued on such ground. But Stevens deemed this too "shadowy" a ground. Proceeding in his review it seemed that the general situation with respect to photographic images was not clear. Citing the Supreme Court in **Brown Chemical Co. v. Meyer** - a man's name is his own property - Stevens wondered why "the peculiar cast of one's features is not also one's property". But he would not draw this conclusion.

Libel by publication did not seem to be involved. The label seemed to cast no aspersion on Edison's reputation. The Vice-Chancellor plunged into reputations and came out dry. Briefly he pondered the right of privacy. Warren and Brandeis in 1890 had published their article in the Harvard Law Review. But Edison seemed too public a figure, his name and portrait too widely recognized to be protected by a right to privacy.

But Stevens issued the injunction, ordering the company not to use the name and picture of Edison in connection with its product. He even ordered the company not to include the word Edison in its company name.

So in **Dandini, Hodecker, Brown,** and **Edison** we are engaged in the game of names. We have the data. What are the rules? We inquire if the judges' opinions help us learn the rules, and here the egg hits the fan.

In **Edison** we have a judge who wished to keep the issue pure, and what do we find? We like his decision, but his grounds were as impure as they could possibly be. It is a matter of fraud, he said. Now Stevens had to make several somersaults to bring fraud into it. If it was fraud, it was fraud against the public, not Edison, and Edison had no right to be in court. If it was fraud, fraud should be handled in a court of law, not equity, and Stevens lacked jurisdiction. If it was fraud, the result should have been prison, or a fine, or damages, not injunction. Worst of all, by calling it fraud he hung up a flag of defeat. Even in fraud there must be injury. So in what way was Edison injured? This was the issue. This was the pure case. What was the loading space that was infringed? And he somersaulted his way out of the tent by calling it fraud.

Stevens said something with which I must agree. At the very moment when he turned his court of equity into a court of law, he maintained his hold on the power of injunction. For this act he claimed precedent. Just a month earlier, in the New Jersey Court of Errors and Appeals, Judge Dill, also illogically, had based a good decision on fraud (I will review **Vanderbilt v. Mitchell** in another context). Dill nevertheless kept the power of injunction in his grip. Both of these New Jersey judges saw fit to paraphrase a New York opinion: "From time immemorial it has been the rule not to grant equitable relief where (the plaintiff) had an adequate remedy at law; but modern ideas... are changing and expanding... it is... coming to be understood that a system of law which will not prevent the doing of a wrong (injunction), but only affords redress after the wrong is committed, is not a complete system...."

The fact is that Stevens knew what he wanted to do and didn't know why. But not to blame. In these matters we are approaching the most critical intersection of politics and human life; the most intangible and abstruse.

In learning the rules of name and fame, we get greater assistance from Judge Bradley's opinion in **Hodecker v. Stricker.** In explaining why he refused to prevent Frederick's girl friend from calling herself Mrs.

Frederick Hodecker, he was a model of precision. "The action is not founded upon any charge of libel or slander.... It rests solely upon the charge that the defendant, residing with the husband of the plaintiff, has wrongfully appropriated... the surname of Hodecker; in other words, that she has taken the apparent relation of wife.... And the plaintiff charges that... this may tend to deny to her, in the community, the enjoyment of the reputation such as she would otherwise have in that relation and name. ... There is no allegation to the effect that any proprietary right or interest of the plaintiff is... impaired by the alleged usurpation..; and therefore the legal principles... of trademarks... have no... application... in the present action. It is said by (plaintiff's) counsel that equity will not suffer a wrong without a remedy. This maxim has its limitation in another known as "damnum absque injuria" (there is no cause of legal action unless there is injury) and further, that... duties merely moral are not the subject of equitable relief. ... The charge... is not that the defendant seeks to impersonate the plaintiff... but that the defendant misrepresents herself by falsely assuming the relation of wife and surname of the plaintiff's husband." (In New Jersey, the judges might have used this reasoning to introduce fraud as grounds!) Judge Bradley then explained that the married Mrs. Hodecker no longer lived with her husband; she did not attribute this circumstance to the defendant; nor did she charge the defendant with alienation of affections. He continued:

"It is therefore difficult to see... that the defendant has invaded any legal personal right of the plaintiff. ... The possibility that others may be misled by... the defendant does not concern the plaintiff, unless by that means some of her property rights (would be endangered); and until then she has no legal cause of complaint...."

Up to this point, Judge Bradley gave water-tight reasons for his decision. His reasons fit the case. His decision was correct. But then he enunciated a statement that can only be characterized as conglomerate.; partly true; partly destructive of the truth; an utterance not harmful to the case at hand, but jeopardizing countless to follow; typifying the failure to define what is property and what is not property in the field of personal relations. Said he, "The question of the identity of the plaintiff as the wife of Hodecker... is merely a social one, and cannot prejudice her legal rights... in the event she survives him. Until then the matters alleged in the complaint present moral questions, for consideration only in the tribunal of conscience."

Bradley's last sentence would have been improved by omission. It reflects an endless and fruitless debate, ineffective except that it fosters his truly destructive phrase: "The question is merely a social one." It is possible he knew what he wanted to say and that he was absolutely correct. If so, he phrased it poorly. What he really wanted to say was, "The question in this particular case is the type of social question that doesn't happen to involve property." Obviously the law does involve itself deeply in questions that are merely social. Why else would Bradley have bothered to mention that "the action is not founded upon any charge of libel or slander." What here is he talking about but reputation; and what is reputation but a social matter - the relation one has with other members of the community. Personal relations.

The truth is that Vice-Chancellor Stevens in **Edison** and Judge Bradley in **Hodecker** had an opportunity to strike to the heart of this important field of conflict. Stevens needed only to ask himself, "What is it in **Edison** that I really want to protect." **Hodecker** presents a different question, to which I devote the next chapter. Stevens was privileged to ask himself what he really desired to protect. He was a judge in equity and, except for the preamble, above the law.

The path to true rules in this field is best gained through **Edison**. The phenomenon is this. One observes a judge wishing so badly to protect something that he turned legal handsprings to accomplish it. And it is obvious that the decision was correct. But why was it correct? To commence the search for the answer, I will ask the following question for him: "What is it in **Edison** that I must protect?" Although we cannot answer it for him, we can answer it for ourselves. We can ask where, as a result of the Polyform company's activity, the harm would fall, and the answer is clear; Edison's reputation would be harmed.

It is safe to say that Edison enjoyed a reputation for integrity that few men enjoy. Most of us must be satisfied if a small circle of friends and colleagues respond favorably to us. But Edison's reputation was nationwide; worldwide probably. He made sure that people got their money's worth when they did business with him. Such reputations are not easy to establish. When they rest upon mass-produced merchandise, it means that the individual's intent has functioned in every person working for him. A bumbler or a malefactor in a factory can destroy the lifework of an employer.

Note that a reputation is both a thing and an objective. As a thing it can be used. As an objective it is pursued. In his day the name Edison could be used to sell a product. On a label the name Edison rang a little bell in people's minds and said, "Buy me." But such a reputation must also be a continuously pursued objective, even by Edison. Though enjoying a tremendous goodwill, he continued to do whatever was necessary to ensure that his products would come up to people's expectations.

So over here in this corner is the real Edison working hard to produce a good reputation, and over there is a false Edison selling a useless liquid under the name and certification of Thomas A. Edison. Are these mutually conflicting pursuits? No. We are seeing a unilateral interference. The work of the real Edison promotes the success of the false Edison, but the work of the false Edison erodes the reputation of the real Edison. The name Edison, you see, is not merely a name. It is a tennis ball with just the right bounce. The Edison Polyform Mfg.Co. is playing with it and at the same time filling it with lead shot. The nature of the interference looks very much like injury; nuisance, with a distorting impact, and so it is. But we will miss a tremendous opportunity if we do not carry the analysis deeper. A name is a different kind of thing than we're accustomed to. Let's see what the format of injury reveals about names in the **Edison** situation. Remember our objective: we are trying to find the rule for attaching the label of property to a name.

1. In this matter is Edison entitled to a certain loading space? What? Loading space? A name is hardly a loading space. But remember that property is granted to a person only in connection with a defined loading space. Well, it is often said that one uses a name. Edison, it might be said, may use his own name on his own manufactures. But again, what do we mean by use? We mean that we do something to a thing, expecting to get a reaction out of it. But names? What do we do to a name? And what reaction do we get out of it? Nothing. Obviously. So how can a name be a thing? Something here is out of focus.

Let us become very particular. What do we mean by using a name? A new manufacturer, in the process of marketing a product, attaches a name to it. In the early stages of marketing, she does not expect a positive buyer response to the name. However if she wishes to really establish the name, she looks forward to creating a positive response to the product and eventually, by association, to the name. The physical letters on a label are not really the important feature in a name. The important thing is the reputation - the association of the name with a product **and** the association of the product with the manufacturer. And this association is not on a label, or in a history book. It is in the minds of individuals.

So, in Edison's situation, what is the project in which he is using his name? What is his loading space, and what is he loading? We must conclude that he is intent on loading human minds - millions of them. His plan is to display machines and appliances in the world of people, hoping his product will be accepted as exchange-worthy goods. To each item he attaches a label stamped Edison, hoping that people will associate item with name and be pleased with both; hoping as competitors come into the field that buyers will favorably remember the item-manufacturer association; hoping also that, as new products emerge from the Edison factories, the Edison tag will promote their acceptance; not because of the name, but because of the manufacturer represented by the name. It is a use of human minds. An intelligent, shrewd, calculating project. Not malevolent. It is a mental induction project in which one uses human minds as subjects. You make an impression on a subject, hoping that the subject will open her purse. Edison's pursuit was highly successful. Millions of minds inclined toward him favorably. To their detriment? Hardly.

In this project was a thing called a name. Sometimes it was represented by paint and, if you looked at, it looked like this: E-D-I-S-O-N. As a thing-in-itself the paint thing was practically useless. You could scratch it with your fingernail and the result was paint under your fingernail. But human minds are strange things. They put things in classes, and two of their biggest classes are "good" and "bad". In the commercial world, the classes are expressed as good buys and bad buys. In general, relative to Edison, everything connected with the name was a good buy. This was something existing only in human minds, but it was a real thing. The reputation of Edison was a special conformation of atoms in each individual mind of a million persons. Now we can return to our analysis under the format of injury.

1. In **Edison** is there a loading space in contention? Yes, and the subjects are millions of human minds. What is the use of these minds? It is putting before them a combined thing stamped with painted scribbles looking like E-D-I-S-O-N. What is the project? The formation of a special atomic configuration in as many minds as possible so that, when a thing stamped E-D-I-S-O-N is placed before them, they will have a favorable "buy" response. Is it an entitled loading space? Evidently. We must say yes. The government allows myriads of projects roughly similar every day, without challenge. With certain restrictions, of course.

2. Is there a loading in this loading space that is (a) adverse to Edison's wishes and (b) charged with the will of the Polyform company? Yes. No issue here. The Polyform company is placing bottles of liquid stamped E-D-I-S-O-N before the buying public. There is a high probability that this activity will decrease Edison's project effectiveness in his entitled loading space, and the bottles on the shelves, so labelled, are the result of the company's will.

3. Is Edison under a servitude or service that takes from him the right to complain of the company's operations? No. He has not assigned the Edison logo to the Polyform people. Even if he had contracted to certify the original product (and he had not) his agreement would apply only to the specific medecine he had sold to the company, not to anything and everything they might produce and market.

4. So is injury present? Is there trespass? Is there nuisance? Or are both parties entitled to this loading space and, if so, is there good reason for the government to favor one pursuit over the other; to draw a property line? And now we must be extremely careful.

If Edison has a right to load people's minds with things painted with funny looking scrawls, why can't the Polyform company load them the same way? Isn't everyone entitled to load the buying person's mind with labelled things, and hasn't the Polyform company bought the paint and paid for it? Now, in this particular case, we might say that we have a case of nuisance, and this would be true. The pursuit of Polyform is interfering with Edison's pursuit to build and maintain a good reputation, and Edison's pursuit in no way frustrates Polyform's pursuit. But what if it so happens that the Polyform liquid is an excellent pain reliever for facial neuralgia. Morphine it no longer contains, but it does the job. Though Edison has not agreed to the use of his name, signature and likeness, their appearance on this exciting product cannot help but enhance his reputation. It may be difficult to show injury through nuisance, but injury exists nevertheless. His loading space has been invaded by trespass.

People's minds, don't you see, are a free space for all commercial operations (with limitations). They are a commons. But Edison, you see, has made his own little clearing in this commons. Diligently throwing good products labeled with his name into this commons, he has cleared and cultivated his own loading space, a space not commons, a creation distinct from commons, this special configuration of atoms in people's minds. It is clear, given goodwill and reputation and nine hundred years of common law, that the government gives title to the creator of this kind of clearing. Consequently if someone else uses this loading space, he or she is using a creation without the creator's permission, and this exactly fits the format of injury through trespass. Whatever loading occurs in this space is entirely under Edison's direction. And Vice-Chancellor Stevens confirmed it, even if he didn't express it quite this way.

Note the similarities and distinctions between **Edison** and **ex parte Warfield.** Both involve the use of human minds. Edison was entitled in a pursuit to cultivate people's minds for honorable commercial purposes. Morris was entitled to cultivate Vivia's mind in a pursuit in marital relations, but only as long as she didn't object. Edison successfully cultivated a favorable relationship - a configuration of atoms in people's brains - between himself, his products, and the people as buyers. This - the favorable configuration of atoms - the Polyform company chose to use to its advantage, without Edison's permission. This the Vice-Chancellor intuitively felt to be trespass, and he evicted the company from the premises.

In **ex parte Warfield,** the favorable relationship established by Morris in Vivia's mind was in a shambles. Morris had hoped to use this particular configuration of atoms for the benefits normally expected from a marriage relationship. Warfield had not trespassed. He had not used this relationship. He had cultivated his own configuration of atoms in her mind, and he was entitled to this pursuit. The difficulty was that the swirling of his relationship in Vivia's mind began to break the atomic bonds of the Morris relationship in the same mind. So the Morris relationship as a subject to be used was no longer reliable. What Morris desired was a chance to rebuild it and, with Vivia's permission, he had every right to make the attempt. But with Warfield constantly injecting his personality into he situation there was no way that Morris could succeed. So would the court help him? Yes, said the court. In a situation like this, the pursuit in marital relations will be given the right of way. This is the rule.

It can be seen that the ground isn't quite solid under the **Warfield** decision, but at least we are building a solid structure on which to base a critique of the rule.

It will be to our advantage to place both **Edison** and **ex parte Warfield** in the class of personal relations. More generally we might call them mental induction cases, the use of human minds, with two general subdivisions; (1) the pursuit to create a personal relationship - a configuration of atoms in a human mind - and (2) the pursuit using the personal relationship as a subject. Both pursuits, where the intentions are honorable, are entitled under the common law; entitled not against the owner of the subject mind, but against the uses and intrusions of all others. In both, the rules of property and injury apply just as they do in any other field of loading spaces. It will be in this general format that we will be able to give a rational structure to class oppression cases. Personal relations is the most important and abstruse field of conflict in which government has intervened.

CHAPTER 26

PERSONAL RELATIONS III: MATERIALITY.
FUNCTION ANALYSIS I

In the previous chapter I left **Hodecker v. Stricker** on the shelf. Using **Edison v. Edison Polyform** as a starting point and drawing upon **ex parte Warfield** and **Brown Chemical Co.**, I began to sketch the substructure of personal relations. This topical matter involves an activity I have termed mental induction. The government seems interested in it. It will protect it. At least it protected it for the defendant in **Brown** and for the plaintiffs in **Edison** and **Warfield**. In **Hodecker** the government did not seem protective in the least. In fact, if one tried to find a consistent rule covering both **Hodecker** and **Dandini**, one would seek in vain. Faced with the same essential facts, the government produced two contradictory opinions. If we are to choose between the two opinions; approving one and disapproving the other, we will need a firmer chopping block, a sharper knife.

Evidently in the field of personal relations, there are two kinds of mental induction projects. There is a pursuit creating a personal relation, and a subsequent pursuit using the personal relation that has been created. The first, in the business world, is handled by the people in public relations. Here the pursuer tries to attract the taxitant; to nurture in her a favorable bent of mind. In the business world, the favorable bent of mind is called goodwill. In the intimate world it is simply called a personal relation. Once it has been established - this favorable bent of mind - the pursuer tries to use it. In the business world it is used for selling goods and services. In the intimate world it is used to satisfy the various social needs of an individual. (Note that in instances this whole activity might not be premeditated; it might be purely instinctive.) In the initial pursuit then we see the personal relationship as the objective of the pursuit. In the follow-up pursuit, the personal relationship is the subject of the pursuit, the thing used.

In both instances, the mind of the taxitant (the taster, the reactor, the responder) is being used. In the initial phase, the originant uses the taxitant's mind to create the personal relation. And where else does the personal relation exist but in the taxitant's mind. So when the good will has been established, and we see subsequent pursuits initiated - a successful sale, a pleasant social companionship, a happy marriage - we see the taxitant's mind - a particular spot in it -   being used in the second kind of personal relation pursuit.

Since the government will protect the honorable pursuit to create a favorable bent of mind, and also the originant's claim on the taxitant's mind, once established (not against the taxitant of course, but against all others) we see in the field of personal relations a set of elements analogous to the elements of real estate. The pursuit to cultivate a personal relationship is like chopping a clearing in the forest. In this pursuit a taxitant's mind, if it does not rebuff the originant, is given the status of a commons. Anyone and everyone may open a clearing here. But, once a particular site is cleared - once the personal relationship is established - it is no longer part of the commons. The government grants exclusive title to the originant. It is an element of the originant's property. It becomes subject to injury. If injury is through trespass, the government will evict the trespasser (witness **Edison**). It, the personal relation, becomes subject to nuisance (refer to **ex parte Warfield**). It becomes subject to harm and damage (thus libel and slander). The personal relation - a thing-of-the-mind as far as the taxitant is concerned - has become a thing-in-itself as far as the pursuer is concerned. It can not be used phenomenally by the taxitant. It can be used phenomenally by the originant. And apparently the government has not been blind to these facts.

In **Hodecker** (the case in which both wife and "other woman" wished to be known as Mrs. Frederick Hodecker), we are looking at a case in personal relations, but we can not equate the situation with **ex parte Warfield**. Anna Hodecker's suit does not represent a pursuit in marital relations. She, Frederick's legal wife, was not interested to cultivate a site in her husband's mind. The old clearing had gone to weeds, and she was not interested in reclaiming it. Her pursuit was social. "Merely" social. And, as I wrote earlier, the government will protect a merely social pursuit.

Anna had clearings in the minds of her social acquaintances. She wished to use these clearings as sources of pleasant social occasions. She wished to cultivate and develop the clearings, and perhaps she wished to make still other acquaintances, nurturing in them a favorable bent of mind. These are healthy desires and pursuits, and the government will protect them.

But another woman, Emma Stricker, was living with Anna's husband, calling herself Mrs. Frederick Hodecker, and this, said Anna, was humiliating. It was destroying the social relations she had established, and it would prejudice other minds, as yet uncultivated, against her. "Unfortunately," said Judge Bradley, "you're not talking about property. There's nothing here I can protect. I can't even hear the case. I cannot attach jurisdiction to the defendant."

In this particular he was in error. For many years personal relations as pursuits had been protected, and personal relations as things had been protected. Honorable pursuits in the exploitation of human minds had been deemed by government to be loading spaces worth protecting. They had been given the status of property. Yet Bradley's intuition was true. Only his reasoning was in error. So what was the truth of the situation? What was his intuition really saying to him? It was saying,

"There is no potential here for harming Anna's social relations. There is no reason to believe that the social relations of the plaintiff can be harmed by the defendant calling herself Mrs. Frederick Hodecker." In denying the hearing, Bradley's instinct was saying that Anna's complaint was immaterial; that it could not possibly be material. A dangerous pronouncement prior to a trial, though probably true in this case. The point is that materiality is essential to a case, whether in law or equity, and the reader must learn exactly what I mean. Unfortunately what I mean does not square with the several definitions of materiality in current legal practice. Unfortunately the definitions in practice are at odds with each other.

Personal relations, as you see, are carrying us into people's minds. We are attempting to establish property lines for pursuits that use people's minds. Tell me where we may find a more boggy field to fence. What is real in a person's mind; and what is unreal? What in this sphere are things-in-themselves, and what are merely figments of the imagination? Indeed, what are the concepts not things at all, that is, what are the non-things?

Take an example. Patriotism. To the patriot, his patriotism is a non-thing. In no way can he use it. He cannot even daydream about it. He perhaps might fantasy about patriotic deeds, and the laurels he will receive. But the patriotism itself is not at his disposal as a subject. But a ruler can use it. The ruler can provide the situation and the right words, and evoke from this patriot the fighting response that the ruler wants. Somewhere in this man's mind there exists a configuration of atoms called patriotism, something responding to situations and words, mobilizing warlike behavior. But you object. "The patriot can use his patriotism," you say. "He can use it to get a promotion." No. this isn't true. He uses his superior's concept of his patriotism, and his superior's own ambition or patriotism, to get the promotion. So in a person's mind we can find certain concepts that are both things and non-things. And we will in later chapters discover something even stranger.

So there you have a taste of this field we are trying to divide into neat little packages called property. What in this field is purely conjectural, and what is truly phenomenal? What are the facts and what are the fancies? In other words we are justified in asking, when we are dealing with human minds, what is material and what is immaterial. This we cannot leave to the philosophers. This we must resolve for ourselves. For law and equity deal only with the material.

I find now I have painted myself into a corner. I have contrived two definitions of the idea of "use" and they are not compatible. Until I have driven this word into a tighter coral, I'll never encircle the idea of materiality. I have implied for instance that we cannot use a name. How can you get a response out of a name? A name can't be a thing; a thing-in-itself. But in an earlier chapter I was more liberal. The color and shape of a vase are things, I said. They can be used by an artist. A song sung at dusk by a shepherd, and echoed through the hills by others, is a thing; even if never noted on paper. It can be used to entertain, oneself or others. And "liberty, fraternity, equality" is a thing, I said. It can be used to inflame a mob.

Anything that can be used, I said, is a thing. More elaborately, I said, "Any concept that can be associated with a pursuit, as a functional element of the pursuit; such a concept is a thing." Why then is a name not a thing; a thing-in-itself; a name like Brown or Edison; or even Mrs. Frederick Hodecker. You see I have climbed to the end of a limb, and now I must back off. I'll do it quickly. A name is a thing. All that now needs discovering are the mechanics of such things. The interactions existing among things. For concepts are things only if we can discover interactions among them.

There is a common thread of consistency running through all my examples on this topic, inadvertent on my part, and perhaps significant. All the examples involve mental induction processes. When we say an artist "uses" a color and a shape, we mean he exerts himself upon a brush, some globs of paint, and a canvas. By means of colored patches on a canvas, he hopes to evoke a response from a human mind; either his own or another's. As for the singing of a song, whether performed for the singer's own benefit or for others, what is this but an exercise in vocal vibrations? In engaging in it, the singer undoubtedly has an objective, and the exercise will have a result, mental perhaps, but real. Then we have the mob-stirring phrase, vocalized by a demagogue; of itself a set of atmospheric vibrations. In each mind of the mob, there is a configuration of atoms energizable by these particular vibrations. At least the orator hopes so. Leave the words unarticulated. The mob will loiter and eventually disperse. But utter them, and the mob will turn and stream in a single direction, as though one body with one will.

There is evidence here that we are observing reactions among concepts, and they can be set in motion by a person. Hence we are talking about things-in-themselves and the fact that they can be used. I got myself into difficulty by being particular but not particular enough. I earlier discussed using a piece of land, having a crop of potatoes as the objective. The land is the subject of the pursuit. You do something to a piece of land; a sack of seed potatoes dwindles; and later, as if by phenomenal magic, you see many sacks of potatoes in the barn. But there are other subjects in the pursuit. I haven't talked enough about the tractor and plow; using them to break up the soil and turn it over.

When the plowing is finished, the tractor and plow are back in the machine shed, a little worse for wear, but have they been used in the same sense that the land has been used? If so, what action did I exert upon them, and what response did I receive from them? The land gives one a response. It has been a subject. But the tools?

Undoubtedly the tools are things-in-themselves. But a different sort of thing than the land. They are a sort of catalyst facilitating the exertion of my will upon the land. Hopeless, pursuing a crop of potatoes with but a tractor and plow; no land. The land's response forms a return to the farmer. The response of the tractor and plow is different. We act upon them and their response is upon the land, not upon us. It would not be easy to describe the physical nature of our actions upon the tools, and their action upon the soil, and the effect of this upon the crop of potatoes. But we know that the system works. It is phenomenally functional. The whole relation, the concepts, the actions and reactions, are material.

How important it is that Justice heeds only the material. If the courts were not discriminating in this respect, we would still be burning witches at the stake. Courts would still be concerned with black cats, poltergeist, chairs moving across the floor, the effect of witchery on the mind of the bewitched. Into this brew, mix the effect of Edison's Polyform on Edison's clearings in consumer's minds. Which of these concepts, these actions and reactions, are material, and which are imaginary?

Gather many people at an exclusive social event, and make it fifty years ago. Note the volume and tone of the hubbub; then mention the name of Henry Ford. Mention it with a certain emphasis signifying he has just entered the room, and as you might easily predict, the sound of the hubbub will change; - Henry Ford is a magic phrase. Suppose he has indeed entered the room, but he isn't the man who manufactures automobiles. Flash this information about the room and again the crowd noise will change. The name Henry Ford has had a material effect.

Yet, magic name that it was, anyone could adopt it. Any woman who wishes may call herself Mrs. Henry Ford.

My father knew a man who started a company to manufacture chemical fertilizers. He wished to call them Best Fertilizers, but, unless he could prove them actually the best, it would have been illegal. So he changed his name to Best and proceeded - legally - to call his product "Best Fertilizers". Obviously he intended to trade upon the ordinary connotation for B-E-S-T. Undoubtedly it was a positive factor in sales, though, as time passed, the name became just another brand in this competitive business. The ink on the sack lost its identification with good-better-best, and became identified in users' minds solely with the worth of the stuff in the sack.

A name is a word, and one finds that a word is the run button of a computer program etched into a human mind. When a word is conveyed to the brain, it starts a little series of meaningful operations in the mind. As such the word is a thing-in-itself. To growers experienced in chemical fertilizers, the word B-E-S-T called a concept to mind - all the memories that they associated with fertilizers, including Best fertilizers. All these memories culminated in an opinion about this product, a reputation; a classification of Best Fertilizers among all fertilizers. The gathering of these associations and their integration into a reputation is like the running of a computer program. It is an actual happening in the brain.

There are difficulties in being strictly definitive in this field. For instance "name" is also a word meaning reputation - "He made a name for himself." So a name is at least two things; it is a button that puts in motion a particular mental program; and it is also an entirely different thing. It is the operating computer program itself. It is the system of recall and conclusion. It is the clearing in a human mind.

And B-E-S-T is something else as well. Being a scrawl of ink on paper, or paint on a sack of fertilizer, or a vibration in the air - Buh-esss-tah - it pushes the Best button in the mind and starts the Best program running. And what do we get out of the name machine? What we get has nothing to do with B-E-S-T as ink or vibrations or button or program. What we get does not connect us mentally with B-E-S-T, but with the crumbly grey stuff in the sack, our reaction to it, our taste for it, our concept of how we can use it and what it can do for us. The mind takes the symbol and transforms it into our comprehension of the thing itself. In short, the symbol and the reputation become one.

Let me hammer on this topic, for it is important that we grasp what is material and what is not, and there will be other chapters later on this most important topic. P-U-R-P-L-E written in letters is ink or paint. That is, the letters themselves are made of ink or paint. The word transmits itself to your brain by electromagnetic vibrations. In sound it consists of other sorts of vibrations - Pah-urr-pah-ll-ah. In letters it is material and in sound it is material. I can make the letters and I can make the sound. I make the letters and you see them, but my basic interest in making them isn't in making the letters. It's that they push the Purple button in your mind and start the Purple program running. My objective is that you see in your mind not PURPLE, the letters, but a color image.

A word is a thing, but it does not refer to itself. It refers to an entirely different thing. A word is a tool, but not for the exclusive use of a single person. A word is not created for the purpose of exclusive use. Given a word, any person can scrawl the letters or vocalize the sound. The use of a word is in everybody's liberty. I may stand on a street corner all day long, repeating the phrase General Electric the whole while, and nobody can stop me - not, anyhow, on grounds of injuring the company. I am forming the vibrations, but I'm not using them. It is like my starting my tractor and running it around the farm all day without purpose, except perhaps for my own amusement. So what do we mean when we say we use a word? We mean exactly what we mean in every activity involving use. We use a word when we associate it functionally with a pursuit. We shape the letters in ink, or the sound in vibrations, intending that they push a mental button and start a mental program running.

I wish to use an arrow to bring down a deer. I fashion the bow and arrow. I release the arrow into the air in a purposeful arc. I rely on the characteristics of the arrow, and the laws of the physical universe, and the properties of deer flesh to accomplish my goal. This is what I mean by use. As an arrow is a tool, a word is a tool. Putting them in motion; disturbing their repose; with purpose. This is what we mean by use. Their turbulence has an interaction with something out there. And if there is a potential for interaction, we are entertaining material concepts.

The letters P-U-R-P-L-E and the sound pah-urr-pah-ll-ah have no value. But their phenomenal function is so valuable as to be beyond value. We Americans as a nation will never sell our rights to use the word purple. More accurately, we will not give up our capacity as a nation to communicate the concept of the specific color. The letters Thomas A. Edison have no value, except that with painstaking care he fashioned them into a material function. Printed on an item of merchandise, they pushed a button in a human mind, and the program ran out a favorable "buy" signal. The function was created under the influence of natural laws, physical, physiological and economic, and it can be harmed, impaired by distorting influences, under the same laws. The function was materialized by a creative hand, and it can be dematerialized by reckless or malevolent hands.

The name Thomas A. Edison as ink on paper, was a thing. As a computer run button in the mind, and as the computer program itself - the clearing in the mind - it was a thing. And as the print-out of the program - the reputation - Thomas A. Edison is a thing. Sometimes by the word "name" we refer to the ink on paper. Sometimes we refer to the run button - mental processing aspect of "name". And sometimes we refer to the reputation, the concept of the thing-in-itself that we associate with the name.

One final extension of the concept of "name". RED is ink on paper, but to a woman who speaks only French it has no run button in the mind. It conjures up no concept of color in her mind. To get the same concept she must see the ink scrawl R-O-U-G-E or hear the vibrations rrr-uuu-zz-hh-ahhh. She has a mental push button that responds to that. Same concept comes out but different name tool, different run button, computer program configuration. The concept is important, and the name tool has no importance of itself. Only as it functions in the total scheme does it gain value. To the Frenchwoman, the nametool RED has little value, but she would not wish to lack the nametool ROUGE. The nametool RED is material, being ink on paper. But to the woman who only speaks French, RED as a phenomenal function is immaterial. For not only is RED a nametool and a namerunbutton-computerprogram and a nameconcept, it is the entire function that I have been describing. When we speak of NAME in its largest sense we speak of the NAMEFUNCTION. If the namefunction is in working order - if it works - it is material. And if it doesn't, it's not.

Anna Hodecker claimed clearings in the minds of her friends and acquaintances. She claimed she had in those minds a name, a reputation. They had a concept of her. There was a name runbutton in their minds, she claimed, that actuated the name program in their minds. This name button, she claimed, responded to the name Mrs. Frederick Hodecker. And she was correct. This was a function that worked. Furthermore it was a name function that she had carefully nurtured. Her pursuit in creating it was honorable, and the function itself, now established, was a valuable asset in her social life. The government would protect both her liberty in the pursuit and the conformation and quality of the function itself. All correct. But I think the time has come to examine **Hodecker v. Stricker** in the format of injury.

1. Is an entitled loading space involved in the case? Yes, with two aspects. First, Anna Hodecker has a right to create name programs - personal relations - in the minds of people, and she has a right to pursue those personal relations without interference. Second, the personal relations, the name functions, are things to which she is exclusively entitled, and the government will protect them against harm, and will protect her liberty in using them in social pursuits.

Now, in the light of our present discussion, we ask a necessary question: are we speaking of a real loading space, real things, functions that work? And the answer is yes. The loading space is real. It is material. Here you see an element - materiality - that must be added to the format of injury.

2. Is there a loading in this space reducing Anna Hodecker's project effectiveness? Is it contrary to Anna's wishes? And is it charged with the will of Emma Stricker? Well, Emma Stricker is living with Anna's husband and calling herself Mrs. Frederick Hodecker. This is a claim of adverse loading, and it is proper to inquire also here whether or not the adverse loading is material. Not only must a claimed loading space be material. The adverse loading - if it is to be deemed injurious - must be material as well. However in this case it will be efficient to defer the question of materiality to step 4, the determination of trespass or nuisance.

3. Is Anna under a service or servitude in the claimed loading space; has she voluntarily granted to Emma the use of the name Mrs. F. Hodecker? An unqualified no.

So we come to part 4 of the format. Usually, if the answers to the preceding questions were all affirmative, we could conclude that injury is present. However we have not settled the question of injury; we have not concluded that the adverse function was material. It is tentative, and we proceed.

4(a). Does the adverse loading constitute a use of plaintiff's loading space? Do we see trespass in the case? Well, how does one apply these terms in this case? Certainly Emma is using the name Mrs. Frederick Hodecker. She is vibrating the air with those syllables, or scribbling the marks on paper, and pointing to herself when she does it. And she is trying to establish a push button in people's minds that runs a mental program producing a certain concept of herself whenever they see the scribble or hear the syllables. This is a project to which she is entitled. She may call herself King Edward of Greece if she pleases.

But is she using Anna Hodecker's reputation to establish herself in society, as Edison Polyform used the reputation of Edison to sell its medecine? No, she is not. Perhaps she is using Frederick's reputation, whatever it is, but he is not complaining. In **Edison** it was to Polyform's benefit that people associate the medecine with the great man. But Emma has no wish to be confused with Anna. Anna's property is a carefully fashioned name function embracing the concept of Anna, and Emma wishes no part of this function. She isn't using it. When she applies Mrs. Frederick Hodecker to herself, she has no wish that people attach to her their concept of Anna Hodecker. Trespass is not a factor in the case. Anna cannot expect the court to evict Emma Stricker from the name tool "Mrs. Frederick Hodecker". Anna did not fashion the tool, she adopted it herself. Anyway, name tools have no value of themselves. What Anna fashioned was the runbutton-mental-program-concept part of the name function. These are things of value, depending of course on the particular concept that has developed. (Note: do not adopt the name of a living actor to use for your own stage career. These name tools are registered.)

4(b). If not trespass, then do we see nuisance in the case? Emma Stricker by using Frederick's name, or so Anna claims, is interfering with Anna's social pursuits. By reason of Emma's activities, claims Anna, "plaintiff has been scandalized, slandered, defamed, humiliated, defrauded, libeled, and otherwise injured among the community, and greatly distressed in mind...." Judge Bradley had no doubt about the distress, but distress cannot raise jurisdiction, witness Mrs. McNamara. Distress can exist in the absence of injury. Witness your distress about the girl-at-the-next-desk's attitude toward you. Of the items on Anna's list of complaints, the judge eliminated all except humiliation. So we come to the true issue. Has Emma's adoption of Frederick's name humiliated Anna? Many a civil rights case has been won charging humiliation. Has Anna been humiliated? Will Emma's use of Fred's name change people's perception of Anna? When the run button of Mrs. Frederick Hodecker is pushed, will a new program be run out in people's minds, with a new print-out, a new concept of Anna, a new taste in their minds, a new reputation?

The question is not whether she is humiliated in her own mind. The humiliation must occur in other people's minds. Suppose your house and the house next door have parlor windows looking right into each other, and your neighbor has placed in her window the ugliest vase that ever existed; a reject from the shooting gallery at the carnival. You are embarrassed when a visitor in your home happens to look out the window. There it is. So we ask, does this humiliation of you exist in your visitor's mind; or only in yours?

We can imagine one of Anna's friends saying to her, "My dear, you should not let her get away with calling herself by a name rightfully yours. People won't think much of you if you do." But this you see, this egging on, is a pursuit of Anna's friend, and is not indicative of true friendship. A court will not respond to this kind of logic. A court cannot respond to an uneducated notion of court functions. No. The court must concentrate on the mechanics of nuisance. Anna wishes people to think highly of her, and this is a pursuit that a court will honor. Anna, speaking in our new terminology, is claiming that Emma's use of Frederick's name is distorting Anna's reputation. But though this might be happening in her imagination, there's no way it can occur in reality. It is different from Polyform's use of the name Edison.

Specify the product of Thomas A. Edison to be a record player, one that performs faithfully year after year. To someone buying it, Edison is the machine and the name. The buyer knows the man Edison only as reflected in the machine. The run button is E-D-I-S-O-N, but the direct generator of the mental program in the buyer's mind is the record player. Now put the name and likeness of Thomas A. Edison on a bottle of ineffective medecine, and the mental program becomes confused. The buy signal becomes weak and tentative. In time the man Edison becomes a different man in the minds of buyers.

But Anna is not a thousand miles from her buying public, and Anna is her own product. Her reputation in the community (the case does not involve libel or slander) is based upon personal contact with the real Anna, not with mechanical products and logos. People will never confuse the real thing Anna with the real thing Emma, though they bear the same name. Though occasionally there will be mix-ups, Anna is available for checking with, and so is Emma, and each will take pains not to be mistaken for the other. In every community one finds duplications in names, and this is no different.

Anna's complaint can be tested for materiality by using a simple function statement, like this: (------> means "we will observe"):

```
(a) If Emma Stricker                      a high opinion
    does not use the name    --------->   of Anna Hodecker
    Mrs. Frederick Hodecker               in the community

(b) If Emma Stricker                      a low opinion of
    uses the name            --------->   Anna Hodecker
    Mrs. Frederick Hodecker               in the community
```

The juxtaposed statements together compose a function; a proposed function. Anna claims statement (b) to be a cause and effect statement; that it is true. However a statement of function is always composed of at least two apposed statements, and the consideration of a function requires considering both statements. Our intuition tells us immediately that the function is absurd. You will never find a witness who will testify with conviction that (1) she has a lower opinion of Anna because Emma is calling herself Mrs. Frederick Hodecker, and (2) she will have a higher opinion of Anna if Emma stops using the name. There is simply no functional relation between this activity of Emma and the loading space that Anna is suing to protect. The function is immaterial. Her claim is immaterial. And a court cannot clamp jurisdiction on a defendant on immaterial grounds.

As for Anna, her goodwill in the community was not based on her being the lawful wife of Frederick Hodecker. Perhaps her "status" was, depending on who Frederick was; but not the actual program that ran in people's minds when they thought of Anna; not her reputation; not her personal relationships. The news of Frederick's affair was abroad for what it was worth, and both sides of the affair had been aired. When it comes right down to it, why should Anna prolong this meaningless fantasy of marital status, particularly if an embarrassment. Judge Bradley put his finger on her problem: "This apprehension of the plaintiff, presumably, is founded upon the fact that she previously cohabited with Frederick Hodecker as his wife. ... it may be that if other persons, by want of knowledge of the situation, treat the defendant as his wife, some opportunity might arise to question that relation of the plaintiff to him, resulting in rumors in the community unpleasant to her. But, upon the facts alleged in the complaint, the plaintiff has her remedy by action for dissolution of the marriage contract, to relieve herself from the relation of wife to him, and from the name she derived from it, and thus from the apprehensions...." For her benefit, Bradley was suggesting that Anna begin to face reality. Truly he was close to understanding why he could not issue the injunction.

CHAPTER 27

A RULE IN PERSONAL RELATIONS
AND A DANGEROUS OPINION

So Justice Peters in **Dandini** was in error. Dandini's new marriage, though his Nevada divorce was void, would not affect Lillian Dandini's societal status as wife. Whatever her status in the minds of her friends, it had nothing to do with being A. O. Dandini's wife; there was no way that Dandini's remarriage could impair Lillian's clearings in the various minds of her social circle. But if this portion of Justice Peter's opinion was erroneous, what harm did it do? After all he otherwise had solid ground for his decision to enjoin Dandini's remarriage. The harm is this. A judicial opinion forms a basis on which future cases will be decided. It seems to state a rule. And this erroneous argument of Justice Peters has been quoted, as expressing California's liberalized rule for injunction.

Justice Peters was confused on two points. First he did not distinguish between the "status" of marriage and the marital relation itself. And he did not distinguish between materiality and fantasy. As far as protecting the marital relation - not the status - a general rule was voiced in 1968. It appears in the opinion of the Supreme Court of Alabama, concluding the case of **Logan v. Davidson**. The court in essence said, summarizing its review of former cases, "In **Knighton v. Knighton** the wife was seeking an injunction against the improper relations between her husband and another woman. But she was also seeking separate maintenance. In fact the husband and wife had agreed to a separation. The injunction was denied. On the other hand in **Henley v. Rockett**, where the wife was seeking an injunction against the behavior of another woman, there was no suit for separate mainte-nance; the wife and seventeen year old daughter claimed to seek the preservation of the marriage, and evidently the court was led to believe them. The injunction issued. We think that this case now in court is governed by the **Henley** case, not **Knighton**."

Note this was not an attempt to justify a rule, but it clearly forms a distinct rule. The government will protect a personal relation that exists at least in germinal form; where there is evidence of a commit-ment to vitalize the substance that exists, ailing though it might be. A court, we are learning, will not issue an injunction to protect a figment of the imagination. The propertied loading space must be material. The mechanics of injury - the adverse loading - must be material. And now what do we mean by material?

By materiality we refer to concepts and relationships between concepts in which we recognize the existence of, or the potential for, phenomenal functioning - systems in which there is a potential for input and a cognizable result. Concepts among which there are actions and reactions.

Now what about rules, principles, in deciding cases in law and equity.

The rule implied by the Alabama high court contradicted Peters's opinion in **Dandini**, pronounced twenty years earlier. It harmonized with **Hodecker** and **ex parte Warfield,** decided seventy years earlier. It also fits **Snedaker v. King** handed down in the Supreme Court of Ohio forty-four years earlier in 1924. We must take a closer look at **Snedaker v. King.** Though the result fits the rule, the coincidence is happenstance, skin-deep, originating from widely diverging lines of reasoning. The Ohio court was listening to a different drummer, and alarmingly the beat is still being heard. It shows how dangerous an opinion can be, even when coupled to a correct decision. The details of the case will seem like replaying a cracked record, but they must be endured.

Jesse Snedaker was actually the defendant, the "other woman", appealing her earlier loss of the case. Grace King had sued for an injunction in the court of common pleas, and her pleading sounded like a carbon copy of Morris's in **ex parte Warfield.** Jesse Snedaker had alienated the affections of Homer King, and Grace King prayed the court to enjoin Jesse from "visiting or associating with the plaintiff's husband, or going to or near him... or communicating with him by word, letter, sign, or symbol... that the defendant... be restrained from interfering with the plaintiff in her peaceful efforts... to regain his love, esteem, support, and conjugal relation...."

The trial court awarded Mrs. King five dollars in damages, diminutive not because the wrong was minor but because Miss Snedaker had no money. Moreover, the court issued the injunction. Taken to the Court of Appeals the award of damages was affirmed but the injunction was overruled.

Said the majority, "The decree (of the trial court) in this case is an extreme case of government by injunction. It attempts to govern, control and direct personal relations and domestic affairs. ... The opening of such a wide field for injunctive process, enforceable only by contempt proceedings, the difficulty if not impossibility of such enforcement, and the very doubtful beneficial results to be obtained thereby, warrant the denial of such a decree in this case, and require a modification of the judgment in that respect."

Said a concurring voice from the bench: "... Under these circumstances it is difficult to see how the court can enforce the injunction... without attaching a probation officer permanently to both Miss Snedaker and King. ... Under this order, what is Miss Snedaker to do if she passes King upon the street? Must she cross the street in order not to go "near him..." ... This injunction should not issue, because an order that forbids a man and woman to see each other or to speak to each other... merely adds fuel to the flame."

Notice that all of the court's objections could be leveled at Henderson's earlier decision in **ex parte Warfield**.

Although Grace King's pleading copied Will Morris's faithfully, there were essential differences between **King v. Snedaker** and **ex parte Warfield**. Vivia Morris was still living with Will Morris. Homer King was no longer living with Grace. Between Vivia and Warfield there had been no sexual relations. Miss Snedaker had fully seduced Homer King and he was hers for the rest of time.

In **ex parte Warfield** the court evidently sensed that Morris was committed to reclaiming and rebuilding what was left of his marriage relationship. But the Ohio court apparently did not receive the same message from Grace King, despite the tender tone of her pleadings. As the court expressed it, the prayer was "based upon the apprehension of the plaintiff that she may in the future be deprived of support, by reason of the alleged alluring conduct of the defendant toward plaintiff's husband."

Given this, that there was no relationship here, no clearing to protect, the court's decision was correct. It fits the rule for which there was adequate precedent. But in presenting grounds for its decision, the Ohio court completely deserted the course of the common law. The concurring judge's objection to an injunction was queer. His remark about attaching a probation officer to the lovers was uncalled for. Grace King herself would be the probation officer, supervising Miss Snedaker's compliance with the injunction, and would carry the news and the evidence back to court if Miss Snedaker acted in contempt of the order. It has the appearance of a counterfeit objection. It is almost as though the court wished to change the course of the law. Let us examine this.

In 1930, in the Kentucky Law Journal, Roy Moreland focused upon the **Injunctive Control of Family Relations**. He cited **Snedaker v. King**. From his review of cases he concluded (1) each spouse has a right to the affections, companionship and support of the other; (2) our legal system will protect the right; (3) the court can find a property right in the "entitlement to consortium" or in the marital "status"; (4) nevertheless, in making an injunction decision, the court may consider the question of how expedient, how feasible, how effective an injunction will be.

Do you see where this leads? Let the government grant a person property; let the going get tough; and the government need not protect the property! This is worse than feudalism. The feudal lord might grant his vassal title, without a guarantee of protection, but at least in the case of **King v. Snedaker** he would let Mrs. King chase Miss Snedaker away with a pistol, and let her use it if necessary. Might as well ask why we fight crime. We catch so few malefactors, convict even fewer. Prison is such a poor environment for rehabilitating criminals. And if you pit the police against the criminal, the criminal will be challenged to even greater crime rather than deterred.

There is yet another school of rules deriving support in the Snedaker-King opinion. Witkin reports that **Dandini** has been criticized "for entering into the undesirable field of injunctive control over family relations." Are these critics suggesting that personal relations are too intangible a matter for jurisdiction; that the government should abandon its attempt to find property in this field of endeavor and conflict; that this is an intrusion into private affairs? Nor do I wish to underrate the importance of such reasoning in deriving an intelligent theory of justice. Why after all does the government bother with such insignificant matters? Yet the fact is that the government indeed has concerned itself deeply, and with resolve in such matters. With this we have once more arrived at the crux of government intervention and judicial decision - the question of justification. Only now we see that justification has two faces. First we might ask how the government can justify to us the people its intrusion into our personal affairs. Second we might wonder how a ruler can justify to himself and his colleagues the bother and expense of intervening in "merely social questions." The answer to the first is easy. The government does not intervene unless one of the parties prays its intervention, and it seems that intervention is continuously sought. It is the second aspect that we never address, unmindful as we are of the presence of rulers in our lives. Why do rulers bother? Rulers again! Yet we will learn the most astounding endowment of equity and the common law when we ask this simple question and find the answer.

But we have merely been trying to discover the rules covering personal relations, not asking for justification. Before we can criticize the rules, we must learn them. The decision in **Snedaker v. King** conforms perfectly to the rules, given the facts of the case, but the opinion supporting the decision is another matter. Such opinions almost persuade us to propose that courts abandon all attempt to explain their decisions.

One more detail of personal relations under the common law can be derived from a case such as **Snedaker v. King.** The truth was that Grace King's clearing in Homer King's mind was obliterated. So loaded was it with weeds and pests, it was no longer suitable for cultivation. In **ex parte Warfield**, Morris pleaded only partial alienation of affections, inferring there was something left to protect. But Grace King pleaded alienation, and the award of five dollars suggests that the court judged there was nothing left to protect. The marital relation projected by Mrs. King was an illusion. It was not material.

So far, so good in our analysis. But what about Grace King's claimed pursuit to establish another clearing in Homer's mind? Suppose these are her true intentions. Doesn't the government protect a pursuit to create a personal relationship? Ah that! But now, you see, we are not looking at an exclusive territory. We are talking about a commons. Let a woman court a man, with his consent, and the government will protect her pursuit against all nuisance in that field, particularly against libel and slander and malicious attempts to defeat it. But other women may also, with the swain's consent, court his favors. Not until one of the women has committed herself to him in matrimony, and he to her, does the government perceive a loading space in which it will grant an exclusive title. And even here, contrary to Moreland in his review, and contrary to Peters in **Dandini**, the government will not protect the "status" of spouse. It must see real commitment in fact, not merely in words.

So Grace King is now on a par with Jesse Snedaker. Each can court Homer if she wishes, and if he consents. As far as this sort of pursuit is concerned, Homer is a commons.

Materiality I have shown to be essential for a personal relationship, if the relationship is to qualify as property. And if a court is to find injury in a case, materiality is a requirement for the alleged infringement. Another essential element of a personal relationship, if a court is to honor a claim in personal relations, is the **consent** of the taxitant to the pursuit claimed by the plaintiff. And **commitment**! Commitment to a pursuit in personal relations! Commitment is now a word in our vocabulary, introduced rather casually. And if we wish it to be significant, it must be made material, a job requiring that we dive deep into the cold, fiery core of the common law. And that we must do now, in the next chapter.

CHAPTER 28

BIOLOGICAL LIFE AND EFFECTIVENESS LIFE

In the previous chapter, regarding personal relations, I introduced the word commitment. Apparently the government favors relationships in which it detects a large input of personal commitment. In closing the chapter, I stated that raising the matter of commitment signified we were approaching the heart of the common law.

As it stands, the idea of commitment is vague. Like the idea of love it requires unlimited qualification. But let us begin with a rhetorical question: what do we mean by commitment if not the commitment of one's life to a pursuit. Now all we need ask is what we mean by life. Next I will remind you of the two directions from which we must attack the question of justifying the law. First, putting it in the framework of **ex parte Warfield,** we have Warfield asking how the government can justify intervening and displaying its muscle in purely personal matters; no "property" is involved. The simple answer is that the government does in fact interfere, and does not bother to explain. It is up to us to figure out for ourselves whether the intervention is justifiable to us the people. So the remaining question is why the government consumes much of its own time in intervention. How can rulers and their cohorts justify among themselves the mental exertion required of them to design and carry out a rational scheme of property and jurisdiction in personal relations. Why get mixed up in family relationships and social affairs? And though we might not think it worth our while to consider it from the rulerly point of view, and though judges sometimes object to the work, the policy persists. It is evident that important people have been giving it their attention. A third question will come to haunt us at this point. When we have found the rulers' reasons for involving their government machinery in this jelly-like field, will these purely selfish motivations on their part satisfy us from our own point of view? And with this we get down to business.

I have been discussing law and justice with the use of a slightly alien language. Property, we find, is occasionally related to marketable assets, but its range extends far beyond assets. In truth, it is the territory of our personal liberty. Beneath the technicalities of law, stripping off the niceties of language, we have sensed the primitive world of human conflict and, underlying everything, it is not difficult to discern two very human elements, will and desire. Now, since basically we are dealing with human emotion when we're dealing with law, and since "the people" are humans, and since rulers are some of the people, we would be shrewd to look more closely at humans. In following this line of reasoning in this chapter, we will find ourselves far from the language of law, yet close to the pulse of law.

In an earlier chapter, I generalized the idea of "thing", and admitted even humans as things - very special things to be sure. Biological facts they are; phenomena that have created law, and in turn they have been shaped by their creation. Under law they are a class apart. Only humans have property; liberty; rights. Only humans can be subjected to servitudes. Servitudes are restraints upon liberty under title, and only humans can hold title.

Only humans are subject to legal restraints - don't kill, don't steal, don't commit adultery. Though you might train beasts not to steal, you can not, by symbols, words, law, instruct them not to steal. Law is communicated in mode abstract, and non-human animals do not deal in the abstract. "If you are a good dog today, I will give you a bone tomorrow." This is a message that will never get a response from Bowser.

Natural principles operate in the jungle. Run or be killed. Kill or starve. Kill or be killed. But only man conceives such principles, or conceives them to be principles, or tries to express them. Though we are constantly amazed at the social lives of beasts, even insects, we understand that reason is absent in those social structures. We find sensible law in a herd of elephants, a pride of lions, a flock of geese, even among cockroaches; but we don't attempt to initiate such creatures as members of our legal community. If by sensible we mean rational, the rationality exists only in our own minds. Otherwise their law is sensible, meaning they feel it. It is practical, but it has no source in reason.

We grant rights to no creature but man. Yes, we will make a wild reserve for deer; but if they become too numerous, we'll thin them out with gunfire. We plead for the preservation of species, but I for one would welcome the extinction of mosquitoes. Or take fish for example. Because a huge dam will threaten the survival of a tiny rare fish, we will drag the dam's construction to a halt. Some of us will maintain that the species has a "right" to its habitat, but the finny individual with gills could care less. Though it will dart and hide to protect itself, it has no thoughts about rights or the preservation of species. All such fond abstractions are in the mind of man.

The squirrel by some instinct will bury a nut, and three months later it will smell a nut and dig it up. But only man knows the meaning of "three months from now". Only man can anticipate in the abstract and, without this faculty, laws would be meaningless. I mean not natural laws, but the kind made by lawmakers. The story of Adam and Eve is a story about anticipation, not sex education. The apple was not from the Tree of Life, but from the Tree of the Knowledge of Good and Evil. A beast knows about sex, but has no knowledge of good and evil. To a social group lacking the capacity to anticipate, a book of law is something to sniff. Anticipation in the concrete abstract is man's greatest blessing, and his greatest curse.

If there are rulers, they are human things. If the masses are their political treasure, their treasure is composed of human things. Rulers are experts in human things; authorities in applied psychology; dedicated observers of their treasure and of each other. As I have suggested, "natural law" in regard to the civilization project, refers to the way humans respond to the acts of their rulers. The common good waxes and wanes in tune with ruler mentality. Consequently an understanding of the human psyche helps us discover the rationale of the common law. A good introduction to this understanding is furnished by the writings of psychiatrist Fritz Kunkel in his book **God Helps Those**. In what follows, I have abstracted some of his ideas.

One needs a little preparation to get on Dr. Kunkel's wavelength, and I'll provide it as follows:

Man acts on subjects. Who then is this man? "She" is not her body, for She uses her own body as subject. Nor is She her brain, for she uses her brain. She uses it to imagine, to predict, to solve, to devise.

She conceivably is her will, for she does not use her will; nor does her will use She. Or She might be her desire, for she does not use her desire, nor does her desire use She. Yet her desire is not identical to her will, for while her will does not use her desire, her desire finds materialization through her will.

Let her lose all desire; let her sit in a corner desiring nothing, willing nothing. Then does She exist? To be sure, the body is living, but if the body eats - yet without desire, it eats because it responds to the will of a custodian. It is not She who is eating.

Desire, if it exists, finds its source in the body. In the material of the body resides at least the **form** of the desire. Probably in the complex of desire lies the **form** of the will. It is probably in this relation - the relation between the material of the body, the form of the desire, and the form of the will that psychology finds its topical matter. A body today can be full of desire and will and, a year from now, display no trace of them. There will be no change in the material of the body that we can detect. Nevertheless a change in the body must have occurred. Now we pick up Dr. Kunkel's train of thought. He says in essence:

"Every human being is subject and object at the same time. As subject he acts; as object he is acted upon. His actions as subject have their results in the world around him, and they fall back upon him and strike him as object." You will notice that the word "subject" will be a bother. Of all the words used to express man's abstractions, none are more important than subject and object, subjective and objective. They are used variously in the sciences; they are used in analyzing sentence grammar; they are used in referring to ruler and commoner; they are used in philosophy; I have used them in relation to projects and pursuits. And evidently we will shift their meaning to denote whatever we hope they might mean. "This is the subject of our discussion. We wish to be objective in discussing it. We are studying that object. John Green is the subject of this clinical study. We will take pains not to interpret his responses subjectively. As subject he acts, and as object he is acted upon. She regards me merely as a sex object, and wishes to subject me to her desires." We have here a linguistic monster that even an international committee will never tame. It was created by the imp of the perverse, and man must learn to live with it, trying despite all obstacles to communicate his most abstruse ideas intelligibly to his fellow man.

By the word subject, Kunkel means the actor, or pursuer, and I have applied it to the thing used in a pursuit. We instinctively sense what he wants to say. His subject and object correspond roughly to their grammarian meanings. "I (subject) caught the fly (object)." The nominative and predicative elements of a sentence, of a thought. A perfectly valid usage in many situations. By subject he means the "She" of my transitional remarks. But I cannot sustain this use of subject in what I wish to develop.

By subject, Kunkel meant the thing from which an act originates, so in the following I will substitute the word **originant** for his use of subject. I proceed to abstract his sense. He illustrates his point:

"A bushman slays his enemy and he is acting as originant; he is slain by the relatives and he suffers as object. A child gets hold of a knife and acts as originant; it cuts its finger and suffers as object. Someone indulges in sweets as an originant; he spoils his stomach and suffers as object."

Object is a good word to express what Kunkel means. In its Latin roots, an object is something or someone whom we obstruct; we throw something in its path; we disturb its passage. In many ways this is the scientific use for the word. In many ways this is the one and only means by which we learn about things. We throw something at them. If a physicist wishes to study the nucleus of an atom, she shoots particles at it and sees what happens. If a general wishes to learn the mind of his enemy, he sends out a reconnaisance in force and observes how his enemy responds. Object as a word may play tricks on us, but we will give it a chance.

Says Kunkel, "It becomes clear that man can treat his own body as an object. And his body in turn has an effect on him; makes him suffer; makes an object of him." Let's put it another way: "It becomes clear that She can treat her own body as an object. And her body in turn has an effect on She; makes She suffer; makes an object of She. In other words, though She is an originant She reacts to things." With this, Kunkel reaches the first stage of his argument; he draws his philosophical - as opposed to his psychiatric - conclusion: "So man as originant is not the body, nor does he dwell in the body. As originant he is nowhere at all in space, since only objects can exist in space. And yet he exists; for he thinks and acts."

Kunkel fails to see the inconsistency in what he has just said; he just previously said that man's body can affect She as an object. However he reaches the same perception that I reached in my transitional remarks. The She of a person is not the body, or even the brain. At least She does not dwell in the thinking capacity of the brain. I would suggest that the corporeal man is the **form** of the She; that She in turn acts through the corporeal man and receives her impressions back through the corporeal man; that through this psyche She, the corporeal mind (she's form) may be changed, and from this new form a new She may arise.

We never see her desires, her will. Only through the words and acts of the corporeal man do we learn something of her desire and her will, and then only by inference. And really this is our idea of this corporeal man, beyond his corporeal physique, our inferences about her desires, her will, and this is the She associated with him. In the final analysis we cannot fault Kunkel's philosophical conclusion. Yes, her desire and her will and She herself arise from the corporeal man, and they act through the corporeal man. But can we maintain that the desire and the will - yes, and the She - are themselves corporeal? There is something very strange here, and it is even stranger than that, as we will presently discover.

Kunkel's philosophical synopsis puts us in a frame of mind for carrying our system of free space to its outermost reaches. This is the creature Man, the She that the legal system proposes to encompass.

His next words lead us from the existential to the psychological:
"All acts have their origin in the incorporeal nucleus of man's being; they arise from that inexhaustible source that we call life." Kunkel says this is important to remember, "for man answers in full for all his acts; for all that arises from the living essence. It is an inviolable law of life that everyone is not only exposed as object to every chance influence from the outer world, but he is the object of the world's reaction to his own originant activity." And it makes no difference whether he's ready to take the consequences or not; even whether he has a comprehension of his vulnerability." Even the child that can

neither judge nor understand its own behavior cannot escape the consequences - "wherefore the answerability of the child's teacher becomes almost immeasurable."

Kunkel observes that the distinguishing mark of man the originant is freedom - freedom from cause; and of man the object the lack of freedom - determination by cause. His psychiatric conclusion is that the successful development of a man's character depends on learning that he is originant and object at the same time; he is both free and answerable; he cannot escape the results of his behavior and "must bear the results even of trying to escape from the results."

Not only is man the originant of his behavior and the object of the consequences, he is co-originant in the family, the class, the nation; and co-object in epidemics, wars, financial crises.... Finally, and inescapably, he is co-originant and co-object in mankind as a whole.

This manifold interdependence carries with it such a burden of consequences and such a demand for personal growth and development that rare is the man who has not lost courage at one time or another, and tried to escape. He who accepts his originant-object set of circumstances acts as an oarsman in the white waters of life whose final plunge into the abyss is known to no mortal.

But he who tries to escape to a safe bank must renounce his own development. He must deny the value of the eternal change of life, and attempt one of two classic avenues of escape. He may try to be originant only; to confront the world as freed from both cause and suffering; and try to screen himself from the results of his actions. Or he may try to be object only; without freedom; without acting; and therefore not vulnerable to the results of his actions.

The first way creates a Napoleon, a person willing to sacrifice everything in order to demonstrate the completeness of his power and his invulnerability. His recklessness is not an expression of courage but of his fear of being object; and this drives him to exaggerate his originancy. He assumes omnipotence until the results of his flight from consequences destroy him.

The second way creates the person who sits mentally on the bank, pretending to be god of the stream, an inactive onlooker, a yes man. He is condemned to disappointment and wretchedness since the course of life will never be corrected by inactive critics. So those who would escape being vulnerable for their own acts must, after all, experience the full effects of their attempts at escape.

In the real world, man cannot be originant exclusively, without being object, for this is equivalent to being immaterial. Nor can he be object exclusively, or he must cease to act, to feel, to grow and develop; he would become a corpse. Both states are impossible in the living man. The conflict between his attempt to escape and the consequences of this attempt put too much stress on him. In both cases we witness suffering upon suffering, increasing and increasing until the error is corrected.

"Whoever suffers must ask himself why and in what way he is trying to evade the living exchange of being originant and object; whether he is trying too much to be only object or only originant. He must try to experience both. He must seek the path of action; and he must seek vulnerability for the consequences.

As esoteric as this may sound, Kunkel has given us the perception that we need in understanding the reality upon which our system of law is based. Here is the human-thing that craves freedom. Here is the She to which we grant titles; on which we lay restrictions and servitudes; to whom we recommend restraint; and to whom we guarantee justice. Here is the She that would be ruler, and here too is the She that is ruled.

We can introduce the law into this esoteric world with just one question. Is the originant a thing? Is She a thing? Remember, we are not speaking of the body; not even the brain. We are speaking of a concept that dwells in a different sphere; closer to the domiciles of desire, and will. Perhaps we are speaking of the ego, or the id. Surely the body has no ego; nor has the brain; though just as surely the ego is generated by the corporeal substance of body and brain.

Remember the definition of thing? A thing is a concept that can be used. There is even a test for usability. A thing is a concept that will react when you "throw" something at it. Thus, although subject and object are not synonymous, the subject of a pursuit must be an object.

Is the originant a thing? From this question radiates a multitude of questions. Can She be used? Can She be owned? As we know, She owns under the common law the uses of her body; her brain. But does She own She? Can properties be mapped on the originant as a subject? Is the originant an object?

We see immediately that She owns things. It is not the body that owns things; it is not even the brain that owns things. It is to Shes that governments grant ownerships. But can an originant own itself? Or, and more fundamental, can an originant use itself?

A person before reaching the age of consent is something of a slave. Given a framework of common decency, all of her uses are vested in parents or guardians. Within a framework of common decency, they may sell uses of her on contract to others. I suppose her parents have the title to possess her as well. And while we like to think their title of possession is limited to her corporeal being (we do not like to think they possess the very She) we nevertheless like to think it's the very She in which they are really interested, when they wish to be her custodians.

When the person attains her majority, all titles in her seemingly become vested in She, the originant. All restraints upon her actions are no longer in the hands of her guardians; they are in her own hands under due process. Nor are these restraints upon the body or the brain. All these restraints are upon She. Nor are these restraints upon the desire. The common law never says, "Do not covet." The restraints are upon the will, making use of her faculty of abstract anticipation. "If you steal, you will be put in jail."

"She" may use her arms and legs to mow grass, but not to hit and kick another person. "She" may use her voice to sing in the shower, but not to sing on the sidewalk at two o'clock in the morning. "She" may sell her body's photographic image to a broadcasting company, though the government might try to restrict how much she may reveal of her corporeal substance. "She" may use her brain and her voice and her signatory capacity to organize a corporation, but not to defraud the stockholders.

When She sells her services as a comedian to a television producer, She will do well to perform them. If She or her body is in Florida at 9 P.M. on November 10, though She is scheduled for a live show from Hollywood, she becomes vulnerable to damages. If her contract provides that She will constrain her body weight to no less than two hundred pounds, She will suffer financially if She does not comply. Even if She falls in love with a pretty girl and wishes She's body were thinner, She will comply, or lose money.

When the television producer buys the use of his body and his voice, the producer is also buying a bit of his She. The producer cannot animate his body, his vocal chords. The producer must depend on She to do it. So the producer uses She to use his body and voice in an entertaining manner.

To an extent She uses her body as She uses pencils and suitcases - as a subject in a pursuit. The uses of her body, within a framework of common decency, belong to She as far as the government is concerned. But two titles of disposition of herself are not granted to She by government under the common law, and later in finding the reason for this, we will learn very much about many things.

A disposition of herself that she may not execute under law is to sell herself into slavery. In the term slavery we can now become more perceptive. By the state of slavery we mean a state in which a wedge has been driven between the desire and the will. It is not quite this simple, and it is not quite accurate, but it is on the right track. In slavery a person is compelled to act in a certain way, though his heart isn't in it. Such a state often occurs in situations not defined as slavery. Certainly it occurs frequently in fulfillments of contracts. All we can say in such an instance is that the contractor's heart was in it when she signed the contract. But in slavery her heart was never in it. The wedge between desire and will was driven firm at the beginning of the master-slave relationship.

As we will observe in later chapters, not all slavery is absolute, and there are slaveries not discerned as slavery. But certainly slavery encoded in and by means of law was what the legislators had in mind when they drafted prohibitions of it in the Northwest Ordinance and the thirteenth amendment. And these enactments have a strange result. You cannot sell yourself into slavery. Interestingly you can sell a portion of your She in connection with a contractual service, and the government will strongly advise your She to comply with the terms. And one would think that by issuing many contractual uses of your She, you could practically let out your whole She. And of course this is your She that is letting out your She.

So why can't you let it all out? Why can't you sell yourself into absolute slavery? Why can't you say to this other person, "I'll sign over my entire She to you"? "If you will pay me an annual salary of $20,000, I will do whatever you want me to do. If I don't do it, you can take me to court." And here we are assuming that the input of the master's will will be within the framework of law; he does not intend to order She to do something illegal. Seemingly here would be a perfectly legal contract, the servant entering freely into the agreement. And really how different is it from slavery? After all, the black slave in America worked under a system of rewards and threats of punishment.

The most obvious mistake in this comparison: you have entered this agreement voluntarily; the black slave had no choice. The second mistake; the slave owner had the full power of government behind him. The power of government would return the runaway; would jail or execute the violent slave; would countenance a limited amount of physical punishment on the part of the owner, spurring the slave to comply with her orders. In other words, the government would aid the owner to compel actual performance, and none of these remedies are available to a contracted "owner" under the common law. Compliance under threat of jailing is precisely the condition of peonage, and this is deemed forbidden by the thirteenth amendment. Physical punishment, except in child discipline by decently restrained parents, is not permitted for any reason. Actual performance under contract is never compelled, and encourageable only by an action for damages. Else by an action called specific performance, not compelling actual performance. And if the non-performer has no net assets, no foreseeable income that might be garnished, the injured party has no relief. Upon each party to a contract the common law places responsibility for foreseeing the possibility of such an outcome. The common law is simply too pure an air for slavery to exist in, providing that jurists recognize slavery when they see it, and what it comes down to is that the government simply will not permit the total delivery of an originant She, a competent She, into the will of another originant.

The other peculiar restriction that government places upon a She is this: Though She may destroy a valuable necklace belonging to her, She may not destroy She. She may not commit suicide. Indeed we will attain a most profound precept if we learn why a person may not, under the common law, commit suicide or sell herself into slavery.

The answers to these riddles are not developed in this chapter. It is the task of this chapter to lay a more general foundation for understanding the human thing. In preparation, I will slightly shift my emphasis. While until now I have been concentrating on the entity of person, the multiple entities of person, the concepts that comprise the person, now I will concentrate on the general description of the human person, the acknowledged characteristics of the person. And of course the predominating characteristic of a person is that she's alive. There is no originant in a dead body and a dead brain. At least law does not presume to extend jurisdiction that far. The three prime protectorates of the common law are said to be life, the body, and liberty. Apparently, life is a topic of interest to rulers. They ponder such matters as murder, capital punishment, suicide and abortion.

If we can ask, "Is She a thing?" "Can She be used?", we might as well ask, "Is life a thing?" "Can life be used?"

A hammer is a concept that reacts to your input. It's a thing-in-itself. A daydream is a concept that can be used to while away the time. But it is obviously a thing-of-the-mind. It cannot be the topic of a lawsuit. So let us begin to frame our question more exactly. Is life a thing-in-itself or a thing-of-the-mind? That is, is it a concept that can be used by the She whose life She represents. Can the life of a person be used by another person? Succinctly then, can the life of a person be the subject of a lawsuit! Or is it a concept; not usable; and therefore not a thing-in-itself?

A title to something is a title to use it. In my fishing pursuit, I use not only my rod but my body. In such a pursuit I use my hands and arm, my eye, and the coordinating tissues of my nervous system. But do I use my life? Or if I sell myself to someone, am I somehow selling my life? Can you sell something that isn't a thing?

Again, is suicide a use of my life? Does a government restriction against suicide mean that the government holds a property in my life? And how can that be? And if I murder another person, am I disposing of that life as I wish? Is this an injury - an invasion of property? If so, whose property is this life that I've disposed of?

Can we answer these questions logically? Do the facts of law fit the facts of science in this sphere, and the facts of a tenable philosophy? And if they do, does this mean that the men of government have traveled these latitudes ahead of us?

The general question then becomes: where does life itself fit into the broad scheme of things and uses, titles, properties, legal freedom - liberty, and loading spaces?

I have found that a good way to approach this analysis is by examining the expression: "He used his life to benefit mankind," and let us make it more concrete, thus: "Francis of Assisi used his life to benefit mankind." Here is a statement coupling the verb use with the noun life and, as we commonly construe it, we know it to be a true statement. But how literal is it? Is it as literal as, "He used his bat to hit the ball"? Or are we seeing a poetic expression, using familiar words to transmit a cryptic message? And here I refer only to the words "he used his life". I am not referring to the more emotional phrase "to benefit mankind". Quite simply, is life a thing; a concept that can be used?

Human life itself is a phenomenon that man cannot create. Though a man and woman, mating, might imagine that they create a new life, they don't. They merely arrange an environment where life might find an agreeable climate for procreating itself. And this it executes in its own manner, according to its own rules, and in its own good time. Medical science's success with "test-tube babies" merely attests to the success of scientists in learning and conforming to life's own rules. And even if man "creates" life from organic chemicals in a laboratory flask, he won't. He will place certain chemicals in the flask and submit them to certain conditions. Then, if everything is to the liking of life, life will begin in the contents of the flask, spontaneously, of its own accord.

All that we call man originates thus; as originant, from the nature of the bodily material and, as object, from the influences impinging upon it. All that a man is, is a display of this living material and, obviously, there is no way a man can use this life that is himself. We might as well say it is the life that uses the man. But rather than quibble over who uses what, we will be on firmer ground to think of a man's She, the originant, and his biological life to be one and the same thing. By biological life, you understand, we mean not the arms and legs; nor even the movement of the arms and legs; but whatever it is that makes the difference between living arms and dead arms, living brain and dead brain.

Most certainly this is not the kind of life that St. Francis used to help mankind. We might as well say that this biological life used St. Francis to help mankind. So here we face a blank wall if we wish to discover what we really want to say about St. Francis and his commitment to mankind.

By "using his life" perhaps we mean that St. Francis dedicated his life to mankind, meaning that the life time allotted to him would be used by him in the service of mankind. However, time is not a thing-in-itself. Nobody will ever use time. There is no way you can throw something at time and get a reaction out of it. So when we say we use time, we definitely mean something entirely different. When we say that St. Francis dedicated his life (time) to mankind, we mean that he made a resolution: in the future he would use his brains and hands and legs in the service of mankind. We might say that he resolved to use his future life for mankind. But of course his future life is not a thing. We never live in the future; - always in the present. It is definite that we can't use our future life.

Nor our past life. As St. Francis used his brain and hands for worthy purposes, his biographical life unfolded. The records of a biographical life have a way of being things. The published material takes on a career of its own, and can in various ways be used to benefit mankind. But this is not what we mean when we say St. Francis used his life to benefit mankind.

So She cannot use her present life; She and her present life are identities. She cannot use her biographical life; it is in the past and invulnerable. Her future life is non-existent. She affects her future life only in the present, the moment it is no longer future. Her present life is the only life She has; and She cannot use it. She can only use her corporeal tissues, and these are not her life.

Evidently, like other words we've met, the word life has several meanings, each valid, and each susceptible to semantic difficulties. Our task here is not to define life as we want to define it, but to discover what we mean when we say St. Francis used his life to benefit mankind.

What we will discover is another kind of life - one of our most precious lives, and we will discover it by wandering a bit, a little aimlessly. Perhaps we can walk around this house called Francis, and peer in through a window or two.

Though we might say that Francis dedicated his life to mankind, we certainly don't mean that he conveyed a deed in himself to his fellow men. He did not assign himself as a slave to mankind. Mankind did not use Francis as a subject in mankind's project. His mission in life was his own personal project. It arose from his own personal desire, and it was immaterial to him that his desires fit mankind's, or not. No. Francis gave no title in himself to mankind; or to his nation; or to his government; or to his pope. And if he did, it was a unilateral promise and not enforceable at law.

Though he was a man of meditation, I take it that he was also a man of action. Though his desires were subliminal, they were supplemented by will; his worthy actions replaced the folly of his youth. His volition must have been dauntless, for 1200 A.D. and Italy at their intersection are not noted for altruism. We gather that every fiber of Francis was oriented in the direction of his godly goals. When it came to golf, or the liberal arts, or marriage, or the Lion's Club, or the school board - unless they furthered his single-minded pursuits - they were not on his weekly calendar. I wonder what would have happened if prince or pope had tried to stop him.

What happens to an enthusiastic person who is thwarted in his pursuits?

Let pope and prince act directly and without subterfuge. Let them cut out her tongue and cut off her hands; now she cannot act or communicate. Her brain still functions. Desire, at first anyhow, is not dead. The will to act might still be alive; it has merely become inconsequential. A wedge has been driven between the will and the potential subject matter of her projects. Have we a different She now; a different originant? And will She remain unchanged?

Or let the men of power act obliquely. By insinuating their operatives into the Franciscan order - it was now a powerful societal force - they insert electrical bypasses in the Franciscan circuits. These men will become his confidantes, by manifold clandestine acts neutralizing his pursuits. Nor is he blind and stupid. He catches the scoundrels and sends them packing. But others have already infiltrated the holy order. A wedge has been slipped between his desires and his objectives.

Nor is it necessary that we implicate pope and prince in these plots. Low and crafty men, eyeing the empire Francis has built, and burning with visions of their own future power and wealth, sidle their way with their minions into the organization, steering it in the directions that suit them. Yes, Francis makes plans and gives orders, but somehow the results are not what he expects. As his antagonists succeed, he fails. Actually this is what happened to Francis and, as his biographical life unfolds, we begin to detect a sick and dying man. When our desire is alive and a wedge driven between our will and the material world, we experience the circumstances provoking the cry, "Give me liberty or give me death!" And with this we have reached a point where we can visualize the life for which we are searching.

Let us expand the field of data that we are examining. Observe a biological life once existing called Ulysses S. Grant; at least study his biographical life; and you will find he was really alive only during the

Civil War. During that period he found himself to be truly effective. No barriers between his originant self and the phenomenal world, his projects materialized magically. Or consider Beethoven, one of the most dynamic and vital of all musical talents. Whatever he wished, musically, would spring into being. I have wondered if his talent did not exactly fit the environment into which he was born - music's stage of development, the political idealism of the day, and I have wondered what he would be if he had been born in our day; with the musical development that we see, and our philosophical tastes. Could he have reached the heights he attained in his day, or would he be just another organ grinder; for creative purposes, a dead man.

What is the life that I'm hinting, and where is it situate? As a first approximation, we might call it the "effectiveness life" closely related to what we call a "sense of effectiveness". In tennis and golf, bowling and basketball, they sometimes call it confidence. So of course we will find the mind to be the matrix in which it is generated.

Every time we commit an act, we put our effectiveness life on the line. We tend to follow those paths of action in which our loadings return the results we desire. If the world likes the music we have written, our effectiveness life blooms. If we fail in business, our effectiveness life might take refuge in a bottle. Remember Kunkel? "Every human being is originant and object at the same time. As originant he acts; as object he is acted upon. His actions as originant have their results in the world around him, and they fall back upon him and strike him as object."

The effectiveness life reflects the relation not between our desire and the world, but between our will and the world. Meaning it reflects the success of our actions; the success of our loadings.

So in talking about the effectiveness life, we are talking about something real, not something imagined. We press the keys of the computer according to a prescribed program. The actions are real. The subject is real. If something unexpected materializes, the world suddenly becomes unreal. Our concepts about objects and their responses turn out to be unreliable. If someone would precede us on our daily round, and transform all our concepts into unreliable concepts, we would be insane at the end of the day. Every time we take an action, we bet on our sanity. The success or failure of that act will have an effect on us; an effect over which we have no control. There is no escape. It is a real function. It is a phenomenon. It is a natural law.

Now then, when we say that St. Francis used his life to benefit mankind, or dedicated his life to mankind, we might or might not be talking about the effectiveness life; but we might as well be, for this was the truth of the matter. To make a resolution - to dedicate your future life - carries no gamble. But each time that Francis denied something for himself, each time he did something for someone else, his She-originant-self took a step into the real world. And, trembling, she watched to see the results. They would affect She. She would grow confident, or she would lose confidence. To act is to gamble. In acting, you commit your originant self to the outcome. If She fails, She might not die, but She might. Most of the time She simply becomes a different She. The effectiveness life is not the biological life. The effectiveness life abides in the She that skips from project to project and pursuit to pursuit. If the effectiveness life feels itself dying, it frequently has an escape. The She - the desire and the will - will change a bit, and the effectiveness life will find an abode in the new She. At all times the She is colored by her results in the real world; by her effectiveness life; by the character of the pursuits in which her effectiveness life has bloomed or withered. An originant self that has succeeded in worthy efforts is very different from a She that has been thwarted in worthy efforts. These effects arise not from the reasoning of the brain; they are phenomenal human responses.

They prevail whether the individual is aware of them or not. They prevail even if the individual is unaware of the particular pursuit in which she has succeeded or failed. They prevail even if She is unaware that she has been engaged in a pursuit. So each of us has two very real lives - a biological life and an effectiveness life. They have such an interdependence and an inter-independence, the one dancing on and living in and infecting the other in such complex patterns that the variations must be left to the imagination.

We cannot use our effectiveness life any more than we can use our biological life. We can put it on the line in undertaking a project. And in so doing we commit it, or use it, in the sense that we commit or use our money in a wager. The difference is that, in life, we cannot escape this commitment; this use. But the effectiveness life is result, only result, and not directly to be manipulated. The biological life - the originant self - acts upon a subject - through the faculties of the body. The subject responds and a result materializes in the real world. Then the originant self compares the result with the desired objective. And in the individual's elation or dejection that follows we catch a glimpse of what's happening to the effectiveness life of the individual.

Note very carefully for future reference. In these last few para- graphs, we have separated a bit from Kunkel's phraseology. That is, we must go beyond his use of the word "object". Man acts as originant; yes. And feels the result as object; yes. But something else is occurring, unless the effectiveness life has indeed become morbid. The She is responding not just as object, but as taxitant!

So we may ask how this relates to government and a standard of justice. Surely the government can not create for Francis a universe of saints, to cultivate his effectiveness life. Or guarantee for Beethoven a musical era to fit his unique genius. Or produce eternally for General Grant the garden of hell required for his flowering. But government projects will foster the personal projects of certain people and thwart the projects of others. History shows that the standards of government have an effect on the character of the nation. A government sometimes finds that its nation has become thriving and prosperous. Sometimes it discovers it has become a government of the walking dead.

In its administrations the government nourishes the effectiveness lives of this group or that. It cannot escape this role. It is reality. We begin to see that the common good in part reflects the effectiveness lives of the population. For the other part, it reflects the climates of mind, the particular fields of exertion, in which effectiveness lives are blooming. If we can find formulas for property and injury with a direct relation to effectiveness lives and climates of mind, we can construct a legal theory, a theory of government administration that has a predictable engagement with reality, a direct effect upon the common good and the rulers' treasure. This will be a formula governing executive, legislative and judicial action having a true functional relationship in the universe of man, actually operating on the basis of natural law.

In the meanwhile we arrive at the point of paradox where we find (1) a man can use his brain, his eyes, his legs and consequently (2) they are things; they can be subjects of title; the government can assign title to him and he can grant uses of them to others; but (3) he cannot use his biological life or his effectiveness life. To him, they are not things. So he can't have title to them, and of course cannot assign title in them to another. This has amazing consequences, and this isn't the end of it. But even at this level of inquiry, one can wonder if this is why under the common law a man cannot commit suicide or sell himself into slavery. He has not the title to his biological life, the originant She. One can pause in these halls and wonder, then, if the government has been here ahead of us. And if so, what sort of minds we glimpse.

CHAPTER 29

THE PONDERABLES OF EQUITY

I have suggested for your consideration the concept of the effectiveness life; the possibility that the common wealth is a reflection of the nation's effectiveness lives. If a person has committed her effectiveness life to a pursuit, and if by protecting her pursuit from intruders the government can nurture her effectiveness life, the government finds its justification for intervening. The rulers but enhance their own treasure.

But you can see how much depends on a ruler's concept of his treasure. Effectiveness lives can be committed to predatory and reckless pursuits as well as productive ones. If the ruler's buddies are committed to predation, and if he nurtures such effectiveness lives by legislation and court decisions, and effectiveness lives committed to productive pursuits are wounded as a result, he chooses the metal of his treasure without considering whether it is lead or gold. People plan and pursue projects in a psychological atmosphere - what I am calling a climate of mind, and it is impossible to separate their effectiveness lives from their climates of mind. The resulting effectiveness life of the nation, and the nature of the common wealth, will find their form in the climates of mind that the ruler favors.

You have probably noticed a coincidence. From the analysis of project spaces emerged the concept of project effectiveness. Project effectiveness turns out to be the criterion by which the government determines injury and assesses damages. Has a person's liberty been infringed? This is the equivalent of asking if her propertied project effectiveness has been diminished by another person.

From the psychological analysis of man himself, of woman herself, emerged the concept of the effectiveness life. Strangely, the two terms developed independently in the course of my thinking. They are terms foreign to legal terminology, yet, though not expressed in the vocabulary of the common law, they exist side by side like right and left ventricles in the heart of the common law. The next question is why; why have they been given such a central position in the structure of law? And there can be only one general answer: something about effectiveness is precious to rulers.

But this isn't the whole story. The government only protects the project effectiveness of a person in her property. The nature of property then is the clue to what the government deems precious. How government determines property will tell us what projects government wishes people to be effective in. And, since people's effectiveness lives bloom in the regions where they find effectiveness, and since there are all sorts of projects, and since projects are pursued in many climates of mind - productive, reckless, greedy, responsible, malevolent - we can tell what climates of mind the government wishes to promote by the nature of the government's legislative and judicial projects. Knowing this, perhaps we can draw general conclusions - general rules - that are guides to correct government action in the spirit of the common law. Evidently the brains of government have explored the depths of human psychology to determine what creates a truly great nation.

So we have graduated from the referee's rule book. We are looking in on the deliberations of the football commission, making the rules, justifying the rules. At the referee level, the rule book asks the simple question: is the project effectiveness of the property owner being reduced? If so, it is injury. At this higher level we ask how these property lines got established in the first place. Property it is that discloses the kinds of pursuits to be protected, the pursuits in which the government wishes us to be effective. And the commissioner in this game of games is sometimes equity, sometimes the legislature.

So why, in **ex parte Warfield**, did Judge Henderson favor Morris and enjoin Warfield from interfering? It is the rule says the rule book. The government will protect a wholesome pursuit in marital relations. But why is this the rule? What justifies this governmental interference with Warfield's pursuit. All Warfield desires is to establish friendly relations with Vivia. I have suggested it is the climates of mind in the opposing parties - responsible, irresponsible - that determines property.

Even so, why does the government get involved in such personal disputes? And I am proposing it does because it once made a policy decision. It decided to cultivate and enhance a certain climate of mind by this means. Why? Because it is part of a government project. What project? This we must learn a step at a time. We know but one thing. It is a perfectly selfish project. And now we must proceed with care.

When a person undertakes a project, I have said, she puts her effectiveness life on the line. In the aftermath of failure she will become a different person than in the aftermath of success. Now in **ex parte Warfield** we see two men, each with his effectiveness life on the line, Morris failing with Vivia, Warfield succeeding. The fact is that Morris's effectiveness in his marital pursuit is rapidly waning, his effectiveness life wounded; Warfield's is blooming. But what difference does it make to government? An ego is down; another is up. If government favors Morris, the see-saw will simply tip the other way. The average national effectiveness will remain the same. Why not stay out of it?

In answering this, some threads must be interwoven stretching back into the early chapters of the book. Since we are in the midst of contemplating personal relationships, I will recall for you something about relationships in general. In Chapter 8 I wrote, "... the designation of property is a legal device engaging the full power of government to enforce the will of one claimant over the other. ... property and the thing are not equivalents... **property attaches to a person's relationship to the thing.** Thus Farmer Brown's land was not his property. His property - his legal free space - lay in his relationship to the land. His relationship to the land was more honored by government than Mr. Anthony's."

It is impossible to overemphasize the importance of relationships for the human mind. The point has been made that everything we do is related to a project. When we pursue a project our success depends on many relationships - our relationships to the things we wish to use (are we strong enough to hoist the sail in this wind); their relationships to each other (is the sail strong enough to withstand the wind); the variability of the relationships (what will happen if the wind shifts); and the reliability of our information concerning the relationships (has mildew weakened the sail since last season). With respect to what we project, or undertake, all that we know in this world (or think we know) are relationships. With respect to our effectiveness in life, our knowledge consists entirely of our inventory of relationships.

So we come to understand that property in person-to-person relationships is perfectly analogous to property in person-to-inanimate thing relationships. What do we mean by freedom if we don't mean facility in exercising those relationships that are precious to us, the loading of this, expecting that. A subject of a project is of no value in itself. It's value resides in a person's relationship to it. An heirloom has several values, depending on the viewer. A rough toy boat, whittled by a boy, is a diamond to two eyes and a shaggy board to others. The question, "What does she see in him?" is generated purely by a divergence in relationships. As Locke said, "The measure of property nature has well set by the extent of man's labour...." And I added by way of interpretation: "The value a woman places on her liberty in a her-thing relationship depends on the nature of the bond holding her personally to the relationship." In fact Locke means much more than that. He is saying that a government is sensitive to such bonds and the various natures of such bonds. When two people are claiming entitled relationships to things, their pursuits relying on such relationships, and their pursuits interfering with each other, the government will clear the space for - will declare property in favor of - the claimant whose life is most deeply invested in her claimed relationship - depending on the kind of bond holding him to the relationship. Fine! Suppose we grant this to be the rule. But why is it the rule?

The question applies to a complex field. A suit in equity is always more complex than it seems. One would think that a well-tailored case, stripped to essential issues, represents a single situation. If there were two situations, there would be two cases. And this is true as far as it goes. But the fact is that every judge in equity, in every case, is looking at two situations; at minimum.

To illustrate, refer once again to Sheila Rienzi crashing her car through Farmer Brown's gate in an attempt to save the little boy Peter. Though warned by Brown not to trespass again, she has set four tires rolling across his pasture, and Brown brings charges of trespass against her. There, one might say, is the case; the situation. If we stipulate that Brown is entitled exclusively to all the uses of the land, then we can say that Sheila has used the land without his permission. In the absence of servitudes or services on Brown's part, justifying her intrusion, she has infringed his liberty. Her act perpetrates injury. Here, as you see, I have not used my big argument. I have not granted Sheila title to this loading space, this loading space composed of Sheila as pursuer, "saving Peter" as objective, and "driving a car across the land" as a necessary loading of an essential subject-element of the pursuit. This of course is the true rule, a use of the land to which all people, not just Brown, hold title.

But I wish to rationalize the rule and, if you'll permit me, I will take a motor car back to sixteenth-century England, putting this case to an English court of law in the early days of property. Real property is paramount. Rescue, as an entitled pursuit, is a non-concept, and due process calls for the court to suspend Sheila's driving license, sentencing her to three days in the stocks. Sheila has trespassed!

But a practiced visitor, a gentleman acquainted in Westminster, happens to be in court observing the trial, hearing the sentence, and he does not like what he sees and hears. Quickly he asks Sheila's permission to represent her. He gains a postponement of punishment and sends an appeal to the High Court of Chancery. He pronounces a point of great moment for the crown and all England. Under his guidance Sheila now claims title to a loading space specifically embracing the land otherwise known as Brown's. She should have title to this loading space; in fact she always has had title if England but adheres to the standard of justice of which England is so proud. What is required is a recognition of title. It is not that the trial judge has made an error. It is rather that the law itself is in error. It has strayed from the principles of equity.

Ah so! Standard of justice! Principles of equity indeed. Now sir, explain.

In the court of law, Sheila was facing the person of those who know the law. Now she is facing the person of those who make the law. A ruler is a body of persons; a person of persons; a massive thing. Sheila's counsellor must prepare a massive argument; brief in words perhaps; but massive in substance. Sheila is in equity. What will her counsellor say to this listening intellect of rulers? That life is sacred? That rulers cannot afford to lose a little boy like Peter? No. Her counsellor will tell them that they can not afford to lose a climate of mind like Sheila's!

In this setting, let me show you that every case in equity involves two situations, no less, and why the chancellor heeds both.

In "Brown v. Rienzi", situation number one takes place far from the courtroom; it occurs in the world of land, rivers, ox-eye daisies and running boys. In that world Sheila made a split-second decision, an act thrilling humanity. Sheila does proud. She was exhilarated by the experience. Let her fail to reach Peter in time; - nevertheless she was exhilarated. She made the effort and her self-esteem mounted.

In this heady state she was summoned to court, and now in the courtroom, situation number two, see how different the situation is. Brown's situation is not greatly different from the field. His eagle eye has become an injured grimace seeking retribution, a climate of mind unchanged. But Sheila's position has been turned inside out, her action of high purpose now to be examined for its "lawfulness". Her mind in the courtroom swirls in a climate vastly different from her sublime spirit in the field. More like Brown, she is complaining, argumentative, sometimes aggressive, sometimes defensive.

The trial court had only the power to look back at situation number one. But in equity, Sheila's counsellor asks the court not only to look back, but to look at what's happening in court right now. Impending is a phenomenon of import to governments. And her counsellor asks the court to look also to the future. Out in the field, in situation number one, the shadow of government was as light as air. Here, in the courtroom, it has materialized; becoming ponderous. This shadow, cast upon the future in the light of these proceedings, will fall dark and heavy across every similar situation in the world of adults and running children. Events in this court will have an effect on things to come, shaping a nation.

In equity, you see, we are not looking at the law peeping from the shelves in a law library. We are looking at natural law operating in the human mind. We are looking at natural relationships. If you do this, you can expect that. Indeed we are looking at the stage on which government speaks to a person and a person responds. This is the arena in which government establishes its personal relationships with each person!

Let Thomas Edison manufacture light bulbs and place them in the market place. Let him advertise them as the best light bulbs in the nation. Nevertheless it will be through the light bulbs themselves - how satisfactory they are - that each person will get to know Thomas Edison. Let Edison address the nation from his fireside every Monday evening via television. So. Nevertheless, it will be the light bulbs that determine how people as individuals will respond to him. Establishing this personal relationship between himself and the public was an ongoing pursuit of Edison. In it he relied on the natural laws of human nature. From these he drew conclusions determining his manufacturing and marketing rules. Thus, and in the same way, natural law fits into the pursuits of intelligent governments.

In getting to the heart of our standard of justice, we are developing a fundamental basis for distinguishing the courts of law and equity. For this, we ask the question, What does blindfold Justice see as she views a case. For the judge at law, we have a definite answer. He sees title, liberty, project effectiveness, and from these sightings he can draw his conclusions respecting injury and damage. On the other hand, the judge in equity sees two conflicting pursuits, both entitled, and must draw a property line around one, excluding the other. This is his task, and the scope of his jurisdiction, and our question becomes, What does a chancellor see in making a determination of property. And what does he weigh? For the practice of weighing is another distinction between the courts of law and equity. In law the judge (or jury) weighs the evidence and the testimony to determine the facts of the case. In equity, having the facts already determined or not, depending on the history of the case, the judge must proceed to weigh concepts beyond the reach of a court of law. The chancellor weighs what he sees in his mind's eye, what he infers about the character of the parties themselves and these facts, I have suggested, subsist in such phenomena as responsibility, commitment, climate of mind and effectiveness lives. Do you see the problem here? We are saying he must weigh such things, having determined their factuality, yet what in the world is more imponderable!

Even so I have not yet brought to light the true complexity of the case. To give you an inkling, I continue to quote from Chapter 8:

"The pioneer clears the land. He associates it with the pursuit of his projects. Now comes another person injecting an interfering will - volo - into this space - into this him-thing relationship - and the pioneer lays a claim of property before a high authority of great power. At a critical point in the authority's decision making process, the authority must ask itself and answer three questions: (1) What is the nature of the bond holding this pioneer personally to this piece of land and (2) What is the nature of the bond holding his antagonist personally to this piece of land and (3) Which of these bonds, if either, should the government honor with the designation of property?"

As you see, this is a neat package, except for a phrase and a word. What is meant by the word "honor", and by the phrase "the nature of the bond"? Without definition, the procedure will be of little practical value. The word honor is easily dispatched.

The question "Which pursuit will I honor over the other", when asked by a powerful ruler, is the exact equivalent of "Will it be better for me personally to favor the plaintiff or the defendant?" There is no reason to put the decision on any other basis. From a ruling point of view, both figism and holonism are rooted firmly in selfishness. Figism is one ruler's response to selfishness; holonism is the other's. Honor and favor are the same words in settling a dispute by a higher authority.

As for the undefined phrase "the nature of the bond", notice what tricks a writer's mind will play to evade a difficult point. As I progressed from the quotation into my discussion of honor, I cleverly modified the phrase to be defined. "Which of these bonds... should I honor...?" These were the words I put in the authority's mouth to begin with. Then I phrased it, "Which pursuit will I honor over the other?" One should be more definite, you see. Is one talking about honoring a pursuit, or is one talking about honoring an emotional bond? But I marched grandly on and again changed the phrasing, thus, "Will it be better for me personally to favor the plaintiff or the defendant?" What a change! Notice. With this I switched from favoring pursuits or bonds - principles, almost - to favoring a live, wriggling person. Almost we are coming back to what Justice should see in a case. Does she see pursuits; does she see emotional bonds; or does she see persons! The answer, I will predict, will be all three!

The stage is not ready yet for putting equity's analysis in a rigorous format as I have done with injury. As a way of beginning, let us run through Sheila's situation in equity on a quasi-intuitive basis. Note first that she is in a learning situation. If equity will not favor her over Brown, she will be punished. It signifies that the government favors the man-land relationship more than the altruistic endeavor. It means that the government does not place a high personal value on what she has done. Alert and learning Sheila, when she next sees a person in danger, will probably turn her head and look at Farmer Toscani's field of cabbage. With such a response by its subject, government has lost the spirit of the helping hand in one of its citizens. It has lost it also in all those observing the outcome of the hearing.

But its specific effect on Sheila can vary. If she is a buoyant person, the court's denial of her appeal will not affect her sense of accomplishment. It will not diminish her sense of personal worth. Her effectiveness life in helping people has been sustained by her rescue effort. A decision against her will not wound her effectiveness life. She will take the penalty in high spirits and shrug them off. She will also shrug off the government. She will have learned that her effectiveness life will find its fullest expression independent of government. Government will have lost Sheila.

But it will gain Brown, and let us look at two different Browns, the first a worse monster than Brown really is, a crony of the court, expecting a figistic favor in the decision. A large portion of this Brown's effectiveness life is invested in his capacity to abuse court procedure, and we may ask if the government will wound his effectiveness life by deciding against him in the case. It depends on Brown and the government. If they both know that Brown will never again win a figistic decision, his effectiveness life in this type of pursuit will suffer and die. His She will have to be reborn in other, hopefully more productive pursuits. But the judge may know that Brown, losing the case, will simply sharpen his tools for circumventing common law justice, and perhaps clip the judge's wings in the process. So can a shrewd judge scheme to keep Sheila as an ally to government, at the same time showing Brown that it will be to Brown's advantage as well? Perhaps the judge, taking Brown aside, can show him what he will lose if the government loses Sheila. He will lose for his community the willingness of a person stupid enough to throw herself whole-heartedly into a rescue mission. Such self-sacrificial stupidity, if we wish to call it that, is material treasure for those who are not so stupid. Might the court point this out to Brown?

In the second version of Brown, we do not see a beast of unadulterated figism, merely an honest, insensitive clod. We have a court seeking an intelligent argument for favoring Sheila, understanding that it won't lose much by losing Brown.

"Mr. Brown, how would you have felt if you had stopped Mrs. Rienzi in her pursuit and the boy had fallen in the river and drowned?"
"I don't know."
"Would you have tried to save the boy from falling over the cliff?"
"I don't know."
"If someone saved you from falling over a cliff, would you appreciate it?"
"I don't know."
"From your responses, I conclude that you feel no compelling interest in saving your own life, and you see no reason why anyone should bother to save a little boy's life. Have you ever heard of heroes?"
"Yes."
"And heroism is meaningless to you."
"That is correct."
"Yet there are heroes. You and I admit there are people who feel that saving lives is important. Evidently they feel some sort of relationship with their fellow man."
"I suppose so."
"But you don't think I should respect that feeling of relationship."
"Not when it means trespassing on my land."
"What is it between you and your land, Mr. Brown. Do you love it?"
"No."
"Then why do you want me to punish Mrs. Rienzi for driving over

your land?"

"Because it's the law. The law says part of my liberty is deciding who will load my land."

"Why is it the law?"

"I don't know and don't care."

"The law must have a reason, Mr. Brown. You call it the law, and it is the law because people like me think it's a good idea. We give you title to the land because you've earned it. Or because someone who earned it gave it to you. We respect the feelings of people who earn things. We respect the feelings of people who commit themselves to projects that tend to benefit everybody, not just themselves. I won't go into why we respect them except to say we feel it is in our interest to respect them. This is why you have any liberty at all in that piece of land.

"Now if you benefit from that policy, and if you want us to protect your use of that particular land - your relationship to that land - there is no way you can tell us to disregard the feelings of those who wish to save a child from harm. If you can show us why we should not give them liberty in that land for that purpose, you will have shown us why we should not bother protecting your liberty in that land. We will let the strongest and cleverest people take it away from you.

"Mr. Brown, in losing this case, you have gained a ruling that actually protects your interest in that piece of land."

"Brown v. Rienzi" depicts an exaggerated situation. Very few people would take the position of Mr. Brown as painted. Nevertheless this fictitious court situation bears noteworthy parallels to real court situations. For instance, the court in this case was not weighing oranges against oranges. It was weighing oranges against nuts and bolts. What do I mean.

The court favored a worthy pursuit, honoring the objective, the pursuer, her energetic action, and her climate of mind; it honored the loading she exerted on the land, but note. Sheila's effectiveness life was not deeply bonded to the pursuit. She had not put years of her life into it, surrendering other pursuits. Surely the pursuit gave her title to that particular loading space, but more importantly it reflected a climate of mind, and it was her climate of mind that the government wished to preserve. It was people with that climate of mind that the government wished to stack away in its treasure house, and it wished to win their affection. A decision like this was evidence of a government pursuit in personal relations, like putting a good light bulb on the market.

But on Brown's side, an effectiveness life was a stake. If we suppose that Brown, like many farmers, lay awake at night thinking about his land, wondering how best to manage the meadow, how best to improve the fertility of the hillside, we are looking at a person who had invested a large part of himself in the land. If the government allowed numbers of people to run roughshod over his feelings about his land, you might soon begin to see a sick and dying man. That court in equity in sixteenth-century England, burdened with an outlandish twentieth-century automobile, was weighing a climate of mind against an effectiveness life. Not an easy task but for one thing; Sheila's climate of mind was admirable. It stood for the common good. And Brown's effectiveness life was for the moment attached to an absurd climate of mind. The decision was really not difficult at all. It was black and white.

So we, the court, ask, What is the nature of the bond holding this person to this particular thing? Do we see that he has committed his effectiveness life to developing a relationship with it. If so, there is undoubtedly a bond between him and it, but what is its nature? If it contributes to the common good; if he has taken raw goods and transformed them into something good for the nation; we can honor that. But if his effectiveness life has been invested in an effort to seize from a creator that which the creator has created, we will, by honoring the bond between the predator and the thing, smother the creative drive of the nation. And this sentiment very nearly states the rule for granting title in the first place.

Given that both parties hold title to project spaces, with their entitled pursuits conflicting, not a simple matter of nuisance, not merely one pursuit interfering with the other, but each interfering with each other, then we must look at each pursuit, and at the climate of mind in which each party is operating. Sheila's pursuit is a pursuit in sociality - preserving life and safety. Brown's pursuit is the preservation of sacrosanct liberty - without reference to any concrete objective - actually an immaterial idea. So we look at the nature of the bond; putting it simply, does the party have title. And we look at the pursuit - what is the objective and what are the loadings, and we weigh them. And we look at each party - defendant and plaintiff - weighing the climate of mind in which each party is operating that he wishes his pursuit to prevail over the other. All are weighed in the gravitational field of the common good. We look at the bond, the pursuit, and the person.

With this I make a proposition, perhaps risky, and it is this: All cases properly in equity are black and white. The correct decisions are as obvious as night and day if.., with but one if, and a very important if. The decisions will be obvious, I say, if (a) the correct entitlements - bonds - for each party are discovered; and (b) the actual pursuits of each are discovered; and (c) the actual climates of mind of each party are discovered. There will be a strength on one side and a weakness on the other that will lift the decision beyond debate. If I am wrong in this proposition, I will not worry, for whoever proves I'm wrong will have found something in our standard of justice that I haven't found.

CHAPTER 30

PERSONAL RELATIONS IV:
WARFIELD RESOLVED; PARENTHOOD

With the vocabulary and understanding of principles gained so far, we can complete our analysis of **ex parte Warfield**, and use it to enter the field of parenthood under the common law. In Chapter 24, I explained how activities such as Warfield's could truly - materially - depress Morris's effectiveness in his own entitled free space - his effectiveness in pursuing his relationship with Vivia - in essence a distortion of his clearing in Vivia's mind - a case of nuisance, and by the rule book this was injury. In Chapter 29, I suggested that Morris's effectiveness life was exposed to serious wounding under the circumstances, but so what? Why does Morris get a grant of property in Vivia relationships, with Warfield absolutely excluded for all time.

It is clear that government entitles everyone to pursue personal relationships of many kinds. Excluded from entitlement are pursuits in which the taxitant in one way or another becomes the prey of the originant - confidence games - fraud - the seduction of minors. Otherwise government probably deems all wholesome pursuits in personal relations to be of equal value to the common good. There is no reason to call a pursuit in marital relations superior to a pursuit in friendship. The things weighed, then, in **ex parte Warfield**, are not the pursuits, and what else might be the issue?

The climates of mind of the parties. Judge Henderson himself mentioned Morris's claim that if Warfield was permitted to associate with Vivia, "it was very likely he would entirely corrupt and lead her astray...." Morris himself, we take it, had the most honorable intentions. But this was a claim, and the judge does not acknowledge it as proved. Yet Henderson gave weight to it, and I think this was improper. We are discussing a determination of property, and I don't see how a mere allegation like this would give Morris a property in Vivia's mind, and exclude Warfield. The only action in which weight might be given to a chance of corruption would be an action for a decree of incompetence, making Vivia a ward of her husband, and this does not seem to have been at issue.

Against Morris's claim of property in his pursuit of marital relations, I think Warfield might have raised the defense of immateriality. If Vivia was inclining toward him and away from her husband, how do we know it was Warfield's fault and not Morris's? How do we know that Vivia will ever again love Morris. Was any evidence presented indicating a future success for Morris's pursuit? We do not hear

Henderson expressing himself on this point. We know that Vivia was still living with her husband, and perhaps the judge talked privately with her and received a positive impression for the future career of the marriage. But against this we have his statement that Warfield was in jail, or close to it, because Vivia had visited him in his boarding house after he had been enjoined from associating with her. One wonders if materiality was thoroughly tested in this case. If Vivia's love for Morris had withered, Morris was back on a par with Warfield. Both had the liberty, given her consent, to pursue a personal relationship with her.

May we turn to effectiveness lives as the means for determining property in this case? In the social field, out where men and women socialize and plan together and converse and make love, if a man and a woman marry, if they are people of integrity - if their inner resolves match their vows - the commitment of effectiveness lives is matchless. Each sacrifices much to the preservation of the marriage. Each puts thought and action into tending the health and contentment of the other. Each surrenders so many alternate opportunities, each limiting her or his per unit time potential to such a degree, that their effectiveness lives subsist not in their own animal satisfactions but in the success of the marriage.

It is possible for this to be a one-sided affair. One of the partners takes for granted the blessings bestowed by the other, yielding nothing in return. But the giving person stakes her or his entire effectiveness life on creating and preserving as much of a marital relationship as might be expected under the circumstances.

Was this tested in the trial of this case? Was Vivia married to an unfeeling boor, and was her effectiveness life in this pursuit finally dead? Was Morris married to a butterfly, his manhood and his future happiness willingly sacrificed to protect a person of little sense and even less sensitivity? Was he preparing to continue this pursuit despite a bleak outlook for marital happiness, in order to keep Vivia's She from complete deterioration? Was Morris's effectiveness life committed to this life-saving program in the field of marriage?

Or was Morris committed single-mindedly to winning his fight with Warfield. Was it an ego trip, an effectiveness life invested in nothing more than winning the suit.

I think I've shown that certain questions should be asked in equity that perhaps were not asked in **Warfield.** Though the questions might not be asked directly, the judge might quietly probe here and there until he satisfies himself as to the answers. I am saying that a probing for facts is appropriate in equity; issues are raised that are not appropriate in a court of law. If the inner person is properly not seen in a court of law, the outer person is judiciously peeled in a court in equity, and the judge must in his written opinion reveal enough to illuminate the principle behind his decision.

But let us suppose that Morris had committed himself to create for Vivia an environment at least safe for her - a home and an attentive husband. In no other pursuit will we find a greater investment of an effectiveness life. Here is the bond tying Morris to his relationship with Vivia, the evidence of loyalty that rulers prize, the spirit of self-sacrifice that generals want in their troops. Here is the commitment that will keep Morris working productively in the economic world, providing for Vivia and increasing the stock of mankind.

In bringing his fight to court, Morris is restraining his desire to wring Warfield's neck. He is trusting government with his effectiveness life. He is responding with spirit to a persistent interference with his pursuit of a magnificent enterprise. Let the government fail to support him, and what will happen in that subconscious mind? Something will snap. Something will vanish. Perhaps something will take its place. The exact nature of the reaction, how it will surface and when, are beyond prediction. Just one consequence of this chain of events is predictable; it will reduce the ruler's treasure.

As for Warfield, let us assume the best of intentions, nothing more than to be friends with Vivia. Her friendship was precious. He put a lot of thought and lunches into it. Even so, he was not deeply invested in it. His sacrifices of fond wishes, his surrender of other pursuits for the sake of this relationship are hardly monumental. Morris, before bring-ing suit, has spoken to Warfield about the matter. Probably irritably and vehemently. Nevertheless, Warfield was informed that his well-meaning pursuit was destroying a marital relationship, and a decent man would withdraw. He would place himself under a servitude. Such an act would manifest the integrity and spirit of self-sacrifice that rulers treasure. Here would be an effectiveness life invested in a great deed. And Warfield didn't measure up.

This is supposition. In **Warfield** many rocks were left unturned. If the facts were actually found, and I hope they were, they weren't acknowledged in the opinion. Perhaps Judge Henderson's intuition found them. They were essential. Now let us extend the principle.

In **Stark v. Hamilton** (Georgia, 1919) we find a case strangely like **ex parte Warfield** but, instead of husband, we find Hamilton to be the father of a young woman who happens to be below the age of legal consent. Stark had been defendant in the lower court, and now he was appealing to the Supreme Court of Georgia. He had been living unmarried with Hamilton's daughter, and Hamilton had won an decree of injunction ordering Stark not to associate with the girl or try to contact her. Stark persisted in the relationship and was cited and sentenced for contempt. Now he was attacking the injunction in the supreme court, his grounds: - his relations were illicit under a state statute providing a penalty. So there being this remedy in law, equity had no jurisdiction; the injunction was improper. Thus spoke due process. But the Supreme Court of Georgia broke this rule, saying:

"The case under consideration differs on its facts from any heretofore decided by this court and from any of the cases cited from other states. It in a sense involves both personal rights and property rights. The father has the right, under the statutes of this state, to protect his minor child, to be protected by her, and to have her reside in his home and with his family and to enjoy the comfort of her association and the advantages of her services.

"It is his legal and moral duty to support her in sickness and in health. Reformation of a wayward daughter is always possible and her father has the legal and moral right to make the effort to save her, and in some measure lessen the reproach to his name and to the reputation of his family. It is difficult to understand that injunctive protection of a mere property right should be placed above similar protection from the continued humiliation of the father and the reputation of the family. In some instances the former may be adequately compensated in damages, but the latter is irreparable; for no mere money consideration could restore the good name and reputation of the family, or palliate the humiliation of the father for the continual debauching of his daughter."

In this opinion are sentiments that one might whole-heartedly support, and others that are difficult to agree with. One sees here the determination of equity to seize jurisdiction if it sees fit. Under my proposition that equity represents those who make the law, one could hardly expect otherwise.

One wonders about the father's right "to be protected by her, and to have her reside in his home... and to enjoy the comfort of her association and the advantages of her services." This sounds curiously like the rights one might have in a bottle of cough medecine, a pretty vase, and a slave, and one wonders if this - even in statute form - is appropriate to the common law. What one sees in this language is, first, the customary loose use of the word right and, second, a complete misconception of a personal relationship in the spirit of the common law.

What does the court mean, the right "to enjoy the comfort of her association?" Does Father Hamilton have government's permission to force daughter to associate with him pleasantly? Suppose by the word right the judge means liberty. We know that liberty under due process consists of (a) our ideal freedom in our property and (b) our free determination of loadings in the space of our property. Recall also that property subsists in a particularized pursuit. So we identify the pursuit of Father Hamilton, the one to which the court refers. Is this a pursuit in personal relations? Does the court mean that Hamilton is legally free to attempt to induce in his daughter an affection for him? If so, of course; he has this right. But almost this is not what the court means. Almost the court implies that Hamilton's daughter has a government mandate to bear a favorable bent of mind toward her father. At least she must display a favorable bent.

One can see that Hamilton's pursuit in personal relations might be frustrated. Stark, painting Hamilton black in the daughter's mind, could destroy any affection she might have felt for Hamilton. In such a case, a court could intervene to protect this clearing. But the daughter herself might rebuff the father, and a court would never, could never compel her to accept him. So what is this right of Hamilton "to enjoy the comfort of her association"?

Is the court speaking of Hamilton's exclusive right to determine the loadings in this pursuit space? Since he has the liberty of pursuing a personal relationship with her, does this mean that no other person has this liberty? Stark in particular? Well, for the most part it seems anyone can pursue a personal relationship with another person, given the taxitant's consent. But perhaps this rule changes in the context of a parent-child relationship. Is there something different about a parent-child relationship?

Before examining this question, I wish to look at another of the court's phrases, "injunctive... protection from the continued humili-ation of the father and the reputation of the family." We are still trying, you see, to find a liberty of the father being infringed - injury; for an injunction may issue only to prevent injury or halt it. Humiliation, reputation; here is a topic with which we are familiar. It is in that subfield of personal relations known as community relations. Everyone has liberty in inducing good relations with the people of a community, and a good relationship becomes a thing-in-itself, a subject peculiar to the property of the originant alone. His name. His reputation. No one may interfere with its creation; no one can distort it to the detriment of the originant; no one may use it without the originant's permission.

No one doubts that the activities of a child reflect upon the other members of the family, and can humiliate them. The activities of a child reflect upon her siblings, due to the commonplace understanding of inherited traits. They reflect upon the parents; the commonplace understanding of parental influence. We are discussing materiality, and we must be discriminating. We are not talking about how an intelligent society should react to the misdeeds of a family members, but about how society usually sees fit to react.

In Anna Hodecker's case, she was claiming that an unmarried woman's use of Frederick Hodecker's name was humiliating her - Anna - and tarnishing her reputation. This claim I showed to be immaterial. Anna and Emma were both at hand in the community. People reacted to them as individuals, not as names. If confusion arose, due to the identity of their names, it would be no more than occurs in many situations where two people in a town happen to bear the same name. As for Anna's claim that the "other woman's" use of Frederick's name was humiliating her, this existed in Anna's mind, not in the minds of her friends. There was no way that Emma's use of Frederick's name could change Anna's image in the minds of her friends.

But now we are looking at the family of Hamiltons. We know from experience that a family connection has a material influence in a community. The activities of a family member can actually prejudice many minds in a community against other members of the family. But we must ask a pertinent question. Are the activities of the daughter harming the reputation of the family, or are they creating a reputation for the family. Are they telling something true about the family. Are they exploding a fantasy that was not accurate. In short, are not these the facts of life? We all bask in the sunshine of the champions in our family, and we must also dwell in the shadows of our black sheep. This is reality. Sensible people in a community discriminate between champions, black sheep, and regular folks. And when it comes to deciding upon marriage, one is never wise to overlook the members of the beloved's family, though they glow in the light of the beloved.

Hamilton was not seeking an injunction against his daughter, restraining her in her escapades. He was seeking an injunction against Stark. Stark, like Warfield, was simply pursuing his own project, but his activities were defeating what Hamilton wanted. Wasn't that injury? Not unless it infringed a liberty of Hamilton. Yes, Hamilton and the other family members as individuals were pursuing honorable reputations in the community. In those pursuits they had liberty, and the government would protect those reputations. And yes, the wayward girl's activities were reflecting upon those reputations through what we might call a "family reputation", but this is not harm, this is reality. You cannot perpetrate injury under the common law, you cannot libel or slander, by telling it as it is. Yes, they are humiliated. But this is not a humiliation that a court can relieve. It can be relieved only by facing reality and establishing their own reputations.

But Hamilton has a case. The parent-child relationship is different from other relationships. Among all its varied aspects, it is a guardian-ward relationship. The court opinion touches upon it, though imprecisely: "The father has the right, under the statutes of this state, to protect his minor child.... It is his legal and moral duty to support her in sickness and in health. Reformation of a wayward daughter is always possible and her father has the legal and moral right to make the effort to save her...."

Here is the whole case. This was all that counted. These rights and duties have been a concern of the common law for centuries, not just in statutory law but in case law. There was no need for this case to go to equity save for the rule that injunction belongs to equity. The Supreme Court of Georgia had but one difficulty, the difficulty of all our jurists; they have not been given the terminology, the depth and precision of concept, to express what they wanted to express. What they had in mind was absolutely correct. They just didn't know how to say it. Let us see if we can say it better.

In the field of parent-child relations, what the common law has gradually wrought over the years is a responsibility of parents toward their children. Here I don't object to the word duty. Actually the government has put parents under a service. Paraphrasing the court's opinion in more precise language, "The father is under a service to protect his minor child. He is under a service to support her in sickness and in health."

Such support applies not merely to the physical and financial, but to her mental and social well-being: "We can always hope for the reformation of a wayward daughter....". Then Georgia provided some of the most beautiful words ever pronounced by the person of government: "... and her father has the right to make the effort to save her."

Note first the depth of understanding - the court did not say he had a right to save her. Her plunge off the precipice might be inevitable. But to stop the father from crashing through the gate trying to rescue her would be injury! The common law says he is at liberty to make the effort to save her. You see that I like the word right to mean, if anything, liberty; as I have defined liberty.

Pause a bit. Look back and see that I started out thus: "The father is under a service to protect her." Then I switched from mode duty to mode right: "The father has the right to make the effort to save her." Observe in the true quotation of the court's words the almost inter-changeable use and sense of the words right and duty. At least it seems so. But the court was merely abbreviating what it wished to say. The mechanics of the situation are these. The government gives parents a duty, putting them under a service. Not a contracted service but more like compulsory military service, parents will be held responsible for a failure in performance. And any time you make a person responsible for a pursuit, it is a law of organization, you must give her full liberty in those loadings necessary to carry out her expected performance. There is no other way to proceed.

So the full statement of the Supreme Court of Georgia was this: "The father is under a service to support the daughter in relation to her physical, mental and social welfare, and to protect her if her welfare is threatened. We don't expect perfect performance and we don't expect success in all cases, but if we see evidence that harm is occurring, that the father is not making an effort to perform, we might take custody of the child. Having placed the father under this service, we also provide for him the liberty necessary for him to act accordingly."

Armed with this, you see, the father may use all lawful means to protect his daughter, and the court must heed his call to evict Stark from this loading space. All he need do is to prove that Stark's activities are decreasing his effectiveness in this pursuit space.

By now you have asked other questions. Has Stark actually interfered with Hamilton's service? Is it possible that the Stark-Hamilton affair is true love, the surest protection for Miss Stark's welfare. And all the other questions. Were they raised in court; were the facts discovered? They are central to a correct decision.

Nor can we neglect materiality in the remedy. True, due process has said a father has the right to make an effort to save his daughter, but can government afford to protect this project space for an ineffectual parent. If Peter is in danger of falling over the cliff, can we give the rescue duty to a pedestrian on crutches? For all these situations, the common law has many sensible answers.

One enters an exciting field of thought by attempting to define the duty of parents. In entering, recall first what I have written about a contracted service. In a contract, I said, the service of a party is to materialize the objective of the other party. This applies equally to a non-contractual duty, the kind that sifts down upon your shoulders from on high. Who is the other party in a case like this? Well it might be " society" or "morality", but more realistically it is those who position themselves as the voice of society or whatever. Result; a service placed upon you from on high is a service to materialize the objectives of invisible authorities. To define the service, we need only to ask the objective. For an answer in the field of parents and children, let me pluck an objective from the air. The service of a parent is to place into society, on the day of her majority, a certain kind of young person. She will have an effectiveness life as vibrant as possible; climates of mind enhancing the common good, if possible. Her project effectiveness in her legal freedom space - on as high a level as possible. Anyone with experience knows that the phrases "as possible" and "if possible" are necessary qualifiers. This job description for parents is not bad, but is it too arbitrary? Perhaps it can be approached from another direction.

How will a parent accomplish her mission? What tools are at her disposal? What are the mechanics of her task? A little thought reveals that she has been given a task in mental induction. Normally, even in the absence of a parental duty, she will pursue a personal relationship with her child. In the happiest of circumstances, a bond will be formed unconsciously between the two, each a pursuer, each a subject or taxitant, each with a complex of objectives that each only dimly perceives. In the happiest of circumstances, the pursuit of the mother will vary little if at all from the performance expected by the higher authorities.

As for her methodology, we expect it to begin with little slaps and enticements. We expect it to graduate into demonstrations, verbal instructions, reasonings, implorings, loving understanding, and even fatalistic resignation. We also expect, knowing human nature, that the effectiveness of her tactics and the career of their personal relation will vary from household to household, from parent to parent, from child to child, from day to day, from phase to phase.

The permission granted by government to parents in their personal relation pursuits with their children cannot be greatly different from other liberties in personal relations. In all cases, I have said, people have a liberty to build personal relations with other people, given the consent of the other people. Always there are restrictions. We are aware of people pursuing mental induction projects for the purpose of gaining an advantage over the taxitant. We are aware of deceitful and fraudulent schemes. We are aware of seductions for personal benefit regardless of the possible dangers for the taxitant. Putting it generally, the government will not favor a mental induction project predictably having an adverse effect on the taxitant - deleterious to her effectiveness life, her climate of mind, and her project effectiveness. We have, you see, strict parallels between all government approved pursuits in personal relations, be they commercial, social or intimate, including the government service imposed on parents.

In a personal relationship we use ourselves of course. Our talents, our charms, our intelligence, our considerateness, whatever it takes to accomplish our objectives. We use the taxitant also. His susceptibility to our charms, his tastes, his intelligence or lack of it, whatever. The government, in giving us a title to pursue a personal relation project, gives us the other person as a subject. And what is the true nature of the restraint the government places upon us in this use? We are placed under a servitude to a master government project. The government, you see, has a project to enhance effectiveness lives, climates of mind, and to enhance the project effectiveness of each and every individual within these climates of mind. Consequently we, in our own mental induction pursuits, find ourselves under servitudes to this master project! The government doesn't tell us this. We learn it by inference from due process. By watching what happens to people who have breached these servitudes, we learn, partly by instinctive inference, partly by reasoning, how to act in similar situations.

Use, remember, is a matter of action and reaction. When one uses a hammer, she swings it in a calculated arc. That is all she does. The rest is left to the momentum of the hammer and the natural relationships between hammer, nail and board. If everything materializes as intended, one gets the result "nail in board". Change a single element.

Use a hammer made of putty. Or use a nail made of spaghetti, or a board of steel, and one gets a different result. Same with mental induction pursuits.

I smile at you as we pass on the street, and you smile back. Sometimes people don't smile back. Of myself I use my face and its muscles. Of you I use your ability to see, and your natural reactions to a face like mine. Really my smile is an experiment. I throw something at you and in turn learn something about you. On your side, in your response, you might use me to establish a relationship. But there are many diverse relationships, and there are ways to initiate them, a congenial, eye-contact smile, a tight-lipped smile with a quick glance away, a glance at my smile then straight ahead with no display of emotion. Thus you use my innate processing apparatus to establish the possibility, the potential, the color of a relationship between us. These are all mental induction pursuits. They are natural. And the government permits them as long as they don't interfere with its master project.

Thus step by step people establish their various relationships with others - loving, friendly, business-like, or cool - each using her own traits and those of the other to construct in the other a set of attitudes and responses toward her. The freedom to load toward a very specific relationship is perhaps the most precious freedom that a person has. And the contours and characteristics of the relationship once created is just as precious. These - the pursuit and the result - are apparently protected by due process - as long as they conform to the master objective of government.

It is in this setting that we return to the situation of the parent. What more could the government ask of parents than to strive for relationships the most productive possible, given the nature of the parent and the nature of the child. Now let's look at the true set of circumstances under which the modern parent labors.

More than anything else, the average parent wishes to have a pleasant companionship with the child. In this the elements of love, pride, economics, play, physical labor, and close association are all involved. Likeness of genetic traits and diversity of genetic traits are involved. Mutual sympathy and mutual antipathy are involved. Peer pressure, mass media, and stylish educational theories are involved.

Of all people who have a channel for input into children, none are more directly affected by child output than the child's parents. If the child causes damage in the community, the parent pays. If the child develops a climate of mind averse to the common good, the parent suffers. If the child marries and divorces, the parent may not only regain the child as a dependent, but the child's child. If the child is unhappy, the parent will be unhappy.

Let us look at all the persons who have an input into a child not their own and are not affected directly by the child's output in life. Mass media produce any material they wish, perhaps over the objection of parents. School libraries may acquire reading material in spite of the objection of parents. Teachers can't teach religion though they are not restrained from teaching anti-religion. They may teach sex independently of morality. They may tell children that their own theories are true, but to disregard the lore of their parents.

Many states say to parents - you must support your child in college if he wishes to go. But the parents may feel the true test is for the child to earn his own way through college.

Say the television people, turn the tube off if you don't want your child to watch it. No one compels you to leave it on. So will you forbid your child to go to his friend's home for watching. "Yes," say the publishers and movie makers, "if you don't want the child to read the magazine or go to the movie, forbid him." And what will this forbidding do to the parent-child relationship, the very relationship that the theorists say is so important.

On one hand the government says to the parent, you are responsible for adding the most effective individual possible to the society. We know that you, by your closeness and innate mental induction apparatus, know this child better than anyone else. We know that you will take the rap if anything goes wrong with the child. On the other hand, says today's government, we are going to let everybody channel anything they wish into this child, even if it interferes with the performance of your duty.

Well said, oh mighty one, except for one thing. No one will put more effort into life than a parent striving to put a happy, effective child into society. No one will fight harder for her homeland than a parent feeling her child to be truly hers - the product of her own love and thought. No effectiveness life is so bound up in a pursuit as the parent in hers - a pursuit of complexity and personal consequence beyond all others. One wonders what now is the master project of today's government.

Put a wedge between this child and the parent, a mental gap, an apathy; distort this material by theory not proven; make the parent wonder if this product is truly hers; bind the parent's hands in this pursuit where nicety of touch is crucial. And take the consequences.

CHAPTER 31

PERSONAL RELATIONS V:
RULERS AS PEOPLE-USERS

I have suggested that property, the legal free space for one's projects, is meted out by rulers on a basis advantageous to themselves. In England and the United States, unnamed princes deemed holonism, tempered with a military duty, the realistic, most effective basis. Or so I have suggested. At least this was true up to mid-twentieth century. I have started to present evidence indicating that holonistic rulers gradually learned to decide court cases according to strange yardsticks: climates of mind, project effectiveness, and investments of effectiveness lives. At least this is the direction in which they seemed oriented - if not by conscious analysis on their part, then by a remarkable intuition. For centuries now, the flags of injury and damage have been raised when a court discovers that a person's effectiveness in her liberty has been diminished by the act of another person. Liberty is defined on property, and when property is in dispute between two persons both operating within their entitlements, equity assigns the property to the plaintiff or defendant by weighing the climate of mind in each, as displayed in their clashing pursuits. A property decision is weighted also by the effectiveness lives that the opposing parties have invested in the project spaces at stake.

As every nation has a common good or common wealth, though it be actually a common poverty, so every person has an effectiveness life, thriving or moribund. This is as true of persistent malefactors as it is of persons of common decency. Yet common law historically does not give malefactors much weight in the scales. Probably our unnamed princes have not placed a high value on their climates of mind.

This is all review and preface to the main task of this chapter, in which the analysis of personal relationships is brought to a climax, a climax incredible in the ordinary mood in which we view the law. In this endeavor we must become better acquainted with the basic elements of slavery. This is necessary if we are to justify to ourselves the rationale of the law of the United States. It is all very well to justify the common law from the viewpoint of rulers. From such a viewpoint is every system of law justified in the final analysis. But if we are willing to accept the fact, can we, we the subjects, be satisfied with the results of their governing decisions? No matter how academic the question is, we feel an overpowering compulsion to know the answer. Are we slaves or are we not? Here we address the theory, not the here and now. If we are ruled according to the principles I have laid before you, are we slaves?

Several trains of thought must be carefully brought together. If for example we enter upon the topic of slavery, we will be pondering the use of an individual by another. We will be examining the use of a biological life.

In Chapter 28, I described three classes of life, the biological, the biographical and the effectiveness lives. The biological life is the complex of phenomena we infer in a living individual. It is a display of material in an operational state of existence. Nor does it exist apart from the material, and here I am not seeking a quarrel with spiritualists. I refer merely to the fact that life does not live or die; it is not life that lives or dies. It is the material of life that lives or does not live. The living material is in some way different from the same material dead. True, circumstances can be arranged in which material will start to live, or continue to live, or die. Nevertheless the phenomena we know as living phenomena, and the phenomenon we know as death arise from the material, and from it alone.

This is the life that is the person. At least it is the only person the law can engage. Not arising from the man; the man if anything arises from it. The biological life is a concept certainly. But is it a thing-in-itself or a thing-of-the-mind? Can it be used or not? To the individual herself, her life is something she cannot use, so to She her life is not a thing. Though She is able to use her arms and brains and voice, she cannot use her biological life. She can't use her desires. She can't even use her own will. For these - her biological life, her will, her desires are She, the originant-as-opposed-to-object She. The She that exists nowhere; for biological life, and desire, and will are **inferences**. We witness the material acting, and we say She's living; She has desires; She has will. Yet the She we refer to is not the material but something originating in and arising from invisible phenomena proceeding within the material. This is the biological life, and also She.

I have dwelt on the subject to make the vocabulary familiar, and to create some awe for this orginant-object we treat so casually; and to introduce the next point. This: that though I cannot use my biological life, you can use my biological life. The biological life that is me can be used by you or any other person who makes the attempt. To you my biological life is a thing, a thing-in-itself, a profound reality to ponder. But think of trying to couple it to the law!

I have already discussed the use of a person in a mental induction pursuit. Now I go to an extreme in depravity. I want an illustration showing the basic elements of slavery. It will serve also to distinguish slavery from captivity - an important distinction as later chapters will show.

I suppose two separate ways to subject a woman to rape, one by binding her helpless; the other by holding a knife at her throat. Both represent humanity at a low level. The two undertakings are alike in their a-legality. That is, their mode in the absence of law is identical to their mode in a universe of law. But there the similarity ends. Upon analysis they are strikingly different. Superficially one thinks of both happenings as the capture of a person, followed by using her as a slave, but this is not true. One is capture, the other enslavement.

A man raping a woman bound helpless, though he is using her - using her anatomy - is not using She. To him she is not originant in the least, she is pure object-subject. But if he is keeping her subdued by holding a knife at her throat, he's using She, the taxitant. He is engaging her desire and her volition in his pursuit; her desire to live and her volition against struggling. In using the tied and bound body, he is using a living corpse. In using a knife, he is using a thinking person - an originant as well as object. Both instances involve entrapment, but the knife method uses the originant, the conscious She as part of the trap. The rope method is not enslavement; it is capture. Captivity simply neutralizes the will of the victim. It ignores her desires. The knife method is slavery. It uses the will of the victim. It pits opposing desires within a victim against each other, and the probability is that the prevailing desire of the victim will fit the desire of the enslaver.

Contrary to some published ideas, the state of slavery does not necessarily involve long-term service. Slavery can be momentary. It exists when the user, by trapping the victim in a predicament, engages the victim's volition in a pursuit of the user. It does not exist unless the user engages the volition of the used. You can put a ball and chain around a person's leg, but this does not make him a slave. If you wish him to hoe cotton, you must somehow engage his volition. He and he alone can will his hands to grasp the hoe and wield it. Unless you can engage his volition, you cannot use him in your project, you cannot use the She of him. These are fundamental considerations in slavery.

So we see the absurdity of the term involuntary servitude in the thirteenth amendment, even if it was Jefferson's. If it meant partial slavery as opposed to black American slavery, as I concluded it did, it meant involuntary service, not involuntary servitude. But even this is ridiculous. There is no way a person can perform a service but by an act of volition. There is no such thing as involuntary service. Even if Jefferson intended involuntary servitude to conform with my puristic definition of the term, it is a senseless conclusion.

But it is of interest that involuntary servitude - my puristic definition, the equivalent of injury - cannot exist outside a universe of law. A servitude of any kind cannot exist unless there are titles. A servitude is a subserviation of title. A slave then is in involuntary servitude if, in the course of his being used, his liberty is infringed. It constitutes injury. Here then was the malevolent genius of American black slavery. Having no property, the black had nothing to be invaded; no liberty to be infringed. So under the slave code, a black could not be injured! How proud our early lawyers must have been, so pure was their theory. Perhaps it was the evaporation of this purity that later was so mourned by low-minded people users.

However, slavery per se is slavery, in or out of a legal universe. You kidnap my beloved child, holding her for ransom. Her you hold in captivity, but you hope to use my She as a slave. You are trying to use my desires and my volition to produce the objective of your pursuit. The methods and the machinery are the same in a primitive jungle or in the United States, whether you wish me to pay in bank notes or in beautifully fashioned arrowheads. In all cases of slavery the enslaver traps the enslaved into doing what she would not usually wish to do. It is a mental induction process. The enslaver uses her desires. Her volition. She.

Having taken the first step, we take another. Suppose our rapist uses techniques more subtle than the threatening knife. With handsome actions and endearing speeches he engages the interest of the female and ultimately her desire and volition. Is she his slave now? Has he not used her? The chemistry that is She? In his pursuit! Are such uses within his property? Indeed what are the rules for such uses? And in his approach to her and her response to him are we not talking about pursuits in personal relations? Mental induction pursuits. You see, we have not strayed from our appointed topic, and thus snugly do the spheres of personal relations and slavery interface with each other.

In distinguishing these classes of pursuits, our courts face the most intricate discriminations to be made in organized society. Inevitably human beings, not gods, must draft the boundaries between them, and it is a natural law that these human beings will happen to be our rulers. In parenthood we stride the same difficult path. When is the child the slave of the parent, and when is she the fortunate taxitant, even originant, in a personal relation with the parent. Even more perplexing is the service imposed upon a parent by the government. In performing her service, does the parent turn the child into a slave of the government? How do we explore these cavernous depths.

We first consider the person who by armed conquest has gained control over another person. In the Norman conquest we are talking about engaging English volition at the keen point of glistening steel. Having conquered, it is now the wish and task of the conqueror to direct and control the actions of the biological life quivering or glowering at his feet. Though he threatens to kill the creature, he does not actually wish it to cease living. He wants it to serve his objectives, building castles, plowing fields, and cooking pastries.

So he sets up conditions under which this life will persist. A certain amount of food. A certain amount of warmth in winter. And now the object-man becomes for the man-user a project all its own. True, the conqueror has ulterior objectives - dreams of tapestries and grand feasts and beautiful ladies and moated parapets. But somehow he has got to form this conquered beast into the efficient tool that will phenomenalize his projects.

His role will be to act toward the creature in some manner or other on the premise that the object-man will respond in one way or another. Indeed, if he wants this man to act, he must contrive that the object responds as originant. Whether the man-user recognizes it or not, he wishes to inspire in his man, by whip or other means, the auto-genesis of a particular kind of biological life. If the man-user is intelligent, he will be the consummate student of his object-originant; a dedicated applied psychologist. Even as the master horse trainer learns the horse - how its desires will conform to the master's own desires, and how he can engage its volition in his pursuit, so the man-user learns his object-originant man. He discovers that the intensity of the creature's volition and ultimately the effectiveness of its performance will reflect the environment in which he immerses this biological life. This She. Really the secret to a successful pursuit in person-using, as in horse training, is to develop the appropriate climate of mind and effectiveness life in the object-originant.

Note the similarities between this pursuit and the projects in personal relations that we are at all times pursuing. To me you say this and that. Toward me you act thus and so, and lo! In me is generated an attitude and a response toward you. An attitude and response appropriate both to your approach and to the biological life that is Mo. Whether we are trying to develop a romantic relationship, a business relationship, a parent-child relationship, a social relationship, even a ten-foot-pole relationship, the give and take rituals have the same essential topography. In the course of such pursuits, the originant learns much about her taxitant. If intelligent, she treats her taxitant as originant as much as object. And the inverse is true; the roles of originant and taxitant are continually and fluidly interchanged. As with the great horse-rider dyad, the horse becomes part of the man, the man part of the horse. In time the originant might conform himself and his projects to fit his taxitant no less than taxitant adapts to originant and originant's projects. This can be the case in ruling and commercial ventures as in family affairs. Here of course we are speaking ideally. In history, speaking now of people-users, we witness a panorama ranging from the most obtuse slave-holder to the most enlightened employer; from the despot to the builder of a high commons. In the used person we see a spectrum ranging from the American black slave, to the slave banker of the Romans, to the slave king of the Egyptians, and on to the new species called Englishmen and Americans - those at least who existed prior to mid-twentieth century.

This relationship between ruler and ruled, is it necessarily a master-slave relationship? Or is there a point, as in an enlightened marital or parent-child relationship, when the relationship is no longer slavery but an interaction raising ruler and people to their greatest effectiveness lives? You see we are not only within our topic of personal relations; we are not far from the field of the common good. On a political level we are talking about natural law. We are talking about the effects of legislation, executive action and court rulings - their effects on the project effectiveness, the effectiveness lives and the climates of mind of the people - rulers and subjects alike. In fact if we include legislation, executive action and court rulings under the term due process, we can give a name to the rulers' loading in their mental induction project. It is called due process. In fact we might call it justice. Intelligent justice.

As subjects, and in our resentments, we are inclined to dwell on our fate as objects in a grand scheme. But it is interesting to consider the fate of people-users as well. Here as in all things, referring again to Kunkel, the user acts as originant and his actions fall back upon him as object. Rulers too have their occupational diseases. The affliction of the unintelligent people-user is brutescence, a slow but certain meta-morphosis into a beast. The ailment of the intelligent person-user is more complex. Perhaps it can be called origino-subjectitis. It is generated by his enlightenment - that climate of mind in which he treats other humans as originants, that they might become subjects in his projects. We can ask if he will ever find a person whom he can trust as originant equal to himself. Will all of his taxitants, high and low, intimate and alien, be originants to him only for his manipulative purposes? And when he sits across the table from a smiling handsome person obviously his equal or superior, must he always ask himself, "Is this person treating me as originant only to use me later as subject?"

Only a ruler would know if the cure for his disease lies in Kunkel's suggestion: maturity. The acceptance of being object as well as originant. "He who accepts his originant-object vulnerability acts as an oarsman in the white-waters of life whose final plunge into the abyss is known to no mortal." The supreme reality for all rulers - figists and holonists alike - is that they risk all; their project effectiveness, their climate of mind, their effectiveness lives, in a word, their She. And there is no safety for them in the middle ground. Nor is the actual ruler (as distinct from the highly visible office-holder) immune from the fate of rulership. I refer of course not to his financial fate or career in power but to the state of his She.

If the common good blooms under his rulership, he blooms. If it

withers, he withers. He and his subjects are one. It is easy to see the
fate of a Nero or Caligula, but in no situation are rulers more tempted to
be self-destructive than in the state mechanism called democracy.
Here the people are taught that the people are the rulers; the elected
officers are their servants. The real rulers, patting themselves on the
back for their cleverness in all sorts of strategems, fail to see the
caverns and fissures yawning beneath their feet. They have not heard
of the sensitivity of climates of mind and effectiveness lives to impure
air.

We begin now to examine the tactile surface where law touches
biological life; this She. Already we learn the biological life cannot be
used by the She that is the biological life. In consequence she cannot
hold title to the use of the biological life that is She. Remember, I am
not speaking of the use of her arms, her voice, her brain. I am speaking
of using the She that feels desire, that exerts will, that breathes
intentional activity into her arms, voice and brain. She cannot hold title
to She. It would be meaningless, for she can't use She.

Yet we run into the peculiarity that She can be used by another
person. Many times do we see someone act upon Her in an instinctive or
premeditated manner, and She responds. This is a use of a biological
life and, under certain conditions, this use of Her is in the liberty of
another person. She is a subject in the property of another person. But,
if She doesn't hold a title in the use of Her, how can she give title of
using Her to another person?

I think the most productive theory is an astounding one. Titles in
biological lives are held by the government! To be lent out under
carefully restrictive conditions, with She - the biological life herself -
as the agent of government in the lending. But the government is
guardian of the biological life, holding legal title on a tight string, with
power to recall title on a moments notice. Who is it after all, who looks
closely into murder. Who forbids suicide. Who commits lives to battle.
Who holds the power of capital punishment. And who outlaws the use
of She under the conditions that spell slavery.

So, supposing that government holds title to our biological lives,
are we slaves of government?

A government, any government, can use its subjects, and use them
as it desires; and does. This is exactly the meaning of government. If it
cannot control its people it isn't a government. If it desires to use them
in a grand figistic scheme, it does. If it desires to use them in a grand
holonistic scheme, it tries. There's no questioning that every government worthy of the name holds the biological lives of the people in its
hands. The question is: Is it slavery?

If it rapes us with a knife to our throat, it is slavery. If it uses us in holonistic projects - treating us as originant-objects, or better, as originant-taxitants, raising us to our highest effectiveness lives - there is no way it can be called slavery. This is exactly our own personal objective. It does not meaning raising us to someone's ideal of what our She should be. It means allowing the She of each person to attain the effectiveness life that belongs to She, within the framework of the common good.

The most general guide to personal relationships under the common law is this: a person may use me in her mental induction project (with my consent) if her project does not clash with the very project that justifies the government's own use of me. This is the very antithesis of slavery. The common law, or the Constitution (given the preamble) does not have to mention slavery by word.

We come to the most intriguing and precious part of this thesis. I have proposed that government holds title to our biological lives, but what is the sense in saying a government holds title in a thing or the use of a thing. For what is government but the agent of the law; and what is the law but the detailed expression of a standard of justice; and what is a holonistic standard of justice but the handmaiden of the common good?

Can the common good hold property? Can the liberty of the common good be infringed? This is ridiculous.

Government. Standard of justice. The common good. Like a species or a class, they are all abstractions. They can hold no title, can own no property. Certainly the "state" can hold no property, though we say it does. The state is an abstraction and can't use anything. More fundamentally, property under the common law is assigned on the basis of effectiveness life and climate of mind, and there is no way that abstractions like the "state" can possess or exhibit an effectiveness life or a climate of mind. As important as are governments, and standards of justice, and the common good of a people, they have no existence or meaning apart from real wriggling humans. Without embodiment in the person of Shes, they are immaterial. How can title and property be held by government? There is but one logical answer. It lies in the proposition that every nation, including ours, has rulers. And when we say government holds title, we really mean that our rulers hold the title.

Individuals, certain individuals, establish standards of government. These individuals, having the power to establish standards, will adhere to the standards or not, as they see fit. And since individuals seize power and institute the law, they are above the law except as they submit to it under their own volition. Therefore the title to rule is above the law; it pivots upon Locke's fundamental maxim of property: "that was his property which could not be taken from him." So what we call the property of government is basically the loading space of those who hold the reins of government at the moment. This true in communism or holonity or anything in between. The organization of personnel that we call government is merely their agent. Our theory then leads us to conclude that the governmental titles in human life actually belong to rulers. Factually it is obvious, even in the absence of theory. Not only under the common law but in all forms and structures of government, even the most despotic, the rulers hold title to the lives of their subjects. The people are in their loading space, their freedom space. The use of the people - any use - is within their liberty. They make it so.

Rulers have climates of mind and effectiveness lives of their own. Existing as they do in a world beyond law, their effectiveness lives are exposed to a more primitive competitive atmosphere than most of us can conceive. Since they determine their own property, they delineate their own liberty - the legal range of their own project effectiveness. In doing so, they even define their own restraints, if any, upon themselves.

Thus the liberties of rulers, as well as the liberties of the people under the justice of the rulers, reflect the rulers' climates of mind. It is to their system of government, their system of justice, that rulers have committed their effectiveness lives. Inspect any legal system, figistic or holonistic, and it will be the result, first, of rulers' decisions and actions. It will be the result, second, of their capacity to maintain power - to hold their property, and to control the system. The property of the people reflects the climate of mind in which the ruler established his own property, though he seized the whole nation by force of arms. Thus do rulers account an invasion of their own property to be injury. Their own project effectiveness and their own effectiveness lives are at stake. In every case of every person entered in court, the ruler's climate of mind is before the bar.

If in a barbaric society a person breaks or blasphemes a barbaric law, she threatens the effectiveness of rulers who are heavily invested in barbaric climates of mind. But if she breaks a law originating in holonism, she reduces the effectiveness lives of rulers heavily invested in holonity. She does that which the rulers do not permit even themselves to do and this, one would think, is a serious offense to rulers.

The most awesome consequence of this theory is the purity of a holonistic ruler's entitlement to his property. If the property of rulers - meaning the uses of things in their realm in which they allow themselves liberty, including uses of human things - if this property is established in climates of mind promoting the general welfare, and if their effectiveness lives are heavily invested in this pursuit, these are precisely the grounds on which they assign property to the rest of us. Even though this ruler seizes this space by force, and holds it by force, and though it is property as defined by Locke in its primitive form, nevertheless it is also property as determined by our emerging standard of justice. Thus is the law common. Thus if we call the people slaves, we must also call this ruler a slave. And what are we all slaves to? - Our own common good. And this, as I will show in Chapter 55, is the antithesis of slavery.

Equity under the preamble operates not only in a court. It is the spirit of a legislative enactment and an executive act. It is becoming apparent that the common wealth and an act in equity compose a unified entity. One is the template from which the other rises, the form of the other. The other is the manifestation and tell-tale yardstick of the one. Together for a nation, equity and the common good spell reality.

If something here relates to the fundamental treasure of rulers, and if this public thing rises from the brain of the High Chancellor, then what greater treasure do rulers have - or the people for that matter - than the Chancellor whose decisions truly promote the common good. It is as though the form of the treasure and the treasure itself interface in the person of equity.

But be not deceived. Never will you find a person who can both design a holonistic project such as I have been describing, and seize and hold the reins of government. One is advisor, the other mover. Not only are the necessary talents and instincts for these functionaries greatly at variance, but each must devote his full time to his portion of the grander scheme. The question becomes, does the potentate have the intelligence to look for and find the advisor who can raise his national treasure to its highest possible level? Indeed, if a ruler has not the holonistic instinct, has he the brains and courage to put his own liberty in the hands of the advisor he chooses. Has he the maturity to be object as well as originant. If so, the people indeed have a treasure in their ruler.

As I stated in an earlier chapter, we are building an arch of justice. But rather are we building the vault of a gothic cathedral. In this effort, I have tried to keep the stones from falling as I place each higher stone at a steeper and steeper angle, hoping to somehow support the structure until that final point where a keystone can be slipped between those stacks of stone leaning so precariously toward each other. The key-stone will be -it can only be - the desires, and dictates, and willpower, and power of a group of Shes - that dominant clique of movers and advisors, the people-users of the nation.

How do we know if we have a holonistic government? We have seen the theory, the arching columns. The keystone itself is too high up for us to examine. So we look at the vault as a whole and ask ourselves, is it leaning, is it tottering, does it soar straight, is it sturdy? And we find there our answer.

At the risk of creating an anti-climax, I should commit another page or two to the interface between the effectiveness life and the world of law. Nothing is more intangible than the effectiveness life. Nothing is more real. It smacks of the manic-depressive. A man succeeding in a little project suddenly feels he can succeed in great projects. But if he feels hamstrung in a really insignificant project, and if he exists in a legal universe - that is to say, his freedom is confined to his liberty - his neurosis will become almost unbearable. He will be consumed by tending his liberties. Let Jimmy Jones walk unobtrusively through Brown's woods and all Brown's faculties will jerk to attention. Other more important projects will be forgotten until he rids his property of this invader.

While it is true that both law-abiding and lawless men have effectiveness lives, that of the lawless man is the less sensitive. It does not carry the burden of restraint observed by a law-abiding man. The law-abiding person, feeling legal bridles upon projects he might like to pursue, feels more keenly the intrusion of others into the loading space designated by government for him and for him alone.

Note that the common law does not list pursuits in the order of their importance to the state. Apart from the climates of mind involved in a pursuit, and the investment of effectiveness life, due process does not weigh the value of one man's project against the value of another's. The hoe of the man in the hovel is as important as the bull-dozer of the subdivider. The investment of effectiveness life in each is the same. Let rulers change the rules of liberty to fit the asset value of projects and you will have the privilege of witnessing the death of a nation.

I have discussed concepts that are both things and non-things. Patriotism is such a concept. A She's patriotism cannot be used by She, but can be used by rulers. Patriotism is a personal relationship between an individual and government. It is like the goodwill of a corporation or the friendship between individuals. It is a configuration of atoms in a person's mind, and nothing is more real. Another concept both thing and non-thing is the biological life. It cannot be used by the very She, but can be used by others, and nothing is more real.

In the effectiveness life we perceive the most ethereal plane of material existence. We have here a concept that cannot be a thing; it can not be used by anyone. Yet nothing is more real. The effectiveness life manifests the symptoms of a hypochondriac. If a person's sense of effectiveness slips the least bit, she begins to feel terminally ill. If she has committed herself deeply to a project only to see her effectiveness drop to zero, she must disengage herself emotionally from the project. Else she will begin to wither in all projects. If her project reflects high purpose for the common good, and her zero effectiveness in it traces to law and the agents of law, the rulers and the nation will in one way or another lose treasure.

The effectiveness life cannot be used by the She to whom it is attached, or by any other person. It is the result of the biographical life and the harbinger of the future life, but there is no way it can be loaded. You can't throw anything at it, expecting it to respond. Like the common good, it is result and only result.

The effectiveness life is so important in human life, it could almost replace Descartes dictum, "I think, therefore I am." It's converse is, "I have no sense of effectiveness, therefore I am not." Indeed, an existentialist might say that a person does not exist if she has no effectiveness life. I, trying to be as realistic as possible, can't go this far. I have said that She exists if the biological life exists. If I hold to this, then the effectiveness life must be a factor coloring She. If She is the desire and the will, then the desire and the will are moderated by the state of the effectiveness life.

But you do not attack the effectiveness life directly. If you are so malevolent as to wish to kill a person's effectiveness life, you must do it indirectly. You must render her impotent in a project to which she has committed her whole self. Likewise if you wish to revive a person's effectiveness life, given that it possesses the minimum essential viability, you cannot do it by stroking it and feeding it. You must engage her biological life with a project to which she will commit herself. Only out of her own desire, commitment and will-to-action will she feel an effectiveness life welling up within her again. A lost effectiveness life, like a lost climate of mind, may be irretrievable, and retrievable only at great cost in time and the project effectiveness of others. When we think in these terms on a national scale, we may have to think in terms of centuries.

It is in this sphere that injury and damage have their reality. They erode and corrupt effectiveness lives and climates of mind. It is to signal these effects that the common law system of property, and infringement of liberty, has been erected.

CHAPTER 32

LAWSUIT LANGUAGE AND TRANSITION
FROM PERSONAL RELATIONS TO CIVIL RIGHTS

We should pause briefly and munch on a minimum diet of court procedure, the mechanics of a judge's thought processes as he peruses a plaintiff's pleadings for the first time.

Over the past nine hundred years, common law jurists have observed the panorama of injury in society, brilliantly placing the varieties of injury into categories of cause. In consequence, the modern lawyer has learned to be very careful in selecting a cause of action when he initiates a suit in court. In what class of cause, he asks himself, will I express my client's pleadings? Will it be trespass, conversion, negligence, breach of contract, fraud, extortion, invasion of privacy, defamation, or what? We lay observers see among professionals a use of certain terms. Cause, theory, action, right of action, injury, remedy.... By constantly using them the professional learns their nuances of meaning, and becomes quite comfortable with them. They confuse only us laymen who attempt to define them precisely. For our purposes then, I will define some of these words and phrases, doing so under this caption: THE CAREER OF A COMPLAINT IN COURT. My definitions may not fit professional usage, but then I am trying to communicate exactly.

A Case. By this word I refer to a situation in the real world; a situation in which a person finds herself complaining against another person. It has nothing to do with legality except that it might be put before a court. I use it in much the same way that a social worker investigates a welfare case, writing up a case history.

An Action is an attempt of a complainant to relieve her situation by acting against her antagonist. In its most general mode it includes actions regardless of legalistic settings - an act of revenge; the siege of a castle by a lord attempting to rescue his captive daughter. In a well governed society, the government usually requires that action be channeled through a court. This is especially true when the action might involve physical force against the antagonist. An action in court is composed of a suit plus due process.

A Suit is a plaintiff's pursuit of relief through an action in court. A suit is the plaintiff's effort in a court action.

The Pleading commencing an action in court, often called **The Complaint,** is a statement filed by the plaintiff to catch the court's attention. The plaintiff's pleading states (1) her complaint and (2) the remedy she seeks. The request for a specific remedy is called **The Prayer.**

A Cause is that set of factors entered into a complaint that, if true to fact, will provide grounds for the court to take action against the defendant. If the complaint shows cause, though it is not yet tested and proven as to the facts, the court system is bound to summon the defendant to court - that is, to seize jurisdiction - and to try the statements of the complaint for their veracity. This government obligation to commence process is ordinarily called the **Plaintiff's Right Of Action.** I think it might more accurately be called a service to which government is bound under due process. If a pleading does not contain statements constituting a cause, a court cannot seize jurisdiction, and will not take the time to hear the case. In some courts, the defendant may **demur**, meaning he may claim the complaint does not constitute a cause. More frequently lately, courts assume power to conclude cause, even if the complaint appears deficient, refusing to permit demurrers to delay proceedings.

If a judge finds a complaint showing cause, the first action he takes is to **Summon** the defendant to answer the complaint. The **Answer** is the defendant's pleading of the case. The summons to appear does not mean he must appear physically before the judge within 30 days. It means he must send in a paper, composed by himself if he wishes but usually by an attorney, giving his side of the case, the basis of his defense. Depending on the case and how he views it, he might claim the statements of the complaint to be false, or that he was justified in acting as he did, or that he was acting within his entitlements. The summons is the court's notice to the defendant that it is about to seize jurisdiction over him. For all practical purposes, the court has already seized jurisdiction. A defendant not responding leaves himself vulnerable to any ruling the court feels justified in making. In response, the defendant either demurs, i.e., denies the jurisdiction of the court, or answers the complaint.

Trial is the court procedure for determining the factuality of the claims stated in complaint and answer. Actually the outcome of the suit is determined by two pleadings, modified as they might be by motions and hearings. If before trial it is shown that the complaint does not constitute cause, or that the answer does not constitute adequate defense, there need be no trial. The judge can base his ruling on the pleadings. And if the answer presents a legal block against court action, the judge without trial will have to deny the prayer of the plaintiff. So if the proceedings come to trial, it is because one party or both have questioned the veracity of the opposing pleading, objecting to its effectiveness, and the trial hopefully will finally provide an accurate set of pleadings for the judge to base his decision on.

Hearing. Appearance of parties or attorneys in person before the judge, presenting arguments on points and motions. A trial is a hearing in which evidence is presented.

Ruling. The court's ruling, finalizing the court's view of the case, consists of either (1) the denial of the plaintiff's prayer, or (2) the court's order to the defendant, designed to give the plaintiff appropriate relief. Depending on the nature of the case, a ruling is sometimes called a decree, an injunction, or a declaratory judgment. A ruling may also be made upon a motion during the processing of a case.

Remedy. If the statements of the complaint constitute cause, and if the defense fails, the court is bound under due process to complete the plaintiff's action against the defendant. Not that it will find the specific remedy sought in the prayer to be appropriate. But it will take appropriate action, and this action is called the remedy. The old maxim, "Equity will not suffer a wrong without a remedy" means "In every case showing true cause, the government will take appropriate action against the defendant." As a suit composes the plaintiff's effort in a court action, so due process composes the court's effort or action, terminating either in dismissal or remedy. When remedy is appropriate it completes the action. It is the tie between due process and results. It materializes the will of the government in the case. To this extent dismissal and remedy taken as a whole compose the scope of justice. Nor is a remedy complete until the losing defendant complies with the court order.

Relief is the effect of the remedy upon the plaintiff. Hopefully it restores the plaintiff's effectiveness in her liberty. Otherwise it represents an equivalent.

Contempt is an attitude of a litigating party toward a court order, implied by the party's failure to comply with the order. A contempt proceedings instigated by the court or an opposing party has the function of laying the executive hand of government upon the recalcitrant.

The task of a judge in reading the complaint is to decide if it states a cause. It states a cause if a learned reader can conclude, assuming the statements to be true, that injury has occurred. More accurately, the claim may be that injury has already occurred, or that it is occurring, or that it will certainly occur in the imminent future.

If the plaintiff seeks damages, a conclusion of cause requires in addition that the judge be able to discern damage in the case. He must be able to see from the pleading, assuming the statements to be true, that (1) the plaintiff suffered harm and (2) both injury and harm found their source in the same contributory act of the defendant.

So, figuratively speaking, one sees on the front of the book the statements of the pleadings - statements of fact claimed to be true. On the back of the book one sees the judicial conclusion that the claims constitute a cause - they represent an occurrence of injury. In the body of the book lies the line of reasoning leading from claims to conclusion. Though the reasoning might be stated in a memorandum of points accompanying a pleading, it exists mostly in the judge's mind, mostly as suggested by the attorneys; and perhaps it will surface in the reported opinion in the case. It is referred to as the **Theory Of The Case,** or the **Theory Of The Pleadings.**

It is clear, if a judge concludes injury (hence cause) he must find in the pleadings (1) A liberty for the plaintiff and (2) an infringement of this liberty attributable to the defendant. Moreover the infringement must pass the test of materiality - the mechanics of the injury must be functional. To see liberty, the judge must see property, an entitled pursuit space appropriately free of servitudes. Unless the plaintiff claims title to certain loadings of a particular subject, the judge will find no legal free space, no liberty to be infringed. This too must pass the test of materiality; there must be a functional relationship between the claimed loadings, subject matter and objectives. A court will pay no heed to a pursuit space in non-functional dreamland.

A main effort in the remainder of the book, in preparing for the task of justification, will be to design a basic system of causes blanketing the entire field of injury under the common law. The design will follow the lead of actual cases, and we will start by looking at cases located at the juncture between personal relations and civil rights. The immediate purpose is to discover the correct grounds for the action taken in **Jones v. Alfred H. Mayer Company.** There should be a more fundamental and less embarrassing cause than "injury under the thirteenth amendment." Slavery was the cause offered and honored in **Jones.** Absurd. In no way do you enslave a person by refusing to sell him a house. Actually the attorneys and the justices didn't even call it slavery. They used the term "badges and incidents of slavery", a term reaching the zenith of its influence in **Jones** and collapsing immediately thereafter.

The concept missing in **Jones** (and most other civil rights suits) is the element of property, the project space in which the plaintiff has liberty. For **Jones** to show cause, we will want a pleading like the following:

1. Jones is entitled to load subject S in accord with objective O. He is under no servitude restraining him in this project space.

2. The Mayer Company's refusal to sell house H to Jones interferes with Jones's pursuit of said project.

3. Both project and interference are material.

No case presents a cause for court action unless it can be expressed in terms like these, in this case comprising nuisance, with the alphabetic symbols filled in with the actual details of the case. Now all we need find in **Jones** is the subject S and objective O, if they exist, and

Jones will have a proper cause. In the first half of the twentieth century, many cases came close to anticipating **Jones**; cases unrelated to racial prejudice. Cases in personal relationships.

In 1937 the Court of Appeals of Kentucky heard the appeal of defendant Nell Reed. She sought the dissolution of an injunction issued against her in **Carter v. Reed**. Miss Reed and Mrs. Carter were sisters, and Miss Reed lived with their mother, who was more than ninety years old, in a house owned jointly by herself and the mother. In her complaint, Mrs. Carter had stated that when she visited her mother in this home, "the defendant had molested her and annoyed her... and had prevented her from conversing with her mother....", and Mrs. Carter had obtained an injunction restraining her sister in this behavior.

In her appeal, Miss Reed stated that the judgment of the lower court forced her to allow Mrs. Carter to come into her home. The injunction, she claimed, underwrote the invasion of a private home. Thus if her contention was accurate, we would be witnessing a government enforced injury.

The appeals court opinion (**Reed v. Carter**) was burdened with the old recital of personal rights versus property rights. And the court reviewed the pros and cons of a contract earlier signed by the sisters. Finally it addressed the true issue. The sole question remaining, said the court, involved the right of Mrs. Carter to visit her mother without molestation. "She undoubtedly has that right as long as her mother desires to see her and does not forbid her from entering upon the premises and, under the facts of this case, it is a right which a court of equity ought to and will protect from interference by others."

Here was a case properly in equity and properly treated by equity. Undoubtedly the court fully understood what it was doing. It was subserviating a title of real property, the title of an owner entitled to determine the loadings in her house. What was the pursuit of Mrs. Carter giving her the mastery of Nell Reed's liberty in her house? Indeed what was Mrs. Carter's cause? What was the liberty being infringed by Miss Reed's annoying tactics? What was this "right of Mrs. Carter to visit her mother without molestation"?

The court did not hedge its position. It did not mention the point that, after all, the mother owned the house jointly with her daughter and had a right to admit anyone she wished. We can be confident that the court would have made the same decision had Nell Reed been the sole owner. I propose that the route by which the court reached its decision was this: It first recognized Mrs. Carter's and her mother's rights in a personal relationship. Apparently the court established to its satisfaction that mother and daughter had established a material personal relation with each other. Each had established in the mind of the other that strange configuration of atoms called love, a desire to be in each other's presence. Each had established a clearing in the mind of the other, and each wished to load that clearing in a manner producing what each desired from the relationship. Certainly the objective was not contrary to the public good. Each was fully entitled to her pursuit, and due process would protect their liberties in this space against nuisance and trespass.

So we have for Mrs. Carter a cause - a liberty and an infringement of liberty - all obviously material. A difficulty is that it isn't trespass - Miss Reed isn't using Mrs. Carter's relationship with the mother. And it doesn't seem to be nuisance! Though Miss Reed is interfering with Mrs. Carter's pursuit, it only occurs when Mrs. Carter insists on using Miss Reed's home without her permission - when Mrs. Carter is trespassing! This is the exact setting for a decision in equity. Two pursuits, both parties entitled, and each intent on invading the space of the other. So in whose property are they operating? This is equity's territory.

What does equity look at? What does she weigh? What but climates of mind and effectiveness lives. Which climate of mind, Mrs. Carter's or Miss Reed's, enhances the common good; one using property to strengthen human bonds, and one using property to build a wall between humans? True, an effectiveness life will be wounded upon any decision the court might make, but if the effectiveness life is invested in a paltry pursuit, hopefully it will rise again invested in more productive pursuits. It is a black and white decision.

If Mrs. Carter was using her visits to harm Miss Reed's relationships with the mother, Miss Reed would have an effective counter-complaint, but the issue was not raised. Nor did the court examine Miss Reed's motives for her actions. Obviously she wished to use her title in her house as a weapon to separate two women. In appealing, she was trying to use equity as a subject, a device in a project unfriendly to the public good. The court became quite frank: Mrs. Carter has the right to visit her mother without molestation "as long as her mother desires to see her... and, under the facts of this case, it is a right which a court of equity ought to and will protect...."

In this decision, the government said by implication, "I hereby put an entitled loading under servitude, when it is being used to interfere with an entitled pursuit in social relations. This," said the government, "is law."

The factor of entrapment must not be neglected. In many cases similar to **Carter v. Reed** the situation could be solved without court intervention. Let the daughter meet the mother at the front door and take her to a more congenial atmosphere for the visit. But in **Carter v. Reed** we are talking about a mother more than ninety years old. Without this factor, the court would not have taken jurisdiction. It would not have heard the case. Entrapment must be part of a cause. There must be no other way for the plaintiff to find relief. A complaint must state it. A judge must be able to conclude its materiality.

It will be instructive to analyze **Carter v. Reed** under the general format of injury.

1. Is Mrs. Carter being frustrated in her pursuit by Miss Reed, and is she entitled to this pursuit. (Answer: Yes.)

2. Are the elements of the pursuit material? (Answer: Yes.)

3. Are the elements of the frustration material? (Answer: Yes.)

4. Is there entrapment? (Plaintiff can find no relief without court action.) (Answer: Yes.)

5. Is Mrs. Carter's pursuit under a servitude to an entitled pursuit of Miss Reed? (Answer: Well, Miss Reed claims that her title in her house masters Mrs. Carter's pursuit in personal relations.)

As you see, it is nuisance, except that Miss Reed's counterclaim forms an issue that throws the action into equity. The issue is joined - right against right. Once settled in equity, similar cases should not have to go back. They are subject to the jurisdiction of law. The property line has been established. "I hereby put an entitled loading under servitude when it is being used to interfere with an entitled pursuit in social relations. "This," said the government, "is law." When a pursuit in personal relations requires the use of a particular house (one of the participants being confined to the house) the other participant may use the house as the pursuit requires. The loadings are defined by the objective. Servitus civiliter exercanda est. A servitude is exercised with as little inconvenience as possible.

But a strange thing has happened. In **Carter v. Reed**, a title of using the house was granted to Mrs. Carter though it was not taken from Miss Reed. As a result, a small section of Miss Reed's total project space became a project space in which they were tenants in common. Mrs. Carter's title, it is true, was strictly limited, but to interfere with her pursuit in this space was injury. Mrs. Carter was in her space, and Miss Reed, as far as the house was concerned, was in her space. But Miss Reed's actions in bothering the other women were beyond her liberty. They constituted nuisance.

I come to a point over which I have vacillated in my own mind. Has the common law completely abandoned the device of servitude, and can it be done without leaving a gaping hole in the system of property. Is it possible to take away title instead of imposing a servitude. In "Hunting Club v. Brown" it seemed not to be possible. Not a bit of Brown's potato growing title was handed over to the hunters. It was put under servitude.

Is it possible, given the concept of nuisance, to say: You do not have title to any pursuit that interferes with an entitled pursuit of another. The entitled spaces of others mark the boundaries of yours. Or more accurately: You have liberty in all pursuits within your entitled space, and your entitled space does not include any pursuit that infringes the liberty of others. I am sorry. My mind is not this fluid. I must say, Here is your entitled space, and you will be wise to restrain yourself in any action, even within your entitled space, that might have the result of infringing the liberty of another.

If government said to Brown, "You do not have title to grow potatoes on the meadow if it will hurt the project effectiveness of the fox-hunters," and if government did not give this title to anyone else, we would see a property without an owner - the potato growing property of the meadow during the period of the lease - and this cannot occur under the common law. Under the common law, every property - every project space - must have an owner. I do not see how the device of servitude can be abandoned without puncturing the continuous fabric of property.

Carter v. Reed has its peculiarities. Miss Reed's original tactic was to pester Mrs. Carter, and the injury was nuisance. But in her appeal we detect a change in her tactics, and we can see it in her counter-complaint. How can it be nuisance, she asks, if Mrs. Carter is trespassing in my house. She is asking the court to exclude Mrs. Carter from her house. Belatedly she has thought, "Why did I pester her? Why didn't I simply refuse to let her in the house?" What is Mrs. Carter's cause in this view of the case?

In a way it is deprivation, like the prankster on the tennis court running away with the balls. It would be putting a barrier or a large distance between the pursuer and the subject of her pursuit, reducing the pursuer's effectiveness in her project to zero. Though it is a different mechanism than pestering, it is still a distortion of project space. Still nuisance. And it gives us an interesting insight into the nature of deprivation - theft. Fundamentally theft is nuisance.

The court has stated a principle. An entitled liberty cannot be used to defeat a pursuit in personal relations. What a powerful statement, and we may appropriately ask how generally applicable this cause is. Does it apply to all pursuits in personal relations, or only the more intimate ones. For example, does Miss Reed have to open her house to an insurance agent who wishes to interest her mother in an insurance policy? I think the answer is yes, under the conditions (1) the elderly woman consents to his visit and (2) his pursuit is honorable.

We have, of course, in a mother-daughter relationship a more highly dimensional pursuit than a commercial conference or a social call. But while one might argue that the visit of a salesman is purely self-centered on his part, not as highly favored in equity as the daughter's visit, one could also argue that excluding the salesman or the social caller would deprive the elderly woman of relationships she might like to pursue. But how one-sided can a relationship be and still win the court's favor? The answer is worth pursuing.

Suppose the mother is indifferent to the daughter, not that she refuses to see the daughter; she willingly consents. We say merely that she does not demand to see the daughter. However the daughter appears to have a genuine desire to be in the presence of the mother from time to time. In such a case, can the court give the daughter a property in the house? Do the Miss Reeds of the world have to admit her?

Does such a situation reflect a true personal relationship. Is the daughter trying to establish a clearing in the mother's mind? Is she trying to use a clearing already established? We must admit a clearing. Though it is true that we do not see in the mother's mind a battery of run buttons and computer programs with an output of obvious affection, we also do not see "No, I refuse to see her." In between these extremes there apparently is a material clearing at least of toleration and condescension.

What is the daughter's pursuit, then? It is to use this tolerance of the mother as an opportunity to bathe in the maternal sunshine, perhaps to feed a fantasy of love and affection that exists only in her own mind. Can we call this a personal relationship? Is it worthy of the name? Is it really material? Would we not be more realistic to see it as a purely self-centered pursuit, unworthy of equity's attention?

First, if the pursuit works - if it satisfies the daughter - it is material. An analysis of abstruse materiality will be made in the group of chapters generally entitled "Delusion". But how self-centered can a pursuit in personal relationships be, and still be given the weight of a personal relationship in law and equity? Well, this is the strange thing about personal relations. It would be difficult to call an insurance salesman's call other than self-centered, though if he is a conscientious person he will serve the client's interests as well. Go further. - All pursuits in sociality are self-centered. If a person derives nothing from a purely social pursuit, she will abandon it. Even marital pursuits, even when true love is present, have their quotas of self-interest in both partners.

When it comes down to it, this is what personal relations are all about, even intimate relationships. They are pursuits using the tolerance or response of another to fill our own needs. In this regard, they are no different than commercial pursuits, except that money is not the medium of exchange. A personal relationship of any kind is evidence of a pursuit of some kind. It means much to the pursuer; her effectiveness life is at stake. And, as the evidence is beginning to show, the government goes to great lengths to protect the pursuit, giving it great liberty.

We have arrived at the bridge between the law of personal relationships and that forum known popularly as civil rights. At the brink of personal relationships, I place **Carter v. Reed.** At the edge of civil rights I place **Jones v. Alfred H. Mayer Company.** I position it there not because it is peripheral or the easiest case in civil rights. I place it there because it is pivotal. The Supreme Court opinion in **Jones** is impertinent. The reviews of the case though brilliant, and coming so close to finding a sound basis for the decision, leave much to be desired. They fail to generate conviction.

Though I place **Carter v. Reed** on the near brink, it is but one of many cases that illustrate the point. As I will show, civil rights finds its attachment to the whole body of common law through the cord of personal relations. Civil rights - the civil rights of the civil rights movements - are no other rights than rights of personal relationships.

Not all public issues classed as civil rights are civil rights issues. The issue of abortion does not come under the topic of personal relations, and it is not a civil rights issue. The same is true of sexual harassment. Such issues have nothing to do with class.

In **Carter v. Reed** the court gave a property in a house to a person who did not hold the deed. In "Farmer Brown v. Sheila Rienzi" a court granted a property in land to a pursuer who didn't hold the deed; it liked the looks of the pursuit. In **Jones v. Alfred H. Mayer Company,** a court gave Jones, a black person, the ownership of a house (Jones of course had to pay the full price) appropriating the title of the house from the Mayer Company by sheer presence of force. In searching for grounds, we will have to find for Jones a pursuit in which he had full liberty, a liberty being infringed by the refusal of the company to do business with him. The case is resolved in the next chapter.

CHAPTER 33

THE TRUE CAUSE IN JONES AND IN CIVIL RIGHTS

We have come a very long way. A person not reading the book to this point will not comprehend the contents of this chapter or any succeeding. The words property, liberty, freedom, projects, injury, damage are now loaded with meanings long neglected. The phrases climate of mind and effectiveness lives are strangers to the legal vocabulary. They have no run buttons and computer programs in the public mind, trained in the law or not, yet we can now visualize them at the foundation of the common law. The term Equity has taken on new dimensions. And the pristine importance to government of a pursuit in personal relationships is beyond ordinary comprehension. It must be viewed from the vantage point of a keen and penetrating intellect housed in power.

We are looking at **Jones.** We are wondering the grounds on which the government can take away the Mayer Company's title to dispose its own house as it wishes, and order the company to sell the house to Jones. Since the universal cause in any case is injury, infringement of liberty, with the subclasses trespass and nuisance, one looks first for the liberty being infringed. In trespass, the trespasser makes a direct loading, intentionally, on a subject in the property of the complainant. He uses the subject. In nuisance, the nuisancer makes a loading, intentional or not, in a space perhaps not the complainant's but having repercussions in the complainant's space. But the nuisancer has no wish to use the complainant's space.

In either case a liberty of the complainant is infringed. In either case the project space of the complainant is altered without the complainant's permission. A subject is altered, or the relations between subjects, or the functional relations between the complainant and the subjects in her space. In trespass, the liberty infringed is the liberty of deciding who will have the use of subjects in the complainant's entitled space. The trespasser uses something in the space without the complainant's permission. In nuisance the liberty infringed is the liberty of the complainant to enjoy her space unaltered, free of distortions caused by people operating outside her space. If the air coming through her window would be fresh and clean were it not for the emissions of a cement factory, a court will order the factory people to clean up the emissions. In **Jones** the court must find a project space for **Jones,** a space to which he is entitled, a space being altered by the refusal of the Mayer Company to sell him a house because he is black. That is, the court must find it if the court wishes to clamp jurisdiction on the company and find an appropriate relief for Jones under due process.

Can we propose for example that Jones's project was to settle his family in a better neighborhood? Would the government favor this pursuit over the time-honored title of disposal? Is it clear that a white neighborhood is the best neighborhood for rearing a black child? Is it clear that a high class neighborhood is more suitable for a family than a low class neighborhood? Are these material functions, or are they figments of the imagination? More important, such a pursuit may represent an idealism not generally accepted by rulers, even holonistic rulers. A ruler almost by definition does not try to escape reality. She does not seek an ivory-tower society for herself. She takes society, human nature, as she finds it and adapts herself and her projects to this grand pursuit space as it exists in reality. No. A ruler might be tempted to honor a pursuer living in an exemplary manner in a low class neighborhood, a jewel in that setting. But a project of moving to a "better neighborhood" has a voice too tiny, in my estimation, for rulerly ears.

Karst in a sensible review suggests that the black person wants a sense of community. Certainly every intelligent ruler wishes this for his people. The sense of community argument, not necessarily tied with racial bias, has been used in attacking educational policy, the policy of placing students in slow or fast sections on the basis of testing. A student has been quoted as saying:

"... but after the tests, there shouldn't be no separation in the classes. ... I felt good when I was with my class, but when they went and separated us - that changed us.

"... You have been from elementary to junior high, you feel great inside. ... You get this shirt that says Brown Junior High... and you are proud of that shirt. But then... the teacher says - "Well, so and so, your're in the basic section, you can't go with the other kids." The devil with the whole thing - you lose - something in you - like it just goes out of you." (Levine).

Yet, though we feel the pain in this statement, and though we would be foolish not to recognize the importance of a sense of community, we have to look for something in a different dimension if we wish a cause in a class oppression case. Let me explain. A sense of community is one of those mysterious spirits like the effectiveness life. It is a most real mental configuration of atoms, but it is result only. Like a sense of effectiveness, a sense of community is never the objective of a pursuit as far as the pursuer is concerned. One never says, "I'm going to join the Civic Club because I want a sense of community." One says, "I'm going to join because I want to learn things and I want to make friends." It might happen that from this activity a sense of community will arise. It depends on how you react to the people and how they react to you.

As a consequence of this characteristic, a government cannot give title to the effectiveness life or to a sense of community. The government gives title to project spaces, pursuit spaces. The objectives must be related directly, functionally, materially to the loadings, not remotely and ultimately. For example, the government gives you no right to make a profit. Given a space of commercial properties, the government will protect your liberties in that space. It will eliminate injurious interferences to your loadings; it will evict trespassers like the Edison Polyform Mfg. Co. If your loadings within this sphere of protection are adapted to profitability, a profit will result. But the government never says to person A, "You must allow person B to make a profit."

The government seems to be engaged in programs to enhance worthy effectiveness lives and senses of community. But since such developments are secondary phenomena, government strategy is to favor and protect project spaces and pursuits from which such spirits arise. Therefore in **Jones** we look for the pursuit or the project space that the Mayer Company is frustrating or distorting, and it is really quite obvious.

Jones wishes to establish certain clearings in the minds of people with whom he mixes in his range of life. He wishes to instill in their minds a Jones run button, and he wishes the associated mental computer programs to reflect his own personal input. He wishes that it not reflect a biased alien input. In short, he wishes the freedom to pursue personal relationships in the community; his guaranteed liberty under the common law.

When a housing developer says - "No, you can't buy a house in my tract. You're black" - he is defaming Jones. He is saying that something is wrong with Jones. He is propagating, without being specific, a statement that Jones, being black, is not a suitable person to have in a neighborhood. He is interfering with Jones's pursuit in personal relations. In making this statement, is he using something belonging to Jones? No; it is not a case of trespass. It is nuisance. He is operating in his entitled space, but his noises are despoiling Jones's pursuit in Jones's space of liberty. What are the mechanics of the injury? The Mayer Company is carrying on its own mental induction program. It is preconditioning people against Jones. By its anti-black policy it is saying, "By his skin color you will know him. It is the clue there is something bad about him."

As a result, the taxitants will not react to Jones's loadings in a manner related to his loadings. They will react to BLACK. Everything that Jones might do will be blotted out by BLACK. In short, Mayer is busy converting the commons, you remember the commons - a subject to which Jones is entitled. We have a case of injury through distortion. Nuisance.

You do not have to take it to equity; the principle is already established. The government will put an entitled loading under servitude when it is being used to interfere with a pursuit in personal relations. Many precedents. Including **Carter v. Reed.**

Take it to equity if you wish. The Mayer Company is trying to use its title, government's greatest gift, to block a pursuit in personal relations. If its attempt should succeed, that use of government grant of title can only destroy effectiveness lives, or generate uncreative or destructive climates of mind. Where lies the common good, the good for Mayer as well as Jones? Does it make a difference that we are looking at community relations rather than mother-daughter relations such as in **Carter v. Reed**? Will the common law go so far as to protect pursuits in community relations?

Melvin v. Reid was a unanimous decision by a California District Court of Appeals. The year was 1931. The appeals court favored Melvin, reversing the lower court's decision. The case was succinctly recounted by Judge Marks:

"It is alleged that appellant's maiden name was Gabrielle Darley; that a number of years ago she was a prostitute and was tried for murder, the trial resulting in her acquittal; that during the year 1918, and after her acquittal, she abandoned her life of shame and became entirely rehabilitated; that during the year 1919 she married Bernard Melvin and commenced the duties of caring for their home, and thereafter at all times lived an exemplary, virtuous, honorable, and righteous life; that she assumed a place in respectable society, and made many friends who were not aware of the incidents of her earlier life; that during the month of July, 1925, the defendants, without her permission, knowledge, or consent, made, photographed, produced, and released a moving picture film entitled "The Red Kimono" and thereafter exhibited it in moving picture houses in California, Arizona, and throughout many other states; that this moving picture was based upon the true story of the past life of appellant, and that her maiden name, Gabrielle Darley, was used therein; that defendants featured and advertised that the plot of the film was the true story of the unsavory incidents in the life of appellant; that Gabrielle Darley was the true name of the principal character; and that Gabrielle Darley was appellant; that by the production and showing of the picture, friends of appellant learned for the first time of the unsavory incidents of her early life. This caused them to scorn and abandon her, and exposed her to obloquy, contempt, and ridicule, causing her grievous mental and physical suffering in the sum of $50,000. These allegations were set forth in the first cause of action. It will not be necessary to detail the other three causes of action which are based upon the invasion of a supposed property right."

Really it will be instructive to learn the three complaints the court did not heed. The first was right of privacy, and privacy did not exist in the case. The unsavory portions of her life had been brought out at the murder trial and were a matter of public record. The other unheeded complaints were invasions of her right first to the use of her name, and second to the use of her life story. The court saw no literary properties in either.

Now look hard at what is at stake. It is the freedom of the press! All that Dorothy Reid and the other defendants intended was to produce a dramatized version of the facts. Defamation was not involved. Certainly the producers were entitled to publish the facts. Or were they?

The $50,000 of course had no relation to the demolition of Mrs. Melvin's social effectiveness. In no way could it be an equivalent. If damages was warranted, justification lay in its training value for movie producers and the media in general. How does it learn to be deprived of project effectiveness? Learn first hand, my dears, what it means to induce damage in the realm! But damage did not exist unless the harm was accompanied by injury - unless liberty had been infringed. What did the court say about it?

"Section 1 of article 1 of the Constitution of California provides as follows: "All men are by nature free and independent, and have certain inalienable rights, among which are those of enjoying and defending life and liberty; acquiring, possessing, and protecting property; and pursuing and obtaining safety and happiness.
"The right to pursue and obtain happiness is guaranteed to all by the fundamental law of our state. This right by its very nature includes the right to live free from the unwarranted attack of others upon one's liberty, property, and reputation. Any person living a life of rectitude has that right to happiness which includes a freedom from unnecessary attacks on his character, social standing, or reputation."

So far, except for stating the right of reputation - personal relationship - the opinion of the court has accumulated to zero. Every statement can be applied equally effectively to support the defendants. They too have a right to liberty, to acquire and possess property, and to "obtain" happiness. Moreover they have a constitutional protection under the first amendment to the federal Constitution - the freedom of the press. But this court has a marvelous sense of direction, and begins to look at pursuits and climates of mind.

"The use of appellant's true name in connection with the incidents of her former life was unnecessary and indelicate, and a wilful and wanton disregard of that charity which should actuate us in our social discourse, and which should keep us from unnecessarily holding another up to the scorn and contempt of upright members of society.

"... This change having occurred in her life, she should have been permitted to continue its course without having her reputation and social standing destroyed by the publication of the story of her former depravity with no other excuse that the expectation of private gain by the publishers."

There might be a difficulty. In **Stark v. Hamilton,** I said that Hamilton's family reputation could not be protected from the effects of the daughter's waywardness. The family members would have to live with reality, and make their own reputations. So is this not true also for Mrs. Melvin? Has she not been living in fantasyland; living a lie? Would it not have been better for her to have built a brick house from the first, admitting her past mistakes to the society she wished to join? The basic question is, is the biographical life representative of reality? And the answer is no. A seasoned investor knows that you cannot gauge a corporation's future performance by its past performance. There is no law saying that a person must tell all her past secrets to her community, and the question in court is materiality, not wisdom.

Mrs. Melvin used her own judgment, and apparently correctly anticipated the reaction of the ladies whom she wished to cultivate, for this was the way they ultimately reacted. She established a favorable clearing in their minds, and it was not for fraudulent purposes. The court does not ask whether she should have cultivated a more down-to-earth group of acquaintances, for this is no business of the court. She was acting within her liberty.

What we have in this case is **Palsgraf** repeated. We have a train conductor operating within his own entitled space - pursuing a project without bothering to consider the risks. Once again we see the world of loaded pistols and itching triggers. Quoting from Chapter 16, "Open your eyes to the harm-causing sequences that surround you. A reckless action may contribute a missing element to an otherwise complete harmful chain of reactions. Direct your actions. Know where your next step will fall if it's to be a safe step. Make sure it falls there." This is the message of damages.

"If you act voluntarily, and if your act contributes an essential element to a causal sequence, you will be held responsible for the consequences. If a consequence of your act perpetrates injury, and if the person whose liberty is thus infringed is harmed as a result of your act, I'll pronounce damage, and I will assess damages against you." This is the voice of due process.

In **Palsgraf** the vulnerable thing was Helen Palsgraf's body and mind. In **Melvin v. Reid**, it was the run button computer program that Gabrielle Darley Melvin had created in her community of minds. It was strong enough as to her present efforts and character, fragile only as to the associations that people might make with her past. The past was immaterial except that people have a way of making these associations; these are real enough. So we are looking at real harm-causing sequences.

The act of the movie producers was more reprehensible than the act of the trainmen. The potential for harm was not hidden in the least, and the fact that they released the film in many states before a general audience reveals that the use of Mrs. Melvin's name was not necessary for financial success. Mrs. Melvin was known only locally. To gain wide attendance, the story and the production itself would have to attract the audience. The libretto, "This is a true story, and the true names have been concealed to protect the present standing of the people in their communities," would have sufficed to satisfy a general audience, and a short statement in completing the drama, noting that the central character later became a model of propriety, would have added a thrill to the story.

If the producers were insensitive to the importance of social relationships; if they didn't have the common decency to discuss the situation confidentially with Mrs. Melvin, the government made certain they had an opportunity to learn. How apt were Judge Mark's words: "The use of the appellant's name... was unnecessary and indelicate, and a wilful and wanton disregard of that charity which should actuate us in our social intercourse." The only inappropriate allusion was his invocation of charity. Due process limits its grounds to, "If you act voluntarily and perpetrate damage, I will assess damages."

For note: though the case might be resolved under equitable principles, climate of mind is not a necessary factor in a **Melvin v. Reid** type of case. This is not a proper case for equity. It is a case of pure nuisance, an automatic decision once the mechanics of injury have been determined. Interference was not mutual. Dorothy Reid's pursuit mutilated Mrs. Melvin's personal relations project space. But Mrs. Melvin's pursuit in personal relationships had no influence upon Dorothy Reid's pursuit. The court's message to the communication media was loud and clear. "Yes, you have title to publish the facts. But title is not property and if in the course of your entitled pursuit you injure another, you have strayed beyond your property lines. You would have been wise to restrain yourself.

We are not far from the **Jones** decision. Protecting a mother-daughter relationship sufficed as grounds for giving Mrs. Carter a property in Miss Reed's home. Protecting pursuits in social relationships provided grounds for subserviating the press's entitled freedom. A comparison of **Jones** with such cases, observing climates of mind and investments of effectiveness lives, clearly provides cause to clear the way for Jones's pursuit in community relationships.

The nature of the remedy in Jones, is like frosting on a grand cake of theory. Why not assess damages? Hasn't the Mayer Company defamed Jones? Well, damages will not relieve Jones's complaint, and there is a remedy that will. The Mayer Company has stated its policy of not selling to blacks. In so acting it has transformed an all-white settlement into an implied statement. Given Mayer's statement of its policy, an all-white settlement on the Mayer tract declares, "Blacks make undesirable neighbors." But I can be more precise. Given the Jones case, a settlement without Jones declares, "Jones is an undesirable neighbor."! And it would keep repeating this, like a statement published in a book, no matter how high the damages a court might award.

The Mayer Company has trapped itself into this position, and the court will not be caught in the same trap. There is but one remedy. Let Jones pay the money for the house. Order the Mayer Company to sign the deed over to Jones. Only in this way will Mayer's injurious project be halted, the statement erased from the book. This is not a new mode of remedy. We will see it again in eighteenth century British chancery.

Having seen the bridge from personal relationships to class oppression situations, the foundations and supports should be thoroughly inspected for soundness. Suppose the Mayer tract already houses many whites not wishing to fraternize with Jones. Does Jones want to pursue social relationships with biased, hostile people? Indeed, having put Jones in the neighborhood, the government cannot compel his neighbors to accept him socially. Under these circumstance, should the government bother to protect his freedom in this unlikely project space?

It is the old question. Should the government keep Willie out of Mrs. Abercrombie's apple tree, if she herself cannot climb it? Should it protect Will Morris's pursuit in personal relations if the outlook is dim? Should it give up the criminal system obviously doomed to eternal failure?

Due process does not ask such questions. It asks, "Is there a property. Is there an infringement of liberty? Is there a mutual interference of entitled pursuits? If so, what can I discover in the way of climates of mind and investments of effectiveness lives? If relief is appropriate, what is the remedy?" Courts relieve infringement and determine equivalents. Other than that they do not try to solve the plaintiff's own personal loading problems in his legal freedom space.

Jones's proper cause was nuisance; distortion of an entitled loading space. The remedy was to remove the interfering loadings from the defendant's liberty. This is the solution of all class related issues - civil rights issues. If they are properly in court, the cause is defamation; nuisance, with distortion of an entitled project space. This is consistent with an eminently monumental commentary (Buchanan) upon the **Jones** decision, an analysis attempting to define the badge of slavery, trying to make of this phrase a solid support for **Jones**. "A person commits an act motivated by arbitrary prejudice when he determines a person's fitness for a particular function primarily upon factors that have no rational bearing upon such person's ability to discharge the function sought." This is a mouthful, but entirely satisfying. However, you see it has no need for the thirteenth amendment or the badge of slavery. In and of itself it states the basic elements of defamation. It states the circumstances of infringement. It describes a reckless act that disregards both facts and consequences.

Justice Bradley was right in the Civil Rights Cases. The exclusion of blacks from places of public accomodation is not slavery. Black people, he said, have the same standing in law and equity as anyone else. If they have been injured, let them seek redress in the courts of their states.

There was a major difficulty in this suggestion; the blacks couldn't afford to seek redress by civil action. There happens to be a very practical reason for using a civil rights act as grounds for suit. The plaintiff will be represented by a government lawyer, and need make no investment in the venture. A civil suit seeking injunction without seeking damages has no attraction for a practicing attorney, unless the plaintiff can afford to pay his fee.

Under current rules of practice, a pure case in equity involves only injury, not damage, and this would hold for the typical class oppression case. Here then is a real limitation to liberty. No money, no liberty. The rule, I believe, is wrong.

My first argument is directed not at the rule but at its consequences - the civil rights acts themselves. They have made legalistic monkeys of our jurists. Their antics in attempting to apply the civil rights acts would be comic were it not for the tragic results. One mourns not only for the supposed beneficiaries, the unrelieved oppressed, but for the credibility of our whole legal system. Examples: two outrageous cases - **Heart of Atlanta Motel, Inc. v. U.S.** (1964) and its sequel **Katzenbach v. McClung.** In **Heart of Atlanta**, the motel had a habit of denying lodging to blacks and, in **Katzenbach,** restauranteur Katzenbach was excluding blacks from his restaurant. The suits won injunctions forbidding the discriminatory practices. This was four years before **Jones**. So the U.S. attorneys had finally broken the back of the **Civil Rights Cases.** How they must have slapped each other triumphantly on the back.

It was a dark day for the black cause as a just cause. It was a low point in American jurisprudence.

In the **Civil Rights Cases**, the blacks' rights to public accomodation were sought on grounds of the 1875 Civil Rights Act, and the act was declared unconstitutional. Specifically it was not supported by the thirteenth and fourteenth amendments. The newer Civil Rights Act of 1964 tried to patch up the defects but, as in the old **Civil Rights Cases**, the appellant in **Heart of Atlanta** challenged the constitutionality of the new act. Once again we see justices and lawyers blind to the presence of real human beings in the court room. Their entire attention was centered not on effectiveness lives and climates of mind but on the question of constitutionality. Believe it or not, the United States attorneys defended the Civil Rights Act of 1964 on grounds of the **commerce** clause of the constitution. The commerce clause is provided in section 8 of Article I, and states: "The Congress shall have power... (2) to regulate Commerce... among the several States....".

Their reasoning? - If the motel denied lodging to negroes, it interfered with interstate commerce! The practice discouraged negroes from traveling! What facts did they present? - Statistics of interstate travel! They won the case!

In the wake of **Heart of Atlanta,** McClung brought his case against Katzenbach; a matter of restaurant accomodation. In the instance of restaurants, it was not easy to find statistics on the number of interstate travelers eating in restaurants, so the attorneys used a new twist. They researched the amount of interstate trucking involved in bringing food to restaurants. They proposed that this traffic would be greater if more blacks could eat in restaurants! They won the case!

Even disregarding the speciousness of their reasoning about truck traffic, the approach brought the odor of sham and legal trickery to the High Court, and we have not heard that the justices held their collective nose. The standard of justice was in shambles. A black learning the truth of the case would be shamed. His liberty in motels and restaurants depended on its benefit to interstate commerce.

Here is the whole contribution of the civil rights acts to the black movement. Failure in the **Civil Rights Cases.** Legal legerdemain in **Heart of Atlanta** and **Katzenbach.** And badges of slavery in **Jones.** At least in the last three cases, the justices came through with good decisions, despite counterfeit grounds. But they threw away their direction finders. A pity. All along, as we now see, the black cause was an infringement of their liberty to pursue personal relations free of defamation. But now with the true cause in view, where does the money for litigation come from? It should come from damages. Damages would not have been an equivalent to relieve Jones's complaint; nevertheless damages in addition to the transfer of property, would have been appropriate.

For illustration, I call upon a remark made by the man who insisted on his amendments to the Constitution, and thereby started our constitutional difficulties. In 1784 George Mason wrote Cockburn: "I have been lately informed that some people intend to open a poll for me at the election tomorrow in this county.... I should look upon such an attempt in no other light than an oppressive and unjust invasion of my personal liberty...." Liberty, I think, is difficult to invade. Liberty is infringed, and property is invaded. However, Mason was not a lawyer, accounting perhaps for his insistence on littering the Constitution with his Bill of Rights. Nevertheless, since he evidently had reliable instincts for liberty, let us see how an infringement of his liberty could be caused by entering his name in an election without his permission.

For readers who have suffered their way through this book it is easy. Willie FitzHugh is in Mrs. Abercrombie's apple tree. The electioneers, without Mason's consent, are using Mason's run button, the one so carefully nurtured in many, many minds. The electioneers are using the mental computer programs in people's minds that print "vote for me" when they see or hear Mason's name. It is a case of trespass, pure and simple. Here is a cleverly schemed project involving a trespass extremely difficult to discern without the analysis we are learning to use.

What will Mason do if the men do not desist upon request? He should go to court and seek an injunction plus damages. Or if he can't commence action in time to stop them, he should seek damages for the deed done. Why? Because they are consuming his time; lowering his project effectiveness.

If his name is entered in the poll, he will have to explain to people how it happened. If elected he will have to explain why he chooses not to serve. The electioneers act is wilful and wanton and disregards Mason's wishes in this space of personal relations. Yet he has no need to explain all these matters in court. In trespass there is no need to give reasons why the plaintiff does not wish the trespasser on his range. The owner of the space has complete liberty in choosing the loadings in the space. But why damages?

If Mason must go to court to stop the electioneers, the very necessity of going to court reduces his project effectiveness in his preferred pursuits. Do you remember project effectiveness? Damages are an equivalent in project effectiveness. Money is a species of project effectiveness. Your project effectiveness is what you can accomplish in a stated period of time. If you wish to spade your garden and someone steals your digging stick, the thief steals some of your project effectiveness. If it normally takes three days to spade your garden with your digging stick, it will now take six days to accomplish the same objective. It will take three days merely to carve another digging stick.

Governments, for all the reasons given in the book so far, do not like dilutions of project effectiveness. If a person goes to court to curtail an infringement of her liberty, it is true that government assumes the burden of protection from that point. Nevertheless, the plaintiff must pay the attorney's fees, her time and thought are distracted from her usual pursuits, she will worry about the outcome of the suit. All these factors will diminish her project effectiveness in the pursuits more precious and valuable to her. People permitted to injure until stopped by a court, and then not slapped with damages can play havoc with their victim's project effectiveness. Malicious people will enjoy an inexpensive vicious sport. I have shown earlier that injury as well as damage is fundamentally a loss of project effectiveness. Injury is damage. The only distinguishing feature is that we tend to associate injury with an active infringement of project effectiveness. We tend to associate damage with the crystallized, irreparable loss following a destructive event. But both constitute injury if viewed in their most general aspect. And both generate damage in the common good.

Given damage, damages are assessed. This is the voice of due process. Given these points it seems to me inescapable. Damages are a basic relief in every case in which an injunction is required to curtail or prevent injury. This will give proper teeth to every suit originating in injury to personal relations, including those cases unhappily pursued under the leaky protection of the civil rights acts.

A person claiming oppression on a class basis must show:
(1) the liberty space being distorted by the activity of the defendant;
(2) that defendant has by sign, symbol, word, deed, literally or by implication, stated (a) that plaintiff is a member of class Z and (b) that members of class Z are characterized by a set T of undesirable traits and (c) that plaintiff is characterized by T;
(3) that (c) is in fact false.
(4) that the mechanics between defendants actions and the claimed distortion are material.

If this is shown, then the remedy, to be effectual, must use in substance the same language in which the statements (a) through (c) were made. In **Jones**, the language of the Mayer Company was in terms of excluding Jones from a house in the Mayer tract in accord with a stated or implied policy. The only possible remedy was to install Jones in the house. There are additional remarks to be made about this cause and remedy, but they will be expressed later under the topic of **Bakke** in Chapter 37.

This approach to the topic of class oppression eliminates the embarrassing dilemmas that have been generated by the civil rights acts. For example a woman cannot use government to force her way into a society of men, and vice versa. Any person, any group can reject the advances of any person on any basis, unless the rejection phenomenalizes as a demeaning statement about the rejected person and is as a statement untrue. A woman's music club rejecting the application of a man for membership in no way defames the man. It merely says, "We don't want men." The same would be true even if the club members were black and the man was white.

However, we are tiptoeing through the avenues of the mind, and must expect to see strange run buttons and computer programs. A white women's social group will have to be fastidious in rejecting the application of a black woman. They will have to show that she personally has traits that would disqualify a white woman as well. I am not certain, however, that the same consideration is true for a social group of black women. I suspect they can reject a white woman because she is white. For all the reasons that history supplies, such a rejection would not constitute defamation. It merely says to all concerned, "We do not want a white woman in our club." Perhaps the day will come when a white association can take the same action against a black applicant. Perhaps that will mark a true social equality of the races. Strange, isn't it.

CHAPTER 34

PSEUDO-INJURY I: USES, VIEWS, AND GAZES
FUNCTION ANALYSIS II

It is becoming clear that pursuits in personal relations have powerful claims to liberty under the common law. In **Carter v. Reed** and in **Jones** they prevailed over titles in real estate. In **Melvin v. Reid,** Mrs. Melvin's claim in personal relations prevailed even over the freedom of the press. The freedom of the press really should be re-examined with a cold eye. Somehow we have given the press a halo. Yet what is the press but human beings, and why should they not be thumped for stepping on cabbages not theirs. Well may we ask some questions. What is their pursuit in this instance? What in this particular project space are their investments of effectiveness life? In what climate of mind are they pursuing this project? Is this particular communication vital to the common good, or is it destructive? These are questions properly put to all bulls frolicking in the china shops of people's personal relations.

But claims in personal relations; so powerful that courts have learned to examine them closely. People can produce quite a theatrical performance in personal relations. Take alienation of affection suits; such a flood of them in the courts; so many of them by a husband and wife pretending to be alienated by a poor goose; and using the courts to pluck the goose. Now the courts have practically banned all alienation of affection suits. Courts dislike being deceived by sham; sham is the word used in legal terminology. Sham is a recognized defense for a defendant answering a complaint. And if she proves sham, the court will throw the case out. But in this three-chapter survey comprising a close study of materiality, I wish to cover many cases in which sham existed unintentionally. The plaintiff was under a delusion.

Mrs. Dandini desired to maintain socially the status of wife; it was delusory, and even the court became confused. Both she and the court missed the distinction between married status and a genuine pursuit in marital relations. To the marital pursuit, the court grants a wide-ranging property. To the marital status, it grants a very narrow property - merely the service of each spouse to the other for purposes of support. And now we shall start a descent into the world of delusion.

In **King v. Snedaker** the lower court issued essentially the same injunction against Miss Snedaker that issued against Warfield in **ex parte Warfield** - "Stay away from the plaintiff's spouse!" But in **King** the higher court caught a different scent in the air. Though the allegations in the two cases were similar, the cases themselves were distinguishable. In **Warfield** Vivia Morris, very friendly with Warfield, was still living at home, and her husband apparently revealed a real potential for rekindling their relationship. But in **King v. Snedaker**, Homer King was no longer at home. He was living with Miss Snedaker. And the higher court sensed that Mrs. King was not truly interested in a reconciliation. In suing, she really was trying to ward off an "imagined" threat to her financial support. On such imagined grounds, the court lacked the power to order Jessie Snedaker to stay away from Homer. Mrs. King's pleading was delusory. Homer King was no longer in his legal wife's exclusive personal relations loading space.

For that matter, going back to **Carter v. Reed,** may one ask if Mrs. Carter was really interested in maintaining relations with her mother? Or was bitter sisterly antagonism the underlying motivation? In visiting her mother, was she chiefly interested in irritating her sister? In **Melvin v. Reid** might one imagine Gabrielle Darley Melvin inwardly to be as tough as nails? To collect $50,000, she feigned humiliation. And in **Jones v. Alfred H. Mayer Company** how do we know that Jones was not a "blockbuster", a person of a minority race moving into a white neighborhood to spoil real estate values, preparing the way for others of his race to buy homes there at depressed prices. Delusion is always a possibility in a case. Sometimes intentional. Sometimes not.

On the law library shelves, we do not find case reports of trials, at least for cases tried in state courts. The case reports are at the appeal level, and the testing for delusion is not usually apparent. But we may be sure that, in the career of the case, judges and attorneys have tested the witnesses for sham and fantasy. Courts take pride in issuing their rulings not on the principles professed by the parties, but on the conformity of principle to the facts of the case.

From 1981 to 1983 in **Shields v. Gross**, a teen-age plaintiff sought a permanent injunction against the publication of two photographs. Taken of her as a child of ten, they showed her standing unclothed in a bathtub. Cuteness might have been the intended effect. In the intervening years the plaintiff had become perhaps the most widely known model in the United States. Moreover she had appeared in several motion pictures. In court she had contended that further distribution of the photographs would impair her professional image and her career. The photographer Gross, in defending himself, claimed the simplest of defenses, and his claim was true: he held title to the publication of the photos.

The complaint recalls **Melvin v. Reid**; - right of publication is not honored when it defeats a worthy pursuit in personal relations. Plaintiff testified she was now embarrassed by the nude photographs. She was more conscious of herself, her body and her friends. She did not want her friends to see the pictures. Her main audience was composed of teenagers and she felt a responsibility to serve as an example for them in their own development. But the facts did not fit her contentions.

Since the time of the photographs she had posed in the semi-nude for a book on beauty. More recently she had appeared unclothed in a movie. And the judge in the federal case stated that some of her recent roles in television ads were physically and verbally suggestive and provocative. All in all, there were no indications that she and her mother had changed their professional strategy. Apparently they intended to use the attractiveness of her bodily image as a source of funds.

It is clear that she basically wished a grant of full liberty in building an attractive program in people's minds. She wished what she wished, and she wished that the government enforce her wishes even over the entitlement of another. But this is serious business. A judge, before he can restrain a defendant in his entitled space, must see a solid connection between the plaintiff's protestations and the facts of the case. Though Miss Shields and her mother might have no wish to deceive the court, they had deluded themselves. They thought they could enjoy the benefits of two contradictory reputations at one and the same time. As we review the progress of the case through the steps of appeal, we see that Miss Shield's plea has not been sustained except in a point. The photographer Gross has been ordered not to sell publishing rights in the photographs to pornographic publications.

Suits in publication rights greatly influenced the development of common law during the nineteenth century. Some authorities even believe that suits in this field were instrumental in defining the task of equity - limiting its jurisdiction to questions of property. Moreland refers to **Gee v. Pritchard** as the decision establishing this principle. To be sure, **Gee v. Pritchard** was heard in British chancery. But to me it seems late in time (1818) to have parented such a fundamental apportionment of powers between law and equity. Nonetheless **Gee v. Pritchard** and the small select group of cases associated with it furnish a rare opportunity to obtain an elemental education in the vocabulary of property. You will have this opportunity in Chapter 41.

Sham played a large part in refining property lines in publication rights. But there is something filmy about publication to begin with. It lends itself to delusion - delusion in general, not necessarily sham. There is something about publication that places it in the twilight zone between materiality and immateriality. We saw this in analyzing the materiality of words. "Brown's Iron Tonic." "Edison." "Purple." Take even the social practice of name-dropping. It employs words calculated to push run buttons in people's minds. Once again we enter the human mind, and indeed how does one distinguish between the material and the immaterial in this domain? The discussion of delusion will cover three chapters, the purpose being to develop a science of the real and the unreal, the crisp and the flaccid, the true and the misleading.

A picture can be used as a subject for publication, and a picture is a strange thing. It is a thing-in-itself, composed of paper and pigment. It has weight. It is material. But in conveying something to the viewer, it does not convey itself, not paper and pigment. It conveys an entirely different concept. The paint daubings push run buttons in viewer's minds. Computer programs start running, and what is their output? Certainly not the paper and pigment of the picture. Not even the pattern of light waves emanating from the pattern of daubing. Rather do those programs convey an interpretation of the pattern. A concept. They convey something of the materiality of the topic of the picture, the thing whose image is called to our minds by the picture, the land itself all silty and weedy, the trees all whispery, the brook all wet. And we might ask - what is there of the material in all this, besides the paper and pigment?

Even the topic of the picture, the things themselves. Things. You remember. Concepts. Concepts that can be used. It appears that the world we live in is not the image so sacredly held in our minds, so precious to our sanity. Yet the machine of law and justice is pledged to deal only with the material. No more daring enterprise than this has ever been undertaken. For centuries now, the legal world has been engaged in discovering the verge of the material. Precisely this is what we mean by the development of the common law. Now it is time to develop the principles evidently guiding our jurists in this venture; to develop reliable tests for materiality. To do this, I have constructed a tutorial sequence of adversarial situations.

But first I wish to treat two topics whose contribution to our thinking will gradually become evident. First I will introduce the matter of publication rights, and then I will finalize a definition for that little verb "to use".

In discussing pictures and landscapes (two different sorts of things), one is not far from the topic of publication. A wonder of nature, say a natural bridge, carved from native rock by rushing stream, is frequently used as photographic subject matter and later used for publication. If a natural bridge exists on my land, and if it can be seen from the public highway, you may stand outside my fence taking as many snapshots of my bridge as you like. You may publish as many as you wish, collecting the profit and paying me not a cent. If on the other hand the bridge is visible only from a point within my fence line - if you must enter upon my land to see it - I can control what you may do in the matter of photographs and publishing. You may enter my land only on the conditions I set, and these conditions may include restraining your right to take pictures and publish them. This is a contractual agreement, and will be honored in the courts.

Now with respect to publishing rights, a thin impenetrable partition separates nature's creations from things created by human beings. If I design and produce a vase, an objet d'arte - a design not imitative but obviously my own - and if I show it to you privately, you do not thereby gain the right to make copies of the vase, displaying them to other people. You can not even make from memory a drawing of the vase and show it to others. This right of a creator to the exclusive display of her creation - its image as well - is known as common law copyright. Nor do I have to take pains to bind you to an agreement to gain such a copyright. It exists under common law, and it is legally operational in the United States as in Mother England.

But on the other hand if I place the vase in my front window for all the passing world to see, I thereby publish it and immediately lose my common law copyright. Anyone may stand on the public street, take photographs of the vase and publish them without paying me, and without my permission. Unless -

Unless I take out a copyright under the federal copyright law, a different device, with a different purpose. Here I must mention a complication, telling you that the common law copyright unfortunately was preempted in the United States by the revised federal copyright law of 1976. But there is much merit, as you will see, in preserving our mental distinction between the two forms of protection as though the common law copyright were still in force, and I will write of it in that vein.

A federal copyright invites publication. It says to the innovator, "Though you have published your creation, I will grant you for a future term the exclusive publication rights." It lures novelty from its hiding place, assuring years of profit for the creator, and providing for the public the blessings of individual initiative and inventiveness. It promotes the common good by protecting the private interest of the inventor. In this sense a federal patent is a species of copyright.

The federal statutory copyright takes effect after publication, but the common law copyright is operative only before publication. A creator wishes to hide some things from general view. An artist wishes to ponder a painting's merit for a term of years before exhibiting it to the public. A letter writer wishes her communication seen by one and only one pair of eyes. Yet there are others - not the creator - privileged in having seen the creation, who foresee a benefit - selfish or humanitarian - in showing the thing to the public.

To prevent publication contrary to the wishes of the creator, the common law copyright was formulated. Yet it advances no principle not already implicit in the common law. It simply reiterates the principle that the owner of a thing has the exclusive use of the thing. You make a fishing pole of material belonging to you and the fishing pole is yours. You can use it as you please in any legitimate pursuit, and no one else is entitled to use it without your permission. The enjoyment of an object of art, the viewing or audition of a composition of any nature, is a use of the thing.

An original lecture, a writing, a sculpture delivered or shown to a privileged few is presumed not published - not given to people generally for their use. This indeed is the essence of privacy - exclusive title of use. And here one sees the basic idea of publication; it is an indiscriminate, unconditional license to use. And in this we see the end of privacy; the evaporation of exclusive title. There is nothing special in these topics of potential conflict. They all fall under the stalwart principles of due process.

Use. Use. Title of use. I wish to use someone's clever remark in a newspaper article. Is this a valid use of "to use"? How can the definition of use be extended to its most general application? A way to discern the verge of materiality is to discover the limits of the word use. For if you can use a concept, it is a thing. And the difference between a thing and a non-thing is the difference between the material and the immaterial.

I have said that to use something is to associate it functionally with a pursuit. This is a true statement, and truly general. But it is absolutely meaningless unless we know what we mean by functional association. This phrase gives a mystic air to the idea of use, and this is not all bad. As I earlier suggested, "to use" partakes of the magical. In using things we engage phenomena that we will never fully comprehend.

We can with skill use a hammer, driving a nail into a board. We can in scientific terms describe how a properly swung hammer drives a nail into a board. But we will never completely understand the magic of the happening. I have also suggested that a use requires an action on our part, and suddenly I find this too narrow a notion. That we act upon a thing and it responds indeed describes some of our uses, and this notion covers more applications that we credit it with. Most of us, for example, do not realize that to jump up in the air, we must push down on the ground. And if the ground does not resist our downward thrust, we will not go up. A great jumper will confirm it and add another bit of information. He will tell you that, under his downward thrust, the ground yields momentarily and then springs back. And it is this resurgence of the ground and his skilled use of it that generates those extra inches needed for a new world record. He acts upon the ground, and it gives him his wish.

One even learns to use things in her personal relations - things not usually considered as things. She prints a succession of suitable words, and they produce favorable impressions in people's minds. She uses the words, and she uses the minds. She acts upon the mind through the words, and it responds. But really this doesn't accurately describe the use of words, does it. When we say we use words, we mean we print them or enunciate them, yet we do not expect the words themselves to respond, do we. Clearly our printing or speaking them has an effect. "Go team go," might work wonders. We are speaking of real phenomena. So there must be a functional association between our printing (or speaking) certain words and the way people's minds operate. We are dealing with a valid use of the word use.

But we commonly use "use" with even greater abandon. There are instances in which we use things - at least we say we use them - yet we initiate no action upon them. Example: "I use the sun to warm me." Yet we exert no action upon the sun, and it certainly has no response to our "use" of it. To show that this is a correct use of use, I will jump into an even more abstruse example. For remember, I am trying to find the division line between the material and the immaterial.

Suppose I wish to meditate, and, in preparing myself for entering that state, I will play soft music on my record player. I will lie on my bed and stare at a vacant area of the ceiling. I will project on that space a mental image of a huge ruby, concentrating on this vision and wilfully eliminating all distractions. I meditate.

One wonders. Would it be correct to say I "use" the music to help me into the meditative state? I "use" the ceiling? Can I "use" my mind to project the image of the ruby? And finally, can I "use" the image itself - a mental image - a mental vision projected into thin air? Note. If we can say we use a mental image, the image is a thing! At least it is if we hold to my definition of a thing (and if the definition is reliable). And note also, in "using" these concepts - music, ceiling, mental image - I am not exerting an action upon them. Nor will they respond to my use.

I will take the fateful step, calling these uses uses, on the basis of the following statement: IF the soft music, the vacant ceiling, my mental ruby are conducive to my objective - a state of meditation - I will say that I am indeed using them. I am talking (observe) about interactions. Yet no action is apparent. Nevertheless the soft music is interacting with something; the projected ruby is interacting with something; and the result is meditation. We do not understand how it works, but it works. And how does one know it works? The answer lies in the idea of functional association.

If I play the soft music and project the ruby, I enter the state of meditation. And if I don't, I don't. Here is the general concept of use - functional association.

In the following examples the symbol ----> means "and we observe that".

Examples:

```
              I don't                    the nail
A.  Form 1:  swing           ---->       remains separate
              the hammer                 from the board

    Form 2:  I swing the hammer ----> the nail pierces the board


B.  Form 1:  I don't play                I remain
              soft music or    ---->      fully aware of
              project the ruby            my surroundings

    Form 2:  I play soft music           I enter a
              and project     ---->       different state
              the ruby                    of awareness


C.  Form 1:  I lie under the   ----> I get chilly.
              beach umbrella

    Form 2:  I do not lie under ----> I get the opposite
              the beach umbrella         of chilly
```

Examples A, B, C illustrate minimum statements of functions. Minimally a function notes two distinctive conditions in each of two distinguishable things. A particular condition in one of the things is associated with a particular condition in the other thing. This is a form of the function. And a function minimally has two forms.

But while this defines a functional association, it does not quite define a use. To satisfy the idea of use, we must add the operation of will - human will, especially if we are working in the universe of legality. Using the term use requires the idea of decision on my part, a manifestation that I have phenomenally elected one of the forms of the function. I have chosen a particular state of the **promotive** variable (the left side of one of the forms), hoping to obtain a particular state of the **dependent** variable (the right side of the same form).

In the chapter after next, I will delve much more deeply into functions, and I anticipate it now by mentioning the word Omega.

Omega is the thing desired by a living creature. It is the objective of its pursuit. Perhaps warmth is the Omega of a dog lying in the sun. But we can never be sure of ultimate Omega; we do not know why a dog wants warmth; and Omega is a slippery thing unless we are very specific.

A dog might want the warmth of the sun but can't get out of the house, and develops an intermediate Omega - an open door. He engages an intermediate pursuit - barking - as a means of getting an open door.

No open door if he doesn't bark. So he uses his bark to get his Omega, intermediate Omega, then ultimate Omega. So we have our definition of use. To use something is to associate it functionally with an Omega. Less exotically, to use something means to associate it functionally with a pursuit.

I wish to devote the remainder of the chapter to a case lying just beyond the verge of the material. Before getting into it, a brief introduction of a case sufficiently material, a case I will thoroughly analyze in the following chapter. Perhaps you remember Andrew Wolcott. He built his three hundred thousand dollar home on a knoll overlooking a valley; mountain beyond. No sooner built than his view was distorted. The world's largest billboard was erected on his neighbor's land.

Wolcott desired to use his view as part of his decor. He wanted to hear his guests exclaim as they first caught sight of it. But more than anything, he himself found great pleasure in it. Arriving at his country estate, the view relaxed him as nothing else did. The view was his Omega; at least an intermediate stage of it. What are the mechanics of this use?

One understands immediately that he did not use the mountain or the valley; and his neighbor's homestead did not furnish him his pleasure. He did not touch the mountain, climb it. He did not lie on the floor of the valley or cultivate it. And he did not sit within the sweet shadows of his neighbor's barn. His view did not consist of buildings and soil and trees and rocks. It consisted of electromagnetic waves - the light waves emanating from all these things stimulated by light rays from the sun. What he enjoyed were electromagnetic waves - a particular pattern of them - impinging on the retina of his eye and stimulating a feeling of pleasure in his mind.

There is no doubt about the materiality of his view. Light rays, as any physicist will confirm, are as real as anything you can find in this world. They are generated in natural phenomena, and can generate responses in other things. The stimulation of an optical system - eye, nerve, brain - is a material happening. Their generation of pleasure (or displeasure) is a material happening. We know it is material because it is functional:

        Form 1. No view ----> No pleasure

        Form 2. View ----> Pleasure

He uses the view for his pleasure; he uses it though he impresses no effort upon it. He only turns his eyes, letting the light rays fall upon his retinas. He uses them exactly as the dog uses the sun's rays for warmth. Both heat rays and light rays are electomagnetic waves. The pleasure is a reaction to them, just as combinations of musical tones, and the pleasure they incite, are brain reactions to sound waves in the air.

You can use a thing - and your use is an act of will - though action is absent. A dog lies in the cool grass while the sun slowly mounts the sky. Finally, bathed in warmth, he opens an eye and realizes the warmth is good. His Omega has come to him without his moving a muscle. Yet his decision to stay there, though a subconscious decision, is an act of will. He is using the sun. It is difficult and perhaps impossible to distinguish decision from will, and either from use, though in a later chapter I will distinguish two levels of will. Of course if I lay in my bathing suit in the shade of a tree, sleeping, while the sun moves and finally burns me, I have not used the sun. Though the forms of the burn function are tortuously real, a use must in some way reflect the will, the decision, the pursuit, the Omega of the user.

Wolcott uses his view and with a slight change his view function is this:

Form 1: a particular pattern of   a high level of aesthetic
        electromagnetic waves   ---->   pleasure for Wolcott
                                           (his Omega)

Form 2: other patterns of   ---->   less pleasure for Wolcott
        electromagnetic waves

We can infer from the function at least two means of separating Wolcott from his Omega. One is by placing him somewhere where his view does not exist. The other is by changing the landscape. Both will change the pattern of electromagnetic waves impacting his retina. Both will change form 1 of the function to form 2, and anything he does to change form 2 to form 1 signifies he is using that particular pattern of electromagnetic waves to attain his Omega.

One more observation before momentarily leaving Wolcott's case. Though the mountain, the valley and the neighbor's homestead are not in Wolcott's entitled space, the electromagnetic waves are in his space. From the moment they enter his real estate space until they make their exit, they are his, and he may do with them whatever he wishes. This is the reason you may build a skyscraper on your land, casting your neighbor's home into eternal shadow. This creates part of the perplexity in cases like Wolcott's, and its solution will be the key to the most perplexing public issue of our day.

Having demonstrated that a view can be material and can be used, I plunge into another case of electromagnetic waves, the fictional case of Miss Engle and Mr. Weatherby. If you will recall, Miss Engle is the comely secretary who walks to work on good mornings, leaving her apartment promptly at seven forty. Across the street behind his fairly clean window, young Weatherby sits with his breakfast coffee, watching her enter the public scene. I suggested earlier that he used her to check the accuracy of his watch; but we know better. He uses her as Wolcott used his neighbor's homestead. Correction. He uses the electromagnetic waves that emanate from her. It provides for him a form of Omega.

This custom of his has been noticed by Miss Engel and she doesn't like it. She wonders if a court might order him to stop. Is it injury, she wonders? An invasion of privacy? Does it constitute nuisance?

Could it conceivably be trespass? We say he is using her. Yet that's merely an expression. We know he is really using the electromagnetic waves that stream from her face and attire. But has she a right to be squeamish? After all, has she not published herself by stepping into the public street?

Nevertheless, she doesn't think it's right. Her instinct tells her there's something wrong about it. She is a private person, and should not be subject to the gaze of people waiting for her to appear every morning. Is it sexual harassment? Certainly it is an intrusion of some sort into her private affairs.

Miss Engel, after reading this book of mine to this point, finally decides it is a case of nuisance. Weatherby is operating within his entitled space; that much is true. But his actions are interfering with a pursuit of hers to which she is entitled. "But after all," her girl friend asks, "what's so bad about it?" She gives it some thought before answering. "It's distracting. That's what it is. It disturbs my train of thought."

It comes to this, she concludes. There's lots of things I want to think about. That's a reason I walk to work. I think good when I'm walking, and his appearance in his window, looking at me, breaks my train of thought. Every morning. There ought to be a law. It's frustrating. It's a nuisance.

But can Mr. Weatherby's gaze be called material? The mechanism of injury must be material. Is his gaze like loud music? Well, it has an effect on her mind. It pushes a run button in her mind, starting a program running and scrambling all her preferred programs. If a word can be material, affecting people's minds, a gaze with a similar effect must be material. Or is it?

Though Miss Engle wishes a judge would order Weatherby never to look at her again, there are difficulties. A court cannot order Weatherby never to look through his window. So when will he look and when will he not look. How will he know when not to look, unless Miss Weatherby has appeared and he has seen her. And how will he know when he may look again, unless he watches to see when she disappears?

Moreover there are rational arguments against restraining the looking of Mr. Weatherby. If the court grants Miss Engel's wish, how many other people can get injunctions ordering Weatherby not to look at them? And why stop at poor Weatherby? Why not forbid everybody to look at anybody?

After all, though Weatherby has perhaps seen Miss Engel sixty times, there might be eyes seeing her once, and feeding a brain capable of greater mischief. As for eyes, what about ears? The blind man selling papers at the corner may eagerly listen each morning for the click of Miss Engel's heels, without disturbing her. Is the gaze of eyes more material than the attentiveness of ears?

A judge often attacks a case like this in a very direct practical manner. Instead of pondering the question of jurisdiction, he researches the conceivable remedies. "Miss Engel," he asks, "I wonder if a restraining order will solve your problem. Suppose Mr. Weatherby at his window is not looking at you when you leave your apartment house. How will you know he's not looking at you when your back is turned?"

"Well I imagine he might, your honor."

"Perhaps I might order him to close his drapes for a brief period, at the time when you would most probably be in view. But how will we know he is not peeking at you from behind the drapes?

"Well I imagine he might, your honor."

"So it seems the only way to assure you he isn't watching is to put him in jail, or to move him to another part of town."

"I can understand this, your honor, so I will change my prayer to that."

"Now Miss Engel, we are beginning to be pretty severe on Mr. Weatherby, and I will ask you to notice something. We are putting him in jail, or moving him across town, because you imagine his eyes on you when your back is turned, and you imagine him peeking at you through his drapes. I am beginning to wonder how much of your distraction is due to your imagination. You are wondering what's on his mind, and you don't like what you imagine you see there.

"Let me remind you that Mr. Weatherby is in his entitled space this whole time. He is using nothing that does not belong to him. He is not using you for his Omega. He is using a pattern of light waves entering his window, and they belong to him the instant they enter his room. He is not using anything to which you are entitled.

"You are claiming his pursuit is interfering with yours, and if I could find a true interference here, I would have grounds for issuing an injunction. It would be a case of nuisance. But I can't see a material chain of cause and effect. You say there is no expression on his face. You merely see his eyes turned toward you. You don't like it. That is understandable. But this court can not support your likes and dislikes by placing a person under restraint in his property. I must see the element of injury in the case. You are saying you don't like the image of Mr. Weatherby looking at you. From every aspect, it seems to be your dislikes and own imagination that are interfering with your mental activities, and this furnishes no grounds on which I may oppress Mr. Weatherby in his own entitled space. For this, I must be able to see a material interference in which you are trapped. Here I see only self-interference and self-entrapment.

"May I also remind you of this. You know Mr. Weatherby is looking at you only when you are looking at him. Rather than ordering him not to look at you, I might as well order you not to look at him."

The judge has resolved the case in a direct and satisfactory manner. We of course must go beyond his solution; we are trying to derive the principles. Basically, the judge is telling Miss Engel that her cause lacks materiality. Is there a more rigorous way of demonstrating it? Let us first express the situation in the language of the format of injury:

Plaintiff has an entitled project space - the thinking capacity of her mind, and it is subjected to load L (defendant's gaze) resulting from his watching pursuit.

The real issue of the whole case is the materiality of Weatherby's gaze; is there a true phenomenal interaction between his gaze and her mental concentration? Interaction is the fundamental test of materiality, and we move to functional association - the test of interaction. Scrutinize the following function; it is the heart of her pleading:

```
Form 1:   Engel sees Weatherby ----> she loses
            looking at her              concentration

Form 2:   Engel does not see    ----> she does not lose
            Weatherby looking           concentration
              at her
```

The judge has shown this claim to be defective. He provoked her to admit that her imagination can make her lose concentration, though the

gazing Weatherby is not visible, and this illustrates the usefulness of
functional analysis. A showing of cause and effect is insufficient if but
one form of a function is demonstrated. Proof requires a demonstration
of both forms.

If we show:
```
          Form 1:    Given A ----> B
```
and also show:
```
          Form 2:    Given C ----> B
```
we have demonstrated that B is not necessarily a result of A. (Engel's
distraction is not necessarily a result of Weatherby's gaze.)

Or if we show:
```
          Form 3:    Given A ----> D
```
we have demonstrated that A can lead to something other than B.
(Weatherby's gaze might lead to a marvelous relationship.) For instance, if you compare form 1 and form 3, you have the basis for the
alternate hypothesis in a criminal trial. The same facts point to more
than one culprit.

Let me try to show by a less mechanical method that Weatherby's
gaze was not material.

If he had leaned from his window and shouted "Miss Engel, I'm
going to break your neck," we can suspect materiality. If "Remember
the Maine" can be material, so can a threat. Our experience tells us
that such a threat might push a run button in a person's mind, initiating
a terror program with dreadful mental consequences. In fact, the
government goes farther; it provides punishment for threats of bodily
harm, and this is significant. It means the government presumes a
threat to be material. By our definition, we also know threat to be a
thing. One can use a threat to obtain an Omega.

But in "Engel v. Weatherby" we are talking about a gaze, not a
threat. Nor will I deny that eyes can speak. There is exasperation in
upcast eyes; smirking in sidecast eyes; demureness in downcast eyes.
And there is something called leering, and a look of ferocity - a threat
by looks. Eyes can communicate, and certain communications can be
enjoined. But in Weatherby we are talking about a gaze; something
wholly bereft of signal power.

A gazer cannot use a gaze except to let the gazed-at know the
gazer is looking at her. Nor will she get that message unless she's
looking at the gazer, and even then her inference may be mistaken. He
might not be trying to give her that message. He might not be looking at
her at all; he might be concentrating on an inner mental image, eyes

resting aimlessly on light waves emanating from her general direction.

A gaze is peculiar. As I have asked, what is the difference between a looking eye and a listening ear. But eyes! Over there I might see a blind man looking ahead and seeing nothing. I might know him to be blind and yet, if that sightless gaze turns toward me, I might become unreasonably disturbed. But I might not be concerned at all by the presence of his listening ear. Some sort of self-suggestion, or lack of it. And the government, if it is not to intrude into every aspect of human existence, must leave us to cure ourselves of some self-induced reactions.

At most, a gaze is an inference about a gazer by another gazer. On the part of both parties, a gaze is purely receptive, transmitting nothing. We can use the sun, ourselves being receptive, because it transmits something material. But a gazer cannot use a gaze. She can use her eyes but not her gaze. Nor can she use the gaze of the gazer gazing at her. If she tries to use her gaze to send him a message, his use of his reception of her gaze depends too much on how he interprets it. Its functionality is too imperfect. And if she tries to use his gaze, she runs into the same functional failure. To her his gaze is merely her mental impression of something that is transmitting nothing. And since his gaze is her mental impression of nothing, he can't use his gaze.

What can be concluded? I first reiterate. A claim of injury lacks materiality if the plaintiff claims an adverse loading that lacks materiality. So what is the test of materiality? For a claimed loading to be material, the function of the loading - the function of which the loading is a form - must be perfect. One must be able to demonstrate both forms of the function.

If we review **Shields v. Gross,** the plaintiff has claimed:

```
Form 1:
   If Gross distributes her            the public will focus
   photograph for publication  ---->   on the attractions of
                                           her body.

Form 2:
   If Gross does not distribute         the public will focus on
   her photograph for publication ---->  her traits other than
                                            the attractions
                                               of her body.
```

Form 2 is seen to be defective. Shields is still acting to concentrate public attention on the attractiveness of her body. She is asking the court to help her achieve an objective incompatible with the objective she strives for in her everyday life. At the moment she seems confused in her Omegas, and in this situation a judge cannot oppress a defendant in his entitled space.

If we re-examine **ex parte Warfield** by this method, we see Morris's claim to be:

```
Form 1:
  If Warfield is involved        Vivia is partially alienated
  in Vivia's life        ---->     from Morris.

Form 2:
  If Warfield is excluded        Vivia will not be alienated
    from Vivia's life      ---->    from Morris.
```

And we see that Morris must convince the court that both forms of the function are material.

As you see, I am treading the sharp ridge between reality and delusion, and there is a good chance for a slip. If I have failed so far, it is due in large part to a failure in language, and this I will try to correct in the chapter after next.

CHAPTER 35

PSEUDO-INJURY II
BILLBOARDS AND VOODOO DOLLS

For the purpose of exploring the verge of the material, the previous chapter dipped into the cool waters of delusion. The present treats entirely of the material, yet delusion remains threatening. I now approach the limits of determining injury when injury nears the indeterminable. And do not think, merely because I practice with clay pigeons, that the real game is not in my gun sights.

In the previous chapter I reviewed the case of "Wolcott v. Billboard" and now I engage it with intensity. I have shown loud music to be a classic example of nuisance, and now we witness Wolcott facing from his veranda the world's largest billboard.

Wolcott's aesthetic hopes are crushed. He has been deprived of his Omega. But won't due process help him? Doesn't this view of landscape belong to Wolcott? Isn't nature there for all to admire? Take it to court and get an injunction. Determine Wolcott's property; define his liberty; and get his view back. Doesn't the billboard pollute the world of nature? Isn't it like loud music? Isn't it a nuisance? Yes, it pollutes the world of nature. And no, it is not like loud music. And no, it is not nuisance.

In differentiating between billboards and loud music, first observe what they have in common. They are both material. Light - electro-magnetic waves - emanates from the wood and paper of the billboard, speeding through space and exciting Wolcott's optical system. We call it "seeing" the billboard, and make no mistake; the light is material. It is as material as the sound waves rolling in from the neighbor's stereo. So haven't we solved it? Surely, just as we have a right to enjoy a quiet conversation in our backyard, Wolcott has a right to his view. And just as our quiet air is disrupted by our neighbor's loud music, so Wolcott's view is disrupted by the invasion of light waves from the billboard. We are talking about material interference with a pursuit. But now let us talk about property.

Where does quiet air originate? Well, it doesn't originate any-where. It is simply quiet - unless it is disturbed by sound vibrations. And space is quiet too, unless it is disturbed by electromagnetic vibrations; - light. Space needs mentioning because light, unlike sound, can travel through space in the absence of air. Left to itself, the space above Wolcott's land would be quiet. And, as surely as quiet air is soundless, quiet space is viewless!

If Wolcott's land were a space capsule launched into absolute space - no stars no planets no anything - it would not only be soundless, except for sounds in the capsule; it would be viewless - all black - except for the electrically lighted interior of the capsule. To Wolcott looking from his capsule window, space is black. No view. Though light escapes from the windows of the capsule - all black; - nothing out there to send the light back. Now to make the point, let's return to earth.

Though we might enjoy quiet air in our backyard, Wolcott would not enjoy quiet space enveloping his veranda. His view would be nothing but black. In saying he enjoys his rural scene, he admits he enjoys disturbed space! And where does this disturbance originate; this pattern of electromagnetic waves - his view? Not - like quiet air - from its intrinsic nature, but from material things - valley and mountain and farm buildings - subject matter in the property of other people. In demanding his view, Wolcott desires nothing less than to dictate to other people the arrangements of their entitled space.

Perhaps you remember Mrs. Cassidy's and Mrs. Quinn's parlor windows. About five feet apart. If you were looking from one, you could look directly into the other. Previously Mrs. Quinn's window held a most charming statuette, one Mrs. Cassidy never tired of pointing out to her visitors. But recently Mrs. Quinn has replaced it with the world's ugliest vase. And now, let us be honest. If Mrs. Cassidy goes to court, she will never induce a judge to order the removal of the vase. Here you see a situation strictly equivalent to Wolcott's, and so the task falls upon us to find the juridical distinction between Wolcott's case and loud music; between loud music and ugly vases. A warning. We have a tiger by the tail.

Having described the mechanistic difference between Wolcott and loud music, let me put it in the form of a diagram. Figure 35:1.

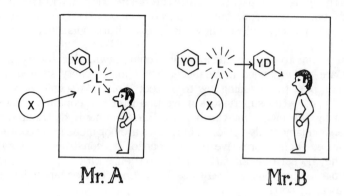

Figure 35:1. Difference Between Nuisance And Pseudo-Nuisance.

In the case of Mr. A enjoying the use of YO (something within his entitled space), YO is spoiled by a loading (L) originating outside his space in source X. YO perhaps is quiet air, and X the source of loud music. Or YO is Jones's entitled space in personal relations, and L the spoiling of this space by the bigoted practices of the Mayer Company.

But Mr. B in the diagram is enjoying YD, a derivative of YO (subject matter in someone else's entitled space), and the adverse loading L intervenes before YD becomes part of his space. Not nuisance. Wolcott's case. Yet if in Wolcott's case the loading should occur after the light waves enter his space, it would constitute nuisance. If from a factory a narrow trail of steam constantly crosses Wolcott's air space, causing no ill effects except to obscure his view, he can obtain an injunction. It is nuisance. But he has no valid claim of injury against the billboard on his neighbor's land. If people could get injunctions against billboards on their neighbor's land, your neighbor could dictate to you the color of your house.

We might sympathize with Wolcott but, if one is seeking the common good, it is important that one not be deluded about what government will protect. A court cannot act unless it sees injury in a case. A court may not permit a plaintiff's desire to prevail merely because the judge sympathizes with the desire. The world is full of billboards and ugly vases, but we cannot rid ourselves of them on grounds of nuisance, unless they really constitute nuisance.

This is not to say we cannot have zoning laws. But zoning laws properly are not grounded in nuisance. Nor should county supervisors enact an ex post facto zoning law to protect Wolcott's scenic view. In passing the law, the supervisors must find that the common good is enhanced by the law; that the benefits are commonly distributed to everyone. Fundamentally, since zoning laws are not measures countering nuisance, their oppressive effects cannot be construed as servitudes. They do not restrain title holders in their entitled space; rather they strip away portions of the titles. This characterizes a restriction, cutting away a portion of title.

So a zoning law is a deprivation of title and we witness here a device entirely distinct from servitude. We are seeing eminent domain. Historically the common law, except for a few carefully defined services to government, never asks a person to perform a sacrifice for the common good. There is an essential difference between servitude, the remedy for nuisance, and eminent domain - stripping away title. The former relieves injury, and there is no reason to reimburse the person placed under servitude. Eminent domain is a direct action in the public good, where the occasion does not involve injury by the person losing title. In such an instance, the owner should always be reimbursed for her loss.

Grave errors can be committed in cases like Wolcott's. A judge might rule against a billboard on grounds of nuisance, though nuisance is absent. This is a sign of delusion. Either the judge miscomprehends nuisance, or she has mis-analyzed the phenomena of the case. A legislature might commit the same error - creating a law protecting a private interest - citing nuisance as grounds, though nuisance is absent. In both instances, a person is deprived of property without being reimbursed. There have been cases of this general nature in which the deprivation was accomplished on delusory grounds of nuisance, though a true cause in eminent domain was available. An excuse was thus prepared for not reimbursing the deprived owner. To such delusions we can attribute the current chaos in several areas of "civil rights", as I will illustrate in succeeding chapters.

As clearly as Figure 35:1 depicts the difference between loud music and billboards, it does not wholly convince us. We admit we cannot force our neighbor to paint his house with our favorite color, yet, when it comes to billboards, we have second thoughts. And when it comes to equal wages or affirmative action, we are lost. In this whole topical area we find ourselves at the shearing edge between injury and non-injury, where the sharp blade of materiality shaves the sharp blade of property, and it will take this chapter and another to comprehend the problem and find the solution.

If the distinction between loud music and billboards, though mechanically understandable, remains instinctively unsatisfactory, let me make it even worse. Let me show that the format of injury itself does not cover the case. For this, I will introduce the voodoo doll. We return to the parlor windows of Mrs. Cassidy and Mrs. Quinn. In Mrs. Quinn's window first a pretty statue, next an ugly vase, and now she places there a voodoo doll, a thing of wide staring eyes pointed always at Mrs. Cassidy's window. It's effect on Mrs. Cassidy is alarming.

Usually a brisk busy person supervising children, husband, dog, and house plants, Mrs. Cassidy, from the day she first saw the voodoo doll, has not been the same person. In the midst of cooking supper her mind goes blank. It is fortunate if the family is fed by eight o'clock. And sometimes while darning socks she quietly rises and peeks at it. She can't restrain herself. The well-organized household begins to disintegrate.

Mr. Cassidy appeals to Mrs. Quinn to remove the doll from her window and meets with a firm refusal. He finds a lawyer who looks into the case. "We have a precedent against us, Mr. Cassidy," says he, ""Engel v. Weatherby" in which a man always seemed to be looking at a woman when she entered the street. It distracted her, but the judge couldn't see materiality in the case. The effect proved to be due to her own imagination, and, since the man was standing or sitting where he was entitled to be, using nothing he wasn't entitled to, and not exerting a true loading on Miss Engel, her case failed."

But Mr. Cassidy explained to the lawyer some facts about Mrs. Cassidy, distinguishing her situation from "Engle", and the lawyer entered a pleading in the proper court:

"Plaintiff is Mrs. Donald Cassidy... etc.etc. On July 13 1949 defendant placed in her window an authentic voodoo doll... etc.etc. Upon seeing it, plaintiff became distracted and has been rendered ineffective in many of her normal entitled pursuits. The effect is real and may be attributed to plaintiff's childhood environment.
"There is no relief for plaintiff without the court's intervention.
"The plaintiff prays that the court order the defendant to remove said doll from said window."

What I wish to construct is a case displaying a real effect in Mrs. Cassidy's space, caused by a loading originating in a pursuit of Mrs. Quinn. I am not trying to portray a supernatural effect in voodooism. What we have here is a woman, who, as a little girl, lived among people immersed in voodooism. Through ear and eye she caught snatches of conversations and sights involving voodoo dolls, and sensed the presence of terror in connection with them. We have here an instance of mental conditioning - the creation of a computer program with a run button, much like the fear of snakes.

I recall a high school occurrence in a town where I once lived. Each class room door had at eye height a small pane of glass, and through this, at odd times, a student in the classroom craned an eyeball to see the passing events in the hall.

One day a prankster in the hallway crouched beneath such a window, gripping the neck of a writhing snake. Suddenly he thrust the snake up to the window, and just then a girl looked out. Suddenly confronted by an electromagnetic pattern of reptilean features, she fainted and fell, and her head struck the concrete floor. When I moved from town two or three years later, she was still in a coma. Was damage present?

Using her optical apparatus was within her entitled space. A loading in the form of a pattern of electromagnetic waves, a loading from the pursuit of another person impinged on that optical system, and was transferred to her mind. Not only did it interfere with the use of her mind, but it had a result that crystallized in her mind. We are talking of a phenomenal interaction as real as a baseball breaking a pane of glass. There was nothing imaginary about it.

This is precisely the effect I wish to depict in the case of the voodoo doll. We have here a material function:

```
Form 1: No display of          Mrs. Cassidy's mind
        voodoo doll    ---->   is composed

Form 2: Display of             Mrs. Cassidy's mind
        voodoo doll    ---->   is distracted.
```

A question. How do we know this wasn't the case in "Engel v. Weatherby"? Was Weatherby in his window possibly a voodoo doll, and not an ugly vase? But I'll leave this as an exercise for the reader. I wish to introduce Mr. Wolcott to the case of the voodoo doll. But first the voodoo doll furnishes an excellent opportunity to complete the concept of entrapment.

Notice that Mrs. Cassidy's complaint carried the statement: "There is no relief for plaintiff without the court's intervention." This is a necessary element of injury. It should be voiced in a complaint. It is actually a statement of entrapment.

But is there no relief for Mrs. Cassidy in the absence of court action? Is she actually trapped? After all there are only the electromagnetic waves. Yes. She can pull down her roller blind. She can close her drapes. She can refrain from looking out her parlor window. But note. This diminishes her freedom in her entitled space. No longer can she use her window for looking out, or for light, or as part of her decor. Does the law require this kind of sacrifice in an effort to abate nuisance? Must entrapment be absolute?

Well, we in our backyard, by constructing a glass dome over the yard, can neutralize the nuisance of loud music. Build it high enough to preserve our sense of spaciousness. Install triple layers of glass with vacuum between for sound insulation. And install air conditioning to keep us from boiling on a sunny day. But be not dismayed. The judge will not insist on such measures.

The doll diminishes Mrs. Cassidy's effectiveness in the use of her mind. Closing the drapes still results in an infringement of her liberty. In one way or another the entrapment is absolute, and, given this example, I think entrapment can be defined thus:

Entrapment in injury exists when all the elements of injury exist, and plaintiff cannot gain relief for herself. At most, she can only gain relief by imposing on herself an alternate curtailment of her liberty.

To attain an all-inclusive definition, we should recall another method of abating loud music - taking our hammer to the neighbor's patio and using it in various ways. It would have undesirable repercussions.

With these varied aspects of entrapment and relief in mind, it must be understood that when a judge reads this claim, "There is no relief for plaintiff unless the court intervenes," he interprets it thus:

"Unless the court intervenes, there is no relief for plaintiff except by plaintiff taking an illegal action, or by plaintiff curtailing her own liberty in some way."

Now what is the point of bringing the voodoo doll into the discussion. Wolcott, you will remember, was frustrated in his litigative hopes. The billboard was not an instance of nuisance. The loading exerted by the billboard was not exerted in Wolcott's space. It was exerted in space belonging exclusively to his neighbor. And now Wolcott and his attorney hear of the case of the voodoo doll, and the lawyer examines Wolcott closely. This is what he hears Wolcott saying.

"The billboard acts like a voodoo doll upon me. I come home on weekends. My mind is tired and needs refreshment. My former view refreshed me, but the billboard inhibits the whole process. The billboard is a voodoo doll. Its pattern of electromagnetic waves produce a real interference in my mind. It is a real function. Yes, my neighbor is acting within his entitled space, but it is producing a loading within my space; a loading upon my mind. It is nuisance."

And Wolcott is not shamming. He is talking about real functions. Furthermore, in his new contention, he has moved the emphasis from (a) the loading of the billboard on the electromagnetic pattern within the neighbor's space to (b) the loading exerted by the altered electromagnetic pattern upon Wolcott's mind. The loading is in his own entitled space!

Will the judge make his neighbor remove the billboard? No, he will not. It is not a case of nuisance.

To develop this sharpness in decision, we must really get down to brass tacks.

CHAPTER 36

PSEUDO-INJURY III:
THE CUT-OFF POINT OF INJURY.
FUNCTION ANALYSIS III

In distinguishing between "Wolcott v. Billboard" and "Cassidy v. Voodoo Doll", we come to the infinitely narrow borderline between injury and non-injury. In the chapter following this, the significance of this cut-off point for contemporary America will become clear. My present concern is to learn how to discern it unmistakably in a borderline case. The skill will be mechanistic, not philosophical. Sign language is the best medium for expressing it. Skip this chapter if you must, but, for a basic understanding of the dividing line between injury and non-injury, we must bury ourselves in the language of functions. Now.

Since a function at minimum describes a system of two **variables**, each having two **variates**, the following sentence expresses a function: A snowshoe rabbit has white fur in winter, brown fur in summer.

In this expression, white fur and brown fur are variates, being variates of something called a variable. The word variable needs some discussion. In the example, one might identify the variable as fur color, and that is proper if one understands that one is considering a much more involved phenomenon than fur color. We might think ourselves more accurate by calling the variable "hair pigment", but really we need to enter an entirely different dimension. Fur color is a parameter for a more basic variable, the variable where the real effects of winter and summer are taking place. Fur color signals a more fundamental process occurring in the tissues of the rabbit. For the real variable we must travel to the site producing the individual hairs of the fur, a submicroscopic biochemical process.

But let us not despise fur color as a parameter merely because it is superficial. After all it is the white fur in winter and brown in summer that hides the rabbit from the eyes of arctic wolves.

Thus we frequently give a variable a name corresponding to the variates we happen to be most interested in, knowing full well that a very simple label may cover an extraordinary family of phenomena.

As white fur and brown fur are variates of a variable, so also winter and summer are variates of a variable. The winter-summer variable we might call season. But season is even further removed from the fundamental variable than is fur color. Scientists would not use season as a parameter unless they were climatologists. They would probably use air temperature and length of day. They would correlate air temperature and daylength with such observations as the tilt of the earth in relation to the sun, and latitude, and density and thickness of the atmosphere. Such a "correlation", by which we really mean "the detection of a functional association" - is another way of saying "we are explaining the variation in a variable". Explaining the variation in a variable is the work of scientists. It is the work of a scientist even if the scientist happens to think of herself as a lawyer pondering variations in judicial temperament, or a housewife pondering the idiosyncrasies of cake flour.

It is well to note that, though temperature and daylength are factors determining the fur color of a snowshoe rabbit, the "interest" of the rabbit species lies not in temperature and daylength but in an entirely different variable - landscape color. It happens frequently that white landscape color is associated with low temperatures and short days. But putting a brown snowshoe rabbit on a white sheet in summer won't turn him white. At least I don't think it will.

By which I mean to say that white fur color does not derive from snow color; for purposes of discussion, I will assume it derives from a certain combination of temperature and daylength. Nor does season depend on fur color, fur color depends on "season". So fur color is a **dependent** variable, and season a **contributing** variable. Brown fur color and white fur color are **derivative** variates, and high temperature and low temperature are **powering** or **promotive** variates. Landscape color, so far as I know, is not a contributing variable, at least in the fur color phenomenon. It is a **coincident** variable as far as fur color is concerned; a very important one for the species. The function between landscape color and fur color in the snowshoe rabbit is not **interactive**; it is **coincidental**. But then the snowshoe rabbit is not a chameleon.

Now I will express the snowshoe rabbit phenomenon more formally, in function language, and you will notice a change from previous chapters in the appearance of the function.

and this functional expression is packed with meaning.

In it, the phrase

is a symbolic expression saying there is a system with variable characteristics that we call winter and summer. The two character sets, winter and summer, are mutually exclusive. When one set is in the ascendancy, the other disappears, and we say one is translated into the other. Loosely we might say that winter is translated into summer and summer into winter, but really we know the phenomenon involves much more. We call this mechanism entity a variable, but we don't even give it an identifying name. I will express it as a free-form cloud, or in text by [v], and unless its fundamentals have been thoroughly demonstrated, we deeply respect its anonymity. Though it be housed in a well recognized phenomenon, the variable itself is more covert, a secret system sending up flags - the variates.

In the expression

Winter

Summer

we suspect that the cloud represents a mixture of temperature and daylength, cold and short in winter, warm and long in summer. At a more basic level, the cloud represents the complex of relationships between earth, atmosphere, and sun - powering or promoting the changes in temperature and daylength.

In the expression

Winter   **White Fur**

Summer   **Brown Fur**

the direction of the arrows tells us that winter promotes white fur. White fur does not produce winter. The swing of the arrows also tells us that winter does not necessarily act directly on fur or on whiteness. It signifies that the underlying system [1] might act on a system [2], a variable, and the result is white fur. Fundamentally something quite complex might be going on, and white fur and brown fur are signals, parameters, of the more basic phenomena.

Generally it is the job of scientists - investigators - to look into the nature of the variable [v] and discover the mechanism of the phenomenon. Occasionally scientists are able to accurately describe the translations of the variable. Given the symptoms of a disease, they can tell you the name of the disease organism. Or, given the identity of the organism, they can predict the course of the symptoms.

Many times however, the basic phenomena, the underlying variables and their variates are a complete mystery. This is true in many
kinds of cancer. Thus we might say in connection with a particular kind
of cancer:

indicating that this person would be alive if she had not developed this
tumor. But it also indicates that the factor promoting the tumor is
unknown. Perhaps a researcher can tell you, given that the tumor has
developed, all the events that translate the variate "life" into the
variate "death". But he can't tell you anything about variable 2 in the
tissue manifesting itself as tumor or non-tumor, and he can't tell you
anything about the factor A-plus or A-star stimulating [2] to develop a
tumor or non-tumor. A-plus and A-star are inferred, not observed. And
he can't tell you anything about the mechanism of system 1 whose
specific activity produces the proposed A-plus and A-star.

Note from what I have said that

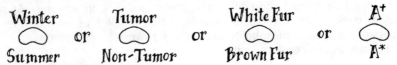

represent **translational** mechanisms, translating a mode of a thing into
another mode of it. A translational relation reflects a variable - a thing
or a bundle of things - in a variety of mutually exclusive modes.
Frequently a variable exists in a mode having particular significance for
us. For instance, we like our car in an uncrumpled mode. And sometimes
our Omega for the evening is a particular mode of moon, say a full one.
Usually when our desires are mixed up with functions, something
translates the mode we desire into an undesirable mode, or vice versa.

On the other hand, the statement

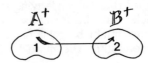

expresses a **powering** or promotive mechanism, operating between
translational mechanisms, a mode of variable 1 activating a translation
in variable 2. And one might say that functional phenomena in the real
world consist of powering mechanisms activating translational mechan-

isms. Very often a powering mechanism is called a cause, or a causal mechanism. I will also call it a **form**, say Form 1, of a function.

Thus B+, the mode or variate, rises from three mechanisms: (1) the translational mechanism having A+ as a mode; (2) the translational mechanism of which B+ is a mode; and (3) the powering mechanism existing between the two translational mechanisms such that if A+ materializes, B+ materializes. These three mechanisms then comprise the form from which the mode B+ arises.

Thus history seems to demonstrate that in government:

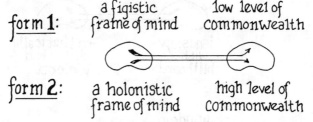

form 1:   a figistic   low level of
            frame of mind   commonwealth

form 2:   a holonistic   high level of
            frame of mind   commonwealth

Our founding fathers preferred to call one of them the Republican Form.

The following series of functions illustrates that a powering variate might also be a derivative variate.

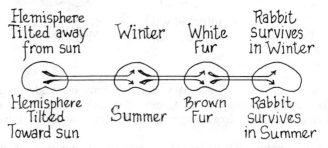

Hemisphere   Rabbit
Tilted away   Winter   White   Survives
from sun   Fur   in Winter

Hemisphere   Brown   Rabbit
Tilted   Summer   Fur   survives
Toward sun   in Summer

We might call the overall statement of the phenomenon a functional sequence.

And if we look at only the upper line of variates:

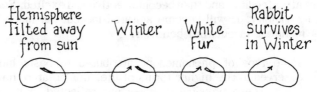

Hemisphere   Rabbit
Tilted away   Winter   White   Survives
from sun   Fur   in Winter

we see what is called a causal chain or causal sequence.

So one should remember that a causal chain or causal sequence is but one-half of a function. If the other half is not demonstrable, one's claim of causal relation is incomplete. Materiality is suspect.

From the observations presented thus far, it may be seen that powering relationships can jump the gap from the external world of our environment into the world of the mind:

In Wolcott's case,

```
landscape              aesthetically
without                   pleased
billboard                 Wolcott


landscape              aesthetically
  with                    disturbed
billboard                 Wolcott
```

In Voodoo doll case,

```
window
without              a composed
voodoo doll          Mrs. Cassidy


window with          a distraught
voodoo doll          Mrs. Cassidy
```

These claims by Wolcott and Mrs. Cassidy have been admitted to be truly functional. Therefore the danger of delusion here is not one of materiality, it comes from imprecision in the concept of injury.

Before further developing the language of function, it will be necessary to tie the discussion to yet another coordinate of structure, our basic drives and desires. In the functions just shown, we see human feelings translated from contentment to perturbation; and one observes similar translations in the lower animals. A starfish remains placid for a few hours after feeding, and then becomes active and excited. Sensing a clam in its vicinity, it will become agitated indeed. An inner hunger becomes manifest in outward behavior.

The same type of phenomenon, attributed to basic biological drives, is observed in the higher forms of life. In a creature having an advanced brain, these physical changes are reflected in its mental processes, and, when psychologists study it, they include its mental changes in their overall observations. At least they make inferences as to its mental inclinations. Thus if an ape lacks daily physical contact with another creature, even a toy doll, it becomes depressed, and this will be reflected in its physical vitality and growth.

These internal translations within a living being, and their relations with its external environment, can be formally and schematically described.

The living thing is composed of networks of interacting systems in a state of constant flux. An organism superficially stable is basically unstable, its various systems shifting from one phase to another; from a charged phase to an uncharged phase, and back. Actually the same shifting occurs in all active phenomena of the universe, living or not. The difference between the living thing and the non-living thing is based on a peculiarity of the systems composing the living thing. Evidently when a system of a living thing becomes uncharged, there is another system that happens to be charged, and the two systems are so related that the uncharged system can "feed" upon the charged system and regain its charge. The contributing system thereby becomes discharged but lo! Another standby system has the capacity to charge it. Ultimately, at the end of this chain of charging-discharging systems, there is a system or complex of systems that, being in a state of discharge, has the capacity to regain its charge from the external environment. Else of course the systems would all settle to their uncharged states, and, being delicate, they might congeal irreversibly in these states, and then the thing could no longer be called living.

These wheels within wheels of charging and discharging systems give the organism its semblance of stability. But really if the organism became stable, it would be dead. This system of stability through interaction I will call kinestasis. And for simplicity's sake I will give the same name to the charging-uncharging cycling of each subsystem of the total organism. I am saying for instance that the hunger-satiation cycle, occurring between lunch and supper, is an example of kinestasis, and to say this is to indulge in both over-simplication and understatement. No one knows, I dare say, how many subsystems are involved in this cycle, each kinestatic in its own right. The transport of food elements into the bloodstream. The feeding of the tissues. The storage and release of sugars in the liver. And the essential alarm systems - "I'm getting hungry.", or, "I'm getting full; don't eat anymore." Each a model of kinestasis. But look at it another way.

The total function of all these working parts is to draw a charge from the external environment; else the whole system fails, and each subsystem fails. So don't look down on hunger as an over-simplification. It is also an understatement. It is hunger that initiates desire, then will (volo). It is hunger that motivates the organism to pursuit - the movement of the organism out into the external world, to bring food back for the internal world. When satiated, the lion lays down with the lamb. When aroused to the point of pursuit, - well.

We discern the same alternation of pursuit and satiation in the sexual drive, again realizing that wheels within wheels are engaged. But the net effect is a buildup of tension - really an uncharged state. A chemical imbalance becomes ascendant. Then there is a quick swing of the pendulum to an alternate chemical phase. We call it satisfaction. All this is internal - without a loading of chemicals from the external world. Yet the total kinestasis is reflected in the mentality of the individual. In the human it can drive a person to buy roses; to develop strategies; to render her or him oblivious to reality; to engage in combat; to engage in careers. It can affect a human's whole life. So it draws upon elements of the external world, though they be elements of an intangible nature. We might say it operates through the medium of the psyche; whatever that might be. Thus we respect it; yet we know not exactly what we are talking about.

In humans we see almost an excess of these abstruse kinestatic systems. There are times when the child seeks the closeness of her mother; and other times when she is indifferent and independent. There are times when Wolcott wants his view, but then he gets his fill. There are cycles of much longer duration. Men there are who can concentrate on hard work for a week or two, and then they must feed on rest and relaxation for a month. For them, driving seems to be a discharging process. There are others who drive, drive, drive for years. Seemingly for them, driving is a charging process. Much we don't know about humans. But everything they do can be attributed to an inner kinestasis.

So we take one such fluxing system in the abstract, calling it W; and W is never constant, continuously being translated from mode W+ to mode W* and back. We can imagine for instance that W+ is a red blood cell charged with oxygen as it leaves the lungs in the bloodstream. W* is its mode after it has surrendered its oxygen to a brain cell, returning to the lungs hungry for oxygen.

Or W might be a complex signaling system. The individual is being held under water by a murderer. The oxygen in her lungs is near depletion, and a chemical alarm system is activated, sending signals to the diaphragm to take a deep breath. By force of will, the victim resists the natural reaction of the diaphragm. Resists. But finally the will of the diaphragm overcomes the will of the brain, and the diaphragm moves. The lungs fill with water. The W system, ordinarily a life-preserving system, becomes a contributing variable in the death of the individual. Thus we have the causal chain:

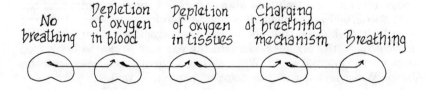

| No breathing | Depletion of oxygen in blood | Depletion of oxygen in tissues | Charging of breathing mechanism | Breathing |

And since it is breathing that normally replaces the oxygen in the system, we get a glimpse of a cyclic nature, such as:

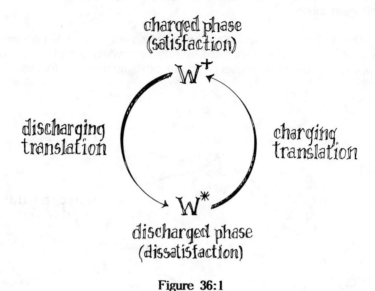

Figure 36:1

The translation from W+ to W* is a self-promoting discharge. On the other hand W* requires a "feeding" for translation back to W+.

It is W*, the discharged phase (at least I call it the discharged phase), that initiates the pursuit mechanism:

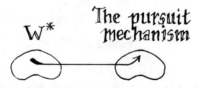

In breathing, perhaps the pursuit mechanism involves the system powering the diaphragm. Another pursuit mechanism might involve systems spurring a physical attack on an enemy. Or in urban society, an inner pursuit system might inspire a person to organize an association sponsoring a symphony orchestra for the community.

The goal of a pursuit mechanism is to obtain and hold Omega for feeding. Omega is the thing desired, the thing in the outside world

that a living thing requires for kinestasis in its inner world. Feeding is
the mysterious process by which Omega is absorbed into the inner
world, and, in one way or another, translates a discharged mode of W to
a charged mode.

Omega for a mosquito might be the blood of a human. For a human
it might be the sounds generated by a symphony orchestra, or a rock
group. The kinestatic sequence might be diagramed as follows:

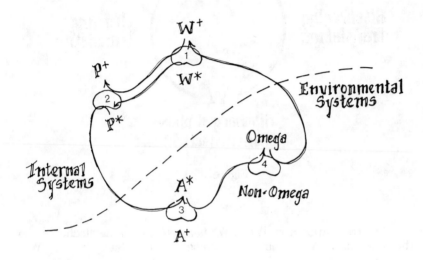

Figure 36:2

Interpretation: [1] is a living organism's system requiring an
Omega from its environment. In its operation, a variate W+ is changed
spontaneously into W*. W* activates [2], the pursuit system of the
organism, changing its status from non-pursuer, P+, to pursuer, P*.
Through the activities of the pursuit system, external mechanisms [3]
and [4] are powered into producing Omega from the environment. In
physical contact with Omega, and stimulated by it, system [1] translates W* to W+, deactivating the pursuit system.

With this understanding of Omega, the thing desired - the thing that the inner woman feeds upon - the objective of a pursuit, I start again using the simplest elements of function language, and gradually build them into sentences adapted to the language of pursuits and property.

(1)

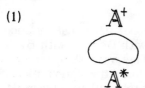

This is a variable. It might be a loading space.

The plus marks and asterisks have no symbolic purpose other than to distinguish the variates. A+ and A* are variates, modes of a variable. Call them A-plus and A-star. Certain loadings upon the variable will translate A+ to A*, and other loadings will translate A* to A+. The cloud represents the variable, that loosely may be called A, remembering that A is neither A+ or A*. It is the mechanism producing A+ or A*, or the thing of which A+ and A* are mutually exclusive features.

(2)

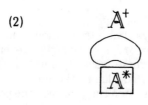

(2) is like (1) except: the box around A* indicates that a translation from A+ to A* is irreversible. Example: A+ is the fresh mode of an egg, A* the boiled mode. Or A+ is a new unspoiled car, A* the same car crumpled.

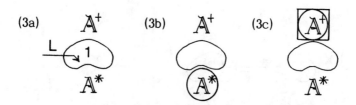

(3a) says, a loading has been exerted on [1] with the power to translate A+ to A*.
(3b) says, A* is the variate in ascendancy.
(3c) says, A+ is the variate in ascendancy, and it is irreversible.

(4)
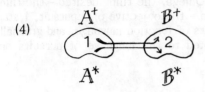

(4) is the statement of perfect (one-to-one) functional variation. It states that A+ is never found associated with B*; only with B+. That A* is never found with B+; only with B*. That a translation from A+ to A* induces a translation from B+ to B*. That a translation from A* to A+ induces a translation from B* to B+; but translations between B* and B+ don't induce translations between A* and A+. Thus we call [1] a contributing variable with powering or causal variates, calling [2] a dependent variable with derivative variates.

(5)
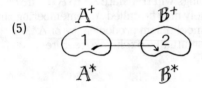

(5) is a statement of semi-function. It says that a translation from A+ to A* will induce a translation from B+ to B*. Yet, though a reverse translation in [1] may be attended by a reverse translation in [2], the translation from B* to B+ is self-inducing, not due to the influence of A+. A wind powers waves on the pond, and when the wind dies the pond will become placcid. But, if a motor boat is racing on the pond when the wind dies, the pond will not become placcid. This is a reminder that there can be form, or cause, or functionality though not perfect (not one-to-one). This is a key distinction in the analysis of nuisance.

(6)
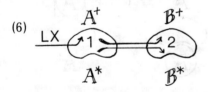

(6) states: a loading has been exerted on [1] with the functional power to translate B* into B+.

(7)

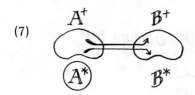

This says: A* being ascendant, we may expect B* ascendant.

(8)

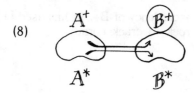

B+ being ascendant, we may infer A+ to be ascendant.

(9)

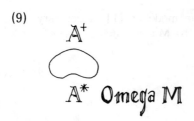

A* is the variate or mode desired by person M.

(10)

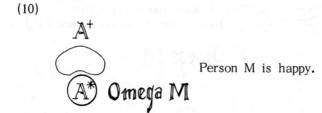

Person M is happy.

(11)

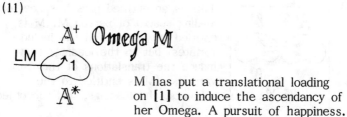

M has put a translational loading on [1] to induce the ascendancy of her Omega. A pursuit of happiness.

(12)

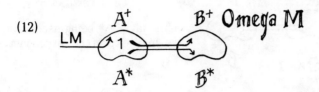

In (12), M has acted to induce the ascendancy of B+. M has used [1] to get B+. M has used a rock to crack corn.

(13)

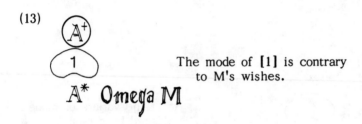

The mode of [1] is contrary to M's wishes.

(14)

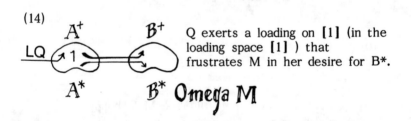

Q exerts a loading on [1] (in the loading space [1]) that frustrates M in her desire for B*.

(15)

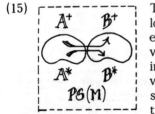

This is an entitled pursuit space (or loading space) of person M. M is entitled not only to all the included variates, but to the loadings that induce the translations of the variates. (M is entitled to the subjects, the loadings, and the objectives.)

(16) 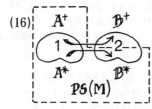 M is entitled to the copper coils [1] and the corn [2], but is not entitled to use A+, the hot mode of [1], to translate B* (corn mash) into B+ (whisky for sale). The necessary translations and powerings are not in his property.

(17)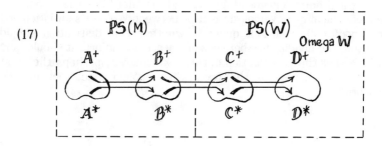

In (17), the satisfaction of person W depends on the ascendancy of a variate in the entitled space of person M. THIS IS THE WOLCOTT SITUATION. The A* arrangement of M's farmstead makes a pattern of light powering itself into Wolcott's space and affecting Wolcott's aesthetic feelings adversely. Wolcott wants M to arrange M's entitled space to fit Wolcott's tastes. Wolcott wishes to use M's space.

(18)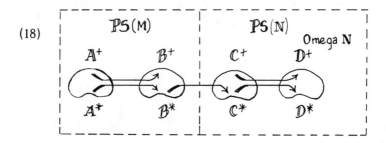

In (18), the satisfaction of person N does not depend on a variate in M's entitled space. However, a variate ascendant in M's space is depressing the ascendancy of N's wishes in N's space. In gaining relief, N is not seeking to use M's space. C* reverts to C+ naturally if [1] is left undisturbed by the powering from M's space. C+ is quiet air, and Mrs. Cassidy's composed mind. Mrs. Cassidy doesn't care what Mrs. Quinn puts in her window - though of course it might upset her aesthetic tastes - as long as it isn't the voodoo doll. In fact to provide relief, Mrs. Quinn can simply prevent the electromagnetic waves from the doll from passing into Mrs. Cassidy's space. She can pull down her window shade or put up a wall. It would put an end to the nuisance.

It is important to understand statements 17 and 18 exactly, and the distinction between them. The difference between them is precisely the difference between nuisance and pseudo-nuisance; one constituting injury, the other a delusion of injury. And now that I have demonstrated the mechanical or physical distinction between Wolcott's situation and the voodoo doll, you still question whether this distinction should constitute the dividing line between injury and non-injury. It should, and I will present the justification in the next chapter, perhaps the most far-reaching chapter of the book when applied to current judicial quandaries.

CHAPTER 37

EQUAL WAGES; BAKKE; TRUSTS
FINAL FORMAT OF INJURY

Having marked the exact division line between injury and non-injury, and having endured the tribulations of function language, it is possible after all to express in simple English the difference between loud music and billboards. In the case of loud music; in our desire for a quiet backyard, we are not greedy. We do not wish to use anything of our neighbors. We merely wish them to refrain from an activity in their space that distorts our loading space - our independently derived loading space. But Wolcott is different. He wishes to use his neighbor's entitled space. He wishes his neighbor to so arrange that space that it will generate his - Wolcott's - Omega. In fact he wishes government to force his neighbor to do it. He is asking government to force his neighbor to obtain his - Wolcott's - objective. This exactly fits the definition of enforced service.

Remember that usable things are part of our potential. They are part of our project effectiveness. I can dig a hole much faster with a shovel than with my bare hand. It is part of the genius of the common law that in creating private property it unites all the elements of project effectiveness - (a) self, and (b) the things one's life is invested in, relative to the common good. The result of law under equity is to make our propertied belongings a part of us; as much a part as an arm or leg. And for government to force us to use our entitled subject matter to please the Omega of another is a mode of slavery.

Within the last year or two, the breakfast newscaster told of a city council enacting an ordinance requiring homes in certain areas of the city to be painted; they could not be left in a weatherbeaten condition. The ordinance was inspired by a certain unpainted house on a certain street, and undoubtedly the council members were acting to satisfy other homeowners on the street. In response, the villain painted his house black with orange trim, and the newscaster closed by saying the council is speedily enacting another ordinance, this time to prevent out-landish color combinations. These acts of council (and many others) contradict the spirit of the common law.

Realize I am not writing of long-range real estate zoning. Buying real estate in a well-planned restricted area is the equivalent of entering a contract. One agrees to help materialize the objectives of other

owners in the area. But the case of the black and orange house
exemplifies ex post facto legislation; forcing an entitled person to serve
the wishes of others.

Let us argue in behalf of owners of well-kept houses. Cannot we
honor their commitment to such worthy efforts, their climates of mind,
the commitment of their effectiveness lives to maintaining high
standards? Here is the case of a single structure marring the perfection
of a beautiful neighborhood. These homeowners having worked hard to
buy and maintain their homes, their efforts enhancing the common
good, do we dare dampen such a spirit? What will happen to their
effectiveness lives if we allow such pursuits to be frustrated by one
slovenly neighbor?

Yes, we sympathize. But if we act on sympathy, we lose the sharp
edge of justice. Shall we construct a hierarchy of preferred tastes.
Pursuit E is more worthy than pursuit F. And when such pursuits clash,
shall we favor them according to rank? Shall we force Farmer Brown to
rent his weed patch for Mr. Anthony's sign?

You realize I am using painted (or unpainted) houses to establish a
fundamental point. That our courts have failed to observe the razor
sharp balance point in the gravity field of injury is the seedbed of their
uneven performance since 1950. That legislative bodies fail to observe it
is nothing new. I will argue my point plausibly, then approach rigor.

Suppose ex post facto a person in a neatly kept house can force his
neighbor to repaint his black and orange house. "This obscene color
scheme offends my tastes. It depresses the market value of my
house." If the judge agrees with this plaintiff and decides in his favor,
where will this kind of judicial sympathy draw the line? Why can't the
owner of a black and orange home make a counter-claim, "Why focus
the judge's attention on the color of my home? What about the
notorious debaucheries that occur in your gorgeous white house! They
offend my taste; they contaminate the environment I wish to create for
my children. They lower the market value of my house."

Historically the common law prevented such a gelatinous state of
affairs by inventing property and liberty and injury. In due process, a
court may not listen to plausible arguments. A judge may hear only the
voice of injury. He may not give plausible reasons as opinions; he may
only relieve injury and cite the law. If he is a chancellor, he may cite
climates of mind and effectiveness lives, but first he must see title.
And a neighbor has no title in his neighbor's land and house unless he
can show a deed or a contract.

City councilmen have a more difficult task. They may listen to
complaints beyond the limits of injury. They must learn to detect the
common good in its largest sense. As a guide, they should note that due

process rebuffs remedies calling for enforced service. This I will expound presently, but for the moment I make the following observation. If an applicant praying for relief in court (or lobbying the legislative; or petitioning the executive) proposes a remedy involving trespass or enforced service, it is a sure signal that the applicant has not been injured. She wishes to use the loading space of another. If you wish, use the language of functions to analyze it. It is a case that a court may not handle, and the other branches of government may treat it only under eminent domain or by outright seizure - appropriation. They may not treat it as injury, though it might wear the delusive aura of nuisance, and in treating it at all they had better achieve optical clarity in the landscape of the common good.

American law traditionally provides very few instances of enforced service, and it is wandering dangerously into that habit. Certainly military service is a traditional example of enforced service, and so are jury duty and witness duty. Men and women are under a service to support a disabled spouse, but not to the extent of personal service, only to the extent of support payments. Parents are under a service to rear their child within a sort of holonistic framework, but not if the performance strains their physical and psychological capacities unreasonably.

But in the disturbed environment of contemporary jurisprudence, it will be easy for government to begin a practice of enforced service. Some months before the air raid on Libya, President Reagan ordered all Americans out of Libya. He threatened non-complying citizens with punishment if and when they later returned to the United States. The correct and mature position for the president would have been to withdraw all guarantee of protection for Americans remaining past the deadline.

I am saying that government-enforced trespass and government-enforced service, though posing as remedies, identify situations in which the government-oppressed person has not injured anyone. Once you have used the courts to force your way into the entitled space of another, the common law's antipathy to slavery has been corrupted. Given such a precedent, a persuasive individual can use court or legislature to do the same to you. Thus marvellously is this legal structure designed. Where better to draw the distinction between injury and non-injury than at the line between slavery and ideal freedom in one's entitled space.

Repeating. Yes, it signals self-interest when you ask a neighbor to lower the volume of her record player. But it signals an entirely different attitude when you try to force your neighbor to arrange his entitled loading space to feed your Omega. And I will soon show how destructive of law the latter attitude becomes if not curbed absolutely. The example of the black and orange house introduces a disturbing fact.

America since mid-century has erupted with the outcries of frustrated Omegas demanding enforced trespass. Though not an unexpected occurrence in legislatures, its appearance in our courts is alarming. It has gone far in destroying our intuition for common law. Perhaps this violent atmosphere is due to the hyper-activity of under-employed lawyers. If so, the much touted overload of suits in our courts is the fault of judges themselves. They should never admit a case that does not in its complaint show cause, does not signal injury.

Under due process, a court does not intervene in every last personal dispute. If it is important to a community that an unpainted house becomes painted, let the homeowners get together and approach the dilatory homeowner on a reasonable and practical basis. They have not been injured, and a court should not hear their plea. If the fellow is a boor, not destitute, refusing to cooperate, let them face the facts of life. They need not feel humiliated merely because their neighbor has an ugly vase in her window. More fundamentally; if you engage government power to force a fellow to serve your wishes, you establish precedents for your own slavery. As for maintaining intelligent climates of mind in ourselves, let us be proud not only of our well-kept homes, but of our resolve not to force our neighbor to use his entitled loading space to serve our wishes. As for the boor, the common law allows every person to act as a mule, as long as the act is not injurious, and we would be intelligent to develop such maturity ourselves.

In spite of these remarks, we have observed what appears to be court-enforced trespass, and I have argued in its favor. Sheila Rienzi used Farmer Brown's land to save Peter. Mrs. Carter used Miss Reed's home for visiting her mother. And Joseph Lee Jones was allowed to dictate the disposition of the Mayer Company house. All government-enforced.

Of course, these so called trespassers had entitled loading spaces. These were cases of intersecting or overlapping loading spaces. People are entitled to save lives, to establish and maintain loving relationships, and to establish honorable reputations. In contrast, in the case of unpainted houses or billboards, we see a government giving title to a pursuit in aesthetics, giving it dominance over a persons liberty in his entitled space, and perhaps gaining the popular support of everyone with the same tastes. But if we wish to establish a rule against enforced trespass, enforced service, a magnificently sharp boundary separating injury from non-injury, why should we endanger the security of our liberty by permitting the exceptions that happen to please us?

Let us note a common thread running through the pursuits of Sheila Rienzi, Mrs. Carter and Joseph Jones. They were reacting to wholesome human bonds. Or they were trying to establish wholesome human bonds. They were exemplary in the grander scheme. They exemplified originant actions in efforts to induce or preserve originancy in others. In addition, there was another common thread in each of the cases. The adversaries were attempting to strangle human bonds, or to frustrate the effort to establish them. At minimum they were insensitive to such bonds. They were trying to reduce people to objects, not in the least concerned with promoting their originancy. And I propose that exactly this opposition of attitudes must be evident in every case in which government makes a property decision favoring one titleholder over another. I think you will find in every such case a notable characteristic. Whenever an owner uses mere title to frustrate a valid pursuit in human relations, you will find in that owner a sordid climate of mind. If so, the boundary between injury and non-injury remains infinitely sharp. Permitting the exception in the pursuit of human rescue or personal relations has not dulled the cutting edge of justice.

We have in this topic - before showing its application to some great legal perplexities of the day - an opportunity to discern the depths of legal theory to which our forebearers plunged. In discussing **Jones v. Alfred H. Mayer Company**, I concluded that the remedy necessarily involved the passing of title from the Mayer Company to Jones. At no time had the company said, in so many words, "Jones, being black, is an undesirable neighbor." It was, under the circumstances, the house-empty-of-Jones that constituted defamation. It was a statement in brick and wood, and consequently there was but one material retraction of the statement - the house-not-empty-of-Jones. To give true relief (not an equivalent), the remedy must utilize the same functions through which the injury materializes.

Of course Jones, having won the case, had to accept the house and pay for it. Not to have done so would have exposed his case as a sham. But what I wish to show is a matter concerning title, and here we touch upon the profound. Note this peculiar situation. We say that the Mayer Company had title to the house, and the title of disposition is on center stage, and I ask, did government really give the title to Jones, and the answer is, not really.

If government had given full title to Jones, Jones could have said to Mr. Green, "Mr. Green I will sell the house to you; I don't want it after all." And we know the government would not permit this if it learned of it. We suspect if Jones moves too soon, if he does not live in that house a decent period of time, the Mayer Company will tattle to government and make claims of sham, perhaps perjury. It would not be feasible in practice or theory that the title of disposition is transferred unconditionally to Jones.

So let us say that the title of disposition is held in abeyance for a reasonable period. Jones meanwhile holds the titles of possession and use. Now, bringing our other cases into the discussion, I earlier suggested that government gave Sheila the title to Brown's land for the strictly limited objective of saving Peter from harm. And it gave

Mrs. Carter the title to Miss Reed's home for the sole objective of visiting her mother. In fact, we might have a more unified theory if we postulated for all three cases - Jones, Sheila, and Carter - that the government took the title for itself in these cases and granted certain people limited uses for specific purposes.

But let us thrust this theory of abeyance one mighty step forward. The government had this particular title of disposition all along, since the beginning - whenever that was - and had never granted it to anyone. For look what we are talking about: Sheila's pursuit to save Peter; Mrs. Carter's pursuit in personal relations; Joseph Jones's pursuit in personal relations. All. All are the government's pursuit. Everybody's pursuit **in her property** is in accord with the government's pursuit. This is the definition of property as far as governments and subjects are concerned. But in holonity, these pursuits in personal relations are **identical** to the government's pursuit - the transformation of objects into originant-taxitants **within their property.**

For such pursuits the government creates loading spaces penetrating every other loading space. All others. The loading space in such pursuits is the She of a person, the biological life. And does not government hold title to the She of each of us? To be let out only with our consent as originant-taxitants and never as objects? Furthermore, government tolerates no other title to interfere with this pursuit. For after all, to whom are titles given but to Shes. Originant-Taxitant Shes.

Thus the apparent abruption of titles for the benefit of personal relations is not enforced trespass. Not slavery. For no one is granted any use that will contravene this government pursuit of originancy-within-property. There are **no** exceptions to the cutting edge between loud music and billboards. There is but one unified theory, pivoting upon the pursuit of the common good. And doesn't our intuition guide us in this direction? Can we honestly feel sorry for Farmer Brown, Nell Carter, and the Mayer Company? Do we feel that their property has been invaded?

The idea of equal rights has impaired our feeling for property, our distaste for enforced service and trespass. In large part this is attributable to inept opinions expressed in court decisions securing for blacks a recognition of their rights. Though certainly a worthy objective, nevertheless this recognition will remain tentative until grounded as rigorously as I am attempting. Actually we seek not equality, but commonalty. The common law has never proposed equality of rights. It proposes to mete justice for all under a common standard. A brief review of the black movement already covered reveals the introduction of "equality" and the proliferation of its influence. And remember, these case were argued not primarily by blacks but by federal attorneys proceeding under the civil rights acts.

The first great victory for blacks was **Brown v. School Board,** the suit that broke the back of segregation in schools. As later for **Jones,** the true cause was defamation, but the opinion based the decision on the equal protection clause of the fourteenth amendment. The courts have never understood the meaning of this clause. In fact it has no meaning in our system. But here is where equality crept officially into court language.

The courts have not been able to shake off the sophistry of equality. It adhered to it in the second case of **Brown** - resulting in a roundabout way in enforced school bussing. The decision rose from the notion that the first **Brown** announced, that segregation was diametrically opposed to equality. But equality had nothing to do with it; school segregation as a consequence of neighborhood segregation casts no aspersion on black people. Neighborhood segregation is in large part the result of human relations pursuits. If economics plays a role in ethnic segregation, we must also admit that ethnic cohesiveness is as much a force in demographics as the publicized villainies of oppressive bigotry.

In a discussion of equality we need not mention the **Heart of Atlanta** case, except as an exercise in crudeness. A cause based on equality would have been a shining beacon in comparison. An insult to blacks, **Heart of Atlanta** said, "even though they are undesirable, still we are going to make you accomodate them. It will be good for interstate commerce." The celebration of **Heart of Atlanta** was a tom-tom victory dance by our federal jurists over the graves of all the great men who conceived and developed the common law.

But the halls of justice are still addicted to equality. Thus we have suits for equal wages, equal admissions to the armed forces, equal admissions to colleges and equal rights to life. The last has surfaced in the indeterminate debate over abortion and in the case known as "Baby Doe" (the services mandate upon physicians and parents in preserving the life of a very feeble and abnormal child's life). It is now my task to show these issues not to be issues of equality. They are questions of "Who is going to use what?".

Equal Wages.

In the usual suit for equal wages, a woman need prove only that she is receiving less pay than a man doing the same work in the same company, due to her being a woman. Given this proof, the court will order the employer to pay her a wage equal to the man's. The practice has been extended by a recent Supreme Court decision declaring that people should receive equal wages if their jobs, though different in effort or product, require equal levels of skill. To judge the correctness of this practice, it will be necessary to analyze the employee-employer situation.

Contrary to many authorities, a job for hire is not a contract. A hiree agreeing to come to work Monday morning need never appear. If he appears and, without maliciousness or malevolence, breaks a one hundred thousand dollar machine, he is not legally liable for the loss. For negligence, laziness, carelessness, clumsiness and churlishness an employer has but one control device - termination of employment.

It is sometimes written that an implied contract begins the moment a hiree enters a job. The time spent by the hiree is said to be the consideration given by the hiree, and the employer agrees to pay the hourly wage for every hour worked. The wage is said to be the employer's consideration. However there are defects in this theory.

The essence of a contract is the predetermination of a property. At a certain future time T, householder H will have her home; the contractor C will have his money. At time T, H's property in her home will exist, whether the home exists or not. C's property in the money will exist whether H can pay it or not. These properties the parties can rely on, for the government will see to it.

As stated in an earlier chapter, this predetermination of property means that each party undertakes to materialize the objective of the other. Quite an undertaking. One never knows when one undertakes a project that the result will indeed phenomenalize the envisioned objective. A wise person devotes much thought to the contractual project before agreeing to it, and this deliberation is referred to by the term "to give consideration". Unfortunately in practice the term is usually applied to the goods or services or money that a party delivers to the other party, it being the other party's objective. As a result of this misapplication, the term loses its powerful significance, that a court will **presume** that each party in entering the contract has given due consideration to her risk, effort and cost in materializing the other party's objective. In a suit involving contract, the court will tolerate no excuse from a party that she did not give the enterprise appropriate consideration.

In making this distinction I am not being academic but practical. For consider the contract in which I give you twenty dollars and you agree to deliver a fresh rosebud to a certain address. You are the only one under contract. In entering the agreement you considered the difficulties you would encounter in materializing my objective. In accepting my twenty dollars, you acknowledged that you had given the project due consideration. If I gave any consideration to the project, I did it before making the offer. Once I gave you the money, I was not under contract. I was not bound to materialize an objective of yours.

And here's the point. Even you are not under contract. What is commonly called a contract in a situation like this is not a contract at all. It has all the elements of a trust. In the most elementary trust, a trustor gives something to the trustee and instructs the trustee what to do with it. If the trustee accepts it, the government presumes that she has agreed to the instructions, and will insist on her performance. The essence of a trust is that a trustor gives something but assumes no burden. In other words, the trustor gives no consideration to materializing an objective for the trustee. No such mission is involved. In the case of the rosebud, you took my money and agreed to transform it into a rosebud delivered to the occupant at 111 Peach Street. If you fail, it is not breach of contract. It is a breach of trust, in some respects more serious.

Rather than being contract, hired employment is a mode of trust. The hiree gives time and perhaps effort to the employer. He may even give skilled effort and a concentration of his attention. But he gives it with certain conditions. A value will be placed on it as it is given, and the accumulated value will be returned to him in material form at a certain time, as at the end of the week, or under certain contingencies, as at termination of employment.

But unlike a person about to enter a contract, the hiree gives no consideration to such points as being bound to a performance. True, before taking the job he may consider his options, but this is not the type of consideration under discussion. He need consider no obligation to the employer. He does not promise even to work for an hour, and having worked an hour he does not promise to work the next. Furthermore, the time and effort spent on the job by the hiree is not the objective of the employer. She looks for some species of productive output from the hiree, and for this the hiree assumes no responsibility. The employer is betting that she will obtain a measure of product from this worker, and she tries to organize the work accordingly. She has but one protection in this situation. She can refuse to accept in trust any more of this worker's time and effort. She can terminate his employment, and pay his entrusted accumulations of time and effort.

On the elementary level, just as the government presumes consideration in the case of a contract, it presumes no consideration on the part of the hiree. To a degree, the device of hired employment covers those who have not the ability to anticipate all the possible difficulties in materializing a set of well-defined objectives. In this group are individuals needing a greater measure of protection. Therefore their time and effort is entrusted to the employer, and the employer is a trustee burdened with the responsibility of returning to them their time and effort in material mode. Every hour on the job adds to his trust fund, and woe to the employer if she does not handle it in a trustworthy manner. If she cannot pay the hiree at the end of the week, it is not so much breach of contract as embezzlement. In a case of bankruptcy, the hiree is more favored than creditors.

There is but one way that this arrangement can be made to work. It is essential that an agreement be reached respecting the value of the hiree's time, and that it be reached before the employer accepts any of the hiree's time. Otherwise the hiree cannot determine what he should receive at the end of the week. If there is no agreement, there will be nothing for a court to enforce if the employer defaults. This was recognized in England soon after the demise of feudalism. English law (Dalton) provided for pre-harvest conferences at which local magistrates or justices of the peace would determine the wages to be paid hired harvest hands. It was understood that the hirelings must have sufficient to live; that this would vary from year to year depending on the prices of necessities.

On a basis of predetermined value, the hiree gives his time, and the employer accepts it if she wishes to accept the conditions that accompany the trust. The hiree has no right to force the employer to accept his time and effort in trust, and the employer has no right to the monetary value of the time, once put into trust.

So for each hour given, the employer must put the wage rate R into the hiree's trust fund. As the R's accumulate, the R+R+R+R... belongs to the hiree. The employer's equity in his cash account dwindles: C-R-R-R-R... The R's belong to the hiree, but the C minus the R's belongs to the employer. For the government to say to the employer, "This hiree wants more of your remainder, therefore give it to him," is to force the employer to use his entitled loading space to please the hiree, and amounts to slavery.

The pursuit of both hiree and employer is the pursuit of money. Unlike the situation with blacks, the lower wages of a woman are in no way a defamation of her as a person or a worker. We are talking about the economic forces of supply and demand. The employer works as hard as the hiree. Her economic heart is as much committed to her pursuit as the hiree's to his. The hiree does not have to give the employer his work, and the employer does not have to accept the work in trust. If you bring the idea of equal into it, why cannot the employer get government to force consumers to give her as much return for her time as her competitor, or even her employee, gets?

In closing the discussion on equal wages, the minimum wage law deserves a brief comment. It is not generally recognized that the minimum wage law injures the hiree. The employer might not wish to accept the hiree's work at the minimum wage rate and, as a result, the minimum wage law deprives the hiree of an opportunity to put his time and effort into trust at a lower rate. In terms of project spaces, it deprives him of an important segment of his freedom in materializing his potential. Since it is usually considered that everyone may work if he wishes, the result of the minimum wage law is this. If there is a potential hiree, wishing to work, but unemployable under the terms of the law, the law deprives him of property. I leave it to you to judge the effect on the common good.

Bakke v. Regents of the University of California.

The topic centers upon a medical school, in particular its admissions policy. As much as any institution, a medical school is an instrument for promoting the public good. In the case of a publically supported medical school, such a mission is the one and only reason for existence.

The school is given the responsibility for the training program. Its name and fame depend on the output of the program, and a big factor in its success is the accuracy with which it selects candidates for training. Many more candidates apply than the schools can train or than the profession can support. The selection process is important. The students chosen are those who, on the basis of medical school experience, will make the best use of medical training. The testing and selection procedure is based on data gathered from generations of medical teachers and practitioners.

A state-supported medical school like the one at the University of California at Davis belongs to the people of the state. The people can build the school if they wish, and staff it and, if they wish, they don't have to admit a single student. It is their property. No candidate has a right to a spot in the student body, just as no hiree has a right to a job.

When the school is turned over to a group of administrators, the powers of use are delegated to them. The arrangement is part contract, part trust. Conditioned by intelligent instructions and the professed mission of the school, they are empowered to use the school as they see fit. No capable administrator would accept the trust on any other basis.

Now comes an affirmative action program, powered with a significant amount of financial muscle, telling them how to run their school. That is, it lays down some guidelines as to the make-up of their student body. Obviously, the guidelines vary widely from the administrators' stated admissions policy, but the guidelines are not entirely implausible. They alert the staff that their admissions policy might exclude certain applicants not because the applicants have less talent for medical practice, but because they have been educationally deprived. They can't pass the tests because they had been raised in poverty-stricken neighborhoods. Fate had assigned them to a below-standard educational machine.

A person thus deprived, though equal or superior in talent to those to whom fate has been kinder, watches opportunity slip away forever. Not only does the nation stand to lose the effectiveness life of this individual, but the advantages of her superior talent. The faculty of the medical school scratch their heads. "Well, maybe we are missing an opportunity. So how might we alter our screening procedure. Obviously we will have to admit some students whom we usually reject. How many?"

Of the new incoming class of 100, the school at Davis admitted 16 who scored below previously established standards. Necessarily this meant that 16 in the very top 100 could not be admitted. The applicant Bakke scored higher than the sixteen variants who were admitted. (The faculty could not demonstrate that he did or did not score in the top 100.) He was Caucasian; the 16 special admittees were all non-Caucasian; and the court decided that the faculty used racial categories in selecting the special students. The California courts, from bottom to top, and the federal Supreme Court declared the admissions program "illegal". They declared that Bakke was entitled to admission. He had been eliminated from consideration on account of his race.

The Superior and Supreme Court of California as well as the Supreme Court of the United States were wrong. No one is "entitled" to be admitted to a medical school. If in a given year the faculty decided to admit but one person, an imbecile with superior motor skills and coolness under pressure, concentrating on him to develop his skill for an extremely delicate brain operation - perhaps an experimental project - no other candidate can sue successfully for admission. The faculty could be asked of course for their letters of resignation but, while they have their positions they - not prospective students - have the use of the medical training machinery.

In the year of Bakke, the faculty was executing an experiment using sixteen subjects. This pursuit was within their entitled loading space and they were attempting to design and execute it within reasonable limits. It was an experiment entirely in the pursuit of the common good. Was their standard admissions policy satisfactory, or was it defective? This was the experimental question. In the experimental design there was perhaps a defect. Conceivably not only non-Caucasians but some Caucasians screened and rejected had been disadvantaged in their pre-graduate education. What of their "equal" rights! But this was error in experimental design if error it was, not legal error.

Baldly stated, Bakke's Omega - what he desired - grew on a tree in the entitled loading space of the medical school administrators, and the court put this space in Bakke's hands. It was an instance of government-enforced trespass and government-enforced service. But wait! Did Bakke after all have a pursuit in personal relations or human bonds, and was the faculty denying him access to this space? Was the school, like the Mayer Company in **Jones**, displaying a sordid climate of mind? Certainly not. No. In no way did Bakke's rejection declare: "Allan Bakke, being a Caucasian, is unfit as a medical student." In no way was it defamation. In no way, as in **Carter v. Reed**, was the school barring him from pursuing a precious relationship. In no way, as in "Brown v. Sheila", was it preventing him from a tremendous exercise of human sensitivity, a rescue of a person materially in distress. In **Bakke** we saw our great courts cater to pure greed. We saw the courts ignore property and the whole spirit of the common law. Why? Why? Why?

With this, I can add the last refinement to the general format of injury. The final outline is this:

(1) Is plaintiff frustrated in an entitled enjoyment by an activity of defendant? (A. Yes.)

(2) Are the elements of the enjoyment material? (A. Yes.)

(3) Are the elements of the frustration material? (A. Yes.)

(4) Is there entrapment? (A. Yes.)

(5) Is plaintiff's enjoyment free from servitude to defendant's stated activity? (A. Yes.)

(6) Does remedial action require a use of defendant or defendant's exclusive subject matter by plaintiff? (A. No.)

An answer to each question is required, and, for a conclusion of injury, the answers must be as stated. The only exception is the case in which plaintiff's pursuit is in personal relations with a third person or class of persons. If, in such a case, the remedy requires a use of defendant's non-human subject matter, the strictly limited use may be ordered.

CHAPTER 38

ABORTION AND A CLOSER LOOK
AT WILL AND DESIRE

Should the government prohibit an abortion that the pregnant mother desires? No question has more deeply troubled and divided the people of the United States. More popularly phrased in the converse, "Should abortion be legalized?", arguments pro and con have been to date conducted only on plausible levels, seeking popular sympathy - none biting into real common law stuff like property and liberty and injury. Allow me to try the common law.

First and briefly separating out a closely related issue - may a physician administer an abortion - I see nothing in our standard of justice preventing it if (1) the mother is entitled to an abortion and (2) she requests the physician's ministrations. It is well settled that an agent may do what the principal may do. Therefore the central issue in abortion is not the entitlement of the physician. It is the entitlement of the mother. Nevertheless a physician has a perplexing problem of his own - what to do with a fetus remaining alive and potentially viable after being parted from the mother. This I will deal with summarily at the end of the chapter.

By historical biological definition, an abortion involves a dead fetus. At least the fetus is no longer viable after the separation process. Historically the word abortion has not denoted a premature parturition, but medical advances have thrown confusion into this distinction. Already, in what we are pleased to call abortions, we suspect fetuses to have been separated who, if they had been treated with current technique, were capable of surviving in the separated state.

For our purposes, I will continue using abortion in its current loose usage - denoting simply the separation of the fetus from the mother. But I will apply a differentiating Roman numeral to three distinguishable situations: Abortion I, the separation of a fetus that has died - no induced separation of a living fetus intended. Abortion II, a wilfully induced separation of a live fetus who, as a result of the separation, has zero expectation of survival. Abortion III, the induced separation that produces a viable fetus, given the technology of the day.

Perhaps someday we will call an Abortion III not an abortion but a PIP - a prematurely induced parturition. And if a prematurely separated but unwanted fetus can be successfully incubated, the legal situation will be indistinguishable from letting a child out for adoption or turning it over to the state. In that day perhaps all Abortions II will have become Abortions III, and PIP will be common procedure. By that time, the term abortion will have reverted to its historical biological application, Abortion I, and we can scrap the Roman numerals.

In this chapter I will conclude that a mother is absolutely entitled - under the common law - to Abortions II and III. Of Abortion I there has never been a question. And what to do with a situation halfway between II and III; what to do with the living separated fetus, the fetus whose survival is uncertain and whose care is strictly experimental and immensely expensive. Here is an issue distinct from the issue of abortion itself. But abortion itself is the topic to treat first and really, the basic problem centers on the Abortion II situation - the wilfully induced separation of a living fetus that will die inevitably as a result of the separation.

Frankly it involves the killing of the fetus, and this we must distinguish as a pivotal issue in itself. Killing a fetus is killing a human despite the biologically ignorant proposal that a fetus is not human, or not human until the end of the first trimester. Biologically the fetus before birth and the baby after birth is the same creature. There is no human, non-human division line between the one-celled zygote and the fully developed mature adult. (On the other hand, a human egg or a human sperm is not a human being.)

Some anti-abortionists think to argue for legal consistency. If a mother can kill her fetus, or pay to have it done - thus goes an argument against abortion - why can't she kill her normally born baby, or even an older child. And if she is permitted to use poverty or danger to mental stability as grounds, well; a child already born can occasion as much economic or mental stress as a fetus in the womb. For that matter, why should she not be allowed to kill a husband who is driving her out of her mind. Pretty telling argument.

Nor can we lean on another mistaken premise. A mother cannot argue that in abortion she is only cutting out a part of herself. Contrary to her concept, the fetus is not part of her body; it is as distinctly individual as an individual can be. But when the mother asks, "Don't I have the use of my own body?", we must pause and consider.

It is undeniable that the fetus is using her body. And if she doesn't want it there, it is trespass, pure and simple. Yes, we say, but is it. Isn't the fetus the result of her own will? And at this point it will be wise to analyze the relationship between will - volo - and kinestasis - Omega.

At a stage in its cycle, kinestasis in a bodily system activates a pursuit system that proceeds to romp in the external environment. Thus, the sexual drive frequently culminates in a sexual act. To this point I have tended to identify act with will - volo. I have distinguished between desire and will. There is desire, and then there is the act. And the difference between desire and act is this inferential operator called will. Well, this analysis may not be sufficient. For instance, I am not sure that the sexual act of a lower creature can be called a function of will. Rather, the inner kinestasis activates the pursuit mechanism, and the sexual act becomes the Omega of the moment. Given this, we will find it to our advantage not to call this sequence by the name will - volo. There is a function in a higher dimension that merits this label.

To proceed with the sexual example, there is no reason to distinguish between the normal sexual act as it occurs in humans and as it occurs in the lower animals. (Not that I wish to debase either.) Thus in humans a married man might desire a woman not his wife and, if the drive is consummated, I think it need not be called an act of will, no more than the act of mating in lower animals. No more, for that matter, than the conjugal act between man and wife.

Humans are not simple. In many situations they are beset with opposing drives. This man in his love affair might have opposing Omegas. He might wish to remain faithful to his wife. Such oppositions we would be wise not to address simplistically. But, simple or complex, a non-consummation with the other woman, though a non-act, is nevertheless a signal of will. At least we may call it such, for it involves an active repression of a potent pursuit mechanism. Even the physicist, I think, would call it an act, for I suppose it to be an energy-consuming phenomenon.

Or a physician deep in his cozy bed on a bitterly cold night might make himself go out to care for a patient. Thus sometimes we say we make ourselves perform an act, and sometimes we make ourselves actually refrain from performing an act. These then are the instances for which we should reserve the use of the label "will".

Do not be misled. On these occasions we are still in the land of desire - still in the realm of kinestasis, pursuit mechanisms and Omegas. We cannot escape the fact, I think, that our resolution of a perplexing situation is still the triumph of desire. Even in the case of a martyr choosing to be burned at the stake, we must conclude that she wants something more than life, more than she wants freedom from pain. We might try to characterize "higher" Omegas and "lower" ones, but I think it best to simply say that some kind of a decision is made between opposing desires, and the act resulting from such a process is the true act of will.

I must dwell on this topic, for its ramifications are immense. In view of its scope, for instance, I must refine my basic descriptions of injury and damage. You run your car over my curb and this is nuisance - injury. In the same act you break my fence - damage. Your will is crystallized in my property; this was one of my characterizations of damage, but note; I am presuming will from action. Yet is will really present? Will, that is, in this higher dimension of decision making. Well, if you premeditated it, running into my fence, you had to give it some thought, and it was an act of will. But what if it was pure accident. You were blissfully pursuing an innocent objective in your car, and the result happened to be not your objective, but a broken fence.

Now follow me. If I call it will - volo - I am claiming you chose to drive into my fence. If I were a judge, I would be presuming your will. I would presume a better way to act - more in the common good. A pursuit in the common good is an appropriate Omega for everyone. This sounds reasonable. To choose such a pursuit despite opposing desires is an act of will. Therefore for you to choose an opposing pursuit - one contrary to the common good - is an act of will. **You should not have done it!**

Notice then where we are. To speak of injury or damage in terms of will is to speak in the language of tort and negligence; you acted thus though you had a duty to act otherwise. Apparently at the point where I cast away the sophistry of tort and negligence, I should have cast away the language of will. Evidently injury and damage can materialize from acts alone; will is not an essential ingredient of a case. The exception would be the case in which you wish to prove malice. Injury and damage can arise solely from kinestasis and pursuit mechanisms; from originancy void of will. Thought and decision are not necessarily implicated. Therefore duty and negligence are immaterial. Evidently injury and damage can rise from the mere fact that one lives and acts, and that one exists in a functional commonalty with one's fellows!

How does this touch the case of the woman pregnant with an unwanted child? Does it permit us to hold her responsible for the existence of the child; may we force her to carry it to full term? After all, even if it wasn't the result of her will, it was the result of her acts, of the kinestasis of her body and brain, of her pursuit mechanisms. And this is sufficient to hold her responsible.

As important as this analysis of will is to the analysis of injury and damage. As significant as it is mechanistically in attaching the responsibility for the child to the mother, we will in the end find it impertinent to the topic at hand. The law is not interested in holding a person responsible for an act unless the act perpetrates injury. Yes, I built the fence at the front of my yard. Yes, I am the cause for the existence of the fence. So you run your bicycle into it, breaking your arm, and sue me for building the fence? No. I am a factor in the existence of the fence, but in doing so I did not invade your property. Yes, the mother is a factor in the existence of the child, and the gods of the common law murmur, "So?"

Fundamentally therefore in the abortion issue, we come to the situation of two human beings, one occupying space within the other. The inner human being is an independent center of kinestasis and pursuit mechanisms, using the outer person as the source of her Omegas. The fetus is using the mother. And against the mother's wishes. Trespass!

For the sake of discussion, for the moment, let us forget about all the statutes governing abortion. Let us situate the issue of abortion within an ambience devoid of statute. The mother has an intruder in her body and wishes to be rid of it. It is her property; this is trespass; and we are talking about a space in which it is her prerogative to determine all the loadings. The child must go.

There is a modifying circumstance; the eviction of the child involves killing a human being, and now we must talk about due process. But in a court action, we must have a plaintiff. Aha! The plaintiff will not be the government; we have stipulated we are not working within a framework of statute. It is not going to be **U.S. v. Mother** or **State v. Mother.**

This is something about which I have been indefinite until now; that every suit must have a plaintiff and a defendant. The judge and lawyers know it, but we lay people tend not to think in these terms, particularly when it comes to the "great" issues. We like to discuss them in terms of what's right and what's wrong. But courts never listen to that kind of discussion. "That's a moot issue," they declare, and dismiss the case. They require a real fighting controversy between at least two live jumping persons. They require a complaining person bringing in a tale of injury implicating a certain human causer. Either that or the situation calling for declaratory judgment; the potential causer comes in seeking to know what will happen if she acts as she wishes to act - will the potential complainer have a valid cause against her? And both plaintiff and defendant must possess the power of wilful human action - they must be mentally competent - and this eliminates babies. It eliminates all whose actions reflect pure kinestatic processes - cleansed of the capacity for decision in the gravity field of law.

Certainly in the case at hand the mother will be the defendant. Someone will seek an injunction preventing her from pursuing her wish to evict the trespasser. There will have to be a claim of injury and there will have to be a plaintiff. The baby not being competent, someone will have to represent her. But first let us find the injury.

The allegation of injury will somehow refer to the imminent death of the baby. For the purpose of injunction a court will listen to allegations of imminent injury. Injury of course must involve an invasion of property, an infringement of liberty, and the best that anti-abortionists have produced to date is "the right to life" - an infringement of the right to life. This must be examined for under the canon I have developed there is no such construction as a right to life, at least as anti-abortionists conceive it, and one does not wish to weaken the plaintiff's case merely by semantic play. Is there a right to life?

The right to life is mentioned in the Declaration of Independence, a paper creating no legal power, and the right to life is not mentioned in the Constitution of the United States. Though the right to life has a degree in philosophic heritage, it is ill-conceived in the context of the common law.

Certainly the common law has the effect of protecting life. If you declare constitutionally for the common good, it will be difficult to achieve a High Commons if each person fends for herself in the matter of personal safety. Property becomes meaningless if the Shes to whom property is assigned can be snuffed out without government reprisal.

I showed in Chapter 28 that you cannot use your biological life, your She. You can use your muscles and your brain, but not your She. We might imagine that She consists of the operations of all your kinestatic systems. Not the substances of the systems, but the fluxing and flashing of electrons among molecules, the chargings and dischargings of the systems, the phenomena that spell the difference between the living material and the corpse. Yes, other people can use your She in their varying pursuits, but you can't use you. If you say you can use your biological life, you might as well say your biological life can use you. It is one and the same.

Therefore your She is not a loading space as far as you are concerned. And what is a right? A right is a loading in which you are propertied. Consequently, you can not hold a right to your life, your She; there is no way you can load you. Your own right to your life would be immaterial, even if postulated in law; and the common law does not deal in immaterialities. In this singular circumstance - particularly since others can use you, and often do, I proposed in Chapter 31 that the government (materially those who control the government) has kept for itself the use of your She. Though due process implies that government has appointed you agent for lending out uses of yourself to others, government can and does maintain in its hands the right to your you, your She, your life.

You are in the property of government. A use of you contrary to government policy, or a distortion of you contrary to government wishes, is an injury to government, the state, the rulers. If someone kills you or anyone else within this dominion, government - the material government - is the injured party, if the killing constitutes injury. We are back where we started. Even in the absence of statute, government after all will be the plaintiff if suit is to be brought against the mother who is intending abortion, or who has already acted in the pursuit. Government will be the defendant if the mother sues for a declaration of right.

So we reach the ultimate expression of the question, it being "Is Abortion II murder?". This is correct, because though it is a killing of a human, there are instances, as in self-defense, when killing a human is not deemed murder. We have a mother who wishes an Abortion II, and the mother and the government will be the interested parties. Either may be plaintiff with the other as defendant, depending on who brings the complaint to court, for we are simply going to seek declaratory relief, meaning a declaration by the court stating the rights of the parties.

Specifically we have a mother who has all the rights to the use of her body, and we have the government who strictly limits all pursuits that will likely end in the death of humans. Here is a true decision in property. There is a right that will prevail and a right that will be transferred or placed in servitude or restricted.

As judge, one of our difficulties is this. Crowds are standing outside the courtroom clamoring, "It isn't right. Killing is killing," and they are striving to gain sympathy for their stance. They are holding up banners proclaiming the "Right to Life". They are showing pictures of aborted fetuses. In these efforts they are trying to act as plaintiffs and, though they have no standing, let us suppose they indeed have standing. What is their cause? It turns out to be pseudo-nuisance.

What we see here are Wolcotts standing on their patios. They don't wish to see abortions. They wish to see mothers loving and nurturing their babies. And they demand that this mother, standing wholly in her entitled space, serve their wishes. She is to be their slave. We are seeing Wolcotts who don't want billboards, and home-owners who don't like black and orange houses, and employees who want the employers money, and people who want to usurp the medical school facilities. We are seeing people who insist that their desires and tastes must prevail over the common law abhorrence of enforced service.

Now transform them into advisors, friends of the court, and this is entirely appropriate. After all, who is deciding the case for or against the government but the appointed agent of the rulers, and she is not seeing an entitled person claiming injury. She sees two entitled persons, one a ruler, one the subject of the ruler, claiming property. In short she must weigh right against right, climate of mind against climate of mind, effectiveness life against effectiveness life. We are in equity.

"After all," say the advisors, "you force a mother to feed and care for her child after its birth, putting her into enforced service no less than carrying the baby to term." The government rubs its chin. "No," it answers. "As long as she keeps the child, I presume she consents to the parental service. And if she protests, I will take over the care and maintainence of the child."

"But what of climates of mind, and commitment, and pursuits in personal relations, and responsibility? If discipline in these qualities is a prime concern of yours, how can you favor a pursuit that flouts each and every one of them?" The government meditates a moment.

"I do not force my subjects to pursue exemplary projects. I do not force my Sheilas to save my Peters. Where I pay attention to climates of mind is where people are greedy to use another person's property, or where they are insensitive to their interference in the liberty of others, or where the use of their own property defeats another person's pursuit in personal relations."

"Well, then, we are engaged in an exemplary project. We wish to save this baby's life. We wish for it to have an opportunity to establish warm personal relationships in life."

"Unfortunately you have no standing in this case. You are neither plaintiff or defendant. You have no title at stake. You have no liberty here threatened with infringement. I see no pursuit of yours, save the pursuit of trying to persuade me to do what you wish me to do. Your claim of pursuit is immaterial. Personally to you this baby is nothing. She is an idea. There is no way you personally can establish a warm personal relationship with her, and I haven't seen you trying.

"There is something you can do, and it does not require an intervention by this court. You can go and talk to this mother. You can put out a material effort to save the infant. Offer the mother a contract for the use of her body. Bring me a contract. Let me see that you have given consideration to an investment of yourself in this project. Let me see a failure of performance on the mother's part or an imminent failure of performance, and you will have standing in this court."

"Then you the government," roars the crowd, "should engage in an exemplary project. Save the baby's life. Make a contract with the mother."

"I am already engaged in an exemplary project. I have the use of the baby's life. But there is no way I can use it. At this point, my idea of using it is a mere matter of principle; it is immaterial. I have the use also of the mother's life, and there are various ways of using it. I can try to convince her to carry the child to term; make a contract with her. But I cannot force her to make a contract; if I did, it would not be a contract. And if I make a contract with her, you will have to pay the bill, just as you would if you made your own contract. For this I will have to get the advice of your representatives in Congress; appropriation is in their power, not in the power of equity. And can I force her to carry the child to term? No, I cannot. My chief use of her is through due process. By this process I train in her the intuition for property, a respect for the property of others. This is in accord with my grand project to promote the common good. This I equate with a project to instill in each person a sense of originancy within her property. This is the effect of the liberty I create under the common law. And this I cannot do by making her a slave to my tastes or yours, by enforcing upon her a service to your and my wishes **within her property.**"

"Right to abortion affirmed."

The doctor and the hospital staff are left with a dilemma, given a living separated fetus. They do not know that they can incubate it into a normally developing human infant. They do not have the money to make the attempt. Shall they feed it? Shall they smother it? Shall they throw it down the disposal shute? Shall they charge the mother for its care until she takes it off their hands? Can she legally smother it?

No one can force the medical people to spend time or money on the child. The government cannot force the mother to care for the child if she notifies the government that she wishes to be rid of the child. But the government has no provision for handling a human at this stage of development.

These are the questions that the government should be facing and has evaded while tangling itself in confusion over the relatively simple question of abortion. It is a situation, as I see it, calling for scientific experimentation with a sample of living separated fetuses, and the humane killing of the others. To permit them to die by starvation or dehydration would be strictly legal, but hardly humane. It is a matter of facing reality, and facing reality as a matter of principle, the anti-slavery principle that lies at the basis of the common law, the principle of establishing a government promoting the highest level of originant-taxitancy in each person within her property. It is a matter in which equity sees two cases, the situation in the field and the effect of its decision on the participants and observers in the courtroom. I have a final word on the subject on the last page of Chapter 53, "Church And State".

CHAPTER 39

PLEADING; LEGISLATED INJURY; ABSCAM

It is true. From chapter to chapter I have gradually modified the general format of injury, and I suspect we are not sure where we stand at the moment.

One can say without error that injury is the life support of the courts. Injury is the only basis on which a court may deliver enforceable commands to a human being. This being the case, a common law court is extremely careful in advancing against a defendant; there is no stress on a person greater than the burden of defending oneself before an omnipotent being. It is particularly true in the case of a particular class of defendant; the one who has always taken pains to respect other people's property. The various responses of such a person to a misdirected seizure by government are not anticipated with pleasure by intelligent rulers.

So the government has devised a format for a plaintiff to follow when she wishes to present in court a claim of injury. It is called a pleading, and the pleading of a plaintiff is often called a complaint and sometimes a petition or bill. Elementally a plaintiff's pleading is comprised of a complaint and a petition. To give it an adequate name, I would call it a "Pleading for Court Action".

To overcome a court's reluctance in seizing jurisdiction over a defendant, the plaintiff's pleading must cover certain aspects of the case - features that courts have learned to look for before summoning the defendant to appear and answer, and I will now outline these components or elements. You of course, if you are intent on commencing a suit, will consult a lawyer or the encoded rules of court procedure. But for my present purpose, I index the plaintiff's pleading in six parts:

Outline of A Pleading for Court Action

Part I identifies the parties and establishes jurisdictional purview. In it plaintiff makes the following statements:

1. Plaintiff is (name of plaintiff) residing at (full address of plaintiff including city, county and state).
2. Defendant is (name of defendant).
3. Defendant lives at (or does business at) (full address of defendant including city, county and state). This statement should make clear to the court that the defendant lives or does business within a geographical area subject to the jurisdictional purview of the court.

Early in the pleading, given the caption (a heading descriptive of the pleading) and Part I, and the early sentences of Part II, the pleading should also make it clear that the subject matter of the case lies within the jurisdictional competence of the particular court. A word or two representing one or more of the following features of the case: the nature of the injury (trespass, nuisance, non-payment of debt...); damage if damage is involved and, if so, the amount of damages sought; the involvement of a certain statute, if it is relevant; the general nature of the prayer (for damages, or injunction, or declaratory judgment...). These are all items that should be stated early in the pleading, almost as part of the caption - one, two, three, four words - enabling the court to determine that it can seize jurisdiction in the case. To this extent they are, wherever they fall, features of Part I.

Part II of the pleading is the actual complaint of injury. It presents the bare bone facts of the case that will support a conclusion of injury. It is Part II that I wish to elaborate in the chapter, but I will first proceed to mention the remaining parts of the pleading.

Part III contains statements of entrapment: "There is no relief for plaintiff without the intervention of the court." Or facts may be stated from which entrapment can be inferred: "The defendant refused to cease her stated activities." Actually entrapment might be inferred without an explicit Part III statement. A Part II statement such as "The radioactive dust from the manufacturing plant settled upon the house and land where plaintiff resides" supports a conclusion of entrapment.

Part IV contains a statement of damage if damage is an element of the case. This will be a statement of facts from which damage can be concluded. It must show (1) that the effectiveness of plaintiff in her property has been irretrievably diminished and (2) that this is a consequence of the very act of defendant that contributed to the injury claimed in Part II.

Part V contains the prayer, the actual petition. This will be a request for specific action on the part of the court. It takes the form of a request for a court order. "The plaintiff prays that the court order the defendant to..." and here follows a statement of the remedy proposed by the plaintiff. Essentially, given the fact that the government will enforce a court order, this is the loading or translation proposed by the plaintiff as the most effective relief under the circumstances.

Part VI comprises the plaintiff's affidavit or verification. Here she declares under penalty of perjury that the statements of her pleading are true - to her knowledge or belief. This required feature of a pleading is a powerful deterrent to intentional sham suits.

In summary outline then, the required elements of a pleading for court action are:

1. Statements identifying parties and establishing jurisdictional purview.
2. Statements establishing injury.
3. Statements establishing entrapment.
4. Statements establishing damage if appropriate.
5. Statements establishing the remedy sought by the plaintiff.
6. Plaintiff's declaration of the verity of the preceding statements.

By its analytical nature, this outline is more rigid than usually required in actual practice. The designations by Part I, Part II..., are mine and would not be expected in an actual pleading. Frequently the elements flow naturally into a pleading and it is necessary only that they be discernible and that the plaintiff adhere to the format prescribed by the particular court.

In response to a pleading for court action - supposing all the required elements to be present - the court will summon the defendant to answer the pleading. Though the answer of the defendant is frequently called simply the "Answer", it is in essence also a pleading. A pleading for what, one might ask. Well, the defendant's pleading also is a pleading for court action, and ordinarily it will pray for an action at variance with the action prayed by the plaintiff. But I will discuss the defendant's pleading in the next chapter. I wish now to focus attention on the central element of the plaintiff's pleading, the complaint of injury.

Having attempted until this chapter to express injury in its most general form, I now reverse this tactic and begin to break injury into categories. I will present injury under two major headings, each having two subheadings. The major distinction is between cases at law and cases in equity. At law I propose two categories - injury through trespass and injury through nuisance. In equity I propose two categories - equitable injury and legislated injury. Thus for Part I of her pleading, the plaintiff will present her case under one of the categories - trespass, nuisance, equitable injury or legislated injury, and will plead them at law or in equity as the case fits.

In meeting Part II requirements, the plaintiff does not say baldly "plaintiff has been injured by defendant". Rather she tells the essential tale as briefly as possible. She does not give her arguments or allude to evidence; she makes statements describing the situation or occasion on the basis of which the judge can draw a conclusion of injury. Naturally he does not thereupon declare his judgment. He will by trial test the factuality of the statements in the light of points raised by the defendant in the defendant's pleading. But if the plaintiff's pleading is complete and the complaint contains the essential elements of injury and if the trial demonstrates the materiality of the statements, the judge can do nothing other than act in favor of the plaintiff and against the defendant. Now I will spell out the elements required in a complaint if the court is to conclude a correct allegation of injury in the case. By "conclude", where a pleading is concerned, I mean the judge finds the elements of injury to be present in the pleading.

From a pleading in **trespass**, the judge must be able to conclude:

(1) The defendant is using a loading space to which she is not entitled and to which plaintiff is entitled.

This is all. Just one element. Trespass is this simple. Mr. Anthony's sign - despite his plausible arguments - was a trespass on Farmer Brown's weed patch by the road. Edison Polyform's use of Thomas A. Edison's carefully cultivated clearing in people's minds for promoting its own products - trespass.

Nuisance is more slippery. In Chapter 17 we first put our finger on it, but it slipped away again in Chapter 35 in "Wolcott v. Billboard", and it took another chapter and baptism in function language to put it back in harness. So.

From a pleading in **nuisance**, the judge must be able to conclude:

(1) Defendant's activity alters a variable in plaintiff's entitled loading space. (The effects of loud music, or of announcing "we will not sell our houses to blacks," or of growing potatoes on a fox hunting course, or of Miss Reed pestering Mrs. Carter visiting her mother).

However this is not all, there are exceptions, and an exception to an exception, which a judge must heed, given situation (1):

Exception 1. Nuisance is not present if plaintiff is under an enforceable servitude to defendant's disruptive activity. (If the fox hunting club had rented land to Brown for growing potatoes, the members could not effectively plead that his potato growing activity spoiled their hunt.)

Exception 2. Nuisance is not present if plaintiff's desired mode (Omega) of said variable derives functionally from defendant's entitled loading space. (Wolcott's Omega derives from his neighbor's land. Our quiet air does not derive from our neighbors space.) But there is an exception to this.

Exception to Exception 2. Nuisance is present if defendant is under an enforceable servitude restraining her from causing the disruption.

When Farmer Brown rents ground to the fox hunting club, his potato growing title is under a contractual servitude to the fox hunting title. Miss Reed's real property title must bow to Mrs. Carter's pursuit in personal relations.)

In Wolcott's case, and also in the case of the unpainted house, the plaintiffs' suits are defeated by Exception 2 of the cause in nuisance. The Omega of the plaintiff in each case is a derivative of the defendant's entitled space. Plaintiff wishes defendant to serve plaintiff in defendant's own space. The same is true of Bakke, and employees who wish part of their employer's money, and people who wish government to outlaw abortion.

The causes in trespass and nuisance are stated in summary form at the end of the chapter, together with the causes for equitable and legislated injury and a list of memoranda to eliminate indistinct areas of the injuries.

Again I mention that a claim of injury may be past, present, or imminent. For relief by injunction, the claim is either present or impending injury; "The defendant is using (or is about to use) a loading space to which plaintiff is entitled." In a suit for damages, a claim of injury is necessarily past tense; "The defendant used my boat without my permission and wrecked it."

If Wolcott learns of the imminent billboard project before construction starts, and threatens to sue his neighbor, the neighbor might wish to ascertain his rights before signing the lease. He might wish a court opinion though no injury has occurred. Notwithstanding, a court will listen to this case, deeming it not moot. A decision now will prevent a suit later if the billboard is erected. And if the neighbor backs away from the project for lack of certainty, his liberty might in a sense be infringed.

In practice today, such a declaratory judgment is deemed in the province of equity, but I see no reason for this. If the court's opinion is based on law, the case should be entered at law. Here I am assuming that the law in the matter is clear, only the parties wish assurance. But having treated trespass and nuisance - cases at law - I come to the province of equity, and here I distinguish two subdivisions of injury - equitable injury and legislated injury. By equitable injury I refer to a claim for which there is no relief at law. And by legislated injury I refer to an injury perpetrated by ill-conceived legislation.

Since legislated injury must be resolved in a court of equity - legislation being law and therefore not subject to scrutiny in law - it is also in a sense equitable injury. The term equitable therefore I apply to a case beyond the jurisdiction of law. This leaves the term "inequit-able" without a home, and I must leave it there.

We will find, I think, that a claim of injury for which there is no relief at law is at bottom a pleading for a declaration of property. This sounds much like a petition for a declaratory judgment. But I will make a distinction between them.

As I have stated before, everything under the common law has an owner. This means that the title for every conceivable use of everything within the ruler's jurisdiction has been assigned to somebody, some person, some class of persons or organization of persons. For the most part, a person's entitled loading space and her property are identical. Thus if Farmer Brown holds title to growing potatoes on a certain meadow, the growing of potatoes there is in his property. Only when the pursuit falls under the shadow of a servitude, as when he leases the meadow to the hunting club, had he better anticipate the effects of growing potatoes on the hunting club space. Under the circumstances, though he retains the potato-growing title, the pursuit is removed from his property. If he exercises his title and distorts the space of the fox-hunt, he will have no defense in court.

So the device called property need come into play only when there is a conflict between two parties who happen to be operating fully within their respective entitled spaces. For instance, our neighbors in playing their music so loudly are operating fully within their entitled space, but they are out of their property. In this case, property is determined automatically under the nuisance formula; it can really be handled at law. A bill in equity should not be necessary.

Undoubtedly there was a time when contractual servitudes and nuisance servitudes, as legal principles, were not yet perfected. Cases like "Fox Hunters v. Brown" and "Quiet Conversation v. Loud Music" had to be presented in equity. There was no relief at law. But once equity began to make consistent decisions in such matters, principles could be abstracted from them, and these principles could be and were considered law, and no further referral to equity need be made in similar cases thereafter. Law could handle them.

Even breach of contract and specific performance can now be treated under nuisance or perhaps trespass. If a building has not been finished on the completion date, or if the contractor used two-by-fours instead of two-by-sixes, he has altered a variable in a loading space to which the prospective homeowner is entitled, a loading space as material as though the house pre-existed the alteration. This is what a contract creates - the objectives of the respective parties - the entitled loading spaces; even though the objectives never materialize!

So ideally the case load of equity, as equity formulates the principles of law, should gradually decrease to zero. Indeed I believe the ultimate stage has arrived. It is my belief that we have at hand all the principles required for handling at law all the cases that will ever appear in a common law country. This does not mean that ingenuity is no longer required in juristic practice, for, as I will demonstrate in succeeding chapters, the discovery of the mechanism of injury in a particular case is frequently as much mental challenge as any man will ever want. Nevertheless, even if equity is never needed again, it will be wise to leave open the category of equitable injury - the dispute for which there is no relief at law. In fact, when we approach a court in equity, we must insert this statement at some point in our pleading - "There is no relief at law for plaintiff."

What is the plaintiff pleading in such a case? First she is admitting that both parties are operating within their entitled loading spaces, and therefore the entitled pursuit of one party must prevail over the entitled pursuit of the other. And the plaintiff is stipulating that nuisance is not a factor; for nuisance she can go to law. Finally the plaintiff is admitting that equity in all its long glorious history has never attained to a principle that establishes a servitude in the case. In short, there are no rules of property that fit the case. What is needed therefore is a declaration of property, and that is not all. The declaration must be accompanied by an opinion stating the principle upon which the property line is drawn. The defendant must be shown that it fits the common good; that he is a winner, though at the moment things look dark.

A declaratory judgment might then be a declaration of property, but it most frequently will not be. Most of the time it will be a conclusion in law, declaring title, declaring property perhaps on a basis of title or nuisance, but drawing its conclusions from principles long since declared in equity. Really I cannot conceive of any case that cannot now be solved at law, given the principles that I have proposed and intend to demonstrate in the remainder of the book. But the category of equitable injury - the pleading for a declaration of property - requires to be kept open. Otherwise the common law system - resting upon equity as its source - would be imperfect.

I hardly know how to frame the complaint in equitable injury. As a first approximation, trying to keep it consistent with my pleadings in trespass and nuisance, I will put it this way:

From a pleading of **equitable injury**, the judge must be able to conclude:

(1) An act of the defendant, acting entirely within her entitled space, infringes the liberty of plaintiff.

(2) It is not a case of trespass or nuisance (i.e., there is no relief at law).

(3) It is important for the common good that defendant's activity be subserviated to plaintiff's liberty under the circumstances.

I cannot offer an example for elucidating the pleading. Furthermore, and most important, I have not introduced the case in which a plaintiff claims a loading space in which rights are not generally recognized. However in Chapter 55 I reach my final word on the task of equity and the principles on which it bases a decision in property.

To complete the spectrum of possible suits, I propose the complaint against legislated injury. It arises from the instance in which legislation violates the principles of the common law, the principles laid down by equity. Since the judge at law should be able to recognize such a violation, I should think he should be competent to declare the law illegal. However, since a statute is construed to be law and therefore legal, it would be appropriate that the question be put to equity; equity being above law.

It might be a pleading for a declaratory judgment. A pregnant woman wishing an abortion might bring it to establish immunity against punishment in the face of an anti-abortion law. As you can see, it is not a proper case for equity. Such a law simply breaches the principle that the common law does not countenance an enforcement of service upon a person. Government-enforced trespass perfectly describes an anti-abortion law. Though we tend to call such disputes "constitutional issues", they are not if they can be resolved under trespass or nuisance. What would most approach a constitutional issue would be a case of equitable injury in which an act of government was perpetrating the injury. The legality of a law under the principles of equity would be at stake, and the pleading would include an appeal to the common good. More precisely, the judge would be asked to refer to the preamble.

From a pleading of **legislated injury**, I think a judge must be able to conclude A or B as follows:

A. This legislative enactment creates a case of enforced service upon plaintiff. Or

B. It creates a case of enforced trespass or enforced nuisance in plaintiff's property. And if the result happens to promote the common good and is thus justified, the enactment fails under the principles of eminent domain to provide adequate compensation to plaintiff.

Eminent domain is the topic of Chapter 50.

Basically I have placed equitable injury and legislated injury in equity because, if you will notice, both appeal to the common good. When a plausible appeal to the common good has no remedy in law, equity must listen. It is for this reason paramount that we discover the exact marrow of the common good. As you are well aware by now, we have long since entered the path to this discovery, and must persist. I bring my search to culmination in Chapter 55.

While on the topic of legislated injury, it will be profitable to review the so-called Abscam cases. These comprise a group of cases initiated in the late 1970's and climaxing in the early 1980's in which the federal government successfully incriminated several congressmen for accepting bribes. Noonan has covered the incident in **Bribes.**

The cases were peculiar, being artificially created by government agents. Government authorities gave the agents money to be tendered to targeted congressmen, purportedly as bribes. In rooms provided with concealed sound and video recording machines, the agents, posing as agents of Arab emirates, sought favors from the uninformed congressmen, to be developed through the congressmen's official capacities, and the money actually changed hands.

Upon indictment, the congressmen in their pleadings claimed to be victims of an "entrapment" scheme, a cause with which I have not familiarized myself. It was not a successful defense, and I believe a proper question for us to ask is whether the bribes were actually bribes. The more fundamental question is whether the government could truly claim injury; if there was no injury - past, present or imminent, the court should not have listened to the case.

The government charges were based on statutes prescribing punishment for taking bribes. The code classifies bribe acceptance as a crime. Having a statute as cause, the case is heard at law. The men were shown to have accepted bribes and were sentenced accordingly. But can a statute create from thin air a condition of injury when no property has been invaded, no liberty infringed, no project effectiveness diminished? Under the common law, for instance, can there be a valid statute providing punishment for a woman who refuses to salute the flag?

I contend a statute cannot make a crime of an act unless the act powers an injury. A theft involves trespass or nuisance or both. So does murder; and in murder we now recognize the government as the injured party. An Abortion II killing must be countenanced, immune to punishment, because an anti-abortion statute would constitute enforced service. And though a government can withhold title to euthenasia - depending on how far it has analyzed the matter - it cannot under statute punish a person for refusing to save a life. This too would constitute enforced service. If the fortress wall of enforced service is once breached, the definition of liberty under the common law will evaporate. Even a criminal is not subject to enforced service. The government will place her in captivity, or will exercise its title to kill her, but it will not force her to act.

But if we insist that crime must involve a true injury, we must take care to thoroughly examine the contours of this field. After all, does the act of running through a red light constitute injury? Who is injured?

This is a question I must ask, for I am about to contend that the acceptance of bribes in the Abscam cases did not constitute crime.

Injury, I have said, is an infringement of liberty. Your liberty is, first, your ideal freedom within your property and, second, your free determination of loadings within your property. So when I ask if someone is injured when someone else runs a red light, we must first determine whose property we are talking about. Really we must first determine who holds title to what. What indeed do we mean by a red light? We mean a signal that you do not have title to the intersection that it governs. Someone else does. If you run through a red light, you are trespassing. But **should** the someone else have the title to the intersection? Well, undoubtedly it is in the common good. But they are not complaining, so who is the plaintiff? Here we see the precise effect of a statute. Under statutory law, the government will assume the role of plaintiff. If at the intersection no one is confronting the trespasser, the government assumes title. Experience shows this to be in the interest of the common good. Undoubtedly there are circumstances, somewhat analogous to Sheila Rienzi's pursuit to save Peter, when the government will grant title to a person facing a red light. But these are the exceptions that prove the rule; the government is interested in the common good.

Let us look at a statute making it a crime for legislators to accept bribes, section 85 of the Penal Code of California:

"Every member of... the legislature... who asks, receives, or agrees to receive, any bribe, upon any understanding that his official vote, opinion, judgment or action shall be influenced thereby... is punishable by imprisonment in the state prison for two, three or four years."

Now if we wish to show injury in a case of bribery, we ask who is injured, and I think we will agree - the people. One remembers that the people is a term including rulers as well as subjects; not only rulers behind the scene but the bribe-taker's colleagues sitting in legislative chambers with him.

Let us recollect also that people are not injured, though we phrase it thus. Injury subsists in the dimensions of the common good, and yet we cannot directly injure the common good. By infringing the liberty of people, supposing liberty to be defined in the beacon of the common good, one erodes the common good. The common good is a dependent variable, its variations powered solely through the functions of human psychology. Injury and the erosion of the common good are identities. This is the scheme of holonism and the common law.

It is presumed that bribery contravenes the common good. We assume that the purpose of a bribe is to induce a legislator to act for a special interest contrary to the common good. In an actual situation of course this might not be the case. The bribe may be intended to induce a wayward legislator to vote in ways promoting the common good. This possibility makes it difficult to define the word bribe. For example take section 7 of the California Penal Code:

"The word "bribe" signifies anything of value or advantage... asked, given or accepted, with a corrupt intent to influence, unlawfully, the person to whom it is given, in his action, vote, or opinion, in any public or official capacity;"

Such a definition, you see, permits a legislator to receive something of value, realizing it is tendered to influence him in his official acts, restricted only thus: the intent of the giver must not be corrupt, or, if the intent is corrupt, the influence must not be unlawful. Such passages are the gift of legislators to people.

By this definition of bribes, the defendants in the Abscam cases did not accept bribes. In the Abscam game, the government agents intended only to entice the defendants to accept the money. They did not intend actually to influence the legislator in his action, vote, or opinion. And since no such intent existed, it couldn't be corrupt and the influence could not be unlawful. Thus might we play with words, and therefore let us get down to fundamentals.

If bribery perpetrates injury, someone's liberty must be infringed in the process. Liberty is erected on property, so one must identify the loading space and the titleholder. One must either find trespass - the wayward legislator is using a titleholder's space in a manner contrary to the titleholder's wishes. Or one must find nuisance - the legislator is in some way distorting a titleholder's loading space.

After a careful search, one will fit together the following picture. The people wish the services of this legislator. By accepting his office he has agreed to represent them in conformity with the common good. One will find then that he holds a position of trust, and one asks what has been entrusted to him. His office? No. The people have entrusted to him all their property - all their loading spaces, including their bodies and brains. For one finds that the whole job of legislators consists of granting titles, and restricting titles, and in transfering titles from one group of people to others. What, for instance is an income tax law, and an assumption of government debt but an appropriation of the bodies and brains of those who will pay taxes and eventually pay the debt with interest, and their labor and the investments of their effectiveness lives? And the whole idea of giving property to a trustee is that he is given only the uses of it that are granted by the trust instrument, and as conditioned by the trust instrument.

The scope of the trustee powers of a legislator is broad indeed.

Read Section 8 of Article I of the federal Constitution - collect taxes, borrow money, regulate commerce, coin money and regulate its value, establish courts inferior to the Supreme Court, declare war, raise armies, and make laws. But remember that this use of us and our property is limited by the objectives of the grand project. Our legislators have these uses only for certain objectives (1) forming a more perfect union (2) establishing justice (3) insuring domestic tranquillity (4) providing for the common defense (5) promoting the general welfare and (6) securing the blessings of liberty to ourselves and our posterity. Any use that our legislators make of us or our property, and any act of theirs that distorts our property or deprives us of it in a manner discordant with those objectives constitutes trespass or nuisance. It is legislated injury. Being trustees, it constitutes breach of trust.

Accepting a bribe does not constitute an abuse of this trust. The only abuse is an act at variance with the stated objectives. There is no functional relationship between accepting the bribe and actually executing the misdeed. This is not true of running a red light. There is always a probability greater than zero that running a red light will cause an accident. But occasionally we see in statutes the invocation of a device known as presumption.

In many states, your appearance within 100 feet of a brook or river and your possession of fishing tackle and your non-possession of a fishing license suffice as grounds for fining you. It is presumed that you intend to fish without a license, and against presumptive evidence you have no defense except to positively prove your innocence of such intent. Most of the time this will be impossible.

It is on the basis of presumption that statutes against bribery are tolerated. A legislator accepting a bribe is presumed to intend misfeasance. If he protests his innocence; he intended to go no farther than accepting the money; he will be asked if he can prove his intentions. Otherwise, as with a conspiracy to commit a crime, the agreement and acceptance of money is presumed to be evidence of malicious intent. Such a policy would seem to be a practical and realistic way to protect the common good.

But Abscam is too much like planting fishing tackle in the pathway of a hiker, beside a stream known secretly by government agents to hold no fish. There is no way that even an intentional poacher can hurt the common good by casting into fishless water. Intent cannot hurt the

common good. The functions between the intended project and the result must be material! The American government cannot convict a
person of conspiring to maim a third person by incantation.

What is the complaint in Abscam? It can not be that Congressman
X intended to impair the common good. It must be that Congressman X
was certainly going to impair the common good, or was likely to, **in the
case at hand.** In such a case injury must have occurred, or must be
occurring, or must be imminent, and in the Abscam cases there was no
way in which the congressman could impair the common good. Was
there?

What then have I said about penal legislation? Only two things.
First, that an act denominated a crime must be an act perpetrating
injury. Second, that the functions of the case must meet the test of
materiality.

If the congressmen had been indicted for true cases of bribery, and
if the verdict pivoted on the credibility of the witnesses, evidence such
as the Abscam agents gathered (if the court would admit it) would serve
to discredit the testimony of the defendants. But Abscam, as a case in
itself, was a sham. What we have is a case in which the defendants
were injured superficially by legislation, but more by judges. However,
given that the appeal has been carried to the highest court in the land
and has failed, one calls it injury in vain. What good does it do to call it
injury if the agents of your rulers don't know what you are talking about.
We cannot call it injustice for it was justice at its worst. We can only
call it judicial error and creep back into our holes.

I will now repeat in summary the four basic categories of causes
and their essential elements. By themselves, stripped of examples, the
statements are not easy to grasp, and the reader is referred to the
earlier parts of the chapter for examples. Appended here, however, are
some very important memoranda that should not be overlooked.

Cases at Law:

From a pleading in **trespass,** a judge must be able to conclude:

(1) The defendant is using a loading space to which she is not
entitled and to which plaintiff is entitled.

From a pleading in **nuisance**, the judge must be able to conclude:

(1) Defendant's activity alters a variable in plaintiff's entitled loading space.

Exception 1. Nuisance is not present if plaintiff is under an enforceable servitude to defendant's disruptive activity.

Exception 2. Nuisance is not present if plaintiff's desired mode (Omega) of said variable derives functionally from defendant's entitled loading space.

Exception to Exception 2. Nuisance is present if defendant is under an enforceable servitude restraining her from causing the disruption.

Cases in Equity:

From a pleading of **equitable injury**, the judge must be able to conclude:

(1) An act of the defendant, acting entirely within her entitled space, infringes the liberty of plaintiff.

(2) It is not a case of trespass or nuisance (i.e., there is no relief at law).

(3) It is important for the common good that defendant's activity be subserviated to plaintiff's liberty under the circumstances.

From a pleading of **legislated injury**, I think a judge must be able to conclude A or B as follows:

A. This legislative enactment creates a case of enforced service upon plaintiff. Or

B. It creates a case of enforced trespass or enforced nuisance in plaintiff's property. And if the result happens to promote the common good and is thus justified, the enactment fails under the principles of eminent domain to provide adequate compensation to plaintiff.

In relation to each of the foregoing causes, the following memoranda are pertinent:

1. For a valid pursuit in personal relations, the government grants a property in all loading spaces with loadings that are absolutely essential to the pursuit.

2. No one is entitled to use a thing for purposes of human killing except when the use is absolutely required (a) to fend off an assailant intending to kidnap or severely harm a human, or (b) to free a person from enforced service or capture.

3. No person, not even the government, is entitled to the enforced service of a person, except that the government is entitled to:

(a) enforce military service upon a person for purposes of the common defense;

(b) enforce service as a witness or juror for purposes of establishing justice under the common law;

(c) enforce service of spouse in behalf of the other spouse, but only by requiring an equivalent;

(d) enforce duties of government-appointed agent (appointment freely accepted) upon said agent - judges, executives, legislators, police, executors of estates, ambassadors, lawyers..., but only by requiring an equivalent;

(e) enforce specific performance of contract, but only by requiring an equivalent.

4. Materiality and entrapment are essential elements of a pleading.

CHAPTER 40

DEFENDANT'S PLEADING AND MENTAL COMPETENCE

In writing about intelligent justice, I simply have been describing the architecture of the common law. I have been claiming intelligent justice not as my creation, but to consist of the quasars and raisins emerging from the observed static and pudding of court cases. Let me show you what I mean. Let me show you an area of law where I find great inconsistency. I do not see intelligent justice. Consequently I can draw no conclusions. I have no solutions for you. It is a field of Brownian motion supporting no theorems in probability. It is the field of mental incompetence. Not that it does not show flashes of brilliance.

Lineweaver is suing Frick for damages. Frick stepped into the path of Lineweaver's car and the resulting delay cost Lineweaver a contract. But before damage can be concluded in the case, the court first must find injury. Lineweaver claims title to the intersection - he had the green light. And Frick usurped his loading space; conclusion, trespass. So Lineweaver's pleading appears to present a case of injury; and the topical matter of the case and Frick himself seem to be within the jurisdictional purview of the court. The court summons Frick; and Frick must now defend himself if he can.

There are various lines of defense, such as the very effective statute of limitations, but for our purposes I wish to concentrate on those directly to the point - logically opposed to the gist of the complaint; the defenses that will effectively uncouple a claim of injury. Actually trespass and nuisance, as I have presented them, allow but two defenses against the complaint itself - I will call them non-originancy and immateriality.

Non-originancy. An answer by Frick that he had been pushed off the curb would be a sufficient pleading to bring the case to trial. If he can convince the judge or jury that his claim is true, it will be an entirely adequate defense. In being pushed, he would have been acting not as originant but as object, and the government, though interested in training people to anticipate harm-causing sequences, is not interested in punishing unguided missiles. To the contrary. To punish a person for simply being an object in a storm-tossed sea would have a negative and confusing effect on the public mind. Evidently a government finds injury only where the defendant contributes as a She to the causal chain - only when her contributory act rises either from her decisive will or from her kinestatic feeding in the external world - only, in short out of her pursuit of an Omega.

Immateriality. If the court is to finally take action against the defendant in the plaintiff's behalf, everything in the complaint must be shown to reflect a material fact. The plaintiff's claim to title must be accurate. The loading space claimed as property - the subject matter, the loadings and the objectives - must be materially inter-functional. And the adverse use, in a case of trespass, or the causal chain claimed as nuisance, must be functional, material, phenomenal.

Any denial that Frick might make of a relevant element of the complaint - that it is false or immaterial - would be a sufficient pleading to bring the case to trial. Basically it would be a claim of sham, delusion - immateriality. He might claim that he, not Lineweaver, had the green light. Or he might go so far as to bring a cross-complaint. "After all," he might say (after leaving the hospital), "we are not talking about red lights and green lights, nor an intersection of asphalt. We are talking about the loading space of my body. He could have swerved to miss me and he didn't. Not I but Lineweaver is the trespasser."

Then Lineweaver would have to show the functions making Lineweaver a non-originant in his disruption of Frick's body. By observing due restraint and the rules of the road, and subjected to the physical laws of momentum, his particular intersection with Frick's body was a purely derivative phenomenon, completely within his loading space. It was Frick who was the originant in the causal chain of the accident.

Thus, you see, the plaintiff's claims and the materiality of the whole situation must be examined in depth and with ingenuity.

Of course, we have reviewed the materiality of situations far more abstruse than "Lineweaver v. Frick" and there are more to come. In this chapter, I merely wish to emphasize that the burden of challenging the materiality of the plaintiff's pleading rests upon the defendant.

Is there a third defense? **Mental incompetency** is a perfect defense for a murderer if it is called insanity. How mentally incompetent would Frick have to be before he could perpetrate no injury; before the government would lose interest in training him? We are entangled somewhat in the coils of our current understanding of psychology. What is an insane killer but a creature of pure kinestasis, no power of restraint. No decisive will. So we hold him not responsible for his crime. Yet a reckless adult, hurtling in his car at full speed, chasing some obscure Omega, pure kinestasis, killing a pedestrian, and we hold him responsible.

Notice in that cell a "hardened" criminal - a killer of several people, though not the cold "hit man" filling a "contract". This man merely kills without reason. When he gets into a quarrel he kills. Pure kinestasis. But this isn't insanity, we say, and hold him responsible for his deeds. Does the government think it can train him otherwise?

If a minor impairs property, not he but his guardian is held responsible. The minor is incompetent. Presumably the guardian will be trained by due process to train the child. So the same minor rents a canoe on a purchase agreement and wrecks it on the river the next day. But this time not even the guardian is responsible. The minor is incompetent and the purchase agreement is unenforceable. A contract is not valid when one of the parties is incompetent. Presumably the canoe dealer learns a lesson, but this particular minor learned of his immunity in high school in a senior studies session on contract. Looking like a young adult, he had the downpayment, and he knew exactly what he was doing. Are minors too young for the government's training project in responsibility? And, the guardian also being immune in this situation, what motivation does the guardian have for training him?

Is there a difference between insanity, incompetence and pure kinestasis? Is insanity equal to non-originancy? It can't be. An insane killer is an originant, not an object.

A man killing his wife's lover in a moment of "passion", meaning anger, is given five years. Pure kinestasis. The hardened criminal is given life for killing in anger. Both men are paroled, one in three years, one in fifteen. Have they suddenly developed decisive wilful restraint? Have they become competent? Is it known that they will not kill again in anger? In fact, their first killing proved their incompetence. For what is competence but the ability to act with restraint, the capacity to rebuff immediate kinestatic impulse for the sake of future Omegas? And if these men are incompetent, where are their guardians?

In paroling killers, has the government released incompetents without guardians? May we infer that the government itself is the guardian of a parolee who is a proven incompetent? Does it hold itself responsible for the damage caused by a released incompetent?

In releasing such people from confinement, people who show a capacity for murder, does the government transfer its title in biological lives to the kinestatic impulses of these people?

CHAPTER 41

PUBLISHING RIGHTS, CLIMATES OF MIND
AND PROPERTY IN BRITISH CHANCERY

In the course of this writing I have praised rigor and censured plausibility, the while advancing grandly on plausible arguments, throwing rigor to the winds. I deem my proposals sufficiently grounded in common law. Still I have used much too many fictitious cases. I have presented too many arguments without authentication, as though they represented accepted doctrine. Many of my claims have been derived from a personally internalized threshing of material reaped from many cases. I have spoken of jewel-like judicial decisions, buried under piles of unconvincing opinions. In presenting my logic, my grounds for many decisions, I rather depreciated the reasons given by the judges themselves for reaching their conclusions.

Well I warned you many chapters ago that we would be raising a Gothic vault; that there would be precarious times when the leaning arches might strain too far the supporting scaffolds. One yearns for that ultimate moment when the keystone itself is slipped into place, and the silly separate unstable components become one secure unified structure supporting not only itself but a whole roof of law as well. In the final analysis, the reasonableness of my proposals will depend on the experience of a nation, the readings of its scholars, and the pragmatic decisions of mature, worldly intelligences.

Whatever arguments I give are bound to be biased, no matter that I assume a beautifully detached attitude. Nevertheless it would be precious to see real cases bringing neatly together the components of the common law as I have been extolling them, and I think we have them in three cases in British chancery - all clustered about the year 1800. We are in equity, and the topical matter is publishing rights. We hear counsel and chancellor using the word property as it was used two hundred years ago. And as fate would have it, delusion and personal relations peer in and out of the sessions like mice thoroughly at home in a Swiss cheese.

We see a judge with his stethoscope unobtrusively checking out climates of mind. We see the Lord Chancellor striving not so hard as the American judge to ground his decision in law. We hear in his words the accent of the British aristocrat, and see the unerring rapier prick masked by the mumble of a typical English understatement.

We are dealing with copyright in personal correspondence - may one publish a private letter that one has received - and also with rights that will be honored above copyright. In 1774, the opinion in **Thompson v. Stanhope** was not the first to enunciate the basic right in personal correspondence, but Lord Chancellor Apsley definitely nailed it down. For literary and sociology students it was significant case, for Thompson and his co-plaintiffs were suing to prevent the publication of Lord Chesterfield's letters to his son. I transcribe the report here, practically unedited. The old typography you will have to imagine.

"Sir Charles Thompson and Others, Executors of Lord Chesterfield, against Eugenia Stanhope, Widow, and John Dodsley, 23d March 1774.

"The Late Earl of Chesterfield had a natural son, Phillip Stanhope, who went abroad and was in a public character. Before Phillip died Lord Chesterfield corresponded with him for many years; in some of his letters drew the character of public persons and wrote upon the subject of politics; in others he wrote upon education, and instructions to his son for his conduct in life; and it was said that those letters formed a complete system of education. On the death of Phillip, his widow Eugenia Stanhope and two sons came over to England in 1769 and were affectionately received by Lord Chesterfield who put the children to school and by his will left each of them an annuity of 100 pounds and also gave them 10,000 pounds.

"The widow delivered up to Lord Chesterfield his drafts of public characters, having first taken copies of them, but did not deliver up the other letters; and after his death in 1772 she agreed with the defendant Dodsley a bookseller for printing and publishing the letters on education and instructions to his son; and public notice was given of it in the newspapers by several advertisements, the first appearing in November; four months ago.

"Here we have a bill by the plaintiffs to restrain the defendants from printing and publishing the letters, and to have the original letters and copies delivered up to the plaintiffs.

"The defendant in her answer said, Being frequently in company with Lord Chesterfield, she one day mentioned to him that she thought the letters would form a fine system of education if published; to which his Lordship answered, "Why, that is true, but there is too much Latin in them;" but he did not express any disapproval in publishing the same; some little time later Lord Chesterfield requested her to restore to him some of his character drafts, characters of particular people, declaring that he intended only to burn or destroy them; and that soon afterwards, about the end of summer 1769, she carried the characters to him, the other letters as well, and that Lord Chesterfield took the original characters but declined taking the letters, or even looking at them, and told her she might keep them. She admitted that she has copies of the characters but never intends that they be published.

"And now the plaintiffs moved for an injunction to stay printing and publishing the letters and characters.

"For the plaintiffs it was insisted, That a person has no right to print and publish letters which he receives, without the consent of the person who wrote them. That his property in the letters does not extend so far. If it did, mischievous consequences would follow in abundance of cases. That the consent of Lord Chesterfield was necessary in his life-time, and of his executors after his death. That neither the one nor the other have given their consent. That Lord Chesterfield taking the characters and leaving the letters in her hands is not evidence of his consent to her printing the letters. He did not choose that the characters be shown to anybody or seen even by chance and therefore burned them. And as to the letters, he told her not that she might make any use of them she pleased, but only that she might **keep** them. That the widow appears to have misbehaved in keeping copies of the characters; and though she says they were not intended to be published, yet she might alter her mind and do it sometime unless restrained by injunction.

"On the other hand it was argued, That the letters contain a system of education, and useful instructions, and would be serviceable to the public. That Lord Chesterfield, if living, would have no objection to their being printed and in fact made no objection when the widow brought the matter up in conversation. That when the Lord Chesterfield declined taking the letters, and told her she might keep them, he meant she might do as she pleased with them. That the executors should be presumed to have given their consent, for they did not forbid the printing nor file their bill till the first of this month, though the advertisements had been in the newspapers since November last. That they ought not to have laid by and permitted the defendants to put themselves to the expense of printing the letters, which is very great, and just as they are going to be published, to interfere and stop the publication.

"Lord Apsley, Chancellor, was very clear that an injunction ought to be granted. That the widow had no right to print the letters without the consent of Lord Chesterfield or his executors. That Lord Chesterfield in his actions did not mean to give her leave to print and publish them. That she did very ill in keeping copies of the characters when Lord Chesterfield meant that they should be destroyed and forgot. That the executors cannot be said to have given their consent though his Lordship thought they would have done better if they had filed their bill earlier, before the expense of printing was incurred. He said it was within reason of several cases where injunctions had been granted, and cited the case of Mr. **Forrester**, of Mr. **Webb**, of Mr. **Pope**'s Letters printed by **Curl**, and Lord **Clarendon**'s Life.

"Lord Chancellor ordered an injunction until hearing, but recommended that the executors permit the publication if they saw no objection to the work upon reading it."

We may assume, since the letters were published the same year, that Mrs. Stanhope, the executors and the bookseller reached an agreement, and I imagine that the executors received royalty payments, adding them to Lord Chesterfield's estate.

After my criticism of American jurists in this book, they might feel better upon noting that even the Lord Chancellor admitted a case into equity that would be more appropriately heard at law, a case very close to the borderline between equity and law and for this reason instructive. Note that his Lordship very properly observed climates of mind in both parties, and nevertheless heeded them not at all in his decision. He treated Mrs. Stanhope's argument for giving her publishing rights - publishing the letters would be in the public interest - exactly as the judge in "Brown v. Anthony" treated Mr. Anthony's plausible pleading to obtain the right to put his sign on Farmer Brown's weed patch. Public good to the Chancellor lay in protecting title, and it was very simple; Mrs. Stanhope had no title in the letters. I must qualify this remark. He made an excellent technical distinction: Mrs. Stanhope had the title of possessing the letters, but not the title of use.

Here is the point to be made. The case was properly at law, not equity, because the question was not of property but of title. A case is not heard in equity unless two entitled pursuits are in conflict, and in **Thompson v. Stanhope** this was not the case. The publishing title was in dispute, and if one of the parties was entitled, the other was not.

But what about the petition for an injunction? By tradition only equity can issue an injunction. Well, this case makes my point; an injunction was improperly sought and inappropriately granted. If a court ruled that the executors held the title and Mrs. Stanhope held none, she would be foolish to publish the letters without the executors' permission. It would be injury, trespass, and the executors could sue her for damages at law. Injunction is necessary only when both parties are acting in their entitled spaces, and one must be ordered to refrain. A court in this case would have properly issued a declaration of title, not an injunction; measurements of climates of mind and effectiveness lives were irrelevant; and the Chancellor actually based his decision on prior decisions - law. It was a case at law.

Aside from these technical flaws, the Apsley's decision was correct, and definitely established the basic principle, that the writer of private correspondence owns the publishing rights to the contents of the letter. The application of the literary copyright to private letters traces back to Lord Hardwicke in **Pope v. Curl**, a case cited by Lord Apsley. The first departure or variance from the basic principle appeared in 1813 in **Perceval v. Phipps**, and in this case we see a true ancestor of **Jones v. Alfred H. Mayer Company.** Vice-Chancellor Plumer in **Perceval v. Phipps**, who was now about to find an exception to **Pope v. Curl** and **Thompson v. Stanhope**, summarizes Lord Hardwicke's opinion about as follows:

"Lord Hardwicke states that letters, though personal, may form a literary composition in which the author retains his copyright. By sending them to a person, the author does not authorize the recipient to use them for the purpose of profit. Though the author parts with the property of the paper, he does not part with the property of copyright in the composition.

The bill or pleading in **Lord and Lady Perceval v. Phipps** stated that between August 1812 and April 1813, Lady Perceval wrote and sent to defendant Mitford several letters of a private nature in the confidence that he would not part with them or communicate the contents to any person or permit them to be published. But Mitford delivered such letters to the other defendant Phipps with publication as the intent. Accordingly Phipps did on May 2 publish one of the letters in his newspaper, announcing his intention to publish the others. The bill prayed an injunction restraining the defendant from publishing the other letters.

When injury is imminent, it is possible for a plaintiff to obtain a temporary injunction or restraining order before the case is heard. The hearing is conducted later, while the restraining order is in effect. The order itself is issued merely upon a reading of the plaintiff's pleading, and for this reason the verification or affidavit of the plaintiff is extremely important, and the plaintiff will be liable for damages if his cause proves to lack merit. Since the order becomes effective before the answer of the defendant is read or even composed, such provision for the defendant's protection is absolutely necessary. In **Perceval v. Phipps** the Lord Chancellor read the complaint and issued the order in restraint of publication, and the hearing was conducted later by the Vice-Chancellor, after the defendant's answer had been filed.

Phipps's answer, as I now closely reproduce the court report stated "that Mitford had come to him purporting to be the confidential agent of Lady Perceval. She wished Mitford to publish from time to time information on a topic of great public interest. Thereupon Phipps asked Mitford to use Phipps's newspaper as a channel for communicating such information to the public, and Mitford afterward brought him a letter purporting to be written to Phipps by Lady Perceval, thanking him for his offer, and Mitford further represented to Phipps that he was authorized by Lady Perceval to tell Phipps that the articles would be sent to him exclusively. Mitford frequently afterward brought Phipps various paragraphs and articles for insertion, declaring them to be in Lady Perceval's handwriting, and they were accordingly inserted."

Phipps answer then went on to state that on April 1 1813 Mitford brought him a paper in Mitford's handwriting written, as Mitford had claimed, for publication at the desire of and in the presence of Lady Perceval. Phipps inserted it on April 4 but subsequently discovered the information therein to be false. When he questioned Lady Perceval, she denied having sent him any such intelligence, declaring that the papers were forgeries. Mitford asserted the contrary and delivered to Phipps several other letters written to Mitford by Lady Perceval materially tending to show that the information published on April 4 came from Lady Perceval, and they further supported the other representations that Mitford had made to Phipps.

"The answer further stated that Lord and Lady Perceval had in public addresses denied that Lady Perceval was privy to the publication of April 4. In consequence, the personal character of Phipps and the value of his newspaper were in danger of falling into public discredit. Phipps submitted that he would be vindicated by the letters last brought to him by Mitford, and under the circumstances he had an interest and property in the letters and ought not be restrained from publishing them. And upon this answer a motion was made that the injunction made by the Lord Chancellor may be dissolved."

It is important for us to distinguish between the three different groups of papers in the case. Group 1 consisted of the articles originally written for publication. Over these, except for the last one, there was no dispute. Group 2 consisted of the last one, the one published on April 4 and then discovered to contain false information. This was the one claimed by Lady Perceval to be counterfeit. But Group 3 were the letters from Lady Perceval to Mitford, not intended for publication, but now claimed by Mitford and Phipps to prove that Lady Perceval was indeed the author of Group 1 letters, including the Group 2 letter containing the false information.

These are essential distinctions to be made for two reasons. First, though Lady Perceval wished to dissociate herself from the April 4 article, she could not dissociate herself from the Group 3 letters, the ones she did not want published. If she had not claimed to be their author, she would have no copyright and could not have applied for the injunction restraining their publication. In fact the Lord Chancellor, before he granted the injunction, insisted upon her affidavit that she was the author.

Second, though the injunction restraining the publication of the Group 3 letters was within the jurisdiction of Chancery, Lady Perceval's claim that she was not the author of the April 4 article was under the purview of law. It was in effect a claim that she had been injured and damaged by misrepresentation, a claim of nuisance, and Chancery couldn't handle it. So in the view of the Vice-Chancellor, the issue was not the authenticity or authorship of the April 4 article, or even the content of the Group 3 letters from Lady Perceval to Mitford, but solely the question of the **use** of the Group 3 letters. Lady Perceval claimed the publication rights, and Phipps claimed the right to publish them for the purpose of vindicating his character. Whose claim should prevail?

After hearing the arguments, Vice-Chancellor Plumer in his opinion did not go unerringly to the point. He covered an issue or two not particularly relevant. But, beyond those points, his language proceeded as follows:

"Being called upon by this motion to dispose of an injunction granted by the Lord Chancellor, I will state how it strikes me at present. An injunction restraining the publication of private letters must stand upon this foundation; that letters, whether of a private nature or upon general subjects may be considered as subject of literary property." (Note his terminology - **subject of property**. Phipps's attorneys in their arguments had said, "This court has never interfered to restrain the publication of letters, unless the petitioner had the sole property in them, the principle of restraint being **the invasion of literal property**." My emphasis.) "Admitting however that private letters may have the character of literary composition, the application of that as a general rule to every letter that any person writes upon any subject appears to me to go a great way; including, as has been justly observed, all mercantile letters, all letters passing between individuals not only upon business but on every subject. If in every such instance the publication may upon this doctrine be restrained as a violation of literary property, the effect must frequently be to deprive an individual of his ability to prove orders for goods, or the truth of his assertions, or agency, or any other fact in the proof of which letters may form the chief ingredient.

"The order made by the Lord Chancellor granting this preliminary injunction considers the letters to fall within this principle. But the case appears materially altered by the answer, the answer representing that the defendant did not deviate from the instructions of his employer and that he had full authority from the plaintiff for inserting what he did. These facts he proposes to establish by the letters. He states that he does not believe these letters were given under any pledge of confidence and, though he may derive a profit from publishing the letters in his own paper, his object is not profit but the vindication of his character from the imputation that is thrown upon it. His object is to prove agency.

"This is the naked case of a bill, certainly, to prevent the publication of private letters, not stating the nature, subject or occasion of them or that they are of any value to the plaintiff. Against this we have the defendant insisting upon his right to use these letters to vindicate his character which he represents as in danger of being greatly injured by holding him out to the public as a person publishing false intelligence upon spurious authority.

"Upon this answer the plaintiffs have failed to establish ground for continuing the injunction. If any case is to be made against the defendant, it cannot be made in a court of equity. The plaintiffs must therefore be left to do what they can at law, and this injunction must be dissolved."

As in **Jones** the house empty of Jones was a statement that Jones was an undesirable neighbor, so the Group 3 letters kept in the dark cast a shadow over the reputations of Phipps and Mitford. As in **Jones** the only remedy was to put Jones in the house, letting neighbors judge him for himself, so in **Percival v. Phipps** the only remedy was to let the public see the letters.

In the **Perceval v. Phipps** decision, due process declares that a title may not be used to frustrate a person in his personal relations. We see a subject of title as a thing capable of being loaded in diverse pursuits. One use of the letters would be to publish them for their literary value. As an entitled space, the titleholder could also restrain all others from using them - copy right. Another use of the letters would be to publish them to vindicate character. The former title under the principles of equity had to be subserviated to the latter. Two conflicting pursuits, both entitled; a proper case for equity, at least until the principle was established.

In the analyses of those professional jurists, there was no pitting of "property rights" against "personal rights". All property rights are personal to property holders. They represent the particular relationship of the particular person to the particular thing. In these analyses, there was no measuring of words and punctuations in a "civil rights" law. There was a quiet weighing of the parties' climates of mind and effectiveness lives in the scales of equity, and the decision was as between black and white.

Five years later, in 1818, **Gee v. Pritchard** appeared in the same court, the perfect sequel to **Perceval v. Phipps** for this tutorial series. The language of property and the definition of equity's jurisdiction is choice.

As it first appeared in court, **Gee v. Pritchard** was an exact duplicate of **Perceval v. Phipps**. Mrs. William Gee obtained a prelimi- nary injunction restraining William Pritchard from publishing certain letters she had written to him. In the hearing that followed, Pritchard moved on ground of vindicating his character that the injunction be dissolved. The very barristers who in **Perceval v. Phipps** successfully got the injunction dissolved were now retained by Mrs. Gee to secure the injunction permanently against Pritchard. We will see the Lord Chancellor, peering through the haze of arguments, taking a firm look at climates of mind. The facts of the complaint were not in dispute. Whose title to the use of the letters would be placed under servitude; this was the issue.

As a boy, William Pritchard was introduced to the plaintiff not long after she married Mr. Gee. Gee told her he maintained the boy and intended to educate him. He wished the boy to live with them during school vacations and eventually he intended to procure him a living in the church or place him in some other respectable situation. Consequently Pritchard was raised at Beddington as though he were Mr. and Mrs. Gee's own son. Over the course of years she had written him many letters, some of a private and confidential nature.

Since the death of Mr. Gee, plaintiff had procured a rectory for Pritchard. She had also given him the sum of 4,500 pounds and other large sums to pay off his debts. From the estate of Mr. Gee he had received 4,000 pounds and a life income from 6,000 pounds. But he was not satisfied and pressed her for a life income from 17,000 pounds in Gee's estate, and this she refused to grant.

On March 18 1818 she received a letter from him containing these words: "I allude to the interest of the 17,000 pounds, which, if you will allow me... to receive... I shall give you no further uneasiness, either by my presence or by further application...."

In April he sent her a parcel of her letters with a letter stating these were her original letters and that, because of her kindness to him, he no longer deserved to be the possessor. But evidently he had made copies. In a letter dated May 14 he wrote: "... My life... at Bedington, together with the grounds I had for being differently situated, viz. your professions contained in your letters, will be published in the middle of June." He conveyed to her the idea that his friends wondered why he had not received a greater inheritance, and he wished to explain the matter so they wouldn't attribute it to some dark misdeed in his past.

On July 9, the co-defendant Anderson, a bookseller, advertised "... the impending publication of **The Adopted Son,** or **Twenty Years at Beddington,** containing Memoirs of a Clergyman, written by himself, and interspersed with interesting correspondence." Mrs. Gee claimed in her affidavit that these letters were wholly her composition and that she had never agreed to their publication. On this ground she was granted the preliminary injunction.

Let us listen to some of the exchanges, minimally edited, between the attorneys and Lord Chancellor Eldon.

Pritchard's attorneys: "... in Hudson's **Treatise on the Court of Star Chamber**... no trace is found of any interference of that tribunal by injunction or otherwise on the subject of letters, unless the publication was libellous."

The Lord Chancellor: "It will not be necessary to trouble you with that view of the case. The publication of a libel is a crime; and I have no jurisdiction to prevent the commission of a crime; excepting of course the protection of infants...."

Pritchard's attorneys: "An attempt will be made by the Plaintiff to sustain the injunction on the ground that the publication of the letters will be painful to the feelings of the Plaintiff."

The Lord Chancellor: "I will relieve you also from that argument. The question will be whether the bill has stated facts of which the Court can take notice as a case of civil property, which it is bound to protect."

Pritchard's attorneys: "The injunction then must rest on one of two grounds: 1. That the Plaintiff possesses in the letters a property either general or literary; 2. That the publication of them is a breach of trust. It will be difficult to establish that letters may be the subject of literary property.... ... Letters not designed for publication may constitute an exception."

The Lord Chancellor: "My predecessors did not inquire whether the intention of the writer was or was not directed to publication.... The doctrines of this Court ought to be as well settled and made as uniform almost as those of the common law, laying down fixed principles, but taking care that they be applied according to the circumstances of each case. I cannot agree that the doctrines of this Court are to be changed with every succeeding judge.

"... I think that the decisions represent the property (in letters) as qualified in some respects; that the writer had given in some cases the receiver a property of **reading** the letter and in other cases a property of **keeping** the letter, yet the gift was so restrained that, **beyond** the purposes for which the letter was sent, the property was in the sender. If that is the principle, it is immaterial whether the publication is for the purpose of profit or not. If for profit, the party is selling a thing a portion of which belongs to the writer. If not for profit, the party is giving it."

Pritchard's attorneys: "... where the correspondent is entitled to retain the manuscript, great difficulty occurs in restricting his right of publication. He can read them to whom he chooses. In this case the

Defendant was unquestionably entitled to retain the letters; and he is now entitled to publish them for the vindication of his character. On the ground of breach of trust, for which there is no evidence, the injunction could not be maintained; this Court interferes with publications only as the subject of property."

The Lord Chancellor: "The question is, what is the conduct of the Plaintiff which by the Defendant's pleading justifies his publication of the letters?"

Mrs. Gee's attorneys: "It has been decided that letters cannot be published without the consent of the writer unless the purposes of justice require the publication. The question here is whether the Defendant has established that he is about to publish these letters for purposes essential to justice. Without that proof he cannot avail himself of the decision in Lord and Lady **Perceval v. Phipps.**"

The Lord Chancellor: "The decision of the Vice Chancellor proceeded on the principle that in that case the publication was necessary for the purposes of justice. The letter of the Defendant, written in April (that he no longer deserved to be the possessor of the letters) is decisive that the publication here is not necessary for those purposes."

Mrs. Gee's attorneys: "The present decision will constitute a most important precedent. If on these pleadings the injunction is dissolved, no man can be restrained from publishing the letters he has received from another; all that will be needed is a quarrel and an assertion that the publication is required for the vindication of his character. When the Defendant returned the originals, clandestinely retaining copies, he abandoned all right of property in them."

The Lord Chancellor: "The Defendant represents that he has never intended to publish the letters for profit. Yet perhaps the Defendant will on reflection admit that if his intention was merely to give these letters to his friend and relations, it was not prudent to announce his intention by advertisement. The advertisement has this effect, that those who see the publication know its nature, but those who saw only the advertisement might be led to believe there was something in the letters more unsettling than they really contained, and I cannot think this a prudent course. The Defendant **Anderson** (the bookseller) has not filed any answer or affidavit; but I am bound by the affidavit of the Defendant **Pritchard** to believe that Defendant **Anderson** (though inserting the advertisement) did not intend to publish the letters for sale either.

"I cannot trust myself with any such question as whether Mr. Gee should have left the Defendant a larger fortune. The provision made by the will is that which this Court is bound to consider proper. From the pleadings and affidavits I take the facts to be these: that the testator had left 17,000 pounds to the discretion of the Plaintiff, intrusting to her a control on the Defendant's conduct; that she had given him various sums of money and he continued to press for more; that the Defendant returned her letters having first taken copies and now threatens to publish them. If it is supposed that by reading the letters I will derive an impression different from that which I am about to state I will forbear to state it till I have read them; otherwise I am now ready to proceed." The counsel for the Defendant intimated that they had read one of the letters and thought it unimportant.

The Lord Chancellor: "I am of opinion that the Plaintiff has a sufficient property in the original letters to authorise an injunction unless she has by some act deprived herself of it. Though counsel for the defense has argued with so much ingenuity that the defendant may yet read the letters to others, yet the Court has never been alarmed out of the practice of granting injunctions simply because it cannot give other relief more effectual.

I do not say that I am to interfere because the letters are written in confidence or because the publication may wound the feelings of the Plaintiff; but if mischievous effects of that kind can be apprehended on principles well established in this Court it would not become me to abandon the jurisdiction which my predecessors have exercised, and refuse to forbid it.

"... In April last the Defendant, having limited properties in these letters, thinks proper to return them to the person having the remaining properties in them, keeping copies without apprising her, and assigning such a reason as he assigns for the return. Now I say that... the Defendant, if he previously had it, has renounced the right of publication.

"On these grounds the injunction must be continued. Motion refused."

I am proud of the Lord Chancellor, and a little disappointed. He could have expressed his reasons more clearly. Yet I suppose they were clear enough to the professionals standing in the court, and that was sufficient while Camelot maintained its integrity. In addition, he faced a technical difficulty that, if precisely expressed, perfects our understanding of equity.

In a way, Lord Eldon lost an opportunity to strengthen the principles of his court. By understatement he reveals his recognition that Pritchard's pleading is a sham. Undoubtedly he saw it even worse than that. Pritchard wanted the threat of publication as a weapon to pry that large income out of Mrs. Gee, and perhaps Eldon wished to tread lightly in that direction; blackmail is in the jurisdiction of law, not equity.

His opinion suggests that it was Pritchard's return of the letters that deprived him of any right of publication. Looking at it in greater depth, especially in view of his earlier comments, one sees the Chancellor concluding that all of Pritchard's acts, and the climate of mind that they betrayed, showed Pritchard's claimed right - the use of the letters to vindicate his character - to be immaterial. This deprived him of any right he might have had.

Now here is the technical difficulty. If Pritchard had no right in the letters, an injunction was not needed; it returns the case to the mold of the Chesterfield letters, **Thompson v. Stanhope**, the fundamental copyright. If Pritchard published the letters without holding title, he would be trespassing. But the Lord Chancellor was in an area that perhaps has never been well charted, and in charting it I must admit another aspect of equity. Though Pritchard ended with no right, showing that the case was not one of entitled right against entitled right, it nevertheless was a case properly in equity.

Pritchard CLAIMED the publishing right as a means of vindicating his character, and this put the case in equity - right versus right. A judge cannot know in advance of trial that a claim is delusory, false, immaterial, sham.

If as a result of the hearing it proves such, then no right need be subserviated to another. No injunction is necessary. The decision in property is not required. The result is a declaration of title. Therefore since equity cannot evade hearing the case, we must place this other duty upon equity, indeed a time honored task - the declaration of title. It is equity's job not only to find principles for subserviating title to title, but to ascertain title itself, and this provides for the development of the common law. If a person in her pleading claims title on some ground, novel but plausible, we see a case automatically in equity. It means she is claiming title to something in which someone else holds a more traditional title. (Remember, everything under the common law is owned by someone.) It means she wishes her new-claimed title to dominate the time-honored title - subserviation. Perhaps she will fail in court - the court may not grant the title, or, if the court grants the novel title, it may subserviate it to the time-honored title. I think equity might correct its compass only as suggested above. - If title for only one party emerges from the proceedings, a declaration of title is all that is required. An injunction is unnecessary and inappropriate.

CHAPTER 42

THE ENIGMA OF SLAVERY

Upon learning that injury is an infringement of liberty, one instantly becomes a legal expert, needing only the meaning of two words (1) liberty (2) infringement. I, having advanced grandly in seven-league boots, retreated modestly in Chapter 39 to classify injury in four categories. Trespass, nuisance, equitable injury, and legislated injury, these four, and now I must be careful. Is this system reliable, or will it fail to detect oppressions that should be relieved?

But first, what does one mean by an oppression that a government should relieve? As if an omnipotent government will do anything it doesn't wish to do. Well, one means an oppression that the government will **wish** to relieve. Relief after all is a government project, a purely selfish action, a process by which a ruler maintains and enhances her treasure. Relieve an oppressed person? Why bother if catching treasure spoilers is not important to her.

Today, the array of causes expounded in legal texts is a series of sieves, designed to separate relief-worthy oppressions from oppressions that government prefers to disregard, and if there are holes in the screens, permitting the escape of plunderers in the queen's treasure-house, well, the closing of such holes spells the history of equity and law.

So we from time to time hear judges quoting Judge Hardwicke's letter of 1759. "Fraud is infinite and, were a court of equity once to lay down rules how far they would go and no farther in extending their relief against it, or to define strictly the species or evidence of it, the jurisdiction would be cramped and perpetually eluded by new schemes which the fertility of man's invention would contrive." And now I wish to test my system for perforations permitting the looters of liberty to elude the guardians of the common good.

Hence for this chapter and a few more, focusing on a leak both wide and obscure, I ask a simple question you might suppose obsolete. Does my system protect a person from slavery? And farther, does our modern law protect us fully from slavery? I hasten to add I am thinking of situations as remote from an ordinary notion of slavery as a space shuttle from a kite, not code-enforced slavery, but slavery created by clever people in an environment supposedly hostile to slavery. I will show you examples of slavery that you do not now comprehend as slavery, protected and enforced by government because unrecognized as slavery - the most elusive operation with which equity and law will tangle.

Slavery is enforced service, and if this seems to put the topic in a nutshell, it reveals our innocence. Most of us do not comprehend the mechanism by which a person forces another person into service. Undoubtedly there is in the common law a strong aversion to enforced service. It is emphatic in the remedy for non-performance under contract. Though you have bound yourself to perform, the government will not force you to perform. It stops short of that extreme, and merely compels you to pay the other party an equivalent.

In Article 23 of Magna Carta we catch a glimmer of the feeling against enforced service: "Neither a town nor a man shall be forced to make bridges over the rivers... " Nevertheless King John and his lords protected their interests: "with the exception of those who from old and of right ought to do it." Long after Magna Carta, many cases of slavery would parade before the courts until the hostile principle prevailed, and still an invisible host of slaves exists, sensible of oppression, but lacking a means of communication. For the basic condition of slavery has never been defined.

As much as we personally chafe under enforced service, we enjoy holding others in that condition; it seems to be human nature. And sometimes we persuade legislators to devise systems of enforced service for our benefit. Witness the city ordinance forcing a homeowner to paint his house to please his neighbors, a legislative infringement of liberty without provision for compensation. Witness those of us wishing to force a woman to contain a fetus in her body against her wish, conforming to our taste in aesthetics and logic. A statute ordering seat belts for minors conforms to the government protection of children, but ordering an adult to wear a seat belt against his wishes is enforced service, and its effect on the common good should be examined carefully.

I have shown that the thirteenth amendment and its flotilla of statutes make poor grounds for relief in many class oppression cases, and, though Joseph Lee Jones found relief on thirteenth amendment grounds in **Jones v. Mayer**, the grounds were irrelevant and immaterial. Though the decision created law, it created poor law. With sham grounds, the resulting case law would provide escape holes for future plaintiffs steeped in sham. Emphatically never was Jones in the enforced service of the Mayer Company, and the "badge of slavery" used by lawyers and judges was an embroidery void of significance in the common law.

So though tradition weighs against enforced service, and the thirteenth amendment explicitly prohibits slavery, there is reason to ask if we recognize slavery when we are in its presence. Are we equipped to relieve it? And a proper question is this. Does slavery fall within the general format of injury? Is it an infringement of liberty? Yes, it is the use of a person without her consent. It is trespass. But I tell you a clever enslaver will slither like quicksilver through this screen.

My definition of slavery was broad and general. I said that slavery is B's engagement of A's volition in B's project without A's free consent. But this definition will play semantic havoc in a courtroom, arising from the term "free consent".

In Chapter 31, I distinguished slavery from captivity by showing the difference between rape at the point of a knife (this being slavery), and the rape of a bound victim (this being capture and trespass); between the plight of a kidnapped child (captivity) and the plight of her parent paying ransom (slavery). We might consider a simpler example, a case of armed robbery. "Your money or your life," expresses it perfectly. The robber gives his victim a perfectly free choice. When the victim hands over his wallet, it is with his free consent. The strategy depends on a general knowledge of human nature.

This exemplifies the essence of slavery. The American black slave could hoe cotton or go without food. Hoe cotton or take ten lashes. Stay on the plantation and hoe cotton or face the dangers of the wilderness with a chance of recapture and twenty lashes. Stay and hoe cotton or run away, never again to see wife and child. Free choice. So we may well ask if slavery is really B's engagement of A's volition in B's project without A's free consent. Well, It is and it isn't. But I tell you, we will have to do better than this or many master enslavers will elude the protective screens of due process.

What in armed robbery is the mechanism of injury? Is it trespass or nuisance? And please don't dismiss armed robbery as trivial - "after all, armed robbery is against the law - it's a crime." We want the theory behind the law. Nor do we dismiss it with, "after all isn't armed robbery simply a case of deprivation?" Yes, the result is deprivation; the victim is removed from his money. But deprivation through armed robbery is not like deprivation through theft. Deprivation through armed robbery is materialized through the victim's own volition and action. It is the act of a slave. Yes, it is not the deprivation that needs understanding, it is the inducement of the victim's voluntary action. We wish to know if the phenomenon of enslavement, yes, even the mere attempt to enslave, constitutes injury. It is the mechanistic elements of enslavement that we wish to learn. We wish to learn them so well that no enslaver can pass off the act of a slave as an act of free choice. We want tools stripping a clever case of enslavement to its bare bones.

It is not easy to show that a mere attempt to enslave constitutes injury. What if the slave-maker fails to enslave his intended victim? Has he then failed to infringe the liberty of his intended victim? Apparently the government does not think so. It will not absolve the robber who stamps away muttering when his intended victim does not cooperate. Attempt at extortion - like blackmail - is everywhere deemed a crime, whether or not the attempt succeeds, and I ask what is blackmail if not an attempt to enslave? Yes, we should enquire how an attempt to enslave constitutes injury.

To see the problem even more clearly, I resurvey Chapter 16, re-analyzing the injury in "Lydia Abercrombie v. Nephew". Under the threats of her nephew, the elderly woman was periodically separated from her money, and, wishing to draw a distinction between the injury and the damage, searching the case for the specific liberty infringed by the nephew, I concluded it to be her liberty to determine the disposal of her money.

Money can be used as a tool. Jingled before a shopkeeper's eyes, she responds by slipping her wares into your hands. It is this jingling that constitutes your use of money. Your entitled loading of it is to jingle it when you wish and in front of the eyes you choose. Your jingling signifies your right to distribute it as you choose. This is your entitled pursuit space with your money as subject, and it belongs to no one else.

So Lydia had the right to choose to whom to give her money and lo! She exercised her right. She chose to give it to her nephew! So how can we say her liberty was infringed? You see, we still haven't grasped the injury in enslavement, the mechanism of infringement. This is the enigma of slavery.

A factor in Lydia's case, as in armed robbery - the threat of bodily harm - perhaps gives us a clue. Such a threat, itself a crime, perhaps helps us analyze the injury in slave-making. A threat involves a loading of the taxitant's mind, much as a pursuit in personal relations involves a loading of a taxitant's mind. As we have a right in a personal relations pursuit to load a consenting person's mind, evidently in contrast we may not load her mind with threats. Nor need there be a specific prohibition against it. Our taxitant simply will never give her consent to such a loading. So? Have we discovered the injury in armed robbery? Is the robber making a loading in which he is not titled?

If you wish to use a person in your project, you must act through her She. Only She can make her hands move, her voice vibrate. You reach She through her mind. You push buttons in her mind and She responds. To push mental buttons you speak words, or smile, or frown, or practice kindly deeds. You jingle money in front of She's eyes, or threaten her with a whip. These buttons print programs into She's mind, or waken programs already printed, or modify them or erase them. You use She by using She's mind. And just as She has title to use She's arms or legs, She also has title to the use of her mind.

And the mind is easy to invade. To perpetrate trespass in a mind is not difficult. The mind is an open, vulnerable thing, connected by at least five senses to She's environment. Though you fail to get her permission to use her mind, you can easily slip within range, push a button, and dash away. And a mental button has mental functions perhaps beyond She's control; real functions; phenomenal; material. Remember Mrs. Cassidy's response to the voodoo doll? Mrs. Quinn's window decoration evidently pushed a button with an unexpected result, a case in which Mrs. Quinn was not trespassing, not using Mrs. Cassidy's mind. It was a case of nuisance, unintentional, and the effect was real.

A threat is the push of a mental button without the owner's consent. It connects her awareness with her capacity to anticipate. Foreseeing pain or distress, she makes a decision, her response. Thus in threat we witness trespass, the use of a mind by a usurper, mobilizing apprehensive programs in the taxitant's mind, inducing her to act in a manner foreign to her nature. Well not exactly. It is foreign except it is natural in view of the new element introduced by the intruder. Here at least is a tottering step toward a theory of slavery. But now let me introduce to you the famous **Slaughterhouse Cases.**

It was heard in the Supreme Court of the United States in 1873, with Salmon P. Chase, Chief Justice, at the end of a remarkable career. Settling in Cincinnati in 1830, he early made a name as a defender of runaway slaves. When later the Democratic party in Ohio endorsed slavery, he defected to help found the Republican party. The **Slaughterhouse** decision came in the year of his death, a five to four decision, with Chief Justice Chase in the minority. As my ancient edition of the Columbia Encyclopedia puts it: "His dissenting opinion in the famous **Slaughterhouse Cases** became in time the accepted opinion of the courts."

New Orleans was a city splotched throughout by nauseous establishments. The family maintenance of livestock in pens, and their slaughtering and butchering for sale persisted as the growing city pushed past the farmsteads of the countryside. Then in 1869 an act of the Louisiana legislature created a corporation named (in brief) the Crescent City Company. Composed of seventeen named persons, it gained legislative authorization to build livestock landings and pens outside the city on the banks of the river. Thus chartered, it was required to build a grand slaughterhouse, and, after its completion, according to the new law, all other stock-landings and slaughterhouses in the area would be closed. Thereafter all slaughtering and butchering would be restricted to the facilities of the Crescent City Company. Any butcher wishing to rent space would be accommodated, and anyone violating the enacted provisions would be fined $250 per violation.

The butchers in association fought the enactment, claiming the statute created a monopoly, reducing them to involuntary servitude and depriving them of liberty and property without due process of law. The cases, of which there were several, provided the first crucial test of the protection afforded by the thirteenth and fourteenth amendments, and no racial issue was involved.

Of the nine justices, five asserted that granting the slaughter-house monopoly lay within the police power of the state. It was simply a matter of establishing sanitary conditions for the city, reducing the offensive aspects of the industry. In their opinion the statute did not deprive the butchers of their right to exercise their trade. It merely defined the location where they would operate.

As for fourteenth amendment grounds, the five justices did not think the statute had deprived the butchers of liberty and property without due process of law. Nor did they think the provisions of the thirteenth amendment were breached. They could not see slavery and involuntary servitude in the case. The thirteenth amendment referred chiefly to American black slavery and was limited to similar conditions - those for instance that might arise in connection with Mexican and Chinese laborers.

Giving the five justices the benefit of the doubt, it cannot be said that the attorneys for the butchers presented a clean sharp case. To do so was perhaps impossible. The case had three aspects tending to conflict with each other. First there was the circumstance that the butchers would be forced unconditionally to cease operations in their own establishments. Was this a valid provision? Well, yes, to the extent that their operations created nuisances. Yet it is not clear that they all created nuisances. And perhaps some might have refined their operations to the point where they ceased to be nuisances. If so, the statute went too far. Forbidding their operations unconditionally was a deprivation of title without due process - legislated injury. On the other hand if the state could show that a complete cessation of butchering within the city, even in the absence of nuisance, was in the interest of the common good, then we still observe a case of legislated injury. It was a case properly in eminent domain, and the butchers should have been fully compensated for their losses.

This first aspect of the case was neglected by the butchers' lawyers, possibly on the prompting of the smaller butchers, and this reflected the second aspect of the situation. Undoubtedly the smaller businesses would collapse under the impact of the statute. For survival, they depended on their neighborhood locations and proximity of shop to home. Not having the means to protect the environment against the effects of their operations, their hope depended on defeating the statute entirely. They did not want police action. They did not want eminent domain. They wanted business as usual.

The third aspect of the case was the statutory creation of monopoly, a target of wrath for the four dissenting justices. But the five justices in the majority apparently could not distinguish the monopoly from the policing thrust of the action. To them it was a matter of constitutional construction. Though it was true that the fourteenth amendment invalidated state laws depriving a person of liberty and property without due process, it was also true that a policing action by the state constituted due process. This in effect was the conclusion of the five.

They overlooked the outstanding facts of the case. First, the incorporators already owned land in the new area authorized for slaughtering operations. Second, there was other suitable land in the same area. Third, when the butchers tried to buy it, intending to build their own slaughtering plants, the attorney general of the State of Louisiana obtained an injunction restraining them from doing so. Fourth, the injunction further restrained the landowners in the area from selling their land for the purpose. So, though no conceivable advantage accrued to the public from establishing a monopoly under the circumstances, the monopoly was bestowed, guarded by the armed might of the state, and upheld by the Supreme Court of the United States. By a vote of five to four. And that was the first half of the story.

In 1879, six years later, after the expensive facilities of the Crescent City Company were built, the State of Louisiana adopted a new constitution with two articles bearing directly on the situation. Article 248 placed the power of regulating livestock slaughter in the hands of local city and parish authorities, and Article 258 abolished, except for railroads, the monopoly features of all corporate charters in the state. By 1881 the city of New Orleans had opened up to everyone, subject to city regulations, the right to build slaughterhouses and engage in butchering. Under the new regulations, the Butchers Union Company organized to do business and, remember, this was in the area bestowed by statute entirely to the monopoly of the Crescent City Company.

Crescent City did battle, and in 1884 the case reached the Supreme Court of the United States. But now the issues did not involve monopoly or slavery or deprivation of property. The Crescent City Company disputed the right of the legislature to violate the provisions of its own legislation. Oh yes, it has the right, said the Supreme Court, as long as it is in the public interest.

So a monopoly that had been created to promote the public good was abolished to promote the public good, and the same Justice Miller who delivered the opinion affirming the monopoly read the opinion breaking it. It need not ruffle his composure; after all, the issues were different.

Salmon P. Chase, who probably recognized slavery when he saw it, was dead. But his fellow dissenters in the earlier case, finding themselves now in the majority, took the opportunity to review the earlier decision.

Said Justice Field, "The act of Louisiana required that the slaughtering be done outside the city of New Orleans and that the animals be inspected. Had the act been limited (to these provisions) there would have been no dissent. But it went a great way beyond them. It created a corporation, and gave to it an exclusive right for twenty-five years, within an area of 1,145 square miles, a place where alone animals intended for slaughter could be landed and sheltered, and where alone they could be slaughtered and their meat prepared for market. In the grant of these exclusive privileges a monopoly of an ordinary employment and business was created."

Said Justice Bradley, with whom Justices Harlan and Woods concurred: "The police regulations proper were hitched on to the charter as a pretext. The exclusive right given to the company had nothing of police regulation about it whatever. It was the creation of a mere monopoly, and nothing else; a monopoly without consideration and against common right; a monopoly of an ordinary employment and business, which no legislature has power to farm out by contract."

These gentlemen were saying that the monopoly was an example of legislated injury. But they did not specify the nature of the injury nor the liberty that was infringed - except that it was "against common right". True, Bradley went on to say, "The right to follow any of the common occupations of life is an inalienable right." And later, arguing that monopolies (with exceptions) contravene the fourteenth amendment, he proposed that the right to follow any common occupation is an essential liberty and property of every citizen, and the grant of the monopoly in question was an example of a state depriving its people of their liberty and property without due process of law.

Undoubtedly these men's intuitions were telling them something, though indistinctly, but let us note a remarkable oversight in the original case. The butchers had sought relief on several grounds; the thirteenth amendment was one. By the majority of justices the thirteenth amendment was interpreted so narrowly as to exclude butchers from its protection. By the minority the thirteenth amendment was practically ignored. Yet the case was as perfect an example of enslavement as we will ever see. Never has the thirteenth amendment been closer to a case so perfectly suited.

The Crescent City people naturally would want tenants for their slaughtering facilities, and where better to find them than among the butchers of the city. "Turn them out of their present shops and we will get 100% occupancy." Here we see the essentials of slavery. To the butchers the legislature said, "Rent the facilities or quit butchering. Rent the facilities or move away from New Orleans. It's your free choice." Here is an exact parallel of "Hoe cotton or go without food." Enforced by state code and government power!

Skilled enslavers don't bother to create absolutes. They work in the sphere of chance and probability. "Not everyone will succumb to the conditions we set up, but some will. And those are the ones we're looking for."

It was enslavement all right and it suggests a question. Were the directors of the corporation and the members of the legislature guilty of a conspiracy to enslave; an attempt to enslave? Well, I won't look into it; I have a more pressing problem. There is a difficulty in my theory. True, the slave-makers in the **Slaughterhouse Cases** presented the butchers with two undesirable options; but they made no threats; no loading of the butchers' minds. So apparently the theory of trespass - mental loading without permission - does not cover all cases of slavery. We have not yet found in enslavement the liberty that is infringed nor the mechanism of infringement; at least in this case.

To begin the solution of the problem, I will describe as broadly as possible the main features of the **Slaughterhouse Cases**, then try to generalize them. The idea is to draft a list of the basic elements of enslavement, and I begin with two characteristics of the situation:

1. The Louisiana legislature acted in such a way that one would expect a number of butchers to finally rent space in the Crescent City slaughterhouse.

2. In the absence of the legislature's action, the butchers probably would not have used the Crescent City slaughterhouse.

This is not sufficient. In those two statements, I might be describing a mere offer of contract, the legislature offering a subsidy to the butchers who rent space in the Crescent City slaughterhouse. A large enough offer will probably induce some of the butchers to use the corporation's facilities, and probably they would not do it in the absence of the offer. So statements 1 and 2 partly describe the situation, but will not completely distinguish an attempt to enslave from a perfectly legal offer of contract. However, the reference to contract is suggestive.

A classic ingredient of contract is "reality of consent". The government will refuse to enforce a contract if one of the parties has been subjected to menace, duress, deceit, or undue influence, or holds a mistaken concept of the provisions. If one of these factors is present in the contracting situation, the party's consent is not "real"; and if this is shown in trial, the government will avoid the contract.

Notice. Though the legislature made no threat calculated to make the butchers use the new facilities, its action exposed them to a duress driving them toward that decision. Only by renting Crescent City space could they use their trade to make a living in the New Orleans area. So though the term "real consent" is but an unimproved substitute for the term "free consent", the magnificent rules of contract have given it substance. Indeed the ideas of menace, duress, undue influence, deceit and mistake somehow fit the phenomenon of slavery. Let's see if we can use them in adding element 3 to the **Slaughterhouse** situation:

3. The act of the legislature introduced into the butchers' decision-making process a factor of menace, duress, deceit, undue influence or mistake.

Indeed it seems appropriate.

Finally the **Slaughterhouse** case had a fourth characteristic to take into account. If the legislature could show that the monopoly was in the best interests of the common good, we could not question the legality of the statute. The government would have the power under the common law to place the butchers under the exact duress in which it placed them. Therefore our description of the **Slaughterhouse** situation must include another characteristic:

4. The legislature's act confining the butchers' operations to the Crescent City slaughterhouse was not required in the interest of the common good.

We can see the reasonableness of the clause. Serving the common good is serving oneself, and cannot be called slavery.

Note that these four analytical statements can be applied to armed robbery.

1. The robber acted in such a way that a number of taxitants so confronted would be expected to surrender their money.
2. In the absence of the robber's action, the taxitant probably would not surrender her money to the robber.
3. The robber's act introduced into the taxitant's decision-making process a factor of menace, duress, undue influence, deceit or mistake.
4. The taxitant's surrender of her money was not required in the interest of the common good.

Given this, I will become bolder and generalize the conditions of enslavement in a format of cause:

1. An act A of the defendant had such a result that many individuals in plaintiff's position would probably decide to perform in a certain way W.
2. In the absence of the situation created by defendant's act A, the plaintiff would probably not perform in way W.
3. The defendant's act A introduced into plaintiff's deliberations a factor of menace, duress, deceit, undue influence or mistake.
4. Performance W was not required in the interest of the common good.

Statement 4 is not essential unless the defendant happens to be the government. An unauthorized person claiming to act in the interest of the public good, cannot get government help to force another person into service. But, when a court is judging a government action, given the government's power to enforce its wishes, element 4 seems critical. Obviously the majority of five in the **Slaughterhouse** decision neglected it. Even if well-regulated slaughter was in the common interest, confining it to the facilities of the Crescent City Company was not.

The four-part format of enslavement has a fair practicality and generality. Not requiring intent on the part of the defendant, it covers the situation in which a defendant by pure accident might introduce menace, duress or mistake into the plaintiff's decision-making process. Thus it distinguishes cases of accident where compensatory damages might be awarded from cases of malice or recklessness where punitive damages might be added.

But it is important to understand that the four elements still do not reveal the basic nature of the injury in slavery. If a court used such a construction as a cause, it would be merely presuming injury and, though this is customary court procedure and practical, our present effort is not to presume, but to discover the fundamental nature of slavery. We are required to justify the presumption. We must demonstrate that, if the case displays the four characteristics of the format, an infringement of the taxitant's liberty has truly occurred.

We have revealed the injury in armed robbery, blackmail, demand for ransom... - threat is an unentitled use of the taxitant's mind. But I have not put my finger on the liberty infringed in the **Slaughterhouse Cases.** Our intuition tells us, as Bradley does, that "the right to follow any of the common occupations of life is an inalienable right". Emotionally compelling, it is not intellectually convincing. If you are a welder and cannot find a job as a welder, do you have a liberty to work as a welder? Must someone employ you as a welder? And what will we say when we get to fraud, - that we have a liberty "not to be deceived"? It is by this piecemeal manner of thinking that one arrives at Lord Hardwicke's conclusion. It is by defining rights piece by piece that we leave holes for thieves of our liberty to creep through. Such thinking has plagued the civil rights movements ("I have a right not to be discriminated against."). Even my format of enslavement suffers from the affliction. How do I know that menace, duress, undue influence, deceit and mistake are the only energizing factors inducing slavery?

We want a general line of attack. When we charge a person with an attempt to enslave, we must demonstrate a liberty infringed.

CHAPTER 43

SLAVERY; TRUSTS; AFFECTION
AND THE HUMAN QUALITY

Somewhere there must be a god of slavery smiling to himself. In some manner, in the wake of Justice Bradley, our "inalienable right to follow any of the common occupations" became incorporated into law. Obviously it didn't happen in the **Slaughterhouse Cases.** It didn't happen in the **Slaughterhouse** sequel, **Crescent City Company v. Butchers Union Company.** It didn't exactly happen in the enactment of the Civil Rights Act of 1964. This act made it a crime to discriminate against a few select classes of people, forgetting to include self-employed butchers. But when it happened, as it certainly did in the aftermath of the 1964 act, it ignited a wild-fire spread of slavery. Since that time we have witnessed people backed by government forcing employers to hire them. The government even forced itself into slavery, forcing its military academy at West Point to admit and serve people whom it didn't wish to admit and serve. All of which illustrates how a well-intentioned intuitive pronouncement, defectively structured, can have disastrous effects.

The mystery of slavery is that we know it is wrong but can't say exactly what is wrong with it. In many cases of enslavement, our jurists have not located the property invaded and analyzed the mechanics of the invasion, and until this is done the god of slavery will continue to twist the tails of our rulers.

By listing four characteristics of enslavement, I have suggested that enslavement is abroad when person A so acts that person B is induced to perform in a way she would not, were it not for A's act. Thus if Leo Karenski accidentally sets fire to Gordon Romanoff's home, and Gordon exhausts himself trying to save his household effects, we see some elements of slavery. If you have read your fire insurance policy, you will know that had Gordon not made a reasonable effort, his insurance protection would be void. Naturally if Gordon sues Leo, he will not plead a cause of slavery, but nuisance with damage. But if Gordon suffers a heart attack while fighting the fire, how can he sue Leo for that? After all, Gordon acted under his own volition. Well, Leo's act, resulting in fire, induced Gordon to perform as he otherwise would not have performed, and it is in this set of circumstances that we must discover the injury making Leo liable for the heart attack.

One understands of course that this case of slavery is not intentional, and therefore is not slavery. Another term will be more appropriate. An attempt to enslave is not abroad, and Leo, unless his act was flagrantly reckless, will not be liable for punitive damages.

An attempt to enslave must display the marks of intention. The perpetrator acts intentionally, expecting to make the intended victim act as he otherwise wouldn't. But this pressure to act, intended or not, must be relieved. At least this seems to represent the spirit of the common law; even when judges don't understand what they are relieving; or why. This is exemplified in two cases to insert in your file before we set our minds resolutely on solving the mystery.

In re Devlin (1925) presents one of the more diabolic attempts at enslavement. Perhaps old man Devlin's actions were inadvertent, but the more one ponders it, the less likely it seems. The judge relieved the intended slave without knowing he was relieving slavery. At least it seems so from the case report. But at least he relieved her. In this case a grandfather, by means of a trust, tried to subvert his daughter-in-law's wishes in the religious training of her son, his grandson.

Thomas Devlin's son had died, leaving widow and small son, and Devlin created a trust, giving 300 shares of stock to the trustees to distribute as follows. They were to disburse the income of the stock for the benefit of grandson Clarence until he was twenty-five. Then they were to give him the stock outright, to use or dispose as he wished. Meanwhile the benefits were subject to certain conditions. Until Clarence was twenty-one, the income was his only if the trustees received yearly statements from a Roman Catholic school certifying that the boy was being raised in the Roman Catholic faith. From age twenty-one to age twenty-five, the benefits were to be given directly to Clarence with no strings attached. But at twenty-five, the outright transfer of the stock to him was again subject to the condition that he had been raised in the faith until the age of twenty-one. When at any time the conditions were not met, income and stock were to be given to other named persons.

Clarence was three when the trust was created. His father had been Catholic, his mother Sarah Protestant, and she had agreed before marriage to Catholic instruction for their children. With her husband's death, Sarah changed her mind and in 1924 she asked the court to avoid the religious restrictions of the trust. Pennsylvania had recently enacted a new statute protecting religious freedom.

It is important to understand that the trust did not and could not compel Sarah to raise her son a Catholic. She was not fighting an oppression of that kind. What she wanted from the courts was a decree ordering the trustees to give the boy the benefits, even if she raised him as a Protestant. Such a request is anathema to trust law as usually construed.

It is a rule of trusts, and there are variances from the rule, that a trustee may attach any conditions he wishes, even frivolous conditions, to the trust benefits. If someone complains, the government will nevertheless enforce the conditions. As far as the government is concerned, the trust involves the trustor's property, something he may use and dispose as he pleases. For example, a trustor may instruct his trustee to give his nephew $300 at the end of each month, but only if the nephew has parachuted from a plane during the month. If the nephew does not take pleasure in parachuting, it would be natural for him to want the benefits without meeting the condition. But the trustees cannot give them to him; they can do only what the trust tells them to do, and he will never get a court to order them otherwise.

But in **Devlin**, the trial court ordered the trustees to disburse the benefits for the boy, irrespective of his religious instruction, and the Supreme Court of Pennsylvania affirmed it, and we ask how the courts reached this decision.

"At the time of the making of the deed," wrote Judge Sadler, "the beneficiary was 3 years old, and it was therefore impossible for him to make intelligent choice of his religious desires. ... The rearing of a child from 3 years of age until he is 21 "in the faith" covering as it does the formative period of life, necessarily bars the exercise of religious freedom, and... such a condition is inoperative and void."

This line of reasoning is nonsense. The judge in talking about the religious freedom of the boy is talking about a non-thing. The boy will not enjoy religious freedom for a number of years. Under any circumstances, his indoctrination will be determined by someone other than himself. But thus did the judge avoid the religious conditions of Devlin's trust. If he had perchance been speaking of the mother's religious freedom, the trust did not bar that either. At no time would the government send out the sheriff and compel the mother to take Clarence to the Catholic school.

Having determined that the religious conditions of the trust were void, how did the judge apply this conclusion to the disposition of the funds? Here are his words: The trust instrument "shows the fund to be used for the education, maintenance, and support of the grandson. The provisions for the religious care... follow." The judge was saying that the conditions of the disbursement were subordinate to the unconditioned disbursement! So, the conditions being void, the benefits were to be given to the boy unconditionally. Thus spake the court, for some reason flouting all the rules of construction.

When creating wills, trusts, contracts... the creators often draft unclear provisions, and later a court might be asked to determine "who gets what" and the conditions under which she gets it. Basically this is a determination of titles and properties, and the court with jurisdiction is traditionally a court in equity. Since the court erects a structure of rights upon the subject matter in question, the task is called construction; and the rules of construction are about as lucid and determinative as the language of tort and negligence.

Conditional clauses in wills, trusts, contracts... sometimes create a tumble of titles impossible to systematize. I am speaking of provisions with iffy results: "I leave to my nephew Carlos a hundred million pesos if he lives two years in my hacienda, lightless at night, together with my pet forty foot anaconda snake free to roam all the rooms at will."

Question: Can Carlos get the money without meeting the conditions?

Question: What happens if Carlos wishes to meet the terms, but the snake dies in the first year?

Question: What happens to the money if Carlos doesn't conform, and can't get the money, and the will provides for no other beneficiary?

These are some of the questions that might be raised in connection with this provision. My advice to you: include conditional clauses in your will only on one condition: that you can retain for the drafting a very old and experienced attorney who is in love with your wife.

Conditions in wills and trusts that inspire unusually erratic court construction are those void because they are illegal. There are several grounds for illegality and I will concentrate on three. One is the condition under which a beneficiary is given something if, for example, he dynamites the capitol building in Washington, perpetrating an injury in carrying out the condition. The second is the condition in and of itself injuring the beneficiary directly; and a third is the condition of and by itself injuring a third person. In **Devlin** the judge thought Devlin's trust imposed the second kind of illegal condition. It had the effect, he said, of limiting the grandson in his religious freedom. An example of the third kind is a provision giving a nephew a hundred thousand dollars if he divorces his wife.

With the first type, blowing up the Capitol, the trustees will smugly refuse to give him the benefits. He can't get at them. There is simply no way he can approach a court saying, "I have blown up the Capitol. Please order the trustees to give me the money." The condition is unenforceable, and we ask who gets the money? Does the trustee get to keep it forever? Well, not legally. The court will treat the gift as though the beneficiary never existed. The amount of the benefit will be given to the person who would get it if the provision were never created.

Nor can the nephew protest, "I am a law-abiding citizen, your honor, and there is no way I'm going to commit such an act. Therefore you should give me the hundred thousand outright." The judge will say, "I'm sorry, my boy. Your uncle wished you to have the money only if you perpetrate this act. Such a condition by its very nature avoids the benefits. Consequently you have no title to the money."

In a type three illegal condition, the case where the nephew gets the money if he divorces his wife, it will be the wife who will bring the case to court. "Your honor," she will say, "my husband's uncle never liked me. Yes, he has the title of disposing his money. But in this manner of distributing it, he is interfering with my personal relationship with my husband." Here is a pleading of nuisance, you see, and we look to the remedy. If the judge avoids the gift, giving the benefits to the next in line, the nephew might become angry at his wife. "Why did you interfere," he will ask. "Now I have lost the money forever." The trust has put the wife in a position where she can't win, and we will see a remedy as we saw in **Jones v. Alfred H. Mayer Company**. The trustor will lose his title of disposition. The government will revoke it and, though the trustor wished the nephew to get no benefits without the divorce, the government will nevertheless give the money to the nephew.

Having illustrated what happens in the first and third types of untenable conditions, it is difficult to find an example of the second type - where the condition injures the beneficiary directly. I have said this type applies to **in re Devlin**, but I said so because the judge said so. Actually it doesn't. The child Clarence Devlin had no potential for exercising a religious liberty. This pursuit traditionally is in the parent's liberty. If as he grew older he decided to embrace Catholicism for its own sake, well, that would be in his liberty. If he decided to take it up for the sake of the trust benefits, that too would be in his liberty. It would differ not at all from accepting an attractive offer of contract.

I can think of an example in which a conditional gift injures the beneficiary. Let there be a retired teacher loved deeply by the trustor's son. When the son was a boy, this teacher discussed the world of ideas with him, opening his eyes to the beauty of nature and bringing to his attention the intriguing mysteries of life. Now in old age the teacher lives in poverty and the trustor's estate of $10,000 is invested at 6% producing an income of $600 a year. This the trustor leaves to the teacher for life, and the corpus of $10,000 will go to the son when the teacher dies.

The son, no longer a youth, is not financially well off. His wife needs an operation they can't afford; but the teacher continues to live. The $10,000 will save his business from bankruptcy, but the teacher continues to live. The son's children could go to college on the $10,000, but the teacher continues to live. Not that the teacher is stupid and insensitive. She knows the situation puts a strain on their relationship. But if each year she will give him the $600 income, it would not be equivalent to the $10,000 in a lump sum. When she talks to him about it, he swears the situation will never affect his love for her.

But this trust provision, conditional on the teacher's death, is a serpent in this personal relationship, tossed there unwittingly by a grateful and affectionate trustor. As it cannot be thrown out or destroyed by teacher or pupil, it is worse than the 40 foot anaconda that Carlos could take or leave. The teacher cannot take it or leave it at will; she can escape it only in two ways, by dying or by surrendering the purity of her teacher-pupil relationship. And if she asks the trustee to give the $10,000 to the son and terminate the trust, the trustee will refuse. He can do only what the trust instrument tells him to do.

Let the teacher take it to court, claiming the trustor has stumbled into a loading space reserved for the teacher. Obviously the will of the trustor has an energy of its own, daily spewing poisonous fumes into one of the most delicate relationships that man knows. And the teacher does not wish it to be there. A case of nuisance. What must the judge do?

He must take the only action that will clear the air, that will throw the snake out of the house. As a general rule, I think we may say that a benefit injuring a beneficiary must be avoided at the petition of the beneficiary.

So if Devlin's trust condition injured Clarence directly, as the judge said it did, the judge should have voided it and passed the benefit to others. Thomas Devlin plainly said he wanted other people to have the money if Clarence was not raised a Catholic. The judge twisted and bent every rule in the book and it was well that he did. He did the right thing. He had an opportunity to create a new development in equity, but he faced a most difficult problem. He had not been given the right words.

Actually Devlin's trust was an attempt to enslave, and it would have succeeded had not the court issued the only order that would free the intended victim. Sarah Devlin it was whom the trust was oppressing, not Clarence. Can we read between the lines and learn what the judges really saw before them in the courtroom? Can we understand the oppression they instinctively relieved?

It is clear that Thomas Devlin, his son dead, anticipated that Sarah would revoke her promise, bringing Clarence up as a Protestant. This she had every right to do. On the face of it, Devlin's trust appears to be an attempt to entice her compliance, an offer of contract. She could accept it or not as she pleased. But his scheme was not this innocent.

Certainly she wanted the money for the boy, and just as certainly she could scorn the temptation if her Protestantism meant that much. But how would the boy feel later, the grown-up boy, the man, upon finding that his mother's decision cost him a large sum of money? No one could predict his reactions, but the antennae of a loving taxitant would tremble.

Thomas Devlin gave Sarah Devlin her free choice. She could bring Clarence up in Catholicism and secure her relationship with him, or bring him up a Protestant and place her mother-son relationship in jeopardy. Having set these conditions in concrete, Devlin determined his own fate under the common law. He would frustrate her right of religious training if she made one choice, and poison her personal relationship with her son if she made the other. Only one remedy will free her from this trap; - give the boy the money on schedule, free of the religious conditions.

Now I am in trouble. We have seen an attempt to enslave, Devlin putting Sarah in a predicament where she could hoe cotton or jump off the cliff. And how does her situation test under the format of enslavement? Well, Devlin's act - his execution of the trust - made it likely that she would act in a way in which she otherwise would not act. And it cannot be said that her performance - bringing up Clarence as Catholic instead of Protestant - was required for the common good. But something is wrong. Devlin did not introduce deceit, menace, duress, mistake, or undue influence into her decision-making process! And the basic nature of enslavement still eludes us.

Before finally solving the mystery, I ask that you insert one more case in your data file; **Hinde v. Pendleton**. Noonan examines it in his chapter "The Virginia Liberators". Noonan in **Persons and Masks of the Law** proposes that judges should see litigants not as A,B and C but as persons, and no case is more appropriate to his thesis than **Hinde v. Pendleton**. It was heard in 1791 by Chancellor George Wythe, role-model of objectivity, mentor of Jefferson.

Wythe as Chancellor in Virginia heard many quarrels between white litigants both claiming the use and possession of some certain black man. Under the Virginia slave code (drafted by Jefferson and himself), Wythe had to be blind to the inner nature of a black person.

Noonan believes that **Hinde v. Pendleton** cleaved the cold impersonal mask of the Chancellor, giving us a glimpse of a compassionate Wythe. He suggests that Wythe in his decision quietly announced the future course of jurisprudence in the slave states. **Hinde v. Pendleton** is, as Noonan says, "The last case in **Wythe's Reports**, taken out of order and set by Wythe himself as a climax." Noonan's chapter masterfully weaves together in one piece the theoretical problems of slavery in Virginia, the role played by Wythe in this lego-cosm, the tragic fate engulfing Wythe in this environment, and, almost as comic relief, Wythe's professional relations with this same Pendleton. I attempt here to focus only on **Hinde v. Pendleton.**

Pendleton as the executor of an estate found it to be the true owner of black people, a woman and her four children, who were mistakenly in the possession of Mrs. Hinde. As executor he ordered them sold at auction, and Mrs. Hinde, having a special affection for them, begged her husband to buy them whatever the price. Pendleton, anticipating that her neighbors would not bid against her, told the agent not to let them go at less than a reasonable price. Toward this end the agent employed a by-bidder - a sham bidder standing in the crowd and pretending to bid - a method of raising the bid as high as possible. As it turned out, the Hindes had to pay the exorbitant price of 52,000 pounds of tobacco to keep the family. But they learned of the ruse, and sued Pendleton for the excess over the fair market price.

By a turn of logic, Wythe judged the use of a by-bidder to be deceit. He also introduced an ancient precept from the civil law, the **praetium affectionis** - the price of affection - "which is unlimited, and which therefore was "What The By-bidder And His Prompter Pleased." To Wythe, Pendleton was the prompter and, as Noonan observes, Wythe himself capitalized the seven words. Apparently the Chancellor was using the same optical lens as we, and from the same observation point. Though seeing that the Hindes had, in the bidding, been neatly impressed into Pendleton's service, Wythe, like us, had difficulty identifying the infringed liberty, and the mechanism of infringement.

To clinch his cause for taking action, Wythe introduced the element of marital relations. Pendleton's maneuvers had injected friction into Mr. Hinde's marriage. Mrs. Hinde's husband, he allowed, was at Pendleton's mercy "to gratify a wife" by buying a family of servants "endeared to her probably by... (their) obsequious attention and faithful ministration... in return for (her) benign treatment and provided care...." Note how carefully Wythe drew the parallel between the blacks' relationship to Mrs. Hinde and the relationship of fawning dogs to their mistress. Wythe was building two causes, an overt one and a covert one, and in his overt cause he intended to stay within the slave code, careful not to establish a human relationship between slaves and whites.

So here was Wythe's cause; the overt one expressed in his opinion; perhaps expressed here a bit more rigorously than he expressed it. Pendleton's deceit operated on Mrs. Hinde, a tender woman ignorant of the ways of men in business and auctions. Terrified by the prospect of losing her black pets to strangers, she importuned, she wheedled, she compelled her husband to bid again and again as the by-bidder raised his bid. Thus Pendleton had engineered a nuisance in Hinde's loading space, and while it had not distorted Mrs. Hinde's mind against Hinde it was threatening. Bidding was Hinde's only means of averting marital deterioration. The whole causal chain produced damage - an excessive price for the slaves - and the damages were calculable in terms of the excess price.

But would the slave code admit affection for slaves as a material factor in such a causal sequence? You see, if a person paid an excessive price for a horse because he loved the horse, the Chancellor would not have ordered the seller to return the excess. And if you bid exorbitantly for a horse, and later tell the Chancellor you did it because your wife loved the horse and you would have lost her love if you failed to bid, he would have ordered the bailiff to chase you out of the courtroom with a long stick.

Well, affection can be defined in several ways and expressed in many ways, and the definition can have various and varying results. The Chancellor didn't go into it, and he didn't have to. His old adversary Pendleton was a lawyer, skilled not only in slave law but enslavement. No one knew better than he that a very good way to chain a slave to a plantation is to provide a wife for him. Every professional within earshot of this trial would admit that affection had a material function in the universe of slavery.

We are seeing in the Chancellor a master at work. No doubt he wished to see the Hindes prevail, if only to see Pendleton lose. Otherwise we might not have seen such ingenuity. In **Hinde v. Pendleton** he erected a landmark, carefully placed deep in the shadows of unspoken law, unillumined.

Wythe's decision was not challenged. Pendleton remained strangely silent; Pendleton who as an appeals court judge, so Noonan tells us, had reversed over fifty percent of Wythe's decisions in Chancery. But Wythe was walking on the surface of a very deep vat of suds.

I think we can throw out his proposal of deceit. After all, Mrs. Hinde's husband was bidding and Hinde, like everyone, had to assume in all business transactions a certain amount of bluffing and sham bidding. As for introducing the element of marital relations, Wythe was simply putting up a smoke-screen. The sound of an auctioneer's gavel finalizes a contract, and a contract is a contract. If in contract negotiations you can demonstrate the effect of deceit, menace, duress, mistake or undue influence, the contract is avoidable. But none of these were present in **Hinde.** For instance, a court will not acknowledge deceit in a case unless the plaintiff's trust in the defendant is reasonable and justifiable, and this cannot be admitted in the circumstances of ordinary auction bidding. Yes, if consent is not "real", a contract is avoidable, but nowhere does the law of contract say that a bid is unenforceable if the bidder claims he bid for the purpose of preserving his marital relationship.

As for the element of affection, what kind of affection was Wythe talking about? It is true that a slave's affection for a loved one will keep him on the plantation. But it is also true that a dog's affection will keep the dog at his master's side. No, a judge will not restore an overage paid at auction by a dog's loving owner, and Wythe himself has compared this slave-Hinde relationship to a dog-master relationship.

But can't we rescue Wythe's argument? In **Hinde**, are we not observing a sort of kidnapping? Weren't Pendleton and his agents holding the slaves where the Hindes could not reach them, threatening to take them far away if the Hindes did not pay the ransom? Wasn't it simply a case of forcing the Hindes into service? Yes, if the blacks were human, but they weren't. For Wythe was expressing his opinion in the context of the slave code. These particular objects at auction had the same legal status as a family of horses.

Kidnapped horses are merely stolen, and must be returned to the owners. The same with slaves. But Pendleton had not stolen these slaves. As executor of the estate, he held legal title in their use and disposition. Given this, there was but one way that Wythe could honestly order Pendleton to restore the excess funds. He had to recognize the slaves as humans; even as slaves - humans. If they were not humans, the Hindes had no property in the excess payments; and this was Wythe's discovery in pure theory. These slaves are humans! This was his tacit announcement to the intellects of the legal world, including Pendleton; and the legal world admitted it, as quietly as possible. How did he reach this conclusion?

We have here, said Wythe, saying it not in his opinion - not by words - but by his decision; we have here a case in which white people have been enslaved. They have been subjected to slavery - material and effective - and it is material and effective because the blacks are human.

I know, he said (not in so many words) that we can legally define blacks as non-human, and we can overlook the pretense and inconsistency of this practice. But in this case, something is occurring that we can't overlook; our definition of blacks as non-humans is permitting us to enslave whites!

Why, asks Wythe (without asking it aloud) did the Hindes pay such an excessive price for the black family? Was it to satisfy their desire to possess them, as a horse lover wishes to possess fine horse? Was it to maintain them as a set, as a connoisseur of glassware wishes to preserve intact a set of irreplaceable goblets? No.

The facts are (and now I paraphrase his actual words) the facts are established that the Hindes do not wish to be separated from the slaves, and **this desire is increased by the "reciprocal abhorrence" shown by the blacks at the thought of being separated from each other.**

This and not the capacity of the slaves for mere affection demonstrated to Wythe their humanity. It is important that we recognize here a relationship that can exist only between humans, and in this we must be rigorously discriminating. I can love a dog, and a dog can love me. And I know in advance that I don't want the dog separated from me. But the dog is incapable of this feeling.

Now be careful. If the dog is separated from me, he might be unhappy. But never in advance of separation will he think, "If I'm separated from this man I will be sad and distressed." It is like the squirrel burying nuts for the winter. Its nature might induce it to bury more nuts than it needs. It might even sense a long winter and bury more nuts than usual. But never will it say to itself, "It might be a colder winter than usual, so on this possibility I will bury more nuts than usual." I am saying what I have said before, that only humans can anticipate in the abstract; only humans are capable of conditional apprehension.

Thus the Hindes were human; they were capable of anticipating their distress at their separation from the blacks. Since the Hindes were white, the court was willing to admit this axiomatically. But the crux of the case was this. The evidence before the court was that the blacks were already in distress. They anticipated that they might be separated from each other! And the Hindes saw this distress, and wanted to relieve it, and their excessive bid was a response to the blacks' conditional apprehension!

Yes, law can be manufactured, calling blacks non-human, but such law is sham. Here was evidence of humans responding to humans, a material fact. The law showed itself to be delusion, immaterial. And a common law judge deals only with the material. My expressed opinion, said the Chancellor, has maintained the blacks at a non-human level, but my decision pronounces them human. And with this, a myth - the purity of slave theory - partly perpetuated by Wythe himself - went up in an invisible puff of smoke. In 1791.

In the course of the next several chapters, we will have to recognize that **Hinde v. Pendleton** furnishes us a unique clue in our search for the principles of equity. In **Devlin,** Sarah fought to preserve two liberties - bringing up her child in the religion of her choice, and nurturing her personal relationship with him. But in **Hinde v. Pendleton,** though personal relations were involved, they were not the issue. Though the sale might separate the families, they would still love each other. Yes, the sale might in separating them deprive each of enjoying their carefully nurtured clearings in each other; but the sale did not separate them after all. So personal relations were not at stake in **Hinde.** On trial actually was Pendleton's particular use of the Hindes' feelings, using them to extract money from them. It was this use that the Chancellor condemned. It was to expose this use and declare his condemnation of it that Wythe had to view the blacks as human, and Pendleton had to concede the point.

CHAPTER 44

SLAVERY NEARLY CAPTURED.
A NEW GLIMPSE OF OUR MARVELOUS ESTATE
UNDER THE COMMON LAW

We have learned that slavery can be invisible, superficially filmy yet binding as steel, abhorrent as death. And to achieve a reliable understanding of its operation, we find ourselves becoming technical in the extreme.

We saw Thomas Devlin make an attempt to enslave, but without success. The wife of his dead son, before acting as a slave, appealed to government and found relief. On the other hand, Pendleton successfully enslaved Hinde. Hinde at auction acted as a slave, bidding as Pendleton wished. Bidding finished, slavery ended, but damage persisted, and Chancellor Wythe's accomplishment was not to relieve slavery. He remedied the financial loss suffered by Hinde acting as slave to Pendleton.

The butchers in New Orleans, those yielding to the might of government and renting space in the Crescent City slaughterhouse, were slaves. The legislature successfully enslaved them, and the Supreme Court, not recognizing slaves standing in its own courtroom, failed them.

Armed robbers and blackmailers perchance are successful in their attempts to enslave; perchance not; it makes no difference. The attempt alone constitutes a crime. So says the government. How far, we ask, must an attempt go before the government calls it a crime, and we find a measure of it in the government's views on conspiracy. A conspiracy to commit a crime is a crime; a conspiracy to enslave is a crime; but there must be at least one step toward perpetration. To be counted a conspiracy, a discussion of the project, and an agreement among the conspirators, must be accompanied by an act. They must have taken at least one material step toward their objective. If they are going to capture their victim, they at least must have bought a coil of rope. One step alone will complete the requirements for a cause in conspiracy, even if the step does not directly engage the intended victim. No injury to the intended victim. No infringement of her liberty. Yet a crime. And what a morsel this becomes for theorists to chew on.

Our task now is to learn the exact nature of the injury in enslavement. We wish to recognize slavery beneath all its guises.

Toward this end, I begin a casual stroll through the barracks of slavery and its environs, catching the distinctions between true slavery and conditions not quite slavery. I bring to your attention, in each and every case of enslavement, the pressure upon the slave to perform in limited channels - a pressure materialized by another person. Never is a person a slave to herself. Though often we say, "She is a slave to her own ambitions", we never expect her to seek relief in court. Nor is an employee a slave to her employer. Though she feels a compulsion to get a job, and though her employer treats her "like a slave", it is not slavery. The pressure to earn money is not occasioned by an act of the employer. It is generated by her own kinestatic drives, independent of the employer.

We take a step in the right direction when we see similarities between slavery and damage. If your small son digs a hole in the shoulder of the road, innocently preparing a stage for my twisted ankle, his act places me in a sort of enforced service. After twisting my ankle, I will go to the hospital emergency room (but I would rather be elsewhere). After the hospital I will stay at home a couple of days (though I'd rather be at the office). Here we see the act of a person channeling someone into a limited set of pursuits.

Is a person responsible for channeling when her act is purely accidental? We come back to the nature of our world and the intent of our rulers. Our world is a jumble of elements only steps from harm-causing sequences. You are walking along a rural highway and come upon a car stalled on the road. At the same time another car shoots recklessly around the curve in the lane of the stalled car. If a collision occurs, engulfing you in its terrible concussions, these drivers will be held responsible for your bruised tissues and broken bones. The injury is nuisance, invasion of your legal free space. In addition, the concussion powers disruption in your bodily substance, and your project effectiveness evaporates. - Damage.

But suppose you see the danger coming and run from the highway, scaling the fence. Running, running, you save yourself, but nevertheless your liberty has been infringed. Under the threatening circumstances, you experienced a rational desire to forego your full potential range of pursuits. You concentrated on one only, and, with this, your entitled pursuit space was diminished. Your actions were channeled, occasioned by the actions of others. Though you acted according to your own free will, in accord with your own reasoning capacity, yet you were a subject of injury. Here is the joker in slavery. A slave always acts in accord with his or her own reasoning ability. It was true even of the American black slave.

This in essence is why the crowd in **Palsgraf** was not held responsible for hurting Helen Palsgraf. Though they knocked the scales over on her, they were acting not as originants but as slaves. In running away from the exploding fireworks, they were responding as best they could to the wilful acts of others.

So, in a sense, if you run from the potential car crash, the injury might be classed as nuisance with resulting slavery. At least we could call it nuisance with resulting channeling. Even if it happens too quickly for you to respond and run, this is your situation for a split second. The conjunction of events makes it desireable for you to take a channeled action, and deprives you of time to take it. The circumstances make you a slave, and simultaneously a captive.

If you notice, we are back to the topic of our effectiveness in our entitled pursuit space. Review Chapters 16 and 18, if you wish, and the part about George Mason in Chapter 33. Remember project effectiveness? It involves what you can undertake in a given period of time. Remember George Mason's letter, 1784? "I have been lately informed that some people intend to open a poll for me at the elections tomorrow in this county.... I should look upon such an attempt in no other light than an oppressive and unjust invasion of my personal liberty...."

What harm have the electioneers caused? It is this.

Mason has been trapped into a perplexing predicament, a decision-making situation. He must do something to stop the electioneers. Else he must face the consequences of failing to do something. He must act or face the consequences; the earmarks of slavery. But what is the injury? Let us briefly review the topic of project spaces. Remember the various species of project spaces?

Again I specify projects E,F,G,H,J,K to be the list of projects in which I am capable. This is my space of potential projects, my time-free potential. But I do not live in a timeless world; I am limited by time; and again I set my thirty day potential at exactly three projects - EFG, FGH, HJK... just one combination of three projects is possible for me in a thirty day period. Mathematically there are twenty of these three-project combinations, and this list of twenty I have called my per unit time potential. And the per unit time potential is peculiar. It does not consist of EFJ **and** FGH **and**... **and** HJK in a thirty-day period. It consists of EFJ **or** FGH **or**... **or** HJK, for if I undertake one of the combinations, I will not be free to undertake any of the other nineteen. My freedom is not my potential. My freedom consists, say, of EJK in the next thirty days if (a) I happen to choose EJK and (b) I can and do undertake it.

Now what if an act of someone else channels you into pursuing project H? How do you express the result in project spaces? It means that each combination of your per unit time potential in the next thirty-day period must contain project H. It means, for instance, that you are no longer free to undertake combination EJK. In fact this channeling has chopped your thirty-day potential in half. There are only ten combinations containing project H.

It does not limit your freedom to choose EFG or EJK... or any combination not containing H. But for a given span of time it removes them from your per unit time potential. Meaning not that you can't choose to do them, but that for a very good reason you choose something else. Meaning they are no longer within your freedom.

So we must eliminate phrases like "without free choice" from our definitions of slavery. In an instance of slavery, you will choose to limit yourself to the channeled set of projects. It is simply that an act of someone has made it highly desireable that you concentrate on pursuing a particular project for the time being. Now, to make this concept more definite, we approach the grandest contrivance of the common law. Your estate.

In legal practice, the word estate is used to describe two distinct concepts. Suppose we have two people, you and I, and just one stone, a stone useful for two purposes, grinding corn and, when heated in the sun, warming our beds. These two uses compose the estate of the stone. Happily there are plenty of daylight hours for both of us for grinding corn. But the stone can be used to warm only one bed at night, and since I'm the bigger, I get that use. So that's the way we distribute the estate of the stone. Since, in a legal universe, we can partition a thing into many uses, it can be the subject of many titles. Gathering all these uses into a systematic bundle, this is the estate that is the thing. An estate of a thing is the legal assembly of all the properties rationally constructable upon a thing.

But I wish to talk about another concept to which the word estate is applied. It is the totality of a person's liberties plus a new dimension. I begin to describe it by the diagram in Figure 44.1.

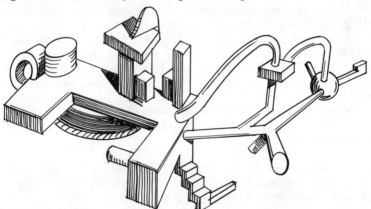

Figure 44:1. A Person's Estate.

This figure displays a series of connected labyrinths in a mountain, through which you may wander and climb at will. It is your free space, your property, your collection of rights, your estate. The rock matrix through which your free space extends is the set of pursuits from which you are excluded. It is the union of all other estates, the estates of other people. If you penetrate the rock, you are invading the property of others. Actually the rock is not solid. It is composed of labyrinths similar to yours, all intermeshed; and hopefully the bounds and interfaces separating the estates have been established by someone with an eye on the common good.

Each segment of your labyrinth is a project in which you are propertied. We might label it E or F or K.... By due process you are at liberty to pursue each project in your estate without interference; and no one else may use it without your permission. And now we discover the sublimating dimension of your estate, the due process statement making the whole greater than the sum of its parts. Not only is your freedom to move within each project protected by due process, but your facility in moving from project to project. More accurately, due process protects your absolute determination of your pursuit within your estate at any moment.

Your per unit time potential of the next moment is precisely one project. If you undertake one, you cannot undertake another. Due process guards your determination of this pursuit - free of any input by another person. This then is the ultimate dimension of your liberty. You have the liberty of your estate.

It is this statement of due process, distilled from the case reports in your law library, that protects you from slavery. More generally, from channeling. The mechanics are quite simple. If, without your consent, the act of a person results in determining the project you will choose to undertake at moment t, that act infringes your liberty in your estate. The mechanism is based on a purely physical fact of reality: if you are personally engaged in pursuit H at time t, you cannot be engaged in pursuit E,F,G,J or K.

We may imagine that the first act undertaken by George Mason, when he heard about the electioneers project, was to think about it. This of itself took his mind from other projects, and constituted an infringement of his liberty. Is it important? It certainly is. There are people who maliciously pursue schemes like this. Unhampered, they will completely destroy a person's effectivness in his estate. It is called hounding, pestering, harassing. Or it may be so subtle we have no word for it. There are other people behaving recklessly, careless of your welfare, the wake of their boats destroying your enjoyment - your liberty - of your estate.

I still have not treated the larger injuries in Mason's case, but need I? Now that we can conceptualize this most subtle injury, the others follow. However, one should not be rash in concluding harassment in every instance of your hectic life. I have mentioned an "act of a person that results in determining the project you will choose to undertake at moment t", but I have not defined the term "determining". By it, I really mean determining, a material phenomenon. I will define it in Chapter 50.

As we close in upon the definition of enslavement, we must be thrice cautious. If we learn to distinguish clearly between slavery and non-slavery, we can dissipate forever the social dynamite buried in such government debacles as the **Slaughterhouse Cases** and yes, **Bakke v. Regents of the University of California,** and yes, the busing of school children stemming from **Brown v. Board of Education** ("Brown II").

It is one thing for the Supreme Court to tell parents and school boards, "No, you may not arbitrarily distinguish school children on the basis of race. In material mode, such segregation is defamation." But it is another thing for courts in the wake of "Brown II" to tell parents and school boards, "You must put your children on buses and transport them to the other side of the city. The population profile of every school must reflect the blended population of the school district as a whole." Segregation of races by neighborhoods is not defamation. One might use "Brown II" logic to transport children from Atlanta to schools in Seattle. It makes the same sense. It is enforced service meeting someone's arbitrary notion of what's good for the nation. It is adverse to the **common** good. It is slavery encoded.

Once we possess legal tools capable of pinpointing slavery, we need no longer rely on intuition for such momentous decisions. But if our tools are faulty, we will see the court's jurisdiction "perpetually eluded by new schemes which the fertility of man's invention would contrive". Moreover we will see men charged with enslavement when slavery is not involved in the least.

On the basis of my discussion to this point, I will as an initial step define slavery thus: "A person is enslaved when she decides to do something as a consequence of an act of another," for example, she runs away from an imminent car crash. In addition, I will want to include the compulsion of time, as "If she does not act quickly and run fast, she will get hurt." The element of time, for instance, is always involved in extortion. The extortioner, be she robber, kidnapper, or blackmailer, always couples her demands to the running of time. "Pay me now." "Pay me at 10 o'clock." "Pay me before Saturday."

The butchers in New Orleans felt the compulsion of time. If they did not rent space in the Crescent City slaughter house, they would have to find another way to make a living (or move to another town), and time would not pause for their decision. The demands of life and the compulsions of time have much in common.

Devlin's trust was stamped indelibly with the element of time. If Sarah's son was removed from Catholic influence at any time before age twenty-one, the benefits would be taken away. Each morning for eighteen years she would have to get him to the Catholic school. Or else! At least these were Thomas Devlin's intentions.

So we have a rudimentary definition of slavery or, more generally, channeling. It exists when (a) you do something in consequence of another person's act, and (b) your time to do it is limited. But the definition is defective.

We see Mr. Wagner offering Eric Neumann a job at six hundred dollars a month, and people have heard Neumann say he didn't want to work for Wagner. But no one else has offered him a job; he is out of money and experiencing the compulsions of life. He accepts the job, and now we ask if Neumann is Wagner's slave. Wagner, you see, has acted in such a way that (a) he has induced Neumann to accept the job and (b) Neumann's time to accept the offer is limited.

Of course, Neumann is not Wagner's slave. Not unless Wagner has trapped Neumann into this predicament. Not unless Wagner, for example, has spread a rumor that Neumann has a wicked temper, not safe as an employee. If Wagner did this, then it would be an act of Wagner that channeled Neumann into his employ. Otherwise Wagner's job offer does not constitute channeling. Rather it opens up Neumann's opportunities; it increases his potential. It is certainly not a case of enslavement.

Slavery, you will agree, will be difficult to define, and we are approaching the critical point. One cannot escape the fact that a person makes a wilful decision in acting as a slave. "I must do this, or else...." This is the tenor of his thinking and, with this, his desire becomes engaged in his master's project.

Since will - volo - is involved, let us complete our thinking on the topic of will. As we have seen, not all human actions can be ascribed to will. At least there are two levels of will - (a) kinestatic pursuit and (b) decisive resolution of conflict, each prompting an action or restraint of action. If we reserve the word will for (b), then wilful powering evolves from a controlled decision, while a pure kinestatic powering develops from a mindless, unrestrained Omega drive. The wrapping of a vine tendril around a trellis wire is an example. However, a pure example of kinestatic powering in an animal might be difficult to find. A desperately hungry weasel attacking a squirrel might represent pure kinestasis. But even here, one might see a fleeting hesitation, a hint of decision; the weasel might remember the sharp teeth of last week's squirrel. To draw a sharp line saying "Here is will. There is kinestasis." may be impossible. And even if one makes that distinction, one must still recognize a sobering truth.

Take two decisions - one to take a pleasure cruise, the other to fight a fire-breathing dragon. Both wilful decisions, they undoubtedly reflect two different levels of will power. Assuredly, the decision to take a cruise reflects desire, hence an Omega, powered by kinestasis. But the decision to fight the dragon also reflects desire, probably desire pitted against desire, but one prevails. Even a decision to sacrifice oneself represents desire. As sublime as these decisions may be, lost in the mysteries of will power, at bottom they are kinestatically powered. In the final analysis we must admit that the act of a slave is not only voluntary, not only his chosen act, but an act rising out of his own desire. These are facts that master slave-makers always use to advantage in arguing their defense.

Now on the threshold of finalizing the definition of slavery, I will bring for your scrutiny a last example of compulsion. Is it slavery or not?

I will name him Sam Harvard. Prone to obesity, he cannot enjoy manly meals and a slim figure at the same time. This year he might be slim and next year indulge, but his wife warns, "Sam, if you get that fat again I'll divorce you." She means it and the question is, is she trying to enslave him? Well, obviously she is trying to channel his actions. Her warning is a threat of sorts and generates, we suppose, at least a modicum of compulsion. Yet somehow we sense that her warning does not constitute an attempt to enslave. How then do we differentiate between slavery and non-slavery and, with this, I start presenting for your examination what I conclude to be the fundamental structure of slavery.

A prime component of slavery is a type of situation to which not one of us is a stranger. It involves what I will call a contra-Omega situation; a situation involving something we don't like; unpleasant; undesireable. This is a negative way of putting it, and perhaps it can be expressed positively, but I don't know how. And perhaps if it were expressed positively, it would lack the conceptual force I wish it to convey. We go to a football game, sitting in a cold rain for two hours, not liking it. But we wouldn't leave the stadium for a thousand dollars. So, though it is a contra-Omega situation, it must at the same time be feeding an Omega of ours. For this situation we consciously or unconsciously strike a balance between our Omega drives. We stay for the game.

But now over the rim of the stadium we see approaching the funnel of a tornado accompanied by angry flashes of lightning, and suddenly the balance shifts; we are caught up in a different kind of contra-Omega situation. It is an action-inducing contra-Omega situation. About as awkward a term as I have yet coined. But this has been my experience with the topic of slavery. To date I have yet to devise a graceful verbal image of the structure of enslavement. Even a magnificent mind defaulted in introducing the phrase "involuntary servitude". It is as though the English language itself is not amicable to a discourse in slavery.

I am discussing a desire to escape a contra-Omega situation, and, against my inclinations, I am approaching a double negative. Human motivation should be expressed positively. Our drives are toward Omegas, not away. But now I am writing about an action away from a contra-Omega (whatever this is)! I might try to cosmeticize my argument and my language. A desire to escape a contra-Omega situation; isn't this basically a drive toward an Omega? A desire to escape hunger; isn't this a drive to feed the entire kinestatic machine? But a desire to escape pain; what is its positive aspect, a drive to live in Nirvana? You see, to escape a double negative we must devise an abstraction, and I think we are wiser to remain in contact with reality. It will be better to talk about specific desires to prevent specific happenings.   In fact I wish to concentrate on an even narrower topic - the situation in which one must act, act, act to prevent the happening.

We meet a grizzly bear in the forest, and we wish not to have pain, and we wish not to have scars, and we wish not to die. What in the world is this term "wish not"? Is it an inverse verb? Well, sometimes we might substitute the verb "fear", but not always, and it creates one too many abstractions to inquire what we wish "for". It will have to suffice that we merely list a set of wish nots or don't wants. And so we take action. I might call this situation a "motivating, stressful situation," but for some inexpressible reason I will adopt the ungainly term "an action-inducing contra-Omega situation", meaning the particular sort of situation in which we must take action to prevent the happening of an event we wish not to happen.

This is the situation in which we cross the street to miss meeting a person we wish not to meet. Again, to avert a contra-Omega situation, we learn to make our beds before our guests come. Or pay our bills on time. On many occasions we act under the influence of an action-inducing contra-Omega situation. It may be upon us at the moment, or merely anticipatory. And in acting thus we do not think of ourselves as slaves, and we're not. I am not saying that all such situations spell slavery. I am saying that an action-inducing contra-Omega situation is an essential component of the enslaving situation.

If you meet a live grizzly in a forest, you do not consider it a case of injury. It is merely nature, and may channel you up a tree. But if some zoo people, having just caged a wild grizzly, are busily hauling it away in a trailer, and if the cage door opens as the trailer passes you on the trail, and the bear bounces out, you have a dreadful case of nuisance on your hands. The zoo people have plunged you into an action-inducing contra-Omega situation. I am saying it is injury. So what is your liberty that has been infringed? And what is the functional description of the infringement? Describe your situations, before and after, pre-bear and bear, in terms of project spaces.

Today, by entering the forest, you have limited your potential. Among your full set of potential pursuits, you have determined your "today" potential. Once in the forest, for instance, there is no way you can get back to the office before quitting time. Nevertheless, at each moment your next moment potential is practically infinite. You can gaze up through the trees at the shining sky. You can playfully hide behind a bush from your husband. You can step from the trail to study a wild orchid. You can sit on a log. You can stride forward along the path. You can retrace your steps to the lodge. You can chat with a binoculared birdwatcher. The number of your entitled loadings in your next-moment potential are, though limited, innumerable. This is your situation, pre-bear.

With the appearance of the bear, your choices of next-moment loadings are strikingly reduced. True, your next action will originate in your personal desire. It will develop out of a perfectly natural action-inducing contra-Omega situation. It is just that the zoo people have contributed toward your engagement in it. It is by their action that you meet this particular bear at this particular moment. An act of theirs plus its consequences have contributed toward a definite channeling of your pursuits in the time-frame of the next moment. They have bumbled into your estate, and, without your permission, have determined your actions in your own estate. Your effectiveness in determining your actions in your own estate has been reduced.

The pressure of time in an action-inducing contra-Omega situation must not be neglected. Without the drive, drive, drive of time, there is never a bit of compulsion in any situation. Therefore an action-inducing contra-Omega situation is a situation in which you feel motivated to act to prevent a driven occurence. Its onset linked to the lapse of time by the laws of nature, its march is beyond your control. Of this there is nothing new, nothing unusual. It is just that we are interested in a special class of action-inducing contra-Omega situation, the one in which you have been involved by the actions of another person. If someone has involved you in this kind of situation, she has powered an injury.

Such an involvement has enslaved you. No, I will adopt a sharper terminology. She has injuriously channeled your pursuits. It is an injury rendering her liable for harm. I think, to call it enslavement, the involvement will have to be intentional on her part. So, let us familiarize ourselves with this idea, testing it as we proceed.

Imagine a high garden wall at a mountain lodge, made of brick, pierced by two entrances, one on the east, one west, and each guarded by very tall iron gates, usually open. To complete the stage, the north wall is breached by a window-like opening, about 3 feet square and four feet from the ground. You and Walter Mathias are making a tour of the surroundings, and he, directing your attention to this window-like opening, offers to wager twenty dollars that Bill Green will jump through it at dawn next day. Walter insists that Bill will do it purely of his own counsel, of his own desire and his own free will, and naturally you counter the bet.

With Bill Green arriving this evening, next morning will be his first morning at the lodge for the summer, and Mathias is confident he will conform to an old pattern of behavior. Lured by a pervading memory-laden fragrance that lingers in the garden just before dawn, Bill will go there and sit in silence on an old slatted bench for a half hour. And Mathias, having been at the lodge two weeks already, knows what Bill doesn't know.

Since Bill was last here, a testy black bear has formed the habit of inspecting the garden each morning at dawn. Lumbering in through the west entrance she checks the roses, and, satisfied, she departs to the east. Like a fortress, these walls; the iron gates, the barriers of a stronghold. They swing smoothly, without squeak or squawk, and perhaps you can design a plan of action as good as Walter's.

I am trying to reproduce the final component in a refined plan of enslavement. You will admit that the meeting between Bill Green and the bear will create an action-inducing contra-Omega situation. But Walter Mathias will have contributed nothing to it. He will only take advantage of a situation that will probably occur without his intervention. He wishes merely to guide Bill to a particular set of actions. For this he need only close each aperture in the wall except the square window-like opening.

So the injury powered by Walter does not subsist in contributing to the action-inducing contra-Omega situation. It is connected with reducing the number of pursuits available to Bill at a critical moment. No doubt it is enslavement. Walter will engage Bill in Walter's pursuit. Anticipating the fun of seeing Bill fly through that opening in the garden wall, and wishing to win the bet, he will establish a mechanism to accomplish it. As, in a water-powered grist mill, the moving water pre-exists the miller (the miller merely takes advantage of the situation), so Walter channels Bill into actions best serving Walter's objectives.

But can we classify the injury as trespass or nuisance? Yes, it is trespass.

Walter Mathias will use Bill Green, and we discover an interesting relationship. Though nuisance might be intentional or unintentional, use is always intentional. The idea of use presupposes pursuit, and pursuit implies an objective. Intentional channeling - though energized by nuisance, or perhaps energized without human agency - is completed by trespass. It involves an originant's use of a taxitant. Some entirely contrived slaveries involve both nuisance and trespass. But how so. How do I get trespass out of it.

Mathias might have had a bit of fun without touching the gates, merely leaving them open. Bill would have executed a neat display of footwork getting to the nearest portal. And though Walter might be entertained by the sight, he would be committing no injury. He would not have introduced the bear. He would not have touched the gates. He would not be using Bill for his entertainment. He would be using the electromagnetic waves emanating from Bill. To use Bill he would have to do something, creating a situation to which Bill would respond.

If Walter was instrumental, intentionally channeling the bear into the garden, he would not only create a nuisance, he would be using Bill. His project would rely on a knowledge of human reactions to bears. He would perform actions having a fair chance of predictable results. He would create a disturbance in Bill's proximity, knowing fairly well how Bill would react, and this exactly fits the definitions both of nuisance and use.

But given the situation as I first described it, he is not content to see Bill exit at random. He will close the east gate after Bill enters the garden, and the west gate when the bear enters. Now, though he is not responsible for introducing the bear, he is going to use Bill; not Bill's reaction to the bear - this is pre-determined - but Bill's reasoning power. Bill will size up the situation quickly, and his hastily formed conclusion will vault him through the window in the wall. This is the final touch of the devil in slavery. The enslaver uses not only the animal nature of the taxitant - her contra-Omega impulses - but her reasoning power; her capacity to look around and weigh her options. This constitutes a use of a person without her permission. Trespass. This is the mechanism of the injury perpetrated by Walter Mathias.

We are glimpsing the full profile of an enslavement. The victim, a taxitant, finds himself in an action-inducing contra-Omega situation, and only a limited number of feasible escape routes. The originant, the enslaver, through devising one or both of two components comprising the total mechanism, has infringed the taxitant's liberty. The **motivating** component engages the victim in a contra-Omega situation -

completing it, or energizing it, or in some manner exposing the victim to it. The **channeling** component restricts the number of escape windows available to the victim, and in this second mechanism the originant utilizes the victim's reasoning ability. The victim's own desires and reasoning ability channel him into an action fitting the originant's objectives.

This was the situation of the American black slave. The master wielded the whip; this was the contra-Omega action inducer: "Hoe cotton now!" This introduced the urgency of time, and opened the only escape route. The other escape routes were blocked by the power machinery of state government, and the federal power machinery established in the federal Constitution, and the color of skin, and the terrors of the frontier, and the potential runaway's affections for loved ones left behind, and a loving owner's apprehensions for the welfare of her freed black in the land of the free. With the black surrounded by this monstrous garden wall, the master put the hoe in the black's hand and pointed to the cotton field, and, under the circumstances, hoeing was the reasonable way to act.

Extortioners, be they blackmailers, kidnappers or armed robbers, all carefully fashion their machineries. They devise their mechanisms for inducing action; they set the time-clock running; they point the taxitant toward her only escape route - the reasonable way for her to act.

The Louisiana legislature closed the butchers' established places of business, exposing them to the perennial wolf at the door, and opened for them a new escape route - the Crescent City slaughterhouse; a reasonable route to take under the circumstances.

The genius who drafted Devlin's trust created a phonograph record with the potential of repeating the same words to Sarah over and over again for the next eighteen years. "You don't want Clarence to lose the money, do you Sarah! You don't want him to hate you, do you? Don't be silly about religion. Look. You've a way out! Take Clarence to the Catholic school, and everything will be great." The government had laws binding trustees to their duties, and Devlin's counselor showed Devlin how he might use the laws to close all escape routes to Sarah, except one. Fortunately the Pennsylvania courts, though not quite understanding what they were doing, were willing to twist all the laws forming Sarah's cage, and set her free.

But in testing this theory of slavery in the case of **Hinde v. Pendleton,** we will lose the case if we are not careful. Hinde no doubt was caught in an action-inducing contra-Omega situation. The slaves would be lost if Hinde did not offer top bid. Each time someone raised his bid, he had to enter a higher one before the gavel fell. Bids and counter bids measure the march of fate in auctions. Nothing but bids will postpone the rap of an auctioneer's gavel. Moreover Hinde's actions were completely channeled. Given the rules of auction, there is only one escape route - bidding.

Nevertheless, given all the components, we still have not established a cause in slavery. In auctioning the slave family, Pendleton was performing his executorial duties, and in removing the slaves from the Hindes' household he had done no wrong. The slaves belonged not to the Hindes, but to the estate he administered. As for devising the means by which the Hindes could regain the slaves and prevent their dispersion, bidding top price at auction was not Pendleton's invention. It was devised by the laws of probate, and the rules of auction and contract. Preserving the family by offering the highest bid for each and all, this was Hinde's only legal escape route.

Now, as we desperately search for a cause, let us propose what Wythe saw, that Pendleton exploited the Hindes' ability to feel compassion. Pendleton's by-bidder bid higher, knowing that the Hindes would raise their bid. Pendleton used them. And at this point we must hone our discrimination to a fine edge. How does a clever horse-trader get a buyer to offer more and more for a horse. He uses the buyer's need for the horse, or the buyer's covetous regard for the horse, or even the buyer's affection for the horse, depending on the buyer and the horse, but the point is, he uses the buyer. Each time he turns down the buyer's offer, he says in effect he will sell the horse to another buyer - even if there's no other buyer in view. This ploy he hopes will bring another response from the buyer - a higher offer, and a shrewd trader will read the buyer's limit in the buyer's eyes. If he misreads and loses a sale, he will start the process all over again next day with another buyer. This is business.

This was the use that Pendleton's agent was making of Hinde. By-bidding is not deceit, as Wythe surmised. It is an auctioneer's method of refusing a bid. And all these techniques are permitted in business transactions. Pendleton in his defense made the very point; people often buy things at extravagant prices, and a court will never require the seller to refund the excess. Wythe himself commented, "... the man who suffers himself to be so much the dupe of epidemical phrenzy or of his own desires... instead of measuring the value of them by their utility to him... can not... be discharged by the court of equity the judge of which neither is the curator, nor hath the power... to appoint a curator, for a prodigal." This comment brought Wythe's cause, up to this point, to zero.

The truth is, a business negotiation is an action-inducing contra-Omega situation with a see-saw character, and a buyer brings it upon himself. He wants the deal, and he doesn't want to lose it. Under the circumstances the seller will use the buyer's need for the object, her acquisitiveness, her craving, her affection for the object... to get the highest price and, with a slight qualification that I'll bring up presently, it is not injury. If you are in this kind of an action-inducing contra-Omega situation, not attributable to the seller, and if your opportunities for escape are limited - they are not his contrivance - it is up to you how high you will jump to get away from the bear; and it is not injury.

So Wythe's opinion totaled zero until he uttered his last twenty significant words: "... he (Hinde) bid the pretium affectionis, which is unlimited, and which therefore was - WHAT THE BY-BIDDER AND HIS PROMPTER PLEASED." He was maintaining, as I have already explained, that Pendleton was exploiting human-to-human affection, human response to distress in other humans, to channel Hinde toward Pendleton's objective, and this could not be favored by a court in equity.

The law of contract itself states specific uses of humans that the common law will disfavor. The devices of menace and duress utilize the capacity of humans to anticipate pain and suffering. The device of mistake uses the capacity of a human to misunderstand the terms of a transactions. The device of undue influence utilizes the capacity of humans to be swayed in their decisions by people close to them. The device of deceit exploits the justifiable and reasonable credulity of people. These are uses of humans disfavored by the common law, even when the taxitant has mired herself in her own action-inducing contra-Omega situation; like a business deal.

For Wythe to include the exploitation of human empathy in this disfavored list was not innovative. Since the beginning of true man, true woman, malevolent men and women have threatened taxitant's with harm or abduction, not that the taxitants themselves will be harmed or abducted, but that other humans with whom they closely empathize will be harmed or abducted. Such a threat is disfavored not because of the impending peril to those who might be harmed or abducted - those are separate injuries - but because it exploits the apprehensive capability possessed only by humans, the ability to feel in advance the distress of other humans. Indeed, Wythe's tacit admission of the slaves' humanity placed them in kidnap - they were not merely stolen animals. It was menace to the taxitant's loved ones, pure and simple. And it will avoid a contract every time.

We have a final case to decide before drafting a final cause in slavery. What will we conclude about Sam Harvard, whose wife will divorce him if he gets fat. Does her threat constitute an attempt to enslave? Well, we can use this fictitious case to clarify the exact nature of the essential components of enslavement.

If I am immersed personally in an action-inducing, contra-Omega situation, I develop a mental image of triggered gun, I pre-sense bear's warm breath at throat, I hear car crash steel on steel, I imagine slashed ear of kidnap victim, as butcher I foresee financial ruin, I feel whip on bare flesh, I feel separation of slave child from slave child, and slave child from mother, and their dispersal into lonely night - unless I act, and act now. All these imminent realities march closer to NOW, unprovoked, not promoted by any act of mine. But this is not an element of Sam Harvard's situation. If he eats a big meal, his wife's time of departure advances. If he eats daintily, it retreats. The advance of the unwanted event is as dependent on Sam as its retreat, and this is not the nature of a tornado - an action-inducing contra-Omega situation.

Aha, even so, you retort. Sam's wife is using Sam's affection to get her way. Yes, but we must assess this affection. Is Sam empathizing for her, or for himself? The emotion of the parent of a kidnapped child is not a feeling of loss; it is concern for the safety and mental state of the child. Morris's wish to clear Warfield out of his territory was not, we hope, a mere desire of possession. It was an apprehension for Vivia's subsequent welfare. If this is not Sam Harvard's feeling toward his wife's departure, then his feeling is hardly more than a desire to possess an unresponsive object, and I find no evidence that the government is interested in favoring this sort of "affection".

If we should go so far as to call Sam's emotion by the name of affection, we still can not say his wife is using him. Before you can use something, you must have a fairly definite idea how it will respond to your input. But Sam's wife has no way of predicting how Sam will act. She has no measure of his wifely Omegas, relative to his eating Omegas. Moreover, we don't really know her objectives. Is she looking to keep Sam slim, or for an excuse to move out? No, her threat is not so much a use of Sam's affection. It is more a test of affection versus caloric kinestatics.

And I think our survey is broad enough to enable us to draft a cause in enslavement.

CHAPTER 45

ENSLAVEMENT; REPULSION CHANNELING; MONOPOLY

So the mechanism of enslavement is comprised of submechanisms. First it requires a repulsion mechanism, an action-inducing contra-Omega circumstance; some kind of threat; an advancing fate repulsive to the taxitant; like the whoops of cowboys in a cattle drive. Second it requires an escape route, the open door that the enslaver opens to the taxitant, the way to escape the advancing fate, like the opening in the box canyon. This implies the third mechanism, one that I have not explicitly discussed, a bottling mechanism, a set of walls barring all exits save the one fitting the purposes of the enslaver. Thus the cowboys surround the herd and whoop on all sides, save in the direction where lies the railroad siding lined with empty cattle cars.

A skilled enslaver need not always devise and activate the action-inducing contra-Omega mechanism. It was not necessary in the **Slaughterhouse Cases.** In the life of the ordinary businessman, the wolf is always at the door. The Louisiana legislature need only close down the shops where the butchers did business, open the doors of the Crescent City slaughterhouse, and forbid butchering at any other location in the metropolitan area. Predictably, the wolf would chase enough butchers into the Crescent City facilities to make the enterprise highly profitable. Yet even with this understanding of the case, it still is not easy to comprehend the injury, the liberty infringed, in the case.

It is easier to see the injury when the enslaver devises the threatening mechanism - the blackmail scheme, the kidnap, the pointed gun. The originant throws the time-bomb into the room with the taxitant, not letting her out until she meets his demands. It is in the first instance nuisance, seizing a person free within her estates - free to exert her desires therein in any direction, and suddenly determining her next-moment set of pursuits - putting distance between the bomb and herself. The originant slices her freedom down to one pursuit, the one he desires. This is the red signal of injury.

It is in the second instance trespass. By the actions of the originant - introducing the bomb, barring the doors and windows, and presenting her with the terms for her release - one can infer he intends to use her. He knows exactly how she will act in response to these pressures; at least he knows how a lot of people would act; and all these features of the case meet the definition of use. He intends to use her without her permission, and this is trespass.

Even if he does not intend to channel her into a particular pursuit - he merely intends to blow her up, we see the nuisance. And even if the bomb is a dud (it doesn't explode), it is a nuisance. The government will not forgive him on grounds of his failure. The bomb was there for the moment, infringing her powers of determining her pursuits. It was injury. And if she cuts herself trying to break out the window, he will be held liable for damages.

If a pedestrian running from an imminent car crash sprains her ankle jumping over the fence, the driver responsible for the crash cannot successfully argue that the pedestrian was merely responding to her own desire and reason. He will be held liable for her costs and losses. He has tossed a nuisance into her estate, into her decision-making process, limiting her channels of next-moment pursuits. Though her choice was freely made, given the circumstances, her liberty in her estate had been infringed.

These injuries, where the repulsion device as a nuisance has been introduced by an originant, are relatively easy to understand. Even when nuisance is absent, as in Mathias steering Bill Green through the high opening in the garden wall, and not responsible for Bill meeting bear, we nevertheless see Mathias's intent to use Bill Green without Green's permission; we see trespass; and Mathias's actions in closing the garden gates, one after the other, provide convincing evidence of his intent to channel. So the closing of escape routes, save one suitable to the originant, given an overhanging repulsion mechanism, is evidence of the originant's intent to use the taxitant, constituting a cause, **attempt to enslave.**

But what if the repulsion mechanism has not been contrived by the defendant, and the closing of escape routes is difficult to detect. These were the difficulties in the **Slaughterhouse Cases**, and Justice Bradley speaking in retrospect could not quite put his finger on the injury. He tried to express it as an infringement of a universal and inalienable right to follow any of the common occupations of life. But this is like saying, as Judge Magruder said in **Richie v. People**, that the privilege of contracting is both a liberty and a property right. It misses the point by an inch. Yes, a person may be free to inquire into an occupation, but no one is compelled to set him up in an occupation. And though a person may attempt to negotiate a contract, no one is compelled to sign it. Getting a job and negotiating a contract are pursuits, **and pursuits are**

not rights unless the subject matter is in the pursuers property, and if the doors shut by the legislature were not within the butchers' estates, how were the butchers injured? How is it correctly expressed?

The legislature took away the butchers' own establishments as escape routes and called it a "police action" - a cleaning-up action - fundamentally a cause in nuisance, and obviously nuisance was not demonstrated in the case of every butchering facility. So this was legislated injury, at least in some cases. And if the shops should have been closed for the common good, even though not nuisances, the suit should have been brought as a cause in eminent domain, and the butchers should have been reimbursed. They were not; another count of legislated injury. Finally, the state attorney general secured an injunction against anyone building a slaughtering facility in the area other than the Crescent City facilities, giving Crescent City a monopoly, the only escape route open for the practice of butchering.

Of these facts, the dissenting judges chose not to consider the illegal closing of the slaughtering and butchering establishments. They gave the police action the benefit of the doubt in all those instances, and concentrated on the monopoly. The monopoly, they said, closed too big a door. But they couldn't express the injury.

Actually the "right to follow an occupation", or the "property of contracting" reflects an intuitive feel, poorly expressed, for a true set of rights, accurately visualized by describing in detail the activities involved in "contracting" or in "following one of the common occupations". What do you mean, for example, when you say you are going to enter the hardware store business?

You mean you are going to walk to the bank - certainly one of your rights. Entering it, you will hold a discussion with the banker (if he consents to meet with you), and attempt to establish a business relationship with him, and certainly this is a liberty of yours (given his permission). If you succeed in getting his support, you will contact people about leasing a suitable store building; you will contact wholesalers in hardware, trying to make business arrangements with them; you will interview people who wish to work as clerks and bookkeepers. And finally, if all these transactions are accomplished to everyone's satisfaction, you will open your doors and do whatever you can to establish goodwill with the people of your community.

In each of these activities you will do nothing outside of your property. You will be disposing your time and assets as you wish, and pursuing many kinds of personal relationships. This range of pursuits and transactions is exactly what goes into "making a contract" or "pursuing an occupation". Even applying for and acquiring a government license, or a chartered monopoly, consists of such pursuits. You are operating fully within your entitled pursuit space; no special right or property - a right to contract, a right to pursue an occupation - needs to be enunciated. This is a commons, and no one may bar you from it, not even a legislature, unless a nuisance rises from your use of it, or unless the revocation of your title is in the **common** interest. This is part of your marvelous estate under the common law.

So the Louisiana statute said to the New Orleans butchers, "You cannot walk upon the public highway, or follow any of your normal pursuits in personal relations, or spend any of your money, if your objective is to butcher livestock anywhere in this 1000 square mile area other than in the Crescent City facilities. It would be bad for the common good." Delusory, sham, it was deprivation without due process, and the legislature was not only closing doors, it was closing them injuriously.

This then is the effect of monopoly, that it deprives people of their ordinary everyday liberties - relative to a particular objective, and for such a drastic action, the only valid cause - **the monopoly promotes the common good.**

I have discussed this at length to make a very important point. Shutting doors can constitute nuisance, even in the absence of an intent to bottle or enslave anyone. All cases of nuisance are, in a way, a shutting of doors, a cutting of liberties. But be careful; enslavers are slippery. The gates that Mathias shut on Bill Green were gates that Mathias was entitled to shut, and a clever enslaver will try to defend himself on this ground. Nevertheless he must be charged with an attempt to enslave. His purpose in shutting the gates took this loading out of his property.

Nevertheless, in enslavement intent is crucial. If, for example, Mathias could show that he shut the gates with the intention of excluding the bear - it was too dark to see Bill and the bear already in the garden - he might be chargeable with nuisance, but not for an attempt to enslave, and punitive damages would be inappropriate.

Apparently there are several levels of refinement in slavery. If for example, for a little fun, Mathias enticed the bear into the garden while Bill was there, and not shutting the gates, he would be trying to use Bill - Bill's simple kinestatic reactions - by introducing a repulsion mechanism into Bill's zone of vulnerability. He would be delimiting Bill's per unit time potential, his liberty within his estate, and it would be injury, nuisance, and the intended use would be classed as an intended trespass. The result would be a low-level channeling, and the undertaking would constitute an unrefined attempt to enslave.

An originant blocking the escape routes of a taxitant, leaving only the originant's preferred escape route open, and taking advantage of a pre-existent action-inducing contra-Omega situation, would be devising a more refined scheme of enslavement. And though the originant might be fully entitled to operate the gates of the escape routes, his title is under servitude when his purpose is to use a taxitant without the taxitant's permission. Such a use is trespass, and its mechanism goes beyond the use of the taxitant's kinestatic reactions. It makes use of the taxitant's reasoning ability. Though the blocking of escape routes might be classed as nuisance, this element of the cause is secondary, merely a matter of mechanics. More importantly, it is evidence of the intent to enslave.

Considering the combinations of mechanisms and intentions reviewed under this topic, we must contemplate a multiplicity of causes. Channeling, generally, can be intentional or unintentional. It reaches into the decision-making processes of the taxitant, reducing her liberty in her estate, and this is the mechanism of the injury. Specifically, it shrinks the number of choices she can make within her per unit time potential. The causes are outlined as follows:

Unintentional Channeling. From a pleading in unintentional channeling, a judge must be able to conclude either (1) or (2) or both:

(1) that the defendant in her activity unintentionally introduced an action-inducing contra-Omega element into plaintiff's propertied environment.

(2) that the defendant in her activity unintentionally reduced the number of options legally open to plaintiff in escaping an action-inducing contra-Omega situation.

Intentional Channeling (Attempt to Enslave). From a pleading in intentional channeling, a judge must be able to conclude either (1) or (2) or both:

(1) that the defendant, intending to direct the plaintiff into a limited set of pursuits, introduced an action-inducing contra-Omega element into plaintiff's propertied environment.

(2) that the defendant, intending to direct the plaintiff into a limited set of pursuits, reduced the number of options legally open to plaintiff in escaping an action-inducing contra-Omega situation.

The reader should observe that these causes add nothing to the four basic categories already established - trespass, nuisance, equitable injury and legislated injury, and the four basic causes hold strong against the injury involved in slavery. The protective screen does not leak.

The profit in perfecting the screen by gaining an understanding of channeling does not lie in devising new causes, but, first, in expanding the concept of liberty within one's estate - free movements among the projects of one's per unit time potential, and, second, in understanding that the victim's acts under channeling, including slavery, involve free choice on the victim's part, perhaps even her reasoning. It is just that her choices have been restricted and determined by circumstances generated by the acts of the originant.

Lastly, the analysis of slavery demonstrates the extraordinary ingenuity sometimes required in discovering a mechanism of injury and the liberty infringed. Rarely, if ever, does common law justice require the formulation of novel rights.

CHAPTER 46

EMBOTTLEMENT

The analysis of enslavement revealed an unsuspected mechanism, successfully eluding juristic grasp, slipping through the protective screens of due process. As I have revealed hidden slaveries abiding in our midst, so also I will reveal another hidden machinery, a set of circumstances I will call embottlement. Capture is a subset of embottlement, but here again I will be seeking the subtler instances, and the idea of being tightly corked in a bottle is apt. When we are embottled, we are aware of what we wish, we see an enjoyment in which we are propertied - we can almost touch it. But our hands can't reach through the glass of our bottle, and we can't dislodge the cork. Each of us, it is true, has an inborn hatred of both slavery and embottlement. Each of us knows intuitively when we are being held in a bottle or used as a slave. And though we tend to classify them together - enslavement and embottlement - they are opposites in effect and purpose.

In slavery - repulsion channeling - the victim is presented with a choice of projects. Of these he chooses a select few, perhaps only one, for immediate pursuit. In making the selection, given the circumstances in which he has been enmeshed, he exercises free choice. What makes it slavery is the activity of another person intending to tangle the victim in the circumstances.

In bottling, it is quite different. Instead of a taxitant driven toward a select pursuit, we see her walled off from a select pursuit. The telltale mark of the bottled victim is her inability to attain a desired goal. Bill Green, finding himself in a high-walled enclosure with a black bear, seeks to escape through the open window, and we call it channeling. But if someone has closed this last escape route, we are witnessing embottlement.

What is the nature of the injury in embottlement, say in the case of a person bound in ropes? It is not merely that the person's ideal freedom has been reduced. It is that her freedom to gain freedom has also been reduced. If you are placed bound and gagged in a closet, it is not the same as being placed bound and gagged in the lobby of the First National Bank on a busy day. The latter is injury, but hardly smacks of embottlement.

This distinguishes embottlement from a simple case of nuisance. Your neighbor playing loud music creates a nuisance. And though we speak of entrapment there is an escape; you can take it to court. A key claim in a pleading of nuisance is, "There is no relief except in court action." But if your music-playing neighbors threaten to harm you if you take them to court, you are seeing an attempt to bottle you up. Even if they make no overt threat, merely exhibiting threatening behavior, we see the outlines of embottlement. True, if you allow yourself to be intimidated, you form a portion of your own bottle, but it is embottlement no less. If you are held captive not by iron bars but by the rifles of armed guards, your reason is being used by your captors no less than in slavery, but it is bottling.

So you see I am focusing on a subtler field of capture - embracing not merely dungeons, chains and armed guards, but circumstances in which you are walled away from something you want (or walled in with something you would like to get away from) - circumstances in which you may be prevented from attaining just one objective; and embottlement is a more fitting term than capture.

Slavery and bottling are alike in this. The mechanisms are as effective in a jungle as in civilization. But in a sense, bottling is stranger than slavery. Given the common law, slavery is always injury. Though sometimes unintentional, repulsion channeling is always injury. But certain instances of embottlement are not injurious. Football team A can be so defensively excellent that it bottles up Team B - Team B cannot execute its plays effectively - and the bottling is not illegal. The manager of Store A, wanting customers, sees people pass his store on their way to Store B, his competitor. By effective merchandising, advertising, public relations, the manager of Store B, doing nothing illegal, creating no nuisance, has put the manager of Store A in a bottle. This is the strange phenomenon of competition under the common law.

Let me put it in a slightly different setting. I will bring St. Francis of Assisi forward into modern times (I have already used his story), and into the universe of the common law. He has established a great volunteer organization, a non-profit corporation, collecting funds from the general public and using them for charitable purposes. He and the workers take practically nothing from the treasury for themselves, and they work out of old warehouses for which the rent is minimal.

Comes now an alien breed infiltrating his organization and quietly assuming control. Though Francis issues his orders as usual, he finds them neglected. Though he has wishes, objectives, and willpower, his objectives fail to materialize.

When we conduct an enquiry, we find the workers no longer willing to do things his way. His personal relationships in his society have deteriorated. But his adversaries have not defamed him. To the workers they have merely suggested other modes of operation. Is it necessary, they ask, that the workers receive no remuneration? Must they labor in old, cold warehouses? Why not solicit greater contributions from the public; advertise on television, build modern facilities, pay wages, provide pensions? In the long run, they suggest, we can provide even greater services for the poor.

Oh, St. Francis will be kept as president for the sake of window-dressing, but there will be a new board of directors, with new policy. Francis, free to move, free to speak, but his hands tied as far as his effectiveness is concerned, is a victim of bottling in his own organization. But he has not been injured.

Francis and his enemies have competed for the minds of the workers, and his enemies have won. Proposing their doctrines under the umbrella of reason, they deprived Francis of nothing to which he had exclusive title; the minds of the worker-members are commons. The schemers embezzled nothing; all the funds can be accounted for. Both Francis and his enemies were pursuing their objectives within their property, and a court will find no basis on which to favor one party over the other.

Francis is frustrated. He has been handcuffed. His effectiveness life in this charitable pursuit will die. But a court of equity or law has no relief for Francis. And from this tale you can model the whole structure of lawful competition under our system of free enterprise. It is non-injurious bottling. But now I wish to concentrate on injurious bottling.

From the shelves of the law library, I have selected two cases, a marvelous opportunity to develop a feeling for embottlement. Moreover they illustrate the inconsistency with which courts operate from time to time. The earlier case is **Holmes v. Connecticut Trust and Safe Deposit Co.**, decided in 1918, all justices concurring, in the Supreme Court of Errors in Connecticut.

A trustor had provided benefits for his two daughters on the condition that they and their husbands abstain from the use of tobacco and intoxicating beverages. The plaintiff was the executor of the estate. The defendant was the trustee of the trust. The executor claimed that the restriction against the use of tobacco and liquors was invalid, and that the benefits should be distributed to the heirs - the same daughters - free of the restriction. The judge of the Superior Court sent it up to the Supreme Court of the State for advice, and the Supreme Court ruled that the condition was valid as to the women but not as to the husbands. The grounds were precisely those I proposed for **Devlin's Trust**, and Justice Prentice's opinion is one of the most signal in the annals of personal relationships.

It is clear that the trust provision as it bore on the women was entirely legitimate. "If you will abstain from alcohol and tobacco, I will give you money," is a mere offer of contract. But involving the husbands in the trust injected into both marital relationships a bizarre set of functions. It would look this way to a husband: "If you will abstain from alcohol and tobacco, I will give your wife some money." And it will look this way to a daughter: "If your husband will refrain from using alcohol and tobacco, I will give you some money." And the Connecticut justices saw still another aspect of the case. They saw the possibility of a husband saying to the wife, "If you don't let me do what I wish, I will start drinking and smoking and you will lose the money." But you should read the very words of Justice Prentice.

"As a general rule," he wrote, "a testator has the right to impose such conditions as he pleases upon a (benefit).... He may not, however, impose one that is uncertain, unlawful, or opposed to public policy. The conditions here attempted to be imposed, in so far as they are made dependant on the conduct of husbands, ... (are) clearly opposed to public policy. ... A situation would thus be created which would be fraught with infinite injustice to (the beneficiary), provocative of marital discord, and conducive of longings to escape from the marital relation. Nor is that all. The husband in such a situation would be furnished with a ready and often times potent means of executing a domination over his wife...."

Note what is happening here in fundamental terms. Prentice is saying above all that a married woman has a right to pursue her marital relationship free from outside input. This is exactly the basis of common law protection against alienation of affection. Let us even assume that the trustor thought he was acting in the best interests of his daughters. He was attempting to give them a weapon to keep their husbands away from tobacco and alcohol in future years. Often in trying to help people, we do more harm than good; we do not consider all the aspects of the situation. What if a husband does not wish to stop drinking or smoking or, perhaps worse, what if he can't! As you can see, a disruptive element has been thrust by an outsider into this deeply personal and delicate situation.

But are we dwelling on mere hypothetical possibilities, immaterialities? Is it actually a fact that either of the husbands drinks or smokes. Is there any chance, given the particular characters in the case, that this trust really will instill friction into one or another of these marriages, or do we have a moot case on our hands? How far should a judge inquire into this aspect of the case? Properly, the Supreme Court took not a glance at this possibility.

One must conclude that in imminent nuisance, a judge need see only a potential for harm; he need not compute odds on the possible results. For materiality it is only required that the functional components of harm be present in the case. If a triggered handgrenade has been thrown through your window, you have been injured. Period. In determining injury or non-injury, a court will not speculate on the possibility that the grenade will not detonate, or that you might escape, or that your furniture is explosion-proof. From this we must infer that (1) if you have an entitled project space and (2) if an element spun from the pursuit of an outsider has entered that space, having a material capability of diminishing your effectiveness in that space, then (3) a court will order the actions required to neutralize any and all disturbing functions of the invasive element.

Notice the potential for embottlement in this case. The trust provision constitutes a nuisance; that much is clear. But note also the "general" rule cited by Justice Prentice - "A testator has the right to impose such conditions as he pleases upon a benefit." This of course is not the general rule but the special rule, the general rule being, "A testator has the right to impose such conditions as he pleases, except those that are uncertain, unlawful or opposed to public policy." So the Supreme Court of Errors in Connecticut fortunately followed the general rule, not succumbing to the too frequently mistaken idea that the special rule is the general rule. If the court had imposed the special rule - if it had held the trust inviolate - then indeed the government would have corked the trustor's daughters in a bottle with a ticking bomb.

To this point we should note several aspects of embottlement. First there are at least two injuries involved, one being nuisance or trespass, and the second being exclusion from relief, or attempted exclusion. If you constantly trespass on my land, and threaten to harm me if I go to the police, you have perpetrated two injuries. First there is trespass. Then in threatening me, you have used my capacity to anticipate harm and to be frightened, a second trespass. With this you have reduced my effectiveness in due process, a pursuit in which I am entitled. So, as in enslavement, bottling involves a multiple injury.

But what if the law itself has put us in the bottle. In **Holmes v. Connecticut Trust**, though the trustor created the nuisance, trusts first and always are creatures of law. By providing the vehicle for nuisance, the government contributes to the nuisance, and, by enforcing the nuisance and failing to abate it, the government binds the injured party to the noisome thing. There is no greater and more direct harm than this to climates of mind and effectiveness lives, and an intelligent group of rulers will be especially displeased with agents who in this manner have perpetrated injury.

The second introductory case in bottling, **National Bank of Commerce v. Greenberg** (1953), was decided by the Supreme Court of Tennessee. Basically the Greenburgs were the plaintiffs, both in the chancery court and in the appeal, but it was the bank, seeking a declaratory judgment, who took the case to court, asking the court to construe the court's duties as trustee under the will of Robert Cohen, deceased. As we saw in Devlin's trust an attempt to enslave, so we will see in Cohen's will an attempt to bottle. In **National Bank**, however, we will see a failure of common law instinct, quite in contrast to the rulings in **Devlin** and in **Holmes v. Connecticut Trust.**

When Eleanor Cohen's father died while she was young and her mother remarried, Eleanor was adopted by the new husband Herbert Greenberg, and her name changed to Eleanor Greenberg. Before her mother remarried, her grandfather made a will providing a trust fund for Eleanor's benefit. Of his estate, $15,000 would be placed under the trusteeship of the National Bank of Commerce, who would invest it in securities, and, for a number of years the income would be accumulated and added to the trust fund. If between the ages of 18 and 25 Eleanor married a man of the Jewish faith, the entire trust fund would be turned over to her. If at age 25 she was unmarried, half of the fund would be given to her, and at age 30 the remainder would be given to her. The provision provoking the lawsuit was the following, in Grandfather Cohen's words:

"In the event that the said Eleanor Cohen is adopted by any person other than a member of my immediate family, and her name is changed, before she is eighteen (18) years of age, then and in those events, this trust shall terminate and the trust fund will then be paid equally to my three children above mentioned, or their heirs."

Undoubtedly the events leading up to the suit occurred in this order: first Mr. Greenberg adopted Eleanor and her name was changed, and then the other beneficiaries, citing the quoted provision, went to the trustee and demanded their money. The Greenbergs protested, not wishing Eleanor to lose the funds, and, to protect itself, the bank took the case to chancery for a declaratory judgment.

Chancery decreed that the conditions providing for Eleanor were breached, and ordered the bank to turn the funds over to the other beneficiaries. Since Eleanor was still a minor, a special charge in equity, the Supreme Court would hear the appeal, and the Greenberg's claims were these: "(1) that the restraint on adoption, as quoted above from the will, is void as against public policy; (2) that since on account of her infancy, Eleanor could not consent to the adoption... that she should not be penalized for such involuntary breach of a condition of the trust." How did the court treat these issues?

As to the first, the court could not find that a "limited" restraint on adoption was contrary to the public policy of Tennessee. "The meaning of the phrase 'public policy' is vague and variable; courts have not defined it, and there is no fixed rule. ... it seems clear that the public policy is to be found in its Constitution, its laws, its judicial decisions and the applicable rules of common law. 'Public policy' is practically synonymous with 'public good,' and unless the (will) is in terms of such a character as to tend to harm or injure the public good, public interest or public welfare, or to violate the letter or the spirit of the Constitution, laws, common and statutory, or judicial decisions of the state, it is not violative of public policy nor void on that account."

Justice Gailor was quoting, and these were pretty good words. He continued, "The provision of a will, or the term of a contract, may be successfully attacked as offensive to public policy, only when such term or provision is detrimental to the public interest or the public welfare or the public good. It must be against 'societal interest,' in the phrase of the Restatement of Law...." Now how did Justice Gailor apply such fine sentiments to the case at hand?

"So, in the present case, if the prohibition against adoption was so arbitrary and absolute that it gave rise to a probability that the result would be to make the child a public charge, it might be argued with reason, that the prohibition was contrary to public policy. We find no such ground for attack upon the limited restriction made... in the will before us here."

This was one year before **Brown v. Board of Education**! If one wished to make **Brown** consistent with **National Bank of Commerce v. Greenberg**, one would argue it would not be against public policy to place a child in a school with other children of her race, keeping her separate from children of another race. Segregation would only be against public policy if it prevented her from entering any school whatsoever. You see, you cannot draw a line between "civil rights" and individual rights.

Having disposed of the first issue, Justice Gailor had no difficulty with the second. - Robert Cohen was entitled to dispose of his estate as he chose, and he chose to do it in the manner expressed in his will. It was the duty of the trustee to follow his instructions.

This was a step backward for equity. The decisions in **Carter v. Reed, Melvin v. Reid, in re Devlin, Holmes v. Connecticut Trust** and many others had spelled out the public welfare. In **National Bank v. Greenberg**, there was a dulling of judicial intuition incredible except that it stands there on the shelf. And this at the dawn of an era in which human rights were supposed to flower. Undoubtedly part of the court's difficulty was the emphasis placed by the attorneys for the plaintiff. Part was caused by the Greenbergs. They, not the bank, should have brought the suit. It was their liberty, not Eleanor's, that was being infringed by Cohen's will, and they should have complained.

A child's welfare is in the hands of its parent or parents. It is not in the hands of a court unless the parents have defaulted in their ministrations. The Greenbergs knew of the clause in the will, yet they arranged for Herbert to adopt Eleanor. Not a sign of delinquency, it was a sign of commitment and responsibility. Though knowing the risk, they must have decided nevertheless that adoption was in the best interest of the child. It would cement the family relationship, protecting the child should something happen to the mother, and dispelling the awkwardness of unmatching names as the child pursued her social relationships. Their interest in the welfare of the child took precedence over the threat of the will.

Note that the will attempted to bottle not Eleanor but the Greenbergs. Adoption would be their pursuit, their entitled pursuit, and the change of names was theirs to make if they wished. So here was a true case for equity, though by 1953 it could have been settled at law. It was title against title. The title of disposing one's funds against the parental title of raising a child.

But this is not embottlement, you say. After all, the parents blew out the cork. Executing the adoption, and changing the name from Cohen to Greenberg, they got what they wanted. Except for one thing.

As we asked concerning Clarence Devlin, we may ask how Eleanor will feel later upon finding she lost $15,000 plus accumulated income? All lost because of a "foolish" notion of her mother and adoptive father. Will she ever forgive them? Here was the snake thrown into the Greenbergs' home by Robert Cohen. But the denseness of a judge can be stupefying. Listen to the last words of Justice Gailor's opinion: "... her mother, before permitting the adoption and change of name, should have obtained a construction of this will before the event rather than after."

The judge is not saying that the court might have decided differently; he is saying he would have made it definite that the child could not have both the name change and the trust benefits. Is he saying this would have convinced the Greenbergs not to change the girl's name? Then indeed he would have hammered Cohen's cork more firmly in the bottle.

In the last analysis, when Cohen's title is up against the Greenbergs', we don't have to resort to the powerful appeal of personal relationships. It is a case of simple nuisance. The Greenbergs in their familial pursuits were doing nothing that infringed the liberty of Cohen. But Cohen's pursuit blew a noxious cloud into their entitled space. As it turned out, the Supreme Court of Tennessee succeeded in bottling the Greenbergs. It condemned them to live in their bottle with the fear of wondering how Eleanor would later feel about their decision, a decision originating in nothing other than love and concern for her welfare, a decision fully within their property.

CHAPTER 47

STATUS

If ever in dealing with government, you sense the presence of omnipotence, you will be merely recognizing a simple fact; your government has an overwhelming ability to enslave and embottle. This of course does not signify a malignant intent to enslave and embottle, but even the best-intentioned government harbors from time to time a few officers and employees not averse to enslaving or embottling, using government power to do it. When such political abuse materializes, and it occasionally does, it is awesome to see how the occurrence surfacing in courts will tie the court system in knots.

The unraveling lies in the judge's instinct for the common good, but occasionally our judges lose their bearings, more and more in recent years. We have seen ascending in the juristic sky a new constellation, a catchy phrase. Lately some cases have been resolved in the light of a new big dipper, "the compelling interest of the state".

Vanderbilt v. Mitchell, being decided in 1907, was light years removed from the influence of this phrase. But an analysis of the case carries us to perhaps the most esoteric reaches and stretches of the common law, and the results make one think about this "compelling interest of the state".

The case grew out of a faulty New Jersey statute, requiring a physician attending a birth to file a birth certificate with the superintendent of vital statistics. The recorded information would be presumed true; the courts of New Jersey would admit it as fact unless proved false by trial.

Into this apparently well-structured legal universe came John and Myra Vanderbilt, living together two months as husband and wife, and not at all after April 1901. About twenty-nine months later, Myra, on October 20, 1903, having lived meantime with another man, gave birth to a son. Calling him William Godfrey Vanderbilt, she named John Vanderbilt as the father, and as soon as John heard the news we find him sending his attorney to the bureau of vital statistics to correct the record.

However Superintendent Henry Mitchell, after reading and rereading the statute, concluded there was no provision for altering the record, and refused to do it.

It is understandable that Vanderbilt, bristling that the child bore the name Vanderbilt, loathed being published as the father, but how far will a court go to relieve irritation in a situation like this, especially in the case of Vanderbilt who was, as I now must inform you, terminally ill. What difference does it make?

Acting through his attorney, Vanderbilt filed his complaint in the New Jersey Court of Chancery. He named Superintendent Mitchell, Myra and the boy as defendants, suing not only to correct the false record but to restrain Myra from further attempts to connect him in any way with the boy. As causes he claimed (1) fraud on the part of Myra and (2) interference with property - diverting the flow of Vanderbilt family funds.

A family trust had been established by Vanderbilt's mother. In addition to providing a life income for Vanderbilt, it also provided at his death a large sum of money for his children. If he had no children, the funds would go to other members of the family. Of children natural or adopted he had none, and now of a sudden he had a child; not materialized naturally or voluntarily on his part, but by a lie, by legislative magic, and by bureaucratic devotion to the letter of the law. And when in the near future he would die, the trustees would be forced by virtue of the vital statistics act to give the Vanderbilt trust funds to Myra, natural guardian of Vanderbilt's "son". The statement of paternity in the bureau record would be presumed true by the courts. So Vanderbilt, citing this diversion of property - this violation of trust intent - sought relief from the court, and **Vanderbilt v. Mitchell** gives us a rare opportunity to watch the legal mind at work.

The defendants demurred. Fraud was a matter of law, not equity, they said, so it didn't subject them to the jurisdiction of the court. As for Vanderbilt's property, the trust was not in it. It was in his mother's property and she, if anyone, was the injured party. Being dead she was not in court and Vanderbilt - not being oppressed in his property - had no relief in equity on this count. Agreeing, the court refused to hear the case, and Vanderbilt, nearly bottled, sent his lawyers to the New Jersey Court of Errors and Appeals.

In that court sat a chancellor named Dill, whose opinion in **Vanderbilt**, together with Henderson's opinion in **ex parte Warfield**, is frequently cited as opening the door to "personal rights". Ordering the case back to the lower court for trial, Dill declared that the court had ample jurisdiction to afford Vanderbilt complete relief. He stated the grounds for his decision and, though I agree with the decision, you will see that he never quite found solid ground. But not until you see the difficulties buried in this apparently straightforward little case will you believe such difficulties possible. And let us not depreciate Dill. In a very few words, in an otherwise over-extended opinion, he came very close to the solution.

Actually he relied not a whit on personal rights, though parading them boldly: "The complainant is entitled to be relieved of the fictitious status of father...." And again, "If it appeared in this case that only the complainant's status and personal rights were thus threatened or thus invaded by the action of the defendants... we should hold... that an individual has rights, other than property rights... which a court of equity will enforce against invasion."

But in the end, several pages later, Dill did not rise to his own challenge. "Whether this bill might be rested on such personal basis alone, without reference to the technical protection of property is not now decided, because the present case present(s) the property feature to an extent sufficient...."

Since Vanderbilt's lawyer had done a poor job of supplying the "property feature", Dill supplied it himself. In the first place, he said, Myra's lie would prevent Vanderbilt from leaving his entire estate to charity (if he wished to). Without children he could do it, but New Jersey law forbade this extreme charitability in a person with children. At least half of his estate must be left to them. So according to Dill, Myra's lie had deprived Vanderbilt of this extremely charitable project. Second, as "legal" father of Myra's son, he was obliged under state law to support and maintain the boy, and the false imposition of this duty was another infringement of his liberty.

But Dill, armed with these proposals of injury, was strangely unprepared to rely on them. Seeking additional cause, he snatched at Vanderbilt's pleading of fraud. It is settled, he said, that on grounds of fraud a court of equity can cancel the certified records of public officers. Well, in the next chapter, I will begin an analysis of fraud, and what a legal maze we will find there. But Dill invoking fraud in **Vanderbilt** violated the precepts of this highly technical cause, and why did he do it? Why did he seek a cause beyond his proposal of plain nuisance - the effect of Myra's lie on Vanderbilt's rights in disposing his property?

The truth is that the proposal was not relevant, and I think he sensed it. To understand what I mean, imagine Vanderbilt to be an indigent; no estate to leave to charity or to heirs; no capacity for supporting and maintaining a child. In such a case, Dill would see no property to protect. Property in assets doesn't exist if assets are absent. As Cardozo might have said, property in assets does not exist in the abstract. You cannot deprive a pauper of his right to eat breakfast at the Waldorf. Lacking cash or credit, he has no eating rights at the Waldorf.

With a penniless Vanderbilt standing before him, Dill's proposals for violations of property would never sustain his decision. A poverty-stricken man bottled up with Myra's lie would not find relief in Dill's court! Given this weakness in his proposed bridge to freedom, he shored it up with fraud.

No true ground in fraud; no relevant ground in property; and he had burned behind him the bridge of personal rights. Knowing only that he must liberate Vanderbilt, he hovered above the courtroom and loosed the pages of his legal dictionary, letting them drift down upon the record as the gentle snow from heaven.

Of course he was burdened by being presented with a poorly drafted pleading. Two separate cases had been rolled together in an insoluble lump, a case against Myra, and a case against the superintendent. Myra had thrown a leaking tank of poisonous gas into Vanderbilt's living space, and the superintendent - or was it the legislature - had not only locked the door, but threw away the key.

The case of nuisance against Myra, such as it was, was dead on arrival. Her injury-causing act - if such it was - lay in the past. Her lie was told. If it had produced damage, Vanderbilt disregarded it; he sought no damages. Looking at Myra, he sought only protection against future chicanery.

The case against the superintendent (or government) was not dead. The injury he perpetrated, if injury it was, was still in progress. In fact it promised to continue forever - as long as the record lasted. And now the confusion multiplies.

If we can indeed implicate the superintendent, we can't hold him responsible. He was obeying not his own will but the will of the law, and we must hold the law responsible. If injury was stalking the land in the shape of the conscientious Mitchell, the injury is traced not to Mitchell but to the law. Law being a creature of government - the will of the law being the will of government - the complaint must be lodged against government - the law-creating government. It is the government with a big G who is perpetrating the injury, and Vanderbilt has brought no complaint against the government.

What if Vanderbilt had brought a fourteenth amendment case against the government. Twenty-three years earlier, in the **Slaughterhouse** sequel, by justices reminiscing about the earlier **Slaughterhouse Cases**, the scope of the fourteenth amendment was stretched full scale. Digressing pointedly from the case before them, they took pains to establish once and for all time that the fourteenth amendment invalidated any and every state law that by undue process deprived any person of any species of property. In **Richie v. People**, fourteen years before **Vanderbilt**, Judge Magruder cited the fourteenth amendment - the Illinois equivalent of it - as ground for invalidating an Illinois statute. Entering a contract, he declared, is a pursuit to which all competent adults are entitled. The statute limiting the workday of a woman to eight hours, was an injurious deprivation of property.

So we have in the fourteenth amendment the principle that a statute must conform to the principles of equity; in this there is nothing new. Therefore the cry "Unconstitutional on ground of the fourteenth amendment" is nothing other than a cry of "legislated injury." But in applying the principle to **Vanderbilt**, there is a difficulty.

Suppose in **Vanderbilt** we name Government as defendant and raise the cry "legislated injury" or "Unconstitutional". Even so, we must demonstrate the particular property of which Vanderbilt was deprived. This is the fundamental question. It haunted Dill, and we must answer it. Knowing that Dill was right in his decision, we don't know why. And remember, a truly sound solution must disembottle not just a Vanderbilt of means but a Vanderbilt with nothing but the rags on his back. What, we ask, was the project space in which he felt frustrated. What was his objective? What were his subjects and loadings? In answer I will propose the following, perhaps the most extravagant proposal I have yet dared to make. He wished to project a true image of himself on the screen of the universe!

That is the proposition in its loneliest, bleakest mode, phrased to meet the special situation in **Vanderbilt**, phrased to meet all such special situations where an individual stands isolated on the brink of the unknowable, phrased to bare the case to the icy charge of immateriality, phrased to pose it quivering before that driest of justicial queries: "Why should I grant title to a project like that?" For we must recognize an eminent characteristic of the common law - its dual nature. At one and the same time, it is both established and developmental, as though due process operates permanently under a dichotomous commission. On the one hand it must be orthodox; it must (a) acknowledge title and (b) mete property on the principles of equity and (c) insist on materiality in every element of a case before it. On the other hand equity has always sensed a compulsion to innovate; it has sensed a duty to see that (a) no truly material loading space is ever denied materiality and (b) no property promoting the common good is left ungranted or unprotected. I mention these points to expose the true weakness of John Vanderbilt's position - not his fundamental position - but his vulnerability before the blasts of courtroom forensics. He is at death's door! This is his weakness in the spotlight of short-sighted interpreters of the common law. If he were hale and hearty, we could receive his brief in the morning mail and dispatch our decision before noon.

A hale and hearty John Vanderbilt would be looking forward to many agreeable pursuits, many of them in personal relationships - social, business, marital and parental. In this broad and important sector of his estate he would wish no obstacle to his progress - no libel, no scandal, no enslavements or embottlements such as we have seen generated by trusts, no lies printed in public records. And in these pursuits, please note, his wish would be independent of assets. A man bereft of worldly goods can have friends, and a father incapable of supporting his child can still maintain a close and enduring relationship with the child. A healthy man has properties far more valuable than financial property, and in pursuing every personal relationship, taxitant willing, he has full liberty. A falsity published in vital statistics constitutes nuisance in his property. Not even the government - definitely not a government observing the common law - may publish a lie about a person.

More fundamentally, the government is eager to free a person corked together in a bottle with something noxious. This legal fact is shouted at us from all the shelves of a law library. Government, operating on the macroscopic stage, sometimes creates rules embottling a person on the microscopic stage, and deems it unwise to leave the person in this condition. No; a judge in equity can not leave Vanderbilt confined by a defective government project to the obnoxious atmosphere of a lie.

And now the question. If we have in Vanderbilt not this hale and hearty individual, but the actual frail failing invalid, we question the materiality of his project space in personal relationships. What are his prospects? A lawsuit and death? Perhaps death before the lawsuit ends? Perhaps no true friends. Who cares, we ask, whether he is or isn't the father of William Godfrey Vanderbilt? If a penniless Vanderbilt having no financial estate to dispose, can find no relief under Dill's proposals, what can Dill do for a Vanderbilt possessing no material loading platform in personal relationships? How can such a person be injured? Where is the liberty to be infringed? Isn't the property delusory; immaterial?

We know of course that the government will wish to amend the false record, and we have taken the extra step to place the government in the shoes of a defendant. But on what basis can the government clamp the Government in its jurisdiction and say, "Government, I order you to change the record on Vanderbilt!"

Well, let us look around. Can we try trespass? Has not Myra Hess used the name Vanderbilt in an effort to gain social status for the boy and isn't this a use of a famous name without permission? A person may label herself with any name she pleases, and why not her child as well? For the following reason. A government frowning on the use of a name, frowns not on the use of the name, but on the use of a personal relationship - the clearing cultivated by a person in the mind of another. In such a pursuit, we see an originant patiently constructing an electronic circuit in a taxitant's mind, creating the delicate function between a mental run button and a mental computer program, and it is this whole device - this name-fame circuit - this run button computer program function, to which the government grants title to the originant.

Assuredly the Vanderbilt name has a run button computer program functioning in the American mind. Though we personally know no Vanderbilt, we visualize everyone named Vanderbilt descending to earth from a golden cloud, and we understand Myra's wish to use this name-fame association for the benefit of her son. And why not? No one holds title to this particular function. It was not engineered by any Vanderbilt you might meet, certainly not by our John Vanderbilt. It is a fancy conjured by our own elves in our own fancying machine. More to the point, it is not a personal relationship. It's an object-object relationship; we mentally associate a cardboard Vanderbilt with a fictitious pile of dollars. Yes, Myra was using the Vanderbilt name. And no; - the court could not order her to stop.

But can't we claim that Myra was using Vanderbilt himself, naming him father, scheming to divert huge benefits to the boy? Nonsense! She was not using him in any sense of the word. She had not pushed a button in his mind, expecting him to react in a predictable manner. To the contrary, she wished him out of the way, bottled if not dead. But mind; Myra was using something without permission. She was using the government's system of records, an entitled project space of the government.

Myra had the right to use the vital statistic records for certain objectives. She had the right to load them with true facts. She had the right to retrieve their contents relative to any search or proof she had in mind. But she used the public record for a personal objective conflicting with the public objective. She used it to preserve a lie. She used it to transform a non-fact into a legal fact. She tried to create a Vanderbilt son from a non-Vanderbilt son. And for this loading, this objective, she held no title.

We have here a strikingly simple solution to Vanderbilt's problem. We can say it without fear of contradiction. To insert error wilfully into the public record is an untitled use; it is trespass. And to insert error by accident is nuisance. The government is the injured party, and we can ask why government policy does not absolutely require a correction as soon as an error is proved. Now that Vanderbilt has claimed error, offering to prove it, why doesn't the superintendent demand a trial, testing the statements of Myra and Vanderbilt?

There is a difficulty; - he hasn't. And Dill has to deal with the flesh he sees before the bench and the pleadings he reads. The superintendent, if bringing a claim in the name of government, should not be defendant but plaintiff, and Vanderbilt should be in court not as plaintiff but as a sort of amicus curiae. So Dill can not use government injury as cause; the government isn't complaining. The result: - Vanderbilt is almost bottled and corked, except that Dill, magnificent soul, will twist every rule in the book, and break the bottle.

He could have accomplished it without leaving the high ground of due process. We should never forget that the Gothic vault of the common law is perfect. In its design, it is impossible for a person to injure the government without injuring a person; and it is impossible to injure a person without injuring the government (i.e., the rulers) at the same time. It was Chancellor Dill himself who furnished the key to Vanderbilt's truly relevant project space. Read again his words as he attempted to inject substance into personal rights; notice the word status. "The complainant is entitled to be relieved of the fictitious status of father...." And again, "If only the complainant's status and personal rights were thus threatened or thus invaded...." We have run against this word status before. In **Dandini v. Dandini** Justice Peters talked about preserving marital status, awkwardly referring under the circumstances to a figment of his imagination.

But status, true status, is a parameter of reality. That at least is the common law ideal. Norman elite and English scum reflect two species of pre-common law status. The Normans assigned status with a sword; the flat of it on a knight's shoulder, and the point of it in a villager's stomach; and this created legal reality. Then later under the developing common law, legal status became invested in a more reliable reality - the nature of things. Reality? Well, for a moment let us concentrate on the nature of things and expose reality for what it is.

To each individual, reality is her concept of reality. True as this is, however, it will not satisfy a scientist, or a judge observing the common law. But a scientist is not, nor is a judge, unreasonable in his demands about reality. He will, believe it or not, admit our concepts to represent reality on a very simple basis; they need merely conform reliably to all-known-concepts-of-things-that-conform-to-each-other. Like it or not, this association of concepts is the only world we know, and the only world to which, as intelligent people, we can subscribe. Moreover, if we wish to remain sane and effective in this somewhat dizzying world, we each must submit our individual destiny to concepts of reality we hope to be reliable. Reality? It is a chief concern of courts. The trial of a case at law is chiefly a matter of deciding which is the true version of two opposing versions of reality, and we find that due process, amazing scientific instrument that it is, will endorse the version exhibiting the more reliable conformity to the largest-body-of-known-concepts-that-conform-to-each-other.

We thus find reality - be it the reality of science, or of the court, or simply the reality of common sense - to be a Gothic vault, standing staunch, but only if each concept supports all other concepts and in turn is supported by them.

So how does status enter the picture? Let us begin very simply and ask this: If status is reality, was Vanderbilt's status changed by Myra's lie? Well plainly he was not the father of the boy before the lie, nor afterward. So what has changed?

His legal status? Let us say his legal status has changed, then ask ourselves what we mean. Indeed what did Dill himself mean when he used the word status? We find on looking it up in **Ballentine's Law Dictionary** that status holds a special place in a jurist's heart. **Ballentine** presents several excerpts from court opinions.

Status. "Position or rank. A legal personal relationship or condition, not temporary in its nature nor terminable at the mere will of the parties, with which third parties and the state are concerned."

"A state of affairs."

"The very meaning of the word "status," both derivative and as defined in legal proceedings, forbids that it should be applied to a mere relation (such as that of marriage). "Status" implies relations, but it is not a mere relation."

Having read the above, you know precisely the jurists concept of status and, in case a doubt lingers in your mind, we will simply push the word toward our immediate objective - using it to label the project space in which Vanderbilt was frustrated, not pretending to define for jurists their use of the word, yet embracing the sense of the **Ballentine** exerpts, and attempting the while to lend substance to Dill's words. Let us propose that your status, referring to your legal status, is your personal relationship with the government. By this I mean that your status is your clearing in the mind of government!

In some ways the idea is familiar. What are the statuses of noble, serf, elite, rabble, if they do not connote personal relationship with government? Watch the black slave and white free man standing before the judge in colonial Virginia. Notice that the judge reacts to their pleadings differentially. They do not have equivalent personal relationships with the government. Though there is something artificial about the distinction, the differences are as real as iron and concrete. Each has a status.

Part of the reality of these statuses is rooted in physical fact; the slave is black; the free man is white. Part is rooted in the index of the justice's handbook: "Slaves - see Negroes." And part of the reality is rooted in the government's ability to enslave and embottle. Note that though slave code and raw power create legal reality, and though the law is based partially on physical fact, the slave law does not conform to total reality. It neglects the laws of psychology. It produces a nation at odds with the objectives of intelligent rulers. Read De Toqueville. Do you see that the aim of the common law has always been to base legal reality on total reality? Or, expressing it in different words, to base status on natural laws.

But isn't this as far as one can go in comparing legal status to a personal relationship? After all, a government has no mind - no mind in which to make a clearing, no electronic circuitry in which to establish a run button computer program function. A government is not a natural person; so how can you have a personal relationship with a government?

Yet in many ways the government is a person to you. When you drive through a red light, the government presents itself in the shape of a uniformed officer. When you are before the bench, a black-robed person looms above you. And when the Internal Revenue Service scrambles your account in its computer, you will envision your status torn in little pieces and flying away like leaves in a storm. Years spent trying to cultivate an honorable personal relationship with government; totally lost. From every act of government you receive a personal impression of government, sometimes heartening, sometimes stomach-wrenching, and when your mind on occasion becomes tortured with the unwelcome presence of government in your life, your anger tends to be leveled not toward "it" but toward "he","she" and "they".

You object to this proposal. This, you say, is how an individual thinks of government, but a personal relationship requires that the government has a concept of the individual, and this isn't the way government operates. A government treats people as a mass phenomenon. It does not contemplate the individual. Oh, but sometimes the government thinks of you as an individual. Your day in court is an example. And government has a mind. It has a memory - the public records. It has systems of operations; we call them laws, policies, regulations, procedures and principles. Public records, systematically processed, equals government contemplating you as an individual.

If you bring your complaint to court, the judge determines your relationship to the court; for instance - are you an adult, and where do you live? He determines whether you are entitled as you claim to a particular project space. He makes a first approximation of your status - meaning his reaction to you as an individual - and he does the same for the defendant. Before the trial begins, he reads your claims, looking up the law and deciding if you will be entitled to relief if your claims prove true. If he decides your pleading has provided a cause for his action, he gives you a special status; you may enter his court on a certain day, and he will give you an opportunity to prove your claims. He will apply the same procedure to the defendant.

During trial, there will be an attempt to establish the true facts. Perhaps reference will be made to public records. Perhaps even a police record will be called into evidence. Perhaps the judge will begin to observe your climate of mind. He will begin to react as taxitant to what he sees and hears. An image of you, and an image of the defendant, and an image of the situation will take shape in his mind. But he will not be permitted to react to you on the basis of his natural feelings; he must react to you only according to reaction circuitry established by government - laws, policies, regulations, procedures and principles. In the process you are being tasted as an individual. It is a marvelous entity, this responsive something or someone who is applying its tongue to you. It is marvelous if it is structured on the principles of intelligent justice. And "Government" is a name for it.

At some point in the tasting procedure this judge, this agent of government, will determine your status (and the status of the defendant) in the mind of Government. One of you will become the chosen one - the elite; the other will be dishonored; and there can be no more expressive personal relationships than these - favored, unfavored.

In completely parallel fashion you can assess your marital status. Actually you have two marital statuses. One is your standing in the mind of government, the other your standing in the mind of your spouse. The same is true of your parental status. And your goodwill as a manufacturer is your status - how you taste - in the mind of this consumer or that. Patriotism, despite government's waving of the Olympic flag, measures the taste of government in the mind and heart of a subject.

Dill talked about status, and he also pondered the lie about Vanderbilt recorded among the vital statistics. A lie is an essential element of defamation, and we can understand that defamation can pose a threat to status. Isn't that how Dill put it? He said (omitting his awkward words about personal rights), "If only the complainant's status was thus threatened, we would declare that he is entitled to a decree establishing the truth about the paternity of the child." In this nutshell he housed his precise cause for action. He need have said no more. It needs only to be clarified.

CHAPTER 48

BASIC NUISANCE; DEFAMATION; MATERIAL DREAMS

In ending Chapter 47, I introduced the problems in **Vanderbilt**. Though Chancellor Dill did not see the solution clearly, he had his finger firmly on it. The injury perpetrated by Myra's lie involved a threat to status, and this needs clarification. In addition I opened Chapter 47 with an allusion to a phrase becoming more popular in legal circles, "the compelling interest of the state", and left it dangling. By the end of this chapter, I hope the phrase is crystal clear.

To clarify the solution to Vanderbilt, I must (1) achieve the ultimate generalization of nuisance; (2) analyze defamation for its fundamental elements; and (3) carry the analysis of status, actually personal relationships, one more step.

To completely generalize nuisance, allow me to use an earthy case, an abstracted example of hundreds of cases appearing over the years, erupting wherever the creeping edge of urban life pushes into farming areas. Welcome to the world of barnyards, whence issue flies and odors, enlivening the atmosphere. Comes now the more fastidious city dweller, moving into a dense tract of houses built by an enterprising contractor, on land adjoining a large hog feeding operation! And now, claim the invading urbanites in court, the feeding operation must fold its tent.

Upon being summoned to court, the hog-feeder usually defends himself on the principle of prior use. He and his predecessors have been there for a hundred and thirty-five years. This is rural America, he says, and barnyards are part and parcel of the landscape. The migrating city folk had every opportunity to see (and smell) what they were buying; their purchases were purely voluntary, and they should be content with what they got. Is it nuisance or not, you ask. How have the courts decided? The courts have decided both ways.

Yes, for generations those barnyard smells have leaped barnyard fences, and in all those years there were but two factors separating them from nuisance. At first there were no human noses on the other side of the fence, and it takes a human nose to register a smell that a court will take notice of. Second, when the noses finally arrived during those hundred and thirty-five years (the early noses) their owners didn't complain.

So we ask if, during all those pioneer years, the smell constituted a nuisance; was the nuisance there in the abstract? After all, the smell was jumping the fence into the space of another person - even though the person might not be living there. And the answer is that the question is moot; the nuisance was immaterial. If nuisance is to be accounted as material, there must be (1) a leakage from one person's pursuit into another person's space; (2) a detectable effect in the space; and (3) a complaint filed in court by the owner of the invaded space. Actually the nuisance exists if (1) and (2) are present, but it is still immaterial to the government. To make it matter to a court, the complaint must materialize.

In **Vanderbilt**, you have seen a person filing a complaint, but the nature of the leakage and the effect in his space are hazy, nor are we sure about the profile of the invaded space itself.

Well, let us propose Vanderbilt's space to be his clearing in the government's mind - his legal status - proposing further that Myra's lie has distorted the clearing; she has altered his status. This proposal poses several difficulties. In this segment of the case - Vanderbilt asking the court to order the change in the public records - the defendant is not Myra but the government. Logically, then, Vanderbilt's complaint reduces to a claim that the government is causing a distortion in the government's mind, like claiming the government is defaming Vanderbilt to itself. Hardly a cause of action. Obviously I can not sue you for harboring in your mind a false image of me; I can only sue you for transmitting it to someone else. As we face this analytical difficulty, it will help to remember that the government is not a natural person but an organizational person.

The government is engaged in many projects. Keeping vital statistics records is one of them. Acting as taxitant is another - selecting from its files bits of information about a person and reacting to them. By this I mean that government assigns status to the person. This brings to our attention an interesting bit of intelligence; the false record involving Vanderbilt was not the status of Vanderbilt; it was an item in the government's memory bank, and it had a capacity to affect Vanderbilt's status. Do you see how correct was Chancellor Dill in his choice of words? "If only the complainant's status was thus threatened...."

Now I am going to connect **Vanderbilt** to the field of defamation, a field well settled in law. If the **Vanderbilt** pattern is congruous upon the pattern of defamation, then indeed the government can find a remedy for his situation. There are problems in making the match, one being that Myra has not defamed Vanderbilt; she has merely told a lie about him. And the vital statistics record does not defame him; it merely preserves the lie, a significant distinction presently explained. The question is, will government enforce a correction in the record of a lie that is not of itself a defamation, and to answer it I have got to strip the cause of defamation to its bare bones.

One thing we have learned is that Myra's lie has not necessarily harmed Vanderbilt's status. It has merely glued a false image of him in the government's memory bank. With this we will with profit switch our attention to a hypothetical case in which the taxitant is not an organization such as the government, but a natural person. We will see that - as in Vanderbilt's relationship to government - so also a personal relationship can be subdivided into its parts. It is composed of two functional mechanisms - a memory bank and a status, and a few pages spent on this understanding will put us on the road to resolving Vanderbilt.

Let us say that while you are sitting with Mr. Dirocco in banker Delgardo's office, you are shocked to hear him tell Delgardo that Frank Venuti is a very poor credit risk. You know Frank personally, recognizing in him the utmost integrity and reliability. Dirocco's remark might be defamatory and might not. Being first a communication and secondly false, it meets two qualifications for slander. If it had been published in more graphic form, something preservable, it would probably fill the requirements for defamation; in this case libel. In libel, a false statement constitutes defamation if it has a potential for harming the plaintiff. In a case of slander, however, the requirements are more narrowly conservative; harm must have actually occurred. In slander, presenting to a court merely the imminence or potential of harm is insufficient to constitute cause.

Thus if Frank Venuti has no intentions of borrowing money from banker Delgardo, Frank cannot successfully sue Dirocco for slander. No harm has been done. We should remember, however, that slander is a tort, an action seeking damages in money. It therefore requires a showing of material damage, and behind all of it we must be able to spy the living spectre of injury. Therefore we should inquire the mechanics and the substance of the injury.

One is tempted to propose that the injury consists of a shriveling of status. It matters not whether we are looking at harm to a social relationship or harm to a business relationship, we see immediately that such a shriveling has occurred in the taxitant's mind. However, the shriveling of status is the harm, not the injury. Looking deeper, then, we find that the injury lies first in the fact of communication and, second in the fact that the communication was false. But these are the parameters of injury - from these the court presumes injury. They do not describe the physics of the injury.

Where is the immediate effect of the false communication? This is the question to ask. Nuisance, remember, requires an effect in the entitled space of the plaintiff. One finds that the immediate impact of the false communication is not on the status of the plaintiff but in the memory bank of the taxitant's mind. In other words, the injury in defamation involves implanting a false image of a person in a memory bank. In a case of slander, the implant is made directly in the memory bank of a living person. In a case of libel, the implant is in the form of a non-human memory bank - a newspaper, a public record, an electronic tape, a cinematic film - something with the power to record the false information and transmit it to any living brain happening to tap it.

So I think we will find that Frank Venuti can obtain a court decree ordering Dirocco to retract his statement to Delgardo. Even if there has been no harm to status - no damage - therefore no slander, there has been injury, and we recognize a hazard of concentrating on tort. In concentrating on tort, a court concluding that damage is absent may conclude that injury is absent. You will see that we have in "Venuti v. Dirocco" a situation in business relations fairly analogous to Vanderbilt's situation in governmental relationships; a false entry has been made in a memory bank. Given this, an experienced system of law will presume that the false entry has projection power, posing a threat to status as long as the file can be recalled and entered in a status-forming program. We see what Plato saw and taught more than 2000 years ago; that the mind is a screen upon which an image of the outside world is cast. It is even more than a screen; it has an amazing capacity to process the image and respond to it. Nevertheless, the process starts with a mental image.

But in what way does Frank Venuti's image in Delgardo's mind "belong" to Frank Venuti? If Venuti can be injured by Dirocco inserting a false image in Delgardo's mind, does this mean that a portion of Delgardo's mind is in the property of Frank Venuti?

This would not be a bizarre proposal in some ways, since Frank's name is attached to the image. Suppose Delgardo had never heard of Frank Venuti; or suppose Frank was not interested to establish status in Delgardo's mind. Even so, at the moment Dirocco spoke Frank's name in Delgardo's presence, sketching his character in a word or two, a memory cell opened in Delgardo's mind, storing this information under the recall button "Frank Venuti". Thereafter, if ever the button "Frank Venuti" is pushed in the banker's mind, the words "poor credit risk" will be pulled from the file, and the banker's status machinery will produce a status for Frank. If ever again, even in Delgardo's casual conversation, the name Frank Venuti is mentioned, Delgardo might find himself repeating what Dirocco had said years earlier, and the falsity would be propagated! No wonder that somewhere in this situation is a loading space in which Frank Venuti is dearly interested, a space in which the government will grant him property. But where is it, and of what material is it composed?

Let us look closer at the portion of a personal relationship called status. Status of course is what an originant seeks during the first part of a personal relations pursuit; she loads the taxitant's memory cells, hoping that the taxitant will respond to the resulting image in her mind by assigning a favorable status to her. Status, like patriotism and like the effectiveness life, is not built up or knocked down by direct external actions. It is an inner response to an inner image that a taxitant gathers and stores from the outside world. It is a very personal thing in that it reflects the taxitant as much as it reflects the originant. Two taxitants we sometimes suppose will have different images of the same originant and I won't deny this; - our fickle senses frequently convey false messages to our memory files. But I think it more helpful to understand that, rather than image, it is the originant's status that varies so widely from taxitant to taxitant. Let Hubert Aldrich act similarly toward Mary and Alice, and let each girl see him mentally as the same person, yet Mary will not wish to date him and Alice will be thrilled. And this reflects not image but status.

I think we may say that status is that part of a personal relationship that is usable. Hubert Aldrich uses his status with Alice to get a date. With Mary he has nothing to use. Edison used his status with millions of consumers to sell his product. The Polyform Company, by attaching Edison's name to its product, used Edison's status for its own purposes. So status, being usable, can be usurped - it is subject to trespass. But being an inner response to an inner image, it is not directly influenced by the outer world, and to that extent it is not the immediate site of the effects of nuisance. In the context of defamation or false personal imaging it is the memory bank, not status, where the direct impact of nuisance is felt.

The memory cells of Delgardo's mind felt the direct impact of Dirocco's false representation of Frank Venuti. Though it cannot be said that Dirocco distorted Frank's image in Delgardo's mind - there being no image there initially - we can say that he prejudiced Delgardo, meaning he inserted a memory labeled "Frank Venuti" in a site accessible to Delgardo's status machinery. Notice that in a natural person the run button "Frank Venuti" powers two operations. First it calls up bits of image from the memory banks and presents them to the status machinery. Then the run button activates the status machinery, producing the status. And now you see how closely this analogy of the human mind resembles due process.

The feature of **Vanderbilt** now becoming prominent is the malfunction of due process under the circumstances, compared to the functioning of an intelligent, reasoning human mind. An intelligent reasoning human mind will readily accept from the outside world a new input involving person A, eagerly processing it to see how well it conforms to its other concepts of person A. It will test the new input to establish it as a real fact. Then it will store it and, if a previously stored item has a conflict with the new fact, and upon reconsideration fails to conform to reality, the mind will erase the old item, replacing it with the new. Lastly, the mind will re-evaluate its person A status.

But in **Vanderbilt**, the governmental procedure - hardly due process - resisted the input of new information, refusing to test it for its conformation to reality, and if ever a run button named "John Vanderbilt" were pushed, the memory banks would deliver erroneous data to whatever status machinery was waiting to receive it. In any case, be the machinery in public or private sector, the status produced would rest not in reality but in fiction. So by several routes we can conclude that, though the damage of false personal imaging lies in the sphere of status, the injury itself lies in the false imaging - the implanting of false intelligence in a material memory bank of some kind. And although in **Vanderbilt** Myra was responsible for the original lie, the government is now responsible for perpetuating it. Loud knocks are being heard on the government door. Loud voices from the real world are saying, "You are storing a false image of a person and transmitting it to anyone and everyone who happens to tap it. By refusing to test our claims for their veracity, you are blinding yourself to reality, encouraging a formulation of status on the basis of a fiction." With this, we are firmly on the path to discovering the true project space in which Vanderbilt was injured. We know it is related to the projection of a false image upon a memory bank of some kind.

I can now proceed with the analysis of who owns this memory bank. Though the image in the mind of a taxitant - say Delgardo - is labeled with, say, Venuti's name, it will be impossible to claim that this particular locus of memory is in the property of Venuti; He does not own the memory mechanism or even the memory filed here. No one can force a taxitant to change her image of a real person, even if it is a false image. The most we can do, with government help, is to make the liar retract her lie, but even then she may retain the false image in her own mind if she wishes. She is restrained only from transmitting it to others. No, the propertied loading space we are seeking for Vanderbilt is not in the mind of the taxitant, but we are now prepared to comprehend what it is and where it is.

We begin to see its scope when we recognize that the only remedy available to government in preventing false imaging is to prevent its propagation. If the falsehood is recorded in non-human form and can be retrieved, the record can be expunged by court order and a retraction ordered. If the falsehood is recorded in a human brain, an enforceable warning against propagation is the only remedy. So propagation is not only injury, it is the very mechanism of nuisance, and the focal point of remedy.

It is as though a simple act of false personal imaging can spread without limit, and all our experience confirms it. There is no effective way to curb it save by threat of punishment, and indeed libel and slander are frequently written into the penal code. If you imprint a falsehood about a person in an accessible memory, you cannot predict or ascertain the extent of its spread. By telling it to one person, or publishing it in a tiny line of print, you have in effect projected it, for all to see, on the screen of the universe!

It is on that screen then, says the common law, that I presume you have projected it, and there on that screen, says the common law, is where I have created a property for each person. If someone projects an image of Maggie there, labeled with her name, it establishes a loading space to which I entitle her. She is the entitled projecter. Her space on the screen is the subject of her property. Her loading rights are her projections of herself, and the entitled objective is the projection of her true image on that space. It is a material project space because it conforms to everything I know about the human race. It has a functional relationship to reality.

Therefore if a crooked beam of light leaks out - is projected - from the pursuit of another person, registering materially on her personal image space, and if she complains, it is injury. It fits the definition of nuisance, and I will find a remedy. And if the false imaging is accompanied by a harm to status, I will declare damage and damages. The injury I will simply call false personal imaging. Injury plus damage will be known as libel or slander or, in general, defamation. Thus speaks the common law from a thousand shelves.

So we have pinpointed the injury in **Vanderbilt**. The false record is continuously radiating a false image of Vanderbilt onto the screen of the universe. The locus of this image is the locus of a property to which government grants Vanderbilt title, and he is complaining about the falsity of the image that the record is projecting into that space. Nuisance and, given this, the government will formulate a remedy. Here, you see, was the exact mechanism in **Jones v. Alfred H. Mayer Company**. The company's house, empty of Jones, given the admitted policy of the company, was a repeating signal beamed continuously on the screen of the universe, "Jones is an undesirable neighbor." Presumably, given the court's decision, the court ascertained this to be a false image, and the court ordered the only remedy that could possibly halt the projection.

This is not the first time we have seen due process create a project space out of a materiality impossible to put one's finger on. You will recall that a contract creates such a property. A house not completed on the contracted date is just as material as a house burned down. They are subjects in the property space of the owner, and the spaces have been distorted. But in these legally projected properties we see spaces possessing a close affinity to natural phenomena. Quite distinct from a legal construction that the emperor's horse is a god, or that a black man is not human.

In starting down this winding trail, I proposed that status - legal status - is your personal relationship with the government, and my purpose was to use the word status as a label for the space in which Vanderbilt was frustrated, the property in which he was injured, but now we must be careful. We have found a pursuit in personal relations to involve a functional sequence. An originant loads the taxitant's memory cells with an image. The image is an objective in itself, but there is a further objective; the originant hopes that the taxitant's status machinery will produce from the image a favorable status for the originant. And there lies beyond status an ultimate project - the originant's wish to use the status for an ultimate pursuit - friendly companionship, or the sale of a product, or marital comradeship. But it is not in this ultimate use of status that Vanderbilt is injured, for we find no taxitant interested in him. So status or the use of status is not the space in which Vanderbilt is frustrated and injured. And in memory bank we find not the site of injury but the mechanism of injury. For when a person beams a false personal image into an accessible memory bank she has in effect projected it onto the screen of the universe, and it is in this latter space, this absolutely abstract yet absolutely material space, that Vanderbilt is injured. This space is not status, and it isn't memory bank. What is it?

I suppose I might call it "personal imaging space". We can't call it fame or reputation, for these are synonymns for status. A physicist might call it a force field. We might define it as "the potential propagating energy of a personal image stored in an accessible memory bank". It is as real as anything that exists anywhere in the universe, as long as there exists anywhere a run button retrieval system that can tap the memory bank. A lie in an accessible memory bank is always a threat to status. This is real. For this reason due process must create the property space, this personal imaging space, to which the government grants title to the person whose image it is. It is a necessary device, implied by all we know to be true.

It is logically necessary that the government create such a space. There is no other way that ground can be laid for slander or libel - no property in which a person can be injured in connection with harm to status. It is also a necessary creation for a government interested in dispensing intelligent justice, and now we are approaching the field to which I have referred as the justification of the law.

Though I have endeavored and perhaps succeeded in demonstrating the materiality of the personal imaging space, it still reduces to a questionable statement, that to each person the government has granted a title to project a true image of herself on the screen of the universe. What meaning or import can this possibly have! Doesn't it still strike a hollow note for Vanderbilt, almost dead, who seems not to matter in society or in the grand affairs of state? Strangely it is precisely here that the importance of this title lies - in the solitude of one human being, unallied, and it gains its significance from two sources.

One we might call ulterior motivation. Picture a woman refusing to steal a diamond ring though she has the chance, and all because inwardly she wishes to preserve in herself a sense of integrity. We are focusing not on mass desire but on individual desire and on a strange phenomenon - the association between an external restraint and an internal pursuit. We have a similar phenomenon in a heroic act, where a person sacrifices herself for love of country. Here she wishes to pursue some sort of self-development in a dream world, and here we witness an external act resulting from an internal pursuit. Though the explanations of a criminal act are varied and conflicting, I don't think its sources are vastly different. Indeed her motives might be as simple as "I see the ring; I want the ring; I take the ring." But a woman taking the ring might also do it because her role-model, her image of herself secretly projected on her inner screen, is a person who can steal without getting caught. So here again we see an association between an external act and an internal pursuit. Indeed, if we look closely enough, we will find a climate of mind to be nothing else than a reflection of an internal pursuit.

We have in this inner dimension of self-realization a project space that we cannot brush aside as immaterial. In these subterranean Omegas originate many of our overt pursuits that we think of as "rational". So what shall we do if we find a solitary person wishing nothing more than "to project a true image of himself on the screen of the universe", a person becoming disturbed if anyone casts a false image of himself on that screen. Can't we afford to close the door of the courtroom in his face, put him in a bottle and shelve him? Has the state a compelling interest in the matter?

Always a judge seated in court is aware of observers sensitive to his every act; his every failure to act. Let there be no one in court but a clerk or bailiff, plaintiff and defendant, and perhaps a lawyer or two; and the judge's every act and failure to act will be stored in as many memory banks as there are people present. He will be assigned a status in their minds and, on his example, each mind will generate an image of government and assign to government a status. Now into this compara- tively empty court bring a plaintiff with nothing left in this world but himself, and very little left of that. In this world with its complement of able individuals avidly trying to grasp what they can, we are apt to find more and more individuals bereft of that financial standing giving them the sheen of independence and the scent of strength. Our plaintiff has but one material thing left of property, an image of himself - a true image - standing on a High Commons, and he comes to court because someone has misrepresented him to someone else. Not only that, the government itself has taken that false image, pasting it in a permanent record for all to see, refusing to remove it, and the plaintiff seeks a court order that it be removed.

The judge will announce his decision, and the faces of the people in the courtroom, save those perhaps of plaintiff and defendant, will betray no emotion, and the judge will know that the mind behind each mask has stored a memory of what it has seen; in each mind an invisible reaction machinery will be in motion. Each taxitant will ask if the judge has created a legal reality from a non-truth. Has he deserted a plaintiff whose case lacks mass appeal. Ancient instincts from feudal days will conjure visions of villagers expelled from the commons on grounds of false rumors, of a loyal subject tortured because of lies fabricated during an inquisition, of a woman burned because another woman called her a witch. Among these silent observers, as the judge knows, there will be divergent reactions. Minds distaining the titles of others will be charmed by what they see; others will be chilled, and the individuals of both groups will share a common thought. "Were I a plaintiff or defendant in this court and in my last extremity, what protection might I expect? What are the principles on which this court operates?"

And just as a small pebble dropped in a pond will impel a ripple to the farthest shore, so the attitudes engendered by this isolated court decision will swell through the body politic. By the laws of human nature even the person excited by the possibilities of Myra's lie will feel a chill at the marrow for she too, in an extremity, will be vulnerable to such treatment.

In the final analysis, a judge's job is to encourage attitudes. It is impossible in the adversarial atmosphere of a trial and within the embrace of natural laws that a judge can hand down a decision without caressing an attitude here and bruising an attitude there. Just as external actions and restraints are derived from internalized pursuits, so internalized pursuits can be redirected by external winds. Thus a judge creates the reality we call the common good, perchance the common bad, and thus a judge in his decision, like a weather vane, always discloses a reality of sorts; for example, the compelling interest of the state.

CHAPTER 49

FRAUD, NEGLIGENCE, AND
THE FIDUCIARY DUTY

Fraud, as malicious tool or legal cause, has an elusive structure, and jurists waver between two schools of thought on the topic. There is a tradition treating fraud very formally, the judge in effect instructing the plaintiff to give him the facts and, if the facts fit a certain check list of ingredients, the judge will declare a case of fraud. Thus many judges have said of fraud, "The essential elements are false representation, scienter, deception and injury." On occasion the list is given as "misrepresentation, scienter, intent to deceive, justifiable reliance, and damage".

On the other hand there is a tradition hunting fraud with a wide-spraying shotgun. Thus if one thumbs through **Words and Phrases** (see Chapter 56), one finds a judge opining, "Fraud is a generic term which embraces all multifarious means which ingenuity can devise and which are resorted to by one individual to gain an advantage over another by false suggestions or by suppression of truth, and includes all surprise, trick, cunning, dissembling, and any unfair way by which another is cheated." And another judge, "the gist of an action for "fraud" is fraudulently producing a false impression on the mind of another party and, if such result is accomplished, it is unimportant whether the means of accomplishment are words or acts of the defendant, or his concealment or suppression of material facts not equally within the knowledge or reach of the plaintiff."

Ultimately in a case on trial the formal treatment prevails, the plaintiff setting forth the facts of the case and judge looking for fraud slithering among the allegations. This suggests there somewhere exists a list of the elements of fraud against which he can check your claims.

For example if a person tells you a certain piece of land contains a valuable lode of gold, knowing it holds no gold at all, he is not defrauding you. He is only lying to you, and lying of itself engenders no injury. However his statement exhibits two elements of fraud: misrepresentation (the falsity of his story) and scienter (his knowledge of its falseness). But more is needed for a conclusion of fraud.

For one thing it is not fraud unless you are deceived - you actually believe the false information - and furthermore it is not fraud unless you act under the influence of your misconception - you sign an agreement to buy the land. In addition, you must have been harmed as a result of taking the action - you paid more money for the land than you can retrieve, due to your misconception. And that still is not all.

It is not fraud unless you have a good reason for trusting him; for believing his information to be true. This is the element of justifiable reliance. If for example the land happens to be his, you will find it difficult to convince the judge that you were justified in believing his tale. To be justified you would have to convince the judge that you are mentally retarded, else that the seller made a special effort to secure your trust.

Thus we arrive at the five classic elements of fraud:
(1) The originant helps crystallize an erroneous concept in the taxitant's mind. This is called **misrepresentation.**
(2) The originant is aware that the concept is erroneous. This is called **scienter.**
(3) The taxitant is fully justified in believing the originant. This is called **justifiable reliance.**
(4) The taxitant acts - makes a loading - on the basis of her misconception; in other words the deception is effective. I will refer to this as **action under misconception.**
(5) The taxitant suffers a loss as a result of her act. I will call this **resulting harm.**

These classic elements need a word or two of explanation and a volume or two of exceptions and variations. For example, suppose the originant does not intend to deceive the taxitant. **Intent to deceive** is sometimes listed among the elements of fraud. But how do you ever know the intentions of a person? If she doesn't wish to disclose them, you must infer them. And certainly if an originant knowing the truth of a situation nevertheless allows a taxitant to develop a misconception, you might infer that the originant has an intent to deceive. Therefore it is arguable that given misrepresentation and scienter, one need not include intent to deceive among the list of essentials as an independent element.

However the intent to deceive is a ponderable in many cases of fraud; there is a recognized class of fraud in which the originant has no scienter and no intent to deceive. He may be a mere blabbermouth, the local villager posing as an expert on gold deposits. He has no personal interest in the land, no propects of gaining an advantage at your expense, but he talks so convincingly about the gold in such glowing terms that he appears to know what he is talking about. You buy the land and lose a small fortune.

His participation in the drama is called reckless misrepresentation, making him liable for damages if the judge or jury is convinced that you were justified in relying on his assertions. But punitive damages is reserved for the intentional defrauder or where the reckless misrepresentation is "wanton", and it is in making these distinctions for levying damages that the intent to deceive becomes an issue.

Of course if this tale-teller is an obvious prattler, the court will not hold him liable. To become liable, he must have assumed an authoritative pose, and you must be convinced of his reliability. But if he is a professional geologist he must refrain from prattling. In the eyes of a court, you are justified in relying on the words of a professed expert, even if he is working for the seller. As a professional he is expected to know not only the difference between fact and fancy but the importance of distinguishing between them in his communications.

The sales agent is in an intermediate position. He is not presumed an expert in anything except selling, unless he poses as expert in the functioning of that which he sells. But he is not allowed the poetic license of the seller. If he simply parrots the seller, "There's gold on the land," there had better be gold on the land. But if he says, "The seller told me there's gold on the land," he's safe. Then if you ask him, "But is there really gold on the land?" he had better say he doesn't know, unless in fact he does.

As the beneficiary of a trust, you may believe anything the trustee tells you. It is justifiable reliance as far as the court is concerned. He is a fiduciary, and so is your attorney, and your physician. And so is anyone else under particular circumstances that I will gradually define. But it is universally acknowledged that the professional, even your stockbroker, talking about a project in his field of expertise and understanding you might pursue the project, must carefully distinguish between fact and opinion. The law considers fiduciaries to be under a special duty to erase (if possible) an erroneous concept they perceive in their client's mind. If they don't adhere to this narrow path, their client suffering as a result, the law constructs and hangs a special charge of fraud over their heads. It is called, reasonably enough, constructive fraud, enabling a court to take remedial action for the plaintiff even if the fiduciary intended no harm.

Though seemingly rigorous, the orthodox analysis of fraud lacks real incisiveness. Simply examine the three elements justifiable reliance, misrepresentation and resulting harm. One sees misrepresentation originating not only in lies, but also in silence. A fiduciary proposing a project for his client - an investment - a legal suit - a heart operation - can not silently watch an erroneous concept of the project creep into his client's mind. A fiduciary has a duty to tell all he knows about the adverse features of the project.

Though the device of duty seems a justified burden to impose on the professional fiduciary - a requirement of his license like imposing the innkeepers law on an innkeeper - the imposition of duty becomes disturbing when we see the law assigning the fiduciary duty to a non-fiduciary. For example, we find the sellers of houses failing to disclose termites to the buyer, or that the dwelling violates the zoning code - and in these cases the courts have found the sellers liable for the buyers' losses. Not that I am excusing the sellers' behavior; I am pointing out an inconsistency. In fraud, the plaintiff's trust must be justified. It is automatic in the case of a fiduciary. Yet here we find a seller, a party traditionally not trusted - caveat emptor - found liable for loss. The condemning court, in constructing a duty for him, has made the seller a fiduciary.

Always it seems that the introduction of duty into the common law spawns a legal guessing game. Once again we find ourselves entering that twilight zone governed by tort and negligence. For instance, among the various species of fraud we find something called negligent misrepresentation; false statements have been made by a person honestly believing them to be true. Hearing there's gold in Hangman's Hill, and having no reasonable basis for believing it, he asserts pure gossip to a prospective buyer as absolute truth; and now he is liable for the buyer's losses on the ground of negligent misrepresentation. One might ask what is meant by a reasonable basis for believing what one has heard, and I will not try to define it, but it is important. For if you have a reasonable basis for your belief - even if the basis is erroneous - you won't be held liable for the buyer's losses! It reduces to this: if you are going to communicate a mistaken belief to someone else, you have a duty to have a reasonable basis for believing it, else you are negligent.

One senses fundamental misgivings about the orthodox treatment of fraud upon studying the last entry in the list of essential elements. It is professionally mislabeled damage, sometimes injury, and you will note that I more puristically labeled it harm. Damage cannot possibly be an element of the list. The purpose of the traditional format of fraud is to spell the conditions under which damages can be assessed. Therefore the whole list adds up legally to damage; damage is not merely an element. Harm must be present if damage is to be pronounced, so harm is the element. The troubling observation is this, and it is called to our attention by misnaming the last element "injury", - no one seems to know what the injury is in a case of fraud. What property has the originant invaded; what liberty has she infringed?

It is simple, you say. That person told me the bridge was safe, but when I drove onto it with my car, it collapsed. And now my car is in five feet of water. Yes, your financial welfare has been harmed, and it is certainly a case of damage - **if you have been injured.** But what is the injury? Did that person have a duty to tell you the bridge was unsafe? Is this a property for you? Does it mean he is a subject in a loading space to which you are entitled? You push his run button, and he must tell you the truth? This is a government-enforced service? Well, we will spend quite a few pages in solving this puzzle.

We have a clue. Given that the fifth and last essential element is resulting harm, completing the cause in damage, then the injury must somehow reside in the first four elements - Misrepresentation - Scienter - Action Under Misconception - Justifiable Reliance. If these elements are present, the law concludes that injury has occurred. The originant has infringed the liberty of the taxitant. But what is the liberty, and what is the property of the taxitant? What is the profile of the taxitant's entitled and invaded space. What is the subject, the loading, and the objective?

Actually we will find that the first four classic elements of fraud do not constitute injury. Rather they signal that injury has occurred. They constitute a parameter of fraudful injury, signaling a judge to presume injury. But what is the injury? We will never gain confidence in our understanding of fraud until we see the injury face to face. We must identify the project space in which the taxitant's effectiveness has been diminished, and the mechanism by which the originant's action has powered this result.

Notice I applied the word "action" to the originant, and this will be a key word. We have learned that a taxitant defrauded has acted under a misconception generated by an act of the originant. But we have also learned that fraud can be found where the originant has failed to act. The injury is functionally associated with a non-act, and as materialists we feel constrained to ask if a non-act can infringe a liberty. Tort tells us it can; the originant has a duty to act, and neglects it. Tort leaves us dangling at that point, but as independent thinkers we must insist on more fundamental instruction. Our analysis begins with the basic facts:

A survey of the field leads one to an extremely basic fact. Fraud always involves a project contemplated by the taxitant. "Perhaps buying Hangman's Hill and digging for gold will make me rich." In the taxitant's projection lies a hidden if - an essential element of every project. "If I do this, I'll get that," or "If I do this, what are my chances of getting that?" It is impossible to undertake any pursuit without having a mental image of (a) the loadings you will make and (b) the results you can expect. Even an O. Henry hero confronting a mysterious green door, bent on grappling with an unknown adventure thinks, "If I open the door, I will find adventure." If upon opening the door he finds an unpainted brick wall, well, his conception was wrong. In each of your contemplated enterprises your mind consciously or unconsciously makes assessments and assumptions about (1) the subjects you will load in the course of your pursuit, (2) the functional relations between your loadings and the subjects' reactions, (3) the chain of reactions from subject to subject in the causal sequence, and (4) how in the course of these reactions your objective will materialize.

If you are climbing into your hammock you expect, rightly or wrongly, that the ropes won't break. Even in this simple transaction you rely on a mental projection of a half dozen relationships. If you suspect that age has weakened the webbing, you will severely test it before applying your full weight.

If someone has secretly snipped a few threads of the webbing, hoping to have some fun at your expense, she has initiated a nuisance, and here I am not referring to the impairment of the hammock, or broken bones. Her pursuit leaking into your project space and having an effect is nuisance. It is a distortion of your space, and fraud is not involved.

Suppose it is not your hammock, but hers, hung between trees in her backyard. Aware of its weakness, she invites you to use it, and you ask, "Will it break?" Due to her answer, "It's as safe as Gibralter," you spend the next month in a hospital bed. Not her intention, nevertheless (1) she misrepresented the functional relationships of the project; (2) she knew it was a misrepresentation; (3) you acted under a misconception thus induced; (4) you were justified in believing her assertions; and (5) you were hurt as a result. A clear case of fraud. But was it damage, and if you claim damage, what was the injury?

Before answering, let me again slightly change the circumstances. As in the previous example, the lady has invited you to eat supper with her in her backyard. The hammock being there, deceptively strong, you climb in on your own initiative and end up in the hospital. First question, is she liable for damages? And the next question, is there a difference between this situation and fraud, and if so what is it?

Before answering, let me once more change the circumstances. A six year old girl living next door has her eye on the hammock. Curious (she has seen hammocks on television) she crawls through the hedge and into the hammock. The fabric tearing, she falls; her arm breaks. Is the hammock-owner liable?

Notice how smoothly these case vary from one to another, yet one case will be tried on fraud and the others probably on the theory of tort-negligence. Indeed three of the more erratically treated cases in litigation are (1) the case of fraud in which the defendant has failed to inform the plaintiff about an adverse feature in a project; (2) the case of negligence in which the defendant has failed to do something that a "reasonably prudent person" would do; (3) the liability of a landowner for children getting hurt while trespassing on his land; and I will add a fourth - (4) strict products liability. This is the liability imposed on manufacturers for harm resulting from defects in the design and manufacture of their products.

What we will discover is that these cases, inadvertently confused under tort treatment, must be analyzed as a continuum to reveal the true distinctions between them.

In **Rowland v. Christian** (1968), an invited guest, while washing in the bathroom, broke the procelain knob of the faucet, and some tendons in his hand were lacerated. Apparently the knob had been previously cracked, and his hostess had asked her landlord to fix it. Upon trial and appeal, the Supreme Court of California ruled five to two that: "Where the occupier of land is aware of a concealed condition involving... an unreasonable risk of harm... and is aware that a person on the premises is about to come into contact with it, ... a failure to warn or to repair the condition constitutes negligence. Whether or not a guest has a right to expect that his host will remedy dangerous conditions on his account, he should reasonably be entitled to rely upon a warning of the dangerous condition so that he, like the host, will be in a position to take special precautions when he comes in contact with it."

Although a case such as this is brought to court under a cause in negligence, note that it could as well be brought under a cause in constructive fraud. As I mentioned earlier, the cause in constructive fraud applies to cases in which the originant does not have a fraudulent intent. She does not necessarily harbor an intent to deceive. In **Estate of Arbuckle** (1950), the court declared, "In its generic sense, constructive fraud comprises all acts, omissions and concealments involving a breach of legal or equitable duty, trust, or confidence, and resulting in damage to another...."

Constructive fraud may be applied to a fiduciary situation. If for example a physician prescribes a drug for his patient, neglecting to mention the possibility of a harmful side effect, he is exposing himself to liability for resulting harm. If the patient is harmed, we see several of the essential elements of fraud: (1) the patient has taken the drug under the misconception that it is safe, so we see **action under misconception;** (2) we see **resulting harm;** and (3) given the fiduciary relationship, the patient's **reliance** on the doctor's prescription is presumed **justifiable.**

What we don't see in the situation is **misrepresentation,** and the possibilities of **scienter** are two: either the doctor knew about the side effects or he did not. But since the court may find the physician liable for the harm, we may infer that the court finds the fiduciary relationship a suitable substitute for misrepresentation and scienter. Here we do not see the physician informing the patient that the drug is safe. We see the patient relying on the physician's professional knowledge and ability to communicate, and we infer he trusts the physician not to direct him into a dangerous undertaking. Evidently the law presumes under these circumstances that if a fiduciary fails to communicate to the patient the adverse features of the undertaking, he in effect represents the undertaking to be safe. This then is misrepresentation. If additionally the physician is aware of the side effects, we see scienter, and the roll-call of fraud is complete.

In some cases a court will presume even the scienter, the physician actually being ignorant of recognized harmful side effects. The court may say he had a duty to know, and the presumption may stretch even further. No matter that side effects are not recognized for the particular drug. Many drugs have been found to have side effects, often after years of use. Therefore a court might say that a physician has a duty to communicate the difference between "knowledge-to-date" and actual fact, informing the patient of both fact and lack of fact, and letting the patient make the final decision.

In the case of a homeowner selling his house, not telling the buyer about the freeway planned through the lot next door, we see (1) the buyer buying on a misconception; (2) the potential for resulting harm; and (3) scienter. But we don't see misrepresentation - the question of freeways doesn't even arise during the negotiations - and we don't see justifiable reliance. The only way then that a court can find the seller liable for the buyer's losses is to drape the mantle of fiduciary upon the seller's shoulders. How can this be? What are the circumstances making him a fiduciary? Can a court create a fictitious fiduciary out of thin air? Isn't that like honoring the marital "status" when the marital relationship has become a fiction? You can see that, unless the idea of fiduciary is strictly defined, a judge can decide a borderline case to suit his fancy. Discovering the factors translating a person into a fiduciary will be an important task for us.

It is clear in **Rowland v. Christian,** the cracked faucet knob case, that the court cast the hostess in role of fiduciary. Given that the hostess knew the faucet was cracked and dangerous, we see Mr. Rowland using the faucet with the idea that it was safe and getting harmed as a result. The court presumes first that his hostess's silence was assurance that the faucet was safe, and second that his reliance on this presumed assurance was justified. So in effect the hostess misrepresented the situation to the guest and the case fits the cause of constructive fraud, and we come to the conclusion that constructive fraud and negligence in performing an "affirmative duty" are one and the same cause.

I think we can ask some questions. Is a court justified in placing a fiduciary burden on a host? If the host sees the crack in the faucet knob, can't the guest see the crack? If the host sees danger in the crack, can't the guest see danger in the crack? If we apply the "reasonably-prudent-person-foreseeable-risk-of-harm" test to the host, can't we apply it to the guest as well? Must we presume all hosts to be administrative and communicative geniuses, all guests to be imbeciles? After all, it is different from the professional fiduciary relationship. The professed professional poses as a person wise in investments, or sutures, or law, and absolutely trustworthy. Does a host pretend to this perfection?

Is it possible that the hostess in **Rowland v. Christian** did not recognize the faucet as a dangerous situation? Really how dangerous is a crack in a faucet knob? It seems to me an extraordinary talent is required to get tendons lacerated by a faucet knob. But these questions were not asked by the court. The danger was presumed and the question of the crack's visibility was left dangling.

We must leave **Rowland v. Christian** for the moment, munching on other cases before solving it. But before leaving it I wish to bring up the topic of landlords. The landlord in **Rowland** was not held liable for the harm, though failing to fix the faucet. Is it possible that the hostess did not mention it to him in the context of danger? When reading the law on landlords, we learn that a landlord does not have to remedy a dangerous situation if (1) he provides sufficient warning of the situation or (2) the danger is so obvious that it serves as a warning in itself.

With the benefit of this intelligence we read the case of **Russo v. Burch** (1964). We read that Michelina Russo, having taken voice lessons from Mrs. Di Tano for over two years, had been to her duplex apartment more than 100 times. On the night in question Miss Russo, having finished her lesson, started to descend the front six steps in pitch darkness and plunged off. It seems that the overhead light was burned out, and in fact the steps were darker than usual. Mrs. Di Tano, intending to leave immediately, had turned out the lights in her apartment, and no light from her windows illuminated the steps.

Paul Burch, the landlord, testified that he always left the outside light burning night and day, replacing burned-out bulbs promptly and visiting the apartment at least twice a week. Contradicting that, Mrs. Di Tano testified that the light had never been on in the two years she had lived there, and she often kept a lamp lighted in her window to light the steps. Miss Russo testified that she had safely descended the stairs in the dark before, even with no light coming from her teacher's window. At such times she put her hands on the house shingles, descending the steps sideways because the treads were narrow, and she started to do the same on the night of the accident.

She testified that she did not trip on anything, did not slip on anything, simply stepped forward, couldn't find the steps, and fell. She testified it didn't occur to her to ask Mrs. Di Tano to turn on the light in her window. A jury found the landlord not liable, but the case was brought to the Appeals Court on the complaint that the trial judge had given the jury prejudicial instructions.

The trial judge had told the jury that "walking through an unlighted, unfamiliar area in the dark constitutes negligent conduct." In other words Miss Russo was negligent in taking care of herself. Aha! said the Appeals Court, this might be true, but the area was familiar, not unfamiliar! (As though one does not have to be careful descending familiar steps in the dark.) And, claimed Miss Russo's appeal, there was a second prejudicial instruction; the trial judge had instructed the jury as to the duty of the music teacher (the invitor) to Miss Russo (the invitee) but not as to the duty of the landlord. The Appeals Court, finding these instructions prejudicial, reversed the judgment, and the landlord became liable for the harm sustained by Miss Russo.

So we see in **Rowland** that the landlord, though informed of the cracked faucet, was not brought into the case as a defendant, and the landlord in **Russo**, though not informed of the burned-out bulb, was found liable for the harm. In **Russo** we see an appeals court picking at a difference between the words familiar and unfamiliar, immaterial in the circumstances since the accident itself proved that descending familiar steps in the dark is dangerous. Finally in **Russo** we see an appeals court reversing a judgment because the trial judge did not instruct the jury on the landlord's duty to Miss Russo. Yet the instructions would have been, if given, that the landlord had no duty, for the danger was obvious in itself. The appeals court, you see, was giving him a fiduciary duty. And how can even a professional fiduciary be held liable if the danger is communicated to the taxitant as clearly through her own senses as the fiduciary could have presented it in words!

Can we extend the principles of this uncertain justice to the world of children, a world already uncertain enough. Examining the case of a child hurt while trespassing, we have at minimum a three-pronged inquiry; (1) does the child herself have responsibility in the accident; (2) to what extent did the landholder contribute to the accident; (3) to what extent did the child's parents (a) teach her to be cautious, (b) teach her the meaning of property and trespass, and (c) restrain a very young child from running at large? The law has withdrawn somewhat from a theory once dominant in the case of trespassing children, the "attractive nuisance" theory of injury. Finding difficulties in applying it, jurists have adopted a rule that omits the involvement of factors attracting a child to another person's property.

Briefly, section 339 of the Second Restatement on this topic says that the landholder is liable for harm to young trespassing children caused by artificial conditions if (1) the place is one where children are likely to trespass, and (2) the condition is one that the possessor is aware of and involves a risk of serious harm to children, and (3) the children because of their youth do not discover the condition or realize the risk, and (4) the possessor fails to exercise reasonable care to eliminate the danger or otherwise protect the children.

Unfortunately the rule produces inconsistent results. In **Helguera v. Cirone** (1960), seven year old John Helguera fell from a scaffold at a construction site. The situation met the conditions of the Restatement. Only in the third element was there a question; does a child of this age realize the risks of climbing? The answer is yes; so said the court. The courts have long decided that a landholder cannot be held liable for risks that a child naturally understands. A court will not unqualifiedly favor a child as though he has no experience or capacity to learn. But there was an additional factor in this case that settled it for the court. The scaffold had a deceptively loose platform board for walking on, behaving something like a trap door, and it was this that caused the child to fall.

In fact, this hidden or concealed trap idea has become almost an essential feature of this cause. It is as though the harm-to-trespassing-children cause has been brought within the framework of constructive fraud. A child undertakes a project under a misconception and gets hurt as a result, the landholder being aware of the true functioning of the situation. All we need do is make the landholder a fiduciary and take the position that the landholder has invited the child to participate in the undertaking. Therefore the child is justified in believing that this particular project space is safe. Under these assumptions, we can draw the conclusion that the landholder has misrepresented the project space to them, and the case adds up to fraud.

This line of reasoning strains my credulity. It shows the weakness of imposing liability on a person without understanding the injurious mechanics of the transaction. If you don't think it has weaknesses, observe the results in **Courtell v. McEachen** (1959). Here a girl less than six years old was severely burned on an empty lot where the defendant's agent had been burning trash. As the girl was walking home from school, some children playing on the lot - children of the man who had burned the trash - called her to join them.

A witness testified that from her home she saw the girl walk to the center of the lot, jump over something and stoop down, and when she got up the back of her dress was on fire. The witness said the fire on the lot was still smouldering at the time of the accident, but there were no flames. The little girl said she had squatted down to pick up a stick, being acquainted with fire only from her mother's stove, and not knowing that embers could set her dress on fire.

Quoted the court, "There are some dangers common in the community which any child of sufficient age to be allowed at large may be expected to understand and appreciate - such are the usual risks of fire and water." The court ruled that the liability of landholders does not extend to those conditions.

When one compares this to the cracked faucet knob and reviews a large number of such cases, one wonders if the courts do not imagine the average child to be more alert and experienced than the average adult, at least the average adult who happens to be a guest. It is clear that a fundamental understanding of the mechanics of injury in "affirmative duty" is lacking.

To illustrate the glaring need to clear the confusion in this entire field, I wish to review a case in detail before commencing the actual analysis. Under the principle known as **strict products liability,** there has been an attempt to reduce judicial inconsistency in negligence cases involving manufactured products. In practice the effect of strict products liability makes every manufacturer a fiduciary to the users of the product. The legal profession has tried to state the principle with absolute incisiveness. As expressed in **Torts Restatement 2d,** the opening clause in strict products liability reads,

"One who sells any product in a defective condition unreasonably dangerous to the user or consumer, or to his property is subject to liability for physical harm thereby caused to the ultimate user or consumer, or to his property...."

It seems that negligence does not have to be alleged and proved. All that needs to be demonstrated is the functional sequence of cause and effect. In 1963 in **Greenman v. Yuba Power Products,** a court in California justified the rule very simply: "The purpose of such liability is to insure that the costs of injuries resulting from defective products are borne by the manufacturers... rather than by the injured persons who are powerless to protect themselves."

Though undoubtedly conceived in the context of negligence, the rule actually lays a basis for constructive fraud. No one occupies such an advantageous position as the manufacturer for inspecting and detecting the defects of the product. From the earliest phase of the assembly, he can test each part and inspect it as to design and manufacture. In the act of putting the product on the market, he signifies that the user may rely on it, indeed may rely on the manufacturer. The thrust of marketing is intended to establish a taxitant's faith and trust in an originant, and traditionally on the basis of this very sort of pretension the common law has construed the originant as a fiduciary.

It is difficult to find any inconsistency between the principle of strict products liability and the spirit of the common law. Subjecting a manufacturer to strict products liability, you might say, is a requirement of the license to manufacture. His placing the product on the market is evidence that he has duly considered the serious nature of his obligation. In this aspect his fiduciary duty may be interpreted as a contractual service to his customer.

However, given the correctness of the principle, one must wonder at the Restatement's manner of expressing it: "One who sells any product in a defective condition unreasonably dangerous...."

First, why did the writers attach "unreasonably" to dangerous? Just plain "dangerous" is dangerous enough. And why use the word "defective" when the lawyers mean a dangerous condition, defective or not. And why use the word "condition" when they intend that the principle will apply to the product's design as well as its condition. Can it be that the writers had something in mind not sufficiently analyzed and expressed?

You can buy a machine that gobbles up tree prunings as you feed them in, turning them into sawdust. Dangerous to operate, it can gobble you up just as easily. But the Restatement writers were not gunning for this sort of danger. The branch gobbler presents an obvious danger, and the manufacturer will usually bring it to the user's attention. Indeed, a user becomes aware of danger by the very nature of the machine, and has every opportunity to apply his mind to it. With a clear mental picture of the risks, he can use the machine and assume the risks, or decide not to use it. So perhaps the Restatement writers, to free manufacturers from liability for this kind of danger, inserted the word "defective".

Now if they had included the word "design", if they had written "One who sells any product with a defective condition or design unreasonably dangerous...", a critic might ask, "What do you mean by dangerous design?" Of course an answer would be that the design was dangerous if the machine as designed was dangerous to use, and this creates a category neatly incorporating the limb-gobbling machine. So the writers omitted the word "design", and lawyers and judges are permitted to assume that design is implied.

This reconstruction of the Restaters' thinking is of course pure conjecture on my part, but surely no more dangerous than the Restatement itself.

I propose that the word they wished to use, and for some reason were paralyzed in using, was the word "imperceptible". Aren't they talking about hidden dangers; not hidden intentionally but by accident of design or manufacture - dangers not overtly presented to the user's consideration as he prepares to use the product. For example, a patient has no way of learning the side effects of a prescribed drug unless his physician informs him. And doesn't the feature of imperceptibility conform to pure theory? Should not a fiduciary be held responsible for dangers not readily recognizable by his client? And should he be held responsible for dangers readily perceived by the client?

So, riding on the Restatement of "strict product liability", we come to **Dimond v. Caterpillar Tractor Co.**, decided in 1976 in a California District Court of Appeal. Roy Dimond operated a towmotor - a transport machine with an elevating arm - in a printer's warehouse. Huge rolls of paper, bound in packages weighing from 900 to 1500 pounds were stacked in columns up to 15 feet high. His job with the towmotor was to stack the rolls, and, upon an order from the pressroom, he would remove a package from a stack and deliver it to the press.

On the night of the accident, Henry Egeland relayed to Dimond an order to deliver a package of a certain kind of paper. Shortly thereafter he and Ralph Allen, hearing a loud "boom" in the warehouse, ran and found Dimond lying face down on the floor behind the towmotor with a 550 pound roll of paper lying across his shoulder and another lying on the floor on the other side of the towmotor. The towmotor was in neutral gear, its engine still running, and, something new, there was a large dent in the top of the protective cage over the driver's seat.

Dimond suffered serious lesions, contusions, concussions and dilacerations, and, particularly significant for the trial, he sustained an amnesia blotting out all memory of the accident. In testifying he assumed he had been in the towmotor when the package began to fall and, seeing the danger, jumped out and tried to run away. He must have done this, he claimed, for two reasons. First, there was a sign on the cage that said the cage wouldn't protect the driver from a very heavy impact. Second, the towmotor's fuel tank, a propane tank, was exposed - not covered or protected from a falling object - and he feared an explosion.

To be accurate, the sign on the cage actually read, "Overhead guard conforms to ASA-B56 safety code and is intended to protect the driver but is not intended to withstand the impact of heavy or capacity loads falling from any height. Obey safety rules." He testified further that when leaving the towmotor he always placed it in neutral gear and turned off the engine.

The manufacturer claimed Dimond did not have a case. Lacking a memory of the actual events, he could not give a recitation of fact; his statement was a selective reconstruction of possible events. As the judge in the trial court expressed it, Dimond, when hit by the rolls, might have been returning from the bathroom. In other words, said the manufacturer, Dimond claimed to be hurt as a result of manufacturing defects, but manufacturing defects were irrelevant or immaterial if he had left the towmotor for other reasons. So the trial court ruled a non-suit and the plaintiff brought the appeal.

The appeals court ruled that the accuracy of Dimond's story was an issue of fact and should have been put to a jury. And the three justices went further, declaring that if the plaintiff's story proved true, the manufacturer should be found liable, all three agreeing on this point though failing to agree on their reasons.

Justice Tamura began his opinion under the rule of strict products liability: "In a products liability case, a plaintiff has met his burden if he establishes that there was a defect in the manufacture or design of the product and that such defect was a proximate cause of the injury."

He and Justice Morris concluded (1) that the warning on the cage was defective and so was the failure to insulate the propane tank from falling objects, and (2) that plaintiff's attempt to separate himself from the site was a consequence of these defects. As to the warning they reasoned that the plaintiff would not have left the cage if the warning had not been there. The warning was defective because the cage actually proved to be safe; Dimond would not have been hurt if he had not left the cage.

Justice Kaufman while accepting the causal nature of the exposed propane tank, did not accept the causal nature of the warning sign. He did not think the accident allowed Dimond enough time to ponder how far he could trust the sign. Further, he contended, there was no proof that the cage was actually safe. Perhaps the impact by the rolls of paper had been glancing, not direct. It is possible that a direct blow might have crumpled the cage and, if that was true the sign was not misleading, i.e., "defective". It was a correct warning.

But Kaufman did not detect the internal defect in Tamura's and Morris's argument. Contrary to their proposition, a thinking man would have left the cage even in the absence of the warning sign and even if in fact the cage was fully protective against falling objects. Overriding all would have been the exposed fuel tank; the fear of explosion would have governed his reactions. But thus can we become swamped with minutiae, and oblivious to the truly prevailing factors in the case.

It seems to me that the giant factor overlooked by lawyers and judges was Dimond's own contribution to the accident. We gather it only by the tiniest of mentions in the report. Tamura mentioned that "the column of paper rolls was about 15 feet high and was directly beneath a ceiling beam." This is significant, but with this statement alone we would never grasp the true picture. Fortunately a footnote is appended, reading, "The evidence indicated that the column of packages and the beam were of equivalent height," and this reveals the true situation. There was no clearance between the top package of the stack and a ceiling beam directly above it, not enough to lift the paper from the stack with the fork of the towmotor, and drag it out under the beam without dislodging it from the fork! Undoubtedly it was Dimond's attempt to complete this maneuver that pulled the rolls from the towmotor's grasp and let them fall. No defect of the towmotor caused the accident. No one but Dimond caused it.

Actually a successful maneuver might have been impossible. Skill and patience were needed to place the paper on the stack in the first place, and we don't know who did it. But it is possible that pushing the package through the narrow space was feasible, whereas pulling it back out was not. It was an operation fully under the control of Dimond. He knew the characteristics of the towmotor claw; he knew the danger of falling objects; he understood the warning sign on the cage; he was aware of the danger of the propane tank. He was working in a tree-limb gobbling situation. He could have ceased operations at any time before the crucial point was reached. He could have stopped his towmotor and conferred with the rest of the crew.

True, the time was between four and five in the morning, a time of dense mental fog, but this had nothing to do with the towmotor's design and manufacture. "This cage is not absolutely safe; don't be reckless." This was the message of the warning sign. Not misleading in the least. Should the manufacturer not have posted such a warning? If the crack in the faucet was obvious; if the guest is fully aware of the danger; if the hostess had said, "Don't be reckless with it"; could she have been held liable for his hurting himself?

It is evident that the justices in **Dimond** felt uneasy in their decision. They groped for additional ground. "The paramount policy to be promoted by the rule of strict liability is the protection of otherwise defenseless victims of manufacturing defects and the spreading throughout society of the cost of compensating them."

"Spreading the cost" is not a job for the court system. Under the separation of powers, it is not within the franchise of a court. In assuming such a power, a court usurps the appropriative powers of the legislature. A court may assess damages, but only in cases involving injury. If a legislature gives a court the power to transfer title in the absence of injury, well, to say the least, it is giving a clerical task to a pretty expensive battery of brains. It had better employ a social insurance commission funded by the official taxing machinery. Spreading the cost in a holonistic government is intelligently assigned to (1) charity, (2) contractual distribution such as accident and disability insurance, and (3) legislative appropriation and entitlement. To assign the task to a court is to confuse the true function of courts. Their job is to detect injury and assign liability for damage.

I think we gain perspective by looking at "negligence" in the format of constructive fraud. In **Dimond** a court striving to adhere to strict liability actually concluded that the manufacturer had misrepresented its product to Dimond, and nothing was farther from the truth. The question arises, can we nonchalantly burden a person with construed fiduciary duties more severe than those we load upon a professed fiduciary? To answer this we must now seek and define the exact characteristics of the situation in which a government wisely charges a person with fiduciary responsibility.

CHAPTER 50

ATTRACTION CHANNELING
AND THE FIDUCIARY EFFECT

The chapter just ended provided examples of tort judgments in effect casting the defendant as a fiduciary, treating the issue as constructive fraud, yet a fiduciary relationship between defendant and plaintiff was problematic if not entirely lacking, and the judges in the cases were not aware they were making this construction of the case. When we analyze the many cases thus decided, we see no consistently applied rule for thus draping the defendants in fiduciary robes, and moreover we see severe liability imposed on these inadvertently presumed fiduciaries under circumstances in which a fully recognized fiduciary would go scot free. Seen in this light, the spectrum of tort cases exhibiting great confusion in practice embraces actual fraud, constructive fraud, negligence, children harmed while trespassing, and strict products liability - all those cases in fact in which lawyers and judges seek precious "duties" for defendants unhappily falling under their jurisdiction.

If a true common law judge consciously recognized the framework into which she was twisting such a case - treating it in a fiduciary context - she would become more cautious. Before proceeding in this vein, she would require a showing that the defendant stood in a true fiduciary relationship to the plaintiff. For example, she would look into such matters as justifiable reliance.

Thus if a fool has been fleeced by a flim-flam operator, a court will not conclude injury unless the operator has taken pains to establish trust in the fool's mind. And why is the same rule not applied in the case of a cracked faucet knob? Deciding in such cases in favor of the plaintiff, a judge consciously or unconsciously presumes upon the defendant the fiduciary burden.

In a broad set of these cases, we will find ourselves concentrating on the element called "affirmative duty". In these cases an originant fails to act and injury results! Stumbling upon this legalistic logic, the scientific mind "misses a beat". How does one distort a project space by failing to act? It is easy, says the legal mind. We give one a **duty** to act.

Well, putting aside the fleeing duty sought in negligence cases, the common law recognizes three classes of duty to act, (1) the contractual duty, in which one might include the duties incumbent upon license, (2) the fiduciary duty, and (3) your few strictly limited duties to government. In the case of the contractual duty, we have seen how a contractor's failure to perform can distort the projected pursuit space of his opposite party. In the case of duties to government - such as military duty and duty to testify - I don't know that we see injury in the non-performance. We merely feel the lash, and recognize the logic of compliance.

In the case of the affirmative fiduciary duty, discovering the mechanism of injury poses an intriguing puzzle, undertaken in this chapter. Once solved, we will find that all affirmative duties consistent with common law will fall in one of the three classes, contractual duty, duty to government, and the duty generated by the fiduciary effect as I will define it. And in accomplishing this, I will raze to ground zero the entire legal mountain called negligence.

It seems entirely appropriate that a manufacturer is presumed a fiduciary to those using her product. In generating the product, she is in a perfect position to test it for defects in design and manufacture. But it is not entirely clear that a hostess should be held responsible willy-nilly for evil befalling her guest. And when it comes to casting a landholder in the role of fiduciary to trespassing children or - if you wish - giving him an affirmative duty to make everything safe for them, well, there is a break in logic here that is impossible to bridge. Indeed there is a solution, but we will find it to lie happily on much sounder ground than "affirmative duty".

In **Rowland v. Christian**, the case of the cracked faucet knob, the Supreme Court of California admitted its ruling diverged from the common law. Under the common law, said the court, "... the general rule is that a trespasser and licensee or social guest are obliged to take the premises as they find them." But, "an increasing concern for human safety has lead to a retreat from this position.... Whatever may have been the historical justifications for the common law distinctions, it is clear that those distinctions are not justified in the light of our modern society.... ... the complexity and confusion that has arisen... is due to the attempts to apply just rules in our modern society within the ancient terminology." To eliminate the confusion, said the court, our modern courts "approach the duty of the possessor on the basis of ordinary principles of negligence." I will at the moment resist comment, but the significance of **Rowland v. Christian** in legal development may be expressed succinctly thus: that the common law did not lay the mantle of fiduciary upon the host, and the modern law does. The correctness of this shift in responsibility will ultimately be judged not on its plausibility but on its wisdom.

It is now my purpose to inquire what creates a fiduciary relationship, and in this I am not thinking of the relationship created by law. I
am thinking of the actual phenomenal relationship developing naturally
between two human beings. We find in the California appeals case of
Wilson v. Zorb (1936) not a definition of the fiduciary relationship, but
at least what it isn't.

Clair Wilson and George Zorb, physicians, had been friends for
many years, closely associated professionally and socially. Zorb's
accidentally shooting Wilson did not impair their relationship, at least
at first. Zorb, begging strained finances, promised Wilson he would take
care of him, paying his expenses until he could resume his practice.
And he would compensate him for his losses as best he could.

After Wilson underwent surgery, remaining in the hospital for
several weeks, he and his wife moved in with Zorb and his wife, and
were well provided for. While there, Wilson signed documents releasing
Zorb from liability for the harm, at the same time agreeing not to sue
Zorb for damages. He later sued but not before Zorb had paid some
$25,000 for Wilson's expenses and $9,000 in compensation. Nevertheless Wilson decided he should have more money, and asked the court to
declare the documents invalid. He claimed he had signed them because
Zorb said he was in financial straits and further claimed Zorb had
obtained his signature while acting in a fiduciary capacity.

It turned out that Zorb had not lied to Wilson about his financial
difficulties, and, though Zorb had agreed to pay all of Wilson's bills and
expenses, the agreement set no time for payment, and the court could
not find that Zorb did not intend to keep his promise. As for the
fiduciary relationship, the court agreed that warm friendship, confidence and affection existed between the parties, yet each person was
self-sufficient and independent. These circumstances, said the court,
do not comprise confidential relationship in a legal sense. It takes
something more to establish a fiduciary relationship.

That is our question. What is that "something more"?

Taking a clue from the court opinion, we apparently do not have a
fiduciary relationship when both parties are self-sufficient and independent. Obviously the court was not thinking about financial dependency,
and we may infer that in a true fiduciary relationship, we see one of the
parties in some way dependent on the other. This I think is sound, but
now we must become more exact.

You will note that each case reviewed in the previous chapter
presented a situation involving a project of the plaintiff. Perhaps he was
interested in a goldmining project; or in climbing into a hammock; or in
washing his hands; or a voice student proposed descending the stairs in
the dark; or a boy ventured to climb a scaffold and tread the platform at

the top; or a little girl was tempted to play among smouldering ashes; or a towmotor operator undertook removing an 1100 pound bundle of paper from a stack 15 feet high. Now observe something strange. In each case, the plaintiff exerted herself or himself in a particular crucial action. Moreover, the plaintiff in each case was hurt as a result of her or his own act. And finally, most signal, the plaintiff wishes to blame someone else! You see, we have stumbled across a most singular classification of cases. They are "hurt myself, blame another" cases, and you will agree that under the circumstances one should proceed cautiously in fixing the blame on the other person.

Mountains of cases are tried under the umbrella of negligence. Of these, by limiting our discussion to "hurt myself, blame another" cases, we can now eliminate a large number. For example, we can eliminate the case in which a person leaves a car stalled on the road and another car roars recklessly around a curve, hitting the stalled car and ricocheting onto a passing pedestrian. Though currently such a case is treated under tort negligence, there is nothing negligent about it. A person drives a car onto the road and leaves it there; this isn't negligence; the car on the road is the result of an act. Another car plows into it, and this isn't negligence, it is action. As a result of these actions, hunks of crumpled steel fly haphazardly into the vulnerability space of a pedestrian and have an effect. It is nuisance pure and simple; - with resulting harm. Many chapters ago we learned this, in the case of **Palsgraf**.

Now having limited the topic to this class of cases in which the plaintiff contributes proximally to her own harm, we can again lop off a large number of cases from the mountain of "negligence". I draw your attention to the defendant's contribution to an accident - the mechanism of the contribution. The pedestrian who, walking at night, steps into an excavation in the sidewalk has made a mechanical contribution to his own harm. His step is an act in which he is fully titled. But of course the hole would not be there in the absence of the hole-digger's acts. It is not a question of the excavator's right to dig there, or his "duty" to take amendatory action. He acted, and his activity distorted the space of the pedestrian, and the pedestrian's space behaved at odds with his expectations. It is nuisance pure and simple.

But what do we see in a case of actual fraud? If I tell you there is gold on Hangman's Hill when in fact there is none, and if you get hurt in acting upon this information, I have not in the least distorted the subject matter of Hangman's Hill. You, however, take action, executing a purchase agreement and transferring your money to the vendor. But this was your act, not mine, and if I had any effect upon the event it was not upon the subject matter of the transaction, it was upon your mind!

So we discover at least two subclasses of "hurt myself, blame another" cases. The first is the case in which the malfunction of the taxitant's act is due to his misconception of his project space - his project space has been distorted by the defendant. The second is the case in which the malfunction again rises from his misconception of his project space, but the misconception is not due to a distortion of the subject matter of his project space, it is due to the defendant's effect upon his mind. The first is nuisance - we need concern ourselves with it no longer. It is the second that generates judicial nightmares.

Notice how easily this little analysis resolves **Dimond v. Caterpillar Tractor Co.**, Dimond basically claiming that the manufacturer gave him a misconception of his operating space. Nonsense. The exposed gas tank was not deceptive. Dimond was fully aware of the danger it posed. As for the warning sign, it said, "This cage might not protect you from very heavy falling objects. Be careful." And how can a government disfavor a manufacturer for posting a sign like that! The manufacturer did not distort Dimond's project space, or his conception of his project space.

We can now exactly pinpoint the element of these cases that will require our attention. In the cases left to resolve, we have a person busily mining a goldless hill, a person climbing into a hammock that won't support him, a person turning a faucet that will break in his hand, a boy climbing a scaffold with tricky planks at the top, a girl stooping in a field of glowing embers. What is the common element in these cases? It is that the pursuit didn't turn out as the pursuer expected. To be sure, everything responded to the pursuer's loadings exactly as it should in accord with the laws of nature, but the project space did not function in accord with the pursuer's conception of it.

This is not true of Miss Russo descending the stairs in the dark. As with Dimond, we can eliminate her case from our troublesome subclass. She knew exactly what would happen if she made a misstep in the dark. The landlord had done nothing to distort the stairs, and he had placed no misconception of them in her mind. In fact she had no misconception of the project at all. As the court itself noticed, she was thoroughly familiar with the stairs. Stairs are stairs, and pitch black is pitch black. If she for some reason was not alert to the danger on this particular night, it could not be attributed to the landlord. I think without doubt we can attribute her fall to her lack of care, not to any failure of the steps to respond in accord with her conception of them.

And now we face the truly troublesome subclass of cases. They are the cases in which the plaintiff will attribute her misconception of a project space to another person. Into this class we can definitely place the purchase of Hangman's Hill. We can place here the case of the hammock-climber whose hostess assured him it was sound as Gibralter. And now once again we will find in these cases nothing less than distortions of project spaces. For what is a project space?

Your project tonight is to feast your guests on a delicious terrapin pie, indeed delicious if you know how to prepare it, and how do you learn? You might learn by experimenting each night for two weeks, placing something in front of your husband, calling it terrapin pie, each night having prepared it differently, or you might follow a well-tested recipe. In preparing terrapin pie, your project space consists of the ingredients, their relation to each other, the response of each to oven heat, and the relation between the finished product and the human palate. The ingredients exist in the real world, and their interrelationships follow the physico-chemical laws of the universe. But your project exists in your mind.

Pursuing your project step by step, you execute an action at each step. But previous to each step, the step is a subproject or project of its own. In your mind you project what you will do, and you project what the result will be. According to our developing terminology, your actions will be your loadings, or powerings, and the results will be the derivatives of functional translations. They are variates reflecting the functional relationships between your subject matter and your loadings.

There are two ways of distorting your terrapin project space. Perhaps the spice in the bottle is not what the label says it is. Or perhaps the recipe book fails to mention an essential operation or ingredient. In either case, your conception of the function space is erroneous. Your project space exists as much in your mind as in your actual subjects and loadings, and error can exist in the internal space or the external, with disastrous results.

A lie is an act. If a person tells you a lie about your project space, or your anticipated project space, we have exactly the same distortion as the failure to finish a house as contracted. If you have trust in the liar or the non-performing promiser, and if there is a basis for such trust, the lie or the non-performance has a material effect on your project space. It is distortion. And this is the exact cause in Hangman's Hill and the misrepresented hammock. The defrauders acted and their acts distorted your project space. If the deception involves a lie, it is not that the liar "neglected" to tell the truth; we have a case of nuisance - action with distortion. And so we have chopped off another hunk of the mountain of negligence cases.

Our concern is now restricted to a very special subsubclass of cases, solely those in which the defendant has done nothing - apparently - and we wish to hold him responsible for harm that we by our own act precipitate upon ourselves; Rowland hurt himself on a cracked faucet in the home of his hostess; John Helguera age seven, trespassing, fell off a tricky scaffold. Is it possible to attribute these accidents to the defendant's effect upon the plaintiff's mind? In placing blame upon the defendant, we are in effect placing him in the role of fiduciary. In the case of Helguera, can we say that the contractor distorted his space, his entitled project space, either physically or by influencing his mind? For to find the contractor liable for damages, we will first have to discover him infringing John Helguera's liberty. In this case it is difficult to sustain either version, and one wonders if Helguera must be placed in still a third subsubclass of cases.

I think that jurists have erred in trying to sweep away the idea of attractive nuisance. We will find attraction at the heart of every project in the world. If in Helguera the contractor had displayed at the top of the scaffold the world's largest most luscious lollypop; had so placed it that a child reaching for it would have to step on the unsteady plank, there is little doubt that the contractor would be held liable for resulting harm. But why?

One first observes that the situation would exhibit all the features of an animal trap, a bait is there, and a relation between bait and trigger, and a relationship between the trigger and the welfare of the taxitant. But is there injury? After all, the trap (or the scaffold) belong to the hunter, not the taxitant. Nothing of the taxitant's entitled space has been distorted. And though trigger and mechanism are inconspicuous, a taxitant with more care might discover them before taking the fatal step. What we will now learn is one of the prime features of the fiduciary relationship. Between a taxitant hesitating to undertake a project, and actually taking a step in pursuit of the project, there is a motivational gap, and a fiduciary in some manner bridges this gap.

In the case of an animal trap, a conflict exists in the animal's mind, cautiousness against curiosity. The bait makes the difference, and with a little thought you will recognize this inner conflict as an element not only in traps but in every project that a taxitant considers or "tastes". We are talking here about a balance between an Omega drive and a contra-Omega hesitance.

Remember we are focusing on those cases in which harm results from a taxitant's own decisive act, and I now assert the following. We can not attribute the resulting harm to another person - the originant - unless we discover that the originant played a determining role in the taxitant's decision to act. Now precisely - very important - what do I mean by "determining"?

I have discussed with you the elements of projects - the subjects, loadings, objectives, - and the projecters themselves. There is never a project without a projecter, or a pursuit without a pursuer, and the

event we are about to study is the phenomenon of a projecter metamor-
phosing into a pursuer; a dreamer changing into a doer; a taxitant
becoming an originant! What is it, I ask, that induces a person to
undertake a pursuit? What motivates him to execute a loading in a
function space? If we trace the transformation of projecter into
pursuer, we observe:

(1) The attention of the taxitant is drawn to the project in
connection with an inner drive - grasping for Omega or escaping contra-
Omega.

(2) Next there develops in the taxitant's mind a concept of the
subject matter in the situation and the loadings she will execute if her
objective is to materialize.

(3) During this period a force and an energy grows within the
taxitant, generated by the attractive features of the undertaking.

(4) At the same time conversely this inner force is restrained, the
energy contravened, by the inhibitions of the taxitant, partly by her
natural reluctance to act and partly by repulsive features of the
undertaking.

(5) The moment arrives when the positive drive overbalances the
inhibitions. Only then does the project turn into pursuit, the projecter
into pursuer; and the critical act is enacted!

We have here a quantitative process, not qualitative, becoming
qualitative only in ultimacy - act/non-act. We have here a supreme
distinction to make, for I hold that a common law court may not make a
quantitative judgment. The 5-4 vote is illegitimate when it comes to
injury. A person either injures another or he does not. And this is what
we are about to determine in this most intangible of intangible events. A
person either determines a taxitant's action or he doesn't. He doesn't
1/8 determine it or 3/4 determine it. And it is this judgment that I wish
to clarify.

To gain an insight into the phenomenon of determination, picture
water pouring from a faucet into a barrel, several holes near the bottom
of the barrel, and water spurting from the holes. You will see that the
ultimate height of the water in the barrel will be determined by the
balance between water pouring in from the top and spurting out at the
bottom. The water level in the barrel represents force and energy, for

the higher the water climbs the more pressure at the bottom. This force and energy we will compare to the force and energy needed for transforming a projecter into a pursuer.

A large drain pipe is joined to the bottom of the barrel, containing a valve preventing a flow of water that would rapidly empty the barrel. The pipe represents a channel directing energy into a human project, and the mechanism is this. The valve is adjusted to open when the water pressure on it is great enough. This of course is attained when the water reaches a certain height in the barrel, and you can see that the critical water level in the barrel represents the force and energy required to turn the projecter into a pursuer.

The water pouring in from the faucet represents an increasing drive in a projecter, induced by the attractions of a project. The punctures at the bottom of the barrel represent factors draining drive from the projecter - her natural inertia and cautiousness, and the repulsive features of the pursuit. Though the drives and deterrents might be related to various parts of the taxitant's body, including the mind, you will agree that the barrel itself - the site where the balancing occurs, if it occurs - is in the taxitant's mind.

Suppose now we wish to charge another person, call her the originant, with determining the taxitant's decision to engage in a pursuit. If we are honest, wishing to relate the originant's liability to reality, we must find two conditions in the situation. First we must find that **in the absence of the originant** the water in the barrel would not reach sufficient height to induce the taxitant's act - we must find that the taxitant would not initiate the act without the originant's input. Second, we may not charge the originant with determining the taxitant's act unless her influence raises the water to the critical level.

The critical level? We can identify it only thus; the taxitant actually makes the loading. No other test will suffice. Law recognizes no fraud, for instance, unless the taxitant takes the critical step. This, in the traditional format of a cause for fraud, is the element I have called "action under misconception." Under the common law there is no cause known as "intent to defraud".

What a judge or jury must see then, if they are asked to charge a person with liability for resulting harm, is a barrel - the plaintiff's mind - in which, in the absence of the originant, the water would not have risen high enough to trigger the valve, and they must see the originant opening the faucet handle wider, or plugging the holes at the bottom of the barrel, enhancing the attractions or minimizing the detractions of the project, causing the water to rise to the critical point.

This is not to say that an eager taxitant herself was not busily enhancing the attractions and minimizing the deterrents of the undertaking. It is to say that despite her entire personal contribution to the water level she would have remained in neutral gear. Without the originant's contribution she never would have shifted into forward drive. These are not matters of principle, you see, but matters of proof calling for the utmost skill of the barrister and his researchers. The principle is that if the taxitant can put herself into motion without a contribution from the originant, we cannot charge the originant with determining the taxitant's transformation from projecter to pursuer.

Have you noticed that once again we have run into the topic of channeling, the originant channeling the taxitant into a pursuit. The parable of the barrel is easily adapted to the mechanism of slavery. Apparently there are two broad mechanisms of channeling. In slavery we dealt with contra-Omega situations - repulsion channeling. Now we are dealing with Omega drives - attraction channeling. In attraction channeling, the originant brings the attraction-repulsion ratio of a project in a taxitant's mind to the critical point where the attraction prevails. It is this that I mean when I say that the originant plays a determining role in the taxitant's decision to undertake the project.

For the next step of the analysis, let me fabricate a situation in which, for the sake of simplicity, the repulsion aspects are negligible, the originant contributing an attractive element to the project. A beautiful woman reclines in a bathing suit on the beach of a river island not far from the river bank, hoping a certain man will see her and swim out to her. And she has just observed an alligator sliding into the waters of the intervening channel.

If harm comes to the man, and if this was her intention, we see all the elements of a trap. She has used the kinestatic drive of the victim as an element of the trap. The function of bait, this, using the prey's Omega to induce him into the fatal step. Knowing something of his mind, or of men's minds in general, she can expect a positive response in a large number of instances.

In such a case where (a) the taxitant was harmed as a result of his own act, and (b) the determining act of the woman functioned through the mind of the taxitant, and (c) she used him - she intended that he respond thus to her determining act, we have an undoubted case of injury. She used him without his permission. It is trespass with resulting harm, and this spells damage.

But what if the woman meant merely to attract him for social purposes. Interested in a personal relation pursuit, she had no mind for alligators. In attempting to attract him she was using him, but for this sort of use she had his full permission. He fully intended to use her in much the same way. Nevertheless the alligator was there and the man was harmed.

We are tiptoeing upon a quivering tightwire. A person can injure another unintentionally. The loud music from our neighbor's yard is not an intentional nuisance, and the railway people in **Palsgraf** did not intend to hurt Helen Palsgraf. They weren't even aware of the "alligator" wrapped in the bundle of newspaper under the boarding passenger's arm. Yet I did not release them from liability. The difference of course is that they did not act through her mind. In fact Helen Palsgraf's role in the accident was purely passive. Nevertheless, in the case of the sociable woman on the river island, her action has an effect on the man's mind, with harmful results. Is she or is she not liable for damages?

To show how close we are to falling from the tightwire, let me bring into focus a slightly different illustration. Instead of an attractive woman on a beach, I now depict for you an attractive man wishing to seduce a pretty girl, and succeeding; and in their intimacy transmitting a venereal disease. Is it damage? It is if he injured her.

I have been plaguing you for two chapters with the question of injury in this subclass of cases. This is the class, remember, where the taxitant has got herself hurt, and wants to blame another person for the harm. In only one instance, the case of the woman wishing a certain gentleman chewed by an alligator, have we identified the mechanism of the injury; trespass; the unauthorized use of a person's mind.

But now we are in the rarefied region where the harm is not intentional. Use of the taxitant's mind by the seducer is involved, but it isn't trespass; the seducer has the taxitant's permission, and the only other mechanism of injury is nuisance. Can we analyze some of these cases from the vantage point of nuisance?

In **Palsgraf** the ignition of the fireworks powered a functional sequence spelling nuisance in Helen Palsgraf's space. She was pelted with panic-stricken people and finally a heavy platform scale. And do you see that if this sort of occurrence kept happening in Helen's space, whenever she waited for a train, even if no harm resulted, she could obtain a court order restraining the railroad people in this sub-pursuit - this business of helping people board who are carrying mysterious bundles? She would have grounds for complaint.

Now in the case in which the bathing beauty is interested socially in the young man, and he in her, her effect is upon his mind but is he complaining? No; he enjoys it. True, he encounters danger as a result, but nuisance is not abroad. In the other case, when he was malevolently lured into alligator-laden waters, admittedly he was enjoying it just as much; he just wasn't aware of the pursuit in which he was being used. Trespass can occur without the knowledge of an owner, but nevertheless he has grounds for complaint.

Shall we accept therefore that the sociable girl in the bathing suit, the man with syphilis, the hostess not warning her guest about the fragile hammock, are not liable for resulting harm; that there was no injury; no trespass; no nuisance? Well, we are haunted with a persistent thought: if the sociable girl knew that alligators were about, if the man knew he had syphilis, if the hostess knew her hammock was frail, should they not have warned their invitees? Ah - should; should not! The affirmative duty. The duty of the fiduciary! And now we have come to the exact point in the narrative when we can appreciate the brilliant invention of the fiduciary device.

The fiduciary device is based upon a very real mechanism, the fiduciary effect. Let me describe the fiduciary effect. An effect that a person has on another person, it obeys the natural laws governing human beings, and it is precisely the effect of a drug. If when you are evaluating Hangman's Hill, reading the fine print of the sales agreement, the vendor puts a drug in your coffee, numbing your ability to think clearly, reducing your inhibitions, you will have grounds for complaint. Putting into your coffee a foreign substance with strange effects comes under the category of nuisance.

Conversely if the drug has the effect of making you see things more clearly and acting more intelligently, you might ask the vendor to administer it, and this encompasses the idea of the fiduciary role. And what is the effect of even the honorable fiduciary? The fiduciary effect is to numb the precautions of a taxitant, making her feel safe in undertaking a project. What the taxitant does not know, the fiduciary knows.

But not wishing to introduce fictions, I must restrict this concept to a real phenomenon. So I ask, what are the circumstances that generate the fiduciary effect; what are the circumstances under which an originant truly gains the position of fiduciary in a taxitant's mind. For only under these circumstances can a government place the fiduciary burden on the originant. The circumstances I propose are these:

First, before we can charge a person with the fiduciary burden, we must see the taxitant facing a particular kind of situation - the taxitant situation - and second we must see existing between taxitant and originant a certain personal relationship - the fiduciary relationship.

The taxitant situation will be distinguished by the following three characteristics:

(1) She is pondering a project space in which she is not wholly knowledgeable. She might think she is but she isn't.

(2) In the course of pursuing the project she will take an irreversible step - she will sign a contract, step on a trap door, her dress will touch smouldering ashes, or she will turn a faulty faucet handle. She will take a step that cannot be retracted without some kind of loss. To put it in function language, the taxitant will execute an action powering an irreversible function. There is no reason to introduce the fiduciary burden into a situation in which the taxitant's circumstances at the end of her pursuit can be effortlessly translated back to her former circumstance.

(3) She will not take the step without an inducement by another person.

You are not unacquainted with the irreversible aspect of the taxitant situation. It happens to be the preeminent feature of a trap. If you think about it, a trap is a functional device that (1) is activated by an act of the taxitant, (2) involves an irreversible translation, and (3) involves some sort of inducement relied upon and often devised by the trap-setter.

We can go further if we wish to be ruthlessly general, and I think we should be. We will recognize that each step in life is a step into a trap. Time is irreversible. If Dave safaries in Africa on his summer vacation, he cannot climb Mt. McKinley in Alaska. If Beth attends Sweetbriar in the fall, it will be difficult for her to attend Vassar as well. If Martha accepts a job with Dow, she must decline DuPont's offer. And Julia can divorce her prince, but she cannot go back to the eve of her wedding day.

Given the dimension of time, each step in life shuts the door on a step one might have taken, and one must take the next step from one's new position, not the old. Fortunately most of our steps produce acceptable results. Life's traps aren't all bad. Thus though a fiduciary situation points toward a taxitant trap, it is not necessarily a harmful one. In using the word trap in this context, I simply mean that your fiduciary, if you have one, is a guardian angel - at least you hope so - under whose watchful eye you feel assured. The trap you are about to enter, you believe, is safe.

That is the taxitant situation, given a fiduciary, and now I direct your attention to the characteristics of a true fiduciary relationship. They are five in number:

(1) The originant claims to have specific knowledge of a function space in a project that the taxitant is considering. It is a function space in which the taxitant is ill-acquainted, and the originant's fiduciary duty will pertain only to the knowledge he claims to have. For example, if you have purchased a fertile island in the south Pacific, and a consulting biologist tells you it has a perfect soil and climate for growing a certain delectable tropical fruit, you can sue him for your losses if his information proves wrong. But (a) you can't sue him if your crop is destroyed by a hurricane, and you yourself knew that the island was subject to destructive hurricanes. And (b) you can't sue him if after producing tons of beautiful fruit you discover that the cost of shipping them to market will swamp you in red ink. He claimed to know only the botanical aspects of the crop, not the economics. The fiduciary responsibility lies only in his specific claims of knowledge in a function space coinciding with a function space in which the taxitant is poorly informed.

(2) The originant assumes a supportive pose relative to the taxitant's welfare. Holonistic justice cannot place the fiduciary burden on a person who obviously shows no interest in the taxitant's welfare. A taxitant himself will feel no security in such a person's advice, and for the government to dub such a person fiduciary, finding him liable for resulting harm, would be to legalize a delusion. For a taxitant to follow such a person's advice indicates that the taxitant was looking for every excuse to do what he had already decided to do, and we cannot conclude that this surrogate fiduciary, dragged in by the heels, actually determined the taxitant's decision.

It is different with the licensed practitioner, the professional consultant. Retained by the taxitant, he may act supportive or take the pose of misanthrope, it makes no difference. He is placed under the fiduciary burden. Even the professional practitioner retained by an interest adverse to the taxitant must answer the taxitant's questions fully and truthfully. Though he need not lay his full knowledge unasked before the taxitant, he will have to answer as a fiduciary if the taxitant asks such a question as, "Are there any aspects of this undertaking that might deter me from engaging in it?" As in the case of a manufacturer putting a product on the market, the common law presumes supportiveness in the professional.

(3) The taxitant believes the originant's claims of knowledge and pose of supportiveness. If a taxitant lacks faith in the originant, we can't charge the originant with determining the taxitant's decision.

(4) The originant sees no indication that the taxitant absolutely will not undertake the project. Other than by this double negative, I know no way to make this point sufficiently strict. If in casual conversation, a taxitant tries to extract information from a person - even from a recognized authority - and pretends to have no interest in using this information, we cannot realistically view this resource person as a fiduciary. If toward you I have acted in a supportive manner, claiming special knowledge of a function space, and if there is a chance you might be poorly informed as to the space, and a chance you might rely on my supportiveness and my claim of knowledge, and a chance you might undertake the project, then I have been given an opportunity to recognize that I might determine your decision. If I am a person of integrity, I will feel a compulsion to warn you of hazards or negative features I know to exist in the function space. On the other hand, if I know you cannot possibly undertake the project, or if you tell me your interest is purely academic I, though a person of integrity, will feel no compulsion from a purely supportive standpoint to go into the details. The situation being placed on a chatty basis, not fiducial, there is no reason to suppose that what I say or neglect to say will affect your welfare one way or the other.

(5) The originant has no sound basis for believing the taxitant is as well informed as the originant about function space F. Space F might be the entire space of the project or a subset of it. It is obvious that if the originant thinks the taxitant is well informed about space F, he will not feel constrained to bring up matters redundant or repetitious to the taxitant.

All in all, then, when we focus attention on the fiduciary relationship, we see a wholly natural human relationship. It is a functioning thing, absolutely material, and its legal counterpart should be no less.

Here in a capsule are the five characteristics of a true fiduciary relationship:
(1) The originant claims knowledge regarding a specific function space F in which the taxitant is poorly informed.
(2) The originant poses as supportive toward the taxitant.
(3) The taxitant believes the originant's claims and poses.
(4) The originant understands there is a real possibility, however remote, that the taxitant might engage function space F.
(5) The originant has no basis for thinking the taxitant is as well informed as the originant about space F.

Now that I have established the characteristics of a fiduciary situation, how are they applied to a case?

Considering the outright falsehood, "The hammock is as sound as

Gibralter," we see all the characteristics of a taxitant situation and a fiduciary relationship. The failure of a hammock under human load precipitates an irreversible translation; so in pondering his hammock project, the guest faces a trap with unknown functioning. In this situation, (1) the hostess asserts reassuring information about the very function space that worries the guest, and (2) surely, unless there is evidence to the contrary, she is supportive of his welfare, and (3) he has faith in her, and (4) there is a possibility he will try to use the hammock, and (5) she has no reason to believe he knows about the hammock's weakness.

Given this we can conclude that her actions have a material effect. In fact we can conclude that they determine her guest's decision to use the hammock. These are actions affecting his mind; actions with an effect; against which understandably he can complain; at least when he understands what has actually transpired and, notice, I have now depicted for you a material mechanism of injury.

We see here the effect of a fiduciary on the mind of a taxitant, and it is the fiduciary relationship that makes it work. It is a drugging effect; the guest starts to load the hammock with his body before testing it as strenuously as he otherwise might. This drugging effect has overbalanced the attraction-deterrent ratio of the hammock project in his mind. He has relied on her assurances and poses. He has felt safe in engaging the function space of the hammock. All in all his hostess has distorted his entitled project space.

This is nuisance, and now you see how brilliant is the concept of the fiduciary relationship. It is this that materializes the whole sequence of events. It is this that materializes the injury. Without the fiduciary relationship, the words of the hostess would have no effect on his mind. If he tried to use the hammock in the absence of any one of the essential characteristics of the fiduciary relationship - (1) hostess's claim of knowledge in function space F, (2) hostess's pose of supportiveness, (3) guest's belief in hostess's assurance and pose, (4) no indication that guest would absolutely not load himself into hammock, (5) guest's obvious ignorance of space F - we could not blame her with determining his decision. There would have been no misconception in his project space attributable to her. No injury.

Now we must take the ultimate step, if we can. We must find the "inviter" liable for her non-action - her "neglect of duty". I mean the hostess who doesn't warn, the alluring girl on river island, the infected seducer. And we still have not solved the case of boy falling from contractor's scaffold, or that of girl's dress catching fire from hot embers on empty lot.

CHAPTER 51

LIABILITY FOR NON-ACTS
ATTRACTION CHANNELING OF CHILDREN
A CLOSING STATEMENT ON FIDUCIARIES
AN OUTLINE OF DAMAGE-RELATED INJURY

In gaining the next level of understanding in this perplexing field, several cases must be juggled together in a consistent framework - the case of the bathing beauty, the case of the handsome seducer with syphilis, and the case of the hostess with the cracked faucet handle. In transition we can profitably linger with the hostess and the hammock - not the case where she lied outright, but where knowing the danger, she held her tongue and watched the guest amble toward the dangerous function space, and failed to warn. And, alas, we still have not resolved the cases of the contractor's scaffold and the little girl whose dress caught fire.

In all these cases, in finding the coactor liable or not liable, we could propose convincing arguments on both sides, else toss a coin. Who is the coactor? She is the person we associate with the harm we have brought on ourselves, the person we are blaming. The defendant. She might be the originant, but only if she truly contributed to the harm, and until we are certain, perhaps the term coactor is better than defendant or originant. As I say, even though we find the coactor not liable - the bathing beauty, the seducer, the hostess, the contractor, the owner of the empty lot - yet each of us will be plagued by an echoing thought. What if the coactor knew about the danger. Should she not have warned the taxitant. That "should"! In the cases at hand, it is the signal of the non-contractual, unlicensed, unprofessional, uncomprehensible affirm-ative duty, definitely a signal of the non-contractual, unlicensed, unprofessional, probably uncomprehending person on whom a capricious tort has frequently placed the fiduciary mantle.

Yet none of these situations exhibited the prime characteristic of the fiduciary relationship. In not one of the cases did the coactor say to the victim of the incident, "I have special knowledge of this particular function space and I can assure you of your safety in undertaking the project you are contemplating." The girl in the bathing suit did not say, "No, there are no alligators in the channel," nor claim to know anything about alligators. The handsome man did not say, "No, I do not have syphilis," nor did he pretend expertise in the subject. As for Miss Christian, we stipulate that she did not bring up the topic of faucet handles. And the out-of-doors hostess silently watched her guest get closer and closer to the hammock.

In the true fiduciary situation, the coactor has professed special knowledge of a project space shadowy to the taxitant. Not leaning on that crutch, "she should have told me about the danger," one simply says, "She claimed she knew all about function space F. She had no reason to believe I was well informed about space F. She had no reason to think I would not try to engage space F. She certainly seemed supportive and gave me every reason to believe I could rely on her support and the accuracy of her information. In sum, her actions made me believe I could pursue the project safely, so I undertook it."

In the outright falsehood - "There's gold on Hangman's Hill," given the fiduciary relationship, we see a specific distortion of a project space. But this is not the fundamental mechanism in which we are interested. We are interested in the acts of the coactor that induce the trust of the taxitant, producing the sedative effect on the taxitant's mind. And these acts, this effect, form the basis of the taxitant's complaint. If the originant intended the effect, we are witnessing trespass; the originant is using the taxitant's capacity to trust. And if the originant is merely a braggard with a talent for instilling trust, we have nuisance. His poses have the same anesthetic effect as the wilful defrauder, and the taxitant has cause for court action.

So, one who has created the fiduciary effect might remain silent about the dangers of project space F. But though a non-act cannot perpetrate injury, she is still on the hook. Silence merely furnishes no antidote against the fiduciary effect, and it is the perpetration of the fiduciary effect against which the taxitant complains. The fiduciary effect then is not the distortion of project space F, but an effect upon the taxitant's mind, making him less attentive, dulling his taste buds, putting his antennae to sleep - in general making him less a taxitant in the project space of his estate, where his mind ranks high as subject matter, and his potential and project effectiveness are at stake. The fiduciary effect in this manner determines the taxitant's decision to act in project space F, diminishing the contra-Omega aspects of the project, allowing the Omega drive of the taxitant to take charge, narrowing his project effectiveness in his estate as a whole, and this is the injury. It is not the fiduciary lie or the fiduciary silence against which the taxitant complains. It is the fiduciary pose of knowledge and supportiveness that has had the fatal effect in the mind, determining the critical water level in the mind-barrel of the taxitant. Is the fiduciary effect necessarily nuisance? No, and neither is the smell from the hog barn. But it is if the taxitant complains!

Where the courts have got into trouble is in placing the fiduciary burden on a coactor who has not professed trustworthiness. This is the situation in each case that we now face. In **Rowland v. Christian**, the California court in effect decreed that a hostess is a fiduciary. If she knows of a danger that her guest might engage, she must warn him. If she does not, she will be liable for the harm that results.

It would seem logical that a court reach this conclusion to be consistent with **Helguera v. Cirone**. The contractor Cirone, probably never seeing Helguera until they met in court, did not promise the boy that the platform would be safe, nor induce trust in the boy. In no consistent way could a court find Cirone liable, particularly when the boy was trespassing, and find Miss Christian not liable, particularly when she had invited Mr. Rowland into her home? Yet there was no justification for the court's placing the fiduciary burden on Cirone, and perhaps there was a plausible argument for calling Miss Christian a fiduciary. She had invited Rowland to her home, a friendly gesture, and perhaps a guest can assume that his host knows all the hazardous functionings of her household equipment. Therefore if Cirone is liable, Miss Christian must be found liable.

Both cases are weak when viewed as taxitant-hesitant situations. True, the boy in facing the scaffold and the man in facing the water faucet both ponder function spaces in which they are not wholly knowledgeable, and they will both get hurt as a result. But it is not immediately clear that their crucial actions were taken in a context of reliance on contractor and hostess, determining their decisions to act.

On the part of Mr. Rowland the court might surmise assurance, given the absence of warning, that the faucet was safe. But this cannot be claimed in John Helguera's case. He needed no assurance for climbing the scaffold. In fact he would probably persist in his adventure in the face of considerable effort to dissuade him.

There were, however, in both situations, two important characteristics of a fiduciary relationship: (a) the coactors - Miss Christian and contractor Cirone - had no reason for believing their respective taxitants would bypass the dangerous function spaces and (b) they had no reason to believe that the taxitants would recognize the dangers in those function spaces. What we can be certain of is that both projects - climbing the scaffold and washing the hands - held sufficient attraction for the taxitants, and what we must discover is whether the coactors determined the taxitant's decisions to take the critical steps. We are back to the question of motivation and determination of decision.

Finally and fundamentally we are facing two questions. First, in determining a person's decision to act, are there mechanisms of attraction channeling other than the fiduciary effect. Is it sufficient, for instance, in the case of a boy, merely to place within his range a climbing challenge? Is its attraction so irresistable that it by itself will determine his decision? If so, then indeed a contractor's pursuit can leak out of his space and have an effect in another person's space. The second question is this, framed for a specific case but with general applications, is it justifiable under the common law to place the fiduciary burden on a hostess?

How can one intentionally induce a taxitant to act? For answer let us look more closely at the hostess who, for fun, would like to see her guest fall through the bottom of the hammock. Though not originating in malevolence, her wish is his falling, and her strategy is that of a fisherman. As all experienced anglers know, not all baits attract all fish at all times, but occasionally some baits catch fish. A trapping device, as in a baited hook and string, does not have to be 100 percent effective to be called a trap. Nor does the scheme of a person have to be 100 percent effective to be called a scheme. Many of our most imaginative schemers do not depend on 100 percent success. They depend on the odds.

Realizing that the hammock might not attract him, but it might; that he might test it before using it, and he might not, that he might climb in and might not; but that if he does, the result will be fun - the hostess merely leaves the hammock within his effective range, and let's nature take its course.

Now look what we have. In the alternate case, he asking if the hammock was safe and she answering in the affirmative, we saw the fiduciary situation completed. Trust was established, and she used not only his attraction for the hammock but his trust. We could say definitely that she determined his decision to use the hammock. It was an abuse of the fiduciary relationship.

But now where she merely watches him move closer and closer to the hammock, can we really say that his trust in her determines his action? An assumption that it might be a factor is an assumption that might be delusory. Just as plausible is a contention that he was attracted by the hammock, and had no hesitance in using it.

Nevertheless, evidence that she wished the accident to occur, will render her liable. By putting the hammock up, or deliberately not taking it down, she used the odds to channel him into the trap. She determined his decision on the basis of probability. She bet that some men attracted by hammocks will climb in without testing them. She used his capacity to be attracted as a means of gaining her objective, as effective a functional sequence as using a sun-heated rock to fry an egg.

Thus in analyzing the most puzzling cases in this field, we can eliminate from study every case in which the coactor intends and plans that the taxitant makes the very step that powers the irreversible translation. In every instance we will find that the coactor has used the taxitant without his permission. Taxitant was hesitant or not, and only when the taxitant is hesitant does the fiduciary effect come into play. In practice, of course, gathering the evidence of intent is what a good attorney and his agents get paid for.

We have become familiar with another kind of determination, repulsion channeling. A striking contrast to the fiduciary effect and attraction channeling, it does not fit the present search.

A court might hear a case of borderline determination, the young man on the river shore wishing to socialize with the girl on the island, but hesitating. He has heard of alligators in these waters. Seeing his hesitance, she makes an impatient and disdainful beckon with her full arm. If he jumps in and gets hurt, is she liable? Has she determined his decision?

In daring him to gamble away his own safety, she has freed herself of all fiduciary bonds. A wave of an arm cannot express both a dare and supportiveness. Her gesture has entangled him in a contra-Omega situation; he must weigh the swimming project against a project with great appeal - personal relations - the status drive. The question is, is it action-inducing; is it determining?

This I think is not a decision in principle or conjecture, not a matter of saying he should have resisted her suggestion. It is a matter of finding the facts. Would he have jumped in without her beckon? Was he naturally reckless? Was he suggestion-prone?

If she was mindful of the danger and he ignorant, we would have a case of reckless trespass. She would be using his attraction to her merely to satisfy her desire for company. But where the young man recognizes the danger and is harmed, and the case comes to trial, he will as a plaintiff be exposed to an embarrassing probe by the opposing attorney. Is he attracted to pretty girls? Well, most young men will admit that. But does he so dearly wish to establish a status of bravado that he will jump into alligator-infested waters?

If he is mentally incompetent, a jury will listen sympathetically as his guardian describes how susceptible he is to suggestion. But if as a mentally competent young man he himself pleads this susceptibility, the jury will see two other ways of looking at it. First, he is trying to get off the hook by hanging the young woman on it. Or second, a young man who exhibits recklessness is indeed reckless, and, though he might have hesitated at first, he might in the end have jumped in without any encouragement from her.

If that is not enough strain on a plaintiff, there is more. A young man with real bravado will wish to claim his bravado as his very own, not a weakness of will under the watching eyes of a girl. He will take his medicine as he took the risk, and I'm saying that many cases of this sort will never appear in court. Of those that appear, a judge or jury will exert an unusual stretch of imagination to believe that a coactor determined the taxitant's action.

But what if the girl reclines on the beach, a conscious attraction for the young man. Mindful of the risk; mindful of the young man's ignorance of the danger; making no sign of invitation; can she be held liable? Can the government place her under a common good service? "If you know of a danger, you must warn the person. You have a duty to warn him. If you don't, I will hold you liable for resulting harm." Can the government place the fiduciary burden on a person when (a) she has made no pretense of specific knowledge and (b) she has made no pose of friendliness and support? Can the law make every person her brother's keeper?

Such a precept would say that every person is entitled to the use of every other person's originancy when:

(a) she has knowledge of a specific function space F, and a knowledge of danger in that space;
(b) it comes to her attention that a taxitant might engage space F;
(c) she has no reason to think that the taxitant is aware of the danger.

Instituting such a precept will of course breathe new life into the negligence theory, promoting millions of cases for the legal profession and making shambles of legal consistency. Over in this courtroom, in a case of fraud, a defendant will be found not liable for fraud. The plaintiff's reliance was not justifiable. Across the hall, in a case of "negligence", a defendant will be found liable for damages on a legal fiction called "affirmative duty", yet the plaintiff had no excuse, no reason in fact, for relying on her. More to this presently.

We face but two cases, **Rowland v. Christian**, and **Helguera v. Cirone**; the cracked faucet and the contractor's scaffold. The case of the girl's dress catching fire was basically identical to **Helguera**, though the California court system saw fit to decide them oppositely. As for the handsome seducer with syphilis, I will leave that case to you.

I have earlier said that justice, to be thoroughly understood, must be viewed from the vantage point of a ruler, intelligent justice from the vantage point of an intelligent ruler. In resolving **Rowland**, in which the court substantially placed a fiduciary burden on the hostess, one might attempt to reach that supreme vantage point.

Analogous to the position of ruler is general of the army or, in the civilian field, the president of the modern corporate conglomerate. You are such a president, holding court in your corporate headquarters. Assembled are your vice-presidents - lingerie, steel, electronics, hamburgers, and international operations.

Minkowski of steel has made an enormous blunder, undertaking a project unaware that function space F was tricky, and incurring a huge financial loss. Realizing that project space F was unclear to him, but deciding that success demanded a full-scale entrance and escalation in the field, he took the risk. Now he's under your presidential microscope.

"I asked all the other v.p.'s," he says. "And nobody discouraged me. "Join the crowd," said Henegan (lingerie). "We all take chances." Said Munger (hamburgers), "You've got to be bold." Electronics said, "You're good, and you are up to any problem you run into." And international operations said, "You've got the best metallurgical crew in the business."

As president, you must say to Minkowski, "Minkowski, that doesn't take the monkey off your shoulders. What they said didn't change the actual picture you had of the project." This you know; that firing Minkowski is not necessarily the solution. A good man fired is a good man for the competition to hire. Your job is the education of good men, and, though as president of a corporation, you don't judge the case from the standpoint of the common good - the common good of the whole United States - nevertheless the common good of each man in the office is at stake.

"I think," you say, "you were all reckless to encourage a man as you encouraged Minkowski. I can imagine some of you enjoying the prospect of seeing him get hit by lightning. But it has hurt the company, and it will reflect on me. And though I am letting you get away with it this time, I am giving you advance notice I won't let you get away with it again. As for you, Minkowski, I think perhaps you made the right decision though the project flopped. However I hope the soft soap these fellows smeared on you did not influence your decision. That kind of vulnerability we don't need."

Later a stupefying piece of information comes to your attention. Henegan of lingerie had previously, in casual conversation on a Riviera beach, learned of the very features of function space F that proved fatal to Minkowski's project. He knew of them when Minkowski had consulted with him. He knew of them when he had encouraged Minkowski to plunge in. Calling Henegan into your office, you storm, "What got into you anyhow? Did you want Minkowski to fail? Did you want me to fail? Did you want the company to take a loss? You seem supportive. You seem to be one of the bunch. Are you a spy for somebody or did you let your own ambition get on top?"

"No," says Henegan, "I was just stupid. The information just did not recur to me at the time."

With this preparation, I must begin to resolve that most difficult of cases, the one typified by **Rowland v. Christian**. What I will demonstrate is that we cannot hold the hostess liable, first dealing with a most telling argument against my position. It derives from the very mechanism of nuisance I have so carefully elucidated.

Let me quickly pose a simple example. A Saturday shopper, having parked her car on a hill, walks down to Main Street, and for one of many possible reasons the car rolls down the hill, crashing into a house. By her actions, the woman has exposed her car to the forces of gravity. Through this contribution to a functional sequence, her project has leaked into the entitled space of another person and had an effect. As you have learned, the accident is not the result of her negligence, it is the result of her actions.

Now quickly look at the case in which Nancy Christian has invited James Rowland to dinner. This has channeled him into a set of project spaces, and there is a good chance that he will at some time wish to wash his hands. It is as natural as gravity. Here is a function space containing a potentially dangerous function and we will stipulate that the faucet gives no hint of the danger. Is this any different than parking a car on a hill? Has not Miss Christian channeled him into this dangerous function space? Isn't she responsible for resulting harm? Well, there is a difference between the two cases.

In the instance of the car crashing into the house, the owner of the house was passive in the event, nor had she welcomed the car owner into her space. But in **Rowland v. Christian**, the project of coming to dinner was as much James Rowland's project as Miss Christian's. Yes, she was for him an attraction, but he's an attraction for her as well, channeling her into the dinner date as much as she channeled him. On this occasion they agreed to eat at her residence. Say if you like that her project leaked into his space, but equally well we can say that his project leaked into his own space.

So, for a cause in **Rowland**, I have eliminated the simplest mechanism of nuisance. Nevertheless (you protest) she knew the faucet was dangerous, and surely she should have warned him. You see, we have eliminated the factor of her being the invitor, and we are simply back to affirmative duty. And what are the characteristics of the situation?

(a) She knows about a specific function space F and its potential danger (we will stipulate this).

(b) She knows that Rowland might engage function F.

(c) She has no reason to believe that Rowland is aware of the danger, and

(d) She has given every appearance of being supportive of Rowland!

Given all this a person can well ask, "Why on earth did she not tell him about the danger," and there is but one answer; - her mind was not working as well as we might wish.

This is the very reason Henegan gave for his failure to tell Minkowski of the joker in his steel project, and in the corporate context Henegan will be fired. A professional, paid handsomely to act as a professional, his forgetfulness has cost the company millions.

But can such high level performance be required in the sphere of unprofessional personal relations? Can a court of law treat a hostess as the president of a corporation treats a vice-president? "She was his friend!" you exclaim. "She should have told him." Ah. But don't you have a dear friend, perhaps the dearest of all, whom you can't count on? She has forgotten to tell you things and you have lost money, or status, or time as a result?

Our difficulty lies in semantics and our solution will lie in definition. Friendly. Supportive. These are the words I have used. Justifiable reliance, the phrase in practice. "If you blame another for harm resulting from your own act, claiming to have relied on her," says the common law, "I will insist that your reliance was justifiable." And now we must inquire into the reason for this insistence.

Let me abandon the words friendly and supportive and turn to the words faithful and trustworthy, and there is a benefit in treating them not as synonyms but as denoting two different sets of human traits.

King Arthur takes to the wars old Fletcher, for years the faithful guard at Arthur's bedroom door. Faithful means never deserting or betraying Arthur; always informing him of danger sensed. Though not intelligent as Arthur, he is an extension of Arthur.

But will Arthur use Fletcher as a spy behind enemy lines? Young Ross is a quicker wit, more resourceful in a tight spot, with the intelligence needed to evaluate the enemy's machinery of war, and as faithful as Fletcher.

A person must have both faithfulness and intelligence to justify your trusting her with certain duties. Two men can be equally faithful but not equally trustworthy. At least we need these separate concepts and this is the way I will use these words. Faithful is or faithful isn't. It is characteristic of a given person, or not. But intelligence varies in degree among persons, even from time to time in the same person, hence trustworthiness varies, and, since intelligence is never perfect, trustworthiness is never perfect. For a given task, King Arthur tries to find faithful retainers, choosing those with the intelligence specific to the task.

If in reporting to Arthur, Ross errs in observation or conclusion, Arthur might next time send another person. But he will not punish Ross, not for a failure in intelligence. This is analogous to your firing vice-president Henegan. Not retributional, the firing merely replaces Henegan with someone whose mind will not go blank at critical moments. Only for a betrayal of faith will Arthur take punitive measures against Ross. Such relations between superior and subordinate are a mark of intelligent control.

The pose of the fiduciary is trustworthiness - not just faithfulness, but also intelligence in function space F. Placing a fiduciary burden on people not projecting trustworthiness by pose or profession is unrealistic on the part of both taxitant and government. In **Rowland v. Christian** we do not see a breach of faith but a breakdown in intelligence, and you can't punish a person for that. To lay on every person an absolute affirmative duty to be smart and remembering, to be the eyes and ears and intelligence for someone about to make a loading under her own volition, to be the surrogate taxitant for a taxitant, is to place too great a burden on the servant. To find her liable merely because she has been friendly is paramount to teaching her to be not friendly.

Remember, in discussing the liability of this person, we are not observing a person who has done something. Here is a someone who has done nothing, yet we wish to blame her for harm we have precipitated on ourselves by our own act in our own project. We wish to find her liable because she has been friendly. We are not talking about the person who has posed as an expert in the project space we are about to undertake, somehow assuring us we may relax and drift comfortably under his guidance. This "expert" has by his pose put a sleeping pill in our soup, playing havoc with our project space. And if harm results, he should pay. But in our hostess, I can find no act that I can call injury; no invasion of my property; and without a finding of injury, I cannot find damage.

Superficially at variance with my stance on nuisance. In nuisance, if harm has resulted, the nuisancer pays. It is a training program, teaching people to anticipate harm-causing sequences. If a person is about to engage a function space in which he is not fully knowledgeable, he will be liable for harm that results. But see; - he is about to act. He is about to set a causal chain in motion. And see how consistent this is with **Rowland v. Christian**? Rowland is about to turn the faucet handle. It is he who will set the causal chain in motion. If he will be liable for harmful results to others, why should he not be liable for harmful results to himself.

We finally come to **Helguera v. Cirone**, a case in which one can find no reason for placing the fiduciary burden on contractor Joseph Cirone. At no time has he assumed the fiduciary pose. He did not tell young Helguera, "Johnny, I know all about that scaffold. It is as safe as your sand box." As to the scaffold, we cannot even burden him with strict products liability. He did not try to sell it to anyone, nor invite the general public to use it. To pin a fiduciary label on him is to fabricate a status with no basis in reality.

In fact, I can find no way in which he has injured John Helguera. John is trespassing. To say Cirone is liable because he attracted John to trespass is to say that the jeweler attracts the thief to steal. I will indeed find Cirone liable for the harm to John Helguera, but let me show first that the contractor can in no way injure John.

Let us examine the various ways in which Cirone can injure John. Since Cirone is not using John for any purpose, we can eliminate trespass, and the injury, if any, will be through nuisance. Nuisance means that Cirone's project has leaked into John's entitled project space with an effect. But to the contrary, Cirone has provided a project space for John, and John likes it! And what is John's project in this space? To explore! To gain new experiences. To climb new heights. Perhaps to taste excitement and danger, and he got everything he was looking for. Nor did Cirone do anything to distort this space in John's mind. John took it as he found it, and his only difficulty, as with a burglar, was in getting caught. But Cirone in no way injured John Helguera.

However some very important people are complaining - John's parents. Bringing the suit in John's name was a mistake, for John was not injured. If anyone was injured it was John's parents. As John's natural guardians, charged with the welfare of the child, it follows that the project of rearing the child is in their property. It is into their property that the contractor's pursuit has leaked. Placing a scaffold in the play space of a healthy boy is like placing gunpowder in a burning building. The variates and functions and natural powerings clearly spell combustion. This is the injury. Parents finding their children attracted to scaffolds, or attracted to glowing embers, can sue for injunctions that will remedy the nuisance. To have a case, the harm is not essential. It is an added feature. Now, you see, we are pleading nuisance in **Helguera v. Cirone,** a leakage into the parents' entitled project space, diminishing their effective control therein. And there happened to be harm to the prime subject matter of that space, hence damage.

There remains the trial, the finding of materiality. Did Cirone's actions actually determine John Helguera's decision to mount the scaffold. Was this child irresistably drawn to the scaffold as a nail to a magnet, or is there evidence of a wilful nature, opposed to heeding the warning of others, opposed to self-restraint. If the scaffold was not there, would John have found other dare-devil projects to chase. For acts determined by such traits, a ruler cannot blame others. As with the young man diving into alligator territory at the beckon of a girl, this scaffold climber will gradually approach an age when a pleading of pure kinestatic attraction will sound hollow to a jury.

The unstable nature of the platform - the traplike feature - is not essential to the injury. I think parents can successfully seek an injunction if a contractor leaves a perfectly sound scaffold unattended and unbarricaded in their neighborhood. At the same time, with a particular child harmed, we will resist a temptation to query the particular parents about their seriousness in this child-raising project. Did they really pursue it, or is this project space as empty as the marital relationship of Mrs. Dandini? Is there evidence that they are training the boy in caution and in respect for the property of others? Or in the final analysis, is this a child of nature untrained in civilization, not the subject of a government-favored parental project? No, we cannot pursue this line of enquiry. True, the invasion is an invasion of parental property - if it exists. But if it is only a hollow fiction, injury remains. The presumed parental pursuit is nothing less than a commission in a government pursuit. In the default of the parents, the government is the plaintiff in the case.

So the cause of attractive nuisance cannot be discarded. Attractive nuisance reflects a real phenomenon, a mechanism of injury not to be despised in modern theory. But negligence is not an element. The coactor has no affirmative duty to perform - only a common good servitude of restraint. He will be wise to devise his activities in such a way that they will not leak into the entitled project spaces of others.

Before closing this three chapter series on attraction channeling, or coactor determination of a taxitant act, I wish to mention something about application in practice. In eliminating some of the confusion in affirmative duty, I have eliminated a significant number of bread and butter cases for the legal profession. But I have also opened the courtroom door for cases rarely brought to court.

Attraction channeling is part of life, only a small fraction of the instances perpetrate injury. Promoters of huge commercial projects, and people selling vacuum sweepers, and people in love rely precisely on attraction channeling to achieve their objectives, and there is always a trap in it for the taxitant. Investing in a joint venture is a trap, as is signing a sales agreement, and engaging in a loving relationship. They all power irreversible translations. Many joint ventures, many purchases, many marriages will be undertaken to the taxitant's detriment, and the coactor will be the determining factor in the taxitant's crucial step. Will the court listen to a complaint?

Was there malevolent intent? Was there reckless induction? Was there taxitant hesitation and a fiduciary relationship? Was there an irresistable attraction? Was there repulsion channeling? These are the critical questions.

I will mention just one significant result of this line of thought. Has a high school counselor advised a student to go to college, a student who should never be encouraged to go to college? Has a high school art teacher advised art school for a student who should never be so advised. And has time and money been lost and a life harmed as a result? Have these advisors assumed a pose of expertise in their fields of advice, and a pose of supportiveness for the student? Does the student develop trust in her advisor?

Are there television programs and advertisements, press publications and government programs with an effect in the parental project space, and are the parents complaining? Under the guise of freedom of press and progressive theories of child development, are we seeing scaffolds erected, burning embers cunningly introduced in the parental space? I have already discussed this in the chapter on parents, but the mechanism of injury has been more clearly exposed.

Even parents encouraging their children to go to college, and state governments forcing parents to support their children in college, are pursuing projects of attraction channeling (and repulsion channeling) that may result in harm. All of us at times are convincing prattlers, professing knowledge that is nothing more than plausible assumption. We present to our audience a faithful and intelligent, supportive and trustworthy facade, and I wonder if we do not infringe the liberty of young people, warping and twisting the conceptual project spaces of their estates. I wonder if we should not be more restrained in our advice, and be taught a stiff lesson now and then.

In closing this series of chapters, the most complex topic yet covered, I will recapitulate the discussion and organize the conclusions. You will note that the topic did not cover the entire field of injury. Rather it focused on injuries associated with harm, the field usually called tort. Actually since tort connotes wrongdoing, and a great fraction of wrongdoing consists of injury in the absence of harm, and another great fraction of wrongdoing has no remedy at law, I see no reason why the term tort can not be discarded. There is injury and, if there is resulting harm, there is damage.

Early in the discussion of this topic, we found that the mechanisms of harm - harm, not injury - can be grouped into two broad classes, (1) those in which the harmful translation is powered entirely by the coactor, the virtual defendant, and (2) those in which it is powered by the taxitant, the virtual plaintiff; it is she whose own action plunged her down the stairs; it is she who touched her skirt hem to the hot embers; it is he whose towmotor maneuvers triggered the bone-crushing accident. Class 2 furnished the topic for these three chapters. It is this class that has caused us - and our jurists - such travail. This is the class of cases in which a taxitant acts, is harmed as a result, and blames another person.

The following outline of causes includes both classes of cases, not covering all kinds of injury, merely those associated with harm; the territory usually covered under tort. Among other things note that trespass - the unentitled use of a subject - is frequently associated with harm, but the mechanism of harm will probably fall under nuisance. Your neighbor using your horseshoe field without permission (trespass) pitches a horseshoe through your window pane. But he isn't using your window pane. So the harm was not mechanistically associated with trespass. His pursuit leaked into your space, and harm was a result. A case with two separate counts, (1) trespass, and (2) nuisance with resulting harm.

Furthermore the following outline of causes results from my conviction that a person cannot injure and cannot harm another person by doing nothing. If we are inclined to blame person A for harm brought on person B in consequence of B's own act, we must find that:

(1) Person A did something, and
(2) Person A's act determined person B's harm-triggering act, and
(3) Person A's act per se - irrespective of harm - resulted in a material, effective invasion of B's property.

Classes Of Injury Functionally Related To Harm

I. Damage Powered By Defendant:

   A. Trespass.
        Example: Defendant used plaintiff's wrench without
                 permission and broke it while using it.
   B. Nuisance.
        Examples:
             (a) **Palsgraf**: Defendant's project: trainmen helping
                 patron board a moving train. Injury mechanism:
                 trainmen's act triggered a mad rush of fireworks
                 and people into Mrs. Palsgraf's personal tactile
                 space.
             (b) **Jones**: Defendant's project: building a tract of
                 houses for white people only. Injury mechanism:
                 this policy distorts people's minds, these being
                 an entitled project space for the personal
                 relations pursuits of Jones. His project space
                 is an unbiased space, blank except for people's
                 perception of his true image.
             (c) **Helguera**: Defendant's project: placing scaffold
                 at construction site. Injury mechanism: young
                 boy was irresistably attracted to climb
                 scaffold. Thus the defendant's act materially
                 invaded the boy-raising property of the parents.

II. Damage Powered By Plaintiff:

   A. Concealed Distortion of Project Space:

        Through trespass or nuisance, defendant alters subject
        matter of plaintiff's property without plaintiff's
        knowledge. Plaintiff acts under misconception with
        resulting harm.
             Example: Defendant's act: defendant digs a hole in
                      plaintiff's property without telling plaintiff.
                      Plaintiff's act: plaintiff steps into hole at
                      night.

B. Mental Channeling:

1. Intentional: (Trespass; unauthorized use of plaintiff's mind.)
   a) Repulsion channeling (enslavement): Defendant by devising or taking advantage of a contra-Omega situation, and in some instances blocking all escape routes save one preferred by defendant, diminishes plaintiff's potential and freedom within his estate.
      Example: **Hinde v. Pendleton.** By employing false bidder at slave auction, Pendleton used Hinde's response to the human feelings of other persons to force Hinde's bid to exorbitant levels.
   b) Attraction channeling:
      Example: Hostess owning a hammock seemingly sound, but known to her to be ready to collapse, used guest's attraction for the hammock to power the functions providing her with some "innocent" fun.
   c) Fiduciary channeling:
      Example: Possessing true fiduciary status, defendant told plaintiff how to drive to a mountain cabin, deliberately neglecting to inform plaintiff that the timbers of an access bridge were rotten. Injury mechanism: defendant, to gain fiduciary status, used plaintiff's capacity for trust and acted to secure it.

2. Unintentional As To Harm:
   a) Reckless induction without fiduciary pose:
      Example: Given all the elements of a taxitant hesitant situation and a fiduciary relationship except the fiduciary pose of expertise (Chapter 50), the pretty girl on the island, beckoning though aware of alligators, induces the unwary young man to dive into the river. She used his attraction for her in a sociable pursuit, and this had his full permission; it was not trespass. But this action powered a harm-causing sequence in his personal project space. Nuisance with resulting harm.

b) Reckless fiduciary pose: Given the taxitant hesitant
        situation, and pretending more expertise and
        trustworthiness than he possessed, though not
        intending harm, school counselor gave student a
        misconception of college and his future welfare,
        and plaintiff undertook college, incurring large
        debts and gaining no benefits. Though not using
        the student, the counselor's acts generated the
        fiduciary effect. Engaged in a pompous though
        innocent pursuit of counseling, the counselor's
        pursuit leaked into plaintiff's estate with
        resulting harm.

   With this, I have completed all my remarks about the mechanics of
injury.

CHAPTER 52

EMINENT DOMAIN

I will not dwell long on the cause called eminent domain, a government procedure for appropriating a person's particularized property, but I will try to depict the topic in several dimensions. The chief characteristics of the cause are these: (1) The government takes away a person's title to a loading space, doing it whether the person consents or not, transferring the title to itself or someone else, and (2) the government or the new owner pays the person an equivalent for the loss of her space, and (3) theoretically the government has a right to do this only if the transfer promotes the general welfare.

We usually think of eminent domain as a case involving real property - a taking of land in the pursuit of a grand overriding project. Someone wishing to construct a dam wants the land for ponding the water. Or someone wishes to decorate the countryside with a new system of electric power lines and supporting towers. A few years ago a highly publicized case of eminent domain involved the evacuation of a whole community - Poletown - in Detroit, where whole blocks of houses, stores, and churches were torn down, generations of social bonds disrupted, all to clear ground for a new General Motors plant.

But there are subtler cases of eminent domain, a case in point: the deprivation of a householder's right to paint his house the color he wishes, or his right to leave it unpainted. But if we argue that his unsightly house spoils the aesthetics of this lovely neighborhood, we forget two important points. First, the city fathers are not paying him for his loss of title; they do not propose a cause in eminent domain, but erroneously brand the house a nuisance. Second, as a case of zoning restriction it is ex post facto, breaking all the principles of equity, and as a result we have a pure case of slavery - the government forcing a householder to load his own functioning space to please his neighbors' aesthetic tastes. The institution of slavery and the promotion of the general welfare are infinitely incompatible.

Taxation is appropriation - the seizing of property, a deprivation of property, and as long as taxpayers receive an equivalent in terms of the common good, they are pleased. In taxing people, holonistic rulers use them as servants of the common good, and in serving the common good the people merely serve themselves, not servants at all, much less slaves. On the other hand, when the money is spent to provide excessively luxurious surroundings and rich pensions for government personnel, and unproductive junkets to all parts of the world; when the construction of highways and bridges and state universities obviously benefits contractors without advancing the public welfare; and when the budget for the common defense obviously benefits the military-indus-trial complex disproportionately to defense capability; when money seized from workers is used to create self-perpetuating classes of political constituencies and the prodigal indolent, then the sensation of being enslaved permeates the creative and productive masses; the glow of self-satisfied slave-masters warms the favored classes, and no amount of fictitious patriotic hoopla can purge the fetid odor of slavery filling the nostrils. The pure air of the common law has been sucked away, and the rulers, cunning as they believe themselves to be, have deceived themselves. Their treasure has become a moldering carcass, appropriation a tool for greed, the mandates of the preamble have been scorned, and the nation - no matter how fast the dollars are spinning - has become moribund. A possibly irreversible translation.

Taking it a step farther, it seems to me that a dead nation - at least its potentially creative and productive segment - will welcome the peace of a nuclear holocaust. This is the true import of Patrick Henry's, "Give me liberty, or give me death." And having rung the carillon of tolls, I wish to observe another aspect of eminent domain.

Note that a cause in eminent domain is not a cause in injury, and therefore is a cause out of tune with the operations of a judiciary. A plaintiff starting an action in eminent domain does not claim that the defendant has injured him. Rather she wishes title to something not hers, and the entitled person does not wish to surrender the title. The plaintiff is not truly a plaintiff, she is an aggressive intruder, and the defendant is truly a defender, defending her property.

There are, for example, many too many electric power lines scattered across the farm lands, ugly, inconvenient for farm operations, hazardous to airplanes. Duplicating parallel lines, many could have occupied one tract of easement, not three or four. Historically courts have presumed that when a power company claims a power project for the public good it speaks with honest authority. To give the power company credit, we will imagine it believes its own claim, but the court's presumption goes too far. Like our restauranteur Mr. Anthony, wishing to erect his sign on Farmer Brown's weedpatch, each of us can argue plausibly why the world should march to the beat of our favorite project.

My only concern here is to question the propriety of a court being burdened with eminent domain. A court's skill lies in determining injury, and injury is black and white; it exists or it does not exist. But injury is not a factor in eminent domain, and I think a suit in eminent domain more appropriately calls for legislative action, or action by a legislative commission, than for judicial action. True, eminent domain is frequently assigned to the court system by legislatures, hence the court is a legislative commission. But a decision in eminent domain is not a black and white decision. It is quantitative rather than qualitative. In the case of dams and highways and university dormitories and county administration centers, and slaughterhouses, the question of the public good may be highly uncertain, speculative, experimental, and rather risky. A political talent, a feel for mass sentiment, is required as much as a feel for property, and by political talent I do not mean the feel for majority greed; I'm thinking of a more deeply streaming instinct for the common good.

Eminent domain is like appropriation; it is not like trespass or nuisance. Like appropriation, eminent domain must give quid pro quo, but the judiciary is not a bargainer. The legislator is primarily a bargainer - not in the sense of scratch-my-back bargaining, this is not in my mind, but in the sense that if the legislator takes quo from a person, he must return a quid. Though he might deprive a person of property, the process will be improper unless the deprivation enhances the welfare of the deprived. And by enhancement in the case of eminent domain, I do not refer to the reimbursement for the property. I am saying that the project for which the property is confiscated must be in the common interest of every person, including the deprived.

But a suit in eminent domain calls for research and investigative work, and may finally require a majority vote for a decision in the common good. Delegating this sort of commission to a judge may eventually dull the judge's mind to the distinction between injury and non-injury, giving him the impression that property lines are fuzzy, that he has more discretion in his true judicial duties than intended under the common law. If budgetary economy is a factor in commissioning the court, eminent domain should be delegated to a city council or a board of supervisors, not the bench.

Another salient remark about eminent domain. The taking of land by the powerful is as old as life itself, but eminent domain in a holonistic universe poses theoretical contradictions. Not far from my old home in California was a large beautiful valley with soil as deep and fertile as any in the world. In the center stood a small community, hardly more than a store and a church. Owned by a few ranchers raising sheep and barley, the land was granted to their great grandfather's under the Homestead Act. They were part of the land, the land part of them.

In abnormally wet winters, a stream running from the valley would swell and flood a small town in the Great Valley, and aggravate the flooding problems of Sacramento itself. So a flood control dam was projected, the valley confiscated, and today a large lake supporting every kind of recreation covers the marvelous soil.

When a family for generations invests its effectiveness life in land, memorizing every variation in the soil, learning to treat each field in accord with its singularity, you witness an investment with no parallel save the investment of spouse in spouse, parent in child, and ruler in nation. Unusual imagination is not required to understand what happens to those minds when that terrain is torn from their care, when that intimate acquaintance becomes useless, the personal relationship with the soil twisted off like the trunk of an oak in a tornado, when they must move to parts unknown, perhaps to buy strange fields with their confiscation money. Or perhaps they will invest the money in sterile securities over which they have no control, into which they have no input. And the tiny community, blasted.

What about climates of mind, effectiveness lives. Where are those high-flying considerations of the common good? Why should these people ever again attach to a worthwhile project, why form the social bonds of a community? In a war, why fight off an invader who cannot take more than their own rulers have taken? This is eminent domain, one of the excruciating tasks of a conscientious ruler, flouting all his principles, perpetrating injury and damage precisely where they dwell.

A ruler can only mention the trade-offs. In times past, he called men from other regions to die protecting this family's relationship to this valley. The family's electricity comes from water power stored farther north in another valley, confiscated in an earlier day. It is brought to them by power lines through easements taken under eminent domain. When they themselves fish at Shasta lake or picnic at Friant Lake, they enjoy waters covering other valleys like theirs, and when their produce goes to market or they go to Los Angeles on the great freeways, they enjoy the use of land torn from other families under eminent domain.

As much as rulers wish their people to love the land, they wish them to love a developing society more. It is only required that the development be intelligent and the reimbursement comprehensive. Perhaps something in addition to a money equivalent - educational programs, recreational programs, new enterprises; not just exile from an old life. - A welcome to a new one. These are humans, and this is not ruthless democracy. It aspires to holonity.

CHAPTER 53

CHURCH AND STATE

As spun from the looms of equity, the structure and operation of the common law is the greatest mental product that I have studied. Its creators, bracing their feet in real estate, and peering through the lenses of trespass and nuisance, turned their attention to the innermost workings of the human mind. After titles in land, their first innovation was to protect a subject's relations to the useful furnishings of this world - things we today unwittingly call property, forgetting that property is our relationship to the thing, not the thing itself. The thing is a subject of property.

You may bathe your dog in your bathtub, and you may use your bathtub to brew a few quarts of alcoholic beverages. But you are restricted in how you dispose the fermented product. Though the barley is yours, at your complete disposal, as well as the water, the malt, the yeast, and the hops - all practically unrestricted as to use, and though the fermentation process is natural - unrestricted by law; the law takes most of your liberties away when it comes to the fermented product. And if you persist in an alcohol marketing project, the law may even empower its peace officers to smash your bathtub. So though you possess a bathtub and some essential ingredients, your property in these things is limited.

Your entitled relationship to a thing, this is what justice protects, or attempts to preserve, and to remedy if breached. And so in history we have seen law and equity extend their protection to relationships hardly imaginable in the beginning - for instance, your name and fame - the protection of your true self in the minds of other people - your image on the screen of the universe, as I have put it. And who are you? You are your She, as I have put it, though you are She's as much as She is yours, and in protecting your life, or in protecting your body from harm, the government is protecting the relationship of your She to the body from which the She arises and on whom She depends. It is your She that holds titles of use. It is your She that the law respects. And, if we are to be realistic, a ruler respects your She not for altruistic reasons but purely selfish ones. A nation of Shes is the only treasure a ruler possesses, and the character of the nation is no other than the integrated characters of her Shes. Shes cannot use themselves - but they can be used, and the ruler, by becoming omnipotent, has assumed for herself title to the use of her subjects - her Shes. She will use them by loading them as she wishes, anticipating that quite often they will respond in more or less predictable ways.

An intelligent ruler learns that some of her subjects are busily using other subjects. They are loading their minds with threats, for purposes of extortion. They are loading their minds with visions of pleasure, for sales purposes. They are loading their minds with visions of heaven, for ecclesiastical purposes. They are loading their minds with promises, for fraudulent purposes. They are loading their minds with images of themselves, to attract them for social or marital or political purposes. They are loading their minds with visions of great careers, for academic purposes. They are loading their minds with diverse philosophic doctrines, for whatever purposes they have in mind. They are loading their minds with trust, intending to use it for some future purpose. They are loading their minds with algebra, history and economic theory for a myriad of purposes. They are loading their minds with feelings of security, because psychologists tell them that a feeling of security is a basic human need.

And the intelligent ruler learns something else: that how a subject person is used will affect her climate of mind. If a ruler oppresses a person, the person will hate the ruler and will start on one of two paths, a path to rebellion, with perhaps a few dips along the way in the pool of lawlessness; or a path to apathy and oblivion. If a ruler abuses the capacity for trust, or the capacity for affection, or the capacity for responsibility, the subject becomes incapable of trust and affection, and incapable of assuming responsibility. Thus the subject becomes a poor tool for the ruler, and the ruler's treasury is impoverished.

Exactly the same results occur if a ruler permits one of his subjects to abuse another. On one side he witnesses a person develop his effectiveness life in the skills of abusing people, blind to his own ultimate good. On the other side he sees people becoming incapable of trust, affection and responsibility - incapable of following a ruler through the impasse of hostile territory, incapable of a transcending patriotic effort, incapable of seizing initiative and taking responsibility for a bold move in an emergency when a bold move might mend a dangerous gap in the ruler's system.

In short, if he does not restrain some of his subjects from abusing others, he wounds himself as fatally as if he himself were abusive. And if he goes farther, favoring abusive groups, protecting them, and nurturing them, he may feel in his hand the delicious power of the lash, but he has lost the infinite power of a nation of trusting, caring, productive, patriotic, responsible individuals, the greatest tool on earth.

In short, the natural law of a governed society is this, the subjects take on the characteristics of the people who dominate them. Given this, the intelligent ruler asks himself, "The masses of my people - whom do I wish them to resemble?" On one hand he views the character of the people most likely to cluster about the faucets of power; on the other hand he projects in his mind's eye a populace of great productive power. And he ponders the various systems whereby, using the one group, he might create the other. This objective is both rationale and motivation for instituting a common law.

So the ruler constructs a system of property, a system of due process. In a woman's property, given the operations of due process, her wishes prevail, purely filling the space of her estate, untouched by the goings and blowings of others. Under equity, property lines are drawn with but one thought in mind, to create the greatest instrument for the ruling group that political ingenuity can devise.

But there is a realm that the rulerly hand cannot reach, in which the king cannot remedy the pain of a heart, a realm not responsive to the mappings of property. A realm where physical armed force has no power; where the heart and the She must heal She's self if She is to be healed at all. The king can do nothing to alleviate Mrs. McNamara's situation. To compel Mr. McNamara to take out the garbage would be enslaving him to her wishes, unleashing a thousand other demons. So what will the court do to preserve Mrs. McNamara's climate of mind?

Nothing.

Mrs. McNamara's climate of mind will have to heal itself. The healing power must come from the nature of the material itself - the body and its kinestatic checks and balances - or from the universe from which the body sprang. The same is true of the person bursting with love and a keen desire to contribute to society, but scarred with a facial blemish that others are embarrassed to look at. The same is true of the person whose children will never be anything but a burden. And with these I mention but a trifle of the million burdens thrust unasked upon a monarch's people, for which a monarch has no remedy. Some burdens he alleviates by taxation and re-entitlement programs. But he cannot cure the source of the aching pain.

Into these situations steps the kindly neighbor, the friend, the loving kin, or perhaps the stranger on the bus. In the past, the matchless healing device has been the strength of religious faith; a more modern instrument the trained psychologist. The intelligent ruler will always welcome the efforts of these people or organizations, complementing the ruler's grand scheme - feeding the caring, trusting, responsible, originant She.

The healer of social heartache can gain such loyalty among his flock that he can effectively compete with the ruler. Nowhere is this felt more than in the despotic state. So it comes about that rulers in the world of property and rulers in the world of pained hearts keep a sharp eye on each other.

In historical perspective, one sees diverse combinations of sacred and secular practitioners. Given a period of despotic rule, a divine might gain such power that he can effectively challenge the despot in his own realm. Or, given the same despot, such a cooperation will develop between him and the religious hierarchy, in unison abusing the people's capacity for fear, affection, self-healing, and trust, that soon nothing remains of the nation but empty husks.

On the other hand, a holonistic ruler might be burdened with self-seeking religious or psychologic practitioners propagating doctrines not healing sick Shes, but turning them to drugs or irresponsible climates of mind, making them insensitive, suspicious, dependent on unrealistic rites and beliefs, and finally disillusioned and sicker than ever. And one wonders how long intelligent rulers can grant these practitioners full liberty in these project spaces. There must be a limit to the tolerance of a holonistic ruler, and I think he must require that a practitioner promote She-healing and not corrode the climates of mind that an intelligent ruler treasures.

To this extent a ruler must be expected to restrict the climates of mind in which healers, or so-called healers, operate, though theoretically speaking, only the truly holonistic ruler would be entitled to make this judgment. And assuming a truly holonistic class of rulers, need there be a separation of church and state?

There is every reason to tolerate a multitude of faiths and psychological doctrines - as long as they heal the sick and produce wholesome Shes. There are as many She ailments as Shes. To prescribe iodine for every physical ailment of humankind would be as intelligent as prescribing one doctrine of life for every She. And requiring every person to adopt a monopolized faith, or one of several state-favored faiths, would be stupid. The strength of nature - the input of the universe - is so self-induced in a number of Shes, that a human mediator is not needed.

There is therefore every reason to keep the rites and indoctrination of organized religions out of the public school, and, by the same token, there is every reason to prohibit anti-religious insinuation on the part of public school personnel. A chief problem of religious indoctrination is that a doctrine well adapted to a person might be poorly adapted to that person's own child. In this perspective it is dangerous to the public health to allow any religion to teach that it is the only true religion. Conversely, the independent self-healer might have a child (or many children if she is a teacher) who might someday need the nurture of religion, and to let her teach, though with the best intention, that there are no true religions, is to endanger the effectiveness lives of those she reaches.

Given holonistic rulers on one hand and conscientious soul-feeders on the other, there is reason to define the domain of the soul-feeders and the limits beyond which they must not tread. Love and the common good do not travel the same road. The soul-feeder teaches, "If you love someone, give him your shirt," or "If someone slaps you on one cheek, show him the other." And in this situation he is teaching that altruism and sacrifice promote self-growth. This is instruction on how to live if one wishes to get the most out of life. But imagine a ruler saying, "I will punish you if you don't try to rescue that small boy running toward that precipice." He is saying, "This is the way I will force you to act so you will get the most out of life." This is the combination of church and state often urged by moralists, but there is reason to believe that teaching moral values and, in contrast, enforcing them, will have divergent subliminal effects.

It is one thing to say, "If you will make the sacrifice and bring the fetus to a natural parturition, you will find your reward in self-development." It is another thing to engage the armed might of government and say, "Whether you like it or not, I am going to force you to carry the fetus full term."

Inciting popular sentiment to force the government to disregard property, to espouse slavery in the name of a moral or aesthetic value, should be off-limits for religious and aesthetic practitioners. And with this we find the true line of separation between church and state. The state must hold dominion where property lines are the problem. And the church, observing the rules of property, will press its objectives in fields not involving property. It is that simple. That simple as long as the state has an intelligent basis for establishing and maintaining property lines.

But given figistic rulers, the topic may take any turn you wish.

CHAPTER 54

TRUST AND ANTICIPATION

Fraud is an abuse of trust. A fiduciary signifies a trustworthy person. Evidently government pays a great deal of attention to trust, and, if government is sound, it deals harshly with breach of trust. But can a person be forced to be trustworthy? What is common law theory on this? We will find it to be unexpected. We can learn it by studying the law of contract.

The law of contract is one of the more remarkable legal devices. If you would read Anson's history of its development, you would get a valid example of the peculiar way in which the common law took shape.

Though a contract is usually considered basically a two party agreement, it is essentially an understanding among three parties, the third party being the government. At some point in history, during the shift from feudal commission to property, the English people began to sense a new signal from government. Though today the signal is usually transmitted by statute, it was initially dim and muddled, and only as it slowly developed through the court process did it become loud and clear. In effect the government said, "If two of you make promises to each other in undertaking a joint project, I will materialize for each of you a phantom property exactly matching the promise made by the other. A failure on the part of one of you to materialize her promise will have the same legal result as though the property was materially pre-existent and the defaulting party had distorted it.

Dams, skyscrapers, and jet airliners are not possible without contract. Hence in effect the modern world reflects not only the power generated by joint enterprise, it reflects the wisdom and power of government in enforcing the performance.

As aesthetically satisfying as it would be to hold that the law of contract is a government program to train the nation in trustworthiness, it is more realistic to admit that the law of contract is silent testimony to a general experience that the world is full of promise breakers completely immune to training in this area.

Speaking of trust, one is reminded of fraud - the taking advantage of trust - and this brings one to ponder a possible relation between fraud and breach of contract. Under our legal system there are two kinds of suit in contract, a basic consideration in analyzing the relationship between fraud and trust. The cause called breach of contract seeks damages and therefore is a case at law. The cause called specific performance seeks a remedy called specific performance, a sort of negative injunction, and comes under the jurisdiction of equity.

A cause in damage requires both injury and associated harm. An injunction seeks only to relieve injury. In either case we are looking at a broken promise, the defendant having failed to perform specifically as she said she would. So what is the difference between breach of contract and specific performance? Very little, except what we might surmise from the plaintiff's prayer.

If damages are sought under breach of contract, we will note that defendant's failure to perform has already caused loss to the plaintiff. But if specific performance is sought, we witness an example of the government program to materialize a person's wishes within his property. As far as the government is concerned, a house contracted for July 9 is a house existing on July 9, a property subject only to the owner's wishes, and, if it exists not, the contractor has infringed the owner's wish space. There might be no loss in the case - except loss of wish space.

If plaintiff has loaned the defendant money, and the contract says the money will be back in his hands on March first, the court will order the debtor to pay. Since the chief weapon of the court for enforcing performance is contempt, with a tacit threat of jail, and since in this case we are in effect looking at debtor's prison, you can see that we are looking at a very special situation. Before a court can issue such an order it must be seeing a case not of inability to pay, but blatant refusal to pay. A refusal to perform as one has promised.

Even if punitive damages are not assessed in the case, the losing defendant will have to bear the costs of litigation, and it is difficult to imagine that this is not a training program. Surely it conditions a person to be trustworthy. If she learns she must pay if she has promised to pay, losing several such cases, she may get into the habit of paying, unless she is an anticipatory moron.

But what if a debt is not involved. What if the defendant has promised to build a tennis court and has not built it? A court of equity will not force him to build it personally, unless he decides to, but will compel him to pay enough to persuade another contractor to do it. This is the gist of specific performance.

If defendant contractor has promised to build the tennis court for

$50,000 and another contractor will not build it for less than $70,000, plaintiff will pay the first $50,000, and the court will order the defendant to pay the additional $20,000. This indeed brings out the true nature of the contractual element called consideration. The contractor bidding $50,000 is wise to consider all aspects of the project, and his $50,000 signature is taken by the court to be prima facie evidence that he has considered all the aspects. What has he considered? He has considered what it will take in organization, time, effort, and expenses, as well as sacrifices of other pursuits, to materialize the project in all its details. This is his consideration.

The prospective owner before signing the contract considers what $50,000 means to him, what he will have to do to get hold of the sum, and whether the tennis court is worth it to him; and his acceptance of the bid is prima facie evidence of his consideration.

A party's contractual promises are not only evidence of his consideration, they are parameters of the immensity of his undertaking. This is an aspect of contract too essential to neglect. If a party in effect promises nothing, it means he had nothing to consider before putting his name on the instrument. How easy it is to sign such a document. If the designated buyer of a house in effect says, I will buy the house if I can get the money, how can there be a contract? A buyer need spend no wakeful nights on a deal like this. No court should hold a seller bound by such an instrument. If the buyer fails to come up with the money, the seller is left out on a limb; and a conscienceless buyer could have a lot of fun signing contracts like this. If a seller seeing the light finds another buyer who will put the money where the words are, the seller should be free to sell to him.

But, returning to the bid of $50,000 for building the tennis court, yes, it might seem severe that a court makes the defaulting contractor pay the additional $20,000 necessary to induce another contractor to build it. But in truth his low bid might have prevented the other contractor from getting the job in the first place. After signing the contract, perhaps he found it was going to cost him $70,000 to build the tennis court, and started to drag his heels. As a result of the contractor's failure to anticipate, the prospective owner of the tennis court is a winner. He gets a $70,000 tennis court for $50,000.

What does specific performance suggest about the theory of the common law? It signifies that the government is not conducting a training program in trustworthiness, but a crash course in anticipation. In the defaulting contractor we see a person who could not anticipate reliably. His considerations were faulty, and he wished to back off from his promise. But the government wants tennis courts. More accurately, it wants the productive power of joint projects. If in the projection of joint enterprises the parties learn to anticipate non-performance, there will never be joint enterprise. Therefore the government enters the

project as a silent partner, and parties can anticipate specific performance.

So our defaulting contractor was (1) malicious, or (2) reckless, or
(3) thoughtless, or (4) an anticipatory moron. If he does not learn to
anticipate, he will go broke. Anticipation will save his skin as well as
reducing waste in the general treasure. And if he is an anticipatory
moron, he had better withdraw from the field for a less demanding
occupation. The common law is a common sense instructor.

Anticipation, given government willpower, is a satisfactory substitute for trust, given that a portion of a population will always be
untrustworthy. But we have the law of fraud and contract and, given the
law, we ask a pertinent question. Who can defraud, who can default on
their promises with impunity? Who but figistic favorites of figistic
rulers. And we ask two more questions before tying it all together.
What are some general classes of promises in the everyday world?
Answer: contracts, fiduciary poses, licenses, oaths of office, professional ethics, trustee acceptance of trust. This gives one an idea of
classes of people in a position to break their promise. Who, for
example, are in the class of fiduciaries? Answer: parties to contract,
any person who has struck a fiduciary pose, lawyers, government
officers and staffs, judges, legislators, physicians, automobile mechanics, TV repairmen, manufacturers, avowed experts.

Let us be realistic. We all live in a great anticipation training school
called life, and we have a talent for learning in this field. Our training
comes not through words but through experience. As originants we act
upon the world, and the world acts back upon us not as objects, but as
taxitants. This is how we learn, and it determines the avenues into
which our effectiveness lives will turn, indeed whether our effectiveness lives will continue to live. This is all intertwined with anticipation,
and with climates of mind. Yes, let us be realistic; the character of
government will in the final analysis generate the environment in which
our genetic forms will develop, determining the characters of the Shes
that are we.

Then who will not receive the government anticipatory training?
Who but these figistic favorites, in effect the ruling class. Who then
will be the anticipatory morons, but the ruling class. Oh, but there
remains nature's training course in anticipation! The masses, the
victims of fraud and breach of contract, will learn to anticipate that
they cannot trust the rulers. They cannot trust them to restrain their
favorites within the law. And the figistic favorites, what training will
they receive? What but training in the anticipation that they need not
heed the law. The top rulers merely show themselves to be anticipatory
morons.

CHAPTER 55

JUSTIFICATION OF COMMON LAW
THE RULER'S TREASURE; COMMON GOOD;
GENERAL WELFARE; PRINCIPLES OF PROPERTY

Having come to the crowning topic and next to last chapter, I must ask what justifies the system I have so laboriously described. While we the people might be satisfied with the system if it promotes and protects our welfare, we must ask a more practical question. We must ask why intelligent rulers, having power enough to work their will on the rest of us, would subject themselves to the same restraints they impose on us. For this is exactly the meaning of the common law.

In treating this topic, we cannot indulge in philosophy or idealism or even in mere logic, we must deal in mechanics. Exactly how does this particular system enhance the common good, and what exactly is the common good.

I am discussing government, only about one-third of government - the department of person-to-person disputes within the population. To give the other two-thirds its due in a paragraph, I will make the excessively general statement that a government's main job is to treat adversarial situations, of which three kinds come to mind. One is the adversarial situation arising between nations, between the rulers of nations. Another comprises the adversarial situations I have elaborated in the book, a matter of property and liberty. The third consists of the adversarial situations that are not interpersonal - the plagues of nature, the limitations of man's potential, even the pitiless tide sweeping over him from the painful evolution of the general welfare itself in which, perhaps without malice, and without injury, the pursuits of some people crush the hopes of others. Particularly in this third sector of the government job does the legislative wisdom of government come into play - appropriation, eminent domain, and re-entitlement - relieving the victims of these impersonal forces, and bursting through the barriers to man's progress.

Anyhow I have been discussing government, and one cannot discuss government without discussing rulers. The ruler, I suppose, when humans were still humanoids, was he or she who could dominate the occasional challenger in head-to-head combat. But at the moment in history when humans emerged as true humans from their primate chrysalis, the ruler became he or she who desired to be ruler, with additionally the ability to plan and mobilize the machinery required for ruling.

Such a person must feel that she, not being ruler, would fare better if she ruled. The expression "would fare better" - what does it mean? It can only signify her unsatisfied Omega drives. A feeling she "would fare better" probably originates from one of two conceivable situations. In one, her Omegas are already in existence within her society, ready for her to acquire and enjoy, but the current regime stands in her way. In the other, her Omegas do not exist. Attributing this to the character of the regime, our would-be ruler proposes to change things, developing an environment in which her Omegas will materialize. These statements could not be more general and abstract, and I leave the details to you.

Therefore the general urge to rule is an absolutely personal and egocentric matter to the would-be ruler, a set of Omega drives to her mind satisfied only by attaining rulership. As to this portfolio of Omegas, one imagines its composition, taking all would-be rulers into account, to be as wide and varied as the range and blend of Omegas taken over the entire human race. To find examples, one might look into the history of ancient Greece and Italy, or into the biblical stories of Israel.

Because attaining an Omega requires pursuits of projects, we always find rulers immersed in personal pursuits. And though you might point to rulers of the past, souls of immobility, I will contend them mere figureheads, serene in the eye of a storm, with covert pursuits of true rulers in full sway; the pursuits are always there. And as we have observed about pursuits, they always have consequences, not always matching the expectations of pursuers. The success of a pursuit depends greatly on the accuracy of the pursuer in anticipating the functions of the pursuit space.

If our would-be ruler achieves rulership, I would naturally advise her to institute the common law, wagering it would produce the highest attainable supply of rulerly Omegas. You lift a quizzical eyebrow, and well you might.

Fortunately for the task of making my advice creditable, it states a form of a function. Remember functions? The full function is this:

Common law   Highest supply of rulerly Omegas

Figist law   Unsatisfactory supply of rulerly Omegas

Then one might identify an intermediate variable, like this:

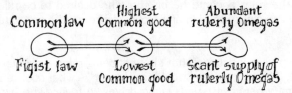

and you should learn to seek the hidden meaning of the clouds.

As you now know, a function is a way of stating a complex of phenomena. At minimum, it states a phenomenal relationship between two phenomena. As we might say in function language, a function states a relationship between at least two variables.

In the example of snowshoe rabbit, one perceives the fur color variable, with variates white and brown, and the intriguing phenomenon is the translation from one to the other. After a series of observations we conclude that fur color is a dependent variable, not changing unless something else happens - an entirely different sort of phenomenon. Fur color changes when the environmental temperature changes, something happening twice a year. As the temperature gets colder, the fur becomes white. Then it gets warmer, and the fur becomes brown. The change in temperature powers the change in fur color, and I have repeated this tale to make the following point.

In diagramming functions, I have used a free-form cloud to represent a variable. In the case of snowshoe rabbits I call the variable "fur color". But I know something basic is happening in the cells of the rabbit, a basic mechanism responding to temperature and producing white fur or dark fur. These inferential happenings are denoted by the little cloud. With this in mind we come back to the function between law and the common good, and I ask the question, what are the clouds? What variables do they represent?

In the case of the dependent variable, the answer is obvious; the cloud represents the common good. The common good - whatever that is - can vary in a range between high and low. But what is the variable (the cloud) ranging from perfect common law to perfect figistic law?

You see, law is not a phenomenon. Law is written in a book. Like fur color, it might be loosely called a phenomenon, but like fur color it is better thought of as signaling a more profound phenomenon. To have an effect, law must pass into a particular human mind, a mind mechanically coupled to a machine with a real effect in the human world. A process called justice. Do you remember my early definition of justice?

"Justice is (a) a series of decisions made by a person, (b) affecting the lives of other persons and (c) backed by irresistable power."

If you are sharp, you will see an inaccuracy in the diagrammed function between law and the common good. Observe a figistic judge operating within a framework of ideal common law, and, exactly as a ray of light is warped in passing through an imperfect pane of glass, you will witness the law warped in passing through this figistic mind. The result will be not enhancement of the common good, but degradation.

Therefore the variable, the cloud, on the left is not law but justice, for justice is a man and a machine. The variates are common law justice and figist justice. The amended chain is:

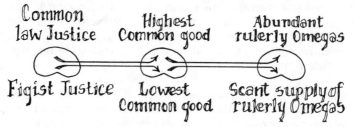

That this is a useful refinement is clear. Figity is chaos, and, if you wish the idea of law to reflect the idea of order, figity is the absence of law. There is only figistic justice and its results.

So justice depends on the character of the man who administers the law, and on the character of the men formulating the law. Hence justice itself is a dependent variable, and how do we express the variable and the variates powering the variations in justice?

At this point we encounter the spectrum of all the Omegas decorating the human race. The cloud on the left is the Shes of rulers; on the right - the Shes of government agents. There is no way of expressing it simply in function language. One uses her imagination and her talents.

Ideal common law justice cannot exist without a perfect theory of common law. Even then, we know that figistic justice can pour from a faucet labeled common law. What then guarantees ideal common law justice, given a perfect theory of common law? Nothing but (1) the will of the rulers that the common law be observed, and (2) the ability of the rulers to control the justicial machinery. So if you witness an outpouring of figistic justice from a system of intelligent law, you can conclude at least one of the two elements is missing. (1) The rulers do not wish the professed law to prevail. (2) The machinery of justice is out of control.

You will now begin to see me wandering in my line of flight, and share with me the experience of progressing in circles. In only this way did I arrive at the first draft of this chapter. To achieve the necessary generality and conclusiveness, many ideas must be kept in mind, and flying in circles is a method of minding and reminding. Long ago I warned that the Gothic arches nearing the summit would begin to lean dangerously, that not until the summit is reached will the construction become meaningful. Then at one moment the parts will unite, becoming a sound and stable whole. This is the fate of every pursuit in inductive inference. When the Gothic arch is made of stone, our minds embrace both theory and structure in one admiring glance, but in an arch of inference, an amount of mental recycling, a wandering retrospective eye, seems required.

Thinking of rulers controlling the justicial machinery reminds one that rulers of a sizable group must operate through agents. The regents of a university operate through a president, and he through a vice-president of finance and a purchasing agent. Directors of a large corporation act through a chief operating officer and he through a thousand subordinates. Generals of the army act through aides and lieutenants, and we need not speak of the rulers of large nations. Even if the people of a democracy were rulers, they might act through representatives. Even judges have agents - lawyers are officers of the court. When the outcome of a case is perfectly predictable they have a duty, occasionally observed, to convince the parties that they should not bother the judge.

Agents, experts in the mechanics of their system, frequently more knowledgable than their principals, can by the sheer exclusiveness of their knowledge gain a sort of immunity from the consequences of their acts. Without them, the machine will simply not operate, and, as organizations mature, they become staffed with these people; bureaucrats. A bureaucrat is someone gaining power through his office, power greatly disproportionate to his responsibility or investment in the enterprise. Thus in mature nations one might find bureaucrats not only in government positions, but branching out into the institutional and commercial sectors of the society. Legislators, generals, judges, lawyers, business managers of universities become bureaucrats. So do corporate presidents not deeply invested in the stock of the corporation, not to mention minor officers handling matters of great importance to the people supposedly served by the enterprise.

Such bureaucrats might form a network not only within the sphere of government or the world of business, but bridging the two. They find ways of faring well personally, careless of the enterprise employing them. People they supposedly serve will be injured, deprived of property in the transaction, but the injury will be hard to trace or define. And when the justicial machinery is finally joined to the network, the participants become immune to the law. Their predations become brazen, multiplying unrestrained. The members of the network become the elite of the society, indeed the rulers of the nation. Britain has had a television series making light of the situation, and Hitler in **Mein Kampf** mentioned this state of affairs as a significant disease of Germany between World Wars I and II.

Without a head, devouring from paw to mouth, or perhaps with a central organization hoping to control the monster, pre-occupied ring-leaders unaware that they have become oligarchs already, the monster strangles the ovaries of the golden goose in the catching. Young eager staffers, hoping to be in control themselves one day, fail to anticipate the true nature of their future. There are pursuits and there are consequences.

Positions of power with immunity from consequences are finally filled with desperadoes. For this reason is the inevitable purging so indiscriminately bloody. When we see in British history a developing system of common law, we are not witnessing the work of dreamers. We are seeing the efforts of ringleaders who have learned something of pursuits and consequences, and whose dominant Omega for the moment is to prevent the suffocation of a nation. Perhaps it is not an Omega. Rather they have found themselves in an action-inducing contra-Omega situation.

To the intelligent and experienced mighty, it is justification enough for a common law. For us inexperienced logicians a more rational argument is required. But for the sake of argument let us suppose movers and advisors to be persuaded of the advantage of property based on the common good, and we are left with an unanswered question. What rules will we institute determining property? Yes, property will be the channel for each person and his little boat, but mete the course of the channel and draft its bounds! Yes, property is based on the idea of promoting the common good. Great. So you are a chancellor in equity, and in your courtroom, before your bench, stand plaintiff and defendant, plaintiff claiming defendant is interfering with his pursuit. Yes, the plaintiff admits, he must use in his pursuit a thing to which defendant is nominally entitled. But he claims the pursuit to be in the common good, and interfering will harm the common good. As chancellor you have never seen or heard of a claim just like this, nor a like complaint, nor prayer. Is he entitled to his project? Must defendant give way?

Well what are the rules of entitlement? And what are the rules of servitude? The two together determine property. If the defendant already holds title, and the plaintiff is now granted title, both plaintiff and defendant will be entitled to their interfering pursuits. This is the cauldron of property.

In your courthouse library, there are no specific rules for granting or denying title or property, but decisions and opinions from which you might glean a set of rules. Sometimes the nature of the pursuit gives the needed title to the pursuer. Sheila Rienzi was granted the use of Farmer Brown's land in a pursuit to rescue a little boy. Mrs. Carter was granted use of her sister's house for visiting her aged mother. Mr. Jones was granted title to a house belonging to the Mayer Company. It was the only way he could counteract a false image of himself projected by the sales policy of the Mayer Company.

So when at the hearing you have interrogated plaintiff and defendant, discovering the facts of the case, you retire to your chamber, and, placing a tablet of paper on your desk, slowly write down the rules of title and property - abstracting the ideas from everything you have ever read on the subject, and this is what you write:

"To acquire property a person must first acquire title, and the following are the rules of entitlement:

"(1) A person acquires title to a thing from a person already holding title, acquiring it by purchase, gift, deed, leases, the owner's permission, or public dedication (as with parks, public buildings, highways).

"(2) A person holds title to the improvements he makes upon a thing he owns.

"(3) By contract a person acquires title to the specific performance of the other party.

"(4) A person gains title to certain pursuit spaces by virtue of the nature of the pursuits. The pursuits that qualify are these:
(a) A person acquires title to the use of another person's mind (the taxitant's mind) in a personal relations pursuit. He must have the taxitant's permission, and his pursuit cannot be of a nature likely to harm the taxitant.
(b) A person gains title to a limited use of a thing if the use is necessary for rescuing a person from harm or capture.
(c) A person acquires title to whatever thing he needs for counteracting a false or questionable image of himself that someone has projected on his personal imaging screen."

Having completed this list, you rub your elbows and decide to grant plaintiff title to the claimed pursuit space, and now, with both plaintiff and defendant holding title to disputed subject matter, you must make a decision in property.

Liberty in the use of entitled space is limited by the rules of servitudes, these operating for both plaintiff and defendant. So you write down a summary of what you know about the principles of servitude, and this is what you write:

"A person is restrained in her liberty in accord with the following rules:

"1. She may not abuse a person's trust in her.
2. She may not distort the entitled space of another.
3. She may not channel another person into slavery.
4. She may not embottle another person (cut him off from legal relief).
5. She may not abuse the machinery of due process.
6. She may not abuse a person's sense of fear or pain or a person's feelings of empathy for another person.
7. (She may not abuse a person's patriotism.)
8. She may not use her title to a thing merely to frustrate another person's use of the thing, given that the other person's pursuit is entitled under Rule 4 of the rules of entitlement.
9. She may not by attraction channeling lead another person into a harmful trap."

In drafting these rules determining title and property, you have helped organize the thinking of the last nine hundred years, but the listing presents two difficulties. First it presents a hazard inherent in the civil rights acts. In the civil rights acts, the legislators listed some classes of people frequently discriminated against, failing to mention women, butchers, homosexuals, ugly people and a million other classes who are for some reason oppressed by other people. As Lord Hardwicke would say, the list is finite and fraud is infinite. A list might leak, its gaps permit misjudgments - titles granted improperly; titles not granted that should have been granted. No. What we need are the principles from which these lists spring, principles forming a continuous membrane separating property from property. Principles serving unerringly the common good.

The other difficulty in the rules; they are presumptive; there is no clear functional link between them and the common good. Yes, we presume that the rules will promote the general welfare. But there is no clear functional path between between these rules and the common good. We have circled back to square one.

Mountain climbers drive spikes into rock. I forget what they are called. As a climbing spike, let us consider the idea that the rules of property must serve something in addition to the common good. They must contribute to the supply of rulerly Omegas. In fact they must serve the ruler's Omegas if they serve nothing else. Indeed, what a coincidence it would be for the rules to serve the common good and the ruler's selfishness in unison!

Oh, for another climbing spike! Well, we have learned that the common law likes interpersonal bonding, and it likes responsibility, integrity, anticipation. It does not like maliciousness or recklessness, and note! We are talking about human attributes. With this you will note another defect in the diagrammed function between justice and the common good. As I refined it, it looked like this:

I neglected to identify the cloud variable giving rise to the common good. Just as the law must operate through a human agent, producing justice, so the common good rises from humans who have responded to justice. The basic variable dependent on justice has something to do with human beings, something to do with human attributes produced in response to justice.

I will list in two columns some cardinal human attributes.

Human Attributes
(Climates of Mind)

Population of Gailax	Population of Mistivan
responsibility, respect for property	irresponsibility, recklessness rapine, greed
patriotism, loyalty	rebelliousness, disaffection, disloyalty
restraint, self-sacrifice	self-indulgence
human empathy	indifference
trust	fear, anger, distrust
integrity	laxity, trickery
industry	sloth, apathy
interpersonal bonding	divisiveness
originancy	mental sterility
affection, love	resentment, hate
sensitivity, responsiveness	insensitivity, autism
taxitancy, anticipation	carelessness, inattention, oblivion

You will note I have grouped one set of characteristics as typifying the community of Gailax, the other the community of Mistivan. Few would wager that the Gailaxers were other than a thriving people, and few would imagine the general welfare in Mistivan to vary from that of wild animals. I have a reason for listing them thus.

If you are of the predatory breed of mankind, more inclined to grab your Omegas from others than to produce, describe the environment in which you will thrive? First, as an aid to grabbing, you will want a band of comrades with your own bent of mind, and next you will want a community of producers upon whom you can prey. Granting that you are clever enough to invade a community by infiltration rather than overt attack, let us suppose you have only Gailax and Mistivan available. Which will you choose? Which will be the easiest to deceive, which the easiest to govern, and which produce the greatest abundance of your Omegas?

If you happen to choose Gailax, and succeed in controlling the government, and permit your gang to rape Gailax by fraud, and by extortion, and by misuse of the courts, how long will it be before the Gailaxers become just like the Mistivanians; just like yourselves?

There are pursuits and there are consequences.

It is possible at this point to distinguish between the common good and the ruler's treasure. But we will have to go farther than that, and I ask you to remember everything I have said about treasure, and common good, and the general welfare. And now I ask you to forget it, for we must be more definite.

Let us look at the real world of a nation. First we see top rulers - movers and advisors - those with ability to organize, seize power, and control the nation to satisfy their Omegas - as far as they can correctly anticipate their Omegas. This group is the personage, I suspect, sometimes called "the state".

Next we have agents of the state, the far flung machinery through which the rulers operate. These, we know, gain a degree of power for themselves, a potential headless state if not controlled.

Last we have the people, those who produce the reserve of Omegas from which rulers and agents draw their supply. But also from the people will the rulers draw their agents. From the people also will come the future rulers, the future state. A ruler's dream of a successor is his dearest Omega, and, unless there is a successful invasion by a neighboring state, his successor will come from the people.

What is the ruler's treasure? It consists of everybody in his realm - his fellow movers and advisors, his agents and his subjects. They are treasure as gold is treasure. Gold, you see, though having an attraction of its own, has greater value as a tool. Gold, poor food, can be used to buy food. Investors these days, hedging against inflation, think of investing in material goods. They think of buying antique furniture, antique cars, coins, stamps, works of art; the list is infinite. Feeling an emotional attachment to the things, or not, their chief excuse for acquiring them is their trading value for the future, and their trading value will depend on how wisely they were chosen, and how intelligently they were cared for. These things are the investors' treasure, worth much or little, but it is all they have to work with. This is the nature of treasure.

So though to this point I have been using treasure and the common good as indefinite synonyms, there is an advantage in distinguishing them. The same will be true of the common good and the general welfare.

Going back to the island castaways, Burl and Scrawn, in that simplest of all examples, we found their climate of mind to be as important to their welfare as the island's soil and rainfall and their stock of corn grains. But notice that their climate of mind is not their welfare. Welfare has to do with faring well, an Omega association. Corn grains are Omegas. Soil and rainfall and stock of seed grains is the subject matter upon which they operate to produce their Omegas, and a cooperative climate of mind is seedbed from which the production and distribution and protection of Omegas will attain its most generally satisfactory level. In other words, the general welfare is a function of a general climate of mind, and it is the general climate of mind that I will call the common good.

So the general welfare is distinguished from the common good. Justice acts upon people and develops a climate of mind, and from this climate of mind emerges the general welfare.

For example, in a human mind there is a complex variable called the capacity to trust. Can we not from experience propose a function like this:

Is it not trust in government that unleashes the creative genius of the people? And if government integrity is translated into government treachery, powering a translation from trust in government to distrust, cannot we predict a domino-like sequence of powerings and translations, industry changing into sloth and apathy, patriotism and loyalty into disaffection and disloyalty, restraint and self-sacrifice into self-indulgence, respect for property into recklessness and rapine. And as these Gailaxers become Mistivanians we will see a deterioration of the general welfare. So we have developed a full functional sequence leading from justice to climate of mind to general welfare.

There are logical reasons for identifying mental attitudes with the common good, but I will not belabor them. I will merely say that when the Supreme Court gave the Mayer Company house to Jones (given that Jones was indeed misrepresented by the company policy of excluding blacks) it was in the common good. It was good for Jones; it was good for the state and the nation; and it was good for the Mayer Company.

The people are the ruler's tools. As he treats them, they will be sharp or dull, warm or cold, creative or inert. Being permitted to develop some of their originancy is merely a crumb falling from a ruler's table. That the crumb is large is evidence of two things. They have an intelligent ruler and he has a real treasure in his agents.

That the crumb under the ideal common law is all that a productive and intelligent person will ever desire is a consequence of the principles of property under the common law, and now we are ready to develop them.

If you feel a circular motion in this discussion, you will feel it accelerate. You have, as chancellor, laid down some guideposts for formulating title and property, and now we must begin to generalize them and regeneralize them. We want something looking like a formula or model, or canon, of justice.

We have first the principle of entitlement, affirming that what a person produces will be hers, and her associated project space will be protected by government. Under such a principle there is no ceiling to a person's productivity save her own limitations.

Giving individual productivity full rein, the ruler next wants the fruits of interpersonal cooperation. So he has drawn up the rules of contract.

But he finds that strictly personal matters - matters not directly related to economic goods and services, matters of frustration in deeply invested personal relationships - can depress the initiative of his subjects. Personal pursuits can be harmed by intrusions of wills and trusts; by the media avid for saleable stories; by inaccurate slights on a person's character; by inaccurate public records; by pasting a name known for integrity on a bottle of ineffective liniment. So the ruler grants the sanctity of property to (a) status, and (b) pursuits in personal relations, protecting them against all intrusions.

Actually we find these pursuits in personal relations to be no different mechanically from any other productive pursuit. Representing creative effort, they produce results dear to the heart of the pursuer. And though not carved in wood or stone and perhaps not valuable in dollars, they are registered in the atoms of a taxitant's mind, as material as anything can be.

We find then that a person is entitled to anything he creates or is given, and this broad generalization must of course be interpreted in terms of modern enterprise, employment, trade, services and agency. His pursuit space - perhaps better expressed as desire space or enjoyment space - is constructed on this subject matter. Anything interfering with his enjoyment of this space is adjudged injury, and this principle places a limit on his own enjoyment of this space. For he is advised not to pursue any enjoyment of his own space interrupting the enjoyment of other people in their enjoyment spaces. The basic principle is not hard to discern.

Where a person has deeply invested herself in a pursuit **that does not intrude into another person's deeply invested pursuit space**, she deeply resents an invasion of her investment space. In a lawless world, she might relieve her resentment by wreaking mayhem on the intruder, but in a law-bound society she is restrained from this kind of relief. If then the state does not find relief for her, the state and its system have in effect rendered her helpless, vulnerable to the recklessness and depredation of others. She is not as effective in productive, commonly decent pursuits as she would be in the absence of state. Her resentment mounts, and her initiative to undertake creative pursuit is diverted or weakened. She is being changed from Gailaxer to Mistivanian.

A person then is entitled to whatever she creates (using subject matter she owns or has permission to use), being restrained from trespass or nuisance. In addition she is entitled to the use of her own body. As for the use of her She - roughly the originant-taxitant part of her - the government keeps title to it, giving her a limited agency in lending the use to others. As a taxitant, she is vulnerable to input from the external world. As a taxitant she trusts, she feels menace and duress, she develops empathy. As a taxitant she develops a feeling for government, the extent to which it is being honest with her, the extent to which it is defrauding her, the extent to which it is separating her from an enjoyment space rightfully hers under the principles of property. As a taxitant she feels her way into the traps of life, both good and bad. As a taxitant anticipating possible consequences of her acts, her antennas are extended for harmful functional sequences, for the possibility of danger when the elements of project space F are not clear. As a taxitant she is sensitive to the image of herself in the minds of others, for it affects her effectiveness in her social pursuits.

So a government that wants her heart, wishing her to be a Gailaxer, does not want these taxitant features abused, especially by its own agents, so we now understand that the state frowns upon and dishonors:

    abuse of trust
    abuse of human empathy
    abuse of fear and sensitivity to pain
    distortion of a person's image on her personal imaging screen.

And finally the state holds for itself the title of killing, letting it out to persons only for very specific situations, those in which it might authorize its own agents to kill. To kill is to snuff out a She, and She belongs to the state.

So you are a chancellor, part of the ruler's treasure, with plaintiff and defendant before you, plaintiff demanding property in a pursuit. What guidelines will you use in assigning the subjects of property to her, or denying them, or issuing an injunction against the defendant, or assessing damages?

I will first propose the following formula that the state can hand to its chancellor in equity. Then I will generalize it to the utmost of my capacity. In most cases the general format of injury as refined in Chapters 18, 26, 32, 37, and 48 will serve. Though the following guidelines cover the format of injury, having generated the common law, they are not so much directed at injury as at pleadings for title where title has never been granted before, or seeking property against persons who have prior title in the disputed subject matter. In what follows, I have not included the essential elements of pleading, speci-fied in Chapter 39, nor do I repeat the mechanics of injury associated with damage, outlined in Chapter 51. They would be essential in any pleading. What I am presenting here is not so much the format of a pleading as the thinking process of a chancellor considering a case properly pleaded in equity. The statements are not in the mode of principles, but I believe the principles - the principles determining title, property, and injury - can be readily inferred from the statements. They are the statements of a ruler, intended as guidelines for his chancellor.

"I respect the following things and relationships as related to my subjects, and there is a certain ranking of respect, and I expect my respect to be observed by my subjects toward all others of my subjects:

"1. I respect a person's functional relationships to things repre-senting investments of her effectiveness life, but such investments must not be in pursuits intruding into invested relationships of other people. I respect her wish to transfer such things or relationships to another, and I respect the transfer and the ensuing relationships of the transferee to the thing. Where the relationship is a personal relationship with another person, and it is frustrated by my protection of a third person's relationship with a non-human thing, the personal relationship will take precedence. And when there is a conflict between the relationships of two persons with the same third person, and the third person is not active in relieving the conflict, the relationship representing the greatest investment of effectiveness life and the most responsible climate of mind will take precedence.

"2. I respect a person's life and body, and her desire for a true image of her character on the screen of the universe. When there is a conflict between her security in these matters and the enjoyment of a person in a non-human thing, her security will take precedence. When a person undertakes to protect another person's life and body, her pursuit will take precedence over the enjoyments of any third person in non-human things.

"3. I respect a person's capacity to trust other people and to trust government.

"4. Any of the foregoing statements to the contrary notwithstanding, I give the highest level of respect to a person's respected freedom in enjoying her functional relationships with her own body (her capacity to determine the powerings and loadings of her body), and I give no respect to the pursuit of another person attempting to control or direct her relationships of this kind by repulsion channeling."

I will now generalize these statements as far as I can, without attempting to support the generalizations by argument. Based purely on the natural drives of man and the principles of mechanical interference, the statements leave all moralizing behind. The generalizations must be interpreted in the light of all the conclusions and qualifying remarks of the book. Construed thus, I think the statements comprise a form, a formula, reproducing the case decisions exactly as I have resolved them. Again, they are presented in the voice of the ruler.

"My pursuit is to create and maintain an environment fostering the highest possible development of originancy and taxitancy among my people. I instruct my courts to dishonor litigating parties whose pursuits and their consequences tend to abuse or inhibit originancy and taxitancy in others, or tend to degrade this environment. I honor pursuits undertaken to induce these attributes in others.

"Injury I define as a functional sequence triggered by the actions of a person, with results tending to dull or kill honorable originancy or taxitancy in another person. Damage is an irreversible consequence of injury tending to perpetuate injurious effects.

"My courts will not intervene in a dispute unless the elements of injury may be inferred from the allegations of the complaint.

"When injury can be remedied by injunction, my courts will issue injunction. When injury can be remedied only by specific performance, my courts will order an equivalent. When damage is discovered, my courts will use the occasion to educate my people in taxitancy (taxitancy being, in addition to all other sensitivities, an awareness of functional sequences in the environment, an anticipation of possible results of pursuits, and a cautious sense of the possibility of unknown factors in a pursuit space)."

I propose this as the spirit of the common law, the constitution of a purely holonisic government. In the context of the Preamble to the Constitution of the United States, this canon becomes the compass for promoting the general welfare.

CHAPTER 56

FINDING AND USING
YOUR LAW LIBRARY

Now that I have stopped, it is your turn, and where do you begin?

Well, first of all, you will discover in this Gothic structure many assumptions that need testing. At this point, science will truly enter the field of justice. On the other hand, there may be a conflict in which you have a personal interest, or a general interest, and you may wish to test my conclusions. In this effort you will first want to discover what the common law has already said in similar cases. You will want to familiarize yourself with a law library. And where is your law library?

In our town it is in a secret place, but the clerk of court told me where to find it. It is on the third floor of the Moose Building, associated with the office of a circuit judge. Though holding a traveling court, he keeps here a secretary and a reading clerk. The library dark and dusty, chairs with no bottoms, open windows for air conditioning, I saw nobody there but the secretary at the times I was there. The secretary, serving as librarian, has pleaded for more space, more shelves, and has given up. The Moose Building has plenty of unoccupied space for rent on the third floor, but, the last time I was there, newly arrived volumes of case reports were piled on the floor, on tables, on chairs (the ones with good bottoms). The shelves were full.

I will presently give you better news, but this quiet place was not a bad place to begin. It housed good sets of **Corpus Juris Secundum** and **American Jurisprudence 2d**, two competing encyclopedias with alphabetically arranged articles and volumes, each occupying several shelves and covering every legal topic, each well-indexed in several volumes. Reading runningly, the text is cleverly composed mainly of excerpts from case reports or journal articles, cited in footnotes. As you read and learn, you collect citations for source material. The first thing you will learn, a matter of self-education, the trial and error variety, is how your topic of interest is expressed in legal terminology. Learning it is the only way you will be able to locate it in the reading material. I learned it primarily from the indexes of the encyclopedias, but then I also found in our public library a copy of Besse May Miller's **The Legal Secretary's Complete Handbook,** a real help.

Abbreviations used in legal citations, exemplified in my index, are standardized. They are explained in the front material of encyclopedias, the bound volumes of case reports, and legal dictionaries; your librarian will be glad to help you get started.

Our law library carries the state code in a set of annotated volumes. A similar set is in our public library. It will be fun as well as important for you to see how your topic is treated in statute mode. Annotated state codes, containing more annotation than statute, present large numbers of one sentence quotes from cited case opinions - another good source of reference material. And, for initiating research, one must not forget **Words and Phrases.** Our law library has a set. In this reference, you will find key words arranged in alphabetical order, words like fraud or trespass or nuisance or contract, but you will find no text. **Words and Phrases** consists entirely of page after page, volume after volume of one-sentence quotes from cited case opinions, distilling a century or so of judicial expression on the various topics of litigation and terminology.

Having gathered a list of citations from these general treatments, you will select some case reports and read them. Today in the United States they are all published by one company in two systematic series of court reporters, a state by state edition, and a region by region edition - Northeast, Southwest, Atlantic, Pacific....., several states to a region. Our law library carries all the regionals.

Case reports comprise the living law, be it recently born or two centuries old. Reading them is the most enlightening and rewarding work in legal research, perhaps in your life. Do not rely on the one sentence excerpts, no matter how attractive for your cause. A sentence is easily lifted from context, and with great violence; and there seems to be a legal tradition to pad new reference material with another editor's old annotations. To rely solely on legal excerpts without looking up the source report is to invite unpleasant surprise.

Our law library subscribes to the Supreme Court reports (lawyers edition), and the **Federal Reporter.** Also **Shepard's Citations.** With **Shepard's** you can trace the career of a case escalating through the courts. Depending on where your citation stands in the history of the case, you can find the results of earlier or later hearings. Or if your citation requires a state reporter, and your library carries only regionals, or vice versa, **Shepard's** will translate one into the other. But **Shepard's** helps you not, if you have no reporter citation - only the names of the parties. In this situation you must search the indexes of the reporters themselves, volume by volume (hopefully you have an approximate date), unless your library takes **West's General Digest.** With **West's General** and a party's name and an approximate date, or with an idea of the specific topic, you can probably locate the report you want to read.

Finally, our law library subscribes to the **Harvard Law Review** and the **American Law Review,** both highly regarded.

Fortunately I live only 50 miles from a law school, in its library abound state reporters, regional reporters, federal reporters and all series of Supreme Court reporters; a room full of the bound law journals of almost every law school in the country; the state codes of every state, and several publications of the federal code and regulations.

The journal articles are erudite commentaries on leading cases as well as expositions of special topics, all liberally bibliographed with case reports and other journal articles. As a guide to journal articles on your topic of interest, the library subscribes to several indexes of periodical legal journals. Other reference aids, of which there are many, I will not mention, save one. The desk has a file of advance summaries of recent Supreme Court decisions. With these you have brought your research up to month. For closer time resolution you will have to use the computer terminals.

The floor above is filled with monographs and texts in every field of law, including the philosophy of jurisprudence. Here too in a dark corner are the bound reports of British Chancery, beginning with the eighteenth century, and rare books are available upon application at the desk.

This library is seldom used by anyone except law students, and during the school year it is well-populated. Critical cramming periods are of course good times for non-crammers to be elsewhere. In summer, there is a scattering of students, the air conditioning is wonderful, the cafeteria is kept open for lunch, and I cannot imagine a better place to spend one's time.

Between these two extreme examples of law library, you will find all sizes and shapes. In decent-sized cities the courthouses, both local and federal, have good law libraries. For access to very old material, I used the rare book department in the law library of the Library of Congress, and that research was a delight. For minutes of the Continental Congress and the correspondence of its members, I used the National Archives. The material is indexed on computer printout, and the staff is very helpful.

It would be remiss of me not to mention Witkin's **Summary of California Law** and **California Procedure,** sets of seven or eight volumes each. I first ran across these works in the Library of Congress, and subsequently sent the publisher's agent the $800 (now $1300) to acquire both sets for myself. It is impossible to overpraise these treatises. Though concentrating on California law, they provide a complete education in all fields of law, and at a fraction of the money and shelf space required for the more exhaustive and general encyclopedias. When I have a question involving federal law or the law of a state other than California, I first digest Witkin's treatment. With that my library research in the more specific law becomes immediately discriminating and efficient. Like many legal references, Witkin's volumes are annually updated with accumulative supplements, and have pockets in the back cover for storing the current supplement.

Witkin is completely objective in selecting cases, and the inconsistency of judicial decision in certain fields, at least in California, becomes conspicuous. For those fields it becomes clear that a judge can find abundant precedent for deciding a case as he wishes. Many cases that I have treated in this book first greeted my eyes in Witkin, and it was his objective reporting in negligence and tort that gave me occasion to find order if order was to be found.

INDEX

Topics, Titles, Cases, Authors, Names

28.15; justification of intervention in personal relations 27.4; what it gains and loses in court decision 29.7-; immaterial per se, basically signifies rulers 31.8; gov't "should" means gov't "wishes to" 42.1; and religious practitioners, many combinations of types in history, examples 53.4; how character of people develop under 54.4; job of, three classes of adversarial situations 55.1; integrity, function with trust of people 55.11; see also conflict; figististic, holonistic
*government, holonistic: see holonistic gov't
*government in England: see Cantor
*government, mixed: defined 21.14; U.S. intended to be 21.14
*government master project under common law: analogous to parental in terms of effectiveness life, climates of mind, project effectiveness 30.9; antithetic to slavery 31.8; identical to personal relations pursuits 37.6
*government protection: 7.4-; see also protection by government, title, property, freedom, or refer to entity protected; gov't protection of title, need to justify to powerful individuals 7.6; of freedom and property, true nature of 12.10; pledge of, compared and contrasted with due process 12.10
*Grant, Ulysses S.: effectiveness life, really alive only during Civil War 28.13-
*guilt, presumption of 39.12
*gun: example of niceties of title 13.2; the world a cocked and loaded _, helpful concept in understanding liability for damage 16.2

*Halderman v. Pennhurst State School and Hospital (1977) 446 F Supp 1295: rights of mentally retarded people 20.11
*Hamilton, Alexander ("The Farmer Refuted," see Works of A.H., H.C. Lodge ed.): on rights and human nature 21.4
*hammock, breaking: illus. various degrees of fraud, negligence, harm to trespassing children 49.6; see also hostess
*happiness, unhappiness: in function language 36.13-
*happiness, pursuit of: ex parte Warfield, 5.5, 5.8, 33.5; in function language 36.13
*Hardwicke, Lord: quote,"fraud is infinite" 42.1
*Harvard Law Review: 56.3
*Harvard, Sam: see fat man
*hearing: material? 34.12; court, see court hearing
*Heart of Atlanta Motel, Inc. v. U.S. (1964) 379 US 241, 85 S Ct 348, 13 L Ed 2d 258: use of commerce clause to relieve discrimination 33.9-
*hearts of people: treasure of king, John Somers quote 10.6

*Helguera v. Cirone (1960) 178 Cal App 2d 232, 3 Cal 64: boy falling from scaffold 49.10-; concealed trap element 49.13; compared and contrasted hostess situation 51.3; final resolution 51.11
*Hinde v. Pendleton (1791) II Wythe 299, Va Ct Chan 354; Decisions in VA by High Ct of Chancery, G. Wythe 1795; 2d ed, 1852 p. 354: auction of slaves 43.7; as slavery, analysis finalized 44.14
*hireling: not a servant 6.9; might be less fortunate than servant 22.6; distinguished from servants and slaves, see Chumbley 22.6-
*hiring: not contractual 37.8; essential to set wages before employment begins 37.9; hiree more favored than creditors in bankruptcy 37.9; how wages set in post-feudal England 37.10; a mode of trust; the trust mechanism 37.9
*Hitler, Blood Purge within Nazi Party 10.7; see also Churchill
*Hodecker v. Stricker (1896) 39 NY Supp 515: marital case, name confusion 25.3-, 25.7-; analyzed under format of injury 26.8
*Holmes v. Connecticut Trust and Safe Deposit Co. (1918) 103 A 640, 92 Conn 507: trust benefits dependent on husband's abstention from alcohol 46.3-; danger for embottlement by court with nuisance 46.5
*holonism, figism, tierism: defined 10.5-
*holonism: requires intermediate theory 10.6 10.10; meaning of 21.15; distinguished from communism and common law 21.12-; entitlement of ruler to his property, purity of theory 31.9
*holonist: characteristics of 10.10
*holonistic government: test of 31.10; need there be separation of church and state 53.4; constitution 55.16
*holony: formidable task of designing and implementing 10.8; must be justified to powerful persons 10.8; and common good, basic problem, King Stanislaus, fictitious example 10.7
*homing pigeon: example of intuitive phenomenon 2.1; research on 4.2
*honor: as verb, same meaning as favor 29.6-
*hostess: see also Rowland, hammock; when liable, fisherman tactics, hammock 51.4; situation contrasted to car parked on hill, non-act v. act 51.8; situation as much guest's project as hostess's 51.8; can court treat her as corp. president treats vice-president 51.9; my position different from my hard stance on nuisance, the reason 51.11
*hot water, child killed by: see Premo
*house: weatherbeaten, black and orange 37.1-; intelligent solution 37.4
*human: as subject of many uses, illus. Mrs. Rinaldo 14.7; see also man, "She", mind, person, originant; no other animal can anticipate in

abstract or has rights 28.2, 43.11; use of, functions through her "She" 42.5
*human actions, origin of, Kunkel 28.5
*human attributes: see attributes, human
*human mind: how used in personal relation project 25.10, 25.12; a commons for general use 25.12; what is real in, what unreal 26.3; see also mental, mind
*human nature: and rights, Alexander Hamilton q.v. on 21.4
*human subjects: see subjects, human
*humiliation: **Hodecker**, must occur in other people's minds, ugly vase in neighbor's window 26.10; Stark, family members 30.5
*hunger cycle: see kinestasis
*"hurt myself, blame another": characterizes difficult cases of fraud, negligence of affirmative duty, harm to trespassing children, strict products liability 50.3-; the other is not liable unless determining plaintiff's act, meaning of determining 50.7-; in absence of fiduciary, examples 51.1; and damage, summary outline 51.17
*hypothesis: atomic, helpful whether or not atoms exist 11.2; what makes meaningful 11.3; alternate, see alternate hypothesis 34.14

*image: see personal image, memory bank
*imaginary project space 7.2; see also project space
*immateriality: usually tested in lower court, testing not apparent in appeal reports 34.2; as defense 40.2
*immaterial law: examples emperor's horse is god, blacks are not human 48.7
*inalienable right to follow common occupation? 42.8; 42.11-
*incompetence, mental: see mental incompetence;
*indenture: example of instrument 22.6; voluntary 22.7
*indentured servants: school teacher 22.6; see Douglas; see service, indentured; see servant; Thomas Jefferson on 22.9; early boat people 22.7
*independent intervening act 19.6
*inference, inductive: progressing in circles 55.5; see also Gothic vault
*infringement: of liberty, injury 15.12; of property, an inappropriate phrase 15.12
*injunction: nature of and implications 5.3; by state court, can it reach into other states 25.1-; power of kept by equity while acting as court of law 25.7; should it issue if difficult to enforce? 27.2; damages also justified, illust. George Mason 33.11; improperly sought and granted 41.4; ineffectuality no bar to issuance British chancery 41.11; see also

restraining order
*injury: general definition, 12.2; not synonymous with hurt or harm 12.2; cannot be inflicted by person on herself 12.2; and damage, illus. by "Nancy v. Timmy", walking and falling 12.7; identical to involuntary servitude 12.8; identified 12.10; claim of, two primary claims 13.2; shooting intruder as example 13.2; not properly a verb 15.1; analogy to sin 15.1; invasion of property 15.12; infringement of liberty 15.12; infringement of property an inappropriate phrase 15.12; and liberty, defined empirically 15.15; and damage in a case, two elements in common 16.2; as cause of damage, unreliable concept 16.2; only possible within property 17.2; many mechanisms of 17.2; infringement sometimes difficult to discern, mechanical analysis 17.3; under feudal law is contempt for lord, analog. to immorality and sin 17.5; in primitive common law, two modes, trespass and breach of service 17.5; concept unified with damage 18.9; by gov't, see government; and damage, true sphere of their effect 31.12; can derive from kinestasis, duty immaterial 38.4; theory of from standpoint of rulers 31.9; if injunction required, damages also justified 33.11; causal loading claimed must be material 34.15; and damage, can arise from kinestasis, devoid of will 38.4; life support of courts 39.1; categories of 39.3; claim may be in past tense, present or imminent 39.5; equitable, 39.5; pleading 39.7, 39.14; legislated, pleading 39.7, 39.14; people are not injured 39.10; occurs in realm of common good 39.10; only occurs where defendant contributes as originant to causal chain 40.1-; discovery of mechanism, ingenuity required, example slavery 45.5; impossible to injure government without injuring a person, and vice versa 47.8; term misused as orthodox element of fraud 49.4; in fraud, not identified in legal texts - resides in first four elements of check list? 49.5; associated with damage, summary outline 51.15; ultimate formula 55.15
*injury, general format of: first draft 17.6; modified, using project effectiveness 18.10; example Hodecker, materiality of claim analyzed, name function 26.8; example of use (entrapment included) **Carter** 32.7; final form 37.13; see also Palsgraf, Edison, Jones, "Loud Music" "McNamara", **ex parte Warfield**
*Inkeles:("Totalitarianism") ed. by C.J. Friedrich; Alex Inkeles **The Totalitarian Mystique: Some Impressions of the Dynamics of the Totalitarian Society** (1954); quotation, logic of random terror 10.9
*innkeepers law 9.4
*insanity: equal to non-originancy? 40.3

attorney, solution 33.9; can a non-act infringe 49.5
*liberty, civil: Blackstone's meaning 21.2-
*liberty, in England: relation to prescription 21.5
*liberty, natural: see natural liberty
*Librador, judge in country of: illust. logic of gov't 10.3
*libraries, law: Chapter 56;
*lie: see falsehood;
*life, biological: see biological life
*life, effectiveness: see effectiveness life
*life: is it a thing, can it be used 28.10; topic of interest to rulers 28.10; where fits into scheme of things and law 28.11; ibid, illus. St. Francis of Assisi 28.11; man cannot create 28.11; one cannot use one's own 28.11; future, can't use 28.12; biographical, use of 28.12; several meanings, each valid 28.12; gov't holds title to 38.6; each step a trap, not all are bad 50.13; burdens which rulers cannot relieve 53.3
*life, right to: questioned 38.5-
*life story: right to use of 33.5
*light (electromagnetic waves) is material 35.1
*light waves: see view, gaze;
*likeness, personal: see **Edison** 25.6; property? 25.6; see also picture
*"Lineweaver v. Frick", illust. of various aspects of damage, car v. pedestrian 12.2-;
*literary property: 33.5; see also publication rights, copyright
*living mechanisms and environment 36.7
*living thing: an unstable organism 36.7; and non-living, distinguished 36.7; charged and uncharged states, see kinestasis 36.8
*loading: as element of project 13.5; transforms project into pursuit 13.7; as term distinct from use 13.7; often the fine touch that is frustrated by intruder 13.8; relation with objective and title 14.2; in property, sometimes defined by objectives or by nature of subjects 17.1; as term, advantage of 17.8; in function language 36.11
*Locke, John **Essay on Human Understanding** Vol. 5 "of Civil Gov't." (1690): quotations 7.6-7.7; verbal trickery 7.7
***Logan v. Davidson** (1968) 282 Ala. 327, 211 So. 2d 461: the general rule for protecting marital relation 27.1. Cases conforming and contradicting 27.2
*logic: contrast with reason and rationality 9.1; plus meaning equals rationality 11.4
*"Loud Music v. Quiet Conversation": introduced 12.9; analysis by format of injury 17.7- in function language 36.15
*"Lydia v. Nephew": extortion, loss of money not essential to injury 16.1

*machine: function of parts and of whole, analog, due process 5.3
*Magna Carta: against enforced service, with exceptions 42.2
*man: see also human, "She", mind, person, originant, taxitant
*man: as both originant and object, Kunkel 28.4; attempt to be originant only, object only, results 28.6
*"Mancowicz v. Smith": Bobby eats only candy, illust. difficulty in instituting holony 10.12
*Mansfield, Lord Chief Justice: 20.7; and John Somers q.v. 20.9; see also slaves, **Somerset**;
***Man Who Liked Dickens**: see Waugh
*marital relation: why given preference 24.9-; when divorce the correct remedy 26.11; protecting, general rule, see **Logan**; materiality of, **Snedaker**, 27.1-
*marital status: Hodecker 25.3-; in various cases 25.4; **Dandini**, q.v. 25.1
*marriage relation: analyzed as pursuit 24.8
*Marshall, John: on constitutionality; see **McCullough**
*martyr: act of, an act of desire 38.3
*Maryland Charter: declaration of rights 22.5
*Mason, George: Virginia's Bill of Rights, provision for slavery 22.9; uninvited nomination, illus. to show propriety of damages for injury 33.11; uninvited nomination analyzed for injury 44.3; see Rowland, K.
*master: see servitude, servant
*master and servant: see Bentham 22.7; master under service to servant 22.7
*material: law and equity deal only with 26.3; importance of 26.5; falsehood materialized by law **Vanderbilt** 47.2
*material effect: girl fainted at sight of snake 35.6
*material freedom contrast to legal freedom 7.10
*materiality: as essential element of case, Hodecker 26.3; ill-defined in legal practice 26.3; defined 27.1; of personal relations, **Snedaker**, 27.2; question of in personal relations 27.4; tested, example **Melvin** 33.6; of gaze, hearing 34.11-; judge's practical test of, example "Engel" 34.12; test of by functional analysis, **ex parte Warfield** 34.16; development of concept, parallel to devel. of common law 34.3; of mental objects 34.7-; functional analysis of, voodoo doll effect 35.6; see also immateriality
***McCullough v. Maryland** (1819) 4 Wheat. 316: constitutionality; opinion used in **Jones**, 22.12-
*"McNamara v. McNamara": husband won't take out the garbage 5.1; the missing claim under format of injury 17.7
*meaningfulness of hypothesis: how achieved 11.2

*medical school admissions: see **Bakke**
*meditation, use of mental objects 34.7-
***Melvin v. Reid** (1931) 112 CA 285, 297 P91: "Red Kimono Case", freedom of press v. personal relations 33.5; mechanical similarity to **Palsgraf** 33.6
*memory bank: and status distinguished 48.2, 48.5; the kind determines libel or slander 48.4; relation to personal relationship 48.8; see also judge
*menace: voids reality of consent in contract, relation to slavery 42.10
*mental: see also human mind
*mental incompetence: field of legal inconsistency 40.2; as a defense 40.2
*mental induction process: 25.10; slavery as 31.3; rape, seduction as 31.4; see also personal relations, fraud, slavery, fiduciary, affirmative duty, embottling
*mentally retarded: see **Halderman**
*mind, human: see human mind, mental, mind (taxitant's; people busy using other people's, summary, examples 53.1-;
*mind, taxitant's: a commons 26.2; clearing in, originant's property 26.2; when a commons in personal relations 27.5; trespass in, not difficult 42.5; unauthorized use of, attraction channeling, trespass 50.10-
*minor person, description as a "She" 28.7 protection of in equity 41.9; defendant, defense in incompetence questioned 40.2
*misconception, action under: as element of fraud 49.2; determining the critical step 50.9
*misconception of project space by projecter, factor in difficult cases 50.5
*misrepresentation: as element of fraud 49.1, 49.2
*misrepresentation, reckless: as element of fraud 49.2; punitive damages? 49.2-
*misrepresentation, negligent: bizarre element of fraud 49.4
*mistake: voids reality of consent in contract, relation to slavery 42.10
*Mistivan and Gailax: climates of mind 55.9
*money:a mode of project effectiveness, analysis 16.11; attractiveness and effectiveness 16.13; a contract 18.1; inadequate textbook definitions 18.1; as project effectiveness, as freedom 18.10; at interface between legal and economic worlds 18.10; evidence of double contract 18.10-; relation to producer's notes 18.10; and pledge of central banking system 18.10-; inflation, banking system failing to meet pledge 18.11; how used as a tool 42.4
*monopoly: under common law, not a general right 21.6; against butchers, see **Slaughterhouse** 22.2; aspect in **Slaughterhouse** 42.7; effect upon liberty 45.4

*moot issue: 38.5
*morality: no status in common law 7.1, 38.8, 53.5, 55.15; and love, paths diverge from common good, example church anti-abortion projects 53.5
*Moreland, Ray: **Injunctive Control of Family Relations** (1930) 18 Ky L J 207: 27.3
*mother-daughter relationship: see **Carter**
*movers and advisors: see rulers

*name: as configuration of atoms in human mind 25.11; as a clearing in human mind 25.12; unmarried woman using married man's name, **Hodecker** 25.3; see also fame, reputation; and fame 25.4; conflict in use of, see **Hodecker, Edison, Brown Chemical**; not important of itself 25.4; connection between name and reputation is important 25.5; property? 25.6; a thing? 25.9; can it be used? 25.10; a thing 26.4; materiality of, illus. name Henry Ford, Best Fertilizer 26.5; as a word, see word; and interference with personal relations, mechanics of 26.10; **Hodecker** 26.9-, **Edison** 26.10; right to use of 33.5; (reputation, status) run button powers two mental operations 48.5
*name function: illus. **Hodecker,** materiality of 26.8
*"Nancy v. Timmy": walking and falling, illus. project, property, injury, damage 12.7
*nation: survival of, king the primary party of concern 6.2; elements of 55.10
*National Archives 56.3
***National Bank of Commerce v. Greenberg** (1953) 258 SW 2d 765, 195 Tenn 217: benefits of trust cease upon adoption of child 46.6, 46.8; inconsistency of opinion with **Brown v. Board** 46.7; a step backward for equity 46.7
*natural law: discussion of term 21.2; Bentham on 21.2; Cicero's meaning 21.4: effectiveness lives and legal theory 28.16; of governed society, in summary 53.3
*natural liberty: Blackstone's meaning 21.2-
*natural principles: operate in jungle society, no source in reason 28.2
*natural rights: discussion 21.3; based on human nature 21.3
*neglect of affirmative duty: same cause as constructive fraud 49.8
*negligence (as cause of action): 17.10; principle of strict accountability 19.6; and principle of duty foster figity 19.11; similar to constructive fraud, liability for harm to trespassing children, strict products liability 49.6; can be treated as constructive fraud 49.7; assumes all hosts geniuses, all guests imbeciles 49.8; classifying under other causes 50.4; see also "hurt myself, blame another"

6.1; personal not class 1.15; v. rights, proper case for equity 3.2; what are rights of person 1.15; what makes a right a right 3.3; how established 3.4; women's, to be drafted into army, illogic of, illust. of difficulties 6.11, 10.11; as word, used only once in original Constitution, criticism of use in Constitutional amendments 3.5; yours depends on other people's 14.8; definition of, preliminary 14.9 defined 15.15; interpreted as liberty or property, ambiguous 15.16; and human nature, Alexander Hamilton 21.4; granted only to "She's" 28.7; only humans have 28.2; in Maryland Charter 22.5; students, see **Rights of Students**; students, slow and fast classes 33.2
*rights, natural: see natural rights
*rights of students: see Alan Levine.
*right to life: questioned 38.5-
*Rowland, K., **Life of George Mason** (1892)
*__Rowland v. Christian__ (1968) 69 C2d 108, 443 P2d 561: harm by faucet knob 49.7; compared and contrasted with contractor's scaffold **Helguera** 51.3; final resolution 51.8; compare and contrast with corporate vice-president situation 51.7-; see also hostess 51.10-
*rulers: U.S. has them 10.1; body of, make-up of 10.2; movers and advisors 10.2; volition and action by, a national requirement 10.1; need for, illust. primitive tribe 10.2; favor-mentality of, shapes legal free space 10.4; picking favorites, essential occupation 10.4 selfish whether figistic or holonistic 10.5 treasure of, figists and holonists contrasted 10.8; as people-users 13.6; experts in human psychology 28.3; mentality, determines common good; ruler a body of persons 29.5; as people users, range of types 31.5; occupational diseases of 31.6; as treasure of people 31.10; investment of own climate of mind and effectiveness lives 31.9; entitlement to property under holonism, purity of theory 31.9; respect person's "She" for purely selfish reasons 53.1; cannot help peoples in large sector of life 53.3; motivation for ruling 55.2; Omega drives 55.2; always immersed in personal pursuits 55.2; must operate through agents 55.5; treasure identified 55.10
*ruler and subject: under common law, slavery or personal relationship? 31.6
*ruling, court: defined 32.3
*__Russo v. Burch__ (1964) 224 Cal App2d 403, 36 Cal 682: woman falling down steps 49.9-; easily resolved 50.5

*school counselor: liable for counsel to student 51.13
*scienter: as element of fraud 49.1, 49.2

*scientific approach: psychology rather than philosophy of science 12.1; see Gothic vault of justice
*scientific theory: see theory, scientific
*scientific method: productive, but never certain 11.3
*screen of universe: 47.7-; personal imaging space, materialized as property, compared to contract 48.7; what is it physically 48.8; importance of 48.8-
*seduction: and rape as mental induction pursuits 31.4; and transmitting venereal disease 50.11
*sense of community: 33.2
*separation of church and state: true line of partition 53.5
*separation of powers: basis for 20.3
*servant: not same as hireling 6.9; under feudalism 6.8-; indentured, nature of contract 6.8; and master, use of master 6.9, 22.7; distinguished from slave and hireling, see Chumbley, 22.6; law of in colonies, see York, Davis, Simpson, Dalton, Boyer, Webb; indentured in U.S., Jefferson on 22.9-
*service: contrasted to servitude 6.9, 6.10; as element of property 14.7; and trespass, gov't enforced, example **Bakke** 37.11-
*service, feudal: modern vestiges 6.9
*service, contractual: does it reduce your liberty 18.4; effect on party in terms of project spaces 18.6; reduces project effectiveness in preferred projects 18.6
*service, enforced: today under common law, kinds of 6.11; undue, example **Bakke** 37.11-; wise for us not to use law for this purpose 37.4; our aversion dulled by idea of equal rights 37.6; criminal not subject to 39.9; Magna Carta against, with exceptions 42.2
*service, indentured: in U.S. stemming from terrible conditions in England 22.6
*servitude: sometimes galling, even when contractual 12.8; device giving complete freedom within property 12.8; a duty of self-restraint, a matter of will 12.6; relation to entrapment 12.6; essential still in delineation of property 6.11; not same as service 6.9, 6.10; effect on title 6.7; general nature of 6.8; roots of, as legal device 6.8; modern misconception of 6.8; as element of property 14.7; in conjunction with title, creates property 14.8; limitations upon 17.13; exercise in civility, common decency 17.13, 17.14; categories of 17.14; in civil law, cannot consist of doing; entirely negative 18.3-; term little used, not mentioned in Blackstone, defined by Dundas, definitions in Johnson's dictionary 22.4; cannot exist outside of law, in contrast to slavery 31.3; can it be abandoned as a device in common law

*topic of property: as element of property 14.6
*tornado: example of action inducing contra-Omega situation 44.9
*tort: 17.10; textbook definition criticized 19.2; case, three parts of 19.2; jury determining injury is court error 19.2-; difficulty of determining duty 19.4; see also duty, negligence, proximate cause, independent intervening act, Palsgraf, Cardozo; hazard as a cause 48.4; as term, can be discarded 51.14
*totalitarianism: see Inkeles
*towmotor, man hurt while operating, see **Dimond**
*trade (barter): a means of increasing project effectiveness 16.13
*translation of variates: 36.3; irreversible, in function language 36.11
*trap: function of bait, attraction channeling 50.10; each step in life is, but not all are bad 50.13
*treasure of king: hearts of people, Somers 10.7
*treasure of rulers: figists and holonists contrasted 10.8; identified 55.10
*trespass: 17.4; feudal times 17.5; violation of title 17.9; and nuisance distinguished, recap 33.1; see also injury, general format of injury; elements of pleading 39.4, 39.13; not in using name Vanderbilt 47.7; associated with damage, in summary outline 51.15
*trespassing children, harm to: see children;
*trial: defined 32.2
*tribe, primitive: illust. need for ruler 10.2
*trust (instrument): and contract distinguished 37.8-; trustor may insert any conditions, even frivolous, with exceptions 43.2-; and wills, see also conditions
*trust (human trait): abused in fraud 54.1; who can default on promises with impunity 54.4; of people, function with government integrity 55.11; function with climate of mind 55.11
*trustee: always a fiduciary 49.3
*trustworthy: distinguished from faithful 51.9
*trustworthiness: is contract a gov't training program in 54.1, 54.2; depends also on talent and intelligence 51.10; anticipation plus gov't willpower a good substitute 54.4

*unconstitutional: legislated injury 47.5
*undue influence: voids reality of consent, relation to slavery 42.10
*undue process and slavery, general nature 24.1
*universe, screen of: 47.5; see also screen of universe
*universe of law: facts of, statutes, court decisions, executive acts 4.1
*"unjust" trial or court decision: pitfall in using this expression
*U.S. v. Morris (1903) 125 F 322: black discrimination relieved 22.2, 22.12

*use: functional definition of 8.5; as term, discussion of 13.6; can be topic of conflict, though always in abstract mode 13.7; as term, distinguished from loading 13.7; as term, correcting ambiguity in, extending concept of 26.3; of various abstruse things, mechanics of reactions among concepts 26.4; scope of word finalized 34.7; without action, analyzed 34.7; of human, functions through "She" 42.5; always intentional 44.12; of person in scheme, negative example **Vanderbilt** 47.7
*utilitas publica: Tacitus 21.4

Vanderbilt v. Mitchell (1907) 72 NJ Eq 910, 67 A 97: paternity falsely recorded, embottling 47.1
*variables: variates, in function language 36.11; defined 36.1; dependent, contributing coincident 36.2
*variates: defined 36.1; derivative and powering, promotive 36.2; ascendant 36.3; translation of 36.3; as parameters of more basic phenomena 36.3; rise from three potencies or mechanisms, example, commonwealth 36.5; powering, may also be derivative 36.5
*vassal: different statuses 6.8; modern misconception of 6.8
*Venn diagram: see Figures; inadequate for describing reduction of freedom 16.7
*"Venuti v. Dirocco": example of false imaging 48.3
*view (landscape): physics and mechanics of 34.9; materiality of analyzed 34.9; see also "Engel", "Wolcott"; an effect of light, analyzed 35.1-
*vital statistics records: everyone has a right to use, but not to insert false information 47.7
*volition: interrelations with will, desire, action, results, 10.2
*voluntary indenture 22.8
*voodoo doll: "Cassidy v. Quinn"; 35.5; material effect of doll 35.6; materiality of effect, functional analysis 35.6; in "Engel", Weatherby a _ or ugly vase? 35.6; effect in function language 36.15

*wages, equal: see pleading, plaintiff's; analyzed as cause 37.7
*wage law, minimum: deprives prospective worker of property 37.10
***Warfield**: see **ex parte Warfield**
*Warren, S.D. and L.D. Brandeis, **The Rights To Privacy** (1890) 4 Harvard LR 193: 25.6
*Waugh, Evelyn, **A Handful of Dust**, "The Man Who Liked Dickens" (1934) (cond. Readers Dig. June 1978): 20.9